BLACKS IN NIAGARA FALLS

BLACKS IN NIAGARA FALLS

LEADERS AND COMMUNITY DEVELOPMENT, 1850–1985

Michael B. Boston

Published by State University of New York Press, Albany

© 2021 State University of New York

All rights reserved

Printed in the United States of America

No part of this book may be used or reproduced in any manner whatsoever without written permission. No part of this book may be stored in a retrieval system or transmitted in any form or by any means including electronic, electrostatic, magnetic tape, mechanical, photocopying, recording, or otherwise without the prior permission in writing of the publisher.

For information, contact State University of New York Press, Albany, NY
www.sunypress.edu

Library of Congress Cataloging-in-Publication Data

Name: Boston, Michael B., author.
Title: Blacks in Niagara Falls : leaders and community development, 1850–1985 / Michael B. Boston.
Description: Albany : State University of New York Press, [2021] | Includes bibliographical references and index.
Identifiers: LCCN 2020044891 | ISBN 9781438484617 (hardcover : alk. paper) | ISBN 9781438484624 (pbk. : alk. paper) | ISBN 9781438484631 (ebook)
Subjects: LCSH: African Americans—New York (State)—Niagara Falls—Social conditions—20th century. | African Americans—Civil rights—New York (State)—Niagara Falls—History—20th century. | Niagara Falls (N.Y.)—Race relations—History—20th century. | Niagara Falls (N.Y.)—History—20th century. | Niagara Community Center (Niagara Falls, New York)—History.
Classification: LCC F127.N8 B75 2021 | DDC 305.896/0730747980904—dc23
LC record available at https://lccn.loc.gov/2020044891

10 9 8 7 6 5 4 3 2 1

I dedicate this book to all who helped make this project possible, especially Barbara Smith, Theodore Williamson, Arthur Ray, Zorie Bell Boling, Eugene Hamilton, Indiana Martin, Carlyle Miller, Eddie Palmore, Helen Reed-McBride, Barbara Williams, and William Williamson.

I heard your voices.

Contents

List of Illustrations		ix
Acknowledgments		xiii
Introduction		1
Chapter One	Community Formation, 1850 to 1914	13
Chapter Two	The Development of the Black Community, Late 1915 to the Early Great Depression Years	51
Chapter Three	The Development of the Black Community, The Great Depression Years, 1930s	85
Chapter Four	Expanded Community and New Realities, 1940 to 1960	123
Chapter Five	The Civil Rights Years, 1960s	167
Chapter Six	Public School Desegregation, 1960s and 1970s	205
Chapter Seven	Urban Renewal, 1960 to 1985: External Change Agents Juxtaposed with Internal Change Agents	243
Chapter Eight	A New Reality, 1980 to 1985	287
Conclusion		293

Appendix A	Template for Interview Questions	299
Appendix B	Sample Institutional Questions Asked About St. John's AME Church	303
Appendix C	Notes on Interviewees	305
Appendix D	Interview Excerpts from Two Recorded Interviews, Barbara Smith and Theodore Williamson	307
Appendix E	Notable Leaders Who Impacted Black Niagaran History	313
Notes		319
Bibliography		393
Index		431

Illustrations

Figures

1.1	*The Mute and the Blind*, c. 1860.	15
1.2	Charlotte Dett, 1900.	25
1.3	Edward Dean Adams Power Plant, 1910.	26
1.4	Rear view of boarding house, 1900.	31
1.5	Antique map of Niagara Falls, 1890.	40
1.6	Ward map of Niagara Falls, 1940.	41
2.1	Benjamin W. Bolden, 1938.	61
2.2	John Magnus Pollard, 1943.	76
3.1	Charles and Alice Hayes, 1960 and 1980.	97
4.1	War map 2 of Niagara Falls, 1940.	131
4.2	Niagara Falls census map, 1960.	140
4.3	Niagara Community Center, 1938.	144
4.4	Niagara Community Center, 1955.	145
6.1	Advisory Committee, 1969.	218
6.2	Mrs. Helen Schoninger, 1970.	233
6.3	Arthur B. Ray, 1970.	240
7.1	Mayor E. Dent Lackey on a horse, 1967.	252

x | Illustrations

7.2	Playground at Unity Park, 1970.	258
7.3	Inside the middle of Unity Park, 1970.	259
7.4	Joe Profit, 1980.	269
7.5	Bloneva Bond, 1992.	276
7.6	Aaron L. Griffin, 1973.	279
7.7	Griffon Manor, 1980.	282
8.1	Census tract map, 1980.	289

Tables

1.1	Black population of Niagara Falls, New York, 1840–1990.	19
1.2	Black workers in Niagara Falls, 1870, 1880, and 1892.	24
1.3	Black workers recorded in the 1900 US Census.	25
1.4	Black workers recorded in the 1910 US Census.	28
2.1	Roomers.	58
2.2	Boarders.	58
2.3	1920 Black population by wards.	60
2.4	Black workers recorded in the 1920 US Census.	63
2.5	1920 marital condition males and females fifteen years of age and over.	65
2.6	1920 household structural arrangement of Black Niagarans.	67
3.1	Black workers recorded in the 1930 US Census.	87
3.2	1930 Black population by wards.	90
3.3	Black Niagaran entrepreneurs, 1900–1940.	116
4.1	Population of city of Niagara Falls, 1840–1990.	124
4.2	Black population of Covington County and Andalusia, Alabama.	127

4.3	1930 and 1940 Black population by ward.	138
4.4	1960 homeowners and renters by census tract.	139
4.5	Population density of census tracts 2, 15, 16, 17, and 24.	141
4.6	The index of dissimilarity, Niagara Falls, 1930–1970.	141
6.1	Niagara Falls 1968 and 1969 Black school enrollment percentages.	224
6.2	1973 racial breakdown of Niagara Falls elementary schools.	233
8.1	1980 Niagara Falls census tract population by race.	288

Acknowledgments

I thank all the extraordinary people who helped me complete this book. First and foremost, I am grateful to the numerous Niagarans who enthusiastically granted me interviews over the years, thereby allowing me to deeply understand the Black Niagaran community. I thank community leaders Barbara Smith, Theodore Williamson, and Arthur Ray, whom I met in 2002, for their commitment to this project, the encouragement they continuously offered, the time they shared with me, and their tremendous patience. I also thank my colleagues who offered helpful comments when I presented chapters of this book at numerous conferences.

In particular, I sincerely thank the Niagara Falls Public Library librarians who aided me tremendously: Maureen Fennie, Linda Reinumagi, Cecilia Driscoll, and Jennifer Potter. Maureen and Linda, now retired, graciously assisted me for ten years, always answering my endless entreaties for help.

Finally but never last, I thank SUNY Press for helping to turn my manuscript into a book, including senior acquisitions editor Mike Rinella, production editor Jenn Bennett-Genthner, and marketing manager Mike Campochiaro.

Introduction

Journey to My Distinct
Research Mythological Approach

At the end of May 2002, I had just completed a visiting professorship at the University of Memphis. While in Memphis, I found it difficult to conduct research and also be a full-time teacher who could give the students the high-quality education they deserved. The summer ahead was a long-awaited time for research. But what could I research? I did not want to follow the path of many historians and rehash what was already known, giving my interpretation of history without contributing to scholarship and knowledge of past events for current and future generations. I wanted to concentrate on African American history, considering it to be a field in need of more intensive work. Major scholars in the field had recently died, including Benjamin Quarles, John Hope Franklin, John Blassingame, Ira Berlin, John Henrik Clarke, C. Vann Woodward, Louis R. Harlan, and Monroe Fordham, leaving extensive records of their important pioneering works. How could I follow in their footsteps?

In mid-June, I found an article that quoted Monroe Fordham, who was both a fine historian and a great archivist. Fordham noted that of all the articles he reviewed over twenty years for the journal he edited, *Afro-Americans in New York Life and History*, none had covered the history of Black Niagarans. He considered it odd. This lack of attention to Black Niagaran history intrigued me. From my graduate training, I imagined that some professionally trained historians might consider such a project unworthy, partly because Niagara Falls, a small city, just can't boast of having the same sort of overtly eventful history as major cities. Yet, the history needed to be told. After all, Niagarans must have contributed to Underground Railroad endeavors; it is common knowledge that fugitive slaves traveled through Niagara Falls on their way to Canada. Surely some of them were aided by local Underground Railroad agents. Some probably also stayed in Niagara Falls rather than relocate to Canada. What happened in the ensuing years? What specific circumstances led to the increase in the Black Niagaran population? Were the experiences of Black Niagarans similar to those of African Americans who relocated to other northern urban locales? Consideration of these and other thoughts ensued.

I went to the Niagara Frontier region eager to engage in some meaningful research to uncover unknown histories. I visited the Earl W. Bridges Public Library in Niagara Falls, thinking that the library would have a profusion of sources on Black Niagaran history. What I found was that few sources were available, not only about Black Niagarans but also about other ethnic groups. There were three or four notebooks full of newspaper clippings that highlighted individuals or events associated with African American history. Over the years, the librarians had recorded a number of newspaper articles written on Black Niagarans from the *Niagara Falls Gazette* (the main local newspaper) and recorded these data in their card catalogue. Also available were the following: a 1950s Niagara University master's thesis, the papers of local resident R. Nathaniel Dett, and a box of papers from the Human Rights Commission from the 1960s and 1970s. Although I had expected much more primary and secondary data, what was available was extremely helpful, and the librarians aided me tremendously.

I began my research by searching the card catalogue. Then I read the articles on microfilm, a process that took years. I noticed that the *Niagara Falls Gazette* had only superficial accounts of events that occurred in the African American community, especially in the years before the civil rights movement. The how, when, and what questions could not always be answered, and connections and generalizations were usually difficult to make. African Americans were definitely on the margins in their coverage. Criminal activities involving Black Niagarans, in contrast, garnered more attention, which helped to perpetuate existing racial stereotypes. By the end of that first summer, I had accumulated enough data, including four interviews, to write an article: "Blacks in Niagara Falls, A Survey, 1865 to 1965." At the time, I had no intention to write a book because the sources seemed too scarce and because researching and writing a book on Black Niagarans would be a long and painful process. I merely wanted to encourage other more experienced researchers to pick up the ball and run with it.

I submitted my article to the editors of the *Journal of Afro-Americans in New York Life and History*, knowing they had not previously published anything similar to it. To my delight, Dr. Fordham agreed to publish it. Several Niagarans read the article, and most agreed that much more work needed to be done on the history of Black Niagarans. William Bradberry, a Black Niagaran lawyer and writer, informed me that he appreciated the article; however, in his view, it did not have the "voice of the people." He further explained that the history lived by Black Niagarans needed to be told through all sources but especially through the voices of Black Niagarans themselves, particularly because the local newspaper did not adequately record their history. I quickly agreed with him, and although I included four interviews in my article, his critique motivated me to seek out more oral sources because the conventional sources were insufficient in the "recording" and "housing" of data on Black Niagarans. Thereafter, I implanted myself in the local community, meeting with many Black Niagarans. My research method makes my study's sources vastly different from those of most African American urban studies. William's critique motivated me to take up the call I had issued to others: to uncover more about the history of Black Niagarans through their own voices.

Veedee Price, a native whose family operated a bar on centrally located Highland Avenue, served as my conduit.[1] At the University of Buffalo in the mid-1990s, he and I had taken a graduate course in education and became friends. Years later we crossed paths again in Niagara Falls. I explained my project to him and that I needed to meet and interview as many Niagarans as possible. Veedee graciously introduced me to some senior citizens who, on his recommendation, granted me an interview. Through Veedee I met several people, including Wilbur Hunt, Edwardo King, and George Hart, all whom I interviewed.

Of these people, George Hart was the oldest, being ninety-five in 2002. Mr. Hart came to Niagara Falls in the mid-1940s. An interesting story he told when he first arrived involved a bar on Highland Avenue. He entered the bar, sat down, and ordered a drink. The White bartender served him. But after Hart finished his drink, the bartender took the glass and violently threw it against the wall. According to Mr. Hart, that was the bartender's way of letting him know that his presence was not desired. Fifty-eight years later Mr. Hart has still not forgotten this incident and has never patronized that bar since.

In my journey to hear the voices of more Black Niagarans, Arthur Ray helped me immensely. Mere words cannot do justice to his contribution to this project. In 2002 someone advised me to speak with and perhaps interview Mr. Ray. Mr. Ray was born and raised in Niagara Falls, and he knew much of its history and current events. From the *Niagara Falls Gazette*, I knew that he was a local entrepreneur who had served on the board of education and that he was well known throughout Cataract City. Upon meeting Mr. Ray, it became readily apparent that he possessed a warm, outgoing, friendly personality. He quickly consented to an interview, and on the same day, he (surprisingly) drove me around, explaining key events that had occurred in Niagara Falls. He spoke quickly, and I attempted to write down as much of what he said as possible. Once he paused and reinforced a lesson that I was already aware of. He said, "You really need a tape recorder to get all that I am saying. You'll never get it all writing it down." His words reminded me that when I took oral history in graduate school, Dr. Michael Frisch had stressed the importance of having the proper equipment at hand and to be prepared for interviews even on short notice. Although I still have those initial notes today, they do not include all the information conveyed to me that day.

Arthur Ray also invited me to participate in the Black Pioneers of Niagara Falls. The Black Pioneers are a local group whose aim is to preserve, record, highlight, and honor the history of Black Niagarans. I joined this group in 2002 and have actively participated in its meetings and festivities, including its annual picnic held on the first Saturday of every August. This organization allowed me to meet and interview many Black Niagarans—particularly senior citizens—who experienced and made history. A few individuals come to mind. At the 2007 annual picnic, I remember interviewing Carlyle Miller, who was a retired factory worker and very generous with his time. We talked at the picnic, at the Wintergarden Botanical complex in downtown Niagara Falls, and later over the phone. He shared a few stories about his family and what made them leave the South. An uncle on his mother's side of the family, for instance, had verbally retaliated against racist remarks directed at him in Mississippi. He had to flee for his own safety. He settled in Cleveland, Ohio, about 220 miles from Niagara Falls. Every three years or so he would show up at the Miller household in Niagara Falls and ask, "Do you have room for me?" Carlyle Miller's parents settled in town, worked hard, and eventually purchased their own home, which was uncommon for most Black Niagarans during the immediate post–World War II years.

Eugene Hamilton's family followed a similar pattern in migrating from the South. Hamilton proved to be an unusual interviewee. He learned how to fly planes in the US Air Force during the Korean War. He eventually became a commercial airline pilot for Pan Am, and his first assignment was to fly passengers to London, England. Hence, Arthur Ray connected me to these individuals and others, serving not only as a host and guide but also as a mentor and friend. Sadly, he passed away on December 7, 2012, with Miller and Hamilton preceding him. Summer 2011 was the last summer we worked together, coordinating activities for the annual Black Pioneers' Picnic.

After I joined the Black Pioneers and met more Black Niagarans, other people asked me to interview people they knew, or they directed me to people they thought would have something valuable to say about the historical experiences of Black Niagarans. Charlotte Harris, also a member of the Black Pioneers, stressed that I should interview Mabel Smith, who attended the 2010 Annual Black Pioneers Picnic. She was visiting from Chicago. Mrs. Smith had met and married her husband and raised a family in Niagara Falls. Thus, she knew many early Black Niagaran families. Born in 1922, she began to be cognizant of race when she began school at age five.

Other introductions led to more interviews. Many Black Niagarans spoke glowingly about Joe Profit and how his political career had advanced the community. Several individuals stated that his wife still resided in the city and insisted that I speak with her. Veedee Price also took me to places where grassroots gatherings of individuals took place, such as a neighborhood bar, a small eatery on Highland Avenue, and some small parks, among other places. James Walker told me that he came to Niagara Falls from Alabama in 1955 on the advice of his parents who already resided in town. Walker told me about Lodge 34 FM and AM, Free and Accepted Masons, a Masonic organization. In discussing Bloneva Bond and the NAACP, Barbara Smith suggested that I speak with Barbara Williams, who had been secretary of the NAACP under Bond's presidency. Barbara Williams and her husband were listed in the local phone book as "Frank and Barbara Williams." When I called her up, Williams gladly consented to an interview.

In responding to William Bradberry's invaluable comments about hearing people's voices, I collected numerous recorded and unrecorded interviews. Most of my evidence is from these interviews and primary source data such as census reports, state and federal reports, and newspaper articles, mostly (but not exclusively) from the *Niagara Falls Gazette*. During the civil rights movement and afterward, the *Niagara Falls Gazette* tended to report more deeply on activities of Black Niagarans than it had in earlier years. Civil rights protest activities compelled local (and national) reporters to dig deeper in understanding the complaints of the African American community to help resolve conflicts and explain events to the broader community. Consequently, these articles often contained more data about local people and events.

Still more pertinent information about Black Niagarans probably exists in the attics and basements of local residents' homes. In searching for more Black Niagaran voices, I remember in 2004, 2005, and 2006 that Arthur Ray and I spent hours searching the Niagara Community Center for records that Black Niagarans left concerning their history. Some materials had disappeared. For many years, the Niagara Community Center functioned as a venue where local residents could learn about Niagara Falls history from a schedule of speakers and events, connecting with the African American community and the broader society.

In addition to conducting interviews, future researchers should seek permission from local Black churches to view their historical records.[2] Most Black Niagaran church histories will not be found in newspapers, libraries, or archives. In my research I examined some of the records of two major Black churches—St. John's AME Church and New Hope Baptist Church. I also consulted secondary sources on Shiloh Baptist Church, Union Baptist Church, Trinity Baptist Church, Second Baptist Church, and a few other churches in the Niagara Falls area. More church records should be examined, considering the fact that Niagara Falls has many Black churches that have been around for decades. This important duty I leave for future researchers, in the hopes that my pioneering work can serve as a foundational study.

How does this foundational study relate to other northern African American urban studies, and why is it important? It is a study that belongs to the genre initiated by W. E. B. Du Bois's groundbreaking work *The Philadelphia Negro*.[3] Like Du Bois's work and most African American urban historical studies, this book underscores the process of community formation at each critical stage of its development—along with sociological themes—examining such topics as early community beginnings, employment, migration, institutional building, intragroup and intergroup relations, and conjugal and family patterns. Like Gilbert Osofsky's well-researched critical study *Harlem: The Making of a Ghetto*, my study analyzes the spatial location of most of the African American community and ghetto formation along with the forces that drove such events: mainly race prejudice.⁴ Although Osofsky's study is an early major historiographical work that encouraged others to write urban historical studies, this study embraces the pattern established by Joe William Trotter in his important work *Black Milwaukee: The Making of an Industrial Proletariat, 1915–45*.⁵ Trotter's work describes the formation and development of Milwaukee's African American community, arguing that African American industrial workers experienced "proletarianization."⁶ More specifically, his portrayal does not depict Black residents or the Black industrial working class as reactive subjects in the construction of their histories; Trotter defines them as proactive agents, planning and shaping their destinies in the Milwaukee milieu they resided in. This study is also specifically written in the tradition of the community formation and development frameworks demonstrated by Richard W. Thomas in his study *Life for Us Is What We Make It: Building Black Community in Detroit, 1915–1945* and Lillian S. Williams in her work *Strangers in the Land of Paradise: The Creation of an African American Community, Buffalo, New York, 1900–1940*.⁷ Both studies support Trotter's approach of underscoring external variables that impacted their respective communities interplayed with internal community agency. Moreover, like Thomas's and Williams's studies, this study represents a borderland community, located next to Canada, through which thousands of fugitive slaves traveled during the days of slavery.

In contrast to the crucial similarities noted above, this study differs from much of the literature on African American urban history. Niagara Falls was/is a small northern city compared to New York City, Buffalo, Cleveland, Detroit, Chicago, and other northern metropolises, whose recorded African American population ranged from 33 people in 1840 to 9,634 people by 1990.⁸ In 1920 and 1950, for example, years that reflected African American population increases for the city of Niagara Falls, census enumerators counted 509 and 3,585 individuals respectively, with Niagara Falls located a little over eighty-one miles southeast of Toronto, Canada.⁹ During much of this study's timeframe, the Niagara Falls economy was driven by the tourist and hydroelectric industries. Peaks in the economy attracted more people to Cataract City, whereas depressions and recessions compelled many to seek employment elsewhere. These economic factors greatly impacted the development and reformation of the Black Niagaran Community. With Niagara Falls being a borderland community whose borders operated as a "fluid frontier," African Canadians and African Americans often relocated to each other's neighboring country or interacted on foreign soil for spiritual, recreational, or business purposes.¹⁰ Unlike the prejudice and discrimination found in large northeastern and Midwestern cities during and immediately following the First Great Migration, Black Niagarans experienced similar forms of racism during and after the Second Great Migration (1941–45).[11] This study rejects the characterization of post–First Great Migration African American entrepreneurs formulated by early studies, beginning with *Black Chicago: The Making of a Negro Ghetto, 1890 to 1920*. Many urban historians incorrectly label many of the successful entrepreneurs as practitioners of Booker T. Washington's economic philosophy because they believed in racial solidarity and the support of African American businesses within a segregated economy, which often was interpreted as a "protected market."[12] Niagara Falls had a local branch of Washington's Negro Business League, whose members supported many of Washington's business ideas. Nonetheless, contrary to popular belief, Washington advocated conducting business in the general "open market" and patronage of businesses that warranted support, not just through pleas of racial solidarity. This was part of his "Indispensable Asset Theory," in which Washington foresaw African American entrepreneurs (and others) as being able to manifest merit to all citizens by offering high-quality goods and/or services. This would contribute toward ending the American race problem, the rationale being that human beings will accept entities that are integral to their welfare. Nonetheless, concerning racial patronage, Washington did believe, partly due to White racism, that African Americans would naturally support entrepreneurs of their own race if they offered high-quality goods and/or services. A different term should be used to define African American entrepreneurs who embraced many of Washington's economic ideas and were compelled, due to racism, to conduct businesses solely in a segregated, "really unprotected market."[13] This foundational study lacks the extensive primary and secondary source base clearly evident in the urban historical studies done on major cities. Therefore, it can be aligned with such studies as *Race and Kinship in a Midwestern Town: The Black Experience in Monroe, Michigan, 1900–1915* by James E. DeVries, *Black Bangor: African Americans in a Maine Community, 1880–1950* by Maureen Elgersman Lee, and *Lord, Please Don't Take Me in August: African Americans in Newport and Saratoga Springs, 1870–1930* by Myra B. Young. These works confirm that all communities have a story that can be conveyed, provided that researchers are willing to use creative or nontraditional methods to supplement small source bases.[14] In embracing this mindset or "inside-out approach" as opposed to the "outside-in approach" utilized by most African American urban studies,

I intermixed within the Black Niagaran community over an eighteen-year period by actively participating in community events, conducting and recording sixty-two oral interviews, as well as by speaking with over eighty Black Niagarans to gain a more in-depth understanding of their history. This approach makes this study vastly different from most black urban historical studies whose evidentiary bases are predominantly from written sources. These interactions assisted me in my efforts to authentically depict the thoughts and voices of the people. Finally, this study utilizes critical concepts to better explicate the history of Black Niagarans, such as borderland, transnational, fluid frontier, self-liberators, collectivist behavior, politics of respectability, institutional building, redlining, an enduring civil rights movement originating well before 1954 and continuing long after 1968, the Cold War's impact on African American movements, and urban renewal as "Negro removal," etc.

Moreover, to interpret the Black Niagaran historical experience, this study uses a conceptual framework that demonstrates proactive leadership in orchestrating community development. Like the power dynamics outlined in most African American urban historical studies, Black Niagarans operated within a broader community setting that they did not control. They mainly sought to live and function within this broader community, becoming an integral part by gaining power and influence as well as by enjoying full citizenship rights on paper and in practice. Racism served as a structural barrier. However, Black Niagaran leadership vehemently refused to settle for a low place within the social stratum.

This study, in essence, conceptualizes community and leadership, offering key characterizations for each term. *Community* is defined by its membership and what said members did to sustain and advance themselves.[15] More specifically, a community consists of two or more individuals who are generally but not exclusively of the same racial and/or ethnic group.[16] This group could include family members, friends, associates, neighbors, or people residing in specific areas. For the community to sustain itself and advance, its members practiced maintenance behaviors, such as working, seeking housing, building institutions, seeking political rights or political power, and fighting against adverse activities, groups, or forces.[17] Black Niagaran leaders usually represented the desires and wants of their racial group. Their racial group influenced them, and they, in turn, impacted their racial group by initiating and heading new institutions, directing established institutions, or spontaneously leading individuals to impact events or to abate crises.

In this study, "[l]eadership can be [broadly] defined as the self-conscious capacity to provide vision and values, and produce structures, programs and practices which satisfy human needs and aspirations and transforms persons and society in the process."[18] More specifically, I assert the following:

1. Regardless of class or gender, and influenced by structural barriers, Black Niagarans arose to proactively serve as leaders, operating "intra-racially" within the Black Niagaran population or "interracially" within the broader community where Black leadership functioned as a minority agent vis-à-vis a community controlled and dominated by a majority White Niagaran leadership. They could also operate simultaneously in both settings.

2. "Leadership . . . proceeded from the collective interests and concerns of people of African descent—including involvement in historical events defined by a 'racial uplift' tradition, and leadership to overcome the impediments to the full enjoyment of every aspect of American life (such as slavery, prejudice and discrimination, institutional racism, and any pattern of exclusion of racial inferiorization of Black humanity)."[19]

3. Most Black Niagaran leaders fit Booker T. Washington's conception of the "captains of industry." They became successful, and then they geared many of their efforts toward aiding others to be successful.[20]

4. Black Niagaran leadership mainly strove to integrate their racial group into the mainstream of the broader community.

5. Black Niagaran Leadership managed activities aimed at building and maintaining institutions, some wholeheartedly supported by the Black Niagaran community and others supported by municipal, state, and/or federal funding.

6. Most Black Niagaran leaders in this study fit middle-class status based on their educational and/or economic achievements. Most migrated or emigrated into the Niagara Falls milieu. All leaders functioned as role models, demonstrating

respectable behaviors conveyed to Black Niagaran community members and the broader Niagaran community. Although a range of epochs existed throughout Black Niagaran history—varying from stormy to calm—Black Niagaran leaders never ceased to agitate for first-class-citizen rights.

7. Alliance leadership existed in which individuals other than African Americans proactively championed one or more issues directly supportive of Black Niagarans (or other African Americans). This could include assisting Blacks in fleeing from slavery or helping them obtain American citizenship and all its privileges and immunities.

Although marginalized throughout most of their existence in the city of Niagara Falls, Black Niagarans, guided chiefly by their leaders, operated proactively to settle in the region, seek and create employment, promote individual and collective advancement, build institutions, confront and overcome racism, and become part of the mainstream of society. They strove to make American democracy live up to the true meaning of its creed. During periods of crisis, their efforts to achieve these ends were accelerated. However, during calmer periods, leaders still arose to encourage Black Niagarans not to be content with their unjust lot, and to continue to strive for their fair share of societal opportunities. This occurred during the slavery era when Black Niagarans and their White allies worked together to ensure that all fugitive slaves traversing the area would be safeguarded in their efforts to reach Canada, particularly if they sought assistance. Black Niagarans also rallied together to protect fugitive slaves if they chose to remain in their community, gathering together at a moment's notice to risk life and limb to ensure the freedom of a member of their racial group. They reasoned that all human beings had a natural right to life, liberty, and ownership of the monetary gains from their labor. Black Niagarans demonstrated this same principle in the Post-slavery era. Like those migrating to California during the Gold Rush (1849) seeking economic fortunes, African Americans settled in Niagara Falls looking for the same. To them, as well as to incoming European immigrants, a fortune meant living a better life than they would have experienced in the places they immigrated from and being allowed to grow economically and materially advance themselves and their families. They wanted to establish institutions that expressed a collective will, being able to proactively participate in creating and implementing laws to govern the city and interact with people from all walks of life. Moreover, parents wanted to see their children get a high-quality education to advance farther in life than they had. These are some of the issues that Black Niagarans, guided by their leadership, strove for in attempting to pull themselves out of obscurity and into relevance, practicing "self-determinism" in shaping the operations of society in more of their "image" and "interest."[21]

To conclude this introduction and begin the journey, this book is divided into eight chapters, which together chronologically discuss historical themes and events that occurred in Niagara Falls from 1850 to 1985. Chapter 1 covers the early foundational years of the Black Niagaran community from 1850 to 1914, the years of slavery to the dawn of the First Great Migration. Chapter 2 highlights several topics, notably the formation of the Niagara Community Center, a well-coordinated collective effort and momentous event in Black Niagaran community history. Chapter 3 examines the Black Niagaran community during an unstable economic era and how it managed to survive and prosper. Chapter 4 examines the Black Niagaran community's efforts to fight against marginalization during decades of economic recovery and stability. Chapter 5 examines the local civil rights movement, the impact of national civil rights events on local events, and other local achievements. Chapter 6 covers another critical era in the history of Niagara Falls—desegregation of the public school system and the plan community leaders and local citizens created instead. Chapter 7 highlights several events and impactful people in Niagara Falls during the urban renewal era of 1960 to 1985. Finally, Chapter 8 discusses crucial issues that arose after the age of urban renewal. Collectively, these chapters present Black Niagaran history through the lens of leadership in effecting community formation and development. They argue that Black Niagarans experienced similar forms of discrimination—especially discrimination related to housing both during and after the Second Great Migration—as those experienced by African American communities in major northeastern and Midwestern cities during and after the First Great Migration. This study also looks at how Booker T. Washington's business ideas filtered into the Black Niagaran community, with the local leadership adhering to a number of these tenets.[22] The study also shows how national civil rights activities, juxtaposed with local issues, helped to fuel local events (e.g., civil rights, board of education decisions, urban renewal protest, etc.), and, in essence, how Black Niagaran leaders operated proactively in creating, developing, and maintaining community—thereby constructing their history.

Chapter One

Community Formation, 1850 to 1914

From 1850 to 1914, striving to improve their plight, Blacks gradually migrated to Niagara Falls, eventually creating a budding community that expanded throughout the city. A progressive leadership arose to represent their group's collective will, although Black Niagarans early on felt they were treated as second-class citizens compared to Whites. But, predictably, due to the minuscule Black population, there was not a significant outcry against racial discrimination.

Underground Railroad and Early Beginnings

Most Blacks who came to Niagara Falls, New York, during the antebellum era (1820–1861) were just passing through.[1] They came from some southerly locale by land, boat, or both, with the intention of reaching Canada safely.[2] Once they set foot on Canadian soil, most were free. If they came by land, many hoped to cross the Niagara Falls Suspension Bridge, which once spanned the Niagara River and connected New York State with Canada.[3] If they came by boat, once they reached Niagara Falls they might hope to be carried to Canadian shores by ferryboat because it was only a short distance across the river to Canada. In 1858 the *Niagara Falls Gazette* commented that Frederick Douglass had guided "four highly colored chattels" aboard the main train at Rochester, New York, planning to reach Canada by way of the Suspension Bridge.[4] At another time, Harriet Tubman, on one of her numerous daring journeys, escorted a fugitive slave named Joe across the bridge to Canada.[5] Upon reaching the Canadian side, Tubman rushed across the aisle, shook Joe with all her might, and shouted, "You've shook de lion's paw, Joe! You're a free man, Joe! Come and look at the Falls."[6] Joe is reputed to have broken down and cried, singing and praising and thanking God. He greatly feared that slave catchers or federal authorities might apprehend him and return him to the hellish life of slavery. William Still, the famous Underground Railroad conductor who was based in Philadelphia, Pennsylvania, received several letters from fugitive slaves he had channeled through the Niagara Falls region en route to Canada. These letters generally expressed great appreciation for the helping hand Still had rendered.[7]

Fugitive slaves who passed through Niagara Falls were often aided by local Underground Railroad conductors who either consciously or inadvertently operated as leaders fostering community development. Unfortunately, much concrete detail concerning their assistance is simply unavailable because aiding fugitive slaves was unlawful and punishable with an extensive fine and a jail term. Consequently, abolitionists did not generally keep written records of their deeds. However, some of this documentation does exist. Records show that W. H. Childs was a conductor in the town, along with Ben Jackson and a person simply known as "P" or "Colonel P."[8] Platt H. Skinner may have been an Underground Railroad conductor.

Colonel P was a wealthy White man with a large farm who lived about two miles from the Niagara River. He employed a female fugitive slave named Cassey. Cassey's owner, Cathcart, came to the area to reclaim his property.[9] Cathcart questioned several Black Niagarans concerning her whereabouts, and because he was aware that Cassey was very religious, he even posted himself outside a church with a known Black congregation. He met a black Niagaran named Ben Davis who purposely misled him by telling him that Cassey lived in Canada. After this, Davis immediately informed Colonel P that Cassey's owner was in the area. For her safety, Cassey was taken to Lockport, the county capital and an abolitionist center. Being doubtful, Cathcart continued to question people. At the front entrance of the bridge, he was told by someone that Cassey resided in Niagara Falls and worked for a Colonel P. Cathcart immediately sought out US marshals, and they went to Colonel P's home. Colonel P predictably anticipated their arrival, and as they neared his home, he took off quickly on his horse and carriage. He rode to Youngstown, New York, and from Youngstown back to his home, with Cathcart and the marshals aggressively pursuing him. Before they caught up with Colonel P, they strongly suspected that Cassey was in his carriage, but to their dismay, she was not. Colonel P informed them that he was merely exercising his horses. "He then invited them all into his house for some refreshments, but they were in no mood for refreshments."[10] However, early on, Cassey had been taken to Canada by ferry, where she continued to enjoy a life of liberty, settling in a country that accommodated many former slaves who valued their freedom.[11]

Platt H. Skinner, like Colonel P, was a committed abolitionist who planned to implement his ideas. He resided in Niagara Falls for about four years, beginning in 1858. He had come from Washington, DC, a major slave-trading center,[12] where he had witnessed firsthand the effects of slavery: slaves being overworked, treated inhumanely, and separated from their families and friends.[13] He had been affiliated with the New York Institute for the Instruction of the Deaf and Dumb. He came to Niagara Falls to establish a school for deaf, blind, and mute Black children, with the intent of teaching its students life skills and Christianity. Skinner, who was a paternalistic, religious person, saw deaf, blind, and mute uneducated Black children as heathens, existing in a life of darkness, of no concern to most people, and destined for Hell in the afterlife unless they received help. However, Skinner believed that before he could teach his handicapped Black children about Christianity, he had to equip them with a means of communication. "We must teach the hand of the mute to perform the office of the tongue, and the eye to perform the office of the ear; the fingers of the blind must be taught to see."[14] Subsequently, Skinner taught his students sign language and braille, as well as other skills enabling them to cope in the world (see figure 1.1).

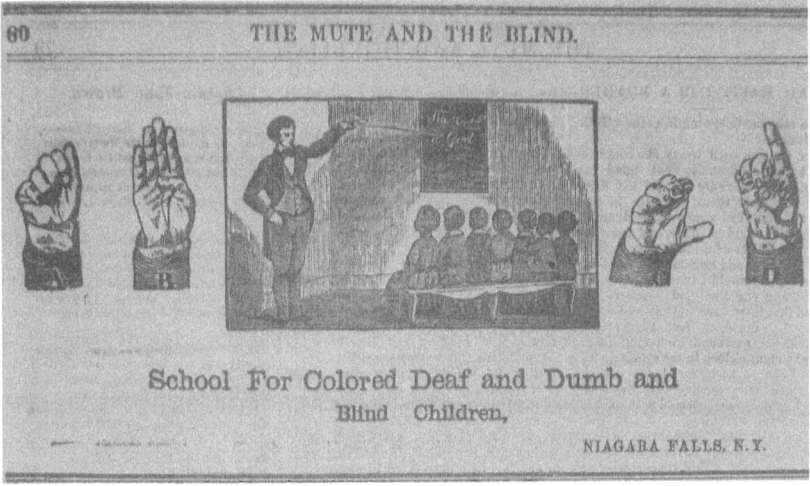

Figure 1.1. *The Mute and the Blind*, c. 1860. Fair use.

In addition to founding his school, Skinner published a newspaper, which he called *The Mute and the Blind*. In commenting on his students' contribution to the paper, he proudly announced, "The editor of the paper was a blind man; the compositors were deaf and dumb; the blind performed the presswork; and the papers were folded by the blind and wrapped by the mute."[15] *The Mute and the Blind* gave Skinner a voice in Niagara Falls and its surrounding counties to inform residents of his work and to raise funds. Skinner established his paper because as a controversial figure he was banned from writing for the local papers in the Niagara Falls area. He criticized these papers, calling them "proslavery" periodicals. Niagara County residents who interacted with Skinner either highly respected him or despised him; there was no middle ground. *The Mute and the Blind* ardently espoused Skinner's philosophy and further conveyed that he was a religious man who believed strongly in the Ten Commandments. Each copy of *The Mute and the Blind* had some moral lesson for parents and children, encouraging children to honor and listen to their parents and encouraging parents to be the parents that God had intended them to be. His paper also offered health advice, such as the proper amount of sleep one needs every night and how to keep up healthy eating habits. Another favorite topic of Skinner's was the institution of slavery. He conveyed its horrors to readers and argued that all of God's creatures were equal and had a right to life and liberty. During the Civil War, he clearly let his allegiances be known, as he kept abreast of and wrote about the successes of the Union Army.[16]

Skinner's activities clearly indicate that he was an abolitionist and activist in the Niagara frontier. He boldly made his views known, and being a promoter of racial equality—while also being a supporter of antislavery activities—he may have been a conductor on the Underground Railroad. For three years he had attended Oberlin College,[17] which produced a number of abolitionists active in the Underground Railroad.[18] He resided at one of the major termini of the Underground Railroad and interacted with fugitive slave communities in Canada, even bringing back some of their children to the States to be educated, with many of these parents worried their children might be caught in the clutches of slavery.[19] In his newspaper he even subtly promoted the harboring of fugitive slaves, asking perplexed readers, "What would the Savior want one to do, return them to their masters or help free them?"[20] By 1862 Skinner had left Niagara Falls and subsequently appeared in Trenton, New Jersey, where he reestablished his school. Although Skinner had left the area, his activities promoted the rights of Blacks, whether free or enslaved, to exist as integral parts of the Niagaran community.

Near the Village of Lewiston, a few miles from Skinner's former residency, a home known as Tryon's Folly is reputed to have been an Underground Railroad station. Tryon's Folly was built by Amos Tryon, who came to Lewiston from Wethersfield, Connecticut, in 1803.[21] Tryon was a successful businessman. In 1818 he married Sally Barton, and they lived in Lewiston. Community lore—traditional local beliefs that are shared and passed on to future generations—states that some years later, without consulting his wife, Tryon had a large stone house built on the banks of the Niagara River, away from the center of town. His beautiful house had a great scenic view of parts of Canada and the Niagara River; it had four cellars built on top of one another, the last one being near the river.[22] He had hoped that he and his wife would move into this house, but his wife refused to move from their residence in town. His miscalculation reflects the name eventually given to his house: Tryon's Folly. For a while the house remained vacant until Josiah Tryon, Amos Tyron's brother and pastor of the Lewiston Presbyterian Church, made use of it. When slave catchers were known to be in the area, fugitive slaves were supposedly hidden in the cellars. When the coast was clear, they exited from the fourth cellar, and Josiah Tryon and/or his associates rowed the fugitive slaves to Canada. At Tryon's Folly, the Niagara River's currents are not as strong as the currents closer to the actual waterfalls of Niagara Falls. Accordingly, many fugitive slaves would have crossed at termini such as Lewiston or Youngstown, especially if slave catchers were closely monitoring ferryboat pilots or the trains crossing the suspension bridge.

Colonel P, Platt H. Skinner, Amos Tryon, and Josiah Tryon were not Black Niagarans. However, they knew of the injustices that befell enslaved people, including those fleeing bondage, and they strove to help them. Their efforts are analogous to Frederick Douglass's characterization of his Underground Railroad experience in Rochester, New York. For Douglass, each time he successfully aided a fugitive slave in gaining his or her freedom, he described it as taking a teaspoon of water from an ocean.[23] However, he simultaneously saw it as monumental because a human being was being freed, and the abominable institution of slavery took a loss. Thus, unlike Douglass, Colonel P, Platt H. Skinner, Amos Tryon, and Josiah Tryon functioned as alliance leaders, similar to the White abolitionists operating in Rochester who knew and worked with Douglass: Amy and Isaac Post, John and Lemira Kedzie, and Samuel and Susan Porter, among others.[24]

These White citizens promoted freedom, fairness, and justice, along with high moral values: all essential elements in a budding and stable community, whether in the United States or Canada.[25] Over time their cumulative audacious efforts helped to eradicate slavery, with the Niagara Falls and Detroit regions serving as major underground railroad termini.

Niagara Falls's Underground Railroad history undoubtedly parallels that of Detroit. Both cities were borderland communities directly adjacent to Canada. Both cities functioned as transnational districts that sheltered fugitive slaves who had fled from or to Canada in order to gain their freedom.[26] Slavery existed in British-controlled Canada until 1833, the year it was officially outlawed by the British government.[27] Thousands of fugitive slaves traveled through each city bound for Canada, whereas some fled to the United States.[28] Both cities were critical destinations: a final Underground Railroad station for fugitive slaves before entering Canada or an entry point for those fleeing Canadian bondage. We may never know which city fugitive slaves traveled through most frequently. Fugitive slaves in Detroit crossed the Detroit River to gain freedom.[29] Fugitive slaves fleeing the United States through Niagara Falls or Detroit entered the province of Ontario (or Canada West). Those escaping from Canada entered territories or states ultimately designated as New York or Michigan.

Not all fugitive slaves traveled on to Canada. Some chose to remain in Niagara Falls (or Detroit) because they felt safe and found employment there.[30] Other Blacks who resided in Niagara Falls during these early years were free and had been born in the area or had moved there. The exact number of Blacks residing in Niagara Falls during the antebellum era will probably never be known; most fugitive slaves would have avoided census takers for fear of losing their freedom. However, an expanding free Black community along with a progressive abolitionist presence may have given them a sense of security and unity, as exemplified in Ben Davis's actions. The recorded Black population of Niagara Falls during early and later years is in table 1.1.[31]

In the 1850 Census 41 Blacks were recorded as living in Niagara Falls: 35 males and 6 females.[32] These forty-one Blacks were probably free and could likely prove their status. In 1850 President Millard Fillmore signed into law the infamous Fugitive Slave Act of 1850, which gave slave owners the right to reclaim their escaped enslaved persons if they were residing in the United States and slave owners knew their whereabouts.[33] This was a harsher version of the Fugitive Slave Act of 1793. The Fugitive

Table 1.1. Black Population of Niagara Falls, New York, 1840–1990

Year	Total Population	Percentage of Population
1840	33	2.60
1850	41	2.10
1860	242	6.91
1865	126	2.00
1870	149	4.96
1880	150	4.52
1890	159	2.89
1900	344	1.77
1910	266	0.87
1920	509	1.00
1930	906	1.20
1940	975	1.25
1950	3,585	3.94
1960	7,038	6.87
1970	8,001	9.35
1980	9,079	12.72
1990	9,634	15.58

Source: Please see page 325, note 31.

Slave Act of 1850 was the result of a compromise between predominantly northern and southern politicians trying to keep the union together. All a slave owner had to do was get a federal marshal to accompany him in apprehending his slave and bring the enslaved individual before a magistrate with one credible witness. In theory, an apprehended person's testimony was not admissible.[34] This helps to explain why Niagara Falls's recorded Black population was small, especially compared to its 1860 figure, as many fugitive slaves almost certainly left the area and fled to Canada after initially being made aware of the Fugitive Slave Act of 1850.

In the 1860 Census, 242 Blacks were recorded as residing in Niagara Falls, an increase since 1850 of 201 individuals.[35] Why the increase? Abolitionist forces had had time to establish their response to the revised Fugitive Slave Act, and many were committed to defying it. Some of these 242 Blacks were perhaps fugitive slaves, who in time once again felt safe in Cataract City. Furthermore, as a reading of slave narratives will readily convey, Black communities, particularly in northern locales, rallied together at a moment's notice to protect their members from the very real threat of slavery and to free any enslaved person in their midst.[36] In 1847 such an incident occurred in Niagara Falls. A male slave owner and a woman from Alabama appeared in Niagara Falls with a female slave servant, staying at the Eagle, a reputable hotel. Somehow, Blacks in the surrounding area discovered this enslaved individual in their midst. They quickly organized and then approached the enslaved servant, asking her if she wished to return to the South. Her response is unknown. Two accounts of this incident appear. One indicates that the group of desperate Blacks was barely fought off with the aid of local White residents, whereas the other states that Black Niagarans were successful in freeing a member of their race from the clutches of slavery.[37] Which account is correct is not the central issue. What is important is how the Black community functioned as a collective unit to free a member of its racial group and to protect itself.

A case that exemplifies the protection issue is that of Patrick Snead.[38] Historians have long discussed this issue.[39] Snead, an escaped slave who had fled from Savannah, Georgia, in 1851, worked two summers at the Cataract House, a major hotel in Niagara Falls. Snead had worked there for two years when in 1853 he was identified as a fugitive slave and arrested at the Cataract House by five constables from Buffalo. After his arrest, he was rescued by a group of Black waiters, also from Cataract House, who assisted him in getting a ferry to Canada. But the constables caught up with the fleeing Snead and called for the boat's pilots to bring their boat ashore, which they did. Snead was again apprehended, taken to Buffalo, jailed for nine days, and finally brought before a judge. Fortunately for Snead, he had good legal representation, resulting in his release. Once freed, he immediately fled to Canada. Although Snead treasured his freedom, he regretted that he had lost his opportunity to earn the much-needed wages that he could have earned at the Cataract House. As with Snead, fugitive slaves often had difficulty finding employment in Canada, especially after 1850, as more of them entered the Province of Ontario. Nonetheless, free Black community members aggressively aided other Blacks.

By 1865, twelve years after the Patrick Snead incident, census takers recorded only 126 Blacks residing in Niagara Falls, a reduction of 116 people since 1850. In 1865 the Civil War ended, which meant that legal slavery was over in the United States. This drastic reduction in the population could mean that many Black Niagarans had been fugitive slaves—or at least the heads of many families were. If so, perhaps the ex-slaves desired to return to the southern regions from which they had fled. Escaping from slavery was a major decision for an enslaved person to make. Despite the risk of being caught and punished, the prospect of never again seeing family members or close friends was an essential issue for fugitive slaves. If it had not been for this issue, more enslaved persons would probably have attempted to flee. Consequently, like recently freed slaves in the South, Blacks in the North were probably seeking loved ones. Another reason for the reduction in population is that many Black heads of household could have found employment elsewhere.

Unlike Niagara Falls's Black population, Lockport's Black population remained relatively constant from 1860 to 1870. Lockport, New York, was a neighboring town only about twenty miles away on the Erie Canal route. In 1860, 209 Blacks were identified as residing in Lockport.[40] In 1865, 240 were recorded, and at least 209 lived there in 1870.[41] Lockport may have had fewer fugitive slaves than Niagara Falls, which would help explain their stable Black population figures. Unlike Lockport, the neighboring city of Buffalo, about twenty-three miles away, exhibited a similar pattern to that of Niagara Falls. In 1860, 809 Blacks were recorded as residing in Buffalo, and in 1870, 696 were accounted for, indicating 113 fewer individuals.[42]

Most fugitive slaves who traveled through Niagara Falls (Detroit or Buffalo) en route to Canada were self-liberators: courageous, proactive people who gained their freedom largely or exclusively through their own efforts. Since the late 1960s, scholars have continuously underscored this issue in their analyses of fugitive slaves.[43] According to one estimate, thirty thousand to forty thousand enslaved persons successfully escaped during the antebellum era.[44] While fleeing they feared two discouraging factors: hunger and the White man.[45] They had to find food to sustain themselves, and because of their fears, escaping slaves intended to flee without any White assistance; thus, most fugitive slaves who successfully escaped were self-liberators. Therefore, we can never know the full history of fugitive slaves and their use (or nonuse) of the Underground Railroad.

Furthermore, portraying fugitive slaves as self-liberators juxtaposed with Underground Railroad conductor histories is critically important. American society (e.g., contemporary popular media, school curricula) still tends to overstate the role of Underground Railroad conductors and minimize the part fugitive slaves played gaining their freedom independently. Some courageously returned to the South to assist other slaves in obtaining their freedom. Wilbur H. Siebert, author of the eminent pioneering study *The Underground Railroad from Slavery to Freedom* (1899) estimated that about five hundred fugitive slaves per year who had settled in Canada during the antebellum era returned to slave territory to assist family members, friends, and others in gaining their freedom.[46]

Conversely, Underground Railroad conductors usually aided fugitive slaves who came to or near their stations. Few ventured into slave territory, like Harriet Tubman, Josiah Henson, John Parker, John Fairfield, Seth Conklin, or Charles Torrey, to liberate enslaved people.[47] Scholars and laypersons should continue to accentuate the self-liberator theme ignited by Larry Gara in his groundbreaking study, *The Liberty Line: The Legend of the Underground Railroad*.[48] This form of courageous slave resistance should be accentuated when juxtaposed with Underground Railroad activities so that each of these historical phenomena can be better understood.

The early Black Niagaran community consisted of free Blacks and an unknown number of fugitive slaves. Unsurprisingly, they abhorred slavery and welcomed support from White abolitionists and White Underground Railroad agents. Leaders arose within their ranks, as heads of households and/or freedom protectors. They proactively organized to protect themselves as well as fugitive slaves, hoping for a better day for their race in the United States and to sustain community growth and development.

Early Occupational Structure

With or without family, or as fugitive slaves or freed persons, Black Niagarans, like most people, had to work hard in order to survive and prosper. Within the small Black population of Niagara Falls in 1865, an even smaller workforce was recorded. According to the 1865 New York State Census reports, twenty-three Blacks were employed.[49] Most of these individuals were low-skilled workers. (From earliest times to the present, Black Niagarans have generally been low-skilled workers.)[50] Nine of these were listed as laborers: one was a drayman, and eight were servants. Five were classified as skilled tradespersons: two barbers, one mason, one tailor, and one head cook. Of the twenty-three people listed as employed, eighteen were male, and five were female. Although Black women historically have had to work to help sustain their families, throughout the timeframe of this study, fewer Black women worked outside their homes than men. Early on, most worked in some domestic service capacity, usually in private homes and occasionally in businesses. Of the eight servants previously noted, five were women, and three were men. Four of the women worked in private homes, and the three men and one woman worked for the International Hotel.

Hotel work was a popular area of employment for Black Niagarans and plentiful because Niagara Falls was a major tourist attraction. In the days of slavery, Blacks were cheap laborers who performed daily menial hotel functions as waiters, bellboys, servants, and janitors. Hotels hired them for the summer but did not use them in the winter.[51] Many of the Black hotel workers "lived in the basements of the hotels and worked all day long and into the night."[52] They continued to labor in hotels beyond the slavery period. The Town and Village 1865 Census for Niagara Falls, for example, listed four blacks working in a hotel, which is, most likely, an undercount. The 1870 Census listed forty, the 1880 Census sixty-one, and this pattern continued throughout the Niagara Falls Town and Village censuses that recorded occupation.[53]

Two of the oldest and most prominent hotels in Niagara Falls were the International Hotel and the Cataract House. These hotels also employed an extensive Black workforce.[54] The Cataract House was built in 1825 and the International Hotel in 1853.[55] These hotels housed and entertained such notable guests as Abraham Lincoln, Ulysses S. Grant, Millard Fillmore, William Boss Tweed, and Li Hung Chang, a Chinese diplomat. President William McKinley had lunch at the International Hotel an hour or so before he was assassinated in Buffalo. The Cataract House (and probably the International Hotel as well) was patronized by rich southerners before and after the Civil War who were made to feel at home by the colored help.[56] During their breaks, Black workers would often congregate near and around the hotel, which was surrounded by a scenic wooded area near the Niagara River.[57] When suddenly needed, they were often summoned by a great bell that hung above the hotel.

Census reports from 1870 to 1892 display similar patterns to the one of 1865, although the recorded Black workforce generally increased with each ensuing decade (see Table 1.2).[58] However, the 1900 Census for Niagara Falls began to display some significant differences.[59] First, four hotelkeepers and three boarding house operators were listed. Robert Dett, Anderson Fayette, T. Franz, and Henry Fayette were the hotelkeepers or proprietors, and Louisa Patterson, James Campbell, and Charlotte Dett (see figure 1.2) managed boarding houses. T. Franz was the sole female hotelkeeper, and two females, Charlotte Dett and Louisa Patterson, managed boarding houses. Charlotte Dett and Robert Dett were the proud parents of famed native son and composer of Negro spirituals, R. Nathaniel Dett.[60] Like their son, both parents were musicians, and Charlotte became

Table 1.2. Black Workers in Niagara Falls 1870, 1880, and 1892

	1870 Numbers & Percentage	1880 Numbers & Percentage	1892 Numbers & Percentage
Males			
Professional	—		
Proprietary	—	1 (1.05)	1 (0.85)
Clerical	1 (1.47)	—	—
Skilled	9 (13.24)	9 (9.47)	7 (5.98)
Semiskilled	9 (13.24)	47 (49.47)	3 (2.56)
Unskilled	35 (51.47)	17 (17.89)	92 (78.63)
Domestic	—	2 (2.11)	3 (2.56)
Total	54	76	106
Females			
1870 Females			
Professional	—	—	2 (1.71)
Proprietary	—	—	—
Clerical	—	—	—
Skilled	2 (2.94)	4 (4.21)	1 (0.85)
Semiskilled	1 (1.47)	4 (4.21)	5 (4.27)
Unskilled	5 (7.35)	7 (7.37)	
Domestic	6 (8.82)	4 (4.21)	3 (2.56)
Total	14	19	11
Grand Total	68	95	117

Adapted from the 1870 and 1880 US Census and the 1892 New York State Census. (See page 327, note 58.)

an effective leader not only in the Black Niagaran community but also in the broader Niagaran society.

Robert and Charlotte Dett had moved to Niagara Falls, New York, from Drummondville, Canada (now known as Niagara Falls, Ontario). Robert was fifty-seven and Charlotte thirty-eight. Their other living son, Samuel Dett, was listed as a clerk at a store. He was twenty-one years old and lived in his mother's seventeen-room tourist home. Anderson Fayette and Henry Fayette may have been related, perhaps son and father or grandson and grandfather. Anderson was thirty-four and Henry seventy-three. Their businesses were in different locations. Early census data reveal that several Blacks boarded with blood relatives and nonrelatives, and their job provided money or some other form of recompense for them to pay the homeowner or landlord. Beginning with the 1900 US Census

Figure 1.2. Charlotte Dett, 1900. Niagara Falls Public Library. Fair use.

report, Blacks were recorded as participating in other skilled trades: a chair maker, a shoemaker, and a dressmaker were among those employed as skilled workers (see table 1.3).

Table 1.3. Black Workers Recorded in the 1900 US Census

Work Classification	All Workers	Males	Females
Boardinghouse Operator	3	1	2
Chair maker	1	1	—
Cook	7	4	3
Domestic Servant	25	4	21
Dressmaker	1	0	1
Driller	4	4	—
Farmer	1	1	—
Hack driver	5	5	—
Hotel owner	4	3	1
Hotel worker	3	2	1
Laborer	105	98	7
Machinist	1	1	—
Shoemaker	1	1	—
Waiter	34	34	—
Total	195	159	36

Adapted from the US Census for 1900. (See page 327, note 59.)

In analyzing table 1.3, census enumerators identified how 195 Black Niagarans earned their livelihood (or at least a portion of it). Of the 195 workers, 159 were men, and 36 were women. Most Black workers were classified as laborers, followed by waiters. Although it is not listed clearly, most of the waiters were probably employed in one of the numerous hotels that operated in Niagara Falls. One Black farmer, sixty-year-old George Martin, was recorded as living in the town of Niagara, which bordered the city of Niagara Falls. Martin was also listed in the US Census for 1910, where he was recorded at the same residence as being seventy years of age.[61]

This expansive labor force can be attributed to the significant increase in the Black population from 1890 to 1900. As shown in Table 1.1, at least 159 Blacks lived in Niagara Falls in 1890. By 1900 that figure had increased to 344. Although this number represented only 1.76 percent of the overall Niagara Falls population, it was a substantial increase of 185 individuals, representing a 116 percent increase. In the period after slavery, this population growth represented the first major influx of Blacks into Niagara Falls, and employment constructing the tunnel is what brought them to the area.[62]

The tunnel was a passage from the Edward Dean Adams Power Plant (see figure 1.3) under the city of Niagara Falls to land below the cataracts. The purpose of this tunnel was to divert water from the Niagara River through the tunnel to a point beyond the cataracts in order to generate electricity at the Edward Dean Adams Power Plant. Construction of the tunnel began in 1890 and ended before 1900. Many workers from various ethnic backgrounds worked on the tunnel, two hundred in the first phase

Figure 1.3. Edward Dean Adams Power Plant, 1910. Niagara Falls Public Library. Fair use.

of its construction and eight hundred in the final phase, with Italians playing a crucial role in laying the bricks.[63] Blacks played a significant role in constructing the tunnel. John Troy, a Black community leader who was highly respected by both Blacks and Whites, was one of the people who worked on this project.[64]

Another Black worker who labored on the Tunnel Project in Niagara Falls and then worked on a similar but smaller project in Niagara Falls, Ontario, compared the treatment of Black workers in both places.

> When we comes along de street [in Niagara Falls, New York] dey runs in de houses and closes de doahs. So fa' as I can see dey's afraid of us, count some of our fellows got such rep' tation for letting blood on dis side. I has to laff' self sometimes, but doan't think we looks over good in our dirty oil skin.[65]

On the Canadian side, citizens did not initially react negatively to the Black workers,[66] probably because the workers were few in number. Also Blacks had not been stereotyped in the way they had been from 1850 to 1861, when they had a more prominent presence and were generally fugitive slaves in Canada.[67] Thus, historically speaking, prejudice did confront Blacks in Canada; however, when compared to the United States, it was not uniform across communities and wholly institutionalized in governmental bodies.[68]

Although early signs of racial distinctiveness existed in Niagara Falls, New York, these would become more pervasive during and after the Second Great Migration (1941–1945).[69] Nonetheless, soon after the tunnel was completed, the 1910 US Census indicated that 266 Blacks were living in Niagara Falls, a decrease since 1900 of seventy-eight individuals. This adds credence to the idea that several Blacks had migrated (or immigrated from Canada) to the area, specifically to work on the Tunnel Project. Table 1.4 reflects some of the changes.

Compared to the census results recorded in 1900, census enumerators identified fewer Black Niagarans who reported how they made their living. One hundred Black men worked, along with thirty-four women. Like the census results of 1900, most employed Black Niagarans, fifty in all, worked as laborers. Domestic servants comprised the next largest group, followed by laundresses. Six entrepreneurs were recorded: two barbers, one proprietor of a rooming house, one farmer, one restaurant owner, and one saloon proprietor. Of the four individuals in 1900 who rented

Table 1.4. Black Workers Recorded in the 1910 US Census

Job	All Workers	Males	Females
Barber	2	2	—
Bartender	1	1	—
Carpenter	1	1	—
Cook	3	1	2
Driver	4	4	—
Domestic servant	15	1	14
Driller	2	2	—
Farm owner	1	1	—
Hotel worker	1	1	—
Laborer	50	47	3
Laundress	14	—	14
Nurse	1		1
Painter	3	3	—
Porter	15	15	—
Proprietor of rooming house	1	1	—
Restaurant owner	1	1	—
Saloon proprietor	1	1	—
Teamster	7	7	—
Waiter	11	11	—
Total	134	100	34

Adapted from the US Census for 1910. (See page 327, note 61.)

out rooms, Anderson Fayette was the only one identified in 1910. In 1900 he was listed as a boardinghouse operator, while in 1910 he was defined as a proprietor of a rooming house. In 1900 Fayette lived in Ward 1, and in 1910 he lived in Ward 4.[70] Ward 1 was in the southeastern section of Niagara Falls. Ward 4 was also in the southeastern section of town but farther east of Ward 1. The census enumerator did not include Charlotte Dett in his count, although she still managed her seventeen-room rooming house. Even so, three skilled tradespersons were recorded: two barbers and one carpenter. One professional employee, a nurse, was listed. For the first time, Blacks appeared in the census as teamsters, seven in total.

Jerry Plato and Arthur Brown were two men who stood out. Jerry Plato was born in Niagara Falls, Ontario, and moved to Niagara Falls, New York, to seek better employment opportunities. He was recorded as being thirty-five years old and a janitor (or laborer).[71] He later contributed greatly toward progressive activities, being an early impactful leader in the formation and development of the Black Niagaran community. He would reside in the city of Niagara Falls for sixty-five years, actively participating in the Masons at Electric City Lodge No. 49, becoming a thirty-third-degree Mason, a founder and member of St. John's AME Church, and a board member of the Niagara Community Center.[72] Arthur Brown was listed in both the 1900 and 1910 censuses.[73] In 1900 he was listed as seventeen years of age, and in 1910 he was twenty-seven. In 1904 he began working for the city as a sanitation worker, a post that by 1949 he still held with no thoughts of retirement.[74] He then was acknowledged as the oldest city employee in terms of service rendered.

Additional Early Signs of Community: Political, Social, and Religious

Unlike the recorded work history of Black Niagarans, information on the social, religious, and political activities of the small Black community is sketchy for the first forty-five years after the Civil War. There are several reasons for this scarcity. First, because the Black community was small and on the fringes of society, there were few records available. As table 1.1 indicates, a small percentage of Blacks resided in Niagara Falls from 1865 to 1910. Obviously, people who lived during that time and who could have been good sources of oral history are no longer alive. Second, the census reports for these early years revealed many individuals labeled as mulattoes (or persons with one White and one Black parent),[75] which could mean they saw themselves as part of the larger community because one of their parents was White. Third, evidence seems to indicate that no distinct Black church existed during this time; no physical church edifice existed that brought Black community members together to worship. Conversely, in neighboring Buffalo, historian Lillian Williams uncovered that Black Buffaloians in 1831 demonstrated early signs of community with the establishment of their first church: the Vine Street African Methodist Episcopal Church.[76]

Other signs of community are evident. In 1872 the Colored Republicans scheduled a meeting for September 26 at Grant's Hall.[77] William H. Johnson of Albany, who was chairman of the Colored Republican State Committee, and William F. Butler of New York City were slated to speak. The Colored Glee Club was on the program to sing some of their favorite campaign songs. Twenty years later, the Colored Republicans held a meeting in Allen's Hall.[78] They were then called the Wide Awake Colored Republican Club. The Colored Glee Club was again on the program. The keynote speaker for the meeting was Buffalo physician Dr. H. H. Lewis, who spoke for about an hour and a half and kept his large audience's attention with serious discussion but also anecdotes and humor.[79] "At the conclusion of Dr. Lewis's remarks the Glee Club rendered another selection and all united in three hearty cheers for Harrison and Reid."[80] Dr. Lewis's presence, along with past and upcoming events, exemplified the connection Black Niagarans had with Black Buffalonians.

Five years later the Colored 400 Dance was held at Crick's Hall.[81] Invitations had been sent out weeks in advance, and guests came from Canada, and from Buffalo, Lockport, and other cities as far away as Cleveland, Ohio. An orchestra played for at least thirty-six dances, from 9 p.m. to 12 a.m. Mrs. Anderson Fayette of Niagara Falls, whose husband was the proprietor of the hotel noted earlier, was nominated belle of the ball.[82] The dance was dubbed a great success and one of the best-managed affairs ever held in Niagara Falls.

In 1893 Niagara Falls, New York, received a family that would contribute significantly to the history of Niagara Falls: the Detts.[83] The family initially consisted of Robert and Charlotte Dett, the parents of Sam, Arthur, Harriet, and R. Nathaniel Dett. It is believed that Charlotte's mother, Harriet Washington, who lived with the family, fled to Canada as a fugitive slave via the Underground Railroad. She was musically inclined and sang spirituals to the children, which they (especially R. Nathaniel) never forgot.[84] She stayed at her daughter's tourist house after following her family to the United States. Arthur never made it to Niagara Falls, New York, as a result of a Halloween night escapade. In 1889 Arthur and his friends played pranks on some of the area merchants, jokingly tampering with some of their property. One merchant, who saw his fence being taken down by a group of children, rushed into his house, got his shotgun, and fired it at Arthur. Arthur was hit and later died in the hospital. This tragedy devastated the Dett family and perhaps influenced them to move to the United States.[85] The Dett's infant daughter, Harriet, lived only two years before she died.[86] Eventually Robert and Charlotte separated. Robert moved away from the tourist home and obtained his own rooming house. The responsibilities of raising the surviving children fell to Charlotte. She, her mother, and the children resided on Second Street, where railroad tracks went past their back porch, and Robert stayed at 333 Main Street, not far from his family (see figure 1.4).[87]

Figure 1.4. Rear view of boarding house, 1900. Niagara Falls Public Library. Fair use.

By 1900 a Black community was strongly evident in Niagara Falls. A Black Baptist group was conducting religious services in Crick's Hall and making plans to build their own house of worship.[88] Leaders of this group were the Reverend B. B. B. Johnson and his wife, who was also an ordained minister. They had recently relocated from Saginaw, Michigan, and had a home on Erie Avenue, in an area where clusters of Blacks were settling. For a long time this area was the main thoroughfare of the Black community. In discussing his prospective role in Niagara Falls, Johnson commented, "I am sure I will find plenty to do in Niagara Falls. There are 300 colored people here and they are greatly in need of a religious revival."[89] Moreover, he felt that within a short time he could bring 125 Black Niagarans to join his fold. African American urban studies often reveal that churches are the first communal institutions that Black citizens establish when initiating efforts to build communities.[90] Churches have always been hubs of Black communities' social, political, and cultural life.[91]

Johnson and his wife were mentioned first in the *Niagara Falls Gazette*, April 9, 1900, after arriving in Niagara Falls on January 5, 1900.[92] The notice stated that the "Negro Baptists" of the city were going to have a service at Crick's Hall, followed by baptisms of fifty people in Loop Drive Lake on the Niagara Reservation. The cornerstone for the first Black church in Niagara Falls would then be laid.[93] The church was to be called the Second Baptist Church of Niagara Falls, located on Twelfth Street. At the actual event, eight people were baptized, and about four thousand people from throughout Niagara County and other areas witnessed the baptisms.[94] The *Niagara Falls Gazette* labeled this activity "a reform movement for the Negroes of Niagara Falls."[95]

Reverend Johnson and his wife emerged as leaders in the Black community. The next month after the baptismal services, the Johnsons made plans to bring Booker T. Washington, D. Augustus Straker, and John J. Jones to Niagara Falls to address residents of the city for the Fourth of July.[96] These were major Black leaders: Washington was the most prominent of the three men and the most influential Black leader. Johnson may have known him personally, because like Washington, Johnson had once lived in Virginia and attended Hampton Institute.[97] Besides having these speakers inform Niagarans about the status of African Americans and how national events affected them, Johnson hoped to generate enough income to pay off the debts of his new church. He had obtained confirmation that each speaker would be present, and he estimated that about twenty-thousand people from New York State and other locales would attend the Jubilee Celebration.

A little over a month later, on June 26, 1900, before the Jubilee Celebration and eight days before the Fourth of July, the *Niagara Falls Gazette* reported that Johnson would give up his pulpit until the debts of the Second Baptist Church were paid. His wife would assume the pulpit until he had raised the funds to pay off the church's debts, some of which he had contracted on his personal account.[98] Johnson told a *Gazette* representative, "It is discouraging to stand up in your pulpit and counsel your congregation to lead an honest life and pay their honest debts, and then have a bill presented to you the minute you step down from the pulpit."[99] Johnson, who had labored hard for the improvement of his race in Niagara Falls, wanted to direct his energy toward eliminating the church's debt. He and others hoped and expected that the coming Fourth of July Jubilee Celebration would contribute significantly to this effort.

The celebration was not the great success it was projected to be, largely because the prominent speakers were unable to attend. Moreover, it rained. Nonetheless, the celebration was partially successful. The event was well attended and began with a parade led by Robert Dett of the

Keystone Hotel. Following Dett was the Tunnel District Blues Band, led by Reverend Johnson, who was wearing his sword and military uniform. The Reverend Hatchet of London, Ontario, spoke at the grounds. Then the Declaration of Independence and the Emancipation Proclamation were read, followed by a patriotic address by Johnson.[100] After the official procedures were over, the visitors enjoyed the games and one another's company.

A small sum was obtained for the Second Baptist Church. Johnson furnished the *Daily Cataract-Journal*, another local Niagara Falls newspaper, with an accounting of income that was raised by his church for the 1900–1901 fiscal year.[101] In July, the month of the Jubilee Celebration, $243 was raised, by far the most money obtained in any single month. According to Johnson, it was still not enough to cover the church's debts.

After 1901, Johnson does not appear in any of the Niagara Falls newspapers. Rumor has it that he left town and kept the funds raised by his congregation that were slated for the church's debts.[102] Even so, for a while he was given credit for ministering to and bringing peace and order in the Tunnel District, a dilapidated, poverty-stricken area located near the Edward Dean Adams plant and composed of newly arrived immigrants, poor native White Niagarans, and African Americans.[103] Had Johnson and his wife been successful in establishing their church, they would have been recognized as leaders of a major community institution.

In 1906 St. John's AME Church became the next Black church established in Niagara Falls. Because the construction of the original Second Baptist Church was never completed, St. John's is the first established, ongoing African American church in Niagara Falls. "Early in 1906, a small number of AMEs began holding service in a home on Eleventh Street."[104] At the request of the members, Reverend Joseph Styles, who was Presiding Elder of the Manhattan District, came to Niagara Falls and organized the church. Reverend A. L. Wilson was appointed pastor. "The congregation [then] moved to 306 Niagara Street, but continued to search for a more appropriate site. The members found property at 477 Main Street, and the church was incorporated as St. John's African Methodist Episcopal Church."[105] As the decades proceeded, beginning with Reverend Wilson's leadership, St. John's continued to grow and positively impact Niagara Falls. Hence, like Reverend B. B. B. Johnson's church, St. John's in these early years served not only as a place of fellowship but also as an all-purpose institution for its members.[106] Adults networked there, encouraged one another, and observed their children socializing with other children.

Early Racial Challenges

Forty-five years after the Civil War and after the formation of St. John's AME Church, no monumental racial problems existed in Niagara Falls, unlike in the South. Southern towns were still experiencing the aftermath of Reconstruction and the early wrath of the Jim Crow era.[107] The reason for Niagara Falls's lack of racial tension was because the Black population was initially only a small percentage of the overall population, and most lived on society's margins.[108] Research verifies this pattern: when Black population figures are low in or near predominantly White living spaces (e.g., neighborhoods, communities, and cities) peaceful race relations usually prevail; however, any noticeable expansion in the Black population frequently fueled racial conflict.[109] In the South, however, where most Blacks lived, they more visibly competed with Whites for a livelihood and in some places made up about one third or more of the population.[110] For example, after 1890, Chicago had an ever-expanding Black population that confronted White fears of black incursion into their claimed spaces. The result was violence, including a major 1919 riot.[111]

Although there were no serious racial problems in the Niagara Falls of 1914, evidence indicates that Black Niagarans felt they were often unfairly treated. A 1901 *Niagara Falls Gazette* article titled "Negroes Object" reported that Blacks in Niagara Falls and Buffalo were incensed by the treatment that was accorded President McKinley's assassin, Leon Czolgosz.

> "Had a Negro shot the President," said a soldier who had fought at San Juan Hill with Theodore Roosevelt, "no power on earth could have protected him from the violence of the mob, and yet here is a man caught red handed in the act and he is protected and will be given a trial and perhaps escape with a sentence of a few years. And why? Simply because he has a white face."[112]

These statements reflect how many Black Niagarans were sensitive to the fact that they were marginalized in society and that a different standard of justice would be applied to them in certain situations, even in Niagara Falls. Furthermore, one *Gazette* interviewee pointed to the fact that a Black man named James B. Parker had knocked down the president's assassin and that this incident should have worked wonders in lifting the prejudice against the Black race.[113]

During the early periods, 1850 to 1914, racial problems existed in Niagara Falls but on a small scale, almost to the extent of not being readily detectable.[114] This fits the pattern of other northern cities when their Black populations were scant compared to their White counterparts.[115] Nonetheless, local newspapers from 1850 to 1985 clearly indicate that Black Niagarans were considered to be of a lower caste than the general White population.[116] This situation appears to have been an accepted "fact," which is evident from the way Blacks were portrayed in the newspapers. Their race was usually mentioned, especially regarding alleged criminal activities. A newspaper reader would get the impression that although Negroes were citizens, it was best to keep an ever-watchful eye on them for the well-being of the community, especially as their population figures grew with time.

Similar to when Black Niagarans quickly gathered in 1847 to free a certain enslaved female in their midst, they rallied together to resist unfair treatment, even for those of lesser stature, which reflected collectivist behavior. Galleon Hobbs's story is a case in point. In 1904 he was characterized as a tramp. He was alleged to have been begging on Falls Street, a major thoroughfare, going in and out of saloons and stores and confronting pedestrians on the streets in the solicitation of alms.[117] One of the people he pestered was the head of the police department, Commissioner Level. Hobbs was taken into custody for questioning and then released. A short time later, he was reported to have been begging in the Tunnel District. Police officers Lalone and Magner approached and questioned Hobbs. Being extremely dissatisfied with his answers and offended by the obvious disregard Hobbs had for them, the officers attempted to arrest him. However, Hobbs resisted. As they tried to subdue him, Hobbs put up a vigorous fight in which "he battled like a tiger and several times attempted to bite Officer Lalone."[118] Officer Lalone eventually hit Hobbs several times over the head with a billyclub, which finally forced Hobbs to relent and allowed the officers to take him into custody.

A few days later a report circulated among Black Niagarans in the Tunnel District. It said that Hobbs had died from his injuries and that the police were attempting to cover up their actions. It further stated that Hobbs's body had been packed with quicklime in the basement of the police station. "The promoters of this subscription list gave it out that the lives of every [N]egro in the city would be imperiled unless the police were taught a vigorous lesson in this case."[119] Many in the community were upset and wanted action. A community representative was sent to the police station to ascertain what specifically had been done to Hobbs. This representative was told that Hobbs was sent to the county jail in Lockport. This person went to Lockport and upon speaking with an authority there felt that he was being misled. With this new information, the Black Niagaran community hired an attorney to ensure that justice prevailed for Hobbs and, in turn, for themselves. The attorney was able to establish that Hobbs had not, in fact, been murdered but had been sentenced to several days in jail. Nonetheless, the Black Niagaran community, with Hobbs's strong consent, brought a civil suit for damages against officers Lalone and Magner, showing that they would energetically fight for their respect and dignity. This collectivist action underscores a budding community refusing to be passive in response to what it perceived as racial injustice. They considered Hobbs, although of lower status, as part of the entire Black community and interpreted an unjust act upon him as an attack on all Black Niagarans. This collectivist behavior manifested itself again during other periods in Black Niagaran history.

Representing national issues and occurring across the border in Ontario, Canada, in 1905, scholar-activist W. E. B. Du Bois and activist William Monroe Trotter organized the Niagara Movement, another assembly for respect and dignity.[120] Twenty-nine men answered their call to gather and organize by participating in a series of meetings in Fort Erie and Niagara Falls, Canada. The aim was to create and implement a civil rights platform. Originally, the meetings were scheduled to be held at a hotel in Buffalo, New York. But the group encountered discrimination, which compelled Du Bois and Trotter to hold the meetings in Canada. This was symbolic because Canada had been a host country that opened its borders to fugitive slaves during the days of slavery and the Underground Railroad. Canada represented freedom for the fleeing fugitive slaves and for the men of this assemblage. The Niagara Movement was diametrically opposed to the hegemonic leadership that Booker T. Washington, a so-called accommodationist, held over Black America.[121] Historians usually describe this as evidence of a major schism in the strategies of Black leadership.[122] Unlike Washington's followers, Niagara Movement participants advocated that African Americans must always openly fight for their civil and political rights until these rights were secured. Members of the Niagara Movement promoted such ideas as freedom of speech and criticism, an unfettered and unsubsidized press, manhood suffrage, the abolition of all caste distinctions based simply on race and color, recognition of the principles of human brotherhood as a practical present creed, recognition of the highest and best human training as not strictly reserved for one class or race, a belief in the dignity of labor, and a united effort to realize these ideals under wise and courageous leadership.[123] After this initial meeting, the Niagara Movement met annually until about 1908. Then the movement disbanded due to internal conflicts and external pressures.

Surprisingly, no Black Niagarans directly participated in the 1905 gathering. Nonetheless, two people who lived near Niagara Falls, New York, were involved. These leaders were William H. Talbert and Nathan Mossell. Organizational discussions had occurred at Talbert's home in Buffalo, which was next door to Michigan Avenue Baptist Church, an acknowledged Underground Railroad station.[124] Talbert was a Buffalo municipal government bookkeeper, realtor, and active parishioner of Michigan Avenue Baptist Church. He was the husband of Mary Talbert, a prominent activist and a dear friend of Charlotte Dett. Nathan Mossell was born in nearby Hamilton, Ontario. His parents, who had been free Blacks during the slavery era, left the United States in 1853 and moved to Hamilton. They later moved to Lockport, New York, where Mossell spent much of his early childhood and teenage years.[125] Mossell was living in Philadelphia, Pennsylvania, and practicing medicine at the time of the first Niagara Movement meeting. He was one of the twenty-nine men who responded to Du Bois and Trotter's call. Years later he would organize a local branch of the National Association for the Advancement of Colored People (NAACP) in Philadelphia. Both men probably frequented Niagara Falls, New York, prior to the 1905 gathering.

One year before the initial Niagara Movement meeting, Mary Talbert visited Niagara Falls, accompanied by Booker T. Washington's wife, Margaret Murray Washington.[126] They traveled together by train from a National Association of Colored Women's meeting held in St. Louis, Missouri. Washington was vice president of this organization and Talbert the secretary. Washington had planned to stay at Talbert's house before traveling on to her summer home in South Weymouth, Massachusetts. With them was Davidson, Margaret's stepson. Because Davidson had never seen the actual waterfalls of Niagara Falls, Talbert escorted her guests to Niagara Falls, New York, where they were swarmed by newspaper reporters who sought interviews from Mrs. Washington.

These contacts between Margret Murray Washington and Mary Talbert underscore the intertwining complexity of relationships between the supporters of the Niagara Movement and those of Booker T. Washington. Mary Talbert worked and socialized with Margaret Murray Washington and therefore had a connection to Booker T. Washington.[127] He held some influence over her, and she greatly respected him. Washington stayed at the Talberts' home on one of his trips to Buffalo,[128] and Talbert gladly served as the keynote speaker at a Buffalo memorial service honoring Washington after his death. She titled her address "Dr. Washington as a Wise Educator."[129] Simultaneously, she had a strong association with W. E. B. Du Bois, which not only involved Du Bois's participation in a Niagara Movement organizational meeting at her home but would eventually involve his participation in the formation of a Buffalo branch of the NAACP. Talbert, much like Mary Church Terrell (also a major figure in the Black Women's Club Movement) was more overtly activist after Booker T. Washington's death, and her actions and influence were felt not only in Buffalo but also in Niagara Falls. These national leaders greatly impacted the local Niagara Falls branch of the National Negro Business League, a division of the national organization founded by Booker T. Washington.

In 1905 African Americans nationwide felt that their best chances for obtaining and maintaining their political and civil rights were through the Republican Party. They generally adhered to Frederick Douglass's stance that for African Americans the Republican Party was the ship while all other political parties represented the sea.[130] This view prevailed until Franklin D. Roosevelt's 1936 presidential reelection bid. In 1900, for example, Republican president William McKinley ran for reelection against Democratic challenger William Jennings Bryan. This was a rematch of the historic 1896 election. McKinley won, mainly due to US success in the Spanish-American War and an overall improvement in the economy. Prior to the election results, two Niagara Falls citizens waged a bet in Terry-Berry's Saloon on Willow Avenue.[131] Black Niagaran Robert Richmond bet Richard Titus, a White patron, that McKinley would win and that if McKinley did not win, he would give Titus a ride around the block in a wheelbarrow. Titus willingly acceded to do the same if he lost the bet. Richmond was thirty-five years old, worked as a teamster, and lived on Pierce Avenue.[132] A newspaper reporter, describing the affair's outcome when the bet was to be paid, wrote:

> A large number of people had assembled when the principals appeared. A wheelbarrow, gaily decorated with bunting, had been furnished, and with the accompaniment of tin horns and a couple of drums, Titus wheeled his victorious opponent over the course that had been selected. Those who had gathered along the route set off a considerable quantity of fireworks

and cheered and encouraged Titus as he wheeled his African brother along with feelings that can better be imagined than described.[133]

An editorial in the *Niagara Falls Gazette* titled "Negro and Democracy" even accentuated that it would be suicidal for colored men to vote for Bryan.[134]

> They have nothing to hope for from the Democratic Party, which has disfranchised them in the [South] and which professes to regard them as unfit for the ballot anywhere. The only chance for the [N]egro is with the Republican Party, and it will be a sad day for the [N]egro when a Republican president will be elected without the votes of [N]egroes having helped to place him in power.[135]

The editorial also emphasized that Bryan approved of African American disfranchisement in the South and that his attitude would not change if he were elected president with African American support, as southern Democrats regarded African Americans voting for their candidate as an endorsement of their treatment in the South. The editorial concluded that "it is impossible to believe that any [African American] who has studied intelligently the history of his race will go into the voting booth and cast a ballot in favor of Bryan."[136] Some years later Charlotte Dett "[would serve] as a Republican committee [member] from old First Ward's second district, . . . [by being] on the Women's Republican Club executive board."[137] Black Niagarans, like African Americans in many places, found it difficult to relinquish their support for the Republican Party. Although the Republican Party had abandoned African Americans during and after Reconstruction, in 1900 most of them were still loyal to the party that they saw as having helped terminate slavery, especially while Abraham Lincoln—its former leader—was still then viewed generally as the Great Emancipator.

In 1900 Black Niagarans were politically organized mostly in the southern end of town. Although they were scattered throughout four wards, according to the 1900 US Census reports, most Blacks resided in Ward 1.[138] Even with this developing community, no ghetto or Black poverty-stricken slum area had developed, as Black Niagarans were geographically scattered throughout the city. The neighboring city of Buffalo experienced similar results. In 1900 census takers recorded 1,698 Blacks residing in Buffalo, constituting less than 1 percent of the population.[139] Many lived east of the downtown business district.[140] However, as in Niagara Falls, they were not restricted to any specific area, living in several wards throughout the city. Even so, with Niagara Falls's first ward containing sections of such major streets as Buffalo Avenue, Erie Avenue, Prospect Street, Falls Street, Second and Third Streets, Black Niagarans daily crossed these streets, interacting with each other and passing on community lore that would be treasured by contemporary and future generations (see figures 1.5 and 1.6).

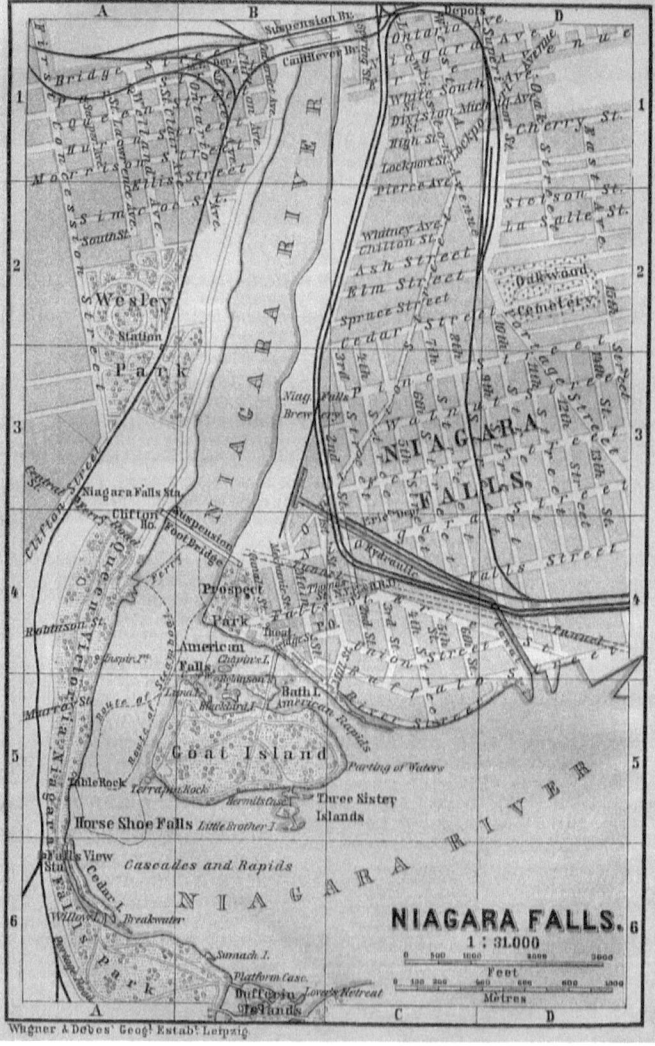

Figure 1.5. Antique map of Niagara Falls, 1890. Niagara County Historical Society. Fair use.

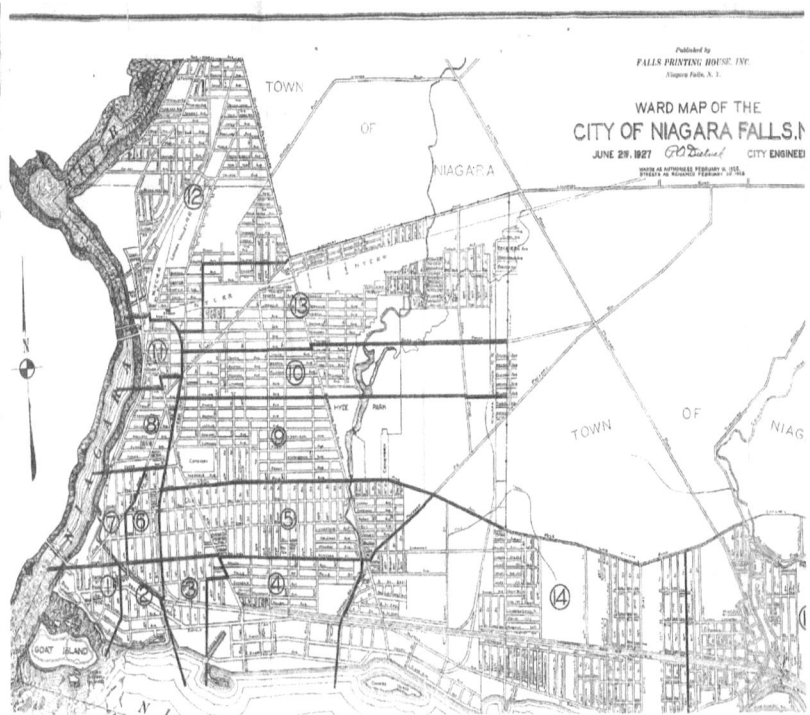

Figure 1.6. Ward map of Niagara Falls, 1940. Courtesy of the *Niagara Falls Gazette*.

Goat Island was near sections of these streets. Elizabeth Brown Coleman, who was a member of one of the early Black Niagaran families who lived during the late nineteenth century, remembered walking on Goat Island as a young girl, when Indians wove leather moccasins and peacocks and rabbits roamed free.[141] Her parents were Charles and Gertrude Brown, who amazingly, had twenty-five children. She may have known or heard of Charlotte Dett, who was influential in local Republican Party politics. She was not allowed in local theaters during these days, due to discrimination; so, she would go to Goat Island where she felt relaxed and happy.[142]

In 1910 the US Census reports listed Charles Brown as being thirty-five years old, living in Ward 2, and working as a laborer.[143] At this time Black Niagarans were still scattered throughout Cataract City but were predominantly in Wards 1, 2, and 5.[144] They were more spread out compared to 1900, though, as indicated earlier, their population figures had decreased significantly. Some of the streets in Ward 1 crossed over into Ward 2, such as Buffalo Avenue and Erie Avenue. Fourth Street through Eighth Streets were also in Ward 2. Ward 5, conversely, consisted of such streets as Monroe Avenue, Orleans Avenue, Livingston Avenue, Ely Avenue, and Dudley Avenue. All these wards usually consisted of a diverse mix of immigrants who had relocated to Niagara Falls. This diverse immigrant population was often in closer proximity to their African American neighbors than to the native White community. In Ward 2, for example, where the Tunnel Town section was located, Black Niagarans lived among such immigrant groups as Syrians, Russians, Russian-Poles, Lithuanians, Italians, German Poles, Bulgarians, Austrians, Austro-Poles, Armenians, and Albanians. Of these the Russian-Poles, Italians, and Austro-Poles were the largest ethnic groups.[145]

In 1910 a man named Gideon Lee lived in Ward 2.[146] He was the son of a respected woman known as Aunty Lee.[147] Aunty Lee came to Niagara Falls from Virginia after the Civil War, and it was believed that she was an ex-slave freed by the North's victory. She made Niagara Falls her home and worked as a domestic servant for part of her life.[148] Aunty Lee may have joined a relative or husband who escaped from slavery and resided in the region. Historians have found that ex-slaves often resided in the counties where they had been enslaved, unless they were seeking to live with loved ones from whom they had been separated or if the place they migrated from was unbearable.[149] Harriet Tubman told Benjamin Drew, a researcher who interviewed many fugitive slaves who fled to Canada, that the fugitive slaves preferred to stay in areas where they were raised but could not do so because of slavery.[150] That was where their loved ones and friends were. No one will ever know what brought Aunty Lee to Niagara Falls, a city in which she felt comfortable raising her son, because the personal records are scarce. But we do know that toward the end of her life she resided at 1107 East Falls Street, and it was said that most residents of the city revered her. She was considered a great citizen, and it was speculated that she was nearly a hundred years old when she died in 1906. A Miss Townsend, a former employer, paid her funeral expenses.[151] In contrast, Aunty Lee's son, Gideon Lee, was not regarded in the same manner.[152] He drove for the William Young Carting Company and was often perceived as an irresponsible drug user. He died about six years after his mother passed. A doctor stated the cause of his death was due to cocaine overuse, which led to heart failure.[153] Unlike for his mother, there was not much fanfare for him when he died. Even still, he was acknowledged as being the son of Aunty Lee, one of the city's best-known characters who had been a Niagaran for many years.

In 1910 Black Niagarans organized a Masonic lodge for fraternal and benevolent purposes.[154] Jerry Plato, John White, Franklin Wright, Royal Palmer, and other community leaders requested from the Grand Lodge of the State of New York a charter of dispensation, which was partly a mandate granting them the right to establish a lodge in Niagara Falls.[155] On May 25, 1909, lodge rooms at the corner of North Avenue and Mark Lane were dedicated. This ceremony was conducted by Henry A. Spencer of Albany, who was the Grand Master of Colored Masons of the State.[156] Masonic dignitaries from other cities, such as Rochester, Buffalo, Troy, and New York City were also present. The name of their Masonic lodge, the Electric City Lodge No. 49, meant that they were the forty-ninth lodge organized in the State of New York and part of the Prince Hall Masonic Order.[157]

Through the issuance of their charter, the Black Masons of Niagara Falls gained a strong identity through promoting respectable middle-class values. Members were required to acknowledge the importance of education and to display public behavioral decorum.[158] The Black Masons were proud members who knew Prince Hall's history and felt that they were continuing a rich and glorious tradition. They fraternized with one another and encouraged others whom they considered worthy to become members. They were even open to establishing a relationship with the White Masonic orders of Niagara Falls. They taught their members about self-help, responsibility, and race progression, encouraging them to be proactive leaders not only in their families and communities but in broader society as well.[159] Members could earn degrees that reflected their knowledge and growth within the Masonic order, the thirty-third degree being the highest one could earn. In 1912, a few years after its formation, new officers were elected. Jerry Plato was elected worshipful master, James Douglass was senior warden, Frank Little was junior warden, John White was treasurer, and Henry Fayette, a hotel keeper, was secretary.[160] Electric City Lodge No. 49 began during these early periods and would continuously grow over time.

Jerry Plato practiced the leadership edict of the Masons by looking out for the best interests of his community.[161] He sought the assistance of a Judge Piper to rid his community of a traveling Black evangelist named Abraham Lincoln. "[Lincoln] operated [in Niagara Falls] . . . was in police court on complaint of a Maggie Johnson who charged him with breaking down the door of her home."[162] Apart from his skin color, he looked like his famous namesake. Jerry Plato, who wanted to make Lincoln's stay in

Cataract City as brief as possible, stressed to Judge Piper that the traveling evangelist, who claimed to be an elder in the African Methodist Church, was an imposter attempting to live off the gullibility of citizens. They had been misused once by Lincoln and were adamant that it was not going to happen again to them or to other Niagarans. Lincoln informed Judge Piper that he had references from prominent citizens concerning his work and character. Judge Piper called Lincoln into his chambers and admonished him for collecting money without authority and advised him to leave the area if he wished to continue his actions.[163] Plato and other prominent community members seemed pleased with the judge's decision. The way Plato and others gathered to protect themselves against Lincoln is analogous to how a number of Black Niagarans organized to protect their humanity symbolized by the Galleon Hobbs case. Excluding alliance leadership, Plato's leadership activities fit all the descriptions of the Black Niagaran leadership.

Familial, Educational, and Recreational Dynamics of a Budding Community

According to interviews and conversations, Black Niagarans like Jerry Plato believed in marriage and the family as crucial dimensions of life and community development. Scholars such as E. Franklin Frazier and Daniel P. Moynihan offered an early paradigm for analyzing and interpreting the postslavery Black American family.[164] They vigorously argued that slavery and generations of racism had harmed the Black family, drastically altering its original structure and causing it to become a matriarchy. Enslaved Africans were brought from societies in which the extended family structure was the norm. These scholars posit that colonial slavery followed by antebellum slavery broke this pattern and made the matriarchal family structure a common, even dominant, prototype. But scholars John Blassingame, Herbert Gutman, Robert Staples, Andrew Billingsley, and many others vehemently disagree with Frazier and Moynihan's thesis.[165] According to the 1910 Census, of 266 Black Niagarans, 151 were men, and 115 were women; atypically, males outnumbered females. Most women of marrying age were in conjugal relationships: of 98 females 15 years or older, 59 were married, 23 were widowed, 2 were divorced, and 14 were single. These data signify that marriage was valued highly among women. Regarding males 15 years or older, 64 were married, 10 were widowed, 3 were divorced, and 53 were single. Marriage was valued highly among men, although the women had a larger pool of available mates from which to choose. Women generally stayed at home and cared for their children. This arrangement was a powerful Victorian value evident in the late nineteenth and early twentieth centuries and beyond. One African American man, for instance, did not fulfill his duties as a husband and provide his wife with consistent living quarters. His wife made a formal complaint before a magistrate who reassured her that he would do everything in his power to make her husband perform his duties.[166] Husbands were considered the breadwinners and presumably heads of their households, which contradicts the idea that the early Black family in Niagara Falls was matriarchal. In all probability, other family arrangements existed, but the cultural norms of the time, census data, and oral accounts do not conclusively point to other family patterns.

Census reports also convey that by 1910 at least fifty-nine youths—nineteen years old or younger—lived in Niagara Falls.[167] Most of those who were of school age probably attended neighborhood schools that were in or near their wards, such as the Third Street School and Niagara Falls Public High School. In these schools Black Niagarans were usually the only African Americans in their classes and one of the few in the entire school. How they were treated often hinged on the learning environment established by their teachers and administrators, as well as their personalities and those of their White peers.[168] Nonetheless, they were exposed to the same education as the rest of the students from predominantly working-class backgrounds.[169]

During the summers when school was out, families took inexpensive outings to Buffalo, Rochester, Lockport, or a similar locale. They continued to venture into Canada. Black Niagarans visited such places as Niagara Falls, Ontario, St. Catherines, Hamilton, Toronto, and other Canadian towns and cities. Many people traveled back and forth from Canada to the United States because they had friends and relatives in both countries. Jerry Plato, for example, had moved to the United States from Canada, but he had a sister in Canada.[170] R. Nathaniel Dett, who was born in Canada, was allowed to finish his secondary schooling there when his family moved to the United States.[171] His family at times still attended the British Methodist Episcopal Church on Peer Street in Niagara Falls, Ontario.[172] This church, built by fugitive slaves, still operates today. Census data for Niagara Falls, New York, clearly show that Black Niagarans married Canadians and resided with their spouses in the United

States. Aside from Canada's proximity, these intimate interactions could also occur because the borders were not nearly as restrictive as they are today, and many people possessed a strong desire to travel outside their immediate surroundings.

Political Involvement and Political Challenges

By 1912 Woodrow Wilson was elected president of the United States. Although he had Black supporters, he did not gain the Black vote. He did gain the support of two prominent leaders who had frequented Niagara Falls—W. E. B. Du Bois and William Monroe Trotter. Wilson gained their support because he had assured them that he wanted to see justice rendered to their race. They were also impressed that he had strong academic credentials. However, when Wilson, a Democrat born in Virginia and raised in South Carolina, obtained his powerful position, it was business as usual for African Americans.[173] Federal buildings and agencies remained segregated during his administration. To protest these actions, a delegation of African Americans led by William Trotter met with the president at the White House. Wilson said that he felt that the separation of races was best because it would reduce racial conflict. Trotter vehemently disagreed, prompting President Wilson, who was visibly annoyed, to state that he would no longer meet with the group if Trotter remained their spokesperson.[174] In the Black press Trotter was venerated and portrayed as a hero.

In Niagara Falls, African Americans continued being loyal Republicans, or they supported what they perceived as a Republican agenda. Black Niagaran Peter Jones called a Bull Moose meeting on September 23, 1912, to organize a Niagara Falls Colored Moosevelt Club.[175] This date marked the fiftieth anniversary of President Abraham Lincoln's signing of the 1863 Emancipation Proclamation, which freed enslaved people in captured Confederate territories. Peter Jones was impressed with some of Theodore Roosevelt's actions, especially his bid for the presidency. When the Republican Party was split, his group did not support William Taft. Du Bois and Trotter differed with Jones because of Roosevelt's actions as president regarding the Brownsville Riot of 1906,[176] his unflagging support of Booker T. Washington, his failure to be proactive concerning the political and civil rights of African Americans, along with his Bull Moose Party's disregard of African American supporters and their concerns. As a matter of record, in a *Niagara Falls Gazette* editorial titled "Repudiating Roosevelt," an anonymous writer in echoing Du Bois and Trotter wrote:

> Theodore Roosevelt made a fatal mistake when he turned his back upon the colored citizens of the South. Not only did he effectually and for all time alienate the friendship and support of the black man, but he also disgusted thousands of whites who believe in opportunity for the [N]egro and a square deal for all citizens of all colors and all creeds. Roosevelt, ever ready to repudiate his closest friend, to elevate himself politically, hoped to win the favor of the Southern whites by his treatment of the colored people, but even they, through the blindness of their great prejudice, have been able to see through the thin veneer of the move and their disgust has more than outweighed their racial prejudices. It was a fatal move for Theodore Roosevelt.[177]

As evidence of further revulsion of feelings that followed Roosevelt's repudiation of the Negro and the enunciation of his platform, the *Gazette* published the following communication denouncing Roosevelt:

> Buffalo, N. Y., August 10, 1912
>
> Editor Niagara Falls, Gazette:
>
> On the evening of July 31, I made a short speech at the International Hotel, wherein I advocated the Progressive cause. Since that date Mr. Roosevelt has issued a statement repudiating the political claims of the Southern negroes. No more retrogressive doctrine was ever enunciated than this; and I cannot support it. Certain socialistic vagaries of the Progressive platform, also, do not meet with my approval, and I have decided, therefore, to support the regular Republican ticket through thick and thin.
>
> Sincerely yours,
>
> Joseph Cronin[178]

Roosevelt won more votes than Taft but lost to Wilson, who became the twenty-eighth president of the United States.

In terms of patronage politics, there are no records of any Black Niagarans being awarded plum jobs or positions during these early years. Because the African American community was such a small percentage of the city's population, the Black Niagaran vote could not have been a critical political factor. Black Niagarans were still on the margins, observing events and hoping for the best for themselves and families and friends. If they worked for city elites, it was usually at White businesses or within households as domestic servants, performing such tasks as babysitting, washing, cooking, and housecleaning. Some Black residents even supported Democrats. Mr. Spencer Vass, an African American who moved from Washington, DC, to Niagara Falls in 1905, was well known in the city for his leadership. "He was a worker for the Democratic organization during campaign time and exercised considerable power among local [N]egroes."[179] What recompense he received for his duties, if anything, is unknown. He perhaps was aware of the early support that Du Bois and Trotter had given to Woodrow Wilson. Like them he may have been frustrated by the false promises and neglect the Republican Party exhibited toward African Americans.

Nineteen hundred fourteen, nonetheless, was a crucial year. World War I started, which reduced the inflow of immigrants to the United States. The African American community was clearly and consistently expanding. Like most other American communities, the Black community had its own class structure. At the bottom were uneducated common laborers. At the top were prominent Black Niagarans, such as ministers, hotel proprietors, skilled tradesmen, and leaders of organizations, some of whom had obtained their positions based on merit.

Charlotte Dett was at the top of the class structure. She was a vital leader, actively involved in local affairs, and not just for Black Niagarans but also for the broader community. Dett was beloved by most people who knew her. She regularly hosted social affairs at her home and participated in Black women's club activities.[180] She seemed to flourish in these settings. For example, she attended, along with Mary Talbert and many others, a 1915 ceremony in Auburn, New York, commemorating Harriet Tubman who had died in 1913.[181] A monument to Tubman was unveiled at the Fort Hill Cemetery by the New York State Federation of Colored Women's Clubs. Dett was the corresponding secretary of that organization. Within this group, Dett seemed to promote and exemplify the "politics of respectability," a belief system, according to historian Evelyn Brooks Higginbotham, that encouraged African Americans to behave honorably and respectfully, publicly conforming to mainstream values of proper decorum rather than challenging those values for their failure to accept differences.[182]

At a 1913 meeting in Buffalo, New York, for instance, which Mary Talbert also attended, the Federation of Colored Women's Clubs criticized women—especially girls—for using tobacco, smoking, and chewing gum in public places.[183] Dett's example and activities ensured her status at the top of the class structure and helped maintain her effectiveness as a leader.

In the history of Blacks in Niagara Falls, New York, 1850 to 1914 was a fascinating era. Blacks were participating in many key events throughout the city. Although records of Black Niagarans during this period are extremely rare, what is available reveals that Blacks had settled throughout the city, mainly in the south end of town. They created and maintained families, formed neighborhoods and institutions, and carved out livelihoods for themselves. Racism undoubtedly existed, but Black Niagarans confronted and adjusted to this barrier as best as they could, generally without significant collective protest. They strove to demand, obtain, and maintain dignity and deference and move from the fringes of society to its core, in pursuit of power, authority, and respect.

According to evidence about the early foundational years (1850 to 1914), the historical epoch impacted the form of Black Niagaran leadership that ascended. During the slavery era, several alliance leaders such as Colonel P, Platt H. Skinner and Josiah Tryon engaged in antislavery activities. Regardless of class or gender, several Black Niagarans responded to specific community demands for leadership. After slavery ended, only a few recorded instances of leadership existed that directed Black Niagarans to unify in the fight against perceived forms of racial injustice. The Hobbs case best exemplifies this point. This was almost certainly related to the small Black Niagaran population figures during the early community foundational years. Only thirty-three recorded Blacks resided in Niagara Falls in 1840, comprising 2.60 percent of the overall population, whereas 266 lived there in 1910, comprising 0.87 percent of the general population. Moreover, early census records indicate that some Niagarans may have defined themselves as mulattoes (mixed-race people), which could have affected how they defined themselves racially. In the early foundational years of Black Niagaran communities, local leaders directed and oversaw activities aimed at building and maintaining institutions. People such as Jerry Plato of the Masons and Reverend A. L. Wilson of St. John's AME Church exemplify such leadership. Their leadership functions and goals not only undergirded the burgeoning Black Niagaran community in their day but also contributed to the future development and progress of the Black Niagaran community in later eras.

Chapter Two

The Development of the Black Community, Late 1915 to the Early Great Depression Years

Due to an abundance of employment opportunities, there was steady growth in the Black Niagaran community from 1915 to the early Great Depression years. The Niagara Community Center was the most profoundly impactful institution that Black Niagarans and their leadership created to advance themselves. It was a progressive association that operated throughout most of the twentieth century. Although Black Niagarans still experienced discrimination, the unfairness they faced, principally in housing, was not as restrictive then compared to later periods. This fact was largely still attributable to the relatively low population figures of Black Niagarans at the time.

Economic Background Setting

By 1915 Niagara Falls was a must-see tourist attraction.[1] People throughout the United States and worldwide visited Niagara Falls on a regular basis and were impressed by the majestic beauty of the waterfalls on both the American and Canadian sides of the border. They debated among themselves and perhaps with others as to which side was most attractive. Upon returning home, they probably told anyone who would listen about the world's natural wonder they had recently witnessed, which most likely motivated others to travel and view the sight at least once. Honeymooners traveled to Niagara Falls in increasing numbers, particularly after the expansion of train services. They rode the trains from the south, west, and north, often arriving in Buffalo, New York, and changing trains there to take the short ride to Niagara Falls. Once in the area, Blacks, unlike Whites, could not generally count on finding hotel accommodations, but they could obtain services offered by Black tourist home operators or private individuals and families.

By the late nineteenth century the tourist industry was no longer the major employer in the area.[2] The economic activity that was generated by the tourist industry was superseded by that of utilities companies, which were overwhelmingly impacted by the development of hydroelectric power. This technological innovation stimulated vast industrial growth in Niagara Falls and its immediate surroundings, attracting a diverse group of firms that could obtain fairly cheap hydroelectric power to operate their companies.

Carborundum Corporation was one of many firms that took advantage of the abundant cheap energy provided by hydroelectric power. Throughout its history, Carborundum hired a notable Black workforce.[3] In 1891 Dr. Edward G. Acheson and a group of stockholders formed the company in Monongahela, Pennsylvania. Dr. Acheson, a scientist and inventor, created the first human-made abrasive, to which he gave the trademark name Carborundum.[4] This abrasive was created in a tiny electric furnace and could cut glass and even diamonds. Dr. Acheson made the first sale of his product to gem cutters. Later he sold an improved version of his product to mechanics who mixed the abrasive particles with an oil or grease carrier and used the resulting compound for the grinding or seating of steam valves.[5] Then he made a grinding wheel, which he sold to the dental profession for grinding cavities and preparatory dental work.[6] Dr. Acheson learned about the hydroelectric power available in Niagara Falls and decided to move the Carborundum Corporation there to take advantage of thousands of units of horsepower of this inexpensive energy. Dr. Acheson and his associates reestablished their company in Niagara Falls in 1895, and by 1915 it was a thriving business.

Union Carbide and Carbon Corporation was another company among many that took advantage of abundant inexpensive hydroelectric power in Niagara Falls, and they, like Carborundum, hired a number of Black employees.[7] Union Carbide and Carbon Corporation was established in 1917 from a conglomerate of four companies: Union Carbide Corporation, Linde Air Products Company, National Carbon Company, and Presto-Lite Company.[8] Each of these companies acted semi-independently, but they combined their efforts in joint ventures for the success of the corporation. For example, Union Carbide and Carbon Corporation produced calcium carbide, which was used to create acetylene gas that could be used in the welding and cutting of metals. Linde Air Products Company produced industrial gases, such as acetylene, hydrogen, and nitrogen, which served as the foundation of the petrochemical industry. National Carbon Company made products marketed under the trade name "Ever Ready." These included batteries for radio, ignition, telephones, call and signal systems, and flashlights.[9] Presto-Lite Company, like Union Carbide and Carbon Corporation, produced calcium carbide by-products. Although the Presto-Lite Company and the Union Carbide and Carbon Corporation had formerly been competitors, they later combined their talents and knowledge to make better products.

The General Abrasive Company, formed in 1913, also used Niagara Falls's abundant hydroelectric energy. It produced abrasive grain, silicon carbide, and aluminum oxide.[10] Census data for 1920 and 1930 indicate that Blacks worked for abrasive companies in Niagara Falls, but there is no indication of which companies these were. The Spirella Company, formed in 1904, capitalized on the use of abundant hydroelectric power. It produced and sold garments, such as corsets, girdles, belts, one-piece items, and brassieres—created to give women natural support and control, as well as to improve comfort and appearance.[11] Whether it hired Blacks or not is unclear due to the paucity of information available. Numerous other companies were in the area by 1915 and benefited greatly from the abundant hydroelectric power available and perhaps hired some Blacks. These companies included Ayers Witmer Lumber Company, Cataract Ice Company, Chisholm-Ryder Company, Double Foundry and Machine Company, Du Pont De Nemours and Company, Maeberle Lumber Company, International Cooperage Company, International Paper Company, Kimberly-Clark Corporation, National Biscuit Company-Shredded Wheat Bakeries, Niagara Alkali Company, Niagara Foundry Company, Niagara Falls Power Company, Niagara Pattern Works, Niagara Steel Finishing Company, Niagara Welding and Boiler Works, Oldbury Electro-Chemical Company, Pittsburgh Metallurgical Company, Russell Manufacturing Company, and Wrights Plating Works.[12] Consequently, these companies underscored that the development of electrical power was critical to Niagara Falls's economic base. Moreover, these companies, especially the Carborundum Corporation and Union Carbide and Carbon Corporation, as stated by many interviewees, provided employment for numerous African Americans, which helped advance the growing Black Niagaran community along with the leadership that would arise.

Niagara Falls's economic structure, like that in most industrialized regions throughout the country, was significantly affected by World War I.[13] The war began on June 28, 1914, but the United States did not formally join the fighting until 1917. As the war progressed, companies in Niagara Falls received numerous job orders from the federal government, which sparked considerable economic growth in the city. The Niagara Falls companies were largely producing chemical products for war, such as mustard gas, phosgene, and chlorine-based substances for explosives.[14] Hooker Electrochemical Company, Mathieson Alkali Company, Niagara Alkali Company, Niagara Smelting Corporation, and the Isco Electrochemical Company all made caustic soda needed by the explosive manufacturers.[15] Graphitized carbon electrodes necessary for the production of chlorine were produced by National Carbon Company, the Acheson Graphite Company, the Republic Carbon Company, and the Star Electrode Company.[16] Niagara Falls industries produced the bulk of ferroalloys needed in the manufacturing of steel.[17] They were the central producers of ferrochrome, an element used in special alloy steels for the engines of airplanes, armor plates, and projectiles.[18] A local company called the Aluminum Company of America manufactured essential aluminum products, such as mess kits, canteens, castings for airplane engines, time fuses on shrapnel, and ammonal—a high explosive.[19] The Carborundum Company, General Abrasive Company, and the Norton Company all manufactured abrasives that were used in the grinding of shells, bayonets, and gun barrels and in the shaping of armor plates for airplanes and trucks.[20] The federal government oversaw the production and administration of these warfare products because they were crucial to an Allied victory.

First Great Migration Activity

The impact of World War I created employment opportunities in America. Black Americans, like Americans in general, took full advantage of these jobs. World War I significantly reduced the steady flow of Europeans immigrating to the United States. These people, mostly part of the industrial working class, resided in ethnic communities often referred to as ghettoes.[21] World War I inspired many of them to stay in their native lands or return to them to assist in the war effort. This helped generate a strong demand for local laborers in northern locales such as Niagara Falls. Employment functioned as a primary positive stimulus for all migrants seeking work.[22] However, for Black Americans obtaining a more acute sense of freedom and a better education for their children functioned as critical secondary stimuli, particularly for the children who not only represented the future but also were expected to advance farther than their parents.[23] Hence, 1914 to 1919 approximates the years of the First Great Migration in the United States, when approximately half a million Black Americans left the South and traveled to northern towns and cities like Niagara Falls.[24] This phenomenon, as noted by historian Joe Trotter, foreshadowed the long-term transformation of Black Americans from a predominantly rural to a predominantly urban population.[25]

By 1920, at least 509 Blacks resided in Niagara Falls, representing 1 percent of the city's population. Compared to the 1910 figure, this was an increase of 243 people. They came from various locales but especially from southern states such as South Carolina, Georgia, and Alabama. Those from the South generally were the children of sharecroppers who worked hard from year to year but usually found themselves in debt to their landlords.[26] They desired a better life for themselves and their families and were willing to move away from their relatives to achieve that. Migration participants commonly traveled north by train from their places of departure.[27] Marie Brinson's family, for example, moved from Quitman, Georgia (southern Georgia, near the Florida border) to Niagara Falls in 1916. Marie Brinson made a life for herself in Niagara Falls.[28] For many years Marie was married to Reverend Arthur L. Brinson Sr. They had eight children. Marie Brinson, who operated as a community leader, was instrumental in establishing the Morning Star Church of God in Christ in 1930.[29] Toward the end of her life, she lived on Twelfth Street and was a missionary teacher and mother of her church.[30] The Brinson family may have traveled by railway to reach Niagara Falls, taking a route almost straight north. Blacks migrating from Mississippi, Arkansas, Alabama, Louisiana, and Texas often made Chicago their destination, whereas those traveling from Florida, South Carolina, Virginia, and Georgia frequently traveled to Pennsylvania, New Jersey, New York, and Massachusetts.[31]

Eugene Miller left Macon, Georgia, which is about 155 miles north of Quitman, and migrated to Niagara Falls. His grandson, Carlyle Miller, believed that his grandfather arrived in Niagara Falls before 1920.[32] John Johnson, his close friend from home, told Eugene Miller about the positive experiences that he had encountered in Cataract City, which undoubtedly encouraged him to move: this was a common pattern among migrants.[33] During the First Great Migration and beyond, Georgia was infamous for its abusive treatment of African Americans and violations of their citizenship rights.[34] Other than close family bonds, it may not have taken much to persuade Eugene Miller and his family to move. Macon, Georgia, located in central Georgia, is nearly 969 miles from Niagara Falls. Miller took up residence near Johnson and actively participated in community affairs.[35] The 1930 US Census shows that Eugene Miller and John Johnson were neighbors, and both worked for an unspecified carbon company (which could have been the same firm).[36] (According to grandson Carlyle Miller, it was the same firm, National Carbon.[37]) They, therefore, helped each other both in their home state and their newly adopted one.

Zorie Bell Boling's great uncle came to Niagara Falls in 1917.[38] He had relatives in Sparta, Georgia, nearly fifty-four miles north of Macon. He had heard about the job opportunities in Niagara Falls while working as a Pullman Red Cap. Red Caps were train porters who wore distinctive red caps and served passengers as they traveled from station to station. Although economically exploited by their employers, Black men working as Red Caps in the early-to-mid twentieth century were highly respected among those in the African American community.[39] Boling's great uncle most likely informed her father, who was one of the relatives that lived in Sparta, Georgia, about the available jobs in Niagara Falls. Boling's father had seen his father labor as a sharecropper most of his life: he hated it and did not want to continue farming as a career. He brought his family, including infant Zorie Bell, to Niagara Falls, New York, in 1925, moving first to MacKenna Avenue, then to Cudaback Avenue, and finally to Eleventh Street (now Memorial Parkway). He worked at the Carborundum Corporation for fifty years.

As revealed in these stories, Blacks were proactive in their migration experiences. In migrating northward, they were separating themselves from an extremely close southern family network.[40] Southern nuclear families lived in a communal manner, akin to an African tribal/ethnic setting, which can be interpreted as a cultural carryover.[41] Great-grandparents, grandparents, parents, uncles, aunts, nieces, nephews, cousins, and children lived in close proximity to one another. A village existed, and the opinions and ideas of the elderly impacted the entire extended family, which worked as a cohesive network to help its members. Nuclear family members babysat for one another, and older children were expected to supervise and help guide younger children. Both young and old were cared for. All able family members, even the elderly, had a duty to perform important tasks such as orally communicating family history to the young or teaching and reinforcing lessons of morality. During the First Great Migration, this was the social network that southern migrants generally left behind when they migrated northward.[42] Consequently, although rampant racism existed in the South and served to push Blacks out, separated families and transformed family interactions were never easily managed.

Richard Ben Stovall, for example, came to Niagara Falls in 1916 from the northeastern Georgia town of Toccoa, near the South Carolina border.[43] He resided at 3335 Ely Avenue with his wife, Addie. Eventually he worked as a janitor in the Elderfield-Hartshorn building. His parents, siblings, and relatives at one time had all lived in Toccoa, where they formed a tight-knit family. However, in time, all the male children ventured out to other places, taking the train from Martin, Georgia, to their respective destinations. Richard traveled the farthest, journeying to Niagara Falls. His brother Early migrated to Chicago, while his brother John moved to Cedartown, in northwestern Georgia. His three sisters lived close to Toccoa: Janie Lewis lived in Lavonia, Georgia, about seventeen miles from Toccoa; Georgia Jones lived nearly ten miles away in Avalon, Georgia, and Elenie Shackford lived eleven miles from Toccoa in Martin, Georgia. The women got married and stayed with their husbands, while two of the three men ventured far from home. The women were close enough to interact physically with their parents and relatives, whereas the two males probably kept in touch from a distance.

Subsequently, extended family networks in the South were generally extremely close, consisting of blood relatives and "fictive kin"—or unrelated people who were considered relatives. These relationships aided family members in surviving and bettering themselves. Migrants attempted to re-create similar social relationships when they moved north and specifically to Niagara Falls. Once they saw and understood the opportunities available to them, they would immediately inform their relatives and friends.

According to historian Gretchen Lemke-Santangelo, all migrants who came to Niagara Falls and stayed generally followed a three-step process in orienting themselves to the milieu.[44] In phase one, they found temporary housing, assisting them in their transition from the South to the North, or perhaps from a rural locale to an urban one. Often, they became roomers or boarders in a house or apartment until they found and held jobs for a specified period until they became comfortable in the new city. When examining the 1920 US Census for the City of Niagara Falls, it is difficult to discern which individuals had participated in the First Great Migration, but inferences can be made. Of the Blacks enumerated as employed, 55 were recorded as roomers and 34 as boarders. Of the 55 employed roomers, 47 were males, and 8 were females. They resided predominantly in Wards 1 and 7, which were adjacent to each other. (See the Niagara Falls ward map in figure 6.) Regarding the employed boarders, all 34 were males who lived primarily in Wards 3 and 4. Age groups of roomers are depicted in table 2.1, while those for the boarders are in table 2.2.

Unsurprisingly, most roomers and boarders were young, aged eighteen to thirty-five, comprising 58.2 percent and 58.8 percent of all boarders and roomers, respectively. The young were often willing to venture out and drastically alter the lifestyles that they and their parents knew. They were the ones unwilling to settle for being sharecroppers, which was really a modified form of slavery, as conveyed in letters of First Great Migration actors.[45] There were no female boarders, but there were eight female roomers, who were predominantly in the eighteen to thirty-five age range. What this meant is unclear; perhaps the roomers rented their lodgings for shorter periods because the norms of the era dictated that women live in some sort

Table 2.1. Roomers

Age Groupings	Males	Females
18 to 35	27	5
36 to 40	7	1
41 to 45	4	0
46 to 50	4	0
51 to 55	3	1
56 to 60	1	0
61 and over	0	1
Unknown age	1	0

Tables 2.1 and 2.2 adapted from the 1920 United States Census. (Please see page 336, note 44.)

Table 2.2. Boarders

Age groupings	Males	Females
18 to 35	20	0
36 to 40	8	0
41 to 45	1	0
46 to 50	0	0
51 to 55	2	0
56 to 60	1	0
61 and over	1	0
Unknown	1	0

of family arrangement. Not all those migrants were residing in temporary dwellings, but undoubtedly some were. The newly employed residents displayed similar behaviors to Black migrants in other towns and cities.[46]

In phase 2, migrants who settled in the area moved from their temporary dwelling arrangement to a transitional situation. Here they found more long-term accommodations in an apartment or other housing. This was better than the temporary arrangement because the migrants were more comfortable. They perhaps had more space and a more attractive neighborhood and living quarters; or they were completely in charge of their own accommodation. However, although this living space was better than the initial temporary quarters, migrants still aimed to find a better permanent home. This usually took time and could require migrants to reside in more than one transitional living place before they found their permanent home.

Permanent quarters signified the third and generally final phase in the housing search. Here migrants found housing they were most comfortable with. They would likely spend many years in these quarters, more than the previous arrangements, attempting to re-create a semblance of the family network they had left in the South. Their children grew up in these dwellings and would remember family and nonfamily interactions. Much Niagara Falls family history was created in these quarters.

The Boling narrative demonstrates that her family followed this three-step process.[47] Her family first moved to MacKenna Avenue, then to Cudaback Avenue, and finally to Eleventh Street (now Memorial Parkway). The MacKenna Avenue rental dwelling served as temporary living quarters, while the Cudaback Avenue apartment functioned as a transitional dwelling. When Zorie Bell Boling's family moved to Eleventh Street, that apartment also served as a transitional dwelling. Boling's family lived in an apartment building in an alleyway, rented from a man named Mr. Oppenheim. The neighborhood consisted primarily of Italians, and according to Boling, every household was like a grocery store, selling fruits, vegetables, and other eatables.[48] This changed because Italians were moving out as Blacks were moving in. The neighborhood was also a red-light district where illegal activities such as prostitution occurred. A horrendous smell from a dead dog's body decomposing under the apartment building's entrance steps was what compelled the Boling family to move. Zorie Bell Boling's mother could no longer cope with the incessant odor and demanded that her family move. They remained on Eleventh Street but moved across the railroad tracks to an apartment in a big, brown house that belonged to a madam who managed a prostitution business. This residence became a permanent home, and it was where Boling's infant sister was born.

The Boling family lived near the actual waterfalls of Niagara Falls. In the 1920s, they lived in Ward 4, where MacKenna and Cudaback avenues were located. Beginning in the 1930s, the Boling family moved west, across the railroad tracks, and up Eleventh Street, which was also part of Ward 4. In 1920 Ward 3 and Ward 4 were two among six wards that housed the bulk of Niagara Falls's Black population. Table 2.3 shows these findings.

In 1910 Wards 1, 2, and 5 contained most of Niagara Falls's Black population. Wards 3, 4, and 7 showed increases in 1920, with Blacks continuing to reside predominantly in the southern section of the city. All the wards in 1920 contained more Black males than females, except Wards 8 and 9. Ward 1 contained the most Blacks, whereas Wards 6 and 10 had none. Although Blacks were primarily in the indicated wards, by 1920 they resided in most sections of the city, with most close to their jobs on and around Buffalo Avenue, the city's main industrial thoroughfare. Consequently, the fact that Niagara Falls's Black population only comprised 1 percent of the city's total population undoubtedly influenced their wider presence.

Benjamin W. Bolden's migratory behaviors contrasted vastly with the norm. Unlike many Black migrants, Bolden came to Niagara Falls from Beaver Falls, Pennsylvania, which is 231 miles away,[49] and he did not relocate from the South. He was born in Pennsylvania in 1895 and was twenty-four years old when he moved to Cataract City.[50] After arriving in 1920, he grew to like it; in turn, many citizens of Niagara Falls liked and respected him.[51] Bolden stayed in the city and made a life for him-

Table 2.3. 1920 Black Population by Wards

Ward	Total	Male	Female
1	113	63	50
2	68	39	29
3	94	60	34
4	52	32	20
5	56	32	24
6	0	0	0
7	58	36	22
8	7	2	5
9	6	1	5
10	0	0	0
11	7	7	0
12	20	11	9
13	28	15	13

Adapted from the 1920 United States Census. (Please see page 336, note 48.)

self, first operating a shoeshine parlor in a barbershop and then raising a family and gaining experiences that would allow him to become a highly respected leader of the local Black community.[52] He does not appear in the 1920 US Census, but he was recorded in the 1930 US Census, where it is documented that he lived on the north end of Thirteenth Street in Ward 9.[53] In addition, he attended St. John's AME Church, which then was located on the south end of Thirteenth Street. Bolden most likely went through the three steps Black migrants followed before establishing a permanent residency.[54] He held many jobs but generally was an independent businessman. Theodore Williamson, an independent businessman himself, said he remembered as a child that Bolden was the first Black businessperson in Niagara Falls.[55] One of Bolden's most well-known jobs was that of owning and operating a souvenir shop on Third Street, "near the main gate to [the waterfalls of Niagara Falls], close to Riverway."[56] An advertisement for Bolden's business read: COMPLETE LINE OF POST CARDS, SOUVENIRS, TOYS, PENNANTS, PILLOW TOPS, MAGAZINES, NEWSPAPERS, BOOKS, STATIONERY, POCKET KNIVES, LEATHER-GOODS, WALLETS, SMALL AND LARGE GIFTS FOR EVERY ELK AND HIS FAMILY[57] (see figure 2.1).

Figure 2.1. Benjamin W. Bolden, 1938. Niagara Community Center.

Many local Black families like Bolden's conducted business to provide a needed service and to generate income. Besides renting to boarders and roomers, Black families rented rooms in their apartments or homes to Blacks who visited Niagara Falls on weekends or holidays. This market developed because Black visitors generally were unwelcome at downtown hotels.[58] This segregation, according to historian Robert Weyeneth, compelled Black Niagarans to create alternative spaces to meet the needs of their racial group.[59] Even so, the small tourist homes owned by Black people such as Charlotte Dett, and Royal and Terrell Palmer (who had a tourist home on First Street), or a Mr. McDonald (who had a tourist home on Second Street), were not enough to accommodate the growing trade. Theodore Williamson and Norwood Hershey Samuel remembered as children in the late 1920s and 1930s their parents requiring them to sleep in other sections of their homes so that their bedrooms could be rented out. Williamson recalled:

> When it got to be a holiday and a lot of Black people were here, people like my mother and father would make us [children] sleep on the floor downstairs and rent the rooms out. That was for Black people who came from New York City and other places. There were no hotels that were open to Black people. They just would not accept a Black person in a hotel.[60]

Like Williamson, Samuel recalled that

> we had a lot to do with the tourist business, and back then Blacks couldn't go into hotels generally, and so people opened their homes in the summer. I remember sleeping under the dining room table a lot because my room had been rented out for the weekend, you know. And the tours, the buses came in from New York [City] or wherever, and people made a little extra money by taking in these tourists.[61]

Black families were largely poor, and an opportunity to bring more resources into households was cherished. Black migrants may have initially been some of these tourists seeking holiday or weekend housing. Even so, employment was still the major factor that encouraged most new Blacks to settle in the area.

Employment

The 1920 US Census for the City of Niagara Falls conveys that most Blacks were laborers or in the lower economic classes, which was similar to the results for 1910 (see table 2.4).

One hundred and twenty-nine Black Niagarans were unskilled laborers. Most Black migrants who gained employment worked as unskilled laborers. They had the dirtiest, most dangerous, and most undesirable jobs.[62] Nevertheless, they most likely saw their occupational status as an improvement from what they had left in the South. Fifteen individuals were skilled laborers: two barbers, two carpenters, one chef, four hairdressers, one machinist, one plumber, three roofers, and one shoemaker. There were two professional workers, a mechanical engineer and a minister. Eight entrepreneurs ran small businesses: three boarding house operators, two hotel proprietors, two poolroom proprietors, one restaurant owner.

Table 2.4. Black Workers Recorded in the 1920 US Census

Males	Number	Percentages
Professional	2	0.75
Proprietary	7	2.63
Clerical	2	0.75
Skilled	11	4.14
Semiskilled	8	3.0
Unskilled	126	47.37
Domestic	68	25.6
Total	224	84.24%
Females		
Professional	0	0
Proprietary	2	0.75
Clerical	0	0
Skilled	4	1.50
Semiskilled	3	1.12
Unskilled	3	1.12
Domestic	30	11.27
Total	42	15.76%
Grand Total	266	100%

Adapted from the *1920 United States Census*. (Please see page 337, note 62).

One individual managed a restaurant. Of the 266 individuals recorded as working, forty-two were females who mainly worked as domestic servants. More specifically, thirty were domestic servants, three laborers, two laundresses, one porter and a dressmaker, four hairdressers, and two boardinghouse keepers. As in earlier decades, most women did not work outside the home. Women who toiled as domestic servants often worked in the De Veaux section of town, which was a part of Ward 12, or in local hotels.[63] Many affluent White Niagarans, who were often the city's elites, lived in the De Veaux section of town. It was an attractive district located near Niagara University.

In comparing the 1920 census data with that of 1910, some interesting findings are evident. The recorded Black labor force increased from 134 workers in 1910 to 266 in 1920. In 1910 census enumerators recorded one professional worker and two in 1920. In 1910 Gertrude Johnson, who lived in Ward 3, was the sole professional, being a twenty-seven-year-old trained nurse.[64] The two professionals in 1920 were Reverend Luther Holloway, who was thirty-three and living in Ward 5,[65] and a man simply listed as Ralph G, who was a mechanical engineer living in Ward 7.[66] Four proprietors (William Bryant, Anderson Fayette, Joseph Venters, and George Martin) operated businesses in 1910 compared to nine in 1920 (Chasa Jackson, Robert Williams, Jack Stiwark, Molen Plarsick, Howard Thomas, Maggie Brown, William Baker, Robert D, and B. Belw).[67] None of the business operators from 1910 appear in the 1920 Census data, which partly indicates that business operators in 1920 may have been recent migrants. Census enumerators recorded no Black Niagaran clerical workers in 1910 but did record two, F. Canes and James Watkins, in 1920.[68] Canes, who was seventeen years old and living in Ward 2, worked as a store clerk, and Watkins, who was thirty-three and living in Ward 7, is listed merely as a clerk. The 1910 US Census reports list six skilled workers (two barbers, one carpenter, and three painters), while the 1920 US Census data display fifteen (two barbers, one carpenter, one chef, four hairdressers, one machinist, one plumber, one paper finisher, three roofers, and one shoemaker).[69] Like the business operators, none of the tradespeople in 1910 appear in the 1920 Census data, which perhaps indicates new migrants undertaking trades. Furthermore, census enumerators counted six semiskilled workers in 1910 (three cooks, two drillers, and one blaster) and 11 in 1920 (five cooks, one dressmaker, one driller, three laundresses, one machine operator),[70] while recording 61 unskilled workers in 1910 and 129 in 1920 along with 56 domestic service workers in 1910 and 98 in 1920.[71] Thus, US Census data for 1910 and 1920 on

Black Niagaran laborers confirm that they were essentially members of the lower economic classes.

After World War I, the economy of Niagara Falls continued to grow steadily through the 1920s until about 1930. New products had been introduced during the war, which created new industries.[72] Although the 1909 US Census listed 156 firms operating in Niagara Falls,[73] the 1919 US Census of Manufacturers conveys that there were 186 firms in Niagara Falls, employing 12,238 workers with a combined annual wage of $15,574,000.[74] These firms manufactured products valued at $89,247,000.[75] In 1929, at the beginning of the Great Depression, and ten years later, Niagara Falls had 123 firms with 13,210 workers who earned wages assessed at $19,870,417.[76] The firms also manufactured products valued at $131,207,000.[77] The fact that there were fewer extant firms in 1929 compared to 1919 was due to several mergers and amalgamations.[78] Subsequently, Niagara Falls's economy functioned to support a steady influx of low-skilled laborers during these early periods. Contributing to the region's economy, manufacturers in the neighboring city of Buffalo even expanded with 1,753 firms in 1909 and 2,093 in 1919 but declined to 1,923 in 1929.[79] With jobs, Black Niagarans focused more on building family and community institutions to enhance their lives, beginning with marriage and family.

Community Institutions: Family, Churches, and the Niagara Community Center

The 1920 US Census reports regarding marriage corresponded to those of 1910. Of the 509 Black Niagarans, there were 298 males and 211 females. As in the 1910 US Census reports, males outnumbered females, which reiterates that the population was steadily growing and that young men

Table 2.5. 1920 Marital Condition Males and Females Fifteen Years of Age and Over

	Total	Single Number	Percent	Married Number	Percent	Widowed	Divorced
Males	258	113	43.8	127	49.2	17	0
Females	155	22	14.2	116	74.8	15	1

Adapted from the 1920 United States Census. (Please see page 338, note 80).

were more likely to leave home and send for their family members and friends once they were settled in a new place. Most marriageable women were in conjugal relationships: of 155 females aged 15 years or older, 116 were married, 15 were widowed, one was divorced, and 22 were single. These data signify that marriage was highly valued among these women. Of the men aged 15 years or older, 127 were married, 17 were widowed, none were divorced, and 113 were recorded as single. The male results also convey that marriage was highly valued, although women had a larger pool of available mates to choose from.

In terms of household demographics, or composition of households managed by Black Niagarans, most consisted of married couples. The 1920 Census for Niagara Falls listed 114 Black Niagaran households (with some Black Niagarans living as servants in White-headed households).[80] Nuclear families existed in 68 of the households, and children lived in 29 of the nuclear family units but were absent in the remaining nuclear family units. Of the 39 nuclear family units without children, 17 of these families had boarders or roomers residing with them; while of the 29 nuclear family units with children, 7 shared their living quarters with boarders or roomers. Hence, whether children were present or not, young, middle-aged, and old couples took full advantage of the opportunity to bring additional funds into their households, aid relatives, or both.

Eleven of the 114 households consisted of extended family units or households with nuclear families with or without children but including relatives.[81] Four extended families included both children and relatives, while seven had relatives only. Census enumerators recorded no roomers or boarders residing with extended families with children, but they did record roomers living with two of the seven extended families with no children present. These results imply that married couples, with or without children, were most likely content to have relatives occupying space within their households, along with the potential contributions they could make, such as money and/or other forms of aid in maintaining the household. In 1920, for example, Jerry Plato, the prominent Black Niagaran leader, lived with his wife Margaret and his younger brother Henry.[82] No children resided in their household. Jerry and his wife likely assisted Henry in improving his life, although in Niagara Falls, Henry never rose to the leadership stature of his brother.

Besides nuclear and extended family arrangements, other household structures, in fact, did exist. In terms of female-headed households, a dominant black matrifocal arrangement did not exist.[83] Of the 114 households, only six fit this arrangement, which is contrary to the findings of E. Franklin Frazier and Daniel Patrick Moynihan and congruent with the findings of Herbert Gutman, Andrew Billingsley, Robert Staples, Lillian W. Williams, and other Black family scholars.[84] More often than not, households with fathers and mothers present made up the prevailing household structure. Moreover, of the six female-headed households, two had boarders or roomers present, with one having three roomers and the other having two boarders. Regarding single-male headed households with children, five existed, with one having two roomers. Sixteen households consisted of single males with no children, while eight were single females with no children. Of the sixteen single-male-headed households with no children, eleven had boarders or roomers, while four of the single-female-headed households had boarders or roomers. Societal norms probably prevented single females from housing individuals that they did not know. Nonetheless, the 1920 US Census household structural arrangements are also conveyed below in table 2.6 as percentages.

The Roundtree family was a well-known nuclear family with children. Several interviewees considered them one of the oldest Black Niagaran families they knew of.[85] William (Bill) Roundtree, who was the patriarch, was thirty-eight years old in 1920 and a laborer.[86] In the 1930 Census, where more information on him and his family is listed, William's age is listed as forty-six.[87] This is unusual because he was recorded as being thirty-eight in 1920: his age should have been forty-eight. An error occurred in either 1920 or 1930. William and his family lived on Allen Avenue; Ethel, his wife, was recorded as being twenty-nine years old and a housewife. William

Table 2.6. 1920 Household Structural Arrangement of Black Niagarans

Household	Percentage of Population
Nuclear Family with Children	25.44
Nuclear Family without Children	34.21
Extended Family with Children	3.51
Extended Family without Children	6.14
Female-Headed Household with Children	5.26
Male-Headed Household with Children	4.39
Single Female-Headed Household Living Alone	7.02
Single Male-Headed Household Living Alone	14.03

Adapted from the 1920 United States Census. (Please see page 338, note 86).

and his wife had eight children at the time. All interviewees that spoke about them commented that they had a large family. The children's names and ages (from oldest to youngest) are listed as follows: Estella 13, Ramon 11, Heredia 10, Elizabeth 8, William 6, Winifred 4½, Timothy 2½, and James 2 months. More children were later born, Ernie being one of them.

One interviewee had childhood memories of the Roundtree family in the 1930s. She referred to the patriarch—William Roundtree—as "old man Roundtree."[88] She stated that he would go around the city of Niagara Falls to collect junk and then place it in his yard. Everyone could walk by and see it.[89] He seemed like a nice man to her. She remembered Mrs. Roundtree as residing in the house with her children, while "old man Roundtree" stayed in their garage, near his junk.[90] In later years, businessman Theodore Williamson remembered more about the children, particularly William and Ernie Roundtree. He remembered William performing a good deed for Black Niagarans. William often went by a fruit vendor's shop at the end of the day, and he would obtain fruit that the vendor could not sell and give it to those in the African American community.[91] Ernie, he commented, provided well for his wife and children, purchasing property and being a quality individual.[92] Ernie later served in the US Air Force during the Korean War and attended the Potters House Church.[93]

Unlike William Roundtree, Samuel Webb lived in an extended family arrangement. He lived with his wife, Orace, and their four children and Samuel's mother. Samuel and his wife were both recorded in 1920 as being twenty-eight years old, which was unusual. According to the 1920 Census, males in conjugal relationships were often older than their wives by as much as five to twenty years. In addition to caring for his family, Samuel participated in the Niagara Falls lodge of Knights of Pythias.[94] His life, unfortunately, was cut short due to an accident he suffered while working as a teamster for the Shipston Coal Company. One of Webb's legs was badly crushed when a piece of heavy timber fell on it.[95] Amputation of the leg was necessary, but due to complications that developed, Webb was unable to withstand the shock of the operation.[96] He died after the operation and was buried in Oakwood Cemetery. At the time of his death, Samuel Webb was only thirty-seven years old.

Samuel Webb's untimely death in 1929 not only made his wife a thirty-seven-year-old widow but also a mature parent (or adult over the age of thirty-five) in charge of a female-headed family, which demonstrates leadership on a micro level. The six female heads of families listed in the 1920 Census, like Orace, were all mature women, which relates to Niara Sudarkasa's thesis that there is a distinct difference between young females who direct female-headed families compared to older more mature women heads of families.⁹⁷ The fact that few female-headed families existed—and those that did had mature heads—indicates that Black Niagarans considered households with mothers and fathers present as ideal; however, more mature women with more life experiences were probably more effective parents. Sudarkasa made her argument to counter critiques of female-headed households, especially those that posited female-headed households as detrimental to the growth and development of male children.⁹⁸ The average age of the six female-family heads was 45.5, with their ages being 38, 38, 38, 45, 54, and 60 respectively. More specifically, four had children they were raising, while two had their adult offspring residing with them. Forty-five-year-old Elizabeth Coleman had six children in her household, and thirty-eight-year-old Josephine Flakes had four children under her care. Mary Jackson, a sixty-year-old widow, had her thirty-nine-year-old son living with her. In the neighboring city of Buffalo in the year 1925, historian Lillian Williams found different results. Black females headed 7 percent of households and were beginning to head them at younger ages, with one out of three being under the age of thirty.⁹⁹ Nonetheless, in 1925, even in Buffalo, a black matrifocal household structure did not predominate.

Of the Black Niagarans who maintained households without children, most were middle-aged, with the average male being forty-eight and the average female being forty-six. Moreover, the oldest male and female were both seventy-eight years old.¹⁰⁰ In terms of young marriageable candidates aged thirty-five years or younger, census enumerators recorded one thirty-year-old female and five males who were 24, 28, 30, 32, and 33 years of age, respectively. Due to the larger number of men than women, these findings reinforce that men had a more difficult task of finding suitable spouses within their racial group, and/or they were recent migrants whose spouses may not have relocated to Niagara Falls yet.

Census enumerators recorded only one mixed-race marriage in the 1920 Census; this is unusual, considering the higher ratio of Black males to females and the fact that many people were listed as mulattoes.¹⁰¹ John and Bertha Niso were married, but they did not fit the pattern of the male partner being older than his spouse. Bertha, who was African American, was recorded as thirty-eight, whereas John, who was White, was listed as thirty-three. They had no children of their own and no boarders or roomers residing with them. It is difficult to determine whether they experienced intense societal pressure for their conjugal relationship. Even so, the fact that they were a married biracial couple and established a nuclear-family household underscores the strength of their bond versus societal pressures.

A prototype of how Black Niagarans conceived of family can be developed based on the numerous recorded and unrecorded interviews of them over the years. They expressed their views explicitly or implicitly when asked about family. First and foremost, they generally conceived of family in terms of blood relationships or consanguinity. Second, and perhaps most importantly, they saw family with regard to household structure and who consistently resided there; consequently, family members could have consisted of mothers, fathers, sisters, brothers, grandparents, aunts, uncles, nieces, nephews, or some fictive kin or nonblood relative(s). Family structures could have been nuclear, extended, augmented, female headed, or male headed. Of course, other family arrangements perhaps existed; however, in documented sources for the period 1850 to 1985, they were not conveyed with certainty, nor orally from 1900 to 1985. Furthermore, Black Niagarans, as a rule, did not describe their families as being patriarchal or matriarchal. They tended to portray family heads as being parties in a unit in which individuals performed crucial roles that served to make their families operable. Some individuals praised their mothers or fathers (or both), and others identified their grandparents as key influential figures, a few even acknowledging older siblings, during their upbringing, as being exceedingly impactful. In short, the concept of "family" for Black Niagarans was not a static term.

At least ninety-six Black children under the age of fifteen lived in Niagara Falls by 1920 and resided in family units, with a few perhaps having been the products of interracial relationships. Children were important to their parents, who had grand hopes for them, especially ensuring that they acquired a good education. Niagara Falls experienced a 48.5 percent surge in its total population during the 1920s, which impacted its school enrollment, causing it to double at 7,889 students.[102] In 1920 the illiteracy rate for Black Niagarans was low at 2.5 percent compared to 7.5 percent for Niagarans generally, which included a 0.2 percent rate for native Whites, and a 16.5 percent rate for foreign-born Whites.[103] Clearly, Black Niagarans took advantage of the increasing resources allocated for education. They most certainly attended neighborhood schools, where they were exposed to the same education as their White peers whose parents were part of the local industrial working class. As in earlier periods, they attended schools such as the Niagara Street School, the Third Street School, the Thirteenth Street School, and the Niagara Falls Public High School. In contrast to later years, their presence did not threaten the racial balance because in all probability they again were the only minorities in their classrooms.

After taking care of family responsibilities at home and school, Black Niagarans returned to developing and maintaining their churches. Black churches have always been essential institutions within African American communities, serving several crucial functions for their parishioners. For example, they have been havens or social places of protection, sole institutions owned and operated by its members, community-based organizations possessing independent incomes, and training grounds for leadership. Scholars such as Albert Raboteau, C. Eric Lincoln, Andrew Billingsley, and numerous others have undertaken extensive studies to validate these assertions.[104] Therefore, it is unsurprising that Black Niagarans would follow this pattern.

Consequently, in 1917 Reverend William Ware organized Shiloh Baptist Church, considered the mother church of all Black Baptist churches in Niagara Falls.[105] Like many Baptist churches, the initial congregation did not meet in a large space; instead they met for worship services over a garage on Pine Avenue.[106] This locale proved to be inadequate, so the congregation then purchased a storefront on Ely Avenue on the east side of town. An oral history conversely states that Reverend H. C. Thomas built the church structure on Ely Avenue.[107] Religious leaders of the First Baptist Church of Niagara Falls visited Shiloh Baptist Church and ordained officers.[108] "The charter members of Shiloh Baptist Church were Deacon and Mrs. W. B. Davis, Deacon and Mrs. Benjamin Stovall, Deacon and Mrs. Hoskins, Mrs. A. A. Scott and Mrs. Annie Ware, who was the wife of the founder and pastor."[109] A year later Reverend Luther Holloway was selected head minister. Benjamin Stovall, Reverend William Ware, and the Reverend Luther Holloway may have migrated to Niagara Falls during the First Great Migration. They appear in the 1920 US Census for the City of Niagara Falls but not in the 1910 Census.[110] They all resided in the Ward 5 as neighbors.[111]

By 1920 Reverend Holloway decided to move his congregation from its Ely Avenue location to Erie Avenue.[112] Some influential members of the church did not agree with this decision and considered it unwise to move from their building (which was paid for) to a rental property. Thus, some members elected to stay at the old address. This controversy split the church. The group that remained at Ely Avenue retained the name of Shiloh Baptist Church, whereas those that moved called their location the Union Baptist Church.

Both churches functioned proactively in offering spiritual guidance and social activities to the Black community. They offered programs such as Sunday schools, Sunday church services, morning worship, preaching services, prayer meetings, choir rehearsals, evening services, and Bible classes.[113] Black families spent much time in church during the early years of the formation and development of these houses of worship and even at St. John's AME Church, which was still consistently offering many services. It was not uncommon for families to be in church on Monday and Wednesday evenings as well as Sunday mornings. Their social worlds revolved around the church.[114] Adult members socialized with each other, and their children played with their peers. These same churches assisted Black migrants who came to Niagara Falls who were seeking spiritual guidance or knowledge about employment, housing, and schools for their children, government agencies, recreation, or the whereabouts of other people from their southern home states or towns.

In 1926 Reverend William Johnson founded Trinity Baptist Church, initially organizing it in Craftsmen Hall on Hyde Park Boulevard.[115] Searching for better accommodations, the congregation a year later moved to MacKenna Avenue, in a section of the city where Blacks had been moving to on a regular basis, forming a "clustering" (or Black community). A minister known as Reverend Reed eventually became Trinity Baptist Church's minister, replacing Reverend Johnson. However, due to some disagreement, the Reverend Reed left this congregation in 1928 and organized a new church at 1007 East Falls Street.[116] This new congregation also became known as Trinity Baptist Church. The dispute over the churches' names eventually ended in 1929.[117] Members of the Trinity Baptist Church who remained on MacKenna Avenue closed their doors and went to the Union Baptist Church's house of worship. After uniting, the two congregations then renamed themselves Second Baptist Church.[118]

In conjunction with the early churches, the formation of a community center was one of the greatest single events that benefited Black Niagarans. It was rumored that Blacks who patronized the local YMCA were told to get their own recreational facility. Regardless of who may have made this statement—White patrons or YMCA representatives—Black Niagarans still maintained an ongoing relationship with the local YMCA. Nonetheless, during the late 1920s, Eugene Ellis, Benjamin W. Bolden, and Reverend Donald B. Barton, who were then leaders of the Black community, approached the Community Chest, a division of the local Niagara Falls government, about sponsoring some social and recreational facility for the Black community.[119] At this juncture Bolden was about thirty-three years old; Ellis was a concerned community leader, and Reverend Barton ministered at St. John's AME Church.

Representatives of both the Black community and the Community Chest agreed that a study should be undertaken to determine the precise needs of the Black community. John M. Pollard Sr. of the Playground and Recreation Association of America was brought from New York City to Niagara Falls to conduct the study. Pollard, who did some graduate work at the School of Social Work at the University of Chicago (which was heavily influenced by the famous pioneering sociologist Robert Park) took several months to complete his study. He administered five hundred questionnaires, made two hundred personal visits, and held six public meetings. On a small scale, his research methods overlapped with those of W. E. B. Du Bois in how he gathered and evaluated data for his pioneering study, *The Philadelphia Negro*.[120] Ben Bolden, who at this juncture was beginning to make a name as a respectable community leader, assisted him.[121] His findings, presented to the Community Chest, confirmed that a community center was needed and would contribute toward the progress of Niagara Falls in general. Furthermore, perhaps reflecting on the Harlem Renaissance (which was in vogue at the time), he envisioned the center as a place for drama and stories, music and plays, dances, baseball and basketball games, swimming, china painting and craftwork of all kinds, forums and debating clubs, study clubs, and an employment bureau to find economic opportunities.[122]

There were mixed reactions in the Black community to the idea of a separate community center for Blacks.[123] One small group felt that separation was counterproductive and that Blacks and Whites, side by side, had to work out the destiny of America: "They [felt] that to permit separation [was] to admit inferiority and because of bitter experience they [asked] for better economic conditions only, and they [were] content to wait for other social adjustments."[124] Another group, still small but larger than the first, felt that with the right kind of leadership, Blacks would integrate into established institutions, even if it meant expanding those existing institutions to accommodate them. The overwhelming majority of people, however, felt that a separate community center was needed to address the social and recreational needs of the Black community. They also felt that the center should be led by well-trained outstanding members of their community.

Although there is no conclusive evidence, the disagreement among the three groups seemed to represent a conflict between old residents of Niagara Falls and new residents who had recently relocated to the city. It really was a difference between two groups, with the first two small groups representing one perspective and the other large group representing another predominant outlook. Most likely, the old residents (or native residents) had been born and raised in Niagara Falls or in the North and had an integrationist outlook. They had experienced forms of racism; however, they believed that racial progress could be achieved more rapidly through a strong working relationship between Blacks and Whites. Conversely, the new residents generally had experienced more brutal, overt forms of racism that were pervasive in the southern settings they had come from.[125] These harsh forms of racism motivated them to leave the South. The farther south their hometowns were, the more overt and dehumanizing that racism was.[126] Therefore, they had no problem with having their own separate community institutions. This conflict between old and new residents represented a common pattern evident in African American northern urban studies that examine intragroup relations.[127]

Pollard's intragroup conflict-evoking study, which was titled "Why Have a Study," also suggested an initial operating budget for the center. For its first year, the center's operating budget was projected to be $5,107. This amount seemed reasonable to the members of the Community Chest; they accepted it without making any adjustments. The budget that Pollard created and submitted to the Community Chest is below:

<u>Suggested Budget</u>[128]

Salaries:	$2,000.00
Wages:	300.00
Other Compensation:	300.00
Total Personnel Service:	$2,600.00
Total Services other than Personnel:	120.00
New Equipment:	1,000.00
Total Equipment:	$1,000.00
Rent:	900.00
	$4,620.00
Total Materials & Supplies:	487.00
Grand Total:	$5,107.00

Most of the funds requested from the Community Chest were projected to cover salaries and equipment. About a fourth of the funds were for rent and services other than personnel. For unknown reasons, Pollard recommended that a woman be hired to head the center and that men volunteer their time until a budget could be secured to support two people.

Several meetings were held to support the creation of the center and to further convince the Community Chest of the worthiness of the project. These meetings were usually well attended, reflecting the majority's view that the center should be separate.[129] Usually, acknowledged community leaders led these meetings: individuals such as Reverend Donald B. Barton, Ben Bolden, Charlotte Dett, and Bessie Palmer, for example.

On October 17, 1928, the leaders met at the Chamber of Commerce to select a name for the new center: "Among the names suggested were: Douglass League (as a tribute to Frederick Douglass, the well-known abolitionist); Dunbar League (in honor of Paul Laurence Dunbar, famed Negro poet); Pollard Center (for John Pollard, who made the survey recommending that a social center for the Falls's Negroes be established); and Nathaniel Dett Centre, in honor of a native son, a composer and conductor of note, and well known [in Niagara Falls]."[130] Besides these suggestions, the leadership welcomed further suggestions from any source. By the end of this meeting no name had yet been confirmed.

By March 29, 1929, a little over a year after Pollard's study was completed, the community center was not only officially organized but also officially named the Niagara Community Center. The objective of the new organization was to promote social, recreational, and cultural activities for the Black residents of Niagara Falls, with special emphasis on programs for young people.[131] Its first home was at 511 Erie Avenue, which only had one large room and one very small one.[132] However, by October 1931, over a year and a half later, its new location was at 637 Erie Avenue. It was moved to provide larger quarters for its members. The community center remained at this location until 1952.

Today many senior citizens still have fond memories of the center at the 637 Erie Avenue location. For example, Indiana Martin, formally known as Indiana Hunt, had fond childhood memories of the community center during its early formative years:

> The Community Center was a house on Erie Avenue. They converted it for us. That was the first place we had to go for children's activities.

It was just a house, but like I said it was turned over, and they had things for us to do in the building. And we would go on hikes and do different things. It really was nice for [us] kids because we had nothing else otherwise.

We used to walk from 24th Street all the way to Erie Avenue. The Community Center, we used to look forward to it every Saturday because we all met different [kids from other sections of the city]; that's where we really started knowing the different kids from the different, well we say neighborhoods. But you know there were different ones at the time. And we all met up at the Community Center, which was like I say we all look back at Mr. Pollard, Mrs. Johnson, Priscilla Glad was our teachers. It really was nice.[133]

Additionally, in accordance with Pollard's counsel that a woman be chosen as the first director of the center, Ann Palmer, who was active in community affairs, was elected. She served from March 29 to May 1929 as the organization's director and secretary.[134] Romania L. Grisby, who was also an active community leader, replaced her, serving from May 1929 to September 1931. She is listed in the 1930 US Census as being forty years old and a welfare work community leader.[135] The third director was John M. Pollard Sr., who had moved to Niagara Falls (see figure 2.2).

Figure 2.2. John Magnus Pollard, 1943. Courtesy of the *Niagara Falls Gazette*.

His directorship began in October 1931, a little over three years after his study. Under his presidency the Niagara Community Center was stabilized, continuously expanded, and became the heart and nucleus of the entire Black community, attracting nonchurchgoers and active church members from the diverse denominations that formed and grew after 1905. The early operations of the Niagara Community Center and its broad reach in the Black Niagaran community are comparable to the impact the all-purpose Buffalo Michigan Avenue YMCA had on the Black Buffalonian community as described by historian Lillian Williams.[136]

John M. Pollard Sr. proved to be an excellent choice to head the Niagara Community Center. He was well read and possessed leadership and administrative skills. He kept abreast of issues in the country and worldwide and reflected on how they might impact African Americans, stating once that "as World War II loomed the world could learn lessons of peace from American Negroes."[137] He studied the lives and leadership platforms of such African American leaders as Booker T. Washington and W. E. B. Du Bois and White leaders such as Abraham Lincoln.[138] Washington's ability to guide his race in arduous times impressed Pollard, who embraced his ideology in operating a budding community center. In writing about the debate between Washington and Du Bois, Pollard subtly allows readers to see where his allegiances were:

> In the life of the late Booker T. Washington, Mr. Du Bois was certain the plan and practices of Tuskegee were all unsound and that no vestige of discrimination in anything should be tolerated for a single moment. He felt and expressed in vigorous terms that Dr. Washington was a traitor and was selling the race to believers in natural inferiority for "gold." Now [in 1934] Dr. Du Bois feels that Mr. Washington was right; that success for colored people must come from within and that prejudice does not matter so much; that colored people must face things as they are and make their full contribution to America, no matter what Americans do. He expresses the change of heart as vigorously as he previously expressed opinions against all forms of discrimination.[139]

Pollard, who respected Du Bois, knew of Du Bois's scholarship and activism and studied both, incorporating many of his ideas into his leadership ideology and practices. He called Du Bois "the most outstanding Negro in

America and one of the best trained men in the world."[140] "[In 1931], after drawing some lessons from 'Black Reconstruction,' by W. E. B. Du Bois, Pollard addressed [a] congregation on "Why Some Things Are as They Are."[141] Pollard also admired President Lincoln's patience in dealing with prejudice, a trait he thought many Americans should demonstrate. In 1939, for example, he spoke on several programs stressing [affable] Race Relations in honor of the birthday of Abraham Lincoln.[142]

In addition to his respect for Washington, Du Bois, and Lincoln, Pollard wanted the Niagara Community Center to be an integral part of the entire Niagara Falls community. Taking the small monetary appropriation from the Community Chest, he operated the Niagara Community Center extremely efficiently. Funds were stretched to their limit, as the citizens who participated in center activities constantly increased. Eight months into his presidency, Pollard issued a quarterly report to the center's board of directors.[143] He wrote that the center had 166 members and that during May, a total of 4,603 contacts had been made (or people who participated once or more in Niagara Community Center activities). He further emphasized that through fundraising that the Community Center had paid a $200 obligation to the Community Chest and that he managed the following fairly new services provided by the Center: a free employment service; a civics department that sponsored lectures, debates, literary activities, health week programs, and Negro history programs; clubs (or groups that met at the center); classes in sewing; Bible studies; handicrafts; dramatic acting; sporting events in basketball, baseball, and track; and a host center for prominent guests, such as Dr. Mary M. Bethune. Any person or group regardless of color or creed that wanted to help advance African Americans was welcome to speak. Edith A. Schwartzeenbeg, for example, of the Child Guidance Clinic, was invited to address the Young Mother's League of the Niagara Community Center.[144]

Pollard, as director of the Niagara Community Center, strove to make his organization a success, and he endeavored to fully incorporate his people into the mainstream of society. In demonstrating his desire, he often spoke in front of both Black and White audiences, informing them of the aims of the community center and its needs.[145] For instance, he addressed members of the Kiwanis Club, the Business Girl's Club, the Sigma Psi fraternity of the Niagara Falls Public High School, and St. John's AME Church. Moreover, during the early years of his directorship, he wrote a column in the *Niagara Falls Gazette* informing all Niagarans and other interested parties about the activities sponsored by the Niagara Community Center. Theodore

Williamson, in reflecting on a few of his childhood memories of Pollard and the Niagara Community Center, commented:

> John M. Pollard was normally called J. M. Pollard. He was a great speaker. He was his own boss. The Niagara Falls Community Center was the first organization that drew blacks together in Niagara Falls.[146]

Later, Williamson, in implicitly echoing W. E. B. Du Bois's thoughts on the importance of community institutions for racial advancement, remembered the following:

> There was a man named, his name was J. M. Pollard, [spelled] P-o-l-l-a-i-d. Mr. Pollard was a man I looked up to because he was the first man that I knew that headed an organization that was going places, helping young people, older people in the community. The entertainment center was the community center. Mr. James [or John] Pollard is the one who headed it, and a woman by the name of Annie Johnson, never married, she worked there as the assistant director. They had all kinds of programs for the kids.[147]

One of the first major successful projects that Pollard undertook was to invite William O. Pickens to Niagara Falls in 1931 to speak to various groups.[148] Pickens was a scholar, educator, and field secretary of the NAACP. At an address before Black and White students at the senior high school, he spoke extensively on the role of Blacks in the making of America, instilling awareness and pride.[149] His addresses were well received according to the *Niagara Falls Gazette*. Under Pollard's management, in 1934 Charlotte Dett sponsored a program at the community center in observance of Negro History Week.[150] Both Buffalonian and local talent were scheduled to appear on the program. Numerous groups used the community center as a meeting place. Activities such as these were ongoing and usually well attended, making Pollard and the Niagara Community Center important and respected names in Niagara Falls and the Niagara Frontier.

The establishment of the Niagara Community Center, along with the other community institutions, signifies that Black Niagarans, despite the examples of early discord, generally had positive intragroup relations.[151] They turned to each other for information concerning employment, housing, recreation, and fellowship services as well as other sources. It was rare that people had many material possessions, which motivated them even more to work together and share their resources. If one individual or family had resources that could be shared with others, they were usually shared. To hear of a Black person owning an automobile and even their own home was uncommon. As past census data show, most held working-class status. They were individuals trying to make it from one day to the next. In essence, Blacks in the area generally came together to help one another.

Interracial Interactions

Interracial interactions between Blacks and Whites cannot generally be characterized as smooth and cohesive like those of intragroup relationships. Blacks behaved proactively in how they functioned in the broader community as well as in their own communities. Those that emigrated from Canada to the United States certainly held some ideas about race relationships.[152] They likely knew about how fugitive slaves had been treated in Canada when their population figures expanded. This was information that would have been passed on from one generation to another. Moreover, some of them had experienced segregation in the Canadian school system.[153] Therefore, although their relatives and family friends may have escaped slavery, they often did not escape racism and discrimination.

Mabel A. Smith's parents immigrated to the United States during the late nineteenth century. Like the Dett family, they came from Canada. There is a possibility that one or both of her grandparents or great-grandparents had escaped from slavery in the United States and settled in Canada. They perhaps knew of Henry Bibb or Josiah Henson. Both men had successfully escaped slavery, resided in Ontario, Canada, and fought slavery from the dominion of Canada. Henry Bibb spoke out and published an abolitionist newspaper called *Voice of the Fugitive*, while Josiah Henson had his autobiography *The Life of Josiah Henson, Formerly a Slave*, published.[154] It is believed that Harriet Beecher Stowe used Josiah Henson's autobiography to create the character "Uncle Tom" in her highly influential novel *Uncle Tom's Cabin*.[155]

In 1922 Mabel's mother gave birth to her in Niagara Falls, New York. Mabel remembered her parents discussing that a great deal of interracial mixing occurred in Canada between Black and White Canadians, producing mixed-race children. Mabel acknowledged that it existed in her family. She also remembered attending school in Niagara Falls and frequenting the Niagara Community Center on Erie Avenue. She had fun as a child and played with all children irrespective of their race or class. However, at around the age of eleven or twelve, she remembered her White playmates not being able to socialize with her as much as they did when they were smaller children. She attributed this to racism and the fact that the White youths' parents did not want their children to get too close to the African American children. She consulted her father about this and remembered him stating that the White children had a right not to speak with her if they did not want to.[156] Mabel also remembered the early to mid-1940s when there was a massive influx of African Americans. She commented that prior to that there were only a few Black families in Niagara Falls, such as the Browns and Webbs. Mabel married William Brooks, who found employment at the Union Carbide and Carbon Corporation. They had children together and remained married for over twenty years. Mabel eventually left Niagara Falls and moved to Buffalo. She stayed there for three years and then moved to Chicago. She remembered Niagara Falls fondly and commented that life had been difficult because she had lost all her brothers and sisters.[157] Yet she was still optimistic, concluding that "you do the best you can."[158]

Unlike Mabel A. Smith's parents, the Blacks that migrated from the South had the most experience with poor race relationships or Whites making the lives of their family and friends very difficult. Many, as is known, left for these reasons, although economics served as the major stimulus. And the Blacks that were born and raised in Niagara Falls probably held some strong conceptions of race and their "supposed place" in the social order, at least as indicated in the 1901 article on President McKinley's assassin.[159] Consequently, in the decades of the 1920s (and beyond), Blacks knew or learned quickly where they were welcome and where they were not, and they simply did not frequent places where they were not welcome.[160] They did not cross the boundaries of the color line.[161]

William Hunt's interview confirms some of these points.[162] Hunt was born on the outskirts of Augusta, Georgia, in 1920. His father, like so many others, was chased out of town by the Ku Klux Klan. Hunt's uncle, who was already in Niagara Falls, had informed his brother about the plentiful well-paying factory jobs in the city. The father came first, organized his family's passage north, and then sent for them. They arrived by train in 1926 and followed the three-step process in finding accommodation. First the Hunts temporarily moved in with their father's brother on Ely Avenue, where a clustering of Blacks already resided. Later they moved to a transitional quarter, a rented house on Twenty-Seventh Street across from the Niagara Street School. However, in 1927, a year after they arrived, their rental house was firebombed, which compelled them to relocate to a permanent location on Mackenna Avenue, in an area where more blacks were settling and living in relative peace. In underscoring facets of race relations and describing the Hunt family history, William Hunt remembered how his father compared Niagara Falls to the state of Georgia. According to his father,

> [White folks] did not want black folks living anyplace else in those days. My father said it was just like living down South except they had jobs. Instead of working out in the hot sun in the fields all day, they worked in the hot factories, doing the jobs white men would not do. . . . Truth is, they did not really want us here either. . . . They just wanted our labor.[163]

Zorie Bell Boling also remembered that there was always a racial divide between Blacks and Whites in Niagara Falls, where Blacks were perceived by Whites generally as inferior, even as far back as the 1920s.[164] Nonetheless, because Black Niagarans made up only 1 percent of the total population, they were not generally perceived as threatening and invasive by the broad White population.[165] Therefore, signs of injustice existed for Black Niagarans, but the racial treatment that they experienced was still better than the treatment that many of them had experienced in the South.

The year 1915 to the end of the early years of the Great Depression was a growth period for the expanding Black Niagaran community. Jobs attracted more Blacks to Niagara Falls. They came from various regions of the United States, while others crossed the border and emigrated from Canada. Ultimately, they worked to maintain their families and to create other institutions, such as churches and the Niagara Community Center. Mainly through the leadership of John M. Pollard Sr., the center operated as a catalyst that brought Black Niagarans together from diverse backgrounds (e.g., class, religious affiliations, recent migrants, early settlers, etc.) and became the central institution of the Black Niagaran community and its greatest collective achievement. John Pollard, like the early ministers (e.g., Reverend William Ware, Reverend Luther Holloway, Reverend William Johnson, and Reverend Reed), helped to form and manage an invaluable institution. He broadly promoted an integrationist philosophy throughout the entire city of Niagara Falls and particularly in the Black Niagaran community, which will be further demonstrated in chapter 3. Notwithstanding effective leadership, Black Niagarans still felt they were being treated as second-class citizens—similar to their experiences during the 1850 to 1914 period. However, the racial barriers, particularly in housing, did not restrict them to the extent they would in later years when their population figures increased significantly. With Blacks progressively working to advance themselves in conjunction with being shepherded by their leadership, the budding community would continue to grow and develop during the ongoing Depression years.

Chapter Three

The Development of the Black Community, the Great Depression Years, 1930s

Impact of the Great Depression on the City of Niagara Falls

During the Great Depression years (1929–1941), many Black Niagaran leaders continued to foster community development, as the Black Niagaran community slowly but steadily expanded. Many Black Niagarans still resided throughout most city wards, but a cluster began to form in specific wards at the south end of town. A race riot in 1930 was the most blatant form of racism they encountered. Under the leadership of John Pollard, the Niagara Community Center continued to flourish as the main institution in the Black Niagaran community, aiding citizens in desperate need, along with facilitating and promoting self-help efforts.

The Wall Street Crash of 1929 precipitated the Great Depression, the worst economic catastrophe the United States had yet experienced. Oral historian Studs Terkel, in his classic work *Hard Times*, chronicled the Great Depression's impact on American society from a range of viewpoints, emphasizing class, race, and gender, with a concentration on people inside and outside of government. Terkel's interviewees eloquently articulated the hardships that they and others encountered.[1] Overnight, people lost everything. People who had never envisioned themselves seeking charity urgently needed it. Men—and now more women—searched for work. Children, through their parents' guidance, did whatever they could to help.

Many months passed before the city of Niagara Falls began to experience the full impact of the Great Depression. This gradual impact was due largely to steady demand for cheap hydroelectric energy generated from the Niagara River and Niagara's waterfalls as well as the city's highly successful tourist industry. Niagara Falls's population expanded throughout the Great Depression years. In 1930, for example, 75,460 people resided in Niagara Falls.[2] By 1940, the year immediately preceding the US entry into World War II, this figure had increased to 78,029.[3]

Once the Great Depression began to take its full toll on Niagarans, economic hardship ensued. The tourist industry greatly declined because fewer tourists visited the city. In 1929 estimates indicated that 3,282,000 people had visited Niagara Falls; by 1932 that figure had dwindled to 1,444,000.[4] The number of tourists who had spent money on high-priced items and world-class hotel accommodations dropped significantly, and vendors were compelled to barter more with tourists over prices. Vendors unwilling to make price adjustments often did not survive. Furthermore, due to the increasing unemployment rate, the number of people who received charity increased. In December 1929, it took $4,525 per month to operate the local Bureau of Charities; by December of 1932, that figure had grown to $66,551.[5] The city government constantly sought aid from the state and federal government.[6] More women sought employment outside of their households. In 1930, for instance, census enumerators recorded 6,788 employed women; by 1940 that figure had increased to 8,529, compared to 24,231 and 25,005 employed men, respectively.[7]

Niagara Falls had a modern, efficient train system. Consequently, hobos and other itinerants illegally rode trains from one municipality to another in hopes of finding food, shelter, and employment.[8] William Feder, who was a child during the Great Depression, later remembered hobos entering and leaving Niagara Falls.[9] He also believed that one of the main reasons his family survived was that they were allowed to live on the Niagara University grounds and receive room and board, provided they worked six days per week for the university. Feder also believed that Niagarans in general were safeguarded from the worst effects of the Depression because many local farms provided additional food for needy families. In this milieu, Black Niagarans, who were mainly poor, proactively worked collectively to advance themselves in a challenging economic epoch.

Community Progress

By 1930 the Great Depression continued to linger. By then more Blacks had settled in the city of Niagara Falls; at least 906 Blacks resided in Niagara Falls, comprising 1.2 percent of the city's recorded population. When compared to the 1920 population figures, this reflects an increase of 397 people and a 0.2 percent increase in Niagara Falls's total population. More Blacks migrated to Niagara Falls between 1920 and 1930 compared to previous decades. As in earlier periods, the hope of finding jobs attracted them to the area.

Just as during the construction of the Tunnel and because of labor needs during World War I until about 1930, there was consistent demand for low-skilled workers. This demand significantly decreased as the Great Depression persisted. Blacks competed with Whites for many of these jobs and performed them with hopes of improving their economic status. Table 3.1 shows the range of jobs that Black Niagarans held in 1930.

Four-hundred and fifty-four Black Niagarans were recorded as working, 336 men (74 percent) and 118 women (26 percent). Most women worked as domestic servants. These figures reflect an increase from the 1920 US Census figures, which showed 42 women working from a total of 266 Black laborers, with 30 females recorded as domestic servants. Most Black workers were unskilled laborers—205 in all. Twenty individuals worked as

Table 3.1. Black Workers Recorded in the 1930 US Census

	Number	Percentages
Males		
Professional	16	3.52
Proprietary	12	2.64
Clerical	6	1.32
Skilled	19	4.18
Semiskilled	16	3.54
Unskilled	196	43.17
Domestic	71	15.63
Total	336	74.0
Females		
Professional	1	0.22
Proprietary	7	1.54
Clerical	1	0.22
Skilled	1	0.22
Semiskilled	9	1.98
Unskilled	9	1.98
Domestic	90	19.82
Total	118	26.0
Grand Total	454	100%

Adapted from the 1930 United States Census. (Please see page 342, note 10.)

skilled tradespersons: three barbers, a bricklayer, a carpenter, eight restaurant cooks, five garage mechanics, a hairdresser, and a painter. Nineteen worked as entrepreneurs: a barbershop owner, a billiard room proprietor, a junk company proprietor, five restaurant proprietors, a proprietor (business not listed), two retail merchants, seven rooming house operators, and the manager of a billiard room. Seventeen individuals labored as professional employees: an engineer, two insurance agents, three ministers, nine musicians, a photographer, and a welfare work-community leader. Although Niagara Falls's Black population by 1930 had significantly increased, trends in table 3.1 conveyed similarities and differences compared to table 2.4. For instance, unskilled laborers comprised the majority of Black workers for both decades, and few Black Niagarans could be found in other work status categories. More specifically, twenty skilled tradepersons were counted in 1930 compared to fifteen in 1920; in 1930 at least seventeen professionals worked compared to two in 1920. Nineteen entrepreneurs operated small businesses in 1930, while nine did so in 1920.

The 1930 Census lists a number of community leaders who contributed not only to African American history in Niagara Falls but also to the history of Niagara Falls in general. Samuel Dett, like his brother R. Nathaniel, made history in Niagara Falls by becoming the first Black postal worker in the city.[10] He was hired in 1907 as a mail carrier, earning about $400 per year. "In a 1947 interview with the *Niagara [Falls] Gazette*, Dett recalled applying for his post office job to gain job security. But there were no Black mail carriers, so Dett needed circulated petitions on his behalf on Fall Street."[11] Enough people signed Dett's petition; he was hired. In 1912 Dett was promoted from mail carrier to special clerk, earning $1,100 annually. His job entailed working more directly with the public, particularly resolving complaints. People respected his service and perceived him as a pleasant, accommodating worker. In addition, Mildred C. Clark, a friend of the Dett family, remembered that [Dett] "was an awfully nice guy, [a] very quiet, polite person who was appreciative of anything that anyone did for him."[12] The 1930 census figures indicate that Dett was forty-five years old and lived on Second Street.[13] He lived in the tourist house that his mother owned. Dett worked for the Niagara Falls US postal service until 1949, when he retired. Dett, who never married, involved himself in the Niagara Community Center and the YMCA, serving in leadership positions. At the Niagara Community Center, he was a member of several committees and the board of directors, and he served as the center president. The YMCA later installed him in their Hall of Fame. During World War I, Dett was appointed an American Red

Cross special lieutenant to help Black servicemen passing through Niagara Falls.[14] Upon retirement Dett's only wish was that his position be filled by another African American. Dett lived for about thirteen years after his retirement. He died in 1962, outliving his famous younger brother, R. Nathaniel, and his mother, Charlotte.

Reverend Donald Benjamin Barton, like Samuel Dett, appeared in the 1930 Census reports, residing on Thirteenth Street near Buffalo Avenue.[15] He lived in his church's parsonage. At this time, he was the minister of St. John's AME Church. By order of his denomination's leadership, he was commissioned to head the church in Niagara Falls. Barton, who had graduated from Howard University, had been in Elmhurst, New York, and relocated to Niagara Falls in 1926.[16] By 1929 Barton led a $4,500 drive to pay off the debts of the church, the debt having been reduced from $6,000 to $4,500.[17] Barton and his helpers called this effort "the Hundred Dollar Club." Barton asked forty-five public-spirited citizens of Niagara Falls to contribute $100 each. Many Niagarans contributed, including the city's chief representative, Mayor William Laughlin. Besides fulfilling his church duties, Barton aggressively sought to broaden his leadership beyond his flock, involving himself in the activities that created the Niagara Community Center. Barton helped create the initial proposal submitted to the Community Chest, and he helped to oversee its implementation by ensuring that competent leadership was selected. He actively served on the center's board of directors, along with Jerry Plato, Royal Palmer, Bessie Palmer, and Benjamin Bolden.[18] All these board members faithfully attended St. John's AME Church.[19] In a speech to Shiloh Baptist Church's congregation encouraging them to actively participate in programs at the new Niagara Community Center, Benjamin Bolden credited Reverend Barton with originating and promoting the idea of having a local community center.[20] Barton also helped increase the membership of St. John's, and his experienced leadership allowed him to meet and interact with Niagarans of diverse creeds, colors, and cultural backgrounds.

Anna Gabriel was also recorded in the 1930 Census reports.[21] Unlike Samuel Dett and Reverend Barton, Gabriel was a young thirty-four-year-old entrepreneur: she operated a rooming house on First Street. Later she moved her business to Erie Avenue, next door to the Niagara Community Center.[22] With the White hotels generally not opening their doors to Blacks, Gabriel saw the need for a place for Black tourists to stay when they visited Cataract City. She may have also rented space to Black migrants who needed temporary housing. Anna Gabriel was one of the few Black entrepreneurs in the city of Niagara Falls and active in Black

Niagaran community affairs. For example, she frequently volunteered to oversee Niagara Community Center activities for young people.[23]

Edison Tucker appeared in the 1930 Census reports as well.[24] Tucker at the time was not a public worker, nor a professional, entrepreneur, or a member of the middle class. He was working class. He moved to Niagara Falls in 1927 and was recorded as being twenty-three years old by 1930.[25] He held a job at Union Carbide and Carbon Company, working with raw materials, mainly as a furnace operator. He worked at the company for forty years and retired in 1968. Tucker regularly attended church and was actively involved, as his leadership operated largely but not exclusively within his church and family. For example, he was a founder of Mount Zion Baptist Church, served on the Deacon board, taught Sunday school, and sang in the church choir. He married Minerva L. Thomas, who may have been his second wife because the census reports indicated that he was married to Helen Tucker in 1930, both spouses being twenty-three years old.[26] Interviewees said that Edison Tucker provided for his family and attempted to be a positive force in his community.[27]

Before or after Black Niagarans had secured their jobs, where did they live as of 1930? Had conditions changed drastically from 1920? Table 3.2 can answer these questions.

Table 3.2. 1930 Black Population by Wards

Wards	Black	White	Black Percentage
1	25	1,642	1.5
2	95	2,629	3.5
3	236	3,997	5.6
4	256	6,341	3.9
5	101	13,809	.07
6	0	3,417	0
7	51	1,834	2.7
8	9	3,061	.03
9	46	9,866	.05
10	0	5,703	0
11	12	1,908	.06
12	33	5,992	.05
13	26	4,793	.05
14	16	6,261	.03
15	0	3,195	0

Adapted from the 1930 United States Census. (Please see page 342, note 28.)

In analyzing this data and comparing it to the 1920 US Census data, some significant transformations did occur. The number of Blacks in Ward 1 decreased to 25; while in 1920, there were 113 Blacks residing there. Ward 3's Black population increased from 94 in 1920 to 236 in 1930. Ninth Street, Tenth Street, Memorial Parkway, Twelfth Street, Thirteenth Street, and Buffalo Avenue were the major streets in Ward 3. Ward 4's Black population ballooned in 1930, increasing from 52 in 1920 to 256 in 1930. Such streets as Welch, East Falls, Cudaback, Mackenna, Allen, Fourteenth, Fifteenth, Twenty-Fourth, and Buffalo Avenue made up Ward 4. The Black population in Ward 5 increased from 56 to 101 people, while the Black population in Ward 6 stayed consistent at zero. Ward 7's Black population decreased by seven. Ward 9's Black population increased from six to forty-six persons. Other wards reflected more increases than decreases, and the city of Niagara Falls added Wards 14 and 15, which had not existed in 1920.

One of the more critical findings illustrated in table 3.2 is that a large cluster of Blacks had formed in Wards 3 and 4. Four hundred and ninety-two Blacks in total resided in those two wards. This represented 54 percent of Niagara Falls's Black population. Moreover, Wards 2 and 5 bordered Wards 3 and 4. Seventy-six percent of Niagara Falls's Black population could be accounted for in these wards combined. Consequently, although Blacks in 1930 lived in twelve of the fifteen city wards, a distinctive Black community had developed. In earlier decades, Blacks resided noticeably in Wards 1 through 5 but were not strictly concentrated in those areas, and their presence did not represent a meaningful clustering. By 1930 they were significantly clustered in Wards 2 through 5 especially in Wards 3 and 4, even though their population percentage in each ward was low.

The rationale for this phenomenon is multifaceted. Racism undoubtedly played a role. There were sections of Niagara Falls in which Whites resented having Black neighbors. These were the more stable areas outside of the Tunnel District that did not receive the constant influx of southern migrants, such as Wards 6, 10, 11, and the De Veaux section of Ward 12. Zorie Bell Boling also remembered in the early 1930s that Blacks and Whites seemed to live apart from one another and that if Whites were in an area where a cluster of Blacks resided, they were usually poor Whites.[28] William Hunt remembered that in the 1920s and 1930s Blacks could live in relative peace only in about three neighborhoods, and Ward 4 was one of them.[29] Even so, the census records clearly convey that Blacks lived interspersed throughout the city of Niagara Falls; some even resided near the waterfalls. In each ward, the percentages of Black residents tended to be low.

Another logical rationale for the clusters is that Blacks were proactive in their housing search. Those who had migrated from other locales felt comfortable living near people they knew or near people of their own racial group. Family members or friends who knew of the benefits of living in Niagara Falls informed their loved ones, and in turn those individuals came and stayed with or near them. Individuals or families who could accommodate roomers or boarders saw an economic opportunity if they were willing to create needed space for migrants seeking temporary accommodations. Barbara Smith's father, for example, migrated to Niagara Falls in 1922.[30] He came from Cayce, South Carolina. Like William Hunt's father and Carlyle Miller's uncle, he was chased out of town because he refused to accept the southern social order of Black subordination to Whites. His brother, H. C. Thomas, had previously informed him about the benefits of Niagara Falls. That helped convince him to join his brother, as he fled for his safety and perhaps his life. He temporarily left his wife and children to prepare their future passage north. He stayed with his brother on Ely Avenue for about a year until he was in a better financial situation to send for them.

Norwood Samuel's parents moved to Niagara Falls largely because they had relatives in the city.[31] Samuel's father migrated from Georgia, while her mother came from North Carolina. Her father's uncle was already in town, and her mother's brothers lived on First Street and operated a hotel called the Palmer House. Terrell and Royal Palmer managed the Palmer House. Eventually, Samuel's parents moved to Center Avenue, where they temporarily stayed with the father's uncle, "old Turner Bryant." Then they moved down the street from Turner Bryant, staying on Center Avenue close to their relative. Countless numbers of these stories exist, which reinforces the idea that although Blacks faced obstacles, they were proactive in seeking and maintaining their living arrangements.

A Works Project Administration (WPA) housing study completed in 1939 uncovered several negative findings concerning living arrangements of Black Niagarans.[32] Most Blacks (87.1 percent) rented living space, whereas 12.9 percent owned their living quarters.[33] This is supported by the 1930 Census reports, which show that only 43 Black families owned their homes, whereas 195 Black families rented.[34] The largest percentage of Blacks lived in dwellings with rent valued at $15 to $20 per month.[35] Nineteen percent of Blacks lived in dwelling units with rents of $20 to

$25 per month, and 12.5 percent lived in units with rents of $5 to $10 per month.[36] The largest percent of Blacks (22%) lived in four-room dwellings, whereas most Whites (24.8%) lived in five- to six-room dwellings.[37] In terms of overcrowded dwellings, 4.9 percent of Black families, compared to 2.7% of Whites, housed more than 1.5 persons per room.[38] Over 60 percent of a sample of 210 Black families lived in substandard dwelling units in need of major repairs or unfit for human habitation.[39]

Before the Work Project Administration study was completed, a discussion forum on housing was sponsored by the local YWCA, held in conjunction with the ongoing WPA study. Supervisor of the WPA property survey, R. R. Pratt; Ernest Curto, a local attorney; chairman of the city's advisory housing commission, Russell G. Larke; and John Pollard spoke authoritatively on housing conditions in Niagara Falls. They predicted that the WPA would find about six thousand substandard homes in Niagara Falls, mainly in poor communities. Moreover, they said Niagara Falls had many slumlords who charged exorbitant rents but did not put monies back into maintaining their properties. As a solution they proposed that city officials support their proposal for the creation and development of a housing authority that would build public housing units. "One of the benefits of better housing," the speakers declared, "[would] be a credit to the community and the appreciable reduction of crime, disease, immorality and the general death rate."[40] The speakers refuted the belief that renters destroy the physical attractiveness of a community; rather, they placed the burden on the landlords' greed and neglect. Their efforts during the Great Depression later helped influence city officials to build minimal public housing (see chapter 4).

Influential Collectivist Leadership during the Great Depression Era: John M. Pollard, Alice C. Hayes, and Dr. Charles B. Hayes

During the Great Depression years, Black Niagarans requested more services from the Niagara Community Center as more Blacks moved to Niagara Falls and searched for living quarters. The center used all its available rooms, including its basement.[41] In the 1930s, the center continued its employment service, which aided many people.[42] Pollard purchased a pool table for $5.63 that was enjoyed by hundreds of boys.[43] An arts and crafts workshop for young people was held in the center's basement despite the congested conditions. They were happy to participate in the activity and to show their family and friends what they had created.[44]

With the steady growth and expanding needs of the Black Niagaran population, John M. Pollard's leadership role became even more essential. Pollard was born in 1883 in Petersburg, Virginia, to a family whose patriarch had been a minister.[45] During his youth, he observed his father demonstrating leadership, which undoubtedly influenced him. He also experienced the Jim Crow South. Pollard earned his bachelor of arts degree from the State College of South Carolina.[46] Then he began his graduate work at St. Augustine's College and ended it at the University of Chicago. From 1907 to 1916, Pollard was dean of the teachers' college of St. Paul's Normal and Industrial School in Lawrenceville, Virginia, an African American institution supported by the Episcopal Church that ranked third in number of pupils and in its endowment, being surpassed only by Hampton and Tuskegee Institutes.[47] During World War I, he did camp community service, followed by serving as national recreations director.[48] Understanding Pollard's leadership philosophy is crucial for understanding his vital role in cultivating community development, which helped uplift the Black Niagaran community.[49] Pollard was the first Black Niagaran leader who operated in a capacity that consistently connected him with the entire Black community. Perceived at first as an "outsider," Pollard awakened hope in others and became well known and highly regarded.

Pollard exhibited some of the leadership traits of both Booker T. Washington and W. E. B. Du Bois.[50] Being educated, a southerner, and the dean of a teachers' college, Pollard knew of Booker T. Washington. During his twelve-year career as director of the Niagara Community Center, Pollard's leadership epitomized Washington's "captains of industry" concept. As Washington counseled, Pollard improved his life through his education and work experiences. Instead of setting himself apart from or above Black Niagarans, he interacted and socialized with them and others, regardless of their class. He passionately strove to improve their plight and serve as a role model.[51] Equally, through his actions, Pollard exemplified Du Bois's description of the "Talented Tenth."[52] Like Du Bois, he was highly educated, having earned advanced degrees. He had acquired high-level research skills that aided him in conducting his 1928 house-to-house survey, the results of which contributed toward the formation of the Niagara Community Center. Du Bois thought that the brightest and best Blacks (or the top 10 percent) should be supported at all costs in their educational endeavors. This was to be a sacrifice and investment for

African American communities throughout the nation. Du Bois's vision demanded that recipients of these momentous efforts go back and help their communities. With support, Pollard fulfilled this role, finding other educated Black Niagarans to help foster community development.

Like Du Bois and Washington, Pollard believed in equality. He was an integrationist who created alliances with the more influential White classes to effect change within and beyond the Niagara Community Center, ensuring its progression specifically and the advancement of his people generally. Hence, during and after the Great Depression, the day-to-day activities of the Niagara Community Center continued.[53] Groups such as Electric City Lodge No. 49, the Neighborhood Council, the Mothers' Club, the Boys' Handicraft Club, the Mary B. Talbert Club, the Harriet Tubman Club, and the Junior Girls' Club met at the center during and after the Depression era.[54] Athletic groups, such as the girls' softball team, boys' baseball team, and men's baseball team, also met at the center.[55] Pollard and his associates also attempted to relieve the hardships of center patrons in grave need through consultation and/or financial means.

In public settings, Pollard articulated that Black Niagarans faced two major barriers in the city of Niagara Falls. One was economics related, and the other was housing related. At a 1939 community-wide meeting, for example, sponsored by the Niagara Peace Council and the Niagara Community Center, Pollard gave an address in which he underlined the economic problems of most Black Niagarans seeking employment.[56] "Most of the problems here are economic," he said, pointing out that "of 1,400 Negro residents, there are only 112 of them on relief, with another third [in] the 'bread and butter line' and the rest with but few exceptions, on the margins between self-sufficiency and destitution, with only a whim of fate needed to bring them to the latter."[57] He further explained that there were plants in Niagara Falls that still would not hire Negroes, and he urged unprejudiced people, particularly the more influential Whites, to intercede to make a change.[58] He concluded his remarks on economics by saying that if Negroes were hired, their wage scale was often many times lower than that offered to White people for the same type of employment.[59] Pollard asked for justice and equality for his constituents.

On housing issues, Pollard articulated the experiences of Black Niagarans that he had often seen and heard as director of the Niagara Community Center: housing was difficult to acquire for recent migrants, and living arrangements were too crowded. In asserting that housing was the second major problem of Black Niagarans, Pollard told the story about ten families who shared a single dwelling and the same lavatory.[60] Concluding his comments on housing, Pollard called for the building of three hundred to four hundred low-rent houses in Niagara Falls to meet the needs of the most desperate Black Niagarans. Consequently, Pollard was one of the first (perhaps *the* first) Black Niagaran leader who urged public officials to use their influence to ensure that Black Niagarans had access to more and better housing. Unfortunately, this plea resonated throughout much of Black Niagaran history. Pollard, like Charlotte Dett and others, was a prominent Black Niagaran leader who was was taken seriously in interracial public forums attended not only by Black Niagarans but also by the broader community of concerned citizens.

When more concerned citizens became aware of who John M. Pollard was and what he stood for (and that he was an excellent speaker), more requests came to Pollard to address audiences on various issues, particularly on how race relationships could be improved.[61] For instance, at an informal forum before St. John's AME Church, Pollard addressed an audience on internal community affairs.[62] At a luncheon meeting of a Council of Social Agencies (probably from Niagara Falls), Pollard presented the housing condition of Black Niagarans.[63] In Auburn, New York, Pollard spoke at an event sponsored by the Cayuga Social Forum at the Chamber of Commerce.[64] Echoing Theodore Roosevelt's words and alluding to how Roosevelt unjustly handled African American soldiers in the 1906 Brownville, Texas incident, he urged that Negroes should be given a "square deal" and not be judged by the criminal behaviors of a few. To accentuate this point, he cited the loyalty of many enslaved persons during the Civil War, stating that many (perhaps most) stayed on farms and plantations to support and protect Whites left behind, while young men were off fighting to keep Blacks enslaved.[65] At some public speaking engagements, Pollard was accompanied by Niagara Community Center singers who would serenade an audience, singing spirituals after his address. Pollard, a southerner, most likely considered this familiar practice to be highly effective. After all, the Fisk University singers had made the practice famous, and other Black schools such as Hampton and Tuskegee Institutes extensively featured singers.[66] In an address at a young people's forum at the Niagara Falls YMCA Branch, Pollard exhibited his religious values from his upbringing by emphasizing to the youth to work hard but to also exercise and value the power of prayers in their daily lives.[67] Therefore, as part of his persuasive approach to win others over to his cause, Pollard used moral arguments to gain support, especially from influential citizens.

In the early 1930s, Niagara Falls received two new major leaders who had a tremendous impact not only on the Black community but also on the entire city: Dr. Charles B. Hayes and Alice C. Hayes. They quickly became strong allies of John Pollard. Originally from Jamaica, Dr. Hayes moved to New York City and attended school there. He graduated from the City College of New York in 1927; then he attended Howard University Medical School, graduating in 1931.[68] He began his medical practice in Niagara Falls in 1934. Alice Hayes graduated from Hunter College, where she majored in social studies. After graduation, she joined the staff of the Russell Sage Foundation, performing medical work at the Harlem Hospital from 1931 to 1935 and social work at the New York State Department of Public Works (see figure 3.1).[69]

During her early years as a social worker, Alice Hayes completed a three-year course in psychology, which was a requirement of all administrators and case workers in the public welfare department.[70] Childhood sweethearts Alice and Charles married, and she moved to Niagara Falls in 1935.[71] Both she and her husband immediately involved themselves in the affairs of the Niagara Community Center, taking on leadership positions. After being a secretary for Pollard, Alice Hayes became president of the board of directors at the Community Center. Of the two, Dr. Hayes had the more easygoing personality.[72]

Both involved themselves in other community activities. Dr. Hayes joined several medical associations, the local Selective Service Board, the International Association of Lions Clubs, and several civic organizations. Alice Hayes joined the Council of Social Agencies and was extremely effective in that organization. Her contributions and skills encouraged

Figure 3.1. Charles and Alice Hayes, 1960 and 1980. Courtesy of the *Niagara Falls Gazette*.

more Whites to assume leadership positions within the Niagara Community Center. Hamilton B. Mizer, a retired publisher of the *Niagara Falls Gazette* who was also an active member of the Council of Social Agencies, recalled that "[Alice Hayes] was well accepted by everyone and that acceptance made it possible for her to serve on many agency boards that blacks did not normally belong to."[73] Aaron L. Griffin, who eventually replaced John Pollard as director of the Community Center, remembered Alice Hayes as having keen executive abilities and being a skilled project manager.[74] Helen Reed-McBride, an African American who was born in Niagara Falls and grew up during the 1930s, remembered both Hayeses and had especially fond memories of Dr. Hayes:

> That's my buddy. What I remember about Charles Hayes, he was a good doctor. He was a real good doctor. I had a sister that got hit by a car. Beulah is what we called her. When the car hit her, [the driver] broke her leg. Dr. Hayes wasn't our doctor then. Our mother said . . . Dr. Hayes said if you give me the case, I will save the leg. All the other doctors wanted to cut it off. Dr. Hayes said I am not guarantying she's going to walk, but I will save the leg. They let him try, and she walked. Dr. Hayes was just an upstart doctor then. When we went to Dr. Hayes' office, it would be so crowded, you would be there half the day, but he was a good doctor.[75]

In another story that demonstrates Dr. Hayes's multiracial patient base and exemplifies Booker T. Washington's concept of not limiting one's patron base exclusively to African Americans, Reed-McBride recounted:

> I remember I used to work for Mary Tatory and John Tatory at the Manhattan Restaurant. They loved Dr. Hayes too. Their daughter Missy was having a baby and she said—this came from Missy's mouth—Missy told me [Dr. Hayes] told me say if you give me the case I'll save [you and your baby]. The other doctors said it was her or the baby. And Dr. Hayes said if you give me the case, I'll save them both. Because Dr. Hayes was black, they were leery about it. But after a while the mother and father said give him the case. So they gave him the case, and he saved her and the baby both. Every time Dr. Hayes went

in their restaurant, they would feed him. They would feed him and everything. He'd come in quite a bit in the restaurant. They loved Dr. Hayes. They would tell you, "We love Dr. Hayes!"[76]

The Hayeses had no biological children, but they adopted a daughter and equipped her with all the tools necessary to be successful.[77]

In terms of leadership philosophies and practices, like Pollard, both Hayeses were integrationists who strongly believed in justice and equality for all people. Since they were relatively new arrivals, the city of Niagara Falls must have seemed to them like a small country town, considering that they had relocated from New York City. For the Hayeses, as young adults, the 1930s was the decade in which they began to demonstrate leadership, which became more evident with each ensuing decade. Booker T. Washington's "captains of industry" concept can also be applied to Dr. Hayes. Most interviewees who discussed Dr. Hayes described him as a consummate professional who made them feel at ease whenever they were around him in any setting.[78] All classes of people, particularly the working class, generally liked Dr. Hayes and felt a personal connection to him.

By contrast, Du Bois's Talented Tenth concept can be applied to Alice Hayes. She, too, was highly educated, and like Du Bois, she appreciated the power of education when used as a "change agent." Accounts in the *Niagara Falls Gazette* from 1935 to 1982 underscore Alice's commitment to improving the plight not only of Black Niagarans but also all Niagarans. She was a very intelligent, strong-minded, progressive, extroverted person who stood her ground on issues if she felt she was right—a trait that all effective leaders must possess. Like Charlotte Dett, she also exhibited the behavioral decorum of the politics of respectability, in that she preferred that Black Niagarans behave honorably and respectfully, particularly in public.[79] Yet some interviewees who did not wish to be quoted thought leadership under Alice Hayes's direction, unlike that of her husband, was of the autocratic top-down style, in which they were expected to listen intently and follow her lead.

Both Hayeses made significant contributions. For example, at a 1936 meeting of the Frontier Chapter of New York State Association for Negro Welfare, held at neighboring Buffalo's Michigan Avenue YMCA, Alice Hayes was elected to the executive committee.[80] At the same gathering, Pollard was elected vice president of the chapter. In these early days, after one of Pollard's formal addresses, Alice Hayes often served as one of his accompanying singers, as she did after a 1937 address given by Pollard in neighboring St. Catharine's, Ontario.[81] At a 1938 meeting before the Missionary Society of the Second Baptist Church of Niagara Falls, Alice Hayes was a guest speaker. She continuously served in many leadership capacities at the Niagara Community Center.[82] Equally, Dr. Hayes, in addition to serving on boards and being a role model, frequently executed his leadership by giving many talks on health issues. In 1935, for example, Dr. Hayes gave a lecture at the Niagara Community Center on the value of the Wasserman Test, then an effective medical procedure for detecting syphilis.[83] Dr. Hayes informed his attentive audience that over a million Americans had syphilis, many unbeknownst to them. Ironically, at the time of this lecture, the infamous Tuskegee Experiment in Macon County, Alabama, was being conducted.[84] Furthermore, in 1937, Dr. Hayes, during "Negro Health Week," spoke to an audience at the Niagara Falls Second Street Baptist Church, appealing to them to hold Negro Health Week every week of the year, so that it might add up to a lifetime of good health.[85] Dr. Hayes also spoke at a 1937 meeting at the Niagara Community Center on the value of cooperation and the ideals of that organization, which among many concerns promoted acquiring an education.[86]

Like Dr. Hayes, Dr. Ezekiel E. Nelson was a physician. They almost certainly knew each other, considering both were two of the few Black medical practitioners in western New York.[87] Dr. Nelson strongly believed in the betterment of his race. Like W. E. B. Du Bois, Nelson espoused cooperative economics during the Great Depression era (and even after) as a strategy for group advancement.[88] For almost four decades (1930 to 1970), he worked with almost fanatical zeal to convince Black residents of Buffalo that cooperative economics and racial solidarity would enable them to escape poverty and economic oppression. Dr. Nelson preached that by working together, pooling their resources, and supporting cooperative ventures, Black Buffalonians could build powerful economic institutions that would enable them to produce many of the goods and services that were needed in their community. Supporting these business endeavors, he felt, would create jobs, particularly for the young, and create a higher standard of living for all. The available sources on Dr. Hayes, including interview testimonies, do not portray him as a champion of cooperative economics; nonetheless, his actions demonstrate that he supported collectivists behavior (or Black Niagarans working together) for group advancement.

Depression-Era Community Dynamics: Educational Experiences, Community Cooperation, Recreation, Racial Conflict, and Self-Help

The educational experiences of Black children in Niagara Falls had not changed much since 1920. Just as in 1920, they attended neighborhood schools, where often they were still the only Black children in their classes. They probably did not have any major problems with their White teachers unless they did not do as they were told.[89] The quality of education they received in reading, writing, and arithmetic was probably adequate. However, the 1930 US Census reports show that the illiteracy rate of Black Niagarans had increased to 3.5 percent.[90] Compared to the 1920 Census, this was an increase of 1 percent. Three and a half percent was still low, considering that the Black population had significantly increased, and some recent migrant children had come from sharecropping families who compelled them to work on farms rather than attend school.[91] For Niagaran school-age children, generally the illiteracy rate was 4.8 percent, for native Whites 0.2 percent, and for foreign-born Whites 11.8 percent.[92] In reflecting on her Niagara Falls school experiences, Helen Reed-McBride remembered some good teachers. She also recalled racial incidents with some of her White schoolmates:

> The schools over there they were nice, and they taught you and everything. But the little White kids over there would call you a jig-a-boo, a nigger; anything they could think of, you just was that. And some of them didn't speak to you. Some of them played with you, and some didn't. Most of the time you was out there by yourself. I had a couple of teachers that I really liked. One was Mrs. Briers. She was my first-grade teacher. And Mrs. Fischer was my high school teacher. She was nice. She was very nice.[93]

Reed-McBride, as a child, also observed how the Black community of Niagara Falls functioned during the 1930s. Being the daughter of the Reverend Thomas Reed helped to enhance these experiences. The Reed family lived on Allen Avenue and then MacKenna Avenue, near Twenty-Seventh Street. They were involved in community affairs.[94] Reed-McBride remembered that a community of Blacks lived in two areas, first in sections linking Allen Avenue, MacKenna Avenue, Cudaback Avenue, and Twenty-Fourth Street, followed by a clustering on East Falls Street, Tenth Street, and on Eleventh Street. In addition to emphasizing education and the growth of the Black community, Reed-McBride also remembered that her community in the 1930s (and 1940s) was really unified: families did not have much in terms of material possessions, but generally what they had was shared.[95] If someone went fishing, other people in the neighborhood received fresh fish; if people grew gardens, their crops were shared.[96] A Mrs. Hampton used to work for a White family that did not eat certain parts of chickens, such as the backs, necks, and wings. They would give their scraps to Mrs. Hampton, and she, in turn, brought them home to be shared with her neighbors. "I remember her bringing big old bags," Reed-McBride recalled. "She'd feed everybody too. She'd give everybody some of those chicken backs and stuff from where she worked at."[97] In the 1930s, as in other periods, Blacks were poor. "Milk and bread were given out. Families picked up metals to sell to Jewish junk dealers."[98] Nevertheless, the Black community was unified and operated as a village, looking out for the well-being of everyone.[99] Tough times were a reality, but Blacks strove to survive and prosper. Helen Reed-McBride's reminiscences demonstrate historian Elsa Barkley-Brown's idea of how the internal dynamics of a Black community can operate, particularly during desperate times, versus how its members may function externally in the broader community when that community offers both negative and positive reinforcement.[100]

Black Niagarans also strove to enjoy life during the Great Depression, despite their economic difficulties. As noted by Gunnar Myrdal, most recreational activities of African Americans tended to be informal, intimate, and sociable, occurring among individuals within their families, neighborhoods, churches, and community centers.[101] In addition, many Black Niagarans looked forward to and planned for the Emancipation Day Celebration picnic at Lakeside Park in Port Dalhousie, Canada. Baseball diamonds, a swimming beach, a skating ring, and cooking facilities were a few of the amenities available to park patrons. The celebration occurred on the first Thursday of every August, beginning in the 1920s and extending well into the 1950s and beyond. People came from such US cities as Niagara Falls, Buffalo, Rochester, Syracuse, Utica, Detroit, and Cleveland—and from Canadian cities like Toronto, Hamilton, and St. Catherines. The Universal Negro Improvement Association (UNIA), led by its powerful, charismatic leader Marcus Mosiah Garvey, initially started and managed this celebration.[102] In reflecting on the great times he had at the Emancipation Day Celebrations, one park patron happily remembered:

> All Black people in Niagara Falls looked forward to [the Emancipation Day celebration]. That was the day when everybody saved nickels, dimes, and quarters, wherever they could save them in a box or can. I had a PET milk can. We all looked forward to getting together as one group of people in Port Dalhousie, in Canada. That was a big, big deal. We would get together in cars. A car that would carry six people, there would be 10 in it. There were no restrictions like now when the police would stop you and say hey you got too many people in your car. There were no restrictions crossing the bridge [into Canada]. Hey, you American [border police would ask]? Yes. See ya [the border police would respond]. We would be mingling with people from Detroit, Buffalo, and of course, Niagara Falls and little towns in between. It was a big, big celebration. We called it Emancipation Day for Black people. You brought your own [food] basket, you know. Anything you wanted to eat, you'd bring it because there was no place to eat. There was a restaurant, but who could afford to go to a restaurant and eat. No one could afford to go and sit down and have a formal dinner in a restaurant. You brought your basket, and you brought your children. And everybody stayed all day and really had a good time. People saved—I did—for one year to the next to go to Port Dalhousie. . . . Port Dalhousie was less than an hour drive away, about 45 minutes, right on the lake [, Lake Erie]. Some people still go there the first Thursday in August, but it is not organized the way it was before. They had a big skating rink there. And where there were no rides as such, and nobody had money to pay for rides anyway, but you could afford to rent some skates for 25 cents, 25 cents, skate all day. Go swimming if you liked; [a] beach [was] right there. Sit down with your family and have a nice dinner. Tell stories about families. People get together and swap stories or lies, whatever you want to call them. It was just a good time. People you hadn't seen in a year [would say:] "Hey I haven't seen you since last time. That's where I've been. Everything

alright in the family? Sure. Everybody healthy? Yes. Oh but Uncle Joe he died you know." People were very cohesive. People enjoyed people. This went on in the 1930s, 40s, 50s, and 60s. Then it started to slowdown Why? People were older. The elders were dying, and young people were not interested. So, it died. Those were some of the good times that I just smile when I talk about it.[103]

Black Niagarans continued to participate actively in YMCA programs during the 1930s. The YMCA had facilities that the Niagara Community Center did not have. Patrons could swim there, play basketball, or engage in other physical activities. Black Niagarans with funds then could go to movie theaters. They could also go fishing. They could visit the waterfalls on the American and Canadian sides of the border. They could also visit historical sites such as old Fort Erie, Lake Ontario, or the church fugitive slaves built on Pier Street in Niagara Falls, Ontario. Many inexpensive recreational activities existed for Black families seeking fun and relaxation.

Intragroup relations and recreational activities were usually positive experiences for Black Niagarans, unifying them and helping them to survive. Race relations during the 1930s functioned differently. They were quite varied and difficult to characterize. Niagara Falls had not yet experienced a major influx of Blacks. Yet they made up a small but significant portion of the population. Blacks were noticeable, but their numbers still did not appear threatening to the general White population, as demonstrated in other cities that experienced a rapidly expanding Black population within a short period.[104] Moreover, as is conveyed in table 1.1, during the Great Depression years, 1930 to 1940, the Black Niagaran population increased by only sixty-nine individuals. The prospect of jobs continued to attract migrants and immigrants to the area. Many immigrants came in search of the American dream: initially they did not know the racial dimensions of American culture. Consequently, Black Niagarans, as featured in the Mabel Smith example, often lived around and among immigrant families. It was not uncommon for their children to play with one another and often eat together. Yet racism still existed. Some of the Whites who migrated to Niagara Falls also came from the American South and brought their prejudices with them. Blacks, who had migrated from the South, also brought their views of southern Whites with them. It was unusual to observe a Black man dating a White American woman (or vice versa); however, periodically, Black men did have relationships with

White Canadian women. Elijah Brown's behavior did not reflect the norm. He experienced intense racism while married to a White woman named Edna Florence Rider for five years beginning in 1933.[105] Brown recalled the social pressures of those days:

> I remember walking down Falls Street. People'd be so busy looking at you they couldn't even shop. People would come up to me and say, "What do you think you're doing?" But they had no right to tell me [that].[106]

Unlike Brown, most Blacks assertively avoided attracting as much overt racism as they possibly could by knowing their place.[107] "Knowing their place" again simply meant that they did not frequent venues in which they knew they were unwelcome or engage in behaviors that would ignite a backlash. Therefore, a racial divide existed; however, during the 1930s, it was not always as clear and rigid as in other cities, particularly major cities.

The Niagara Falls race riot that occurred in August of 1934 underscores the racial divide issue. Tensions existed, according to police, because many in the Polish community resented Blacks increasingly settling around East Falls and Twenty-Fourth Street, a "contested space" or a section that the Polish community claimed as their own.[108] The International Labor Defense sponsored a rally in the area for Alphonso Davis, an African American who had been arrested on a charge of attacking a White girl.[109] A large number of Blacks participated in this rally. According to Indiana Martin, members of the Polish community seemed content in allowing Blacks to have their rally in peace.[110] Then a Black man showed up with a White woman. This, according to Martin, ignited the fury of many Polish men who then set out to not only disrupt the rally but to stop it as well.[111] They chased this Black man for several blocks, caught and cornered him in an alley, and nearly beat him to death.[112] He, in turn, according to Martin, nearly killed one of his attackers, and for that he had to serve a long prison sentence.[113] Martin further noted that the only thing that prevented the Polish men from further pursuing and attacking more Blacks was the presence of Italians, who stopped the mob from pursuing Blacks up Eleventh Street, which was a stronghold of the Italian community. The Italians pushed the mob back to Twenty-Fourth Street and dared them to come back up Eleventh Street.[114] Theodore Williamson, a child during the riot, remembered being told by his parents to stay in the house.[115] Helen Reed-McBride remembered White males driving around her neighborhood in a truck shouting "I don't like a nigger no how!"[116] She also remembered her mother telling her and her siblings to get on the floor as rocks were being thrown at their windows.[117] Their windows—unlike their neighbors'—did not get broken. During the riot and a few days after it, Blacks generally did not come out at night. Reed-McBride further noted that the riot stopped because an African American man called "White Hand" took a truck and brought many African American men from Buffalo to assist local Black residents.[118] Police records indicated that at least three people were seriously injured, and many others suffered minor wounds.[119] Gunshots had been fired, but no one was hit. A Walter Korpolinski, forty-five years old, was in Memorial Hospital with little hope of recovery from a knife wound in his abdomen.[120] His alleged assailant, William Fisher, thirty, a Black man, was also in the hospital with cuts and a possible skull fracture.[121] Another man, forty-five-year-old Joseph Buckford, who police believed had been injured in the fighting, was also in the same hospital suffering from a possible concussion.[122] One report estimated that three thousand people had participated in the riot.[123] Later in October, Alphonso Davis was sentenced to twenty years in Auburn prison.[124] This verdict may have pleased the Polish community, but it angered the Black community, making them feel that justice would not prevail for them.

Fueling tensions between racial groups, fascist racial theories of White supremacy became more common during the Depression era and permeated the Niagara Falls community. Internationally, Adolf Hitler's book *Mein Kampf* (My struggle) proclaimed Aryan superiority and the right of Aryans to rule over the lower non-Aryan Whites, Blacks, and Asians.[125] Locally, Reverend Joseph M. Noonan, president of Niagara University, told enrolling students that he was prepared to immediately break the contract of any professor defending theories of racial superiority.[126] He felt such ideas were wrong before God and man.[127] Still, the Race Riot of 1934 occurred during the Depression era, impacted by the desperate economic state in which many Niagarans found themselves. Records indicate that no other riot between Blacks and Whites occurred in Niagara Falls. Five years later, in 1939, Joseph Williamson, David Rice, Austin Haynes, Alexander Daniels, and Harry Thomas formed the Niagara Civic and Protective Club.[128] The specific role of this organization is unknown, but its formation could have been influenced by the riot of 1934. Joseph Williamson was president, David Rice vice president, Austin Haynes treasurer, Alexander Daniels secretary, and Harry Thomas general advisor. They usually met on Allen

Avenue, where most of them lived. These grassroots leaders seemed to be proactive regarding community and civic safety matters.[129]

Although the Great Depression affected relationships within and between racial groups, and the initial demoralizing effects of the Depression did not impact Niagara Falls as quickly as other parts of the country, the results, nonetheless, were significant.[130] In the year 1933, about four years after the Wall Street Crash of 1929, public welfare and relief fund costs reached $1,236,952.[131] These rising welfare costs quickly outran the city's projected budget, causing the city to seek loans from the state.[132] Black Niagarans, as highlighted by Reed-McBride, unified even more as a community to help one another survive. Many of them grew gardens on land loaned to them by the city, sometimes growing from 45 to 50 percent of the food their families consumed.[133] Moreover, having and managing a garden came easy to many Black Niagarans simply because they had grown up on farms.

Depression-Era Black Niagaran Politics

Black Niagarans also demonstrated self-help efforts in politics. Nationally, Blacks began to disassociate themselves from the political party of Abraham Lincoln, which impacted their political alliances and affiliations. By the late 1920s, Herbert Hoover, the Republican president whom many Americans blamed for the Great Depression, supported the lily-white Republican movement in the South to exclude Blacks from positions of influence and leadership. Hoover also supported the confirmation to the Supreme Court of John J. Parker who was reported to have said that "the participation of the Negro in politics is a source of evil and danger to both races."[134] Nevertheless, many Black voters still thought that the Republican Party could fight more vigorously on their behalf and would give them more in exchange for their loyal patronage. Given a Republican Party that mistakenly took the Black vote for granted and with newer generations of Blacks of voting age, Black political party alliances began to shift.

Democrat Franklin D. Roosevelt won the presidency in 1932 as the Great Depression's effects lingered on. His presidency was responsible for a significant portion of the shift. He won the 1932 election without major Black support. During his "fireside chat" radio broadcasts, Roosevelt assured Americans that they had nothing to fear but fear itself. He implemented his New Deal program, which helped Americans in general, including

African Americans. As Roosevelt's tenure as president progressed, along with his wife Eleanor's strong public stance against racial injustice, Blacks, both nationally and locally, slowly began to shift their allegiances from the once-beloved Republican Party to the Democratic Party. This was an extremely difficult but necessary move due to African Americans' long attachment to the Republican Party.

In Niagara Falls, like other towns and cities, changes occurred. Where once Blacks generally supported Republican candidates, this tradition became contested. Arthur W. Mitchell, an African American Democrat, ran for Congress in 1934 and won, replacing Republican Oscar DePriest of the First Illinois District. Mitchell's victory made him the first African American Democrat in Congress. John Pollard, who was politically astute and a scholar, in his *Niagara Falls Gazette* column praised Mitchell's victory and its implications. He noted: "First, the tremendous vote cast for [Mitchell] and for the Democratic party by colored people of the second ward in effect is a declaration that the colored people of Chicago as voters are no longer slaves to any traditions of the past as they may relate to party politics. Henceforth, the Negro in Chicago will use the bargaining power of his vote so as to obtain all the political recognition that other racial groups have received and are now receiving."[135] Two years later, in 1936, Pollard permitted William J. Reefer, a Democratic African American leader, to address Blacks at the Niagara Community Center. Reefer strongly criticized Republicans for exhuming Abraham Lincoln from his tomb every four years to hold the Black vote in the Republican ranks.[136] He urged Black Niagarans to support the Democratic Party nationally and locally.

Reefer had arrived by motor caravan with other African American leaders and a quartet of singers. Concerning President Roosevelt's work in aiding African Americans, Reefer further proclaimed: "It was the first time during the present century that the Negro has received something more than mere promises. He has been given a chance to earn an honest living without begging for it."[137] A sizeable audience observed this event.

Although the Democrats had made significant gains, the Republicans aggressively attempted to maintain some leverage by again reminding Black Niagarans that the Democratic Party supported the racist South. "Negroes who vote for Democratic national candidates in next Tuesday's election will be betraying their race," announced Dr. W. E. Rakeshaw, of New York City, to Niagarans at Republican headquarters on Third Street.[138] Furthermore, he noted, "the Democratic [Party] is hamstrung to the southern states, where colored citizens are oppressed and live under conditions of slavery as deplorable as those which existed before the Civil War, and no Democratic president will dare displease the south."[139] Local leaders W. A. Garey, John Fillman, and Jerry Isom stayed committed to the Republican Party, although residents of the city of Niagara Falls voted overwhelmingly for Roosevelt in the 1936. Black Niagarans, along with other Americans, gained many benefits from the Democratic Party in general and FDR's administration in particular.[140] Nonetheless, the Republican Party by 1933 began to lose the stronghold it held over Black Niagarans during the days Charlotte Dett served as a Republican committee member for the old Ward 1.

The Declining Years of an Early Influential Leader: Charlotte Dett

During this political transformation, Charlotte Dett steadily progressed toward the twilight of her life. Despite the Race Riot of 1934, she tried to pull people together of different political affiliations, races, ethnic backgrounds, and creeds. In the closing years of her life, she enjoyed and exhibited great pride in the success of her children, and she continued to manifest her strong social and organizational skills. By this time, Charlotte's son, R. Nathaniel Dett, had made a name for himself. He grew to be recognized nationally and internationally, specializing in the creation of spiritual music. He had graduated from the Oberlin Conservatory of Music, being the first African American to do so. He taught at Lane College, Lincoln Institute, and Hampton Institute. At Hampton Institute, he taught from 1913 to 1931, first as director of vocal music and choir director, then as director of the music department.[141] He matured and developed there as a teacher and artist and created some of his best musical works, such as "Listen to the Lambs," "Don't Be Weary Traveler," and "I'll Never Turn Back No More." He gave numerous concerts in which he highlighted both standards and his own original spiritual compositions, showing the vocal abilities of his choirs. In 1930 through the aid of George F. Peabody and other benefactors, he took his Hampton Institute choir, three chaperones, and his mother on a concert tour of six European countries: England, France, Switzerland, the Netherlands, Belgium, and Austria.[142] The tour lasted six weeks and strove to favorably enhance European views of Black people because several of these nations possessed African colonies and held negative views of people of color. This tour represented the apex of Dett's professional career at Hampton Institute.

The *Chicago Defender*, a prominent Black-owned-and-operated newspaper, mentioned that on April 26 Charlotte Dett, the mother of R. Nathaniel Dett, had set sail for Europe.[143] It also indicated that she would visit England, Germany, France, Belgium, and Switzerland and that she was a member of one the oldest and most respected families of Niagara Falls.[144] John Pollard kept track of noteworthy news on respectable citizens such as the Dett family, and he ensured that it appeared in the *Niagara Falls Gazette*'s weekly column about the Niagara Community Center news and also in other media. Furthermore, it was Pollard who sent this noteworthy news to the *Chicago Defender*. He and other friends of Dett wished her a happy trip.[145]

A few months after her return, Dett and her famous son were entertained and honored by Niagara Falls branches of the Unity, Phillis Wheatley, and Mary B. Talbert clubs at the Niagara Community Center.[146] Members of each club came to meet the Dett family. R. Nathaniel Dett spoke enthusiastically about his trip abroad and about the recent convention of the National Association of Negro Musicians that he had recently attended.[147] Charlotte Dett sat proudly as her son recounted recent events. Dett was honored again two weeks later at the Niagara Community Center. About fifty women attended the reception. "Dett was introduced by the president of the Mary B. Talbert Club, after which Dett told very interestingly of her experiences abroad with her famous son, Dr. R. Nathaniel Dett."[148] Dett stressed that the Hampton choir tour was not only a decided artistic success but also a great adventure in interracial understanding.[149] Irene Byrd and Vivian Ellis performed a musical selection. Mabel White, who served as president of the Unity Club, responded to Dett's address and expressed the clubwomen's high esteem for her.[150]

In August of 1932, Dett visited her son in Hampton, Virginia, and had a wonderful time. R. Nathaniel by this time had married and had two daughters. Charlotte Dett wrote back to Niagara Community Center members, stating that she was having a great time with her son and his family.[151] Her son had been on a leave of absence from Hampton Institute when his mother visited. That same year, he came back north and spent time in Rochester, New York, studying at the Eastman School of Music, where he ultimately earned a master's degree.[152] He was forever a student, willing to work hard to advance his talent. Dett and her son Samuel also visited R. Nathaniel in Rochester and saw the music studio he worked in.[153] He had been training a racially mixed choir that consisted of vocalists from the Rochester broadcasting station WHAM.[154]

Charlotte Dett continued to enjoy the respect and admiration accorded to her, which she had earned over the years. She involved herself in Niagara Community Center affairs, giving speeches of encouragement to young and old, serving as a hostess at social affairs, presiding over important meetings, taking on administrative duties, offering advice when needed, and being a fundraiser.[155] Dett's talents, as underscored earlier, spread beyond Niagara Falls. In 1933, at the Michigan Avenue Baptist Church in Buffalo, she was one of three people asked to speak at a memorial service in honor of her dear friend Mary B. Talbert.[156] Accounts indicate that Dett thrived in these roles, giving an excellent presentation to those at the memorial service.

By 1932 Charlotte Dett began experiencing bouts of illness.[157] By 1935 she was having long periods of illness that marked the breakdown of her health and eventually forced her to become bedridden.[158] R. Nathaniel Dett returned to Niagara Falls from Washington, DC, so that he and Samuel could be at their mother's bedside to comfort her.[159] By 1937, Dett had grown frail and did not get around much, which was contrary to her extroverted personality. Reports indicated that she had grown quite ill, although she still welcomed friends to see her.[160]

On April 8, 1937, after being ill for two years, Dett died at seventy-five years of age. Funeral services were held at the First Presbyterian Church of Niagara Falls. "Tributes to her memory came from many sources as persons in all walks of life spoke of her outstanding character and ability while they reviewed her many accomplishments attained under handicaps which made them truly remarkable."[161] Besides raising two upstanding children, Charlotte Dett was cultured and possessed natural leadership qualities, always taking the keenest interest in her people and also attaining a high place in fraternal, civic, political, welfare, and social circles.[162] An editorial further remarked:

> For years she was an active leader in many societies and fraternal organizations. For five years she was Republican committee woman for the second district of the first ward. She was a past chairman of the ways and means committee of the National Federation of Women's clubs; past vice president of the Empire State Federation of Women's clubs; president of the Phyllis Wheatley club; member of the Unity club and member of the

Golden Rod Sewing club. She was also the organizer of the former Coolidge and Dawes club here.

In fraternal circles she was a member and past officer of the Order of Eastern Star, member of Bison City Court of Calanthe, No. 28, Knights of Pythias; member of Eureka Circle, No. 289, Companions of the Foresters, and member and past officer of Queen Esther Household of Ruth, I. O. O. F.[163]

Both her sons were, of course, deeply saddened. R. Nathaniel Dett wrote a friend expressing his grief, stating that his mother was his main source of inspiration, motivating him to do more and better work.[164] He expressed that he would miss her unspeakably; however, he was glad his mother did not have to suffer anymore because during her last days she was in great pain.[165] Years after his mother's death, Samuel paid for a statement to be published about his mother in the memorial section of the *Niagara Falls Gazette*. It read as follows:

CHARLOTTE DETT

In loving memory of my dear mother Charlotte Dett, who passed away 22 years ago today, April 8, 1937. As I gaze on your picture that hangs on the wall, your smiles and your welcome I often recall; I miss you and mourn you in silence unseen, and dwell on the memories of days that have been: Dear is the grave where mother is laid. Sweet is the memory that never will fade; flowers may wither, leaves fade and die. If some do forget you, never will I. Sadly missed by, Son, Sam.[166]

Charlotte Dett was buried in Fairview Cemetery in Niagara Falls, Ontario, next to her son Arthur.[167] Canada was her country of birth. Her ex-husband and the father of her children—Robert Tue Dett—died in 1921 and was buried in Oakwood Cemetery in Niagara Falls, New York. Samuel continued to work at the post office and live in the tourist house that had once belonged to his mother.

Increased Reliance on the Niagara Community Center

The Great Depression continued after the death of Charlotte Dett. Black Niagarans, who were predominantly poor, did the best they could to survive. For the first time in Niagara Falls history, a significantly higher percentage of Black women had to seek work outside the home to assist their families.[168] This motivated Black families to continue to function in a collectivist manner, like an African village. Every able-bodied person, from children to adults, had a role that contributed to entire families operating as one.[169]

The Niagara Community Center continued to aid community residents. From 1929 to 1938, its representatives found 691 jobs for Black citizens, and, according to John Pollard, the relationships established between employees and employers had generally been satisfactory.[170] The center relieved sixty families in severe distress.[171] It established a charity fund that persons of means could contribute to.[172] It continued to promote good race relationships and to publicize the discrimination that Black Niagarans encountered to churches, civic associations, and government bodies.[173] The Niagara Community Center's leadership emphasized that Black Niagarans usually behaved as upstanding citizens contributing to the well-being of the city but that the press tended to give undeserved emphasis to crime and other problems of the Black community.[174]

By 1938 there was even greater demand for the Community Center and its activities. Many continued to incorrectly perceive it as a relief agency. As explained by Pollard: "It is difficult to make those who are in need understand that the Center does not have money to give cash relief. When money is given from the office of the director it is his own personal offering and so here instead of having a treasure chest with which to help we have only a sheaf of promises to [re]pay by those whose need was too urgent for the request to wait for the law to move."[175] During the Depression era, the Niagara Community Center became an even more vital institution for the Black Niagaran community.

Additional Self-Help Efforts: Families, Churches, and the Local Business League

The main factor that enabled Black Niagarans to survive the Great Depression, in conjunction with the aid they may have received from the Niagara Community Center, the federal, state, or local governments (or from their neighbors), was the support they got from their churches and families.[176] When attending church services, their religious faith was reinforced with their belief that no matter how difficult life seemed, things would get better. As in the days of slavery, particularly regarding the Invisible Institution,[177] churches served as places of refuge and bonding, giving parishioners the faith to continue on.[178] Moreover, families extending acts of kindness to their members gave them the support to carry on. Longtime Niagaran Vivian V. C. Thompson, who was a leader in her church, is a case in point.[179]

Vivian's parents, who were founding members of New Hope Baptist Church, brought her and her siblings to church services at young ages.[180] Vivian, who was the goddaughter of Charlotte Dett, grew up in the church and enthusiastically participated in church activities, learning to play the piano and organ and eventually becoming her church's organist. Church for Vivian, who ultimately became a lifetime member of New Hope Baptist Church, reinforced and expanded lessons taught in the home: honoring one's parents, treating others how one would like to be treated, understanding the Creator and his forgiving grace, learning to forgive and not hate, and praying for those who spitefully used you.[181] Vivian and her family consistently attended church before, during, and after the Depression era. She socialized with church members, children as well as adults. Each time a church program took place, her family attended; whenever the church doors opened for any religious purpose, they were there. All this strengthened Vivian and her family, through pleasant and difficult times, enabling them to proceed in life. Interviewee Indiana Martin supported Vivian Thompson's explanation of how Black Niagarans survived hard times: " 'When you don't have nothing, you don't miss nothing' and [community members] put their few dimes and nickels together to make things work."[182] Anthropologist Jacqueline Mithum referred to this behavior as "cooperation and solidarity as survival necessities."[183] In essence Indiana Martin stated that Black Niagarans were routinely poor, particularly during the Great Depression as brought out by Helen-Reed's 1930s community description. They had nothing and therefore were accustomed to trying to make something out of nothing.

In this study "middle class" is defined as a social status between the upper class and the lower class, determined by such factors as income, occupation, education, or value system. Many Black Niagarans, as alluded to by Indiana Martin above, historically often failed to qualify for middle-class status based on their income, occupation, or educational level. However, many met middle-class standards based on a belief system that incorporates and exemplifies such ideas as high moral values, dignified public behavior, respect for education, self-help, and a disdain for being content with remaining in an occupationally low labor status throughout one's entire career.

In further promoting self-help along with spirituality for overcoming problems, Reverend Jesse Nash Sr. of Buffalo and pastor of Michigan Avenue Baptist Church, reinforced Vivian Thompson's example. At a 1935 event cosponsored by the Niagara Peace Council and the Council of Mother's Club, Nash informed his listeners that Americans focused too much of their energies on material gains.[184] While acknowledging that this had advanced the mechanical and industrial aspects of civilization, Nash counseled that these efforts would not ultimately make humans happy. Similar to what Vivian Thompson's example implies, he counseled spiritual faith and development as a means of overcoming the hardships of the Great Depression and obtaining real peace and happiness. Many Black Niagarans heard and seemed to appreciate Nash's remarks, and after his address, they honored him with a dinner at the Niagara Community Center.[185] Black Niagaran churches constantly reiterated the theme of relying on a spiritual being.

In addition to help provided during the Great Depression by families, churches, the Niagara Community Center, and governmental agencies, a local branch of the National Negro Business League (NNBL) operated in Niagara Falls.[186] Booker T. Washington had organized the NNBL in 1900.[187] It was a national organization that functioned to stimulate African American business development throughout the nation. As characterized by historian Richard W. Thomas, it was a form of economic nationalism.[188] Washington taught that if African Americans would become entrepreneurs on a massive scale—fulfilling the needs and wants of all American consumers and thereby making themselves indispensable assets to their respective communities and the nation as a whole—then the race problem would solve itself naturally.[189] Given his stature as a prominent national leader, Washington was able to disseminate this message throughout the nation, particularly through the network of the NNBL. By 1915, at its height and in the year of Washington's death, the NNBL had about three hundred local branches nationwide, with most of the local branches being located in the South and the major cities in the North.[190]

After Booker T. Washington's death, the NNBL continued to operate effectively until about 1955, at the dawn of the modern civil rights movement, vigorously continuing Washington's pervasive message.[191] In 1931 Black Niagarans formed a local NNBL branch.[192] This occurred sixteen years after Washington's death, and neighboring Buffalo and Rochester also established local leagues.[193] T. J. Ireland was instrumental in the league's operations from its beginning until its end in about 1941. He does not appear in the 1930 Census for the city of Niagara Falls, but he was in Cataract City by 1927.[194] For several years, Ireland served as president of the local league, coordinating meetings and public forums and representing the league before city officials. Frank W. Holloman, Henry Patterson, Fredrick Johnson, William Martin, Ray Waters, and W. H. Davis actively participated in league functions and took on leadership positions. Of these men, Henry Patterson is the only one recorded in the 1930 Census.[195] He was listed as being twenty-six years of age and living on Twenty-Second Street in Ward 4, the area that had the largest number of Black Niagarans. Census enumerators recorded Patterson as being a laborer, performing furnace work at a carbide plant.[196]

Evidence indicates that the local NNBL functioned most effectively in encouraging its members and operating as a job referral agency but not in implementing Booker T. Washington's ultimate aim—the fostering and expansion of business development among Black Niagarans (table 3.3).[197]

The local league tended to meet regularly on Monday evenings at the Niagara Community Center where John Pollard actively participated in Local League functions. Dr. Charles B. Hayes took on leadership positions.[198] The Local League held an annual banquet that members and other interested parties attended. This was a smaller version of the banquet given at the annual meetings of the NNBL held in various cities throughout the nation. At the annual meeting, events were planned that always included a banquet. During Booker T. Washington's presidential years (1900–1915), his annual address was always the apex of the national gatherings.[199] At

Table 3.3. Black Niagaran Entrepreneurs, 1900–1940

Year	Black Population	Percentage of Total Population	Male Entrepreneurs	Female Entrepreneurs
1900	344	1.77	6	3
1910	266	0.87	6	0
1920	509	1.00	7	2
1930	906	1.20	12	7
1940	975	1.25	13	8

Adapted from the United States Censuses from 1900 to 1940. (Please see page 349, note 197.)

these local league annual banquets, members heard encouraging comments from fellow members.[200]

At a meeting held in 1932, the Local League visited the Men's Club of Niagara Falls, Ontario.[201] W. B. Davis gave a history of the local league, and T. J. Ireland expressed hope for its future operations.[202] A Frederick Jones led a discussion on Negro leadership.[203] This sparked an intense debate on what type of leadership could advance Black people the farthest. The groups juxtaposed Booker T. Washington's leadership against W. E. B. Du Bois's. For the attendees, this must have brought back memories of the Niagara movement, which used Niagara Falls, Ontario, as one of its meeting sites. Their discussion became so intense that concerned leaders agreed to table the debate for the next meeting. Both groups agreed that aggressive leadership was needed to advance the cause of Blacks, whether in Canada or the United States. However, each side thought that the leader they supported—Washington for the Black Niagarans and Du Bois for the Black Canadians—best represented the most progressive form of leadership needed.

As did Booker T. Washington, the Local League's leadership attempted to establish relationships with White elites within the Niagaran community. League leaders attended city council meetings and invited city officials to address their organization. In 1932, for example, Frank A. Jenss, the mayor of Niagara Falls, addressed their meeting, informing them that the structure of city government needed to be changed for the betterment of Niagaran citizens.[204] In 1934, local Judge Thomas B. Lee gave an address before the league, in which a mock trial was conducted to further inform league members of the operations of the judicial system.[205] In 1935 Francis D. Bowman of the Carborundum Company, one of Niagara Falls's larger employers, addressed the Local League, whose members attentively listened to his talk.[206] At a meeting before the city council and mayor, the league successfully got city officials to formally denounce discrimination in any form.[207] In establishing these contacts, the Local League believed that these men could aid them in their future endeavor(s). Booker T. Washington came to believe that creating alliances with what he termed the "better classes" of whites could foster more progressive changes for African Americans.[208] The Local League's actions verify that they also embraced this concept.

Contacts with White elites during the Great Depression years aided the Local League in assisting Black Niagarans in their search for work. They held Niagara Community Center labor forums, in which league members offered their advice on how job seekers could best obtain employment.[209] Pollard advised job seekers to train themselves to fill a spot that was not already filled.[210] Furthermore, he instructed them that if they went after a job hard enough, they would obtain it.[211] These maxims coincide with teachings of Booker T. Washington, when he posited that if there was no door opened to obtain an opportunity, then make one.[212] In another incident, the Local League heard reports that some local industries would no longer hire Black employees because of bad experiences they had encountered by granting a few Black Niagarans job opportunities.[213] The Local League informed local industries that for every bad Black employee they could come up with, the Local League could supply data on numerous successful employees. Moreover, they informed local industries that they would serve as an employment agency for the industries, placing the Local League's credibility on the line. These statements in conjunction with their alliances seemed to have had an impact. "T. J. Ireland president of the Business League announced [in May of 1936] that eight men [had] been placed at the Union Carbide and Carbon plant within the past week through the cooperation of the personnel department of [that] company."[214] Local League members speculated that more jobs would soon become available, and they organized more meetings at the Niagara Community Center to further encourage the unemployed to seek jobs and training and to advise them on how subpar work performance would adversely impact their racial group.[215]

The Local League welcomed a visit at the Niagara Community Center from Reverend Sydney O. B. Johnson of Buffalo, minister of the Lloyd Memorial Congregational Church, a social activist, and later editor of the *Buffalo American*.[216] Reverend Johnson held the post of National Youth Administration representative (NYA) for Erie and Niagara counties.[217] The Roosevelt administration created the NYA as another New Deal policy to combat and overturn the effects of the Great Depression:[218] as a report in the *Gazette* stated, "Through the efforts of the [Local Business League] . . . six NYA jobs [were] offered to colored youths, four boys and two girls."[219]

The Local League stayed abreast of the national organization's proceedings and thought about how national planning could help Black Niagarans. For example, in 1929 the NNBL decided to form and promote a cooperative grocery store chain in cities throughout the nation, identifying this effort as the Colored Merchants Association (CMA). Albon L. Holsey, who was a Tuskegee Institute employee and a key leader within the NNBL, orchestrated these activities.[220] The CMA's goal was to organize African

American grocers into cooperative buying units, create a standardized store service, promote cooperative advertising, and use the Local League chapters as coordinating agencies. This idea excited Local League members: "While the program of the [Local League] Monday night, February 15, [1933] was chiefly of a business nature, inspiring talks were made by Ray Waters, Frederick Ford, T. J. Ireland and W. H. Davis. The subjects under discussion were the [CMA] and the National Negro Business League."[221] Although at the height of the CMA, twenty-five cooperative grocery stores existed throughout the nation, with central headquarters located in New York City, Local League members did not establish a CMA grocery store within the city of Niagara Falls.[222] Nonetheless, they continued to be receptive to ideas from the national office, and they made plans to send at least one representative to an annual gathering to be held in Atlanta.[223]

How can the Depression-era Niagara Falls Local Business League Branch be ultimately assessed? It had effective leadership. T. J. Ireland was a driving force behind the operations of the Local League. He actively participated in activities from the Local League's inception until its end, consistently maintaining pivotal leadership positions and encouraging others to get involved.[224] For the most part, the Local League welcomed Black Niagarans regardless of their class or educational backgrounds. T. J. Ireland, for example, worked as a laborer at Hooker Chemical Corporation for twenty-two years, retiring in 1949.[225] Many others also worked as laborers for local industries, and the Local League attracted its share of formally educated members. However, the key ingredient for membership seemed to have been a willingness to improve one's racial group status and, in turn, improve one's own condition.

Criticism of the Local League centers on two issues. First, the role of women was minimal in Local League operations. Women were not in leadership positions and may not have been active members. In the published materials from the Local League, women's names are absent, but women did assist with the annual banquet. This is contrary to NNBL principles. Although women generally were not in leadership positions in the national organization, they were active leaders in local branches throughout the country, particularly in the South. Women often gave Booker T. Washington and other men effective advice on how to improve the operations of the league.[226] When Washington formed his organization, the requirement for membership was not gender but engagement in an entrepreneurial activity.[227] Second, in terms of promoting business development, the Local League had little success. Local League members passionately discussed economic development, as underscored in the CMA example, but no concrete result ensued. In fairness to the Local League, the Great Depression was a major structural barrier to entrepreneurial activities. Nonetheless, Booker T. Washington's philosophy had been disseminated, compelling many Black Niagarans to consider economic development as a means of self-help for improving their—and their group's—plights.

Like the Niagara Falls Local League branch, a range of clubs consistently met at the Niagara Community Center during the Depression to stimulate self-help and give its members and others encouragement. This includes the Harriet Tubman Club, Sunset Lodge No. 295, Electric City Lodge No. 49, the Girl Reserves, the Red Cross Sewing Club, the Quilting Club, the Mary Talbert Club, and others.[228] The Quilting Club, for example, placed their first completed quilt on exhibit as a marketing tool.[229] They planned to sell their quilts and donate the proceeds to the Niagara Community Center so that its community services could continue.[230]

Finally, John Pollard and other Niagara Community Center representatives believed that if they could instill racial pride within Black Niagarans, especially children, it would do much to increase self-help efforts. During "Negro History Week," a remembrance period started by Carter G. Woodson in 1926 to honor the historical accomplishments of people of African descent, several events were held.[231] Center representatives taught patrons about Ancient history, African history, world history, and American colonial and antebellum history, in conjunction with contemporary affairs.[232] Pollard intoned: "Every week is Negro History Week at the Community Center; however, these boys and girls are taught those facts of their own cultural heritage which will enable them to keep their self-respect in the face of misunderstanding attitudes on the part of those who do not know that students of world history are bringing to light many things that Negroes may be proud of."[233] Community center representatives supported the adage that with more self-knowledge, individuals would search inward for solutions to their plight.[234]

A larger stable Black community existed in Niagara Falls by the end of the 1930s. It had expanded considerably since 1920. The likelihood of obtaining employment continued to attract Black migrants to the area. Once employed and making a respectable wage, adults sought to further stabilize their families, which partly meant ensuring that their children obtained a good education. Black Niagarans also sought to re-create institutions with which they had been familiar. During the Depression the Niagara Community Center continued to function as an essential entity for Black Niagarans. Guided by John Pollard, it brought together members of all religious faiths and people from all walks of life. As it had in earlier decades, racism still existed, and Black Niagarans fought it. However, racism would become more pervasive and threatening in ensuing decades, as greater numbers of Blacks migrated to Cataract City.

The Depression years also encouraged several Black Niagarans to become or remain leaders, and several residents began their leadership during this difficult period. Some fit Booker T. Washington's "captains of industry" concept (e.g., Samuel Dett, Benjamin Bolden, Charles Hayes, and T. J. Ireland), and others fit W. E. B. Du Bois's "Talented Tenth" (e.g., Alice Hayes and John Pollard) or demonstrated a combination of both leadership approaches (e.g., John Pollard). Alongside the Black Niagaran community expanding markedly from 1920 to 1930, Black Niagaran leaders concentrated their leadership activities more toward the advancement of their racial group while still valuing multiracial associations, coalitions, and partnerships. Consequently, they all seemed to support an integrated racial society free from the racial barriers that restricted their racial group's progression. The expanded population further compelled Black Niagaran leaders to increase their efforts in directing and managing community institutions, beginning first with their families and churches and then with the Niagara Community Center.

While enjoying the positive dimensions of their environment and working against the negative ones, many Black Niagarans continued to improve their lives. Although this effort would continue in ensuing years, the Second Great Migration severely restricted the spatial location of the expanding community.

Chapter Four

Expanded Community and New Realities, 1940 to 1960

The period from 1940 to 1960 is a monumental one in Black Niagaran history. The African American population expanded more during this time than in any other twenty-year period. The Niagara Community Center continued to grow, and its leadership proactively sought a larger facility to house its operations. Black Niagaran leadership continued to promote integration into the mainstream of society, working intra- and interracially, managing institutions, and working for the collective well-being of Black Niagarans.

This midcentury era is also critical because it represents a time in which Black Niagarans would experience more intense forms of racism, particularly related to housing. With African Americans rapidly relocating to Niagara Falls in unprecedented numbers, White property owners, realtors, and community neighbors prohibited new Black migrants from filtering into their residential districts. This exclusion restricted the migrants to recently established enclaves, which contributed to overcrowding. This phenomenon coincides with the findings of other Black urban historical studies that examined the impact of the First Great Migration on major northeastern cities.[1]

Unlike the large and major northeastern cities that initially experienced Black housing impediments from 1915 to 1920, Black Niagarans experienced those barriers more intensively after 1941. In expressing their personal histories, several Black Niagarans remembered this epoch and how they lived through it. These Black Niagarans and their leaders strove to tear down these barriers.

Migration, Housing, Bigotry, and Community Voices

MIGRATION

Adverse effects of the Great Depression abated in the city of Niagara Falls soon after the United States declared war on Japan in 1941. Major local industries, such as Du Pont, Hooker Electrochemical, Carborundum, Union Carbide and Carbon, and Bell Aircraft transformed from peacetime operations to wartime production, with the Allied powers being their principal consumers. With an almost endless demand for labor, people from other locales rushed to the city of Niagara Falls. In 1940, census enumerators counted 78,029 Niagarans; by 1950 that figure had increased to 90,875, reflecting a difference of 12,846 (see table 4.1).[2]

With an ever-increasing population of new industrial workers, an acute demand for housing arose. Federal and state governments attempted to meet this demand by building adequate housing for war workers and their families. In 1941, for example, the federal government purchased land from the city of Niagara Falls to build three hundred housing units for war workers.[3] They called this housing complex Griffon Manor. In 1942 they added 450 additional units to the purchased land, bringing the total

Table 4.1. Population of City of Niagara Falls, 1840–1990

Year	Number of People
1840	1,277
1850	1,951
1860	3,500
1870	3,006
1880	3,320
1890	5,502
1900	19,457
1910	30,445
1920	50,760
1930	75,460
1940	78,029
1950	90,875
1960	102,394
1970	85,615
1980	71,384
1990	61,840

Adapted from the United States Censuses 1840 to 1990. (Please see page 351, note 2.)

number of Griffon Manor housing units to 750.[4] The federal government also negotiated plans for other housing arrangements in attempting to accommodate the influx of war workers.

With the flood of war workers, Niagara Falls simultaneously experienced a significantly high influx of Blacks between 1940 and 1950. The Second Great Migration, also sparked by the high demand for factory labor during World War II, ignited this. At least 975 blacks resided in Niagara Falls in 1940. By 1950 census enumerators recorded 3,585, which was 3.94 percent of the total population and well over a 300 percent increase.[5] As in the First Great Migration, Blacks arrived from locations throughout the South. They came by bus, car, and train, seeking employment and a better life in the North. In traveling to Niagara Falls, they often carried their meals in a shoebox, with such food items as fried chicken, collard greens, potato salad, biscuits, and cake due to their poverty and the railroad segregation customs of the South.[6] Economic factors pushed them out of the South and pulled them to the North. There was plenty of low-skilled work for all who sought it.

Bell Aircraft Corporation eventually hired a large number of Blacks during the war, especially after A. Phillip Randolph's 1941 March on Washington activism, which agitated for an abatement of defense industry discrimination in conjunction with working toward the defeat of the Axis powers. This collective effort was known as the Double V-Campaign.[7] By December 1942, they employed 9,000 workers, of which 4,500 were women.[8] Their Niagara Falls plant operated next door to the Niagara Falls Municipal Airport. Bell Aircraft made fighter planes such as the Airacobra and Kingcobra along with jet-propelled fighters for the US military.[9] Zorie Bell Boling, who worked at Bell Aircraft during the war, remembered Tuskegee Airmen in uniforms visiting her plant and how handsome they looked.[10] Factory laborers were in high demand, and good wages were offered. John Pollard, for example, resigned from his post as director of the Niagara Community Center in 1943 to take a job at Bell Aircraft.[11] He had served as director of the Niagara Community Center since 1931. He worked for Bell Aircraft for two years.[12] Then Carborundum Company employed him in its plant protection department for a year and a half.[13]

The Carborundum Company hired Blacks during and after World War II.[14] With their job orders increasing, they constantly sought out new employees, regardless of creed or color, to meet the demands of the war. To encourage workers to be on time, work diligently, and not to be absent unless absolutely necessary, the Carborundum Company in its worker publications stressed that their labor was needed to supply soldiers on the battlefield with excellent equipment and supplies to fight the Axis powers (Germany, Italy, and Japan). They stressed that the United States required a united effort to be victorious in the war. Bloneva Bond, a longtime resident who came to Niagara Falls with her husband in 1943, remembered that when she moved to Niagara Falls, Carborundum was paying fifty-two cents an hour, which was better than the $100 a month she earned as a teacher in North Carolina.[15] Her husband, Harwood Bond, got a job working for the Hooker Electrochemical Company (now Occidental Chemical Corporation) as a chemist.[16]

Union Carbide and Carbon Corporation, a major corporation during and after the war, also hired many Blacks (possibly more than anyone else) compared to other firms.[17] Most Blacks employed by Union Carbide and Carbon, like those at other plants, worked in low-skilled jobs. Nevertheless, from their perspective, this was an upgrade from sharecropping, migrant farm work, and other work for low wages in the South.

One of the most difficult and dangerous jobs that Blacks did at Union Carbide and Carbon was shoveling metal materials into open-hearth furnaces. Blacks did this type of work, some believed, because Whites could not stand to be exposed to the extreme heat.[18] Men had to wear special shoes and aprons to protect themselves from the gases that spread once materials were thrown into the furnaces. They had to rush back about nine feet in order to avoid the hot gases. Many Black men began their careers at Union Carbide and Carbon doing this hot and dangerous work. Other companies also employed Black labor, such as Du Pont, the Vanadian Company, Presto-Lite, and the Pittsburgh Metallurgical Company. Black Niagarans' presence in industry expanded due to World War II, expanding the black industrial working class.[19]

Community lore indicates that factories employed several methods to recruit Black labor.[20] Agents traveled to southern locales and actively recruited workers, promising them jobs and assistance in adapting to their new environment. Andalusia, Alabama, was one place from which agents recruited labor. Andalusia is in southern Alabama near the border with Florida, a little over ninety-one miles south of Montgomery and nearly ninety-three miles north of Pensacola, Florida. Many Black Niagarans believed that most Blacks who migrated to Niagara Falls during the World War II era came from Andalusia, Alabama, or nearby areas.[21] Companies offered war bonds or cash to employees who recruited workers who successfully completed sixty to ninety days of work. They also aggressively canvassed other western New York regions in attempting to meet their labor needs (see table 4.2).

Table 4.2. Black Population of Covington County and Andalusia, Alabama

Year	Covington County	Andalusia, Alabama
1930	7,078	1,809
1940	6,912	1,789
1950	6,086	2,107
1960	5,747	2,294
1970	5,043	2,102

Adapted from the United States Censuses 1830 to 1970. (Please see page 352, note 21.)

Comparing the Black population of Andalusia, Alabama, to that of Covington County it can be determined that its decadal changes, for the most part, do not coincide with community recollections (table 4.2). However, from 1930 to 1970, Covington County's population steadily decreased, which was probably the result of the relocation of many rural migrants to Niagara Falls (and other locales). Many Black Alabamians also migrated to the neighboring city of Buffalo.[22]

As they did during the First Great Migration, Black migrants were proactive on their own behalf. They came to Niagara Falls, usually independently, stabilized themselves by obtaining jobs and maintaining them, and then sent for their family members. Willie C. Fields Sr., who became a prominent local Black entrepreneur, first migrated to Niagara Falls in 1939.[23] He came from Baton Rouge, Louisiana, and would eventually return. Then, following a cyclical pattern described by historian Peter Gottlieb, he came back to Niagara Falls in 1940 and found employment at Bell Aircraft.[24] As a laborer, he eventually worked for the city of Niagara Falls as a parking meter fee collector. Like Dr. Charles Hayes, he married his childhood sweetheart, who joined him in 1942. Mrs. Fields was brought from Baton Rouge to Niagara Falls by her father. Another migrant, Eugene Cook, left Holt, Alabama, to seek employment in Niagara Falls.[25] He arrived in 1943 and worked for the Carborundum Company for the next thirty-seven years. He also helped establish institutions, being a founder of New Hope Baptist Church and Mount Zion Baptist Church. Religious fellowship deeply inspired his life.

Wendel O. Akers, who was born in Floyd, Virginia, migrated to Niagara Falls in 1949 after serving in the US Army during World War II.[26] Akers came a few years after the Second Great Migration (1941–1945) but close enough to be associated with it.[27] He worked for the W. T. Grant Store from 1950 to 1967, mainly at their warehouse. After meeting his future wife, Helen M. Warren, in Niagara Falls, they married and had six children: four sons and two daughters.[28]

The Second Great Migration attracted numerous individuals to Niagara Falls. Aaron L. Griffin, for example, moved to Niagara Falls in 1943 to serve as new director of the Niagara Community Center after John Pollard resigned.[29] He was born in Natchez, Mississippi. His parents were there for six years and then moved to St. Louis, Missouri, where Griffin grew to young adulthood. After completing high school, due to segregation, Griffin had to leave his state in order to attend college.[30] He chose to attend Ohio State University and earn a bachelor's and master's degree in education. Before coming to Niagara Falls, Griffin had taught in high schools and colleges in Texas, Indiana, and Ohio. After being offered a job in Niagara Falls, he quickly accepted the position at the Niagara Community Center and settled in Niagara Falls. He held the directorship of the Niagara Community Center longer than anyone else, retaining that post for over thirty years (1943–1976).

Like John Pollard, Griffin was a major influential leader during the ongoing growth, crisis, stability, and progressive years of the Black Niagaran community. During the decade he spent as director, the Niagaran population expanded significantly. This, in turn (much like it did for Pollard), enlarged Griffin's role. He must have felt some pressure to do superlative work in administering the Niagara Community Center, considering that he replaced Pollard, who had placed the center on a solid foundation and was highly regarded throughout the city of Niagara Falls. Throughout his career, Griffin strove to uplift and integrate Black Niagarans into the mainstream of society, which also included making critical alliances with influential Whites.[31] In time he, too, became respected and beloved.

Bloneva Bond, when she arrived in Niagara Falls, had hoped to continue her career as a teacher.[32] Like Griffin, she would eventually become one of the most (if not the most) impactful Black Niagaran leaders in her community. She applied for work with the Niagara Falls public school system, but she was not hired.[33] Only years later did the Niagara Falls public school system hire its first teacher of African descent, Elizabeth Young, whose family had immigrated to the United States from Canada.[34] This experience did not discourage Bond; it motivated her to use her talents in other realms. Although Bond was unable to continue her teaching career, her husband obtained a professional position at Hooker Chemical, which, for the era, was unusual.[35]

Bond obtained work at the Niagara Community Center in 1943, being appointed the girls' work director and working closely with Aaron Griffin.[36] In this role, Bond felt needed, and she enjoyed the duties assigned to her, growing into the leader she would ultimately become. "She like[d] working with young people and stayed at the Community Center for eight years, planning camping, cooking, and other activities for girls"[37] before pursuing other career opportunities.

With Bond networking with all classes of Niagarans at the Niagara Community Center along with her propensity for leadership, what kind of personality did Bond possess and what shaped her political outlook? Considering her vast historical influence on the city of Niagara Falls, this is important to evaluate. She was extroverted, a go-getter, a stately businesslike woman, and a pioneer willing to make something out of nothing. A practitioner of Booker T. Washington's "captains of industry" concept, she possessed a dominating, fearless personality that defied cultural norms of patriarchy. She could be ladylike if she chose to be, thus demonstrating the politics of respectability in her public behavior.[38] Moreover, she was highly intelligent, well-read, and outspoken, able to ask penetrating questions that would make many uneasy.[39] If she thought she was correct on an issue and was opposed, like Alice C. Hayes, she did not back down. As one interviewee mentioned, "She was tough as nails."[40] Her critics, conversely, would accuse her of always trying to run any organization that she actively participated in, while her allies would counter this charge.[41] In sum, all interviewees who knew Bloneva Bond spoke of her with veneration.

In terms of her political outlook, Bloneva Bond was a product of her times. She was a civil rights activist who strove to ensure that African Americans obtained their full citizenship rights in law but especially in practice. She strongly supported the integration of African Americans into all facets of American society, which included gaining their fair share of economic opportunities in the public and private sectors. From her experiences with marginalization, she also empathized with the plight of the poor, regardless of their color, creed, or religion, and she strove to make changes. Bond's crucial leadership activities will be covered more extensively in chapters 5, 6, and 7.[42]

William F. McClendon, who knew and may have worked with Bloneva Bond, relocated to Niagara Falls in 1942. He came from Graceville, Florida, his place of birth. He began his working life in Niagara Falls as a laborer in the construction industry for the Vanadium Company. He later entered a partnership to form the Federal Blacktop Company and in 1953 started his own business.[43] Over time, his business flourished where McClendon employed both Black and White employees, which he felt was good for generating business. McClendon was reputed to have been one of the best and most successful blacktop workers in Niagara County.[44] In addition to being a local entrepreneurial leader, who practiced the credo of catering to the open market, McClendon served in leadership capacities in his masonic lodge, Electric City Lodge No. 49, and St. John's AME Church.

Blacks who migrated to Niagara Falls during the Second Great Migration and all ensuing migration movements followed the pattern that First Great Migration travelers exhibited.[45] Jobs attracted them to the area. Men often traveled first and did so alone; they sought out jobs, labored in them, had housing arrangements where they often became roomers or boarders, and eventually sent for their families (wife, children, parents, brothers, sisters, and others). They also related their experiences to their friends, encouraging them to leave their home states as well. Migrants and their loved ones generally resided in transitional living quarters until a permanent suitable living arrangement could be found. Most migrants followed national trends of being unskilled laborers, southerners, and often former farmers who were eager to experience the benefits of the North, especially considering that discrimination had stifled their lives in the South.[46] Unfortunately, with their steadily expanding numbers, recent migrants encountered intense forms of housing discrimination that would restrict most of them, along with other Black Niagarans, to a few locations, which would soon become overcrowded. This phenomenon replicated the experiences of many Blacks in larger northeastern and Midwestern cities during and immediately after the First Great Migration. White communities historically have responded to increasing numbers of Blacks filtering into (and around) their neighborhoods and communities in search of living space.[47]

HOUSING

Before World War II, most Black Niagarans, who could be found in wards throughout the city and who were predominantly new migrants, were clustered in four areas of the southern end of the city: (1) the Erie Avenue area, (2) the Buffalo Avenue area, (3) the East Falls Street area, (4) and the Twenty-Fourth Street-Allen-MacKenna Avenue area.[48]

Reverend James Banks, who was the pastor of Emmanuel Baptist Church of Niagara Falls and a Niagara University graduate student, explained the area's parameters:

The first area included part of Erie Avenue between Eighth Street and Fifth Street. The Second area consisted of that part of Buffalo Avenue between Tenth and Thirteenth Streets. The third area is that part of East Falls Street between Tenth and Thirteenth Streets. The fourth area is bounded on the south by Buffalo Avenue, on the west by Twenty-Second Street, on the north by MacKenna Avenue and on the East by Twenty-Seventh Street.[49]

Of these four areas, which are conveyed below in Wards 2, 3, and 4 of Ward Map 2, Erie Avenue was the main business district and the entertainment center of the Black community (see Figure 4.1).[50]

Figure 4.1. Ward map 2 of Niagara Falls, 1940. Courtesy of the *Niagara Falls Gazette*.

The Niagara Community Center was located on Erie Avenue, as was at least one church. Ann Gabriel and Almed Cheatham had tourist homes on the avenue. Jerry Plato owned and operated a boardinghouse there. Wesley Parker ran a restaurant/boardinghouse called the Parker House. Also there was the Sunset Club, which had New York City–style entertainment for people over the age of twenty-one. Murphy's Grill, which had twenty rooms for rent upstairs, was a popular restaurant. A man by the name of Torran operated a poolroom on the avenue, and Emmett Ashford and his wife managed a beauty salon and barbershop.[51]

During and after World War II, some Blacks left the previously mentioned areas and moved to the northern end of the city. By 1947 about 61 percent of Black Niagarans resided on the northern end of town.[52] The section that they relocated to was in Ward 12, just below the Lehigh Valley Railroad site (see Ward Map 2 in figure 4.1). This population shift resulted from the building of Hyde Park Village and Center Court, which were both public housing projects and in response to the large influx of African Americans migrating to Niagara Falls. The federal government sponsored the building of Hyde Park Village, and New York State funded the building of Center Court.[53] The former was built in 1943 and the latter in 1944. Hyde Park Village was originally built to be temporary quarters for World War II military personnel and therefore was not an attractively built unit. It was hastily assembled and projected to be dismantled soon after the war. Center Court was more appealing and as decent as a public housing unit could be. (For one, it had manicured lawns.) These two housing projects represented efforts by federal and state government officials to address migrant war workers' desperate pleas for lodging.

Hyde Park Village was located at the extreme northern edge of Niagara Falls, bounded by James Street, the New York Central Car Lines, Lafayette Avenue, and Hyde Park Boulevard.[54] Many Second Great Migration migrants settled in Hyde Park Village, which offered tenants two-, three-, and four-bedroom apartments, along with a kitchen and living room. These units were constructed with cheap cinderlike red bricks about four or six inches wide, which was the thickness of the walls of the buildings.[55] Tenants used potbellied stoves to heat their apartments, and wood and coal ranges were used for cooking. Hyde Park Village was the most unattractive public housing unit operated by the city of Niagara Falls and generally considered an eyesore. There were no sidewalks built connecting each housing unit; there were just dirt walkways that turned muddy when it rained. Its thin walls were made of unplastered cinder blocks, and floors were just bare concrete.

In addition to Hyde Park Village's dilapidated environment, adjacent to it was a bar known as "Bucket of Blood." It was a small bar located on the corners of James and Highland Avenues. Hyde Park Village residents and those from other areas patronized Bucket of Blood. It was known by this name because violence frequently occurred there, usually on Friday and Saturday nights. It became a place that could regularly generate a "bucket of blood" because patrons often fought and stabbed each other. Besides the stabbings, at least one person was murdered there. Respectable families, consisting of some who believed in the Politics of Respectability, told others to stay away from Bucket of Blood.

The Sugar Hill and Johnson apartments, near Hyde Park Village but even closer to Center Court, also housed Black Niagarans. People who aimed to profit from the housing shortage owned and rented these units. Community lore indicates that Sugar Hill was given that name because it existed near a hill on Hyde Park Boulevard, which at one time was referred to as Sugar Street. Delivery trucks that drove by dropped sand that resembled sugar.[56] The first seventeen Sugar Hill units were built in 1940 on Birch Court, Elm Court, and Michal Court, followed by eleven more built in 1955 on Twenty-Third Street.[57] These units were one-floor flattop-roof houses consisting of two separate apartments, each with two bedrooms, a kitchen, and a bathroom. The initial renters were Whites who in all probability moved out once the flood of Blacks surged into the area. Richard and Jack Johnson had the first Johnson apartments built in 1952, consisting of two eight-unit apartments and two six-unit apartments, both on Twenty-Second Street.[58] These apartments, unlike the Sugar Hill rentals, contained two stories joined by stairs.

Redlining, a practice that contributed to the restriction of African Americans or other citizens deemed undesirable in specific city sections, most likely occurred in Niagara Falls, although no conclusive documented evidence is currently available.[59] It occurred in numerous other cities throughout the nation, particularly after the massive movement of African Americans to northern urban locales. The Home Owners' Loan Corporation (HOLC) and the Federal Housing Authority (FHA), established in 1933 and 1944, respectively, by President Franklin D. Roosevelt and his administration, issued millions of loans to American citizens either to refinance their mortgages to counter the adverse results of the Great Depression or to purchase new homes.[60] These policies, along with the Veterans Administration (VA), significantly increased the number of White Americans who owned homes and contributed toward the expansion of suburbs such as Levittown in New York State and Pennsylvania.[61] The HOLC, with the aid of local realtors, created maps that ranked city sections from one to four.[62] City sections labeled as four commonly consisted of all or a high percentage of African Americans. HOLC planners highlighted these map sections in red, which signaled to financiers (federal or private) not to issue loans to residents in these sections because they were considered too risky.[63] Banks and other lending institutions used the HOLC maps to help determine who they would issue loans to.[64]

During World War II, Black Niagarans began to be restricted to earlier areas and to new areas on the north end of town. Racism undoubtedly played an integral role in this process.[65] If Black Niagarans after 1941 had been able to obtain federal (HOLC, FHA, VA) loans, their housing market still would have been limited to Black enclaves.[66] Because of social pressure, and at times independent actions, White realtors refused to rent or sell properties to Black Niagarans outside of restricted areas.[67] As the population of Blacks residing in Niagara Falls increased, the density in the areas where they resided significantly increased. The natural tendency was for the overflowing population to spill over into surrounding communities, but this process did not occur. Instead, Blacks found themselves competing with one another for limited living quarters.

Black Niagarans attempted to conquer (or perhaps cope) with the housing crisis. In surmounting these obstacles they undertook several strategies.[68] They attempted to sublet properties that they rented. This functioned well in Hyde Park Village but not in Center Court, where housing authorities were more vigilant in preventing subletting. In Hyde Park Village families allowed extended family members or friends to live with them until they were back on their feet financially. Another form of subletting occurred when a legitimate family moved out and moved another family into their old apartment but kept the apartment in their name, allowing the new tenants to pay the rent under the name of the old tenant. Because veterans and war workers had priority in renting housing units, a woman and a veteran or war worker sometimes went to sign up for an apartment. After the apartment was obtained, the veteran or war worker collected the fee for their services of having the apartment established in their name. Later, a couple lived in the new apartment and paid the rent under the veteran or war worker's name. The veteran would then move on. Another form of subletting occurred when a qualified individual rented an apartment and then rented rooms or space in his apartment. A person would place two or three cots in every room, perhaps except the kitchen, and rent them out. Some individuals thus capitalized on the housing shortage in Niagara Falls. Considering the subsistence patterns of Black Niagarans, these arrangements probably occurred in the Sugar Hill and Johnson apartments.

By the mid-1950s, the demolition of Hyde Park Village began. In 1952 twenty-eight residents of Hyde Park Village were granted a thirty-day stay by Judge Thomas B. Lee after they had been ordered to vacate their dwellings.[69] Most of the adults had received eviction notices and testified that they had tried in vain to find other accommodations throughout the city; however, their efforts were to no avail. The judge informed the City Council that there was no housing shortage in the city, and he unhesitatingly informed the Black citizens before him of this fact.[70] He was correct, but he apparently was unaware that realtors and homeowners refused to sell or rent to Blacks in certain sections where housing was available. Most of the adults who received eviction notices had come from Alabama, having been enticed by local industries to work for them.[71] However, these industries made no effort to ensure that housing would be available for their recruited employees.

In addition to their testimonies before Judge Lee, perhaps what helped the twenty-eight evicted tenants receive a stay is that they had support from a Judge J. D. Carr, who was a mediator from the Civil Rights League, Inc., of Buffalo, and James A. Lafferty, who was the Hyde Park Village project manager. Lafferty told Judge Carr, "The tenants [were] illegally in possession of the units but that it was his view that for these same people there [was] an acute housing shortage."[72] Lafferty may have reached this conclusion based on the numerous African Americans who applied and pleaded for living quarters at Hyde Park Village.[73]

Once these tenants finally evacuated Hyde Park Village, they generally crowded back into the older areas in the southern end of town. Or they moved to Center Court, where a closer watch was kept on tenants to prevent them from allowing relatives and friends to double up in their apartments as many had done in Hyde Park Village, which helped to produce a slumlike atmosphere. A few were allowed into Griffon Manor, which was an exclusively White federal housing project. There was, however, still an urgent unfulfilled demand for housing among the ever-expanding Black population.

The leaders of the Niagara Community Center constantly spoke out against the housing discrimination that confronted Black Niagarans.[74] They also supported studies that further underscored the housing problem. In the mid-1950s, their complaints and the studies' findings calling for the development of more housing for Black Niagarans fell upon deaf ears in the city council. The need for more and better housing was not seriously considered until a fire took the lives of many children housed in an old overcrowded, dilapidated apartment building.[75] This fire embarrassed council members and other city officials into providing more public housing for Black Niagarans and silenced all opposition.

The fire, a major calamity, occurred at 4:30 a.m. on Saturday, November 16, 1957, at the Moonglow Hotel, at 2449 Allen Avenue. William Dietz, a local police officer, owned the hotel. The Moonglow Hotel had three floors with twelve small apartments per floor, totaling thirty-six apartments. Only one bathroom and one kitchen existed on each floor. Many Black families who had been forced out of Hyde Park Village or who had desperately searched for limited housing may have lived at the Moonglow Hotel. The Moonglow Hotel had only one door for entering and exiting the building. The hallways were dark, and the rooms were small and crowded.[76] It was known that parents would have many children in each room often stretched across a single bed; in fact, most occupants of the Moonglow Hotel were children.[77] Most people obtained their own cooking and heating utilities, which consisted of oil or gas burners.[78] Because so many people resided in the Moonglow Hotel there was a steady flow of people at all hours of the day and night. One of the best descriptions of the fire's impact was written by a *Niagara Falls Gazette* staff writer, quoted in full:

> From dawn until dusk Saturday, people came to look. They watched as firemen carried blanket wrapped bundles from the second and third stories of the burned out shell of a three-story building. If they counted, they got up to 17. They watched as the building's owner William Dietz manned his own steam shovel to knock apart the paper-thin walls of the most damaged portion. They watched as officials toured the building looking for the cause. They watched as knots of officials—fire, police, housing—discussed the fire and its implications.
>
> It was about four hours after the first alarm sounded that the last of the bodies was taken from the building. Firemen went from room to room in their search, methodically looking for the victims, many small children and infants. It seemed they would never end their search. They kept finding more.
>
> The building itself was a simple structure—a frame dwelling that housed at least 25 persons and in the past had been home for many more. It was a refuge for some families who used to live in Hyde Park Village. What was it like to live there? One of the onlookers yesterday was eager to tell.

Mrs. Bertha Faulk qualifies as an expert. She lived there for six years until moving out in August of this year. She and her husband paid $10 a week rent for two rooms in the basement. She told spectators that it was common for sewage from the upper stories to back up on the floor of the apartment—to come up through the drain and bubble in the sink. She said she had been warned by a city building inspector that she would be wise to leave. So she and her husband, Henry, employed by the City's Department of Public Works, moved to 109 24th St.

Was Mrs. Faulk ever afraid of fire? "Yes sir, I was," she said. She charged the basement apartment had one small window and a single door as means of escape. How many people lived there when the building was fully occupied? Mrs. Faulk was stumped. She mentioned names she knew but could come up with no figures. Were there as many as 60? "Lord, sometimes there were 60 children alone," she said.

As near as anyone knows, there were about 25 living in the building at the time of the fire. Owner Dietz said he had been attempting to evict the two families there until yesterday.

The people came and went. Those who were not there when the bodies were being discovered missed the impact of the disaster. After that, there was only a frame building, a gutted, charred structure. And mud. And tired men wondering what can be done to keep this sort of thing from happening again.[79]

In responding to this tragedy, the city council authorized the Niagara Falls Housing Authority to proceed with its plan to construct fifty dwellings units near the present Packard Court housing project. The council ordered the reactivation of the City Housing Advisory Committee and instructed it to make an immediate study of the city's housing needs.[80] City officials made Griffon Manor more accessible to Black Niagarans. In 1961 Richard and Jack Johnson had four more eight-unit apartments built next to their earlier rental units.[81] (In 1972 they built two additional ten-unit apartments, and in 1982 one final thirteen-unit apartment, all near their first units.) Some Niagarans felt that this gesture was too little, too late. Ben Bolden, for example, reemphasized to city officials that he had informed them in 1937, twenty years earlier, that places such as the Moonglow Hotel were unfit for human habitation and that "members of the City Council should hang their heads in shame, go into the woods and not come back until conditions in the city like those that existed at the Moonglow Hotel [were] eradicated."[82] His words had not initially been taken seriously. Nevertheless, concerning the current tragedy, Bolden emphasized that he sent letters to the city manager, mayor, and city council urging that immediate action be taken to correct other deplorable housing conditions in the city to prevent another catastrophe.[83] Obtaining suitable housing during and after World War II served as a constant challenge for Black Niagarans.

By 1940 Black Niagarans' residential patterns had not changed drastically since 1930 (see table 4.3). With a population increase of sixty-nine people, Wards 2 and 3 grew significantly, whereas Ward 5's population decreased. Black Niagarans continued to be absent in Wards 6 and 10, and three Black Niagarans made Ward 15 their home. As in 1930, Black Niagarans continued to make up only a small percentage of all the wards they resided in (less than 8 percent),[84] and their highest concentration remained in Wards 2, 3, 4, and 5.

The 1950 US Census, unfortunately, did not record Black Niagarans by wards. This would have shown a greater concentration of Black Niagarans in specific wards, considering that the 1940 Black Niagaran population had drastically increased from 975 to 3,585 by 1950. Moreover, for conveying housing patterns, by 1960, the federal government had abandoned ward labeling with the encouragement of local government; they adopted a census tract system that divided the city of Niagara Falls into twenty-five census tracts and labeled Niagarans in general terms as either white or

Table 4.3. 1930 and 1940 Black Population by Ward

Ward	1930	1940	1930 Percentage	1940 Percentage
1	25	30	1.5	1.6
2	95	142	3.5	5.2
3	236	302	5.6	7.7
4	256	232	3.9	3.7
5	101	65	.07	.05
6	0	0	0	0
7	51	66	2.7	3.4
8	9	3	.03	.01
9	46	32	.05	.03
10	0	0	0	0
11	12	6	.06	.03
12	33	55	.05	.08
13	26	16	.05	.03
14	16	23	.03	.03
15	0	3	0	.01

Adapted from the 1930 and 1940 United States Censuses. (Please see page 356, note 84.)

non-White. Within the twenty-five census tracts 7,664 non-Whites existed, 3,791 males and 3,873 females.[85] Hence, census enumerators recorded 7,038 Black Niagarans by 1960, which means that of the 7,664 non-Whites, 626 (or about 8.2 percent) were not African American. A consensus of local politicians posited that citizens would gain better representation, since an expansion of census tracts compared to the smaller number of wards would increase the number of representatives in city government.[86] However, this arrangement accelerated the trend in which Black Niagarans would be confined or isolated strictly among themselves in relatively few census tracts. Table 4.4 partially illustrates this pattern, underlining non-White household heads who owned or rented the dwellings they resided in.

Table 4.4. 1960 Homeowners and Renters by Census Tract

Census Tract	Total Number of Owners	Total Number of White Owners	Total Number of Nonwhite Owners	Total Number of Renters	Total Number of White Renters	Total Number of Nonwhite Renters
1	1,235	1,234	1	330	327	3
2	562	291	271	681	105	576
3	462	458	4	105	102	3
4	608	607	1	400	396	4
5	532	529	3	1,064	1,038	26
6	533	533	0	600	586	14
7	930	930	0	326	326	0
8	251	251	0	205	204	1
9	684	682	2	649	637	12
10	929	928	1	618	616	2
11	360	359	1	993	965	28
12	599	598	1	813	805	8
13	623	621	2	824	813	11
14	720	718	2	428	425	3
15	205	197	8	1498	1411	87
16	391	351	40	1,178	860	318
17	640	614	26	838	722	116
18	701	672	29	187	178	9
19	467	463	4	207	206	1
20	872	868	4	245	244	1
21	1,024	1,023	1	155	152	3
22	1,168	1,163	5	387	386	1
23	897	893	4	281	280	1
24	958	956	2	734	591	143
25	561	560	1	175	174	1

Adapted from the 1960 United States Census. (Please see page 356, note 85.)

In 1960 most non-White homeowners and renters predominantly resided in five census tracts: 2, 15, 16, 17, and 24. Census tract 2 contained the most non-White homeowners (271) and renters (576), followed by census tracts 16, 24, 17, and 15. More specifically, 65.61 percent of the non-White homeowners resided in census tract 2. Census tract 2 also contained 41.98 percent of all non-White renters, and 47.45 percent of all combined non-White homeowners and renters. Census tract 2 existed on the northern side of Niagara Falls and contained the Center Court project, and Hyde Park Village had been there. Census tracts 15, 16, and 17 were in the southern section of town, containing such streets as East Falls Street, Allen Street, Thirteenth Street, and MacKenna Avenue, while the LaSalle section of town contained census tract 24, where Griffon Manor was located. The 1960 census tract map (figure 4.2) shows where each census tract was located.

For aggregate census tract population figures, Table 4.5 below details racial groups more specifically, which allows the number of White, Black, and other races in census tracts 2, 15, 16, 17, and 24 to be examined more critically. Of the five census tracts, 16 and 2 contained the highest percentage of Black Niagarans, tract 16 having 23.72 percent and tract 2 holding 72.92 percent.[87] Census tract 2 also contained 56.32 percent of Niagara Falls's total African American population, and census tracts 2

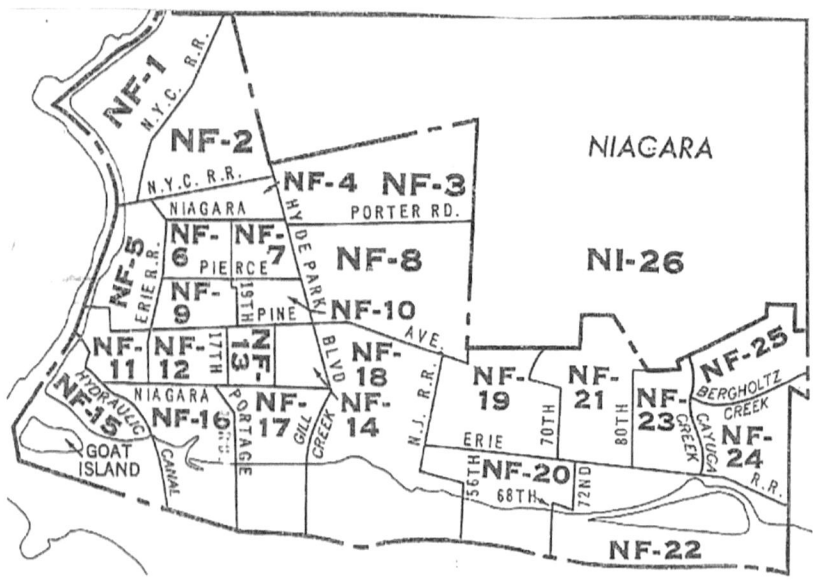

Figure 4.2. Niagara Falls census map, 1960. United States Census. Fair use.

Table 4.5. Population Density of Census Tracts 2, 15, 16, 17, and 24

	Census Tract 2	Census Tract 15	Census Tract 16	Census Tract 17	Census Tract 24
Total Population	5,436	3,467	4,988	4,777	6,967
White	1,464 (26.93)	3,135 (90.42)	3,761 (75.40)	4,150 (86.87)	6,233 (89.46)
Black	3,964 (72.92)	231 (6.66)	1,183 (23.72)	605 (12.67)	688 (9.88)
Other Races	8 (0.15)	101 (2.91)	44 (0.88)	22 (0.46)	46 (0.66)

Adapted from the 1960 United States Census of Population and Housing. (Please see page 356, note 87.)

and 16 contained 73.13 percent.[88] In each ensuing decade, census tract 2's Black Niagaran population continued to increase.[89]

The significant expansion of the African American population after 1940 increased residential segregation and strengthened a pattern whereby Black Niagarans were relegated to certain city sections (e.g., wards or census tracts). Table 4.6 depicts the computed indices of dissimilarity from 1930 to 1970.

The Index of Dissimilarity value ranges from 0 to 100 percent. A value of 50 percent or higher is more indicative of the existence of residential segregation.[90] For Niagara Falls, the Index of Dissimilarity value increased after 1930, had declined by 1960, and then had increased again by 1970. This difference may have had something to do with city officials opting to use a census tract method of dividing city sections as opposed to wards. In 1940, Niagara Falls had fifteen wards; by 1960, it had twenty-five census tracts. Moreover, from 1940 to 1960, Niagara Falls's Index of Dissimilarity values notably decreased from 0.5825 to 0.5089, as was shown in Karl and Alma Taeuber's list of twenty-five northeastern cities

Table 4.6. The Index of Dissimilarity, Niagara Falls, 1930–1970

Year	Dissimilarity	Black Population	% Black
1930	0.510	906	1.20
1940	0.5825	975	1.25
1950	N/A	3,585	3.94
1960	0.5089	7,038	6.87
1970	0.6635	8,001	9.35

Adapted from the 1930 to 1970 United States Censuses. (Please see page 356, note 92.)

in the same period.[91] Even so, Niagara Falls undeniably followed a trend of increased residential segregation with its expanding African American population.[92]

Obtaining housing continued to be a major problem for Black Niagarans, even after the Moonglow Hotel tragedy.[93] Low-skilled jobs were plentiful, and African Americans arrived in steady numbers to seek those opportunities. From 1950 to 1960, their population figures nearly doubled, increasing from 3,585 to 7,038 (see table 1.1). Black Niagarans persistently and desperately searched for dwelling units throughout the city, but realtors continued to rent or sell properties to them only in the noted five census tracts, where a large, ever-expanding group of Blacks had been living.[94]

By 1956 a few Black families were renting units in Griffon Manor. One of the local newspapers reported that there was no housing shortage in Niagara Falls due to available rental units such as Griffon Manor. A desperate phone caller contacted the manager of Griffon Manor and told him that he had read in the newspaper that a hundred Griffon Manor units were vacant. He informed the manager that if he rented any of those units to colored people, he would be physically harmed.[95] He also indicated that the past housing manager had kept them out and that he represented a group of concerned citizens who had a large investment in property around Griffon Manor. When told to come to the Griffon Manor office to discuss the matter, the caller, speaking in broken English, refused to comply, repeating his warning several times to the effect that if the manager did not keep out colored people, he would be "taken care of." This threat was reported to the police.[96] No recorded acts of violence exist concerning this event.

Some professional people wanted to purchase housing in Niagara Falls but could not buy into the neighborhoods they desired.[97] Some of these people purchased homes in Buffalo and commuted to their jobs in Niagara Falls. Reverend H. Edward Whitaker, head of the New Hope Baptist Church and an upcoming civil rights activist, told his fellow clergymen at a 1959 Niagara Falls Christian convention that fifty members of his congregation had to commute from Buffalo to Niagara Falls because they could not find decent housing in the city.[98] The convention members unanimously supported a resolution for fair housing for everyone without regard to race, color, creed, or national origin.

According to community lore, before World War II, Black Niagarans did not experience any considerable racial problems in Cataract City until Blacks arrived from Andalusia, Alabama. This belief also highlights that prior to the Second Great Migration, Blacks generally could live in peace throughout the city of Niagara Falls, even living among other ethnic groups.[99] In support of this notion, one African American woman proclaimed: "When I was growing up my family lived all over the city. We lived where we wanted to."[100] She cited an all-White section of Cudaback Avenue as an example.[101] "When I was 8, my family lived there in a double house with a Polish family. We got along fine. But I couldn't live there today."[102] Some older residents believed that Andalusia Alabamians brought their backward country ways to Niagara Falls—a northern cosmopolitan city. They spoke differently, dressed differently, their families were usually large, their education level was generally low (below the standards of New York State), and they were often uninhibited in public (e.g., talking and laughing too loudly on public conveyances). These behaviors and others not only shocked the sensibilities of the Whites but also the Black Niagarans who had been longtime residents. This phenomenon was not exclusive to Niagara Falls; it occurred in city after northern city that experienced the impact of the migration movements from the South.[103] Hence, after 1941 racial issues involving housing became more acute and intertwined with the rapid expansion of the Black population.

During the 1940s and beyond, largely due to racial barriers, most Black Niagarans rented living space.[104] Of 1,785 housing units occupied by non-Whites in 1960, 1,372 were renter occupied and only 413 owner occupied.[105] It was difficult for Blacks to own property. Properties for sale were limited in the areas that Blacks were confined to, and realtors continued to be discouraged from renting or selling properties to Blacks outside three general districts. By 1943 the First District was the East Falls Street area around Eleventh Street; the Second District consisted of Pine Acres, Hyde Park Village, and Center Court, and the Third District became the Griffon Manor area, which throttled the efforts of the aforementioned desperate phone caller. The Black community within Buffalo in 1912 to 1940, according to historian Lillian S. Williams, experienced similar housing impediments.[106]

Those few Blacks who did own their homes were usually old residents who lived throughout the city of Niagara Falls and had generally established their residency before World War II. Since their numbers were small, they probably were not perceived as a threat by their White neighbors.[107] One or two might be in a predominantly White neighborhood, and their family heads worked and were perceived as respectable community members. William Rudolph, for example, was the first Black bricklayer in Niagara Falls.[108] He owned a home on Livingston Avenue; the Goffeny family and the Hershey family owned their homes on North Avenue.[109] Blacks also owned homes in the Tennessee Avenue and Twenty-First area and on Ely and Dudley Avenues. Their properties usually were well kept and attractive.[110] These Black Niagaran homeowners lived outside the three city sections where most of their racial group resided.

Even so, more Blacks were steadily migrating to Niagara Falls (see table 1.1) and more arrived from Andalusia, Alabama. Their presence placed an even heavier strain on the Niagara Community Center.[111] The house at 637 Erie Avenue was not large enough to accommodate the increasing number of people who wanted to patronize the center (see figure 4.3).[112] After a request for further assistance from the Community Chest, another study was conducted to convince the Community Chest of the center's needs. This study was titled "Survey of the Niagara Community Center Association of Niagara Falls, New York."[113] Edward G. Lindsey, who was the executive secretary of the Council of Social Agencies for the city of Niagara Falls, conducted the study and completed it in 1948. He found that since the war the center's paid-up membership had grown from 50 to 1,357.[114] Twenty-nine groups were meeting at the center, members had participated in programs 19,302 times, and its leadership had promoted

Figure 4.3. Niagara Community Center, 1938. Niagara Community Center. Fair use.

racial harmony. His study supported and advocated for building larger quarters.

To obtain funds to build the new building, in May 1949, the center launched a $120,000 fundraising campaign, which was approved by the Community Chest. Leaders of the Niagara Community Center wanted to move it from the southern end of town to the northern end, where about 60 percent of the Black community resided, preferably next to the Center Court project where many youths lived. Through the influence of board members such as a Mr. Van Liew, the city council and the Niagara Falls Housing Authority donated five lots of land adjacent to Center Avenue and Fifteenth Street,[115] which was next to the Center Court project. In 1952, amid a festive celebration, the Niagara Falls Community Center relocated to its new home (however, it was inoperative as of 2010) (see figure 4.4).

Figure 4.4. Niagara Community Center, 1955. Niagara Community Center. Fair use.

Bigotry

Aside from the relocation of the Niagara Community Center and the growing trend of Black Niagarans being largely concentrated in a few census tracts, the fact that Black Niagarans were expected by many Niagarans to exist in certain spaces on the fringes of society is confirmed by another incident. Florence Lovell Dyett, who resided in Jacksonville, Florida, and was head of the Elementary Education Department at Bethune-Cookman College, in 1946, responded to an advertisement from the De Veaux School of Niagara Falls, an all-boys school largely consisting of children whose parents were affluent.[116] The advertisement declared that any child of a deceased minister who possessed an outstanding academic record could qualify for a scholarship at De Veaux (called the Samuel De Veaux scholarship) and was worth $1,000 per year. It paid all charges—tuition, room, board, and laundry.

Mrs. Dyett applied for the scholarship on her twelve-year-old son's behalf. Reverend William S. Hudson, headmaster of the school, corresponded with Dyett. He found Ernest's academic record very impressive, and school officials quickly voted to issue Ernest the esteemed scholarship. More correspondence ensued between Dyett and Reverend Hudson, who congratulated Ernest on being chosen as a scholarship recipient, as plans were being made to get Ernest to school. Dyett informed Reverend Hudson that she would not be able to deliver Ernest to school herself but that a friend would do it for her. When Ernest and his chaperone arrived at the school, Hudson bluntly told them that Ernest could not enter the school because he was colored. Hudson then escorted them to the train station and paid their fare to Philadelphia.

When Mrs. Dyett was informed of what had happened, she was angry and concerned about the psychological damage that might have been done to her son. In a follow-up letter, Reverend Hudson informed Dyett that during their correspondence he had not been told that Ernest was Black and that had he known he would have spared all parties the embarrassment. Moreover, he surmised that Dyett might have assumed that racial prejudice was nonexistent in the North because she lived in the South. He further informed her that parents would withdraw their children if they knew a Black student attended the De Veaux School. He then subtly reprimanded Dyett for not informing him that Ernest was Black.[117]

In response, Mrs. Dyett contacted Walter White, head of the NAACP, for advice concerning this matter.[118] White had one of his legal aides,

Franklin H. Williams, contact Reverend Hudson and hint at a lawsuit if Ernest was not allowed entry to the school and awarded his scholarship.[119] Reverend Hudson consulted with the school's board of directors who decided that because Ernest had been awarded the scholarship, he should be admitted to the De Veaux School. This information was conveyed to the Dyetts and the NAACP.[120] Knowing that he was not initially welcomed, the psychological damage of attending the De Veaux School, a private religious institution, may have been even more damaging than his first encounter with Reverend Hudson.[121]

Despite the initial discrimination, Ernest Dyett did attend the De Veaux School. He later remembered that the Pullman Red Cap porters on the trains from Florida to Niagara Falls looked out for him.[122] He attended because he did not want to let his mother down. He also did not want to disappoint Dr. Mary McLeod Bethune, who was president and one of the founders of Bethune-Cookman College.[123] Specifically, he did not want to give Dr. Bethune, who was a strong civil rights advocate, the impression that his mother had raised someone who did not have backbone. Dr. Bethune told Ernest that she would visit the De Veaux School to give him support. Ernest remembered the school headmaster (probably Reverend Hudson) assuring his mother that he would be integrated into the flow of life at the school. The school was a military academy for young men, required school uniforms (among other rigorous measures) for its students. School routines were regimented, with classes held and tasks done at specific times. Ernest attended the De Veaux School for less than a month. Being a Floridian he had a difficult time adjusting to the cold, and he became homesick.

In terms of being the only Black student at the school, Ernest said that his memory of discrimination was vague. He was seventy-six years old when interviewed about his experiences at the school. Nonetheless, he could still recall some older White boys teasing him and making racial jokes about his skin color and hair being different from theirs. Although racism existed, Ernest felt it was not as flagrant as in Florida, where he came from. He also made a point of stating that he, like Dr. Bethune, was fearless and willing to fight anyone who bothered him, which may have prevented some of his schoolmates from picking on him. No records indicate whether the local Black community or its leadership was aware of the Ernest Dyett case. It may have been a private matter between the NAACP's national office and the De Veaux School, although a local branch of the NAACP had been formed in Niagara Falls in 1943. The De Veaux School closed in 1972 and is now part of De Veaux Woods State Park.

Another case that exemplifies discrimination but also opportunity is the story of the Marigold Restaurant, which was located on Second Street. It opened in 1925 and came up repeatedly in interviewees' stories.[124] A White woman from Niagara Falls—Mary H. Baldwin—was the restaurant proprietor. When she first opened her restaurant, she operated it in Niagara Falls during the tourist season, summer and fall, and closed it in the winter. During the winters, she operated a similar restaurant in New Orleans.[125] Her restaurant specialized in southern cuisines common to African American culture, such as fried chicken, biscuits, vegetables, and sweet tea. It was a popular restaurant that attracted a steady flow of patronage from most Niagarans. Other than the waitresses, however, the Marigold Restaurant's working staff consisted of Blacks, some who had come from Louisiana to work for Baldwin. Pristell Anderson, for example, moved from Alexandria, Louisiana, to retake his position as chief kitchen worker, a position he held for Baldwin in New Orleans.[126] Several parents, their children, and other relatives also worked at the restaurant.

Although Blacks worked at the Marigold Restaurant, they initially could not be served in the dining area. That was an unwritten policy. Helen Reed-McBride, who was an employee of the Marigold, related another story from her childhood.[127] A White woman patronized the Marigold with her children and the family's Black maid. She sat in the dining area with her children and her maid and was ready to order a meal. An employee approached her and said that she and her children could eat in the dining area but not her maid. The woman defended herself and her maid sternly by stating that her family and maid would eat together. The employee insisted that a place in the kitchen could be reserved for her maid. The woman flatly refused the arrangement and stormed out of the restaurant with her children and the maid. This woman, like other women, was willing to speak up against overt forms of racism.[128] Perhaps due to the customs of the North, constant resistance (or both) Eddie Palmore, a Black Niagaran and future leader, indicated that when he moved to Niagara Falls from Andalusia, Alabama, in 1947, he ate meals in the Marigold Restaurant's dining area and that he thoroughly enjoyed them.[129]

COMMUNITY VOICES

Accounts presented in this section are from a few of many people interviewed over the years. Their testimonies convey the voices of the people, or the views of many, if not most, Black Niagarans. Their voices allow us to

Expanded Community and New Realities | 149

understand more of the internal community dynamics, which reflect social history.[130] These people conformed to Booker T. Washington's philosophy of pulling themselves up then reaching back to help others. They lived from 1940 to 1960 (and beyond), with each ultimately functioning as a leader. They are unique—yet common—because their narratives reinforce many of the points made throughout this chapter: triumphs over obstacles, and the will to overcome, reflecting community realities.

Barbara J. Smith's family, like the Rudolph, Hershey, and Goffeny families, resided in Niagara Falls before World War II.[131] Her father, John Daniels Sr., arrived in 1923 and soon found employment at Bell Aircraft Corporation in the janitorial department. At the time, according to Barbara, these low-paying jobs were the only ones usually available to Black Niagarans.[132] John Daniels Sr. worked for nearly a year, saving up funds to send for his family, which he did, later in the same year of his arrival. With money for train passage, Barbara's mother, sister, and two brothers traveled to Niagara Falls. Barbara had not yet been born and would not be until 1938. The children were Daisy, John Jr., and Alexander. By 1930 Barbara Smith's family lived on Twenty-Seventh Street.[133] John Daniels Sr. was 48, Annie 37, Daisy 20, John Jr. 18, and Alexander 11.[134] There were three other children Frank (five years old), Bernice (three and a half), and William (one and a half). Barbara and two other children would be born later. In all, Barbara had six brothers and two sisters.[135]

By 1943 Barbara's family had moved to Allen Avenue near Twenty-Fourth Street. She remembered her neighborhood being multiethnic. Two houses were in front of the house where her family resided. Her family lived in the rear of the two houses. She lived directly next to Polish, Italian, and German families. Many of these ethnic group members had recently come to the United States, and some could not speak English. Many family heads ideally wanted to live near Buffalo Avenue and thus close to the plants where they worked. Everyone was generally poor, trying to advance themselves in the land of opportunity. Barbara played with children from various ethnic backgrounds having one thing in common: they all wanted to have fun.

Barbara noted that despite living so close to each other, very little race mixing occurred.[136] The Black Niagarans she knew married members of their own racial group. If a mixed-race couple existed in the area, it might be a Canadian and a Black Niagaran. Barbara partly attributed a Canadian willingness to marry a Black Niagaran to the fact that their conception of race differed from that of US citizens because slavery had not been as pervasive in Canada. She also observed that European emigrants soon became mindful of American racial dynamics. In summing up her remarks on race mixing, Barbara commented that Black Niagarans did not go to places where they knew they were not welcome, such as bars, political and social clubs, hotels, and restaurants.

As far as European emigrants being aware of American racial norms, Barbara cited an example concerning her sister Daisy. Daisy had been one of the first seven African American females hired at the Carborundum Corporation during the early 1940s. Located on Buffalo Avenue, this company became one of the largest employers of Black Niagarans. Daisy started off doing janitorial work, but she was promoted to working on the plant production line during World War II. Along with the six other African American women, Daisy made some of the European women emigrants uncomfortable. They approached management about providing separate restroom and lounge facilities for them and the African American females. When Daisy and the other African American females found out about this, they became extremely upset, and some wanted to physically fight the complainants. Management did not concede to the immigrant workers' request. According to Barbara, "Daisy and the others felt that here were foreigners who were considered as nothing in their former countries coming to the United States and thinking that they were better simply due to the color of their skin."[137] Moreover, they felt these women could not even speak English properly; yet they had quickly embraced an attitude of racial superiority. Even so, Barbara's sister Daisy worked thirty-three years at the Carborundum Corporation.

Barbara also said that although racism existed at the Carborundum Corporation, intragroup tension sometimes operated as well. She explained an example involving her brother John Jr., the second oldest child who traveled on the train with her mother from Cayce, South Carolina. John Jr., like his father and sister, obtained employment at the Carborundum Corporation. With the passage of time and advancements in civil rights, the Carborundum Corporation began to try to operate as a more equal opportunity employer. The fact that Daisy could move out of janitorial work to a better-paying job in the plant attests to this attitude. After a job notice had been posted at the Carborundum Corporation, John Jr. told other African American employees that they should apply for the position. Several of the African American employees told John Jr. that it would be futile because the company's personnel department would not consider a Black employee for this position. John Jr. did not take their advice. He applied for the job and got it. Several of the African American employees were envious and angry with John Jr. Some told him that they should have gotten the job because they had more seniority than he had, according to Barbara. John informed them that they did not get the job because they did not apply for it.[138] Regardless, they still expressed their resentment to John Jr. who was willing to see if his employer would grant him an opportunity.

Barbara Smith keenly remembered the large influx of African Americans who arrived in Niagara Falls during World War II. Men stood out; they seemed to arrive in droves. Many lived as boarders in homes or other living quarters. They came to work in the plants, according to Barbara, because of the high demand for labor. Many of the men came alone, much like her father had; then after they had saved enough money, they sent for their family members. She also noticed that African Americans began to settle in the North Side neighborhood of Niagara Falls. Originally a clustering existed on the East Side, where she lived, and on the South End; however, Black Niagarans had lived throughout the city. Now they began to settle in Hyde Park Village and in Center Court, forming a more intense cluster. Her father, sister, and brother began to meet new coworkers who sought their advice on a range of subjects.

Barbara also saw Black Niagarans engaging in entrepreneurial activities. At the time she did not perceive them as entrepreneurs or as unique entities within the community. She remembered Dr. Charles B. Hayes as being the first doctor of African descent in the city. She remembered Little Joe's Café, which the Williamson family owned and managed. She remembered Inez Caver's restaurant, on Thirteenth Street near Buffalo Avenue. Caver's restaurant was one of the eateries that catered to the laborers who worked at the plants on Buffalo Avenue. Many of the new southern migrants frequented Caver's place for a good homecooked meal. Barbara also remembered Billy Carter's soda fountain store, which she frequently visited to buy candies and other treats. She remembered that Black Niagarans had barbers and hairdressers. Barber Claude Martin cut hair in the East Side neighborhood, cornering that market, with his barbershop on Erie Avenue. On legendary Erie Avenue, she recalled discussions about the Sunset Club and the Parker House. Black Niagarans had several small businesses.

In analyzing Black Niagaran families when she grew up, compared to local businesspersons, Barbara Smith was more insightful. She stressed that stability existed in families. First and foremost, she commented that jobs were plentiful in Niagara Falls. Her family, as alluded to above, lived near Buffalo Avenue, which was a thoroughfare that contained numerous plants. Buses operated twenty-four hours a day, taking patrons to and from work. Restaurants conducted business near the plants to capture that market by accommodating hungry and weary workers. If they chose to, workers could leave one job and find employment at another plant. Although Black Niagarans generally had low-level plant jobs, they earned a paycheck, which went toward the welfare of their families. For Black Niagarans, like John Daniels Sr., who had recently migrated from the South, plant labor was far superior to southern farm work.

According to Barbara, a steady income contributed to family stability.[139] She observed men sticking by their families and being the breadwinners. This certainly applied to her family. Her father worked at least eight hours per day, while her mother worked at home, taking care of the children. Her father ended his employment with Bell Aircraft because the Carborundum job paid more, which provided extra needed money for his family. Barbara's father worked to maintain and advance his family until the day he died. He envisioned a better day for his children and encouraged them all, including his girls, to advance themselves educationally.

In the southern farming families from which most recent migrants had come, children had duties within families.[140] African American southern farmers usually had large families like John Daniels Sr. had. Children had to help their parents cultivate the crops. If they were teenagers, they might have helped their parents plow; or if they were too young to plow, their job might have been bringing water to thirsty older workers or removing bugs from certain plants or even feeding some of the farm animals. As a matter of survival, family heads needed all available laborers to manage and maintain their households.[141] African American migrants brought this training to northern regions such as Niagara Falls. Older children in Barbara's family had to help monitor younger children, perform household tasks, or even work outside the home. These tasks included babysitting, preparing or helping to prepare meals, regularly taking the garbage out, washing dishes and clothes, shoveling snow, and raking leaves. Some later obtained employment at the Carborundum Corporation to help pay family expenses and doing whatever it took to help maintain and advance the family. Barbara saw her siblings John Jr. and Daisy fulfilling this role; they were adults by the time of her birth.

Desiring to make a family contribution and following her father's educational directive, Barbara attended Niagara Street School. In these early years, most Black Niagaran youth attended the Niagara Street School, Barbara recalled. She excelled in school and was usually the only African American in her classes. If another African American was present, according to Barbara, it was often a relative. She loved to read and learn; she also "credited one of her teachers, Lucy Rainville, for serving as her academic mentor, encouraging her to keep her grades up and to aim high."[142] Barbara graduated from Niagara Falls Senior High School in 1956. Then she attended Buffalo State College and earned her bachelor's degree in 1960. Her older sister, Daisy, paid much of her college tuition and fees. Barbara made her family proud, being the first to graduate from college. She earned her master's degree in elementary education, also from Buffalo State College, which was then known for its strong elementary and secondary teaching programs. Inspired by Gussy Wilson, an early African American teacher in the Niagara Falls public school system, Barbara taught elementary education for forty-two years, first at Thirteenth Street School, then at her old Niagara Street School, and finally at Henry F. Abate School.[143] Barbara taught over a thousand students, many of whom later became successful. She remained a strong advocate for all children.

With the completion of her education, along with teaching in the Niagara Falls public school system, Barbara noticed that several Black Niagarans saw her as an elitist. Her college training certainly fits W. E. B. Du Bois's description of the Talented Tenth and what one should do after acquiring her/his education. Some people felt that she should not be in certain places or do certain things because they now perceived her to be of a higher status. Barbara, on the other hand, commented that she saw herself as a human being willing to associate with anyone who was a good and respectable person.[144] Her education, along with observing earlier community leaders helped her to be a more effective leader. Barbara went on to serve as president of the local Niagara Falls NAACP branch. At the end of an interview on May 17, 2002, I asked Barbara if she were writing a history of Black Niagarans for future generations, what points would she emphasize? Barbara responded that she would accentuate the drastic changes that have occurred.

> Many physical changes have occurred in the area. For example, factories were here. Now they are gone. Strikes existed in the past. Unions were growing. Niagara Falls was a working-class town. A lot of young people have left.[145]

In 2002 and in 2010, the year of my last interview with Barbara, Niagara Falls certainly was not the expanding, bustling, and cosmopolitan city that Barbara knew in her childhood and young adulthood; yet she still called it home because she and her family had not only planted roots in Niagara Falls but made history there as well. Consequently, for her there was "no place like home."[146]

Joe O'Neal, like Barbara Smith, remembered many crucial facets of Black Niagaran history.[147] At the age of eighteen, Joe migrated from Florida to Niagara Falls, arriving in 1950 after the Second Great Migration. He arrived in December and had to get used to the cold weather; it was hard, but Joe adjusted. His older brother, who had earlier come to Niagara Falls and sent for Joe, told him about the abundance of available work. Joe quickly came and soon found employment at the Union Carbide and Carbon Corporation. He initially stayed in a home that Bloneva Bond owned. Joe expressed his high admiration for Bond in his interview.

Joe was blue collar, or working class. When he started working at the Union Carbide and Carbon Corporation, he knew that a person could leave one plant job and get employment somewhere else rather quickly. Even in 1950 his plant and many others were still in great need of workers, so much so that they often found it difficult to meet some of their job orders on a timely basis. Joe commented that Union Carbide and Carbon and other plants sent personnel employees out to recruit workers, and he heard that during World War II plants sent staff workers to the South to recruit labor. "They would show up to a farm area with a truck, for example, and ask if there were individuals that wanted to work, if so to get on the truck. They would provide passage to Niagara Falls, provided their prospective employees promised to work."[148]

Joe worked at National Carbon, the main plant on Highland Avenue and one of Union Carbide and Carbon's three local plants. The common laborers had to perform difficult and dirty work. Joe started his career on the Green Floor, where the assignments were the dirtiest. An African American and a White worker might begin their workday with different skin colors; by the end of the day, they would all be one color—black, from the dust. The Green Floor also had an open-hearth furnace. Men threw materials into the furnace to make certain products. Joe commented that it was mainly African American workers who were assigned this work. Joe also noted that most of the workers in his plant were African Americans and that the management treated them fairly.

When Joe started as an employee, Union Carbide and Carbon provided him with no benefits, although as time progressed he did receive health insurance. He earned fairly good wages, which allowed him to take care of his family. The company was not unionized and tried to treat the workers well so that they would not unionize, granting them perhaps a fairer deal in most arrangements. The workers eventually did unionize, however.

Joe commented that if a young person were coming into his plant to work, with the knowledge he had now he would tell them not to work there. He would tell them that if they had to work in a plant to go work for DuPont or General Motors. Joe stated that he got stuck in his plant because he put in many years and obtained seniority. It was harder to leave and start somewhere else with the experience he had accumulated. Moreover, when he started working at the Union Carbide and Carbon Corporation, Joe admitted that he did not have the knowledge to make the best decisions for himself regarding employment. He also stated that many of the African American workers in his plant were uneducated because they did not have the opportunity to attend school in their youth: many had to work rather than go to school. An African American man who was promoted to a supervisory position, for example, frequently came to Joe privately and asked him to write things down for him because he could not write. Joe, who had graduated from high school, graciously aided his coworker and friend in private.

Within the broader Niagaran community, away from work Joe did experience racism. Regarding housing, Joe stated that Black Niagarans were confined to certain areas of the city and that the *Niagara Falls Gazette* even advertised housing for "Colored Folks," indicating that by 1950 only certain sections of Niagara Falls were available to them. He distinctively remembered some bars on Highland Avenue that did not want Black Niagarans to patronize them. Joe found this out when he and a few of his African American friends wanted to see a Sugar Ray Robinson fight. They had to go to one of the bars to see the fight, so they chose one of the Highland Avenue bars. Although the bartender did not throw their glasses against the wall after they finished their drinks, he let them know that he did not want them there.

Joe's comments on housing substantiated another story told by Theodore Williamson.[149] During the early to mid-1960s, Williamson had diligently saved his money and wanted to move his growing family into a larger home. He had decided to purchase a home in Lewiston close to the Niagara River, near the gorge area that was by the Niagara River's waters that emptied into Lake Ontario. Lewiston was an affluent community near Niagara Falls. The home was beautiful and a vast improvement over Williamson's Tennessee Avenue home, a neighborhood Williamson had moved to from a previous address. A salesman agreed to sell Williamson his home. When the prospective neighbors found out about the arrangement, several frantically worked to stop it. They persistently sent Williamson letters to discourage him.[150] One letter emphatically stated that if he moved to the Lewiston location his children would certainly be harmed. A furious Williamson had a house built in the Town of Niagara rather than risk harm to his children. Years after this event, Williamson still admired the beauty of the area where he and his family, under different circumstances, might have lived.

Joe was also disappointed in the busing situation. The Niagara Falls board of education selected his children (and others) to be bused away from their neighborhood school. He said he was not in favor of this because there was a good school right down the street from his house at 1221 Beech Street, and his children's new school was too far from home. The children could not come home for lunch and would get home at a later time. Joe and his wife had a more difficult time establishing an ongoing relationship with the school. Previously, they could readily pick their daughters up and interact with some of the teachers and other personnel. Their daughters could even walk home from school. Busing ended that. Despite this busing problem, when Joe discussed his family, he glowed. He and his wife had married young, raised three daughters, and provided educational opportunities for them to move into the middle class and do better than he did financially. This made him proud.

With seniority at the Union Carbide and Carbon Corporation, Joe functioned as a leader among his fellow workers. However, our interview began with Joe presenting an extensive oral history of his church, Emmanuel Baptist.[151] Practicing his religion and maintaining his spiritual faith governed Joe's life.[152] He explained its early beginnings with the Reverend Millard Fillmore Clay, continuing into contemporary times. In 1925, for example, White Niagarans organized Emmanuel Baptist Church. Its first home was in the basement of a building on Hyde Park Boulevard and Tennessee Avenue, with the initial congregation being all white. In time it became mixed, with white and Black parishioners, and ultimately became all Black. In 1950 the Reverend Millard Fillmore Clay began serving as minister, and the church grew under his leadership. Reverend Clay held his post until 1957, followed by a succession of ministers. Joe knew his church's history well and could have elaborated even further on what he initially said. He happily shared a written history of his church. His church clearly played a pivotal role in his life. At the time of this interview, Joe fulfilled another leadership role, being a deacon in his church.

Eugene Hamilton and his family came to Niagara Falls seven years before eighteen-year-old Joe O'Neal, arriving in 1943.[153] Eugene's parents brought him and his siblings from the South. They came from Docena, Alabama, which was a coal-producing town, about ten miles north of Birmingham and 187 miles north of Andalusia. Limited available opportunities there motivated Eugene's parents to leave. Eugene was about eleven years old when his parents came to Niagara Falls. He recalled the South but did not then totally understand the full dynamics of that region and the Black Belt section that Docena was in.[154]

Eugene's father quickly found a job working at the Union Carbide and Carbon Corporation and as Joe O'Neal mentioned, Eugene's father also saw that a person could leave one job and quickly find another. Docena, Alabama, certainly did not afford African Americans this privilege. African Americans worked in the dangerous coal mines, farmed, or did both, and it was difficult for them to advance out of poverty. Eugene's father was proud of being able to earn a paycheck on a regular basis and provide for his family. Eugene stated that his father worked for the Union Carbide and Carbon Corporation for twenty-five years.

The Hamilton family initially found living quarters in the Center Court housing project. Center Court had recently opened, and Black Niagarans rushed to fill the vacant family apartments. Eugene remembered that his family stayed in apartment 15B. As a youngster, Eugene thoroughly enjoyed the Center Court apartments and later had fond memories of them. He remembered playing all sorts of games with his playmates: kick the can, baseball, running, and wrestling. The Hamilton family did not stay in the Center Court housing project long; it was a transitional living space. After a year, they moved to 3208 Highland Avenue, not far from the Center Court apartments. Both places were on the north side of the city, an enclave opened to new Black migrants.

Eugene's father came to Niagara Falls and, in a relatively short period, owned his home on Highland Avenue or had a mortgage on it. Home ownership showed that Eugene's father practiced frugality and believed in the southern cultural concept that landownership was an urgent requirement for families.[155] This is important because, as noted earlier, most Black

Niagarans then rented property.[156] Homeownership then, was considered by Black Niagarans to be a major accomplishment. When thinking of Highland Avenue, Eugene had fond memories of the name itself. He construed that the word symbolized something big—high land. He commented that he placed the word *highland* on many documents, contemplating that he was writing something important, especially if he were in a different town or city and people had no knowledge of Highland Avenue.

Eugene remembered the first playmates that he met at his new home: Johnny and Pappy Martin. He liked these two people immensely and enjoyed playing with them. The Martin boys had musical talent and wanted to form a band. Eugene wanted to play in the band, and initially Eugene's parents leaned toward allowing him to do this. However, when Eugene's mother saw some of the Martin boys behaving in a way she disapproved of, being a practitioner of the Politics of Respectability, she told Eugene to forget it. He could not join the band. Johnny and Pappy Martin went on to become fine musicians, gaining respectable reputations and performing at numerous venues throughout the nation, including the local Ontario Club. Johnny played the saxophone and became known in many circles as Johnny "Spider" Martin. He performed with such musicians as Dizzy Gillespie, Charlie Mariano, and Lee Konitz. Pappy Martin played the trumpet and became well known. Eugene hinted that had he joined the band he, too, may have been a serious musician.

In addition to the Martin boys, Eugene fondly remembered his trips to the Dietz farm, which was in Ransomville, near Lake Ontario. His father knew and appreciated farming. They went out to the Dietz farm to cultivate some crops that they grew there and to help Mr. Dietz with his own crops. Eugene remembered the farm being a great place for children to run and play. He fondly remembered Six-Mile Creek, where he and his family fished. Mr. Dietz also had a vineyard where white grapes were grown, and Eugene loved to eat them. He told about his wife purchasing a new product that the Welch's Grape Company made: a white grape juice. Eugene explained that he tasted the juice and knew right away that it had been produced from Niagara grapes. He told his wife that the grapes—Niagara grapes—had been grown in Niagara County as the juice container stated. Eugene visited Dietz Farm up until he was thirty.

At age eighteen, Eugene sought a steady job, making enough income to maintain the car that he owned. He obtained employment at the Carborundum Corporation. On his first day at work, his supervisor gave him the task of sweeping two floors, each about a hundred yards long. Eugene finished it quickly and did a good job. The supervisor then gave Eugene a third floor to sweep. Eugene finished this job and performed it well also. The next day the supervisor gave him three floors to sweep. Eugene swept these floors again rather quickly, and like the previous day's work, the supervisor had no complaints. In spite of this, the supervisor told Eugene that working at the Carborundum Corporation was not the place for him and fired him. Eugene was flabbergasted. He could not understand why he was being fired for working hard and performing well; he certainly had not been underworking, which is usually the most common reason for a person to be fired. Eugene later realized that his work performance was well beyond the norms established by the Carborundum Corporation's management and laborers. He showed too much ambition, and for that, he lasted only two days.

Disheartened but not defeated, Eugene went over to Union Carbide and Carbon Corporation where his father worked, and he found employment there. His daily duty consisted of removing pins from loaded trains so that their contents could be lowered into containers on a lower floor. Staff brought the trains in about every two to three hours. Eugene never had more than three trains per day from which to remove pins. He earned about ninety-five cents per hour, which was good money in 1949, enough for the average person to support himself and a family if he had one. Eugene enjoyed his wages and used them to pay expenses. Because it only took a short while for the trains to be emptied and no more than three were brought in per shift, Eugene had much free time. Rather than just sitting around eating cherry pies (like one of his coworkers), Eugene explored the plant to see how it operated. He saw the job his father did in the plant as a furnace tapper. Eugene also figured out how all jobs within the plant related to its general purpose. Eugene said that he had an inquisitive mind.

Eugene did not stay long at Union Carbide and Carbon Corporation. The Korean War started in 1950, and Eugene decided to join the army. He went down to enlist at the US Post Office, where recruiting officers were. The officers had Eugene and others take an assessment test. After thirty or forty minutes the recruiter asked, "Who is Eugene Hamilton?" He said, "You don't want to go in the army." Eugene again was flabbergasted. He came to join the army, and the recruiting officer told him he did not want to join. He told Eugene to go see an air force recruiter who was also at the post office. The air force recruiter also gave Eugene a test. After the recruiter scored the test, he told Eugene that he was going to go to aviation school. Eugene did the training and decided that he wanted to be a pilot. He went through weeks of training before the air force agreed to train him to be a pilot. This training forced him to compete with an auditorium full of people of which only two were selected, Eugene and another man. Eugene had scored the highest of everyone in the auditorium.

The air force sent him to navigation training. He completed the training and graduated first in his class. Then they wanted to send him to the West Point Military Academy. Eugene said that he was flattered, but he wanted to be a pilot. The air force supported his dream. Before he went to pilot training, he had to serve a "tour of duty" as a navigator, which he did. Then he went to pilot training and graduated nearly first in his class. He was a pilot in the military in the US Air Force for fourteen years with six years in the US National Guard.

After his years as a military pilot, Eastern Airlines expressed great interest in him as a pilot for the Eastern Shuttle. With Eastern Airlines, Eugene did not like the flight schedule, which consisted of flying from Boston to New York City, then to Washington. He contemplated working for them, but he ended up flying for Pan American airlines instead. As mentioned in the introduction, Eugene flew to London on his first flight for Pan American. It was what he wanted—to fly and travel on nonroutine routes.

Eugene treasured his time in Niagara Falls, viewing it as providing a foundation for all that he had accomplished. He met some wonderful people who made a positive impact on his life, such as his Boy Scout leaders Bill Wright and Benny Brown. He was also proud of the high-quality education he obtained from the Niagara Falls public schools. Eugene characterized himself as a maverick, a person willing to aim high, take risks, and follow his dreams, even if they took him to the other side of the world. As a leader and role model, he left this adage for future generations: "Dream and pursue your dreams and never stop learning."[157]

Eddie Palmore knew Eugene and his family when they lived on Highland Avenue. Eddie stated that they were one of the few Black Niagaran families to own a house during the late 1940s and 1950s. When Eddie migrated to Niagara Falls in 1947, his younger brother traveled with him. Some of Eddie's relatives already lived in the city and told him to come up because he might be able to gain employment since jobs were so plentiful. Eddie had originally only intended to work for a short while in Niagara Falls and then go back home to Andalusia, Alabama; but he would remain in Niagara Falls most of his adult life. Commenting on his first impression of Niagara Falls, Eddie remarked:

I thought it was magnificent just to see the Falls itself, and the City of Niagara Falls was hustling and bustling at that time. The people were here.[158]

When Eddie and his brother arrived, they stayed with relatives who lived in the Center Court housing project. They could only stay there briefly and had to find their own living quarters. Their relatives' apartment served as a springboard for them to enter the Niagara Falls environment, learn it, and then operate independently. Unfortunately, like other new African American migrants, finding living quarters turned out to be extremely difficult for the Palmores. More and more people arrived daily to Niagara Falls, adding to already overcrowded city enclaves, searching for *Lebensraum* (or living space), as denoted by social scientist St. Clair Drake and Horace R. Cayton.[159] Realtors directed them to saturated areas. Eddie stated that people rented out basements, attics, or any other available space attempting to accommodate the high demand for housing.

Eddie Palmore had another relative—an uncle—who lived in Hyde Park Village. Being a southerner and used to having ample space, Eddie was not at all impressed by Hyde Park Village. His uncle was not pleased with Hyde Park Village either, but considering the competition for housing, it was the best he could do at the time. Before residing in Hyde Park Village, Eddie's uncle rented a room on the 1200 Block of Buffalo Avenue near where New Hope Baptist Church is today. Eddie and his brother, although new migrants, fortunately had a network of relatives to consult and depend upon if needed, like the southern milieu they had left in Alabama.

Eddie first worked at the Pittsburgh Metallurgical plant on Highland Avenue, which made some of the ingredients for making steel. He had a difficult entry-level position that involved throwing materials in an open-hearth furnace. He described this work as hot and hard. Eddie performed this job for about a week and quickly decided that it was not for him, reasoning that he could do better. He had not finished his high school education, planning to finish school when he returned to Alabama. Eddie found out that he could earn his high school diploma by attending Niagara Falls Senior High School, so he did. Then he enrolled in Bryant and Stratton Business Institute to study business administration. Eddie always wanted to advance himself, especially educationally. Later after college, Eddie's brother learned that a White Irish gentleman at 2801 Highland Avenue wanted a work partner. He told Eddie about this, who, in turn, spoke with the Irish gentleman. Eddie established a partnership with him that lasted from 1950 to 1960. They called their business Kelly's New and Used Furniture and Radio Store. The partners adopted this name because it was the name Kelly originally had and was known by. Their partnership ended in 1960 when Kelly died. In reflecting on his entrepreneurial activities, Eddie described historic Erie Avenue and some of the businesspersons and their families who resided in the area:

> It basically catered to us [African Americans and African Canadians], and it was very good. . . . On the south side of old 3rd Street was old Falls Street there. And there is where the tourists all basically came. And this was basically on the north side of 3rd Street in that area, called Erie Avenue, and it was kind of a short street from 3rd Street. And it went on down to 10th Street. And that's where it stopped at. There used to be a big canal that came through there with the water flushing from the Niagara River going through to—I guess—turn the turbines for the power at that time. But that particular block was very busy because that is where we had our black entrepreneurs at that time. When tourists came to town, they looked for some of that activity that they enjoyed. They went there to Erie Avenue. That is where they exactly went.[160] And then we had some old pioneers that lived in the area at that time too. We had the Young family. They had what used to be called tourists homes. A lot of the blacks that came here as tourists, they didn't go to the hotels; they went to those houses that people accepted tourists. The Young family down there and the Ford family lived in that particular area. I am trying to think. There was the Reynolds [that] lived in that particular area. They were all down in that highly tourist area at the time. But I had heard and I knew Brother Palmer [Royal Palmer]. They [Palmer and his family] were supposed to have had a hotel. But they had lost that hotel when I arrived in the area.[161]

In addition to remembering Erie Avenue and the early families that lived near it, Eddie noticed that Black Niagarans really supported each other and worked together, particularly to end injustices. The NAACP existed and acted proactively to earn the respect of Niagarans in general. Eddie commented that the NAACP could rally Black Niagarans and their supporters if a problem arose and articulate its views on issues commandingly.[162] Eddie saw Aaron Griffin as a very effective community leader, first operating the Niagara Community Center on Erie Avenue, then in Center Court in the 1950s and beyond, offering numerous programs and activities to patrons and supporting uplift activities for Black Niagarans.

Eddie, like Barbara Smith, also remembered Black Niagaran families being stable during the 1950s and 1960s. Families, Eddie remarked, generally had both mothers and fathers present. Some mothers worked outside the home, but others stayed at home. The parents supported their children and encouraged them to earn their educations. Parents created rules for their children and demanded that they follow them. "Families had to struggle to improve," Eddie commented, "and they had that initiative and drive that they wanted to do something. People showed more aggression."[163] Families worked as a team and looked out for one another.

Besides his relatives, the Masons served as a close-knit family for Eddie. Old Turner Bryant, who was a Mason, stopped by Kelly's New and Used Furniture and Radio Store to speak with Eddie. He invited Eddie Palmore to a Christmas party. He attended and noticed that most of the men at the party were Masons. This was in 1950. By 1952 Eddie had joined the Masons along with Dr. Charles B. Hayes. The experience with the Masons profoundly affected Eddie. Other members included Royal Palmer, Jerry Plato, T. R. Davis, Johnny Taylor, Edison Tucker, Ollie Mason, Arthur Ray, and Henry Patterson. The lodge provided a strong support system that emphasized self-help and benevolence. Some of their adages that Eddie remembered and cherished included the following:

1. People say an opportunity only comes once in a lifetime. This is not true. An opportunity comes as often as you can see it and take advantage of it.

2. The best interest that a person can have is invested interest. If you invest your time and energy into something, that project that you undertake is going to be done well. Therefore, always have invested interest.

3. Look out for human beings in need.[164]

In 1957 when the devastating fire occurred on Allen Avenue in which seventeen people lost their lives, Robert Garey, a Mason whose family had been deeply involved in local politics,[165] stated that the Masons had to do something to help the families of the victims. The Masons did. They raised money to contribute toward the aid of the families. They did not broadcast their deed; they just did it humbly. In time, Eddie moved up the ranks in the Masons, acquiring the post of "worshipful master." At this rank, Eddie proudly remembered helping his lodge brothers obtain a permanent building to hold their meetings, located on South Avenue. This took place in 1959. Eddie's Masonic experience helped groom him to take on other leadership roles.

No one highlighted in this section, except Barbara Smith, was born in the city of Niagara Falls. They migrated to Niagara Falls on their own, or their parents brought them to the area. All the interviewees knew their family history well, meaning histories of their parents, aunts, and uncles, siblings, and exactly how they or their parents came to the city of Niagara Falls. All the interviewees radiated joy when discussing their own histories or that of their families.

All the interviewees conveyed that within the setting of Niagara Falls they had to contend with prejudice or racism. No one used it as an excuse for not achieving and doing the best that he or she could do. It was simply a fact of life. They acknowledged it and dealt with it but progressed regardless. Some even mentioned White Niagarans who helped them to succeed. Barbara Smith and Eugene Hamilton, for example, mentioned White teachers who encouraged them, and Eddie Palmore cited a Jewish man who encouraged his entrepreneurial activities. This help and encouragement they would always treasure.

These interviewees experienced Niagara Falls during its boom years from World War II to around the mid-1960s. They described Niagara Falls as an even more attractive town then. More people lived in town, jobs were plentiful, and married women did not always have to work outside the home. Many could stay home to look after their children; families seemed to have enough income to take care of their basic needs, and as Eddie Palmore mentioned, Black Niagaran families largely appeared to be working and striving together as a unit. People typically seemed to have pride in themselves and their families. Problems, however, existed. Black Niagarans, for instance, had a very difficult time finding housing. Yet these interviewees accentuated what they attempted to do to improve themselves, their families, their racial group, and the broader community. Most accumulated experiences that would contribute to their development as future leaders.

The decades 1940 to 1960 were decisive years in the history of Black Niagarans. They made progress by obtaining employment, continuously caring for their families, expanding existing institutions, and networking with individuals and organizations throughout the broader community. Conversely, this period also signifies the years that housing segregation became more deeply entrenched. The Black population expanded significantly from 1940 to 1960, increasing from 975 individuals to 7,038. White realtors (and others) operated more aggressively and tactically to ensure that Black Niagarans generally only resided in certain sections of the city, which served to expand existing enclaves or create new ones. This form of discrimination and others, in combination with national forms of racial injustice, encouraged the leadership activities of Reverend H. Edward Whitaker, Bloneva Bond, Aaron L. Griffin, Alice C. Hayes, Harwood Bond, Eddie Palmore, Barbara Smith, and many others in inspiring Black Niagarans to fight against injustice, particularly during the ensuing civil rights years, the public school desegregation crisis, and the era of urban renewal.

Chapter Five

The Civil Rights Years, 1960s

Within the original thirteen colonies and the United States, racial barriers have always been problematic. Throughout their history, African Americans have ceaselessly demonstrated agency (or self-help) in attempting to remove racial barriers, while simultaneously fighting to transform their historical and contemporary status from that of enslavement and second-class citizens to that of first-class citizenship in law and praxis—a status not yet fully obtained. The modern civil rights movement, as Jacquelyn Dowd Hall has argued, did not occur independently. Events continued after 1968, the date denoted by many as the final year of the movement.[1] Although Hall conceives the birth of this movement during the New Deal era (1932–1941), this study conceptualizes the movement as beginning during slavery but especially after passage of the Thirteenth Amendment. As Hall did, I construe the civil rights movement as continuing nationally and locally beyond 1968, enduring via movements to desegregate schools, revitalize cities through urban renewal, and advocate for police reform in 2020. Activist leaders, such as Malcolm X, have referred to it as a "human rights" movement—a campaign for human dignity and respect.[2]

During the early civil rights era, many Black Niagaran leaders, men and women, arose to direct the advancement of their people. Like the diverse range of leadership evident in the national movement, the local civil rights movement showed a similar diversity. Most leaders continued to promote integration into the mainstream of society; however, that pervasive outlook would be challenged. Nonetheless, the aim of the local movement, like that of the national one, was to establish allies (including alliance leaders) and to draw more attention to forms of racial injustice (e.g., housing, employment, education, etc.) by disrupting the status quo and effecting change, all with the intent of removing racial impediments on the Black Niagaran community.[3] Thus, leadership would continue to be proactive in promoting community development.[4]

The US Constitution had not benefited all Americans.[5] It was a document that many of the nation's leaders touted as part of a great American legacy and a symbol of freedom. However, since 1787, African Americans knew from difficult experiences that the Constitution was just a series of fine-sounding words that had no complete legitimacy when applied to them.[6] Nevertheless, after actively participating in the nation's efforts to defeat the Axis powers during World War II, African Americans throughout the nation were inspired to gain their rights in practice and to fight injustice in all its forms at home.[7] They had fought for freedoms abroad, and they would also earn them at home, aiming to make the Double V Campaign a reality.

African Americans received encouragement for embracing their proactive stance. World powers came together after World War II and formed the United Nations in 1945. They had seen the devastation of World War II and were now ready to prevent a similar future catastrophe. Woodrow Wilson had worked diligently to form such an international body (the League of Nations), but his efforts were not wholeheartedly embraced. The United Nations promoted humanity and justice for all human beings, which coincided with objectives of the modern American civil rights movement.[8] African American leaders applauded the United Nations' efforts to examine racial injustice in South Africa, some with hopes that the UN would eventually turn its attention to the racial climate within the United States (and other lands, such as Rhodesia and Australia).[9]

The Soviet Union operated as an influential member of the United Nations, often supporting issues for racial justice and equality. The Soviets had been significantly weakened by World War II, suffering a significant percentage of the war's casualties. Miraculously, after the war it began to grow as a world power whose Communist belief system was diametrically opposed to that of the capitalist United States. By 1946 the Soviet Union and the United States, although allies during World War II, had become open enemies engaged in an undeclared conflict called the Cold War. The Soviet Union's existence, and how it critiqued the United States (which proclaimed itself a great democracy), served to strengthen and support the activities of American civil rights activists.[10]

Africans who witnessed the global cry for freedom, justice, and democracy struck out for the independence of their nations. First, Ghana gained its independence from Britain in 1957, ridding itself of direct colonial rule. Dr. Kwame Nkrumah led Ghana's independence efforts and was supportive of civil rights activities within the United States. He had spent many years in America, earning undergraduate and graduate degrees and familiarizing himself with the racial environment of the United States.[11] Zaire, Somalia, Dahomey, Ivory Coast, Chad, Nigeria, Sierra Leone, and other African nations followed suit, gaining their independence, which further served to encourage civil rights activism within the United States. Studying African independence activities, Dr. Martin Luther King Jr. stated that the Freedom Movement in America was creeping at a horse-and-buggy pace, while those movements in Africa moved at jet speed.[12] According to political historian Azza Salama Layton, these and other events impacted national events, which in turn encouraged civil rights activities on local levels throughout the country and within the city of Niagara Falls.[13]

Directed by their leadership, Black Niagarans refused to sit idly by while national civil rights events permeated television, radio, and other forms of popular media—events such as the *Brown v. Board of Education* decision, the murder of Emmett Till, the Montgomery Bus Boycott, the formation of the Southern Christian Leadership Conference, the Little Rock school desegregation crisis, and other events. They observed African Americans in other locales actively confronting injustices, with some people even courageously risking their lives. This encouraged them to be more cognizant of injustices in their own community and to fight, if necessary, to make drastic changes in employment, social discrimination, housing discrimination, and school desegregation[14] as well as offering support for civil rights activism that occurred in the South.[15] Niagara Falls's civil rights activists, like those on the national level, fought to make the operations of society fair and equal.

In striving for equality, Black Niagarans from the beginning demonstrated their support for movements against southern racial injustice. Most of them had migrated from the South, had family in the South, or had heard about racial discrimination prevalent in that region. So it was easy for them to empathize with their southern counterparts. In 1956 Dr. Martin Luther King Jr. came to Niagara Falls during the Montgomery Bus Boycott.[16] H. Edward Whitaker, the pastor of New Hope Baptist Church, invited him to speak on July 22 at a Sunday service called Men's Day. Whitaker and Dr. King were old friends who had attended Crozer Theological Seminary in Chester, Pennsylvania. Reverend Whitaker received the note below from Dr. King confirming that he would address the New Hope Baptist Church congregation:

30 January 1956

[Montgomery, Ala.]

The Reverend H. Edward Whittaker
1122 Buffalo Avenue
Niagara Falls, New York

Dear Horace:

This is just a note to say that I will be happy to preach for you on the dates that you have designated. I have already placed this engagement on my calendar. Please feel free to contact me concerning necessary details. I am looking forward with great anticipation to a rich fellowship with you and your fine members. With every good wish, I am

Sincerely yours,

M. L. King, Jr.

MLK: lmt

P.S. The bus situation here in Montgomery is keeping me so busy that I hardly have time to breathe.[17]

On Saturday, before Dr. King's Sunday sermon, Whitaker gave him a tour of the city of Niagara Falls, focusing on the cataracts. Dr. King was greatly impressed by the waterfalls, expressing that they manifested the majestic power of God.[18]

At Men's Day, Dr. King gave two sermons, one in the morning and the other at an afternoon service. Dr. King titled his morning sermon "Going Backward in Order to Go Forward." He warned of a breakdown of ethical principles and morality and stated that the solution was to go back to God, who gave people life and basic principles of right and wrong.[19] This would help one progress well into the future. Dr. King's speech for the afternoon service was "The Montgomery Story."[20] In it he outlined and discussed the Montgomery Bus Boycott and its objectives, which were to treat all passengers on a first-come, first-served basis and to offer more courteous treatment of African Americans by white drivers and provide African American bus drivers on lines catering to African American passengers.[21]

Mildred Isom, a longtime member of New Hope Baptist Church and resident of Niagara Falls, heard both sermons and mentioned that her church was nearly full to capacity.[22] Initially she did not know much about Dr. King, and on observing him in person, she commented: "I thought he was someone who thought he was a little better than everyone else."[23] Nonetheless, listening to Dr. King gave her inspiration. She reflected on his words for a few days and wrote down her thoughts. What she had written she stored away and then forgot. Nearly fifty years later, in January 2004, her daughter found her comments and reminded her mother of what she had written.[24] After 381 days, the Montgomery Bus Boycott ended, and Dr. King ultimately involved himself in other civil rights struggles (in Albany, Birmingham, St. Augustine, Selma, and elsewhere) and became the acknowledged leader of the modern civil rights movement. His visit to Niagara Falls, along with his leadership, not only deepened Isom's view of Dr. King but also served as a model for Niagara Falls activists.[25]

On February 1, 1960, nearly four years after Dr. King's visit to Niagara Falls, four students at North Carolina Agricultural and Technical College decided to desegregate local restaurants by sitting at the lunch counter at a Woolworth five-and-dime store in Greensboro, North Carolina.[26] They felt that if their money was welcome in all other sections of the Woolworth store it should also be welcome at the lunch counter. The actions of these four freshmen students set off the sit-in movement throughout the American South. Southerners held sit-ins, and many Northerners demonstrated to show their support.

On April 2, 1960, Leeland Jones, field representative of the New York State Commission against Discrimination, spoke in favor of the student sit-in movement at the fifteenth annual dinner of Frontier Chapter no. 21, Order of the Eastern Star, Prince Hall Affiliation in Niagara Falls. Jones encouraged his audience to morally and financially support the dedicated young people in the South who were fighting segregation: he suggested they contribute to the legal defense fund of the NAACP so the organization could investigate what happened to students expelled from school due to their activism.[27] He criticized Black Niagarans for their apathy and false sense of comfort, and he emphasized that the students desired equality in their lifetimes, not in the dim, nebulous future.[28] Jones even proclaimed that the students were actually fighting the battles of older adults, who in his view should have been more proactive. "They say," Jones declared, "a little child shall lead us."[29]

Reverend Whitaker, perhaps taking his cue from Jones but certainly from the youth sit-in movement, organized picketing demonstrations at four local variety stores linked to southern chain stores that discriminated at their lunch counters—a Woolworths, two Kresge stores, and a W. T. Grant. Whitaker, who was also a local NAACP leader, followed the national directive to boycott such stores.[30] Under his leadership on April 19, 1960, Black and White community members picketed the four stores in shifts, carrying signs that read, SEGREGATION IS IMMORAL and SUPPORT THE NAACP, underscoring the injustices occurring in the South. The picketing, however, bewildered some White community members.[31] One man claimed that the problem being protested was thousands of miles away and that he could not understand the merit of such a demonstration in Niagara Falls, which did not adhere to such unfair practices. One teenager yelled that the picketers should be run off the street; instead, he was chased away by a police officer. A sympathetic store operator stated that the picketers had a legitimate complaint and perhaps needed to picket in order to work out their frustrations.

Picketers, sometimes thirty at a single store, spaced themselves out so as not to block customers from entering a store. Their aim was to simply register a complaint with the chain stores' leadership—that all American citizens should be treated justly and fairly. People accompanying the picketers passed out pamphlets to interested onlookers that read in part:

> We are picketing this store because we want:
>
> 1. To demonstrate our full support of the Southern Negro students' protest against Jim Crowism in the South.
>
> 2. To focus public attention on the discriminatory policy of the chain in which this store is a link, and
>
> 3. To rally support of all elements of the community in behalf of the gallant stand of Southern youth for freedom.[32]

Reverend Whitaker visited each picketing site to ensure that objectives were being accomplished. Dr. Benjamin F. Bullock, a local dentist and a member of the executive committee of the Niagara Falls chapter of the

NAACP, picked the Reverend Whitaker up at one of the Kresge stores and took him to another site.[33]

About seven weeks after the student sit-ins began in Greensboro, another national civil rights leader came to Niagara Falls. Daisy Bates, who was the head of the Little Rock, Arkansas local NAACP branch and the guiding hand behind the desegregation of Little Rock's Central High School, was invited to give a few addresses to the general Niagara Falls community.[34] In one address she stressed that in the South, Blacks were fighting for their constitutional right to vote, but in Niagara Falls Blacks could vote but were not taking advantage of their rights and opportunities.[35] She also reprimanded Black Niagarans for not writing their congressmen about the racial injustices going on in America and the lack of effort by Congress to create a strong civil rights bill. Some Niagarans hinted that because she was an outsider, Bates's criticisms of Black Niagarans should not be taken too seriously. However, long after Bates left town, members of the Black community rushed to defend her, saying that her criticisms were legitimate.[36]

In 1961 or 1962, a religious group entered the Niagara Falls area, but unlike the prominent civil rights activists, it vehemently opposed the civil rights movement, viewing its ultimate goal and strategies as unwise, docile, and remarkably detrimental to the freedom and progression of African Americans.[37] That group was the Nation of Islam.[38] Bill Murphy, who was a White staff reporter for the *Niagara Falls Gazette*, viewed them as fanatics.[39] Members from the Muslim temple in Buffalo, Temple 23, came to Niagara Falls to recruit members into the Nation of Islam and perhaps to establish a temple in the area. Some of the recruiters may have come from Rochester, New York, because a temple was located there as well.[40] Although most Black leaders, such as John Pollard, Ben Bolden, Bloneva Bond, Aaron Griffin, and H. Edward Whitaker had been seeking to integrate Black Niagarans into the mainstream of the community, the Muslims sought, among other goals, to convert the Black community to Islam, implement racial separatism, and develop an independent economic base within the Black community.[41] An early account indicates that they held meetings on East Falls Street.[42] Malcolm X, the charismatic national spokesperson for the Nation of Islam, came to Niagara Falls to help spread his group's teachings.[43] By the mid-1970s the Muslims were still operating there. They no longer called their place of worship a temple but a mosque, which was then located on Highland Avenue.[44] The Muslims gained few converts in the area, probably because most Black Niagarans were Baptists or Methodists who vigorously opposed considering any religion other than Christianity.[45] Moreover, Jabril Shareef, a former minister of the Niagara Falls mosque, noted that many Black Niagarans believed many aspects of the Muslim doctrine but were afraid to profess their beliefs publicly out of fear of reprisal by influential Whites, employers, or landlords. Despite the mixed reception, Shareef attested that the lives of many Black Niagarans who embraced the Muslim teachings had been improved. Conversely, at a 1963 NAACP forum on civil rights at the Niagara Community Center, for example, when Bloneva Bond was asked if the NAACP should join forces with the Muslims on a project that could benefit the entire Black community, she responded: "No. Ours is a democratic organization operating within the Constitution. We believe in the equality of man, which the Muslims do not."[46] Aaron Griffin also did not view the Muslims as a helpful force within the community.[47] In several circles such as Christians, the White community, and police departments, Muslims were perceived as a cult that impeded the progress of the struggling Black community.[48] The local police department, for example, was aware of the Muslim presence and monitored their activities and influence.[49]

Notwithstanding the police and civil rights community's response to the Muslims, adherence by more Black Niagarans to some of the Muslim teachings might have helped to further advance the Black community.[50] The Muslims preached community economic development, the pooling of economic resources, and the development of an enterprising mindset.[51] Booker T. Washington had promoted these same ideas years earlier, as had the local branch of the National Negro Business League, but these ideas were not generally embraced (or practiced).[52] Accepting some of these principles might have been a tremendous help to the Black community, which was struggling economically, especially during the early 1960s when the effects of the postwar economic boom had waned.

In 1963, for example, the NAACP conducted a survey of employment of Black Niagarans and found that 17.6 percent of the heads of families were unemployed.[53] Thus, adherence to Muslim economic principles perhaps might have helped to establish a stronger, more advanced economic structure and a sorely needed enterprising tradition within the Black community. Nevertheless, the very presence of the Muslims locally (and of course nationally) served to aid the civil rights movement by making their demands appear more reasonable to the power structure.[54]

With the Muslims operating on the fringes of the Black community, Black Niagarans continued to promote and support the strategies of the civil rights movement. Motivated also by national events such as the sit-in movement, the Birmingham Desegregation Movement, the March on Washington, and other civil rights protest activities, the local leadership continued to voice their concern about housing and employment, making stronger demands.

Before leaving to assume his new ministerial post in his native Virginia, Reverend Whitaker, in a 1962 interview with a *Niagara Falls Gazette* reporter, continued to emphasize that the housing available to Black Niagarans was limited and that they were more or less restricted to certain sections of the city.[55] As a minister in Niagara Falls for ten years, he acknowledged that some racial progress had been made in that decade. Because of improvements in race relations, he generally considered Niagara Falls a good place to live, but there was still much work to be done. He said that discrimination was subtle in Niagara Falls compared to that in the South, where it was more blatant and open. He believed that each region had its own styles of racial discrimination but that through strong leadership, racial problems could be eliminated.[56]

In January 1963, ten of Niagara Falls's Black churches, led by their ministers, participated together in planning to get more Blacks hired in local supermarkets and department stores, preferably in customer-service positions where they would be readily visible to the public.[57] A twofold plan was the result of their discussions. First, they would send fact finders to specific stores to determine if any Blacks worked there. If no Blacks were employed, the surveyors would discuss with the owner or manager the importance of hiring Black employees and suggest that a boycott of the store might ensue if no Blacks were hired, especially if many Blacks patronized the store. The second phase would be the actual boycott, where ministers would tell their congregations not to patronize a specific store until Black employees were hired.

The ten Black church ministers pledged that their church members would relay the message to their nonchurchgoing friends.[58] Although the conditions in Niagara Falls were not as desperate as in the South, the national activities of civil rights organizations had made the ministers determined to make some improvements within their city; one minister even predicted marches if concessions were not made to the Black community's satisfaction.[59] Plans by these churches did not lead to any immediate changes, but they got people thinking more about the importance of action over rhetoric, as a proactive attitude began to permeate the Black community.

Amid this situation, a young progressive leader by the name of Otis Cowart, a Wilberforce University graduate, arose as a Black community spokesperson. He was the president of the Niagara Falls branch of the Congress of Racial Equality (CORE), which, among many other ideas, promoted hiring equality and immediate action when confronting cases of hiring discrimination.[60] Believing that unequal hiring practices existed at the local W. T. Grant Store, Cowart and other CORE members conducted a four-day survey of the store at 2116 Main Street.[61] They sought to determine how many Blacks were employed by the store and to get an estimate of how many Black people patronized the establishment.

In their survey, CORE found that only one Black worked at the store and that he worked in the store's warehouse.[62] They also found that 466 Blacks had patronized the store during the four-day period of their study, whereas six thousand Whites had also done so. After questioning the Black patrons, they estimated that within the last year, Blacks had spent a total of $46,381 in the store, many of them having accounts there. With this information, Cowart contacted Frank Carmichael, who was the manager of the W. T. Grant store, and informed him of the survey results and stressed that the store should hire five Blacks within the next six months or face picketing. It was demanded that the Blacks be hired in visible customer service roles, such as sales personnel or clerks, and as a good-faith gesture at least two Blacks should be hired by Monday, three days after these demands were issued.

CORE argued that since January 1963 several Blacks had applied for employment, but none were hired, while two Whites were hired permanently and twelve temporarily during the previous Christmas season.[63] Cowart informed Carmichael and local authorities that CORE's picketing demonstrations would be nonviolent and that they would not prevent store patrons from entering and exiting the store and that their picket signs would display such messages as DON'T BUY WHERE YOU CAN'T WORK, FULL DEMOCRACY IS COMPLETE FREEDOM, NO QUOTAS, and NO TOKENISM.

On August 28, 1963, the same day as the March on Washington, about twenty-five picketers began their protests. They started at 10 a.m. and continued until the store closed at 5:30 p.m.[64] Arthur Ray indicated that he participated in the picketing not only because discrimination was wrong but also to ensure a better future for his children and grandchildren.⁶⁵ By Wednesday one hundred people were picketing in front of the W. T. Grant Store, several of them White (as CORE during this period was a multiracial civil rights organization).⁶⁶ Cowart, who had given workshops on nonviolence and was constantly coaching them as they picketed, had warned store officials that the pickets were determined to stay on until Christmas and beyond, until CORE's demands had been met. In a story on the picketing published in the *Niagara Falls Gazette*, Cowart acknowledged that the W. T. Grant store just happened to be the first store chosen for picketing and that there would be other stores targeted if unfair hiring practices did not cease. In response, the management of W. T. Grant issued a published statement in which they declared that W. T. Grant was for equal opportunity and hiring equality but that they refused to hire strictly based on race, which they considered discriminatory and contrary to sound personnel policy.⁶⁷

To strengthen their picketing efforts, and in disregard of W. T. Grant's stance, at a community rally at Trinity Baptist Church, Cowart asked community members who had patronized the store to do four things:

1. Not to cross the picket line and buy [at W. T. Grant];

2. To turn in their charge plates, if they [had] any there;

3. To notify the store that when their current bill [was] paid the account [would] not be reopened; and

4. To encourage others not to buy there.⁶⁸

The Black community was overwhelmingly supportive of Cowart's request and CORE's crusade to ensure equal opportunities and equal hiring practices in Niagara Falls. Many young Blacks were leaving the area due to limited employment opportunities, and the community wanted to support efforts to change this situation. They donated funds toward the endeavor, giving $108 at one meeting.⁶⁹ Their support and unity tremendously aided CORE's campaign because after three weeks of picketing a settlement was reached, in which W. T. Grant agreed to ensure that Blacks were given equal employment opportunities at their store.⁷⁰ Other details of the settlement were not disclosed to the public. Nonetheless, with the settlement, the picketing was called off on September 21 at 5:30 p.m. W. T. Grant hired Ramona Bradberry as its first Black Niagaran in a visible clerical position, accelerating the acceptance of Cowart as a legitimate community leader.⁷¹

With the famous March on Washington occurring on the same day that picketing began, 32 Niagarans—31 Blacks and one White—left together, departing from St. John's AME Church, then at 917 Garden Avenue.[72] Delegates represented such local organizations as the NAACP, the Congress of Racial Equality, the Niagara Falls Ministerial Council, and the Niagara Falls Cosmetology Club, which was a women's beauty society. The Reverend David Reiehert, Charlette Bennett, Ariel Davis, Gloria Fields, Rosie B. Smith, Alexander Carr, Walter Searcy, Juanita Payne, Geraldine Isom, Hazel Isom, Richard Allen, Patricia McClain, Helen Davis, Virginia Wesby, Bloneva Bond, Joe Profit, Leamon Mills, Guy Gainor, Charles Towns, Elizata Haugabook, Ulysses Diggs, the Reverend Glen Raybon, Olivia Davis, Vera Tremier, Charles Gipson, Diane Echols, George Mabry, Ralph Thorton, Barbara Cook, and Sadie Martin were some of the attendees.[73] Several local leaders came to St. John's AME Church to offer prayers and wish the marchers well: Harwood Bond, who was in charge of the farewell program, Reverend Edgar Huff, pastor of St. John's AME Church, Reverend Paul F. Thompson, who was pastor of Emmanuel Baptist Church and president of the Niagara Falls Branch of the NAACP, and Niagara Falls's mayor E. Dent Lackey.[74] The delegates left by chartered bus at 7:22 p.m. Tuesday and were scheduled to arrive in Washington by 8:30 a.m. on Wednesday.[75] They took packed lunches with a plan of stopping for breakfast in Baltimore.

The delegates participated in this historic gathering, organized by A. Phillip Randolph and Bayard Rustin. Dr. Martin Luther King Jr. gave his "I Have a Dream" speech, one of the most timely and profound speeches of the twentieth century.[76] About 249,968 other marchers joined the thirty-two Niagarans. All had attended the event to support passage of the Civil Rights Bill of 1963, a major piece of legislation that was being filibustered by southern senators. Local marchers said they expected to be provided with signs in Washington designating them as the Niagara Falls contingent.[77] Many of them may not have fully realized how the events of that day would overwhelmingly impact the nation and world.

The local NAACP branch strongly supported the March on Washington and the passage of the 1963 Civil Rights Bill. Of the civil rights groups that operated in Niagara Falls, the NAACP was the most pervasive and persistent. Progressive activists created the NAACP in 1909 in New York City.[78] The Springfield Race Riot of 1908 had sparked its formation.[79] The death and destruction experienced by the innocent Springfield African American community compelled progressive activists to act. Oswald

Garrison Villard, the grandson of nineteenth-century abolitionist William Lloyd Garrison, issued "The Call," a document requesting that individuals who wanted to make the Constitution applicable to all Americans meet and form an organization. Several people attended the first organizing meeting, including the great scholar W. E. B. Du Bois, who had been instrumental in creating the Niagara Movement. The NAACP strove to ensure that African Americans received their civic and political constitutional rights. They would use judicial and legislative bodies to ensure that this occurred and promote the formation of local branches throughout the nation.

Specific details concerning the formation of the local Niagara Falls branch are sketchy at best. Nonetheless, Black Niagarans created it in 1943.[80] That year coincides with Black southerners relocating in droves to Cataract City. Millard Fillmore Clay and and Dr. Charles B. Hayes were early NAACP presidents. The era of the modern civil rights movement (1954–1972) was when the Niagara Falls NAACP branch was busiest. Reverend James Banks, Reverend H. Edward Whitaker, Reverend Paul F. Thompson, Casper L. Jordon, Harwood R. Bond, and Bloneva Bond were some of the civil rights–era NAACP presidents. These and other people worked hard to ensure that Black Niagarans could take advantage of all their rights and opportunities.

Reverend Banks, for example, was president of the NAACP when the local branch sponsored a 1959 membership drive. Gloster Current, who was national director of branches, came to Niagara Falls and spoke at New Hope Baptist Church. Current desired to encourage the local branch to increase its membership from two hundred to five hundred. Current had expertise in this endeavor. "He [had] served as executive secretary of the Detroit branch from 1941 to 1946, during which time the branch's membership reached 24,500 members."[81] With Current's advice, Banks hosted and coordinated activities. Reverend Whitaker, near the time he promoted picketing of stores in Niagara Falls, also opened an NAACP public meeting, held at the Niagara Community Center. Two hundred and fifty individuals attended. The gathering successfully raised $500 for southern students engaged in sit-in activities. Bloneva Bond chaired the rally.[82] At a 1963 Emancipation Proclamation celebration sponsored by the Niagara Falls NAACP branch, Reverend Thompson promoted another membership drive. He noted that the branch currently had five hundred members, but it aimed to gain another five hundred members. This celebration marked the twentieth anniversary of the Niagara Falls Branch of the NAACP.[83] The Branch, under Jordon's leadership, sponsored a 1967 forum entitled

"You and the Law" to highlight the importance of understanding the law.[84] Earl Bridges Jr., then a Niagara County public defender, was the guest speaker. His lecture began a series of educational addresses for the public sponsored by the NAACP. Harwood and Bloneva Bond worked as a pair, both participating actively in NAACP activities. They rose through the NAACP leadership ranks, taking on lower positions of responsibility, and both ultimately becoming NAACP presidents. Harwood, as president in 1970, pledged the NAACP's support to a multiracial group that wanted to work with the Niagara Falls Board of Education to select textbooks for public school students.[85] They desired to increase multicultural education. The group called themselves Understanding Each Other. Meanwhile, in 1972 Bloneva coordinated Niagara Falls's local branch activities to select delegates to attend a Detroit NAACP national meeting.[86]

All the NAACP local branch presidents knew about housing discrimination in Niagara Falls. They had heard stories about housing discrimination and could see with their own eyes the sections of Niagara Falls where Black Niagarans were clustered and confined. The civil rights movement further influenced them to demand changes. At a 1963 NAACP rally at St. John's AME Church, for example, Dr. Clayburn Booth, a physician who then was a vice president of the Niagara Falls branch of the NAACP, affirmed that he believed that housing discrimination existed. More specifically, he asked:

> Is it purely coincidence this city is divided as it is? Is it by accident the Negro lives in certain areas of this city? Is it by coincidence the Negro predominates [then] in Griffon Manor, Center Court and Jordan Gardens and the whites in Parkard Court?[87]

To encourage drastic changes, the NAACP local branch, in conjunction with the CORE local branch, sponsored a February 8, 1964 march and rally to protest housing discrimination.[88] About 125 marchers participated, most being African American, but some were White. Demonstrators began their march at Bath Avenue and Whirlpool Street and marched to the YWCA, carrying a banner that read: CORE AND NAACP MARCH TO FREEDOM.[89] Reverend Glen Raybon, who was chairman of CORE's advisory board and pastor of Trinity Baptist Church, served as master of ceremonies. Mayor E. Dent Lackey, Democratic Party member and the principal speaker, told the demonstrators, "You must be inspired by love and guided by knowledge."⁹⁰ He further informed the demonstrators that the civil rights movement nationally and locally within the city of Niagara Falls had deeply inspired him. While underscoring this idea, he had to pause to wipe tears from his eyes. Reverend Paul Thompson informed the demonstrators and observers that the march and rally occurred "not because [demonstrators] like parades or because they want to foment strife or ill will but because [they believed] in the cause of freedom."⁹¹ Otis Cowart ensured all that current and future protest activities would convey more action and less talk. Further describing this point, Cowart announced: "We shall walk softly and carry a big stick."⁹² He called the "stick" one of nonviolence, with a razor edge coming in the form of people.⁹³ These people would fight continuously until freedom, justice, and equality were obtained. "We want to be free and we want it now," Cowart asserted.⁹⁴ Reverend James M. Bradley of Mount Erie Baptist Church supported Thompson and Cowart, proclaiming "the time has come for us to take a stand."⁹⁵ At the close of the rally, civil rights representatives passed out housing committee cards. Many of those present filled out the cards, indicating whether they wanted to rent, buy, or sell property.⁹⁶ From the cards a clearinghouse was established to bring together buyers and sellers or renters and landlords. The NAACP and CORE strove to obtain quality housing for Black Niagarans outside of restrictive and often unattractive areas.

The NAACP local branch operated consistently throughout the civil rights era. Over two years after the march and rally, the NAACP local branch involved itself in another protest activity.⁹⁷ Then-president Vera B. Tremier had replaced Reverend Huff, who had accepted a pastorate of a church in New York City.⁹⁸ She had been associated with the NAACP local branch for fifteen years, serving as first vice president before obtaining her new position. She also had been employed as an assistant food manager for the Clark Food Service operating at the De Veaux School. Two reporters from the *New York Times* interviewed Norman J. Schreiber, executive director of the Niagara County Welfare Department. In the interview Schreiber allegedly stated that he once threw a "nigger" out of his office.⁹⁹ One of the reporters published this information. Schreiber also supported a New York State welfare policy that compelled able-bodied welfare recipients to work in order to receive their monthly benefits. Apparently, Moses Pickett of Niagara Falls, who was the father of four children, refused employment as a landscaping aide after completing his job training. Accordingly, this violated Section 145 of the Social Welfare Law of the State of New York, which stipulated that "any person who . . . does any willful act designed to interfere with the proper administration of public assistance shall be guilty of a misdemeanor."[100] The framers of this act hoped to force able-bodied individuals to work for their daily bread and to demonstrate to all their get-tough policy. For violation of this act, Pickett was dropped from welfare and sentenced by Nunzio Rizzo, the Acting City Court judge, to thirty days in jail.

National, state, and local branches of the NAACP took exception to Schreiber's alleged comments and the jailing of Pickett.[101] Roy Wilkins, executive director of the NAACP and Dr. Eugene Reed, state chairman of the NAACP, demanded an immediate public apology from Schreiber and called for an investigation by State Social Welfare Commissioner George K. Wyman. When no public apology or an investigation occurred, the NAACP local branch demonstrated twice in front of Schreiber's home at 1211 Ferry Avenue. Tremier indicated there was a threefold purpose for calling the NAACP's demonstrations:

1. To protest the alleged racial slur attributed to Norman Schreiber;

2. To protest the constitutionality of the New York State Welfare statute which enforces involuntary servitude; and

3. To protest "the Get-Tough policy" of the Niagara County Welfare Department.[102]

At 11 a.m. fifteen demonstrators marched slowly around Schreiber's two-story home. They carried placards, some of which read: INVOLUNTARY SERVITUDE IS UNCONSTITUTIONAL; LINCOLN FREED THE SLAVES OVER 100 YEARS AGO; and WHAT COLOR IS COMPASSION?[103] Periodically they sang verses of the civil rights movement's anthem, "We Shall Overcome." Neighbors of Schreiber and onlookers generally watched the marchers in silence, while only a few hecklers expressed their disapproval. One man who did not live in Schreiber's neighborhood joined the marchers at the end of their line. He also carried a placard that supported Schreiber. "On one side, his placard read: NO WORKEE, NO EATEE. On the other side it read: GREAT SOCIETY NEEDS WORKERS, NOT LOAFERS."[104] This person joined the march for about fifteen minutes and was largely ignored by the other marchers. The demonstration ended at noon. Still, after no further satisfactory response, the NAACP local branch scheduled a second protest march.[105]

Schreiber denied that he had made the racial slur, proclaiming that "nigger" was not part of his vocabulary, whereas Ralph Blumenthal, one of the *New York Times* reporters, stood by his statement.[106] Schreiber publicly appeared emotionless and under control despite the intense scrutiny focused on him. Nonetheless, Earl W. Brydges Jr. represented Pickett and even challenged the constitutionality of New York State's welfare law. Brydges won. The New York State Court of Appeals overturned Pickett's conviction.[107] This was a victory not only for Pickett and Brydges but for the NAACP local branch as well.

In addition to being proactive in the city of Niagara Falls, the NAACP local branch, just as it supported the sit-ins and the March on Washington, supported every other major national civil rights event highlighted in the media. These events, in turn, would continue to impact local civil rights activities. For example, Medgar Evers bravely headed the NAACP branch in Jackson, Mississippi.[108] Civil rights activists described Mississippi as a closed society during the 1960s because of its negative racial policies that could be considered the worst in the nation.[109] Medgar Evers openly led the Jackson, Mississippi NAACP branch, despite receiving numerous death threats. When the murderers of Emmett Till were on trial, Evers aided the African American witnesses, protecting them in court and safely transporting them out of town after the trial.[110] Many African American citizens of Jackson avoided Evers, a World War II veteran, out of fear that they could be harmed. On June 12, 1963, harm did come to Evers. Byron de la Beckwith, a Greenwood, Mississippi White Citizen's Council member, murdered him after he exited his car in his driveway. De la Beckwith shot Evers with a deer rifle.

The assassination of Medgar Evers saddened the Niagara Falls NAACP local branch members, reminding them of the price that often had to be paid for freedom. However, they refused to stop demanding justice and equality. They paid tribute to Evers by organizing a meeting in his honor in 1967.[111] They also coordinated with NAACP state officials to ask their city government to boycott products produced or processed in Mississippi.[112] Their boycott list consisted of more than eighty items.[113] In 1972 Charles Evers, the brother of Medgar, visited Niagara Falls. Medgar Evers's example and bravery undoubtedly aided his brother. Mayor E. Dent Lackey gave Charles Evers and his family a tour of Niagara Falls.[114]

Charles Evers was then also the mayor of Fayetteville, Mississippi, which made him the first African American mayor of a Mississippi municipality since Reconstruction.

The Birmingham desegregation movement had begun a little over two months before the assassination of Medgar Evers. The Southern Christian Leadership Conference (SCLC) orchestrated the activities of this movement. They implemented Project C, which included (1) sit-ins, (2) adult marches, and (3) children's marches. Theophilus Eugene "Bull" Connor, the Birmingham commissioner of public safety, had firemen spray civil rights demonstrators with firehoses. This sparked general outrage throughout the nation. In that year of 1963 Dr. King composed his famous "Letter from a Birmingham Jail," which became the manifesto of the civil rights movement. The SCLC, along with the support of its allies, gained a critical victory: the successful result of which catapulted Dr. King to international prominence. He was awarded a Nobel Peace Prize in 1964. Dr. King's Birmingham nemesis, "Bull" Connor, was not pleased with the announcement, nor was J. Edgar Hoover, director of the Federal Bureau of Investigation.[115]

Repercussions from the Birmingham movement generated negative results. White racists bombed the Sixteenth Street Baptist Church in Birmingham on September 15, 1963. The Sixteenth Street Baptist Church had served as an organizing center for the SCLC during the Birmingham movement campaign. Demonstrators filed out of the church to protest segregation and inequality. The bombing caused the deaths of four girls and injured twenty-three people. "Sunday school classes at the church were just ending a lesson on 'The Love That Forgives' when the explosion tore out concrete, metal and glass."[116]

> The four girls apparently were in the lounge in the basement of the old brick church. One, Cynthia Wesley, 14, was hit by the full force of the blast and could be identified only by clothing and a ring. The others were Carol Roberson and Addie Mae Collins, 14, and Denise McNair, 11.[117]

The event outraged many Americans, who called for action on the part of government officials and law enforcement agencies. The Niagara Falls NAACP local branch actively participated in a memorial service held for the four girls at Mount Erie Baptist Church.[118] In addition the Niagara Falls NAACP local branch sent telegrams to President Kennedy, Birmingham's mayor Albert Boutwell, and Sixteenth Street Baptist Church's pastor, John Cross. The telegram to President Kennedy noted "the slayings were a bitter testimony to the need for the passage of his civil rights bill"; "[the] one to Mayor Boutwell registered the members' shock and urged the apprehension of those responsible for the bombing"; and the one to Reverend Cross "extended the personal and collective sympathy of the local NAACP members to the bereaved families of the four slain girls."[119] The National Office sent a telegram to all its NAACP local branches, asking them to organize a silent march on the day of the funeral for the four girls.[120]

After the Birmingham Movement the SCLC led another protest movement in Selma, Alabama. This movement fought for voting rights. It was the last movement that the SCLC participated in that gained a major immediate victory—the Voting Rights Act of 1965. SCLC leaders organized several demonstrations. At one demonstration held on a Sunday, six-hundred civil rights demonstrators marched across Selma's Edmund Pettus Bridge. When they got to the end of the bridge, they were met by fifty state troopers wearing gas masks. The troopers rode horses, while others stood with billyclubs in their hands. Major John Cloud gave the marchers two minutes to disperse. The state troopers attacked and beat the marchers because they did not move. According to one account, "Television coverage of the police assault interrupted the networks' regular programming."[121] This historical event has been labeled "Bloody Sunday." Citizens throughout the nation were once again outraged.

Black Niagarans knew the racial climate of Alabama well, since many had recently migrated from that state or had family members that had done so. Wilbur Hunt, for example, lived on the outskirts of Montgomery, Alabama, during the Montgomery Bus Boycott Movement. He remembered racist Whites driving their cars throughout the countryside at night, firing their guns in the air to intimidate and subdue the African American community.[122] Black Niagarans, therefore, adamantly wanted justice done. Gerda Swensson, a member of the Niagara Falls NAACP local branch, said she had been bombarded with calls from local citizens concerned about how they could contribute toward the medical expenses of the beaten marchers.[123] The NAACP local branch established a fund and had citizens send their contributions to the SCLC via St. John's AME Church, the home base of the Reverend Edgar Huff, who then was president of the local branch after returning to Niagara Falls. Swensson strongly urged residents to send telegrams and letters of protest to President Lyndon B. Johnson and Alabama governor George Wallace.[124]

On March 14, 1965, Reverend Huff doggedly organized a local protest march that attracted over four hundred multiracial participants. Marchers started at the Prospect Street state parking lot at the foot of Falls Street and marched for twenty-three minutes, arriving at City Hall in snowy wet weather.[125] Led by Reverend Huff, the marchers sang songs such as "We Shall Overcome" and carried placards that stated, STOP POLICE BRUTALITY IN ALABAMA, HOW MANY MORE MUST DIE?, EQUAL RIGHTS FOR EVERYONE, WE SHALL OVERCOME, CONDEMN VIOLENCE, IS THIS OUR COUNTRY?, and FREEDOM IS ON THE LINE NOW.[126] Once at City Hall an hour-long rally began at which many speakers of various faiths and political views vehemently expressed their outrage.

E. Dent Lackey, mayor of the City of Niagara Falls, addressed the marchers: "When things like what has happened in Selma can happen, it is time for national tears and national repentance. Let each of us promise we will do better."[127] An article in the *Gazette* reported the following: "Reverend Dr. Andrew S. Turnipseed, pastor of St. Paul's Methodist Church and an Alabama native, in his invocation prayed for the blessings of Almighty God upon Gov. Wallace, Alabama Sheriff James Clark, who has been leading attempts to frustrate Negro voting drives in Selma, and upon those there, who take no stand, who know better and should be protesting."[128] Huff "declared that the civil rights crisis is not exclusively a Negro problem but a problem that affects the total citizenry of our society and that the shame of Selma is the shame of America."[129] The *Gazette* also reported that "Reverend Theodore L. Menter, pastor of St. Paul's Lutheran Church and president of the Niagara Council of Churches, said that prayer can help solve the crisis."[130] The Reverend J. Donald Johnston, pastor of First Unitarian Church, observed that the audience was the most mixed group he had seen since he had been in Niagara Falls.[131] Reverend Walter M. Echols, the new pastor of New Hope Baptist Church, said, "It is not a dream to believe that we in this country can live together as American citizens and that I wished the day would come when [Americans] would not look at each other as black and white but as one family under God."[132] Rabbi Alan L. Penn, spiritual leader of Temple Beth El, said, "The ages-long prejudice against the Jews has given them a sympathetic understanding of the Negro's plight in America."[133] He further stressed to all that rights are won not by sitting, waiting, and hoping but by struggle.[134] Otis Cowart called what happened in Selma a tragedy and that it would be an even greater tragedy if all Americans could not exercise their right to vote.[135] Alice C. Hayes, who represented the Women's Social Clubs and Organizations in

Niagara Falls, said: "We march because it is downright disgraceful to be identified with a nation that dares to tell Viet Nam and other nations how to treat their people and yet can do nothing in Selma, Alabama."[136] Other speakers spoke on similar themes. The Niagara Falls NAACP Local Branch collected $550 at the rally for the injured Selma demonstrators, while local donations to the SCLC reached $190.[137]

The Niagara Falls NAACP local branch did not just respond to civil rights events highlighted in the national media, although the civil rights era certainly impacted them. The local branch organized and managed many local events because they were a strong unit. This was a common pattern of NAACP branches during the civil rights era.[138] "No other [civil rights] organization," according to journalist Denton L. Watson, "contributed more to making the U.S. Constitution responsive to the needs of all citizens."[139] Barbara Williams, a longtime NAACP member and official, explained more concretely what made them effective: they were a multiracial organization, received advice and guidance from the national and state offices, had a constant stream of funding, retained a number of first-rate lawyers (e.g., Thurgood Marshall, Robert L. Carter, Jack Greenberg, and others), were meticulously organized, and could mobilize a massive number of people to protest injustice at a moment's notice. Individuals constantly joined the NAACP, bringing their intelligence and resources. Governmental bodies and officials along with corporate America responded to them, and on moral racial issues involving inequality, they were usually right.[140] During the civil rights era, these and other qualities made the Niagara Falls NAACP local branch a feared and respected organization.

Casper L. Jordon, who was educational chairman of the Niagara Falls NAACP local branch during the Selma campaign, managed and promoted a local artistic event. He wrote a play that underscored the literary and musical historical contributions of African Americans.[141] The play's debut was on February 1, the start of Black History Week at Wilberforce University in Ohio.[142] Actors and actresses performed roles that featured the works of Phillis Wheatley, Benjamin Banneker, Frances Watkins Harper, Paul Laurence Dunbar, Langston Hughes, and Niagara Falls's own R. Nathaniel Dett.[143] Jordon wanted to convey some of the contributions to society that African Americans had made and particularly to raise the self-image of his people. Jordon was ahead of his local contemporaries in broadly promoting self-awareness to the Niagara Falls Community.

Jordon eventually became president of the Niagara Falls NAACP local branch. However, before obtaining that post, he continued to serve in other capacities, unceasingly working for the benefit of Black Niagarans. He involved the Niagara Falls NAACP branch in another local struggle concerning a $36,820 grant that President Johnson's Great Society program allotted for the aid of the poor in Niagara Falls.[144] A Community Action Program unit had been established with a board of directors comprising mainly white-collar professionals.[145] The board of directors selected Alice C. Hayes to be director of the Community Action Program, which received strong disapproval from the NAACP and CORE.[146] Moreover, Jordon led a community group that called themselves the Citizen Committee for an Effective Community Action Program. They created a list of sixteen grievances that they sent to the Community Action Program and demanded a response.[147] Some of the complaints they had were the following:

1. Mrs. Hayes was appointed to the directorship on January 24th, while individuals were instructed to come to an interview on January 24th;

2. Mrs. Hayes, while being head of the Board of Directors, was present while they discussed her candidacy, and once being selected as director Mrs. Hayes should have resigned her post as chairperson of the Board of Directors;

3. The Community Action Program had not responded to three neighborhood policy proposals that had been sent several months [previously];

4. That the Board of Directors did not have the voice of the poor because no poor individuals were on it.[148]

The Citizen Committee for an Effective Community Action Program let it be known that they were not attacking Hayes herself but the improper personnel procedures of the Community Action Program. When the Community Action Program issued no response, the Citizen Committee dispatched telegrams to R. Sargent Shriver, War on Poverty Director and New York Senator Robert F. Kennedy, and Congressman Adam Clayton Powell, chairman of the Education and Labor Committee.[149] This recieved a response in which the Community Action Program agreed to consider the grievances and invited community members to a forum to articulate their complaints.[150] One hundred and fifty people attended the forum as speaker after speaker stood to air their grievances. Hayes and other board members sat silently listening. However, Weldon R. Oliver, superintendent of schools and new acting chairman of the board of directors, assured the audience that the Community Action Program wanted to work with all concerned citizens to guarantee that the aims of the federal legislation would be enacted.[151]

During and immediately after the Citizen Committee's critique of the Community Action Program's operations, the Niagara Falls NAACP local branch constantly stayed active, attempting to implement the Great Society programs for their constituency and the general community. Responding to the frustrations and steady demands concerning obtaining suitable housing, for example, in 1966 the NAACP local branch asked Matthew P. Flanagan, who was president of the Niagara Falls Area Board of Realtors, to speak to them and address some of their concerns.[152] Flanagan consented and spoke at St. John's AME Church. He informed his African American audience that his organization supported and promoted open occupancy as mandated by New York State law.[153] He stated that he disapproved of low-income housing because it was socialistic and contributed to the formation of ghettos. Attempting to dispel notions that he was a racist, Flanagan argued that he thought all families deserved to reside in private homes. Flanagan further noted that his organization had a grievance committee that accepted alleged discrimination complaints in written form.[154] When asked if a complaint had been filed, Flanagan answered no. Casper L. Jordon then interjected that "there are many realtors in the city who are evading the law through subterfuge."[155] Jordon further stated that "the issue of racial discrimination in housing boiled down to one point: 'The Negroes are forced to live in certain areas . . . the white people are not.'"[156] Flanagan responded by "[saying] that he could not speak for other real estate firms, but that his firm, M. P. Flanagan & Son, does not list a house for sale unless it is for open occupancy."[157] Flanagan apparently did not convince his African American audience that housing discrimination was not rampant in Niagara Falls. Still, the NAACP local branch seemed pleased that it was networking with an influential realtor, which signified that change certainly could occur to quell some of the unceasing cries for decent housing.

Black Niagarans, like African Americans in other urban locales during the civil rights era, regularly (and justifiably) complained about housing and employment discrimination.[158] Lack of response from city and industrial officials frustrated them and made them resentful. This common urban pattern became a powder keg for violent outbreaks. In

1964 Rochester, New York, had a riot. A riot took place in Watts in 1965, as did many others in 1967, including similar uprisings in Newark, New Jersey, and Detroit, Michigan.[159] Fueling these riots were overcrowding, unemployment, reported police brutality (but also police inaction in the face of many Black Niagaran complaints), lack of concern from government officials, and school segregation, among other issues. Buffalo, New York, Niagara Falls's neighboring city, experienced a riot for many of the same reasons as the other cities. Buffalo's riot began on June 26, 1967, and lasted until July 1. This impacted many African American teenagers in Niagara Falls.

On June 28, two days after the start of the riot in Buffalo, Niagara Falls experienced another riot. The initial cause of the riot is unclear. Nonetheless, one account states that an incident occurred at a Highland Avenue bar. A woman called police to register a complaint. While the arriving police officer listened to the woman, teenagers came from a nearby housing project and began pounding on the police officer's vehicle, shattering a back window. A second police car arrived, and soon it had a broken window.[160] About thirty additional police officers were called in to disperse the swelling crowd that traveled up Highland Avenue, breaking a few store windows and throwing rocks at police officers.[161] Police described the rioters as youths between the ages of fourteen and nineteen.[162] Unlike the earlier riot, no one was hurt, and only one arrest was made. Black Niagarans rioted on Highland Avenue again the next night. Teenagers and young adults participated, throwing bricks, stones, and bottles at cars and police officers.[163] Concerned local African American leaders offered specific reasons for the two-day riot. Reverend Walter Echols attributed the riot to a lack of jobs and recreational facilities for youth. Vera Tremier thought that school segregation had contributed to the outbreak, and Alice Hayes said that she had information that at least two people from Buffalo were partly responsible for inciting the youngsters to riot.[164] Eddie Palmore, who at the time worked at Harrison Radiator and had an income tax business on Highland Avenue, commented that his business was not damaged.[165] Elaborating further, he remarked:

> I think the vandalism occurred because of what happened in Buffalo. It was contagious. But I also think the firing of [Joe] Profit by City Manager O'Hara was a contributing factor. It certainly added to the situation. The Negro community is still unhappy about the murder of Washington Nunn. While the two

Canadian men accused of the murder of Gorton Plampton were hunted down and brought back here, nothing was ever done about Nunn. We see this as unjust handling of police cases.[166]

Palmore concluded by asserting that although the race situation in Niagara Falls was stable compared to other cities, there were near riots in 1965 and 1966. "In both instances," he stated, "Joe Profit was instrumental in averting them."[167]

On Thursday, the evening of the second night of disturbance, about thirty people crowded into the City Hall office of Mayor Lackey to discuss the nature of the Highland Avenue conflagration.[168] Some citizens represented the African American community, and others were city officials. A consensus existed among those present that none of the adults could adequately represent the rioting youth and that the youth could only represent themselves. Evidently no youth spokesperson attended the meeting or perhaps even knew about the meeting. The African Americans convinced the mayor that the youth rioted due to frustrations, and more specifically, because of inadequate recreational facilities and no jobs. Mayor Lackey strongly embraced this idea and pushed those present to offer strategies to solve the current problem. When someone remarked that the youth should not be rewarded for creating a disturbance, Mayor Lackey commented:

> Let's be honest. We wouldn't be here in this office tonight if they weren't out there on Highland Avenue last night. Let's be honest. This community has been neglected.[169]

With the assistance of the attendees, Mayor Lackey developed a twenty-two-step agenda to address employment and recreational needs of the youth. Regarding employment, these recommendations were made:

1. Check with the Niagara County Welfare Department because boys are penalized if they get jobs while the family is on welfare;

2. Look into job discrimination and foster permanent job programs;

3. Make contact with the personnel departments of industries and businesses to encourage hiring and take advantage of federal training grants that have not been utilized;

4. Hire 82 persons shortly by the Niagara Community Action Program is expected.[170]

Concerning recreation, ideas included:

1. Lighting of the basketball courts at the Center Avenue park area;
2. Finding a location for an athletic club that would be supervised by police officers. Instructions in judo, boxing, and wrestling would be provided;
3. Checking the possibility of renting either the old Lincoln Store building or the old Liberty Bank building in North Main Street as a site for recreational activities such as ping pong, cards, pool, and the like;
4. Conducting outdoor boxing at Center Court.[171]

Mayor Lackey spoke at an impromptu gathering that Friday night after the disturbance. He spoke near the Niagara Community Center and Center Court to a crowd of about six hundred people.[172] The audience displayed no excitement about Mayor Lackey's jobs-recreation plan. They politely applauded and then expressed their feelings to the mayor. "It's like throwing a few peanuts," one woman told him.[173] "You didn't talk about the things that are important—decent housing and being able to get a job."[174] Another woman informed the mayor that recreation was not the answer. Pointing to her fifteen-year-old son, she added: "He's going to go to school first and then play."[175] Questioning the mayor's sincerity, one woman asked: "How long have they been integrating the schools?"[176] "Four years and nothing yet has been done."[177] Mayor Lackey informed the woman that it was the job of the board of education to integrate the schools and not city government.[178]

In addition to Mayor Lackey's address, baseball great Jackie Robinson had been invited to speak.[179] That may be the reason why nearly six hundred people had come. Mayor Lackey asked Robinson to speak to Black Niagarans after being informed that the Black baseball hero was scheduled to address rioters in Buffalo. Robinson consented. New York State Governor Nelson A. Rockefeller had asked Robinson to help quell the racial tension in Buffalo. The Niagara Falls audience waited an hour to hear Robinson, who was escorted to Niagara Falls by former Niagara University basketball great Al Butler and then-current star, Calvin Murphy. Murphy introduced Robinson, who promoted communication by all parties, real employment and recreational initiatives by governmental and industrial entities, and self-help on the part of Black Niagarans.[180] Robinson told the audience that the state was committed to solving racial problems, and he warned city government officials to be sincere in initiating solutions. Robinson's words seemed to please those present.

After Robinson left, the Niagara Falls NAACP local branch organized a planning session to discuss the Highland Avenue disturbances and to create a more formal set of grievances and demands to present to City Hall.[181] This meeting imploded. Like the meeting at Mayor Lackey's office, a consensus prevailed that indicated it was best that the citizens in the Highland Avenue/Center Court housing project neighborhood create the grievance-demands list. This accentuated class issues. Most of the local NAACP branch leadership, due to their educational levels or gainful employment, had middle-class status. They had college/university degrees or higher education training or perhaps decent paying jobs (or even both). Citizens in the Highland Avenue/Center Court neighborhood were of lower economic status. Neglect and poverty surrounded them. All the same, interested residents organized a grievance-demand meeting, calling themselves the Jordan Garden session.[182] They created a "Negro Manifesto" highlighting their complaints and demands, which was to be presented at a city council meeting. The manifesto incorporated grievances of Black Niagarans about employment, welfare, recreation, housing, education, sanitation, and allegations of police brutality in hopes that collaborative solutions could be created.[183]

The Jordan Garden session held a rally in the Jordan Garden apartment complex to promote the Negro Manifesto, allow residents to air their complaints, and to inform residents of the next day's city council meeting in which the Negro Manifesto would be presented. Class issues arose at this gathering as well. NAACP officials and ministers spoke, such as Reverend Huff, Reverend Glenn Raybon, Harwood Bond, Thomas Pettaway, and Donald Lee, but the grassroots leaders such as Jimmy Miles, William Marshall Jr., Joe Profit, Glover Jones, and Reid Hart elicited a boisterous response from the four hundred people in the crowd. Someone asked Hart, a young bystander, to speak. "At first demurring, then agreeing to speak, the youth started to rhetorically question the crowd and soon had the rally participants responding with vigor. He showed a natural sense of oratory and almost perfect timing."[184]

Can a Negro boy get out of summer school and get in a plant like a white boy can?" "Noooooo!" "We been asking for picnic tables at [Center] Court for years and years. Nothing. But we went out on the streets and we got them there now!" "Yeaaaaa." "We got somethin' going now, and if we have to, we can bust a few more windows." "Yeeaaaaahh!"[185]

Hart, like the other speakers, wanted justice and equality for Black Niagarans.

The next day, Clover Jones represented the Jordan Garden session and most Black Niagarans at the city council meeting. About 425 spectators packed the City Hall Chambers, most of them being Black Niagarans.[186] Jones spoke for twenty-two minutes in a bold, articulate voice, accentuating the Jordan Garden session's seven-point manifesto. A door-to-door committee had been established to solicit grievances and demands from African American community members, mainly but not exclusively from those who lived on and around Highland Avenue, East Falls Street, and Griffon Manor, enclaves where Black Niagarans had been living. Led by Jones, and using the information collected at other events, they created a seven-point, seven-page manifesto that highlighted their grievances. Jones titled his presentation "The Declaration of Intentions and Motives of the Negro Community of Niagara Falls."[187] It echoed ideas and behaviors of the contemporary Black Power movement because Jones did not plead the cause of Black Niagarans like earlier leaders had done.[188] He demanded specific responses from city government and industry and business leaders. Jones warned city council members that if White community leaders did not respond, Black Niagarans would participate in more violent demonstrations. The African American spectators interrupted Jones thirty-two times with sustained applause.[189] Jones ended his speech by shouting the following:

> We proclaim one truth! We are not the slaves of slavery that dehumanized our fathers. We demand human behavior. We claim only one right—and that is to demand human behavior for all people. We have assessed our identity in a world of transition, and we choose not to slumber in the ghetto. We do not seek glad-handed sentiment. What is to prevent us from violence when we are cheated, shunned, insulted, and outraged beyond human endurance? There are solutions to our reasonable demands—peace and tranquility are at stake![190]

The Black Niagarans gave Jones a standing ovation; the city council members were silent.

Jones told the city council that he represented the African American community, which through him spoke as one voice. City Manager Donald J. O'Hara doubted that. He mentioned that he had received a phone call from a prominent African American community leader who urged him not to allow himself to be bullied by the Jordan Garden session, which he said was full of hoodlums.[191] If what Manager O'Hara said is true, it clearly highlights class conflict. The caller evidently felt there was a better way to represent and solve racial problems in Niagara Falls.

Mayor Lackey spoke immediately following Jones's presentation. He promised Jones and the Black Niagarans there that real answers would be found expeditiously.[192] He further reiterated his earlier proposals and asked not for total agreement but for a continuing dialogue to be established in lieu of demonstrations and violence. He praised Black Niagarans for coming before the city council and noted "that they should have come . . . a long time ago."[193] Although evidence considering a counterview is limited, some individuals probably felt that the mayor pandered to the demonstrators. Nonetheless, "it was the hour of the Negro" (or Black Niagarans) who embraced a wait-and-see stance concerning what Mayor Lackey had told them.[194]

Nearly two weeks after Clover Jones presented the seven-point manifesto, Reverend Raybon held a rally at the Jordan Garden housing complex.[195] Fewer than a hundred people came. Reverend Raybon threatened to lead demonstrations in front of downtown stores because some store managers had agreed two weeks earlier to consider employment prospects for some Black Niagarans and to discuss this issue on a specified date. These things had not happened. After consultation with community leaders, including Clover Jones and city officials, Reverend Raybon decided to end his protest efforts and allow more dialogue to improve the status of his people. Mayor Lackey stressed to Jones that steps were being taken to effect change.[196] He had, for example, categorized the grievances he received and distributed them to the relevant departments within his city administration. The disturbance on Highland Avenue had pressured city officials to promote equality for all and to realize that their actions would be scrutinized by Black Niagarans and their leaders.

The assassination of Dr. Martin Luther King Jr. heightened racial tensions even more in Cataract City as well as in other municipalities. Dr. King taught that African Americans should use nonviolent means to obtain their freedom; he urged Black people never to hate anyone, since hate damages a person from within.[197] He taught that racist behaviors and beliefs had been inculcated into people's minds, and as a result such attitudes and behaviors could be deprogrammed. He taught the world about the brotherhood of man and that people should be judged by character rather than by skin color. He emphasized to the nation that more of its wealth should be shared with the poor rather than hoarded by a wealthy minority. Yet the "drum major for peace" was assassinated.

Many Americans and people throughout the world were stunned and deeply sad. Many sought revenge. About 125 riots occurred throughout the nation in response to the news that Dr. King had been assassinated. Many people were hurt and killed. In neighboring Buffalo a riot ensued; yet in Niagara Falls, surprisingly, there was no riot.

However, in commenting on the slaying of Dr. King, local leaders discussed the racial changes that had to be made in Niagara Falls. Mayor E. Dent Lackey, at the fiftieth annual dinner of the Niagara Falls Area Chamber of Commerce, called for an end to discrimination in the city and characterized racial prejudice as the "eternal crucifixion."[198] Bloneva Bond, who at the time was vice president of the Human Relations Commission, stated that it was despicable that a person could be killed for his views and that in Niagara Falls the Human Relations Commission was fighting to ensure that all Americans' rights were guaranteed.[199] She also mentioned that she had met Dr. King eight years earlier when he had spoken in Niagara Falls at New Hope Baptist Church.[200] Student organizers orchestrated a walkout in all area high schools in honor of Dr. King and to protest the slight they felt they had received from Weldon R. Oliver, the superintendent of schools.[201] They referred to the superintendent as a "double cross."[202] The pupils met with Mr. Oliver, board of education members, police officials, and black and White civic leaders later in the day to discuss their complaints.[203] All in all the death of Dr. King was an even more obvious signal that drastic changes had to be made throughout the country and in the city of Niagara Falls.

Six days after the assassination, Congress passed the Civil Rights Act of 1968, partly to honor Dr. King. This law made it a federal crime to discriminate in the sale and rental of housing. Federal, state, and civic agencies began to respond more to the cries of justice and equality from African American communities. The city of Niagara Falls demonstrated this in several ways. Progressive-minded individuals created the Friendship House immediately following the assassination of Dr. King. It also was a response to the call for more recreational facilities for youth in the Highland Avenue section. The Niagara Community Center still operated under Aaron Griffin's leadership; however, young people wanted more recreational facilities.[204] The Niagara Ministers Council, understanding this, organized the formation of the Friendship House. They convinced the board of education to allow them to use the abandoned Center Avenue School building, located at the intersection of Center and Highland Avenues. The school board also agreed to contribute up to $15,000 for a year of janitorial services and to cover utilities, hoping that a projected state grant would reimburse their contribution.[205] Under the Urban Education Act, New York State appropriated a grant of about $180,000 to be dispersed through the Niagara Falls Board of Education over two years.[206] The city of Niagara Falls gave Friendship House $11,800 in start-up funds. The funds had been provided from the seventy-fifth municipal anniversary sale of commemorative coins and memorabilia by the Niagara Falls Area Chamber of Commerce.[207] Councilman William M. Paterson suggested that the proceeds be used to help establish Friendship House.[208]

The Niagara Ministers Council envisioned the Friendship House offering educational and recreational services to ghetto youth,[209] programs such as a Teen Drop-In Center, a study hall with reference materials, and a sports department that the city police department's community service would run.[210] They selected Willie Shine to be the director. Shine graduated from Trott Vocational High School; he had been a high school football star who also flourished as a running back at the University of Buffalo. Shine played professional football in Canada, one year with the Edmonton Eskimos and two with the Montreal Beavers, ending his career only after his arm had been fractured and doctors advised him not to play any longer.[211] Shine also had a background in youth social work and had worked for the East Central Citizens Organization in Columbus, Ohio, a federally funded youth poverty project.[212] He hired a staff, including a secretary and assistant director, and coordinated Friendship House's programs under the supervision of a board of directors, the board of education, and the State Education Department's Division for Intercultural Relations. Arthur B. Ray, who was a partner in the firm of Palmore and Ray Income Tax Consultants, and who had been elected as Friendship House's treasurer, assisted Shine in managing the organization's finances.[213]

The Friendship House was fully operational by summer 1968, and by autumn, Shine was proclaiming that recreational and educational activities had been a success.[214] A swimming program existed; youth participated in a teen picnic at Fort Niagara State Park; the staff organized two dances that drew more than six hundred youth; more than one thousand people used the newly blacktopped playground behind the Friendship House Building; a course in Black history had been offered; grade-school youths took advantage of tutorial classes; and a significant number of teenage girls viewed a film on sex education. The future seemed bright for Friendship House. Willie Shine managed it for about twenty-one months, and then Reverend Raybon administered it for nearly a year.[215]

Joe McCoy administered a federally funded program for adults interested in learning a skilled trade. He called his program "Training for Construction."[216] This was also a government response to the assassination of Dr. King along with the late 1960s demand for jobs. McCoy, who was born in Arkansas and was a twenty-two-year army veteran, coordinated with local skilled tradesmen to come up with the requirements for his training course. The program was opened to adult minorities (e.g., African Americans, American Indians, and Latino Americans) who wished to join an eighteen-month accelerated training program leading to journeyman status in a trade union.[217] Completion of the program, along with the approval of a committee of established skilled tradesmen, made a person a fully qualified journeyman. To apply, applicants were not required to have experience. This program placed some people in jobs; however, most were not placed because unions and contractors would not hire them.[218] Ultimately, the Training for Construction program ended when the federal government did not renew its grant,[219] as not enough trainees had been placed in jobs. McCoy saw the end coming but knew his program could be more successful provided his grant was renewed, and local unions and contractors held to their pledge to hire minority trainees.

NiaCAP's (or Niagara Community Action Program) creation and implementation was also a response to the complaints and needs of the poor and neglected.[220] The federal government awarded grants to NiaCAP, which, in turn, provided services to poor minority communities, offering such programs as Head Start, child daycare services, tutoring for youth, and legal services.[221] NiaCAP began as a Great Society program that catered only to citizens of the city of Niagara Falls; then it expanded, catering to those within Niagara County. NiaCAP successfully aided a number of citizens.

Despite these concessions and others not covered here, Black Niagarans still felt that they were treated as second-class citizens. Finding suitable housing and employment, along with not being granted the respect they warranted, continued to trouble them. Anger existed and could have turned to fury. On August 19, 1969, anger turned to rage—Black rage.[222] About three hundred Niagarans sat in the Strand Theater, apparently enjoying the movie, an Edgar Allan Poe thriller called *The Oblong Box*.[223] A scuffle ensued between Whites and Blacks, and soon the show was stopped and the theater emptied.[224] Theatergoers were enraged that they had paid their money and now had to leave. Police had to be called when three hundred people stood in front of the theater and refused to move. Police made several arrests and dispersed the crowd. Many Black Niagarans angrily headed to the East Falls Street area, breaking a few downtown store windows as they left. When they reached the East Falls Street section, others joined them in breaking windows and throwing firebombs at stores, targeting White-owned establishments, such as Los Tiempos Pharmacy. One Mr. Miles, an official of the Human Rights Commission, commented: "[Blacks] regarded the store as one of the places where they were mistreated."[225] He said there had been frequent complaints of overcharges, insults to Blacks, and a failure to hire Black salespeople.[226] The owner did not plan to reopen. Youths threw rocks and bricks at passing cars and assaulted three White Canadian men in a car in the East Falls Street area. The Canadian men were treated at a local hospital and sent back across the border under police escort.[227]

From East Falls Street the rioting spread to the Highland Avenue section of Niagara Falls and lasted for two days. Community leaders such as Ronnie Cunningham and active NAACP members walked throughout the community for several days, talking to many residents and convincing them not to riot.[228] City manager Donald J. O'Hara enacted several measures. He had his police officers work double shifts and expanded his police force, incorporating reinforcements from the Niagara Frontier State Parks Commission and about forty Niagara County sheriff's deputies. This gave O'Hara 130 police officers to place on duty to suppress the riot.[229] He finally imposed an 11:30 p.m. four-day curfew on the East Falls Street and Highland Avenue sections of town to prevent the riot from spreading in the revenue-generating tourist areas. This angered Black Niagarans of all classes.[230] "If he [Mr. O'Hara] doesn't call it off," said a civil rights worker who had helped calm the area Wednesday night, "he'll have another Detroit on his hands tonight and I'll be out there helping to throw the bricks."[231] When O'Hara announced at a meeting with fifteen community leaders that he was lifting the emergency curfew, there were no cheers. "[O'Hara] made his announcement at City Hall to the group of black leaders who had helped keep the slum areas calm the previous night on the promise that this would lead to the lifting of the curfew."²³² Several Black Niagarans complained about the treatment they had received from police, especially from those added to help the Niagara Falls Police Department. A man complained that he was arrested while going to lock up his bar after being advised to do so by city officials; another man stated he was returning from an Elks Club meeting to his home in the curfew area when he was pulled out of his car by policemen, handcuffed, and called a "Black bastard." Another man was on his way to work with a lunch bag when a police officer stopped him and asked him why he was on the streets. He informed the officer that he was on his way to work. The officer searched his lunch bag, gave it back, and then informed him to stay off the streets, allowing him to go on to work.²³³ Bill Williamson remembered how police had effectively cordoned off and contained the entire African American community where no one could leave or enter without their consent.²³⁴ City authorities along with the assistance of some community members ultimately defused the disturbance but not the feelings of the African American community. Black Niagarans still felt injustice and inequality concerning employment, housing, and their citizenship status, reflected in a comment again by Mr. Miles: "A key problem is recognition. . . . We tried to start a storefront museum with the art works and theater for the black community so we could show tourists our contributions to society, but no one was interested."²³⁵ Evidently, much more work had to be done.

In 1970 Frank Mesiah, an educator and active Buffalo NAACP member and leader, attempted to address the recognition issue; he sought to bring the Black museum concept back to the city of Niagara Falls. The civil rights movement and the Black Power movement (1966 to 1975) had made many Americans more empathetic to the importance of being aware of a multicultural history. Moreover, many people in authoritative positions felt compelled to respond to pleas and demands from the African American community. Mesiah orchestrated his project before the publication of Alex Haley's classic work, *Roots*, which got Americans in general thinking about their family history. The idea for a Black museum that would feature artifacts highlighting the African American experience developed in the minds of residents in Cooperstown, New York.²³⁶ However, they did not want a Black museum in their area.²³⁷

Undaunted, Mesiah decided to try to implement the museum in the city of Niagara Falls. He reasoned that Niagara Falls was a good international location, only a few hundred miles from Black population centers like Cleveland, Chicago, Detroit, and New York.[238] The museum could serve as an attraction for tourists who preferred to stay on the Canadian side of Niagara Falls because of the number of shops and exhibits there. Mesiah particularly thought that both Black and White Americans could benefit from it: "White people needed to know more about the contributions of blacks so they could correct some of the misconceptions they have about black people," Mesiah noted, "and black people needed to know more about their own contributions for their own 'self-esteem.'"[239] Mesiah also listed some historical reasons for the selection of Niagara Falls as the museum site:

1. The Niagara movement, forerunner of the oldest black civil rights organization in the country, the National Association for the Advancement of Colored People, was founded on the Niagara Frontier;

2. The area is full of "underground railroad" stations used by escaped slaves as resting or hiding places on their way to Canada and freedom;

3. Black sailors served on the great lakes in the War of 1812;

4. Black troops maintained order among the quarreling Irishmen who built the Welland Canal, connecting Lake Erie and Ontario.[240]

The Niagara frontier, according to Mesiah, held tremendous importance to the development of many aspects of Black history and culture.[241]

About $3.5 million had to be raised to make the project operational. The Committee on Black History and Culture, headed by Mesiah and supported by the Niagara Falls Board of Education, had to raise $3.5 million and convince the Niagara Falls City Council to give them an option agreement for land near the actual cataracts of Niagara Falls.[242] First and foremost, a plan had to be refined to persuade people of the worthiness of the project. The committee developed a plan and spent about three years refining it. The museum would house sculptures, paintings, and other artifacts and also a research department containing books, manuscripts, publications, and microfilm.[243] The museum would also have a multimedia, multisensory exhibitory component that would give museum patrons a realistic "you are there" experience.[244] They would be thrust in the middle of an attack on Fort Wagner during the Civil War, or in the middle of a slave revolt, or on one of Harriet Tubman's Underground Railroad journeys, experiencing sights, sounds, odors, dangers, and seeking out the North Star. Patrons would be given previsit and postvisit tests to document that learning had occurred. The museum would also have a souvenir shop and a few other amenities.

Robert Coles, a Buffalo architect, designed the museum, detailing every aspect of the building's structure: the number of floors, offices, meeting rooms, bathrooms, entrance and exit doors, and exterior landscaping. In addition the committee spent eight weeks creating a financial plan that could adequately answer questions of prospective donors and other interested parties, calculations were done down to the penny. They also created a booklet that named the museum and professionally highlighted the museum and its objective. Organizers named the museum the National Black American Museum and Cultural Center. Committee members subsequently gave numerous presentations to businesses, governmental agencies, educational groups, and people who could impact the museum's existence and success.

All aspects of the National Black American Museum and Cultural Center seemed to be in order. Enough entities had made financial commitments so that project funding was ensured. General Motors had agreed to make the largest contribution.[245] Members of the Committee on Black History and Culture were extremely optimistic. All their earlier objectives had come to fruition. The only remaining need now was to obtain land close to the American Niagara Falls area. This could only be obtained from the Niagara Falls City Council.[246] The committee requested the option for land from the city council, and several meetings occurred with Mayor Lackey. However, even with more requests, the city council never acted on the option for the land. The committee informed them that if the project did not work then the land would go back to the city. This still made no difference. Mesiah remembered Mayor Lackey "slipping" when he said that "he did not see any black in the rainbow," with regard to the National Black American Museum and Culture Center idea.[247] Mesiah further remembered that Mayor Lackey for some reason associated the museum with African cuisines and dancing girls.[248] The city council never acted on the option agreement to purchase land, and the donors would not continue to disperse funds unless the option was granted. "Once the funds stopped," Mesiah remarked, "I closed my Niagara Falls office and left town."[249] Mayor Lackey and the city council's actions angered

Black Niagarans. During the next mayoral election, they did not support Lackey.[250] Had the National Black American Museum and Cultural Center been realized, it would not only have served to make amends for past injustices but also would have been a pioneering effort.

Other civil rights activities occurred in the city of Niagara Falls. For example, Jesse Jefferson, a student at Utah State University and a local resident, helped form a group called the New Black Society.[251] That organization strove to create a community center in the East Falls Street neighborhood similar to the Friendship House and the Niagara Community Center both located in the North End section. They argued before the mayor and other city officials that the growing population in their section warranted a facility to accommodate the influx of newcomers. Furthermore, they demanded control of the facility. The NAACP continued to be active and effective. Toward the end of the civil rights movement, Harwood and Bloneva Bond became presidents, Harwood first and then Bloneva. Attica prisoners asked Bloneva to be one of the outside negotiators during the Attica uprising. She consented and enthusiastically negotiated with them at Attica prison.[252] A progressive organization calling itself the Black Employees Club formed in 1968 alongside the civil rights movement. They fought against all forms of discrimination, keeping pressure on city authorities and encouraging their people to be proactive.[253] Fred Brown, a community businessman and activist, promoted civil rights activities on the streets of the African American community, especially on Highland Avenue. He demonstrated leadership and always supported progressive efforts.[254]

The civil rights years profoundly impacted Americans in general. Some writers have marked the beginning of the civil rights movement as Rosa Parks's refusal to give up her bus seat to a White male passenger.[255] Her defiant act ignited the 1955 Montgomery Bus Boycott. But considering Parks's act as being the spark that ignited the modern civil rights movement has been vehemently challenged. Some scholars posit that the murder of Emmett Till was the decisive event that led to the 1950s–1960s civil rights movement.[256] Others argue that the *Brown v. Board of Education* decision served as the catalyst. Although this debate may never be resolved, the nationwide events of the modern civil rights movement influenced communities throughout the nation, encouraging local leaders to accelerate their long-standing activities against racial injustice and to initiate protest.

During the civil rights movement, Black Niagarans, guided by their collectivist leaders, acted progressively to improve their status locally and nationally. After World War II, Black Niagarans continued to work hard trying to change their fortunes. In attempting to advance their community, Black Niagaran leaders, like African American leaders in other municipalities, strove to end racial injustices and elicit change within their own city, thereby helping to make America better as a whole.

Chapter Six

Public School Desegregation, 1960s and 1970s

Civil rights and public-school desegregation motivated many Black Niagarans to organize around issues of race in advancing their racial group and contributing to community development. And Alliance leaders such as Helen Schoninger and Donald C. Johnson joined forces with them. Black Niagaran leaders Glover Jones, Harwood Bond, Arthur B. Ray, and Casper L. Jordon strove to make the Niagara Falls school desegregation process efficient and peaceful so that the educational experiences of Niagaran children could be enriched. Housing discrimination continued to be a critical factor in preventing desegregation, but Black Niagarans and their leaders needed to compel a reluctant board of education to create and implement a viable desegregation plan.

In 1896 the Supreme Court legalized the separation of racial groups in *Plessy vs. Ferguson*, which would remain officially in force for about sixty years.[1] Charles Hamilton Houston, a Black Harvard-trained lawyer representing the NAACP, enlisted a cadre of young lawyers, including Thurgood Marshall, who chipped away at *Plessy vs. Ferguson* until it was finally overturned.[2] In 1954 the Supreme Court proclaimed unanimously in *Brown v. Board of Education* that separate but equal education was inherently unequal. *Brown v. Board* made such practices illegal in schools and strengthened the cases of groups or individuals arguing against segregated education.[3] The *Brown* decision excited and encouraged many people, including civil rights activists. However, like numerous cities and towns, the city of Niagara Falls did not enforce it immediately but only when pressured by Black Niagarans and their supporters.

In 1963, nine years after the *Brown v. Board of Education* decision, New York State Commissioner of Education James E. Allen Jr. mandated that all state public schools should correct their racial imbalances.[4] Allen required all state public schools to be truly reflective of their city or town populations. At the time, Niagara Falls's elementary schools were racially imbalanced. Most African American grammar school students attended schools in their segregated neighborhoods. Common complaints among Black Niagarans were that they did not have the best teachers, school curricula, and school facilities. Moreover, the schools were overcrowded, and students did not have teachers from their own racial group to emulate. Another complaint indicated that students were at first forced to try to operate in a monoracial culture: that is, "children who someday [would] get out and work in a biracial world [were] preparing for the day the wrong way."[5] Because realtors maintained segregated housing, the neighborhood schools mirrored the all-Black neighborhood population. Center Avenue School, Thirteenth Street School, and Beech Avenue School, for example, had predominantly African American student bodies.[6]

The charge that they were maintaining segregated schools shocked northerners in general and White Niagarans in particular.[7] When they thought of racism and discrimination toward African Americans, they thought of events in the South, thousands of miles away.[8] But when data showed that northerners also practiced racial discrimination, White Niagarans were taken aback.[9] The Niagara Falls Board of Education had to act or have its funding curtailed. Commissioner Allen demanded that the imbalanced status be rectified immediately. What should the board do? How could they proceed? How could balance be achieved most effectively without causing major turmoil? Could mayhem be avoided? These and other questions arose for the Niagara Falls board to resolve.[10]

Black Niagarans constantly pressured the Niagara Falls board to create and implement an effective integration plan.[11] The local Niagara Falls NAACP branch led the movement. Glover Jones, who had issued the Negro Manifesto of the Black Community of Niagara Falls, also held a leadership position in the local NAACP branch.[12] He chaired the Education Committee. At the August 23, 1967 board of education meeting, four years after Commissioner Allen had issued his decree, Jones questioned the board as to when they planned to create and implement an integration plan. Jones had listed segregation of schools as one of the grievances in his 1967 manifesto that if not resolved could cause upheaval in the city's African American districts.[13] William F. Collins, the newly elected board president, gave no concrete answers, stating that the issue would be dealt with at the next board meeting. Not satisfied with this response, Jones sought a commitment from the board and kept inquiring: "Have the administrators done anything yet?"[14] and "Have any plans been discussed or given by the administration yet?"[15] Jones still received no concrete answers—only that the integration issue would be discussed at the next meeting and that the board had been grappling with it the past three or four years. Still dissatisfied, Jones commented, "You have not answered my basic question."[16]

Initially, the Niagara Falls Board of Education promoted a plan that called for building three large school complexes in the North End, the South End, and the LaSalle sections, each facility being large enough to accommodate the populations of at least three schools. Moreover, as an addendum, they proposed that no school within the city of Niagara Falls would have an African American student body greater than 25 percent.[17] Although the board's leadership proposed the codicil, it was just an oral statement and not a written policy.[18] With this percentage, they argued that no school would be segregated. On the surface this plan seemed reasonable. However, by August 24, 1967, when NAACP and Human Relations Commission representatives questioned board members about its details, it became evident that not much thought had been given to the project, reflecting a half-hearted commitment to integration. Glover Jones doubted that the North End School's African American student population could theoretically be just 25 percent or less, due to the high concentration of Black Niagarans in the area.[19] He estimated that the African American student population would be 37 percent.[20] Paul H. Reid Jr., chairman of the city's Commission on Human Relations, predicted that African Americans would make up more than half the new school's enrollment by the time it opened its doors for classes in 1970.[21] Jones asked board members if they had a study to support their plan—one that accounted for growth projections of the African American community—so that reasonable estimates could be made about how many Black Niagarans would attend the North End Elementary School. No study had been done. Harwood Bond, vice president of the local NAACP branch, suggested creating a large campus school that could accommodate a vast number of students. This, he felt, could ensure integration. Joseph Chille, vice president of the board, discouraged this idea and stressed that many parents did not want neighborhood schools ended.[22] Bond replied: "What is so sacred about the neighborhood schools?"[23] Weldon R. Oliver, superintendent of schools, strongly supported neighborhood schools.[24] Thus, for the board, by August 23, 1967, the early integration plan was secondary to maintaining neighborhood schools.[25]

In implementing this plan, the board proposed to close several schools and to change school boundaries. On the city's North End, Ashland Avenue, Center Avenue, and Twenty-Second Street Schools were slated to be closed. School boundary changes would be made at Maple Avenue, Cleveland Avenue, Seventeenth Street, and Hyde Park schools.[26] On the South End, Thirteenth Street, Tenth Street, and Fifth Street Schools would be closed.[27] To the chagrin of the local NAACP branch, the board planned to close Center Avenue School by September 1967 and Thirteenth Street School by September 1968. Both schools had a primarily African American student body: Center Avenue being 99 percent and Thirteenth Street approximately 80 percent Black, respectively.[28] Students at Center Avenue School were scheduled to be bused to various predominately White schools. Beech Avenue School, a fairly new school with an all African American student body, was to receive forty gifted and talented White students. The board planned to bus a similar number of Beech Avenue School Black Niagarans to a mostly White school. The local NAACP branch, along with the Commission on Human Relations, vehemently denounced these plans by the Niagara Falls Board of Education.

The local NAACP branch felt that a more effective desegregation plan could and should be developed. The board had no studies or survey results to justify its plans. The NAACP also argued about the unfairness of one-way busing or the busing of only African Americans to achieve integration. In closing Center Avenue School along with future projected changes, the NAACP reasoned that Black Niagarans would be making most of the adjustments.[29] The daily school procedures of White elementary school children would generally be the same, but those of African American school children would be vastly altered. They would ride the bus to and from school, adjust to their new school environment, and eat their lunches in school rather than at home as they had done before. A significant number of African American parents enjoyed the amenities of the neighborhood school and disliked the busing idea. Their children, too, could awaken at a later hour, walk to school, come home for the hour-long lunch break, interact with a parent and perhaps other siblings, and then walk back to school for afternoon classes. For some students, this break from school may have aided the learning process.

The local NAACP branch, under Casper L. Jordon's leadership, demanded consistent communication with the Niagara Falls Board of Education, and the board responded to the NAACP's request.[30] Under Collins's leadership, after reading a press release that the NAACP disapproved the board's integration plan, the board invited the executive committee of the local NAACP branch to attend its August 1967 board meeting and present their views.[31] Besides being democratic, an additional reason that the board had an open-door policy toward the NAACP was that one of its members, Arthur B. Ray, was African American. Ray had been elected to the board in 1964, being the first member of his racial group to obtain that post.[32] H. Edward Whitaker had sought a seat earlier but was unsuccessful in his election bid. The Niagara Falls African American community greatly respected Ray and saw him as their voice on the board.[33]

At a September 21, 1967 board meeting, NAACP representatives questioned the board about its statement that no Niagara Falls public school would maintain a student body of greater than 25 percent African American. The NAACP learned that the 25 percent rule was not really a policy; it was a statement board officials made after consulting with Albany State Educational officials.[34] At the meeting, when the NAACP pressed the board to commit to their 25 percent rule statement, board members refused. This understandably angered NAACP representatives, who in turn threatened to ask the State of New York to coordinate the integration process in the city of Niagara Falls.[35]

Responding to intense pressure from the NAACP and the State of New York, Superintendent of Schools Weldon R. Oliver, with board approval, committed to a 28 percent rule.[36] New York State Department of Education defined "imbalance" as any school that had 50 percent or more non-White students.[37] To remedy the imbalance, Oliver proposed a plan that coincided with state guidelines. "The State Department of Education urged Niagara Falls to set a goal for racial balance at no more than 10 [percent] above the over-all [African American] enrollment in the school district."[38] At that time, Niagara Falls's African American student enrollment for elementary schools equaled 17.7 percent. Rounding 17.7 to 18 and adding 10 points to the number 18 is how Oliver obtained the 28 percent rule. Twenty-eight percent is three points higher than the original 25 percent measurement, which meant that less pressure would be on the Niagara Falls Board of Education to reassign students to other schools, so that all their twenty-two elementary schools met the 28 percent criterion. To a large degree, Niagara Falls's junior high and high schools did not have these imbalances, although North Junior High School was 28.7 percent African American.[39]

White parents showed displeasure with the board of education's initial school integration plan, which operated on a trial-and-error basis.[40] Like most towns and cities, Niagara Falls had not had to wrestle with such an intricate problem nor please so many groups and individuals. At an August 14, 1968 meeting at Beech Avenue School with White parents whose children were to be bused, Superintendent Oliver made several comments to these parents; some of his comments could now be construed as racist. The students being bused were the forty White gifted and talented students who originally came from Twenty-Fourth Street School. Oliver, accompanied by Harry F. Abate, deputy superintendent of schools, and Geraldine Mann, assistant superintendent for elementary schools, told parents that the move of their children to Beech Avenue School was not part of school desegregation and that the switch was made because of additional space available at Beech Avenue School.[41] He further informed the parents that their children would be academically isolated from the mostly Black Niagaran student body. They might only interact with other students in gym or during auditorium programs. Their classes would be designed to enhance their advanced intellectual abilities because the children were in a gifted and talented program. "It doesn't matter where the students are brought, they are by themselves," Superintendent Oliver said.[42] Some parents still complained and expressed concern about their children psychologically adjusting to the new setting. Milton Anglin, a school psychologist, expressed the view that the participating students were exceptional enough that they would adjust without any serious emotional problems.[43] Oliver followed that up by expressing that if any parents were not satisfied with the setup they could withdraw their children.[44] Several parents still criticized the school administrators for poor implementation of the plan. Further, Oliver informed parents that a reading center had been scheduled to open at Beech Avenue School and that about thirty former Beech Avenue students had been transferred to Hyde Park School, fostering the desegregation that the state had mandated.

Neither Superintendent Oliver nor school psychologist Anglin ever discussed (or perhaps considered) the psychological impact that the forty gifted and talented White isolated students in a predominantly African American school would have on the mostly African American student body.[45] Would the African American students think they were being treated unequally? Would they understand the intent of isolation? Would the African American students feel a sense of inferiority? Was a sense of inferiority being ingrained in them? Did they think that school officials granted the forty gifted and talented students special privileges? Eddie L. Ashely, an African American parent whose child attended Beech Avenue School, said that his first-grade daughter could not understand why the White children at school had received new desks and the African American children had not. "I know it's bothering her," commented Mr. Ashely, "because she's asked me twice now, 'Daddy, why did the [White] kids get new desks?' "[46] These unfair practices further angered Black Niagarans, while perhaps reassuring the parents of the forty gifted and talented students.

By September 1968, notwithstanding constant complaints, the Niagara Falls Board of Education had accomplished some of its initial objectives.[47] They had closed Center Avenue School and Thirteenth Street School by the projected dates. The board bused students from those schools to predominantly White schools. Moreover, they had shifted some students to and from schools to correct racial imbalances. As a result, all elementary schools met the 28 percent rule, except Beech Avenue School. Board members felt a sense of progress and believed that they would eventually meet Commissioner Allen's mandate.

Black Niagarans and their leadership, on the other hand, did not share the board of education's sense of progress.[48] They expressed anger and resentment when the board transferred thirty-one African American students from Cleveland Avenue School to Twenty-Second Street School.[49] Some reasoned that African American students had been transferred to make room for kindergarten students who had turned to the public school after Sacred Heart School closed its kindergarten in 1967.[50] On September 10, 1968, twenty-three parents, led by Reverend Glen Raybon, protested the board's plan by keeping their children out of school for five days.[51] The parents expressed their old grievance that Black Niagarans were the only ones making sacrifices and adjustments for the integration of public schools. Wilbur R. Nordos, director of the state education department's Bureau for Intercultural Relations, came from Albany to respond to the complaints of Black Niagarans. Parents told Director Nordos that their children had been arbitrarily assigned to inferior schools and that many of their children had attended three different schools in the past three years because of integration shifts.[52] They also expressed the view that only busing African American children and closing only predominantly African American schools to achieve integration was unfair. Director

Nordos heard their grievances and seemed to empathize with them. He encouraged them to file a grievance with the commissioner of education if they were dissatisfied with the way that the Niagara Falls Board of Education had been managing the integration process. He advised them not to build their case strictly on the thirty African American students transferred from Cleveland Avenue to Twenty-Second Street School because the board had a right to assign students to particular schools. Harwood Bond, who was now president of the local NAACP branch, interjected that the NAACP could and would use its lawyers to develop a case to present before James E. Allen.[53] Director Nordos also advised his audience to enter a dialogue with the board so that the African American community's concerns could be integrated into the board's planning. With this, he encouraged them to attend the board's next meeting to express their concerns and to ask pertinent questions that could perhaps convince the parents to end their boycott.

Black Niagarans followed Director Nordos's advice. They attended the next board of education meeting on September 11, 1968, to air their grievances. The board closed the meeting, admitting only their members, the African American community, the superintendent, and the deputy superintendent of schools. They also voted to remain silent and listen to the complaints of the African American community. Black Niagarans asked the following:

1. Why weren't the parents consulted on busing?
2. What is going to happen to Beech Avenue School?
3. What is the justification of the Board of Education for placing the full burden of integration on the Negroes?
4. We want intelligent answers, and we should get answers.
5. Who formulated this busing plan?
6. You have slapped the Negro community hard. It has been a slap to the dignity of our pride as black people in a black community.[54]

The board did not respond to the questions and comments, provoking community activist and entrepreneur Fred Brown to say the board was passing the buck.[55] He pointedly told them: "You know the answers to questions asked tonight, but you want to wait to give answers with a painted picture so it looks good."⁵⁶ The truth of this statement unsettled a few board members who felt compelled to speak. The board demanded that members uphold their decision to be silent and just listen. Arthur B. Ray, the board's first and only African American member, said to his constituents:

> I think the board should come up with some answers for these people, but not necessarily what's to be done tomorrow. I've been harping on this fact of one-sided information. It's been a one-way street and it's not good. These people want to hear our ideas. I think 22nd Street School maybe should be closed, and maybe there should be more busing—bringing Whites into the black community. This program is not as good as I first thought. Maybe we don't have to build these new schools either.⁵⁷

Black Niagarans applauded Ray for his comments, but board members ended Ray's speech by reiterating the board's vow of silence. The dialogue that Director Nordos promoted did not happen, igniting more anger and frustration. Before leaving, Black Niagarans threatened a citywide boycott of schools if the board did not implement drastic changes, including truly integrating Beech Avenue School and dropping the current arrangement established by school administrators and the board.⁵⁸

On September 11, 1968, Director Nordos, as a New York State representative, consulted with African American parents and Niagara Falls board members, along with school administrators. In advising board members and school administrators, he strongly recommended that they bring the Niagara Falls community into their dialogue and decision making, nurturing favorable public relations.⁵⁹ He discouraged them from creating policies and then forcing them on the public. He advised them to have open forums in which school representatives could explain potential policies and get the reactions and input of community members, allowing them to feel that they had an impact on policies and that their needs and wants had been respectfully considered. At this point, educational representatives seemed not to adhere wholeheartedly to this advice, which made their complicated job even more difficult.

Superintendent Oliver continued to promote the activities of his office and the Niagara Falls Board of Education, regardless of the barrage of criticism.[60] Perhaps now taking Director Nordos's advice, on October 16, 1968, Oliver sponsored a community forum on the integration at Cleveland Avenue School. In addressing his audience, he first traced the history of school integration in New York State since 1963. He then emphasized that local educational leaders had worked extremely hard to create the integration and that the mandate of Commissioner Allen was being followed. To date, he announced, no child in Niagara Falls had been hurt by integration, a statement that some audience members strongly disagreed with. One mother resented the way the school district's integration program had affected mostly Black Niagarans: "Despite what Mr. Oliver said, my children have been hurt by integration."[61] A Black father remarked that "[his] daughter had been 'tormented' by the way adults—White and Black—had been fighting over the situation."[62] Oliver still maintained that good work was being done. Educational leaders had been working overtime, he asserted. Commissioner Allen knew their timetable, along with their accomplishments, and would approve of the progress being made. Oliver also compared what was being done in Niagara Falls to what was happening in New York, Washington, Detroit, and Buffalo and said that despite Niagara Falls being small, it had accomplished more than these bigger cities had. He called for goodwill and understanding from parents as educational leaders worked for integration.[63] In concluding, Oliver expressed his sincere commitment to school integration, noting that communication regarding school integration may not have been the best, but it had been honest and sincere.[64] "We are not interested in children because they are black, white, red or yellow," exclaimed the superintendent.[65] "We are just interested in children."[66]

Superintendent Oliver's flowery but sincere words did not deter Black Niagarans from following through on their initial threat.[67] On October 16, 1968, they staged another boycott. Parents at Beech Avenue School kept home 50 percent of that school's Black student body. Black Niagarans in front of Beech Avenue School informed bewildered and concerned parents of the boycott. At Niagara Falls High School, South Junior High School, and Gaskill Junior High School between fifty and one hundred disgruntled African American students walked out of their schools. With the students' departure, the Niagara Falls public school system lost state funding and would lose more for each day the students were absent. Black Niagarans reiterated their demands. They wanted Beech Avenue School truly integrated, not a program that isolated White students from the African American student body. They demanded two-way busing, not just the busing of Black Niagarans to acheive integration. They also demanded that the proposed reading center at Beech Avenue School be canceled. They saw it as a ploy to appease White parents who had gifted and talented students at the school. After walking out of school, many of the junior high and senior high students went to Superintendent Oliver's office to register their complaints. They also wanted African American history to be taught at their schools.[68] They did not want it to be incorporated into a general American history course. They wanted a separate course taught by a qualified instructor, preferably an African American.

In response to the boycott, Superintendent Oliver and the board decided to abandon plans to establish a reading center at the Beech Avenue School.[69] Oliver also stated that a supplemental African American history curriculum had been developed for eighth- and eleventh-grade students. Parents, however, repeated their desire for a separate course using a top-rated textbook, taught by qualified teachers and, if possible, by African Americans.[70] After the African American parents ended their three-day boycott, Oliver and board members agreed to integrate Beech Avenue School with two-way busing of Black and White students.[71] Hence, the pressure that Black Niagarans and their leaders exhibited produced results from educational leaders.

By contrast, many White Niagarans vehemently disagreed with the board of education's decision to bus Whites to achieve integration.[72] The board, with the assistance of the Human Rights Commission, scheduled an open forum to allow citizens to be informed of the board's plans, express their views, and offer helpful suggestions. The meeting took place at Hyde Park School's auditorium on October 21, 1968, with about seven hundred Black and White Niagarans attending. Perhaps weary of the constant battles over school integration, Superintendent Oliver had made plans to retire when his contract expired in June 1969. Therefore, the board was also actively searching for a replacement, willing to consider internal and external applicants.[73] Shouts and boos were tossed back and forth between Blacks and Whites until order was restored by the presiding officer, John W. Acosta, executive director of the Human Rights Commission.[74] White parents vigorously stated they would not allow their children to be bused, and they would keep their children home if the board's plan went into effect. They said that they had worked hard and paid high taxes to be in certain neighborhoods so that their children could attend specific neighborhood schools. Conversely, members of the African American community argued that it was not fair that only their children should be the ones making significant adjustments. A White father said he felt people should have the right to send their children to any school they want.[75] Harry Abate replied, "There is only one body in this city which determines what schools children go to and that is the Board of Education."[76] Some parents realized that an impasse had developed between Blacks and Whites, and therefore they encouraged cooperation between the groups. A few parents offered peacemaking solutions. A White mother said busing to achieve integration was the next best thing to open housing.[77] A Black mother suggested busing only older children and letting younger children attend neighborhood schools.[78] A Black father asked for understanding, but he noted that many Whites were teaching their children to hate Blacks.[79] A dialogue ensued, but problems concerning the integration plan and specifically, two-way busing, were far from being solved.

These public forums, in conjunction with Director Nordos's advice, greatly assisted the board of education. The board created an integration committee that initially consisted of twenty-seven independent citizens from the community. New Superintendent of Schools Henry J. Kalfas first charged them to create a plan, using two-way busing, to integrate Beech Avenue School.[80] The board was now proactively incorporating the voice of the community into their decision making, despite the threats of a boycott from the White community.[81] Committee members agreed to meet weekly to draw up a feasible plan by April 1, 1969.[82] They also solicited community members to submit viable integration plans for consideration and quickly received ten proposals. To evaluate the proposals fairly, the committee labeled them by number according to the order in which they were received. The Niagara Falls Federation of Teachers proposal suggested improving the overall quality of Beech Avenue School and permitting only voluntary busing.[83] They reasoned that if it was an exceptional school, parents would sign up in droves to have their children placed there. Helen Schoninger, principal of Beech Avenue School, suggested a detailed plan in which many students would be transferred out of Beech Avenue School, while students would be transferred in from other schools by specific grades.[84] Carol D. Cody, a local citizen, suggested a pupil exchange between two schools involving only grades four through six; kindergarten through third grade students would attend their neighborhood schools.[85] Ralph R. Meranto suggested floating (or changing) boundary lines allowing Black and White students to walk to schools outside their present boundaries.[86] More plans were forthcoming. The Advisory Committee on Integration had much work to do but not much time to accomplish its mission.

In the midst of controversy to bring about true integration at Beech Avenue School, those in favor of integration gained a strong ally—the Niagara Falls Teachers Association.[87] On February 6, 1969, the association embraced total integration of Niagara Falls public schools and urged the Niagara Falls Board of Education to completely integrate schools by the opening of the coming school year, using busing of Black and White students on a limited basis. They also agreed with school critics that students generally received a distorted and unilateral view of American society and history using existing curricula and textbooks.[88] A new pedagogy had to be employed. Literary segregation, they maintained, helped to develop feelings of inferiority in Black children while creating feelings of false superiority in White children.[89] They strongly supported the African American community's argument for the teaching of African American history in schools. Moreover, they stated that more African Americans should be hired as school personnel professionals: teachers, guidance counselors, school administrators, and so on. Association president Gerald McGlynn read the association's statement, with which the board unanimously concurred.

Unity existed between the Niagara Falls Teachers Association and the Niagara Falls Board of Education. This same accord did not exist on the Advisory Committee on Integration. As time progressed, more members joined this committee, and by February 1969, it had forty members. Donald C. Johnson, managing editor of the *Niagara Falls Gazette*, functioned as chairman, while Harwood Bond of the local NAACP branch served as vice president.[90] The members generally seemed to be liberal minded. They agreed with Superintendent Kalfas and the board of education that integration had to be instituted at Beech Avenue School, and later, throughout the district at predominantly White schools. However, disagreement ensued over the issue of compulsory busing. Most members appeared to be in favor of compulsory busing, if needed, to achieve integration (see figure 6.1).

A few members bravely articulated their views against involuntary busing.[91] Mrs. Thomas Pendergast wanted to resign from the committee. She "read a statement in which she said she could not continue to serve on a committee some call 'stacked.'"[92] Pendergast also informed the committee

Figure 6.1. Advisory Committee, 1969. Courtesy of the *Niagara Falls Gazette*.

that she headed the Committee of Parents, a group organized to oppose compulsory busing of White students for integration purposes.[93] Up to a thousand parents, she claimed, supported her group. Several Advisory Committee on Integration members attempted to persuade Pendergast to stay because they felt a range of perspectives was needed in order to develop the best integration policy. When pleaded with to stay, Pendergast commented that she would give it considerable thought.[94]

The Advisory Committee on Integration, with its diverse outlooks, intensively reviewed eighteen proposals before making a recommendation to the board. Members had spent four months meeting weekly and painstakingly examining various proposals. On June 16, 1969, two and a half months after their April 1 deadline, they recommended the Gaskill Sector Integration Plan to the board as the strategy to be employed to integrate Beech Avenue School by September 1, 1969.[95] The Advisory Committee on Integration named its plan "Gaskill" because that was a section of Niagara Falls near Beech Avenue School that was mostly White. Some of the White children could be bused to Beech Avenue School. According to the Gaskill sector proposal, children in kindergarten through grade three would attend the Twenty-Fourth Street, Thirty-Ninth Street, and Hyde Park Schools, and children in grades four through six would attend Beech Avenue and Niagara Street Schools.[96] Rumors circulated that the board intended to approve this plan.

On June 16, 1969, the Advisory Committee on Integration sponsored an open forum at Beech Avenue School to inform interested parties of the details of the Gaskill Sector Integration Plan. About two hundred people attended.[97] Many White parents expressed their disapproval of the plan and said they would not send their children to school under it. They accused the committee of trying to jam the plan down their throats, calling it unfair and detrimental to their children if enforced.[98] Although many in the audience vehemently denounced the plan, the Advisory Committee on Integration still intended to offer it to the board as a solution to the Beech Avenue School integration problem.

Opposing parents encouraged their state legislators to formulate laws to prevent compulsory integration by busing. Months earlier, on February 16, 1969, State Senate Majority Leader Earl W. Brydges, the former Niagara County public defender, had told the Associated Press that state Republicans, who then controlled state government, would pass an antibusing measure.[99] Under Brydges's leadership, Republicans wanted the state constitution amended to forbid the state and all school districts from considering race, color, religion, or national origin in assigning children to schools.[100] The Advisory Committee on Integration voted 18–2 in support of efforts to kill the antibusing bill, which if passed would take administrators years to bring about complete school integration.

With antibusing activities in the State Assembly serving as a backdrop, the Niagara Falls Board of Education held its regularly scheduled meeting on June 19, 1969. Parents thought board members would discuss and vote on the Gaskill Sector Integration Plan, which was referred to as Plan 18. Probably anticipating grave disruption, the board announced before the meeting that the recommended plan would not be covered at that meeting. Nevertheless, parents attended in full force. An overflow crowd of about four hundred parents warned the board that they would boycott schools, withhold taxes, or take a legal fight to Albany to prevent involuntary transfer of students for integration.[101] The Niagara Falls Teachers Association, which had denounced the fact that Niagara Falls students had been only exposed to knowledge from a Eurocentric perspective, disapproved the Gaskill plan. Speaker after speaker informed the board of their disapproval of compulsory busing. Dan Thomas, the author of Plan 18 and an engineer at Carborundum Company, tried in vain to explain Plan 18. He even stressed the morality of the plan and how it would aid Black Niagarans to have Blacks and Whites attend school together, granting all pupils a quality education. Parents shouted him down and stated that he did not even live in Niagara Falls nor have children in the Niagara Falls public school system. Therefore, as far as they were concerned, he had no business speaking. In fact, Thomas had two children, one of whom was slated to enter Ashland Avenue School in the fall.

Harwood Bond accused the Niagara Falls Teachers Association (NFTA) of stirring up trouble. He said the NFTA had mailed letters to parents telling them to come out and oppose Plan 18. Bond made his statement after Rodney S. Rhodes, president of the NFTA, read a statement saying that the NFTA would like to see a modified version of Plan 17 used, rather than Plan 18, which it opposed.[102] The NFTA also supported an earlier plan—Plan 7, which called for voluntary busing.

At an Advisory Committee on Integration meeting on July 11, 1969, Dan Thomas indicated he wanted to revise Plan 18, incorporating suggestions from the board, terming the revisions a "'valid' version of his plan."[103] Critical aspects of the changes included

- making pupil school assignments a grade-per-year move from present school to new school;
- retaining one class each of kindergarten, first, second, and third grades in selected grammar schools for nearby resident children with physical defects; and
- emphasizing in different classes certain needs such as reading, geography, or arithmetic to help pupils weak in these areas.[104]

With these changes, all members of the Advisory Committee on Integration still did not think enough had been done to make Plan 18 acceptable to the broader community. The aggressiveness of parents demonstrated at the last board meeting made some committee members skeptical. Richard L. Covatta, a local citizen, predicted that a boycott would ensue if Plan 18 were implemented in its current state.[105]

The Advisory Committee on Integration had analyzed twenty integration proposals, and a consensus of its members considered Plan 18 the best proposition. By the end of July 1969 the board had not selected a plan for integrating Beech Avenue School. To give themselves more time and perhaps to appease many parents, the board voted to indefinitely postpone the integration of Beech Avenue School specifically and the broader district in general. Two board members voted against postponement: Reverend Ray Hallin, who was the minister of Bacon Memorial Presbyterian Church, and Arthur Ray. They characterized the postponement vote by the board as a delaying tactic. In addition to following his convictions, Reverend Hallin may have been influenced by critics. Casper Jordon, past NAACP local branch president, criticized Reverend Hallin for a statement he made in the *Niagara Falls Gazette* indicating that the school board should not bear all the blame for segregated schools in Niagara Falls. Jordon wrote Hallin that the board is mostly at fault because they had done nothing since Commissioner Allen requested desegregation in 1963.[106] Ray's vote reflected the will of many of his constituents who demanded true integration without the entire burden being placed on the African American community. Board members supporting postponement cited the changing population characteristics of the city, new housing plans that would change individual school attendance totals, and the district plan to build the North End school complex.[107]

To the consternation of some Advisory Committee on Integration members, the Board of Education voted to establish another committee to review integration proposals. This time the committee consisted of fifteen people, five board members to be selected by Board President Joseph Chille, five administrators named by Superintendent Kalfas, and five teachers named by the Niagara Falls Teachers Association.[108] Board President Chille sponsored the motion. He had originally thought it best to have Advisory Committee on Integration members on the new proposal committee, but he changed his mind after speaking with a few of these members.[109] The task of reviewing integration proposals and offering suggestions was removed from the hands of taxpaying citizens—many of them parents—and became the responsibility of "so-called professionals." Reverend Hallin also considered this decision a slap in the face of the Advisory Committee on Integration and its tireless work.[110]

Black Niagarans demonstrated their anger concerning the board's decision to postpone integration indefinitely. About a week after the board voted for postponement, about sixty to seventy-five Black Niagarans met on August 7, 1969, at the Niagara Community Center, to discuss the ramifications of the board's actions. They formed a Black Coalition, composed of the NAACP, members of the city's Human Relations Commission, the New Black Society, the Niagara Coalition, the Niagara Community Center, and the Niagara Community Action Program. Reverend Daniel Porter, assistant pastor at Our Lady of Mount Carmel Roman Catholic Church, was the central spokesperson for the Black Coalition. After the

Black Coalition meeting at the Niagara Community Center, nearly all the participants went to the board meeting later in the day to express their discontent. Father Porter addressed the board, informing them that the African American community had been lied to by the board, who had promised to integrate Beech Avenue School by September 1, 1969. He remarked firmly that the African American community was fed up with games the board had played with integration and that Black Niagarans would have no further part in it. He branded the proposed voluntary busing program for Beech Avenue School "tokenism" and demanded that the board create a desegregated system.[111] Board members sat silent and did not respond to Father Porter's comments. Days later, the Black Coalition requested that the acting state education commissioner, Ewald J. Nyquist, investigate the Niagara Falls Board of Education's action immediately and issue a ruling by September 1.[112]

September 1 came, and the new academic year began. The Niagara Falls Board of Education had not created an effective integration plan and was still under intense pressure. Black and White Niagarans still closely scrutinized all board activities, examining them to ensure that their children did not get shortchanged during the integration process. Some board members and school administrators seemed optimistic that a new voluntary busing program at Beech Avenue School could partially solve the integration crisis and relieve some pressure. Surveys had been sent out, and more than one hundred White parents indicated that they would be willing to voluntarily allow their children to be bused to Beech Avenue School. From survey results and enrollment data, school administrators made projections for the academic year. They estimated that 140 White students would attend Beech Avenue School alongside 345 African American pupils: this meant 71 percent African American students and 29 percent White students.[113] School administrators and board members also made plans to change the student body dynamics of Beech Avenue School. All the gifted and talented students, except for one class, would be sent to Maple Avenue School or Niagara Street School. Class sizes would be approximately twenty-five students per class with a maximum of twenty-eight, and no African American students would be bused to other schools, except for seven students whose parents volunteered them for enrollment elsewhere. Bused White students would not be isolated from the other students, and the lunch hour would be shortened to encourage African American students (who would normally go home for lunch) to stay.[114]

After the first month of school, the integration status of schools throughout the city of Niagara Falls paralleled the previous year's figures. Most schools met or nearly met the Niagara Falls Board of Education's 28 percent rule, except Beech Avenue School and Tenth Street School.[115] African American student enrollment equaled 65 percent at Beech Avenue School and 44 percent at Tenth Street School, which was 37 percent and 16 percent, respectively, above the established rate. North Junior and South Junior High Schools' rates had increased, taking them slightly over the 28 percent mark. Cleveland Avenue School's African American student body also increased, keeping it slightly over the 28 percent mark. The African American student body at Ninety-Ninth Street School decreased from 1968 to 1969, reducing from 19.4 percent to .01 percent. Conversely, LaSalle Senior High, LaSalle Junior High, Ashland Avenue School, Cayuga Drive School, Twenty-Second Street School, Twenty-Fourth Street School, and Seventy-Ninth Street School all had African American student bodies of less than 10 percent, with Seventy-Ninth Street School having the lowest percent for elementary schools at 3.0 percent and LaSalle Senior possessing the lowest rate, 4.1 percent, for high schools. See table 6.1.[116]

By January 1970, the special board committee on integration had made progress in achieving racial balance in the Niagara Falls public school system. Like the Advisory Committee on Integration, they also examined the twenty submitted plans, including Plan 18, which the Advisory Committee supported. They proposed Plan 21, shaped mainly by Principal Helen Schoninger and Paul Brown Jr., an African American teacher coordinator for racial balance.[117] Plan 21 concentrated on the racial imbalance in elementary schools, although it could be applied to high schools as well. This plan proposed establishing a marker on a street in front of an imbalanced school and at the midpoint in that school's property line and then drawing a circle perimeter around that area and the surrounding neighborhood. Thus, an 80:20 ratio of Whites to Blacks was found.[118] Students within the circle perimeter hypothetically could attend the school, and those living on blocks outside the circle were subject to reassignment to another school, which could mean being bused. Plan 21 did not operate in an absolute manner. It incorporated six mandatory provisions:

1. Every attempt will be made to allow children who have already been moved to achieve racial balance (such as those from the former Center Avenue and Thirteenth Street Schools) to remain at their present schools.

Table 6.1. Niagara Falls 1968 and 1969 Black School Enrollment Percentages

	September 1968			September 1969		
School	Enrolled	Black	Pct.	Enrolled	Black	Pct.
NF High	1947	289	14.8	1929	320	16.6
LaSalle Sr.	1675	70	4.1	1768	74	4.2
Trott High	524	73	13.9	506	86	17.0
Gaskill Jr.	1387	183	13.1	1362	200	14.7
LaSalle Jr.	1222	52	4.2	1224	40	3.3
North Jr.	882	244	27.6	896	253	28.2
South Jr.	813	214	26.3	740	210	28.3
Elementary						
Ashland	262	9	3.4	251	15	6.0
Beech Ave.	386	340	83.4	465	302	65.0
Cayuga Dr.	342	31	9.0	342	41	12.0
Cleveland	518	147	28.3	535	153	28.5
Ferry Ave.	419	83	20.5	424	91	21.4
Hyde Park	626	78	12.9	579	69	12.0
Maple Ave.	552	101	19.7	497	87	17.5
Niagara St.	883	224	25.4	786	196	25.0
Pacific Ave.	496	58	12.0	477	72	15.0
5th St.	320	56	16.8	307	52	17.0
10th St.	260	98	37.3	247	109	44.0
17th St.	571	73	12.7	533	69	13.0
22nd St.	265	15	6.7	266	27	10.0
24th St.	393	34	9.4	374	30	8.0
39th St.	456	79	18.4	400	96	24.0
60th St.	466	74	16.3	447	76	17.0
66th St.	553	57	10.3	503	65	13.0
79th St.	628	18	3.0	603	26	4.3
93rd St.	607	73	12.0	603	84	14.0
95th St.	587	95	16.1	553	66	12.0
99th St.	344	64	19.4	247	2	.01

Source: See page 375, note 115.

2. So far as possible, special education classes for the [students with disabilities] will remain at their present schools. Each class will reflect the racial balance of that school (an ability questioned by some committee members).

3. Wherever instituted, lunch and playground programs should be integrated.

4. Racial balance at school openings each September [would be maintained] on the basis of annual enrollment projection (made the previous winter). If any school becomes unbalanced during the school year, correction will be made the following September.

5. All children should have equal time and instruction (gym, swim, library and special services) even though "equal facilities may not be available." The committee has held that length of instruction and type of instruction are more important to a child's learning than facilities.

6. Every attempt will be made to allow children who have been "voluntarily enrolled" at Beech Avenue School to remain at that school.[119]

Provided Plan 21 would be approved by the Niagara Falls Board of Education, new proposal committee members argued that the plan could be operational by September 1970.

On March 12, 1970, the board tentatively approved Plan 21, subject to comments, criticisms, and suggestions from the community.[120] Although President Richard Nixon spoke out against busing, new proposal committee members received inspiration from former New York State Education Commissioner James E. Allen. In a speech presented in Atlantic City with excerpts published in the *Niagara Falls Gazette*, Allen made the case that educators, not the courts or the Justice Department, should be leading the effort to provide equal educational opportunities to all pupils—Black or White.[121] Dr. Morton Sobel of New York State's Bureau of Intercultural Relations discussed Plan 21 with members of the appointed integration committee and school administrators. "The plan is fair and equitable," Sobel said. "It encompasses both Blacks and Whites. It guarantees equal educational opportunity for all. The continuing pattern of the plan means that these city-wide guidelines will be able to be applied when a school becomes racially unbalanced."[122] In addition to Drs. Allen and Sobel's encouragement and praise, Niagaran education planners received national plaudits. The Kerner Commission Report, a study President Lyndon Johnson authorized to explain the cause of urban turmoil after the Detroit Riot of 1967, mentioned that Niagara Falls was one of two school districts in the country working toward achieving integration.[123] New Integration Committee and Niagara Falls Board of Education members felt Plan 21 was their best option to present to Niagarans.

Niagara Falls Conservative Party officials had learned the details of Plan 21 before it was presented to the public. They quickly wrote a well-conceived position paper that vehemently opposed busing for integration of schools in general and to the school board's Plan 21 in particular.[124] Clayton R. Miller, who led their protest and was chairman of the Conservative Party, pointedly stated that they opposed busing solely to obtain racial balance in the city for the specific reasons listed below:

1. The Board of Education should not take a stand on a political and moral issue of such great importance without benefit of a public referendum.

2. The Department of Education at Albany directed the school system to integrate. The New York State Legislature passed and Gov. Rockefeller signed a law banning nonelected school boards from busing for the sole purpose of racial balance. This law, in essence, put the decision strictly at the disposition of locally elected school boards. Since this is the case, the decision of the Board of Education should reflect the will of a majority of the people since they are their elected representatives. The need to bus is not mandatory by law in this city since our schools are not segregated because of race but rather is due to de facto housing [segregation].

3. The President of the United States, in his release of Tuesday, March 1970, specifically endorsed the concept of the neighborhood school and ruled out busing for the sake of racial balance in the classroom.

4. Civil rights laws such as fair housing, equal opportunities, and others, along with local urban renewal relocations, will over a period of time reverse the trend of de facto segregation in our schools.

5. We cannot embrace the opinion of the deputy school superintendent Charles Long to the effect that Plan 21 will have no effect on property values of those homes existing outside of the perimeter of attendance circles. Citizens here have historically selected homes under the concept of neighborhood schools. Homes which now fall outside the attendance circle will not be subject to the neighborhood

concept. As a result, these properties will not command the same value as those within the circle. The mere fact we have de facto segregation in Niagara Falls strongly points to this.[125]

At a meeting on March 26, 1970, Conservative Party members articulated their disapproval of Plan 21, emphasizing that the board of education spent too much time on racial mathematics and not enough on quality education.[126] A Mrs. Barrett characterized the integration plan as a waste of money when so many children throughout the city needed remedial reading help and third and fourth graders at Seventy-Ninth Street School still had not received their social studies textbooks.[127] Moreover, she said that her child would not be able to come home for lunch and interact with the family at midday.[128]

The board of education stuck to its plans regardless of the strong criticisms by the Conservative Party. Beginning on April 22, 1970, it had open forums at the eight racially imbalanced schools to explain Plan 21. Parents generally listened and demonstrated great concern. No overwhelming expressions of disapproval arose at the meetings. Plan 21 had been explained in great detail to board members, school administrators, teachers, and other school staff. Many people affiliated with the Niagara Falls public school system seemed to support Plan 21. Therefore, when board members discussed it at open forums, parents' questions and concerns were addressed by board members, school administrators, teachers, professional school staff members, community activists, and state officials.

For example, the Niagara Falls Board of Education held an open forum at Beech Avenue School on April 22.[129] Led by Superintendent Kalfas, board members explained Plan 21 and its ramifications to about seventy parents.[130] Several teachers expressed strong support for it and were roundly applauded. Some White parents who already had children in Beech Avenue School spoke about the good experiences their children had there. At the end of the forum, school administrators gave parents a tour of the school. Although many Niagara Falls Public School teachers supported Plan 21, the Niagara Falls Teachers' Association, representing 1,038 instructional personnel, did not initially support the plan, taking a wait-and-see attitude.[131]

Many other groups and individuals strongly supported Plan 21, including the local NAACP branch,[132] as well as the YMCA board of directors, the Friendship House, the Human Relations Commission, the

Niagara Community Action Program (NiaCAP), the Religious Fellowship and the Ministerial Association, the Council of Churches, Rabbi Irvin Dick of Temple Beth Israel and Rabbi Alan Ponn of Temple Beth El, Reverend Donald Peck of St. Paul's United Methodist Church, and Reverend Joseph Carlo, assistant pastor of Our Lady of the Rosary Church.[133] Some of these groups and individuals agreed to participate in a nine-member steering committee to undertake an intensive campaign to generate public support for Plan 21.[134]

The Niagara Falls Board of Education tentatively strove to implement Plan 21 by September 1, 1970. With that, Deputy School Superintendent Dr. Charles M. Long informed interested parties that the projected September date could be financially feasible. He noted that at the time it had cost $66,000 to annually transport 861 students to various schools; he and his staff projected it would cost about $49,000 to finance reassignment of 420 additional pupils: $15,000 for additional busing expenses, $20,000 for twenty playground-lunch aides, $12,062 for thirty-seven lunch tables, and $1,730 for five milk refrigerators.[135] A total of 1,281 pupils would be bused for integration purposes.[136] Dr. Long's forecasts also included 127 volunteers to aid in the integration process.

When the controversy first arose in 1967 concerning balancing Niagara Falls's public schools, Mayor E. Dent Lackey was silent at first. As the Niagara Falls board neared the date scheduled to decide on Plan 21, Mayor Lackey was urged at a city council meeting to state his position on the integration plan.[137] He stated that he would express his views not as the mayor but as a private citizen. He reasoned that the council should not interfere with the board's work. He opposed integration through compulsory busing. He favored neighborhood schools and voluntary busing. "In a statement . . . the mayor said he believe[d] in the traditional concept of the community school and added that the schools should not use children to force integration upon the community."[138] "Forced busing for integration," the mayor remarked, "will breed more virulent racism, and in my opinion, is illegal."[139] The mayor saw imbalanced schools as a product of housing and job discrimination. "Open housing for all without racial discrimination must be enforced," he said. "Equality of opportunity for work must be achieved and maintained."[140]

As a highly experienced city administrator, he was aware that what he proposed would take several years, and that Plan 21 was a more viable option for complying with the State of New York's mandate. Therefore, his statements can only be interpreted as politically driven and disingenuous.

The *Niagara Falls Gazette* called Mayor Lackey's statement "odious" and "opportunistic": these harsh words upset the mayor.¹⁴¹ Moreover, at a meeting, Reverend Raybon accused the mayor of bringing politics to its lowest level and charged that under the mayor's administration there had never been an effort to pass an open housing resolution.¹⁴²

In early June 1970, the Niagara Falls Board of Education approved Plan 21. About 270 people attended the meeting when the board voted. Assigned police officers also attended to ensure that no disturbances occurred. Before the vote, thirty-seven people shared their views on Plan 21; twenty spokespersons supporting the plan's general concepts, thirteen opposed it, and four declared no position.¹⁴³ Those in favor of Plan 21 expressed a range of ideas to support their points. Those against the plan either emphasized their opposition to compulsory busing or the cost of busing. When the time came for the board to vote, members voted in alphabetical order. "[A]pproval was stated by L. Paul Bash, James R. Caprio, David K. George, Rev. Ray K. Hallin, J. Bradley Harrison, Arthur B. Ray and Board President Joseph Chille."¹⁴⁴ Mathew V. Buchalski disapproved, and William F. Collins abstained. Commenting on their votes, Bash expressed his hope that Niagara Falls as a school system and community could promote racial harmony; Caprio stated that he approved the precepts of the plan with the assurance that further refinement would be made to see that reasonable recognition of isolated pupils was considered; George proposed that the Special Board Committee on Integration meet in August to make sure the intent of the plan would be implemented; Reverend Hallin regretted that the decision was needed; Harrison noted the great strength of the plan and its flexibility; Ray said he was proud to see his colleagues meet their responsibility; Chille remarked that he was convinced of the benefits of school integration and felt that busing was safer than walking as a means of pupil transportation; Buchalski, who supported the construction of a downtown school complex as a solution, read from a prepared statement that recalled his dissent in a 6–2 approval of a previous board policy on school integration in October 1967; Collins, in abstaining, was requesting that the board temporarily delay its vote until it could determine from the Niagara Falls Housing Authority when and what effect Griffon Manor housing project would have.¹⁴⁵ Overall, the board voted as follows: seven for Plan 21, one against, and one abstention. Plan 21 became the operative integration plan of the Niagara Falls Board of Education. Superintendent Henry Kalfas pledged to do all in his power to ensure that all Niagaran children regardless of race, class, creed, place of residence, and socioeconomic background received an equal quality public education in the city of Niagara Falls.[146]

Plan 21 went into effect on September 9, 1970, when schools opened.[147] Niagara Falls public school teachers did not show up on the first day of school. They went on strike to demonstrate their disapproval of Plan 21 and compulsory busing. Although the Niagara Falls Teachers Association had representation on the New Integration Proposal Committee, they still orchestrated the teachers' strike. On the first day of school, children waited at designated areas to be transported to schools. Bus drivers refused to cross the picket lines, and hundreds of elementary school children were stranded at bus stops.[148] School Superintendent Kalfas went on the radio as soon as he learned of the strike and advised parents either to keep their children home or to take them to school themselves.[149] He and Chille were served a show-cause order designed to stop implementation of Plan 21. This measure, which sought a temporary injunction, was signed by State Supreme Court Justice John H. Doerr.[150] Nearly 302 substitute teachers covered for the striking teachers, who were supported by the Committee for Neighborhood Schools (CFNS).

The parents of two children, who attended Ninety-Fifth Street School but were assigned to Beech Avenue School, Mr. and Mrs. Michael Udut Jr. sought a bid for an injunction against Plan 21. The CFNS asked the Uduts to file the action.[151] The Niagara Falls Teachers Association also strongly supported the Uduts' bid for an injunction against Plan 21. After hearing arguments from both sides, Supreme Court Justice Michael Catalano of Buffalo dismissed the case.[152] The teachers who had been on strike for four days had their pay docked. "Approximately $135,000 was deducted from salary checks of 737 Niagara Falls school district teachers . . . for being absent from duty during the September 8 through 13 teacher strike."[153] Moreover, striking teachers faced postponement of tenure by one year for probationary teachers and a one-year probationary period for tenured teachers, as well as the right of the State Public Employment Relations Board to end the dues deduction status of the Niagara Falls Teachers Association.[154] The CFNS filed a notice of appeal.[155] Regardless of the views of many parents, the Niagara Falls Teachers Association, and the CFNS, Plan 21 would not be overturned. The courts ruled it constitutional.

Many White Niagarans resisted desegregation, particularly those in the LaSalle sections of the city.[156] But board members remained committed to its implementation. Both racial groups now experienced busing. Black

Niagarans saw White students being bused into schools or out of city sections to obtain racial balance. One-way busing of only African American students no longer existed. Bused students seemed not to mind being bused; they accepted busing as routine. Bused students, neighborhood students who walked to school, teachers, and administrators all had to adjust to each other and to new arrangements. The busing process, although not perfect, was successful, as reflected in comments Niagarans made three years after Plan 21's enforcement:

1. White families who have had children bused into Black neighborhoods say that most of their early fears proved unfounded. While many would prefer the old neighborhood school concept, they acknowledge that busing has in no way harmed their children.

2. White families whose children have not been bused into black neighborhoods repeat many of the same fears voiced in 1970 and insist they would fight every effort to include their children among those bused.

3. Black families report general acceptance in the White communities into which their children have been bused, at the same time registering some complaints that teachers have not always treated Black students equally.

4. School personnel state that the implementation of the busing program has gone even smoother than they had optimistically hoped.

5. Teachers admit their profession is not free from the biases of the overall society but stress that attitudes and acceptance of busing for integration are definitely improving with experience.

6. Reaction to the possible extension of Plan 21 integration into the secondary schools is mixed. All but two schools—LaSalle Junior and Senior High school—already meet state requirements.

7. Both Black and White families agree that the ideal path to an integrated school system is open housing.[157]

The McConnaughey family is a case study of a White family who benefited from Plan 21. Dawn McConnaughey, the daughter of Charles and Garnet McConnaughey, originally attended the Seventy-Ninth Street School; however, due to Plan 21, she was reassigned to Beech Avenue School. Her parents vigorously protested this decision and attended several board of education meetings to register their complaints. Dawn's parents had heard the stereotypes about African American children, such as they are intellectually inferior and that being educated with them would reduce the quality of education that their daughter would receive. According to the stereotypes, Blacks are violent, often fighting among themselves, involved in gangs, inclined to carry knives (especially to school), and known for being bullies, particularly toward White children. These perceptions made Dawn's parents unhappy about her attending Beech Avenue School. Her parents frequently visited the school to observe its operations and to speak with Principal Helen Schoninger, who allayed their fears. Dawn, who had not had much contact with Black Niagarans, rode the school bus daily and did not encounter any racial problems. She grew to love Beech Avenue School. Academically, she performed extremely well, making her parents acknowledge that they had been wrong about many of their earlier perceptions. Regardless of the success, Mr. McConnaughey still felt that he and his wife, as parents, should have the right to decide whether or not their child should be bused.[158] In three years, the only problem Dawn encountered was with a White girl on the school bus who tried to tell Dawn which students she should be friends with, a matter Principal Schoninger promptly resolved in her office.

Plan 21 surpassed the hopes of most backers. It even made a believer out of a board member who at first voted against the plan.[159] Mathew Buchalski said that he would oppose rescinding Plan 21. In 1970 he voted against Plan 21 because he thought that predictably changing housing patterns in the LaSalle and North End areas warranted a delay until new enrollment breakdowns could be determined. The LaSalle housing did not cause the mass movement and disruption he envisioned. On August 27, 1973, Buchalski demonstrated his new support for Plan 21: "I have not heard of serious problems—nothing as great as I expected—and things are going well."[160] By 1973 Plan 21 had generated racial change, as demonstrated by table 6.2.

This table shows that all of Niagara Falls's public elementary schools in 1973 met the board of education's racially balanced criteria, which were

Public School Desegregation | 233

Table 6.2. 1973 Racial Breakdown of Niagara Falls Elementary Schools

School	Black Percentage
Beech Avenue	27
Cayuga Drive	12
Cleveland Avenue	29
Harry F. Abate	25
Ferry Avenue	18
Hyde Park	12
Maple Avenue	13
Niagara Street	22
60th Street	17
24th Street	16
39th Street	22
66th Street	13
79th Street	19
93rd Street	17
95th Street	10
99th Street	29

Source: See page 377, note 161.

determined by calculating the African American citywide student enrollment percentage for all schools (elementary, junior high, and secondary) and adding ten points to that figure (see figure 6.2).[161]

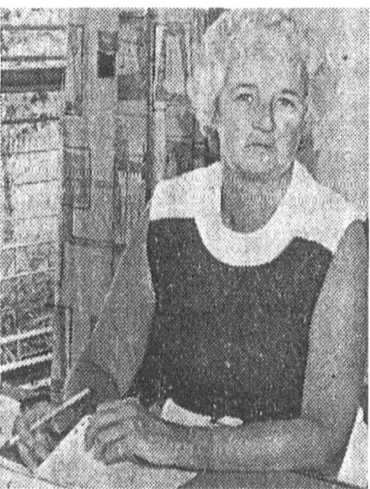

Figure 6.2. Mrs. Helen Schoninger, 1970. Courtesy of the *Niagara Falls Gazette*.

For Niagara Falls public schools for 1973, that figure was 19.6 percent. Adding ten points to 19.6 percent yields a 29 percent rule. Analyzing the racial breakdown table further, Beech Avenue School's African American student enrollment had decreased from 65 percent in 1969 to 27 percent. Beech Avenue School, Cleveland Avenue School, Harry F. Abate School, Niagara Street School, Thirty-Ninth Street School, and Ninety-Ninth Street School all had African American enrollment above 20 percent. The mean African American enrollment of all the elementary schools was 18.8 percent.[162] The above data clearly convey that Plan 21 had been effective in integrating elementary schools in the city of Niagara Falls, although secondary schools remained racially imbalanced.

Principal Helen Schoninger, an alliance leader, demonstrated excellent leadership in creating and implementing Plan 21. In addition to being principal of Beech Avenue School, she served on numerous committees related to creating and operating Plan 21. She managed Beech Avenue School amid its transition from a racially imbalanced school to a racially balanced one. She kept order when parents of both racial groups expressed their disapproval of how the board managed the integration process. She ensured that Beech Avenue School maintained high academic standards and that all students behaved appropriately. Several parents testified that their fears were relieved after speaking with Principal Schoninger.[163]

Black Niagarans observed aspects of the integration process that they considered unfair; yet they did not bemoan these issues. The Niagara Falls Board of Education required significantly more Black Niagarans to be bused compared to White Niagarans.[164] About one in three Black Niagarans participated in busing compared to about one in every thirty White Niagarans.[165] "The nature of any integration program shows that it is the minority group which bears the heavier load," school superintendent Henry Kalfas said.[166] Black Niagarans accepted this idea and were pleased that some White Niagarans had to be bused.[167] They also had faced standardized tests with a bias toward White middle-class students. Some White teachers either resented having African American students in their classes or were insensitive to their needs. Teachers often did not involve themselves with the African American community beyond school hours. Many Black Niagarans called for better preparation of teachers for work with African American students or familiarity with African American environments.[168] Black Niagarans observed problems but truly felt they would be rectified in the near future.

With Plan 21 operative Black Niagarans complained about the limited number of their racial group employed within the Niagara Falls public school system. They argued that the presence of more African American school professionals would make Plan 21 even more effective. The local NAACP branch, shepherded by Harwood Bond, argued that professional employees within the Niagara Falls public school system should reflect the ratio of Black to White students. They stated that Black Niagaran students in 1973 composed 17.9 percent of the student population but had less than 4 percent African American faculty and no African American administrators.[169] The Niagara Falls Board of Education applied for $2.6 million from the US Office of Education, under the Emergency School Assistance Act (ESAA) of the Department of Health, Education and Welfare. Federal governmental officials designed ESAA funding to give minority group youngsters in schools help in four areas: mathematics, language arts, human relations, and career education.[170] The local NAACP branch wanted more African American professionals hired by the Niagara Falls public school system with some of the requested funds. Niagara Falls was eligible for part of $17 million allocated for New York State communities that had desegregated their public education system.[171] The local NAACP branch wanted ten minority administrators hired at a cost of $164,030.[172] Moreover, the local NAACP branch pledged to fight to prevent any federal funds from being granted to the Niagara Falls Board of Education because a local advisory community had not been allowed to review the board's application as mandated by the federal government. The local NAACP branch wanted budget lines for the ten minority administrators included in the board's proposal. The board claimed that the NAACP's request would be an amendment but would not be sent to federal officials at the same time as the overall proposal.[173] It would be sent later. At a Beech Avenue School two-week teacher training workshop, Bloncva Bond, who by then had replaced her husband as head of the NAACP local branch, stated that part of the problem for Black parents and their children was the absence of any recognition at the top level of the school district.[174] "There are 1,000 teachers and only 33 are black," Bond remarked, noting that all principals were White and that there were no Black assistant principals, guidance counselors, or any activity ongoing to correct the situation.[175] Bond suggested that rather than make pawns of children for desegregation board of education members should intensely discuss this issue and correct it.[176]

Protest by the local NAACP branch attained results. In 1973 the Niagara Falls Board of Education hired its first African American administrator, Lillie P. Stephens, formerly a physical education teacher for the Niagara Falls public school system since 1957. Funding for Stephens's post came from the Emergency School Aid Act (ESAA) that the board of education had received. By December 1974, the board had ramped up its hiring of African American teachers. From 1973 to 1974 the number of African American teachers had increased from 3.3 percent of the teaching force to 5.1 percent (going from thirty-three to fifty-one African American teachers) with most teaching in elementary schools.[177] This was far short of the 17.9 percent demanded by the local NAACP branch, but it was an increase. The local NAACP branch, under the leadership of Bloneva Bond, required further changes. They argued that the school setting should truly reflect society, providing role models not only for White students but also for other racial groups as well. These goals would be achieved at a later date.

Along with the increase in the African American teaching force, in 1974 Black Niagarans lost their consistent voice on the Niagara Falls Board of Education. Arthur B. Ray did not win his reelection bid. Fourteen candidates ran for three seats. During this election, Ray was not the only African American to run: John Q. Stephens also ran. The election deposed Ray, who finished fourth in the balloting with 1,489 votes. James Caprio, Bo Erias, and Carmen Morreale were voted into office.[178] Stephens finished fifth, with 1,380 votes.[179] Many Niagarans attributed Ray's loss to a low percentage of African Americans coming out to vote. About 18 percent of the registered voters appeared at the polls.[180] Some analysts indicated that two African American candidates on the ballot split the African American vote. The LaSalle section of Niagara Falls, which had been strongly against busing, supported newcomer Stephens. The Niagara Falls Teachers Association also supported Stephens over Ray:[181] "Despite declarations of support for [Stephens], there [was] some sentiment that the ulterior motives of some in the White community who supported the challenger were to split the Black vote and reduce the number of Black school board members to zero."[182] Ray had been on the board for ten years.[183] His presence would be sorely missed because he had a way of making all his constituents—both Black and White—feel comfortable approaching him about issues or informing them of events occurring with the board of education. He was a people person, very accessible, extremely intelligent, and articulate. For his service over the years, the Niagara Falls Board of Education honored Ray with a Citizen Service Award.[184]

Under Arthur Ray's leadership, the Niagara Falls Board of Education developed and implemented an integration plan relatively quickly compared to its neighboring city of Buffalo. Several factors explain why. In 1970, the year Plan 21 went into effect, Buffalo was a much larger city than Niagara Falls. Buffalo's population was 462,768, compared to Niagara Falls's 85,615.[185] Both cities had earlier peaked in population growth and were on the decline. Buffalo then had principally 98,401 African Americans, whereas Niagara Falls had 8,001.[186] Buffalo's integration process involved more people and was much more complex operationally than that of the city of Niagara Falls.

Leaders in Niagara Falls, unlike those in the Buffalo, understood and more readily accepted New York State Commissioner of Education James Allen's mandate to desegregate all public schools in the State of New York. Commissioner Allen had defined a school as imbalanced if it had a minority enrollment greater than 50 percent. He informed all local boards of education to report to his office which of their schools had minority enrollment greater than 50 percent.[187] He also required a plan to correct the imbalance. This met the 1960 board of regent's policy statement urging the desegregation of the public schools of the state.[188] No Niagara Falls board member challenged Commissioner Allen's directive. No court order had to compel them to do what was inevitable. Willingly or unwillingly, they acted. In a speech on the Senate floor, Republican Senator Jacob K. Javits glowingly spoke of how Niagarans achieved integration successfully without violence.[189]

The Buffalo Board of Education developed a few plans to desegregate schools that were unacceptable to the new education commissioner. One plan called for the hiring of a commissioner of integration, the development of middle schools that would be integrated, and no forced busing of White students.[190] Finally, in January 1972, Commissioner Ewald Nyquist ordered the Buffalo Board of Education to create an acceptable desegregation plan by April 1, 1972.[191] In turn, the board voted 4–3 to inform Commissioner Nyquist that they were unable to create a plan.[192]

Niagara Falls board members seemed to be greatly concerned about losing state funds by not following the mandates of Commissioners Allen and Nyquist compared to Buffalo's board, regardless of the pressure they faced from local citizens. Niagara Falls board members generally acknowledged the state education commissioner's power over them. Buffalo's board prior to 1974 did not always exhibit such behavior.[193] The fact that they did not create an integration proposal despite two requests from the education commissioner verifies this.

All nine Niagara Falls board members who voted on Plan 21 embraced the idea of integration. Everyone agreed that the Niagara Falls public schools should be integrated and that integration was the law. They supported the idea that public education should be a multiracial experience, but they differed as to how integration should be achieved. Listening to their constituents, several hoped for an alternative to compulsory busing. However, busing was an inevitable solution because open housing did not exist in Niagara Falls or Buffalo to achieve integration with neighborhood populations, which would have supported the neighborhood school concept. Beginning in 1962, the Buffalo Board of Education had a strong opponent of desegregation and busing: Alfreda Slominski, who fulfilled a five-year appointment.[194] After this appointment, she ran for an at-large seat on the common council and won. She also ran for mayor of Buffalo in 1969 but lost. While on the council, she vehemently supported neighborhood schools and denounced forced busing. She even led a fight to prevent construction of portables, the trailerlike buildings built to further enhance the ability of schools to accommodate more students.[195] Portables were needed to accommodate African American students who had agreed to participate in a voluntary busing program to foster integration. Among their members, the Niagara Falls Board of Education had no one to spearhead a movement against desegregation and busing.

During the school integration years, Niagara Falls had an elected board of education. They operated independently of the city council and other city units, such as the Housing Authority. They treasured their independence. Therefore, city council members may not have supported the decisions of the Niagara Falls Board of Education, but technically they could not alter the board's decision. Before 1974, Buffalo Board of Education members were appointed by the mayor and confirmed by the city council; they had no sense of autonomy. Work of the Buffalo Board of Education could be abated by the council's refusal to fund a particular activity. The council did not approve of the portable school option. Alfreda Slominski supported a charter change within Buffalo that required board members to be elected; an elected board would reflect the views of the majority of Buffalonians, who were White and predictably favored neighborhood schools while opposing desegregation and compulsory busing. In 1974, under the charter, the seven-member appointed board was replaced by a nine-member elected board.[196] Contrary to projections, after this the city of Buffalo, led by African American board president Florence Baugh, made significant strides toward integrating Buffalo's public schools.[197]

Civil rights organizations in Niagara Falls and Buffalo put constant pressure on their boards of education. In 1964 the Congress of Racial Equality (CORE) submitted a detailed report to the Niagara Falls Board of Education underscoring several needed improvements involving raising the quality of education, renovating the physical condition of old buildings, ending discrimination in schools, replacing inadequate curriculum materials, and banning brutal methods of disciplining youngsters.[198] CORE not only highlighted problems but also recommended solutions. A specific measure that CORE recommended emphasized training teachers to understand and effectively operate in classrooms composed predominantly of African American students. They also encouraged the board to develop and implement a plan to end racially imbalanced schools in the city. The Niagara Falls NAACP local branch constantly confronted the Niagara Falls Board of Education to ensure that they adhered to Commissioner Allen's 1963 mandate. If it seemed the board was not moving progressively enough or created plans that appeared unfair, the local NAACP branch informed the board that they would complain to state officials in Albany. The Buffalo NAACP local branch behaved similarly. The branch, along with other citizens, began the process of pushing the Buffalo Board of Education to begin creating a desegregation plan.[199] The Buffalo board did not act upon their request. They, in turn, appealed to Commissioner Allen to compel the Buffalo board to desegregate Buffalo schools. He concurred and ordered the Buffalo Board of Education to adopt a policy to racially balance the public schools.[200] The Niagara Falls Board of Education initially and consistently responded to civil rights groups, although sometimes reluctantly.

With Buffalo being a much larger city than Niagara Falls, the separation of Black and White racial groups operated more rigidly, although racial separation existed in both cities. In Niagara Falls, Black Niagarans mainly lived in the North End or the East Falls Street section, largely but not exclusively living in clusters or enclaves. Black Buffalonians predominantly resided on the East Side, also in clusters or enclaves. Few interactions occurred between Buffalo's African American community and other ethnic communities, especially in sections of south Buffalo, where Irish Americans lived. This pattern also existed in the early twentieth century, when Black Buffalonians resided around Michigan Avenue and William Street.[201] Although in Niagara Falls, Blacks and Whites generally resided in separate communities, especially after the Second Great Migration, community borders between White and Black communities were often fluid. Blacks and Whites moved within and between the border areas, interacting with one another and sharing each other's culture. Roosevelt Bradberry, for example, remembered that Black and White youths did not have many places to go to have fun.[202] He stressed that public outings often involved Blacks and Whites appreciating one another's company.[203] Hence, in Buffalo, racial exclusion may have operated rigidly, but racial and cultural boundaries were more porous in Cataract City; this phenomenon contributed more to resistance to desegregation and compulsory busing in Buffalo than in Niagara Falls.

The leadership of Arthur B. Ray is a final crucial factor that contributed toward Niagara Falls schools desegregating sooner than Buffalo's. His tenure on the Niagara Falls board began soon after Commissioner Allen issued his decree. Most Black Niagaran adults either knew Ray or knew of him. He was someone they looked up to with pride.[204] He was proactive at board meetings and kept himself and his constituents apprised of important issues. African American community leaders such as Fred Brown, Harwood and Bloneva Bond, Charles and Alice Hayes, Casper Jordon, Eddie Palmore, Joe Profit, Father Daniel Porter, Reverend Glen Raybon, and others consulted Ray for his knowledge and insight.[205] With Ray present, the Niagara Falls board had to operate fairly and judiciously (see figure 6.3).

Figure 6.3. Arthur B. Ray, 1970. Courtesy of the *Niagara Falls Gazette*.

Buffalo's situation was different. Until 1974, when the Buffalo City charter had been changed to require board of education members to be elected, no African American presence existed. Black Buffalonians had no voice on the board. They were not privy to what had taken place behind closed doors. That changed when three African Americans (one man and two women) were unexpectedly elected to the board in 1974.[206] Florence Baugh had run as an at-large candidate and received a plurality of White votes and the endorsement of some of the Lutheran church leaders in south Buffalo.[207] She was extremely bright, articulate, and affable; she epitomized the Politics of Respectability and was forceful when she needed to be. Ms. Baugh became president of the Buffalo Board of Education. Her presence greatly aided the public school integration process within the city of Buffalo.

School desegregation in Niagara Falls, as in Buffalo and other towns and cities, occurred because of the US Supreme Court's ruling in the *Brown v. Board of Education* case. This law stated that separate public educational facilities were inherently unequal. It also contributed toward outlawing de jure segregation in the South and de facto segregation in the North. After the Supreme Court issued this decree, it would be several years in many locales before the law would be enforced. Nine years after the Supreme Court's momentous decision, the New York State Commissioner of Education mandated that imbalanced schools within the state should be desegregated. Even with this law on the books, the Niagara Falls Board of Education did not move speedily toward adhering to the commissioner's order. They had to be pushed, threatened, and constantly watched to ensure that they were following the law. Embracing a collectivist approach, Black Niagaran leaders and organizations served as a unified catalyst to move the board members faster than they would have progressed on their own. The Niagara Falls Board of Education first proposed the closing of schools with predominantly African American student bodies. Then they planned and implemented one-way busing of African American students to predominantly White schools to rid the city of racial imbalance in education. They may not have been aware of the unfairness of one-way busing, but Black Niagarans, guided by their leaders, wasted little time in informing them of the injustice. They then incorporated two-way busing—and to the extreme disapproval of many in the White community. As much as they may have wanted to slow the process to curb relentless criticism, Black Niagarans, in conjunction with the state mandate, compelled the board to develop a fair integration program that would end racially imbalanced public schools in Niagara Falls. A few years after the implementation of Plan 21, several board members spoke positively about the plan and its results, including the sole board member who had voted against it. Had Black Niagarans not undertaken a progressive role, change would have been skewed and community development hindered. Frederick Douglass once said, "Power concedes nothing without demand. It never did and it never will."[208] This idea most certainly applied to public school desegregation in Cataract City.

Chapter Seven

Urban Renewal, 1960 to 1985

*External Change Agents Juxtaposed
with Internal Change Agents*

From 1958 to 1981 urban renewal actions were occurring within the city of Niagara Falls, beginning at a planning stage and ending with an implementation phase. These plans and activities would impact the entire city in some form, but the Black Niagaran community would be affected the most. Once more, Black Niagaran leaders would proactively strive to represent their group's interest by directing their energies toward continuously sustaining and advancing their community's development. Housing discrimination would be one of the crucial issues that continued to plague Black Niagarans. Yet, they would unceasingly fight to overcome this impediment. Conversely, during the urban renewal era, Black Niagarans gaining political power would be one of their greatest accomplishments.

In examining how Niagara Falls's urban renewal policies and procedures impacted the Black Niagaran community, external change agents are interconnected with internal change agents. The urban renewal plans and practices of federal, state, and (principally) local government officials served as external change agents that impacted the broader community but especially the Black Niagaran community. How Black Niagarans operated in their community on a day-to-day basis in conjunction with how they proactively responded to urban renewal mandates made them important agents of internal change. Assuredly, the city of Niagara Falls's urban renewal project, like those of other municipalities, overwhelmingly impacted the Black Niagaran community.[1]

In the early 1960s, during the civil rights movement years but before public school desegregation, Niagara Falls's municipal leaders began intense discussions on how to revitalize their city economically.[2] Like many US cities, Niagara Falls expanded economically during and after World War II.[3] African Americans continued to arrive, as did immigrants from abroad. Jobs paying livable wages were plentiful. According to community lore an employee could leave one factory job and find another relatively quickly.[4] The city's population increased, and many residents clustered in areas where their ethnic group predominated. However, from the 1960s and beyond, Niagara Falls experienced industrial decline, which led to jobs lost and a steady reduction in population.

City leaders attributed the economic decline to the catastrophe that befell the city in 1956: Schoellkopf Power Station flooded and then collapsed. Parts of the station fell into the Niagara Gorge and sank into the Niagara River.[5] This plant had generated cheap hydroelectrical power for the city of Niagara Falls and other areas in Niagara County. At the time, Niagara Mohawk Power Corporation owned the plant. Several local businesses could not operate due to the sudden loss of electrical power. To accommodate its patrons, Niagara Mohawk Power Corporation diverted electrical power from some of its other electrical facilities. This catastrophe convinced federal, state, and local officials that another means of generating electrical power had to be created, preferably a publicly controlled facility. Accordingly, in 1957, the Federal Power Commission gave a fifty-year license to the New York State Power Authority to build and operate the Robert Moses Niagara Power Project.[6]

Construction of the Robert Moses Niagara Power Project initially buoyed the adverse effects that the end of the Schoellkopf Power Station had on the local economy. From 1957 to 1964 Robert Moses Niagara Power Project officials hired thousands of temporary laborers to complete construction of their plant, hiring over nine thousand workers in 1958 and two hundred in 1964.[7] Laborers in Niagara County and beyond gained employment at the plant. However, at the completion of this project, the Niagara Falls economy again began to decline. Many firms that had been obtaining cheap and efficient hydroelectrical power from Schoellkopf complained about the new rates they had to pay in order to continue operating their facilities in western New York. Several company officials threatened to relocate elsewhere if drastic changes were not made. Some firms ultimately left. Vanadium, Union Carbide and Carbon Corporation, Hooker Chemical Corporation, International Paper Company, Aluminum Company of America, E. I. DuPont de Nemours and Company, and Bell

Aerospace Company left or ceased operations, driving up the unemployment rate and diminishing Niagara Falls's tax base.[8]

Economic decline placed Niagara Falls in a precarious position. To progress, city planners knew that creative strategies were needed to guide their city. Some realized that they needed to work harder with local industry leaders to convince them to stay in the area. Seeking solutions, city leaders observed and examined activities that other municipalities had undertaken. Many municipalities had successfully gained federal funds for "urban renewal projects," which was part of a governmental program created to revitalize urban areas and eliminate blight or to clear slums.[9]

In 1958 the city of Niagara Falls initiated an urban renewal program with the federal government, initially focusing on "slum clearance" and restoration.[10] Many Niagara Falls leaders strongly supported the concept of urban renewal and strove to implement it throughout their city, impacting all residents. E. Dent Lackey, for example, true to the zeitgeist, aggressively responded by running as the Democrat candidate for mayor. Lackey, an ex-Methodist minister and a former public relations manager for the Carborundum Company, articulated that he held a vision to guide Niagara Falls back to prosperity and to make it a world-class city on par with its natural gifts—the cataracts of great Niagara. Lackey's message convinced voters, as he won the 1963 election. In short, Lackey would strive to revitalize not only "industry" but "tourism" as well: this was his double-edged sword to help Niagara Falls progress into the twenty-first century.

Time and experience, however, made city officials such as Mayor Lackey cognizant of opposition to urban renewal. For instance, some argued that government-funded urban renewal programs were socialist, contrary to the natural law of economics, unduly expensive, and prone to skyrocketing costs, which could encourage graft. Other critics cited the demolition of functional buildings as needless, and a failure to prevent blight, clearing one slum only to relocate it to another section of the city.[11] These criticisms impacted the activities of city planners.

External Change Agents: Urban Renewal Plans and Implementation, Additional Housing, and Community Responses

Through research and planning, Niagara Falls city officials first negotiated with the federal government about removing major slums from the city and redeveloping the land.[12] Their slum clearance proposal had the most significant impact on Black Niagarans, adversely affecting community development by directly or indirectly relocating Black Niagarans from one segregated black enclave to another. African Americans were made to suffer at the whims of city officials, and the main economic thoroughfare of the Black Niagaran community was demolished. [13]

The Allen-MacKenna neighborhood served as their top priority for slum clearance. It was home to many African Americans, some of whom had lived there for generations. The Allen-MacKenna neighborhood was a poverty-stricken community. James Banks, who knew the neighborhood well, described it as such:

> The Twenty-Fourth Street-Allen-Mackenna Avenues Area has a large junk yard as one of its attractions, but when one visits the area and even casually observes it, he sees the entire area as one great "junk" yard. Untidy piles of old bricks and old lumber, scattered pieces of worn out furniture and household equipment, old and broken down automobiles, parked in front of houses, dirty streets littered with paper and unpainted and dilapidated houses are a "sore spot to the eye." With the exception of the East Fall Area all of these areas are in the midst of industrial plants and the front grounds of many of the homes on Allen Avenue of the Twenty-Fourth Street-Allen-MacKenna Avenues serve as parking space for two large chemical plants in the area.[14]

By 1961 Niagara Falls city officials had finalized negotiations with the federal government to begin the first of three urban renewal projects, which they named the "Allen MacKenna Avenue project." Through the use of eminent domain, city officials took possession of private properties from the twenty-second block of Allen Avenue to the twenty-seventh block.[15] All of the houses and most of the buildings, except for an apartment building and a small factory, would be torn down.[16] Spot clearances on MacKenna Avenue, which paralleled Allen Avenue, were scheduled to take place, with the intent of demolishing businesses in addition to the homes.[17] Former property owners would be compensated fairly with federal funds and assisted in moving to other neighborhoods. Families who rented would also be aided in their relocation to other sections of Niagara Falls. Unfortunately, government representatives offered no financial assistance to single renters. Men were the largest single renter group.[18] Federal, state, and city government officials reasoned that these "transient individuals," as characterized in the main local paper, could fend for themselves.[19] City officials informed private property owners and relocated residents that their land was being expropriated for the improvement of the city. They intended to redevelop the area and sell plots for light industrial use. The federal government agreed to pay most of the expenses, provided that the city of Niagara Falls paid a portion. In response, the Niagara Falls City Council unanimously passed a resolution authorizing the sale of $200,578 worth of serial bonds for financing the city's share of the $1,381,770 Allen MacKenna Avenue project.[20]

With the civil rights movement proceeding in conjunction with urban renewal projects throughout the country, the New York State government reacted to the critiques of urban renewal.[21] They created policies stipulating that municipalities receiving public funding cannot clear a slum area only to relocate citizens to another slum area or another area on the verge of disintegrating into a slum. For the most part, the city of Niagara Falls tried to adhere to this policy; however, ultimately urban renewal officials, due to unwritten discriminatory housing polices, helped to relocate Black Niagarans mainly to segregated Black enclaves.[22] William Bradberry noted that he first became mindful of this as a child:

> When the City Fathers finally decided to designate the area for "slum clearance," our house and all the others on Allen Avenue were purchased by the Urban Renewal Agency and demolished. Most of the former residents wound up in public housing, but some, like my family, just moved one block over to Mackenna Avenue. A few families bought houses around Highland, some moved over to the East Falls Street and Erie Avenue area, and that is what has been bothering me ever since. Everybody was forced to move into certain areas while other, nicer neighborhoods remained "off-limits" to our people.
>
> I could not then, as a little boy, understand why we did not move to the nicer neighborhoods just a few blocks north of us, like Welch Avenue, for example, where I went to school at Our Lady of the Rosary.
>
> The houses were so much nicer there, I remember. They had been built solidly of fine bricks and mortar. Their lawns actually had grass and big trees in front of them.
>
> Why didn't we move there, I wondered. It could not have been because we were poorer than the people who lived there. They all worked at the same plants, doing the same thing my

father was doing, presumably for the same wages. So why couldn't we live there?

My mom's answer was short. "There aren't any 'coloreds' there because it's a white street," she said. "You'll understand when you grow up, son." My dad just nodded in agreement and that was the end of that conversation. But it was just the beginning of my understanding of racism and the segregated life we lived.[23]

Of course it could be argued that Black Niagarans selected the homes they moved to or that city segregation patterns should not be blamed on urban renewal officials, which is true.[24] Nonetheless, during the period of urban renewal, as conveyed in Tables 4.4 and 4.5, and supported by the findings of sociologists Douglass S. Massey and Nancy A. Denton, Black Niagarans generally could live only in specific sections of Niagara Falls, which through overcrowding and neglect by absentee landlords, city officials, and inattentive residents, often turned into slum areas.[25]

Although many considered the Allen-MacKenna Avenue area an eyesore, residents had mixed feelings about being forced to move. Some renters were delighted to be moving out of a poor area. Homeowners were the most disappointed; although many perceived their neighborhood as unattractive, they still considered it home. Some houses had been passed down from an older family member to a younger one. One woman said her brick house had been in the family since 1905.[26] Residents usually felt strong ties to their neighborhood and were accustomed to knowing the people there. They also often lived near their jobs, as nearby Buffalo Avenue was the site of several industrial plants (e.g., Carborundum Company, Edward Dean Adams Power Plant, Shredded Wheat Factory, etc.). Therefore, although urban renewal representatives, city councilmen, and James Banks saw the Allen-MacKenna neighborhood as a slum that was ripe for clearance, homeowners did not wholeheartedly embrace the idea.[27]

Niagara Falls Housing Authority representatives sent information to prospective displaced Allen-Mackenna Avenue residents about the new Jordan Garden housing project, which was adjacent to Center Court.[28] Harry S. Jordan, for whom the complex was named, had formerly been president of the Niagara Falls Housing Authority. Largely in response to the Moonglow Hotel tragedy, city officials had this project complex built to make public housing more accessible to large families. Designers built the complex to consist of one hundred units. The manager, John F. Merino, advertised the apartments in the local newspaper, stating that they would be available for rent on Monday, February 26, 1962.[29] He further surmised that 90 percent of the units would be rented by April 1, which underscores the great demand for the apartments. To obtain residency, applicants had to turn in their applications quickly. They also had to be considered low income and renting for family occupancy. For successful applicants, rent would vary according to the income of the occupant, the minimum rent being $38 per month; the size of the family would also be a factor in determining the amount of rent to be paid.[30] Manager Merino, after reviewing several applications, predicted that his complex would house five hundred to six hundred children and that a bus system would have to be created to get the children to and from school.[31] Besides a manager, Niagara Falls Housing Authority representatives also hired an account clerk, a maintenance man, and a staff assistant to help operate the complex.[32] Zorie Bell Boling, who later lived at the Jordan Garden complex, spoke favorably of the apartments.[33] She said she and her husband Floyd raised their sixteen children there. She obtained one of the few large apartments, which had five bedrooms, two bathrooms, and a large living room and dining room. She commented that "the arrangement was nice" and that there were only about five large units like theirs in the entire complex.[34] Jordan Garden housing project was built in the town's North Side neighborhood amid a growing cluster of Black Niagarans.

The Jordan Garden apartments also served as an option for Black Niagarans displaced by Niagara Falls's second major urban renewal project, the Highland-Hyde Park Industrial Urban Renewal Project. City officials planned and executed this project during the early 1960s, estimating its cost at $1,075,815, most of which the federal government covered.[35] Planners set for demolition and restoration the area north of the Pittsburgh Metallurgical Company, bounded by Highland Avenue, James Avenue, Hyde Park Boulevard, and Massachusetts Avenue.[36] The plan called for the city to acquire all the property except for some land owned by General Abrasive and Pittsburgh Metallurgical Company and to demolish as many as one hundred buildings. Towers for Niagara Mohawk Power Corporation transmission lines and a Pittsburgh Metallurgical Company transformer building were the only structures to remain.[37] Black Niagarans constituted 40 percent of the residents who had to be relocated. By 1968 most businesses and residents had been relocated, and Pittsburgh Metallurgical Company had purchased most of the restored light-industrial property.[38]

City officials again attempted to adhere to the state's urban renewal mandate that Black Niagarans not be moved from one ghetto to another. They inspected homes or rental properties that they recommended to displaced residents to ensure that the properties met accepted standards. City officials could thus argue that they were not contributing to slum development. Moreover, the truth of novelist James Baldwin's conception of urban renewal made them cautious in their actions.[39] Baldwin eloquently noted that "urban renewal meant Negro removal."[40] Most Black Niagarans in the Highland/Hyde Park area relocated to Black enclaves.[41] One family successfully integrated into a white neighborhood, although a petition was circulated to prevent this. Another family was ultimately happy not to have to deal with the heavy pollution from the area plants; others did not want to live in public housing.[42] Similar to homeowners in the Allen-MacKenna neighborhood, former residents had fond memories of the area.[43]

With the two urban renewal projects proceeding to the satisfaction of several city planners, Mayor Lackey felt that more effective leadership was still needed for urban renewal and the economic advancement of the city.[44] He had campaigned on a platform supporting massive redevelopment for the city of Niagara Falls. To support his tourism idea along with the local economy, he established an urban renewal agency, made himself chairman, and supported a parallel organization, SPUR (Society for the Promotion, Unification and Redevelopment of Niagara Falls), which was led by William H. Wendel, president of Carborundum Company.[45] In a short time, Mayor Lackey and his allies developed and presented the third major plan sponsored by the city. They called their plan "the Rainbow Project." Seeking to advance uniquely beyond how Canadian officials had developed activities around the sections of Niagara Falls that they controlled, this plan called for the construction of an eighty-two-acre downtown development that would include a huge new $35 million international convention center.[46] Mayor Lackey successfully sold this idea and gained support from local citizens, state and federal governmental agencies, and international sponsors. He envisioned the convention center as being a multinational facility that would appeal to all, hosting entertainment, athletic competitions, cultural celebrations, political conventions, national and international events, and religious and humanitarian services.

In 1969 construction workers began building the Niagara Falls International Convention Center and completed it in 1974. The Wintergarden botanical complex, the turtle-shaped Native American Center for the Performing Arts, new corporate office buildings, and the Rainbow Centre shopping mall were built near the convention center.[47] Local African American citizens had wanted a Black museum built near the convention center, but city officials objected.[48]

Mayor Lackey envisioned that the Niagara Falls International Convention Center and the developed structures around it would draw businesses and tourism. Businesses would see the opportunities in Niagara Falls and come in droves. Tourists would frequent the convention center and walk a short eighteen-hundred feet to the world-renowned waterfalls. The convention center would be a funnel, moving people in two directions: tourists would leave from the convention center going to the waterfalls and then walk to the convention center or to the other buildings around the convention center. Time has shown that this plan did not work, and it certainly did not help revitalize Niagara Falls.

Old-timers often speak of a glorious period for Niagara Falls before the 1960s, when Falls Street stretched throughout neighborhoods and close to the actual waterfalls.[49] On Falls Street, numerous stores bustled with activity and served as an outing for residents and tourists. Both groups congregated in the Falls Street area—local citizens and tourists shopped while tourists headed to and from the area of the waterfalls. The Niagara Falls International Convention Center and the structures that surrounded it stood more or less apart from the neighborhoods rather than being an extension of the communities. These ideas reflect points Jane Jacobs made in her renowned book *The Death and Life of Great American Cities* (1961). She noted that comprehensive, aggressive urban renewal polices often destroy the social cohesion and quality of life of urban neighborhoods.[50] Her book critiqued ideas of planners such as Robert Moses who created structures that seemed to be independent of neighborhoods and communities. Her ideas are strongly applicable to the Rainbow Centre Project.

Mayor Lackey, who lived to see the Niagara Falls International Convention Center completed, felt proud of his early urban renewal efforts and of the progress that had been made.[51] He remembered the slow progression of urban renewal activities from 1963 to 1966, due to an initially unimaginative and unproductive Urban Renewal Agency. In an August 6, 1975 interview, reflecting on his legacy and the changing pace of urban renewal, Lackey declared:

> I went to New York City myself, and was told that whoever said our plans wouldn't be approved was a damn liar. I came back and fired the whole staff of the Urban Renewal Agency. There were no consultants, no discussion—they were fired.[52] This was a

turning point in the life of Mayor E. Dent Lackey and in the life of urban renewal in the city of Niagara Falls (see figure 7.1).⁵³

Many Black Niagarans lived on and around East Falls Street, which was a landmass that urban renewal officials wanted to be part of the eighty-two-acre Rainbow Centre Project.⁵⁴ Once more, perhaps sensing conflict because the civil rights movement was at its apex, the local NAACP was strong and active, and because Black Niagarans had recently rioted in the area, urban renewal officials invited African American citizens to participate in the revitalization of their neighborhood.⁵⁵ City manager Donald J. O'Hara asked the city council to establish an advisory committee that would incorporate Black Niagarans who would work with planning director Harvey N. Albond.⁵⁶ To receive federal funding, the area would have to be redeveloped as residential. Who the area would be redeveloped for understandably weighed heavily on the minds of local residents. They pondered whether it would be redeveloped for them or for higher-income citizens.⁵⁷

Figure 7.1. Mayor E. Dent Lackey on a horse, 1967. Courtesy of the *Niagara Falls Gazette*.

At a December 8, 1969 city council meeting an idea was introduced to build low-income housing in the area.[58] City council members strongly disagreed with the idea because they felt that low-income housing near the Niagara Falls International Convention Center would diminish its attractiveness and international appeal. Simultaneously, the East Side Professional and Businessmen's Association and the Pulaski Civic League actively supported the city council's stance. Each of these organizations presented letters to the council to articulate their views. Matthew Fiener, president of the East Side Professional and Businessmen's Association, read a three-page letter to the council in which he advocated construction of high-rise apartment houses immediately adjacent to the Rainbow Centre.[59] The council also received a letter from the Pulaski Civic League, signed by its secretary, Matthew Fiener. "The League said it felt low cost subsidized housing would detract from the city's convention center and that East Falls Street [was] a 'prime location' for substantial development of hotels, motels and high-rise apartments to compliment [the] Rainbow Centre."[60] The NAACP, which at the time was led by Harwood Bond, rallied to be a voice for Black Niagarans who lived on and around East Falls Street. They sent a telegram to the council expressing the East Falls Street African American community's views, which read in part: "We take the position that this is another attempt to appropriate a potentially desirable area for purely selfish gains at the expense of the poor and not a subtle effort to coerce social governmental officials to aid and abet in their race's endeavor to remove the blacks from the area in the holy name of economic feasibility."[61] Harvey Albond, representing city government, responded that things were at an exploratory stage and that people need not become alarmed. The committee to evaluate whether the city of Niagara Falls should apply for federal funds for residential development of East Falls Street, he noted, had not been formed yet. Even if this committee had been formed, according to Albond, it still would take about two years before funds would be granted. He also emphasized that there was no guarantee that the federal government would approve funding for the project. This defused tensions (at least briefly), and the city applied for federal funds.

By 1970 there was still a demand for housing among Black Niagarans, including those who lived on the south end of town and knew that they might be relocated from sections of the East Falls Street area. Responding to this demand, city of Niagara Falls planners arranged to build another public housing complex: it was a housing unit that many Black Niagarans perceived as a corral to keep them from the redeveloped downtown area.[62] Led by Mayor E. Dent Lackey, city planners called this complex "Unity Park." Mayor Lackey claimed that he wanted integration to work in the Unity Park complex specifically. He also wanted a bridge built between the North Side African American community—which included Highland Avenue, Center Court housing project, and Jordan Garden—and the De Veaux section, one of the more affluent sections of the city.[63] In selling this idea to the community, Mayor Lackey obtained support from several people, including the Reverend Glen Raybon and Aaron Griffin, both highly influential Black Niagaran leaders. He also sought the support of Eddie Palmore, who was an active member of the Niagara Falls Housing Authority.[64] Palmore did not support the mayor's idea, disagreeing also with two of his friends who strongly supported it. Palmore felt that the proposed type of housing would not work in Niagara Falls, although he was aware that a similar housing structure had been successful in Pittsburgh, Pennsylvania. Instead of a housing complex or project, Palmore argued, as did realtor Matthew P. Flanagan, that building independent houses for local citizens would be better for the residents and for the city of Niagara Falls. He thought that if people owned homes, they would take more pride in them and work hard at their upkeep. For the city, he argued, a tax base would be created whereby the city could increase its operational income. Furthermore, Palmore argued that the housing units would not last because of their poor structure and quality. He remembered that he lost the argument, as the mayor vehemently responded, "No! I want that Unity Park built."[65] Hence, in the long run, Palmore felt vindicated.[66]

City planners did not initially call their project Unity Park. When planning grew intense after January 1, 1970, they first named it the Lehigh Project.[67] For many it had been known as the old Lehigh Valley Railroad site, an abandoned railroad yard that consisted of about fifty-nine acres south of College Avenue between McKoon and Highland Avenues. The project's location was arguably the only remaining area in Niagara Falls where a large housing complex could be built. City planners hired the architectural firm Bazemore & Grove to design the large $6.5 million housing complex. Support also came from the State Urban Development Corporation and the Interfaith Housing Corporation, a group of seventeen local churches interested in integrated housing.[68] All agreed that the new complex should not be labeled as a project, although it was near two public housing projects, Center Court and Jordan Garden.

Bazemore & Grove proposed that housing be half townhouses and half garden apartment rental units. Planners held neighborhood meetings in which citizens, predominantly Black Niagarans, partially agreed with Eddie Palmore in suggesting that detached home sites for private purchase be created. In essence, the Highland Avenue Black community, represented by a "Committee of Fifteen," felt what was being promised was only an extension of the ghetto, or a continued herding and corralling of blacks. The committee members and Black community residents wanted single-family detached homes, less density, and participation in the planning and construction of Lehigh housing.[69] City planners, along with Bazemore & Grove, incorporated these ideas into their plan and proposed building fifty such structures, increasing the prospective housing unit total to 450: 200 townhouses, 200 apartments, and 50 independent single housing units.

The Committee of Fifteen, representing local African American residents, made other suggestions besides separate housing units that they wanted to be taken seriously, which included the following:

1. Provide more access from De Veaux as well as Highland Avenue to avoid "boxing in" the project area as a separate community.

2. Plan for fireproof siding in various colors.

3. Scatter the housing the entire length of the proposed property.

4. Provide for meaningful employment of Black workers at all levels of construction and that this stipulation be included in the contract that Interfaith enters.

5. Rule out any commercial or private business in the development.

6. Add a gymnasium and swimming pool to the day care center, physical fitness facilities, and recreational facilities already planned.[70]

Additionally, the Committee of Fifteen posed questions to city planners and Bazemore & Grove. They wanted to know, for example, why basements would not be offered or how the Niagara Falls Board of Education would provide for racial balancing of schools with the large influx of children expected to reside in Unity Park. The second question did not initially get answered. However, Bazemore & Grove did answer the first question by stating that adding basements would considerably increase the total cost of the project.[71] The Committee of Fifteen seemed satisfied that they had aggressively expressed their views, although they doubted that city planners and Bazemore & Grove would seriously consider all of their suggestions. They reasoned that time would tell in most instances.[72] Conversely, city planners and Bazemore & Grove felt that the Committee of Fifteen's apprehensions would prove unfounded in the long run.

With plans formalized, city officials hired local construction firm Wright & Kremers to build the Unity Park housing complex. City officials set October 1970 as the date when construction was to begin.[73] The Human Relations Commission, a citywide group that tried to ensure fairness and equality in all city operations, cautiously approved the proposed Unity Park Housing Development plan, making it clear that the commission would watch construction, rental practices, management, maintenance, and any other areas where there might be a possibility of discrimination against anyone.[74] Joe McCoy, head of the new Training for Construction, voiced concern that Wright & Kremers should hire minorities to participate in the building of Unity Park.[75] A representative of Wright & Kremers said that 15 percent of their workforce was Black. Upon being told this, Bloneva Bond, who served on the board of the Human Relations Commission, remarked that she would like to know if that was true.[76] McCoy said: "If they have 15 percent we need to find out what work they're doing and how much they're paid."[77]

City planners, led by Mayor Lackey and the Interfaith Housing Corporation, envisioned that Unity Park would be an integrated housing complex, perfectly complementing the complex's name. They also did not want the complex to be exclusively a lower economic class unit. Planners designed Unity Park to house low-income and moderate-income residents: moderate income groups were to be allotted 70 percent of the units, while low-income families were granted the remaining 30 percent.[78] Black Niagarans' concerns were not that Unity Park be integrated; they simply wanted safe, comfortable, quality housing.

Some Black Niagarans still did not like the proposed project. They echoed the pervasive theme of being corralled and caged in, and they resented it. At a public hearing on the progress of the Unity Park complex, attended by all the key city planners and Interfaith Housing Corporation members, Larry Myles, a local resident, expressed his strong opposition:

"You got all the blacks caged now, and then if a riot arises, you call in the militia. They aren't going to set me up anywhere—I can get it myself just like you got it."[79] Members in the audience interspersed shouts of "Right on!" following Myles's comments.[80] Myles clearly remembered when Black Niagarans rioted in Niagara Falls in the late 1960s. In the riot areas where Black Niagarans lived, police had the section blockaded at every exit and entrance.[81] Myles continued his protest in an editorial published in the *Niagara Falls Gazette*:

> It is plain to see the total picture of what is going to soon happen. East Falls St., 24th St. and Erie Ave. will be closed off to blacks because of the plans of the Urban Renewal Agency. All the blacks will be forced into the Highland Ave. neighborhood where they will be fenced or caged in when "necessary," they won't be able to come out.[82]

Unity Park's architects acknowledged that they had received phone calls from White Niagarans interested in potentially moving into the new complex; however, they did not want to be hemmed in by Blacks.[83] Residents of the De Veaux neighborhood expressed their displeasure with the Unity Park complex being so close to them. Perhaps to prevent accusations of racism, they couched their disapproval in complaints of increased traffic flow. At the same public meeting where Myles announced his opposition, Arnold Littlewood, a resident of McKoon Avenue, presented a petition to city officials.[84] Sixty-five De Veaux residents signed the petition, objecting to the planned construction of a six-foot-wide walkway connecting Unity Park with McKoon Avenue. The petition stated that McKoon was currently a raceway where several traffic accidents had happened and that the proposed plan would only worsen conditions. Many children lived on and around McKoon Avenue, and petitioners feared that they could be harmed. City officials at the public meeting told concerned citizens that their comments and suggestions would be considered.[85]

These community responses paralleled those of other northern cities that experienced expanding populations, whereby older White communities strove to maintain the racial makeup of their neighborhoods by excluding encroaching populations they deemed undesirable.[86] Conversely, the excluded population—Black Niagarans in this case—were ever mindful of the high population density of their neighborhoods and the need to obtain more living space by filtering into other city sections, chiefly those they were surrounded by. Larry Myles articulated this; and the De Veaux community, through its representative, made it clear that they desired no opened pathway between their community and Unity Park, along with the projects around it.

Nonetheless, Bernard Goodman, the manager of Unity Park, began accepting applications for housing units by March 1972.[87] Eighty units were then available for occupancy, and twenty-five families were expected to be in residence by the end of March. The Human Rights Commission, as it stated earlier, did monitor the activities of Unity Park. They invited Goodman to a meeting to discuss Unity Park's method for selecting prospective tenants. At the meeting, commission member Ashlan Harlan wanted to know why the actual number of residents was far below the number of applications made.[88] Goodman told her that although well over four hundred applications were made, not all applicants were eligible, and not all the applications had been processed.[89] This response seemed to satisfy the commission members. Unity Park then operated to fulfill its mission of being a place that would meet the standards of any upright, self-respecting person who worked hard for a living (see figures 7.2 and 7.3).

City and state leaders continued to proclaim their opposition to ghetto formation and development. They claimed that Unity Park was designed to clash with factors that stimulated slum development. Unfortunately, organizers allowed an event that contributed significantly toward blight.[90] Wright & Kremers created a twenty-five-foot mountain of dirt behind one of the Unity Park housing units and also behind a section of the Jordan Garden and left them there for over a year. They used the area as a dumping ground, covering it with boards full of old nails, broken

Figure 7.2. Playground at Unity Park, 1970. Courtesy of the Niagara Falls Public Library.

Figure 7.3. Inside the middle of Unity Park, 1970. Courtesy of the Niagara Falls Public Library.

glass, tile fragments, and other trash. Water, as much as two-feet deep in some places, surrounded the mountain of debris. Children used makeshift rafts to ride around in the water; there were no fences to keep them away. Adults feared that children would get hurt. The twenty-five-foot dirt pile was supposed to be a sledding hill when the property was developed as a recreational area for Unity Park.[91] Residents in Unity Park, Jordan Garden, and the Highland Avenue neighborhood bitterly complained and demanded that city officials do something.

George Smith owned a dry-cleaning business at 3120 Highland Avenue that was also his home. He complained for over a year that water, mud, and ice ran onto his property and damaged it.[92] One woman remarked that the dirt pile wasn't put anywhere near De Veaux.[93] Other neighbors also complained, with some initiating lawsuits against the city, including Smith. With no immediate actions taken, residents felt discriminated against and appealed to the Human Rights Commission. Responsible parties seemed to abdicate responsibility and placed the blame elsewhere. Wright & Kremers claimed that they placed the dirt pile there at the behest of the landscape and ecological consultant, R. T. Schnadelbach of

Philadelphia, an employee of Bazemore Architecture and Planning; Mr. Bazemore, president of this architectural firm, said something would be done.[94] Yet nothing had been done for a long time. The city of Niagara Falls was scheduled to take title of the property but had not done so; at the time, the Urban Development Corporation, a state-operated agency, owned the property.[95]

The responses from all parties involved sent unhealthy messages to the African American community that they were considered unimportant, that their constant complaints could be ignored or placed on the backburner, and that if lawsuits were filed they would most likely not be seriously considered or would be deemed frivolous by the judicial system. Although the dirt pile was an "eyesore" and perhaps dangerous, expedient actions might not be taken because the community would soon deteriorate into a slum. In this case, Black Niagarans were treated as second-class citizens. The twenty-five-foot dirt pile would not have been left in or near the De Veaux section.[96]

With Unity Park's construction near completion, the city of Niagara Falls received a $1.2 million grant from the federal department of Housing and Urban Development (HUD).[97] HUD issued the grant for city planners to fulfill the first year of their East Falls Street urban renewal plan. The first-year plan called for the acquisition, clearance, and sale of land along sections of Erie Avenue and Memorial Parkway.[98] This alarmed Black Niagarans in general but particularly those who resided in the South End neighborhood near the Niagara Falls International Convention Center. They knew that the grant was for the redevelopment of their area, but they did not know the specifics of the city's plan, such as which street blocks would be demolished and which would remain. To get answers, the leadership of the African American community called a public meeting on July 12, 1972, at the Niagara Community Action Program (NiaCAP) center at 1412 East Falls Street.[99] Three community organizations sponsored the meeting: the NAACP, the Human Rights Commission, and NiaCAP. Bloneva Bond then headed the NAACP; Reverend Daniel Porter, who had strongly supported school desegregation, now led the Human Rights Commission; and Anita Lingo served as chief coordinator of NiaCAP. About sixty individuals turned out for the meeting, which was held at 7:30 p.m. on a Sunday evening.[100]

At the meeting, community leaders and other outspoken people, who were well-informed of their rights, advised residents of the East Falls Street area to press the Urban Renewal Agency for information on what was specifically planned for the future of their neighborhood.[101] If the Urban Renewal Agency did not give satisfactory answers, residents were instructed to contact HUD, especially because HUD required that receiving grants required city planners to involve and inform local residents about the destiny of their community. Urban Renewal Agency officials, led by director Daniel Collins, had been invited to the meeting to answer questions but refused to attend. Collins said that he would not deal with the group holding the meeting but only with the Project Advisory Committee, which consisted of eleven people, led by Reverend Randall McCaskill, who claimed to represent the interests of East Falls Street residents.[102] Somehow, the Project Advisory Committee did not pass information back to community residents. Reverend McCaskill also did not attend the public meeting and indicated that he thought the three groups sponsoring the meeting were creating a panic.[103] Bloneva Bond, the most impactful NAACP leader the city of Niagara Falls had had to date, informed the audience that she had asked the Urban Renewal Agency about guidelines to distribute to the public and was told that a booklet would be furnished (but hadn't been written yet).[104] She also concurred with Larry Myles by accusing the Urban Renewal Agency of using urban renewal work on East Falls Street to force residents to move to Unity Park, a development that East Falls Street residents generally did not want to move to.[105] She felt that people should not be bulldozed into a designated locale.

Miscommunication persisted. Using eminent domain, city officials planned to seize two streets in the East Falls Street neighborhood: the west side of Memorial Parkway between Falls and Niagara Streets and Erie Avenue between Fifth Street and Quay Street.[106] Residents had not been properly informed, and rumors were rampant. Daniel Collins and several of the Urban Renewal Agency members probably felt better dealing with the Project Advisory Committee; it was small, although one of its members felt that it should have been much larger to truly represent the interest of East Falls Street residents.[107] The Urban Renewal Agency and the Project Advisory Committee did not host community forums to inform and encourage participation of all concerned community members as mandated by HUD. This made East Falls Street residents feel neglected, disrespected, resentful, angry, and like pawns manipulated by outside interests. Reverend Daniel Porter and Bloneva Bond both spoke up forcefully for the African American community, frequently making those opposed to their ideas uncomfortable.[108] Consequently, if the Urban Renewal Agency wanted their plan to be implemented quickly with minimal conflict, it is not surprising that Reverend Porter or Bloneva Bond were not members of the Project Advisory Committee.[109]

Reverend McCaskill accused the three groups of creating unnecessary tensions; yet the three group representatives proclaimed that they did not seek to compete with the Project Advisory Committee and that they were concerned because they represented the community under siege. Moreover, they wanted residents to know their rights: they had the right to be informed and participate in urban renewal planning, obtain moving expenses if required to move, recieve supplemental assistance if relocating from a lower-priced rental unit into a similar but more expensive structure, and to have an office in the proposed restructured area to aid displaced citizens, for example.[110] Echoing Joe McCoy's earlier request, Bond also wanted Black Niagarans and other minorities to be hired in all phases of the demolition and reconstruction.[111] All attendees at the public meeting knew that more meetings were ahead.

Regardless of the public meeting and the media attention it received, the Urban Renewal Agency maintained that it would not deal with the general community—only with the Project Advisory Committee.[112] They evidently felt justified in their actions. On the Wednesday after Sunday's public meeting, the Urban Renewal Agency and the Project Advisory Committee met privately. Reverend McCaskill had informed the *Niagara Falls Gazette* of the meeting that Wednesday morning. When a *Gazette* reporter, along with Republican candidate for city council George Poulos, attended the meeting, they were asked to leave.[113] These events were vastly different from the actions of the board of education, a group that hosted many community forums before Plan 21's creation and ultimate implementation, as articulated below by a concerned Niagaran:

> Plan 21 for the integration of Niagara Falls schools is a perfect example of a plan that was formed with broad public participation. The Board of Education and the superintendent of schools could have drawn up an identical plan in the seclusion of their offices, and they probably would have been tarred and feathered when they put it into effect. Plan 21, nearly two years in the making through the messy, stormy process of public participation, was generally accepted. It's not universally beloved and it has its flaws, but it works—and has worked, right from the start.

The Urban Renewal Agency and its Project Advisory Committee would do well to do likewise. They might be pleasantly surprised to learn that ordinary people can be quite intelligent, quite constructive, even quite willing to make sacrifices—when they know what's going on.[114]

Due to the secrecy and the exclusion practiced, the NAACP made plans to contact HUD and inquire whether the procedures of the Urban Renewal Agency complied with their rules. Their understanding of HUD's policy indicated that for a public-funded neighborhood project, the funded group had to involve the affected community in the creation and implementation of any proposed urban renewal plan.[115] Additionally, the NAACP planned to inform HUD representatives that the Niagara Falls Urban Renewal Agency had no Blacks on its staff.[116]

The pressure that the NAACP and the other groups exerted had a decisive impact on the Urban Renewal Agency, though they tried to stick to their original plan of working largely, if not exclusively, with the Project Advisory Committee. They unanimously voted to approve a $30,000 budget for the Project Advisory Committee to establish an office at New Hope Baptist Church at 1122 Buffalo Avenue.[117] This was a HUD mandate as articulated by Reverend Daniel Porter. The Urban Renewal Agency finally informed East Falls Street area residents that the office would be established to answer individuals' questions, assist people in the relocation process, and act as a liaison among the Urban Renewal Agency, the landowners, and tenants in the Neighborhood Development Project area.[118] Contributing to the pressure, HUD informed Bloneva Bond that they would investigate her complaints and asked her about specific meetings and dates the public had been excluded from, as well as a list of Project Advisory Committee members.[119] Bond thought that HUD should have asked the Urban Renewal Agency for a list of Project Advisory Committee members.[120]

Even with the Project Advisory Committee operating an office and ultimately interacting more with the public, the organization still had its critics. Residents perceived it as a rubber stamp agency, one with no real power, that did the bidding of the Urban Renewal Agency at the expense of East Falls Street area residents.[121] Conversely, the committee, under Reverend McCaskill, vigorously defended themselves.[122] McCaskill denied that the committee was a rubber stamp agency devoid of decision-making power and stated that they could consult HUD directly if an impasse occurred between them and the Urban Renewal Agency.[123] He also called his critics "ignorant and devious," motivated solely by self-interest. To buttress his claims, he cited examples of people his committee had aided. William Brooks, who was a conservative Black Niagaran, a strong supporter of Reverend McCaskill, a former deputy director of the local Affirmative Action office, and a relocation aide for the Project Advisory Committee, accused NiaCAP, the NAACP, and other organizations of failing to eradicate poverty, since he thought that enough antipoverty money had been spent in the area over the previous five years.[124]

Even with evident tensions, city officials took possession of Erie Avenue and Memorial Parkway properties that were adjacent to the Niagara Falls International Convention Center.[125] Urban Renewal Agency officials planned to convert the Erie Avenue properties into a parking lot or recreation area. They would also demolish properties on Memorial Parkway in order to build new upscale residential properties for those who could afford them.[126] Historic Erie Avenue, where the first Niagara Community Center once stood, and several African American businesses, would ultimately be demolished by the Urban Renewal Agency. People who lived in the area had to relocate, and businesses had to move or close. As time progressed, Black Niagarans grew to miss and appreciate Erie Avenue even more; it had been one of the few streets in Niagara Falls where any citizen could walk and see several businesses owned and operated by African Americans.

Prior to the demolition of Erie Avenue, on November 20, 1968, Mayor Lackey hosted a demolition ceremony there.[127] Construction workers planned to begin their Erie Avenue demolition project by tearing down sixteen buildings. Event workers had set up a stage for city officials, and a good-sized crowd gathered to observe the ceremony. In his speech, Mayor Lackey predicted that the tearing down of sixteen buildings was only the physical beginning of South End redevelopment.[128] It was an ending, but the mayor foretold a bright beginning and future. In his own words, Mayor Lackey believed it was more than the demolition and reconstruction of a small area: "It [was] the revitalization of the entire city."[129] Immediately following the ceremony, Niagara Erection Company workers demolished a small house on Erie Avenue, as people witnessed the end of a historical epoch.

Most people in the crowd probably did not realize or value the significance of Erie Avenue to many Black Niagarans. Though pockets of blight might have occasionally appeared in or around it, Erie Avenue was important to many. Old-timers remembered it from their youth as a street they frequented to get to the Community Center. Out-of-town sightseers could remember staying at an Erie Avenue inn while visiting Niagara Falls. Partygoers would remember the good times they had at the Sunset Club, Murphy's Hotel & Grill, Fifty-One Club, Parker House, or other establishments. Teenagers could recall the fun they had on a Saturday afternoon with friends at Busy Bee Grill, Otey's Café, New Royal Restaurant, or a local pool hall. Shoppers might remember Levy Brothers Furniture Warehouse or the Salvation Army store. Erie Avenue represented a district that enhanced their lives by bringing them joy and pride in their hometown.

Internal Change Agents

Community Restructuring and Development

To reclaim the destiny of their community, nondisplaced East Falls Street area residents organized roughly seven years after the demolition began on Erie Avenue to gain urban renewal funding to rehabilitate aspects of their neighborhood.[130] They called themselves Rebuild East Side through Cooperation, Unity and Effort (RESCUE).[131] They also renamed their neighborhood, dubbing it "The People's Side of the Convention Center." This was an attempt to distance themselves from how the media often characterized their district, stereotypically overexaggerating violence and mayhem as common characteristics of the area. Niagarans of all colors united, backing both Black and White leaders to represent them before city officials. White Niagaran Robert Narkiewicz and Black Niagaran Ruby Howard served as key representatives for the group.

RESCUE knew of the Community Development Act, a federal policy that dictated how funds allocated for urban renewal projects should be used. In part, the act mandated that funds could be used for providing decent housing, healthy living environments, and greater economic opportunities for persons of low or moderate income levels.[132] Perhaps in an attempt to quell their enthusiasm, Angelo Massaro, the new Urban Renewal Agency director who had replaced Daniel Collins, informed a gathering of seventy East Falls Street residents at the Echo Club that urban renewal rules had changed and that funds were no longer granted for projects with a limited reach. He told the residents that if they expected to be seriously considered for funding, their neighborhood project had to benefit the entire community.[133]

In spite of director Massaro's admonition, RESCUE created a proposal that competed with similar intended plans submitted by Highland Avenue and LaSalle Avenue residents.[134] If fully funded, RESCUE planned to ensure that low-interest guaranteed loans would be available to residents to improve one-and two-family houses. The old Thirteenth Street School would be acquired through donation or sale to be used as a community center. A gymnasium would be added, costing between $250,000 and $300,000; and an all-Black rent-paying organization would be allowed in the newly refurbished community center.[135] Moreover, RESCUE would ensure that still-useful East Side buildings were not demolished and that the city strictly enforced its housing code violations not only to generate funds for this necessary service but also to concurrently eliminate some of the slumlords on the East Side.[136] Director Massaro seemed to have been correct because no records indicate that any of RESCUE's proposals received federal funding. East Falls Street area residents, guided by their leaders, tried to impact their neighborhood proactively rather than strictly reacting to the directives of the Urban Renewal Agency and its use of eminent domain.

A little earlier, in 1974, prior to RESCUE's efforts, Black Niagarans sought to get a community center for children built within the East Falls Street neighborhood. The East Falls Street Boys Club closed in 1974 due to deterioration, which meant unsafe conditions for children. They hoped to obtain urban renewal funding, but it never materialized. As a result, they sought other means to obtain funds. A group called the Black Employees Club, led by Eugene Walker, orchestrated the efforts to gain a facility for the nondisplaced children in the South End neighborhood.[137] Black Employees Club members estimated that five hundred or more children lived in the East Falls Street neighborhood.[138] They reasoned that if a community center continued to exist, it would assist in reducing crime and contribute to the progress of children.[139] Black Employees Club members and other supportive East Falls Street residents were well aware of the expanded social-recreational institutions on the North Side available to children: the Niagara Community Center, and a new unit called II Betterment Inc. Friendship House had recently closed.

Black Employees Club members circulated a survey to twenty-five East Falls Street area residents concerning an ideal center and the kind of programs they would want. Results indicated that residents placed the highest priority on the establishment of a gym, with health and social services also high on the list.[140] Concurrently with seeking other avenues for funding, the Black Employees Club sought other prospective sites to house their community center. They attempted to obtain the Old State Theater near the Niagara Falls International Convention Center; however, the East Side Professional and Businessmen's Association, like their earlier protest against low-income housing being built in the area, strongly resisted this effort. They argued for preserving a section of East Falls Street for commercial projects that were expected to thrive on business generated from the convention center.[141] They also opposed the community centers being Black owned and operated, stressing that it should be under the control of the general community. The area had an enclave of African Americans but also a mélange of other ethnic groups. Discouraged but not defeated, the Black Employees Club gained use of the old Thirteenth Street School from the board of education. The club had hoped that the board would deed the property to them, but the board's attorney informed them that that would be illegal.[142] Instead, the board granted them use of the first floor of the building, which contained a gymnasium. Black Employees Club members estimated that the structure would be available for use in about eight weeks, especially with the financial support they had received from the Frank E. Gannett Newspaper Foundation, the United Presbytery of Western New York, and independent contributions from their own members.[143] By 1975 East Falls Street neighborhood youths once again had a recreational center, at least for a while.

William Brooks, who served on the Urban Renewal Agency's Project Advisory Committee, also worked in the East Falls Street neighborhood. He operated a one-man business called Falls Products at 201 Thirteenth Street, making concrete decorative building blocks and cement flowerpots and planters.[144] He had established his business in January 1967, employing workers, especially but not exclusively African Americans, and having his business be a concrete self-help example for his racial group. Brooks foresaw his business expanding to employ twenty-five people. Epitomizing elements of Booker T. Washington's "captains of industry" concept, Brooks preached to all who would listen that the only salvation for African Americans in general (and Black Niagarans in particular) was for them to seriously adopt a self-help mindset. He counseled people not to rely on government aid. Intelligent, responsible Whites who heard Brooks's message applauded him, perhaps because some responsibility for the plight of Black Niagarans was taken off their shoulders, regardless of past acts of discrimination and White racism, and placed squarely on the shoulders of Black Niagarans themselves. Brooks did not shy away from articulating Black Niagarans' faults publicly, where the broader community could hear them. Many Black Niagarans who heard Brooks's message considered him an "Uncle Tom"[145] and a self-righteous man who was using the oppression of his race for his own ends.[146]

Brooks aligned himself with the urban renewal ideas of the day. He promoted slum clearance and the beautification of the East Falls Street area. The building that housed his business could have been described as a dilapidated old warehouse, but Brooks proudly emphasized that it was clean. Brooks's business was initiated from the work of the East Side Progressive Club, a biracial group organized to combat filth, vandalism, crime, and juvenile delinquency on the East Side.[147] This group cleaned the streets and alleys regularly, installed flower boxes, and dressed up the areas in front of businesses.[148]

Brooks's conventional message and example fit the American creed. It was a "pull yourself up by your bootstraps" philosophy. It seemed to imply that Black Niagarans were held in contempt by many Whites because they were at the bottom of the social order. Brooks claimed Blacks were not discriminated against due to race but because of their low economic status: if African Americans would only pull themselves up, Brooks insisted, their plight would change, almost overnight. Brooks proclaimed: "The best way for the Negro to help himself is to industrialize in this growing America,"[149] further asserting that "God Almighty can't help you if you don't help yourself. And millions and millions of laws will help only if we help ourselves reach the top of the ladder."[150] Brooks's message also alerted White employers that they should not deny jobs to qualified African Americans because of their race. He also noted that African Americans should not be given jobs or expect to get them unless they were qualified. Although many truths were evident in Brooks's messages, many Black Niagarans viewed him with skepticism, and they refused to see him in the same light as established Black Niagaran leaders such as Aaron Griffin, Bloneva Bond, and Arthur Ray. His leadership message seemed out of step with the popular message of the times: self-help in conjunction with governmental societal oversight to ensure justice and equal opportunities for all (along with some governmental restitution to minorities for massive past and current discrimination).[151] Although conservative, Brooks, in his own way, proactively strove to improve the plight of Black Niagarans.

Political Leadership

In 1953 Joe Profit came to Niagara Falls from Montgomery, Alabama, when the population of African Americans was still rapidly expanding.[152] In 1950 the US Census enumerators recorded 3,585 African Americans in Niagara Falls; by 1960 the figure was 7,038.[153] Comparing the two decades shows a difference of 3,453, as African Americans flocked to Niagara Falls seeking employment. Profit left Montgomery shortly before the Montgomery Bus Boycott occurred, which catapulted Rosa Parks and Dr. Martin Luther King Jr. to national acclaim. Sylvia Love, Joe's wife, also came from Montgomery, Alabama. Profit, like many other Niagarans, saw the results of urban renewal agency planners' actions and how they had altered neighborhoods such as the East Falls Street section and Hyde Park/Highland districts. Profit, who resided on Highland Avenue, was one of several Black Niagaran leaders who acted progressively to advance his community during the urban renewal era (see figure 7.4).

At some point Joe Profit decided to return to his home state to visit relatives and friends. While he was in Montgomery, Alabama, he had a

Figure 7.4. Joe Profit, 1980. Courtesy of the *Niagara Falls Gazette*.

problem with the local police chief and did not like the way the chief had treated him.[154] Profit was most likely discriminated against and therefore, dehumanized, considering the Montgomery Bus Boycott, the Birmingham Desegregation Movement, and the Selma Voting Rights Movement that had occurred in segregated Alabama. The discriminatory actions of the police chief ignited a fire in Profit that drove him not only to make a change in his own life but also to help advance his racial group.[155]

Joe Profit approached two respected friends whose advice he valued: Eddie Palmore and Arthur Ray.[156] He told them he was going to run for supervisor of Ward 12 for the Democratic Party. Concerning their reactions, Profit commented: "I remember when I told Art [Ray] and Eddie Palmore I was going to run. They thought I was joking. When they laughed at me that really made up my mind."[157]

Perhaps they laughed because they knew it would be difficult for an African American to be elected supervisor for Ward 12, located on the north end of town. Although an enclave of African Americans resided in Ward 12, most were not registered to vote in 1963 when Profit ran, and many were not registered because they reasoned that most of the candidates, Republican or Democrat, had not represented their interests in the past and would fail to do so in the future.[158] Ward 12 had not had a Democrat as supervisor since 1949, when the Highland Avenue neighborhood was incorporated into Ward 12, coexisting with the De Veaux section of town.[159] Moreover, earlier Black Niagarans had run unsuccessfully. James Marable ran in 1949 and lost to incumbent Howard Palmer, 1,561 to 641; Eddie Palmore ran unsuccessfully in 1955 against George K. Boyer, and Hewer K. Seals tried and lost in 1957.[160] Seals ran unsuccessfully again in 1959, opposing Republican Stanley Grossman.[161] Members of the Garey family had been actively involved in local politics, but family members had died, some at early ages, and others had not run for political office.[162]

Eddie Palmore gave a similar but more detailed account of how Joe Profit told Arthur Ray and him, members of the Niagara Falls Civic and Social Organization, of his intent to run for political office and their reaction to the news:

> Joe Profit said "I am going to run and win." I told Joe Profit to join the Niagara Falls Civic and Social Organization and we will support you. And we supported him and by luck he won, and that made "a great difference in our political activities here within the City of Niagara Falls." Until that time basically all the

Blacks were registering as republicans. They did not want to be bothered with Democrats because everything was Republican. The way we got Joe Profit elected, Mr. Ray worked, and we all was working together on the situation. Two Whites that lived in the De Veaux area, one was called Mr. [Frank] Flay. He ran as a Democrat. Stanley Grossman, a Jewish fellow, had been a supervisor in the 12th Ward for years. Joe Profit ran against Frank Flay in the Primaries, and Joe beat him in the Primaries. But Flay also ran on the "Liberal and Conservative Line." Flay decided that since he was beaten as a Democrat, he would run on the [Liberal and] Conservative Line. Grossman ran on the Republican Line, and by Flay and Grossman "splitting the vote," Joe was able to win. That gave the African American community great political strength in our area. At that time we had wards with supervisors. They call them legislators today. When Joe Profit ran they had 42 supervisors. At the present [2010], you only have 19 legislatures through population shifts and censuses. That's what actually happened.[163]

Joe Profit's victory, as conveyed by Eddie Palmore, had a tremendous impact on the Black Niagaran community, contributing to their self-deterministic uplift agenda, as promoted in the William Brooks story.[164] In his own way, like baseball star Jackie Robinson, Profit was a leading light of integration. He awakened a desire within Black Niagarans to use electoral political power more for their advancement and the progression of their community. For example, Profit encouraged Arthur Ray to run for the Niagara Falls Board of Education.[165] Ray had great respect for Joe Profit. Profit encouraged other Black Niagarans to serve in municipal positions. He influenced Reverend Edgar Huff to serve on the Niagara Falls Housing Authority. When the leaders of Reverend Huff's Methodist denomination required that he leave Niagara Falls to pastor a church in New York City, a vacancy was created. In September 1965 Joe Profit asked Eddie Palmore to fill that vacancy.[166] Palmore willingly served and stayed on the Niagara Falls Housing Authority for many years.

Joe Profit performed well as Ward 12 supervisor. As a good council member, he responded to the concerns and requests of his constituents regardless of their race, color, class, or creed. He was not a silent voice in city government. He consistently placed requests before the city council, informing them of what Ward 12 residents needed to operate efficiently and to feel secure. For example, on January 10, 1964, he asked the city manager to have three lots on the east side of Twentieth Street between Center and Calumet Avenues changed from R-3 (multifamily residential) to C-1 (commercial) to allow construction of retail stores and businesses. On January 20, 1964, he requested that the skating rink at the Maple Avenue School be reinstated. On July 6, 1964, he requested that two streetlights be installed on Washington Street between College Avenue, and on Morley Avenue; and on January 20, 1965, he requested that streetlights be installed in various places throughout Ward 12.[167] Profit proposed similar activities throughout his tenure on the city council.

Profit served his two-year term as Ward 12 supervisor, but he was not reelected in 1965.[168] The splitting of the White vote allowed him to win the 1963 election. By 1965, Ward 12 voters, particularly those in the De Veaux district, united to unseat Profit. Nevertheless, Profit had a strong aptitude for politics and had gained allies in city government who helped him obtain political appointments and move up the ladder in City Hall. City manager Edward Connell, for instance, awarded him an inspector's job in the Department of Public Works; sixteen months later, Perc Weaver, a new city manager, promoted Profit to a foreman's position in the city's street division.[169] By 1970 Morton H. Abramowitz, then the city manager, appointed him head of the Department of Public Works, replacing the retired Onofrio Murphy Pafazzo.[170] Profit's advancement and leadership outlook fit Booker T. Washington's "captains of industry" idea. Although his formal education was limited, he was self-educated, and he used his influence to lift up others.[171] Moreover, Profit had immense influence on Black Niagarans, especially those of the working class. In his bid for Ward 12 supervisor, many people that voted for Profit had been working-class Blacks who had relocated to the newly constructed Jordan Gardens due to the Allen-Mackenna Avenue Urban Renewal Slum-Clearance Project. Jordan Gardens was populated predominantly by Blacks.[172]

As head of the Department of Public Works, Joe Profit created a legacy, becoming even more well known throughout the city. If bulk garbage needed to be picked up, residents contacted Profit's division, which worked in tandem with Urban Renewal Agency officials to beautify the city: the agency worked in the three designated sections and Profit throughout the entire city. People attested to seeing Profit all over the city, all year round, with a team of men fixing something or adding to the city's physical structure.[173] He did not sit in his office and direct his crew to repair problems; he generally led his multiracial staff because he could talk to his men and influence them to work hard and follow his lead. A bus driver witnessed a road resurfacing job that Profit and his crew started and completed. He was so impressed that he wrote a letter to the local newspaper, "expressing that he had to give credit where credit was due."[174] He commented that the job Profit and his staff did was a work of art and a pleasure for him and his fellow bus drivers to observe as they traveled their daily routes: the road resurfacing had not been an inconvenience at all to the traffic flow and was a good use of taxpayers' money.[175] There is a strong consensus among many Niagarans that no one has kept up the streets of Niagara Falls as well as Joe Profit—either before him or after.[176]

Black Niagarans generally looked up to Joe Profit and perceived him as one of their leaders. He involved himself in community affairs, stayed abreast of local issues, pulled others up as he gained a number of promotions, and made the African American community aware of its political strength. However, some politicians in City Hall did not appreciate Profit. Around 1972, concrete opposition arose against Profit's position as head of the Department of Public Works. According to the Black Employees Club, Councilman Murphy J. Pitarresi began to make inquiries about the Department of Public Works, questioning their extensive purchases at the Town of Niagara hardware store.[177] Councilman Pitarresi felt that taxpayer money had been wasted. Moreover, there appeared to be complaints among one or more subordinates in the Department of Public Works. Many Black Niagarans believed that the intense scrutiny Joe Profit faced stemmed from the fact that he was Black and that several city officials felt that a white man should be head of the Department of Public Works. Notwithstanding, the city council changed the requirements for a person to be head of the Department of Public Works. The new requirement stated that a candidate for head of the department must have a professional engineering degree, which Profit did not have; thus, he lost a job that he loved and had performed admirably in. In response, he filed a discrimination suit against the city for a million dollars and reinstatement of his former job. Besides being discriminated against, Profit felt that he was targeted because he took city business to new vendors.[178] He lost the case. City officials offered Profit a deputy's job in his former department, which he rejected because he believed it was offered to him because he was Black.[179] Profit continued to serve as a community leader, mainly in an advisory role, and he ran unsuccessfully for various political offices. Profit died in 1987, and because of the important work he had done for the city of Niagara Falls, city officials named a street in his honor:

"Profit Lane." In remembering Profit's personality and political style, Bill Gallagher, during his early days on the city council, remarked about an encounter he had with Profit:

> Joe Profit always had keen insight on how the political world operated. In my early months on the Council, I brought a neighborhood problem to the attention of a low-ranking supervisor in the public works department. Joe got wind of it and explained that he was the "shepherd" of his department. "Bill," he said, "don't you be dealing with no sheep. I'm the shepherd. Get the shepherd on your side and all the sheep will follow." Another Profit insight was on political power. "If you got the power and don't use it, you don't deserve to have the power," Joe used to say.[180]

During the age of urban renewal, besides awakening Black Niagarans to their budding political strength, Joe Profit, through his example, left a roadmap for his successors: these included Robert Anderson, Renae Kimble, and Charles Walker, all of whom later served in political capacities.[181]

In 1971, a short time after Profit was promoted to head of the Department of Public Works, Arthur Ray decided to run for a common council seat. Profit had encouraged and supported him; he even wore a T-shirt around City Hall that stated, VOTE FOR ART RAY.[182] Some aspects of Ray's political platform coincided with Mayor Lackey's. Both embraced the urban renewal idea of industrial retention and a brighter future for the city of Niagara Falls. Unlike his victory for a board of education seat, Ray did not obtain a high percentage of the white vote, he believed, because of the Attica prison uprising, which had polarized both Black and white Niagarans.[183] Black Niagarans tended to support the inmates, whereas most white Niagarans supported Governor Nelson Rockefeller, New York State Commissioner of Correctional Facilities Russell Oswald, and police who were on standby to take back control of the prison from inmates. Ray believed that had the Attica prison uprising not occurred, he would have won and been the next Black Niagaran to hold a city government post.[184]

During the Attica crisis, inmates called upon a select group of non-prisoners to aid in negotiations between themselves and prison authorities. One of their leaders read their list of negotiators on television, and Bloneva Bond was one of the people they turned to for help.[185] Other people that the prisoners sought help from were Tom Wicker of the *New York Times*,

New York State Assemblyman Arthur O. Eve, Minister Louis Farrakhan of the Nation of Islam, Black Panther Party Minister of Defense Huey P. Newton, *Buffalo Courier-Express* reporter Richard J. Roth, and Clarence Jones, a writer for the *Amsterdam Press*. Bond felt honored to be requested in the company of such distinguished individuals and wondered how the prisoners even knew of her. She suspected that copies of the *Niagara Falls Gazette* had been smuggled into Attica prison. (It could have been an incarcerated inmate from Niagara Falls that knew about Bond's long activist career in the city of Niagara Falls that suggested her as one of the outside negotiators.) Bond willingly agreed to serve and do all she could to help end the crisis peacefully. In addition to the nonincarcerated negotiators, the prisoners wanted complete amnesty, meaning freedom from any physical, mental, and legal reprisals; speedy and safe transportation out of confinement to a nonimperialistic country; intervention by the federal government so that they would be under direct federal jurisdiction; and reconstruction of Attica prison by inmates and/or under inmate supervision.[186] The Attica prisoners had other demands, such as being allowed to take showers more often, being given an adequate supply of toilet paper, and being granted an opportunity to acquire a sound education. Inmates had written to the Buffalo NAACP branch in the early 1930s with these same grievances.[187] Bond diligently negotiated to help resolve the impasse. In evaluating the Attica prisoners' demands, Bond thought that some of these demands were reasonable but that others were not, such as safe transportation out of confinement to a nonimperialistic country.[188] The peaceful solution Bond had hoped for did not occur. Police and New York State troopers, with the approval of Governor Nelson Rockefeller, regained control of the prison by deadly force.

Forty-six community action leaders throughout the state, including Bloneva Bond, met in Niagara Falls and charged that President Richard Nixon, Governor Nelson Rockefeller, and State Corrections Commissioner Russell G. Oswald were personally responsible for the premeditated murder of Attica inmates.[189] They created a resolution and sent it to the charged individuals. The resolution stated, in part, that "we are appalled at the indiscriminate use of gas and fire power on prisoners, your [Gov. Rockefeller] refusal to meet with the negotiating team, your [the governor's] refusal to allow more time for negotiations (and) an endless barrage of insults and lies by absent prison officials."[190] They also selected Bond and six other people to present their concerns at the State Advisory Council of the regional office of the Federal Office of Economic Opportunity.[191]

Bond showed righteous indignation at how the crisis was solved and did what she could to see that the prisoners and their families received some justice. Her response to a call for aid stretched her leadership beyond Niagara Falls and further endeared her to many Black Niagarans, principally those who may have had relatives and/or friends in Attica prison (see figure 7.5).

ENTREPRENEURIAL LEADERSHIP

Like Bloneva Bond, Arthur Ray, and Joe Profit, Fred Brown demonstrated effective leadership skills. Black Niagarans remembered him as being bright, hardworking, outspoken, and a community and family man.[192] Fred Brown came to Niagara Falls in 1956 from Tuscaloosa, Alabama, arriving with his wife, Alma, and their two children.[193] Brown began his

Figure 7.5. Bloneva Bond, 1992. Courtesy of the *Niagara Falls Gazette*.

work career in Niagara Falls as a laborer at the Carborundum Company, starting first as a low-level worker, then being promoted to machine operator and, later, to an inspector. He also strongly supported union activity and became a union steward. Brown left the Carborundum Company in 1968 and established a business of his own, which was his long-held dream. This move was risky because Brown's expanding family needed food and shelter. At first, he was not successful, but he persisted until his hard work improved his life.

Brown, who had forcefully confronted the Niagara Falls Board of Education, coordinated his entrepreneurial activities with the Urban Renewal Agency. In reflecting on city planners' aims for urban renewal, Brown told *Niagara Falls Gazette* readers: "We have to stop thinking just about dollars the tourists bring in and start thinking about the people who live here."[194] In making this statement, Brown wanted Niagarans and especially local leaders to make a true commitment to revitalize the whole city and not just specific sections to attract tourists or industry. He wanted planners to be more visionary and to focus not just on the areas they worked and lived in but on the entire city.

The urban renewal era also stimulated Brown's entrepreneurial philosophy. He desired to uplift the Highland Avenue community, where he lived. As underlined in CORE's 1963 boycott of the W. T. Grant Store, young people left Niagara Falls, during and after the urban renewal era because they believed that no economic opportunities existed. Brown told the story of his nephew who graduated from Howard University with a degree in pharmacy and who did not plan on returning to Niagara Falls because no jobs existed there.[195] Brown attempted to convince his nephew to return so that they could open a pharmacy together. Brown believed that economic opportunities existed in one's surrounding community/environment and that a person had to seize them. Brown remarked: "I feel that we have to make our own opportunities and if we can build up this area others will follow."[196] In other words, quality businesses would attract people.[197]

Fred Brown implemented this vision for his community: the Highland Avenue neighborhood. He foresaw Highland Avenue as a thoroughfare consisting of a series of African American entrepreneurs providing much-needed goods and services for a consumer market. He visualized his area as contributing to the success and revitalization of the entire city. Brown contributed to this process by starting small and gradually building his business. With the aid of his wife Alma, Brown opened Brown Delicatessen in a small six-by-six structure. The business was highly successful.[198] Brown always wanted his business to grow, and he wanted to provide jobs for members of his community. He next opened a B-Kwik grocery store and eventually hired seventeen people. Brown met the goal of making himself an indispensable asset within his community by providing consumer goods that his community valued, furnishing employment for a number of people, contributing to the city's tax base, and serving as a role model.

During the urban renewal era, Brown actively participated in many organizations, taking on leadership roles. His life could not have been easy, considering that he and his wife cared for their seven children and one adopted niece. He had been chairman of the Black Museum Committee, treasurer of NiaCAP, and a member of the Niagara Coalition, the Human Relations Board, Human Rights Commission, Niagara Community Center Board, and St. Luke's Masonic Lodge.[199] People counted on Brown to express his views because he was an extremely outspoken individual.[200] People may not have liked him, but they could not easily dismiss what he had to say. Like Bloneva Bond, Brown could make individuals who publicly opposed his ideas feel uneasy or defensive.[201] Brown continued his many public engagements throughout and beyond the urban renewal era.

INSTITUTIONAL LEADERSHIP

Like Joe Profit, Bloneva Bond, and Fred Brown, Aaron Griffin strongly supported the economic development of the Black Niagaran community. If the downtown section of Niagara Falls was to be redeveloped by urban renewal actions, he, like Fred Brown, also desired to see the local Black Niagaran community benefit from the revitalization efforts.[202] He had strongly supported the building of the Black Museum downtown near the Niagara Falls International Convention Center.[203] With the passing of years and all the ongoing activities continuously occurring around him and within the Niagara Community Center, Griffin decided that it was time to retire. He had performed his duty well for a long time. In 1973 he decided to step down.[204] Griffin actually retired in 1975 and was replaced by Robert E. Laster.[205] Laster resigned in the spring of 1976. To bring about stability, Griffin came back as interim consultant until September 1976, when another replacement was found (see figure 7.6).[206]

The selection committee chose Sandy Perry to replace Griffin. Griffin was a strong foundation for Niagara Falls's Black community. He played a key role in keeping the Niagara Community Center active by

Figure 7.6. Aaron L. Griffin, 1973. Niagara Community Center.

orchestrating fundraising, recruiting volunteers to help run the center's numerous programs, and joining boards in the broader community so that he participated in activities affecting the entire city and networked with people who could help improve the center. For example, he was active in the NAACP, Electric City Lodge No. 49, Sunset Lodge 295 of the International Benevolent and Protective Order of the Elks of the World, the North End Safe Streets Act Group, the Niagara Falls City Charter Commission, and the Niagara Frontier Transportation Authority.[207] Many interviewees spoke of the great impact Aaron Griffin had on the city of Niagara Falls.[208]

Eddie Palmore, reflecting on impactful individuals, spoke of how Griffin aided him when he first arrived in Niagara Falls.[209] In one incident, Palmore had received a check from the federal government and went to a local bank to open an account and cash his check. Bank officials questioned him intensively, wanting to know how he came to have the check and what he was doing with the large sum of money. They did not want to cash Palmore's check because they did not know or trust him. Palmore thought hard about a good reply for the bank officials. He told them he knew Aaron Griffin. They told Palmore if Griffin vouched for him they would allow him to open an account. Griffin did indeed give the recommendation, and Palmore cashed his check. Palmore said that after that event he became heavily involved in Niagara Community Center activities and grew to respect Griffin even more.

Barbara Williams also spoke highly of Aaron Griffin (or "Mr. Griffin" as many called him).[210] She shared that periodically the local NAACP branch would meet at the community center and that Griffin always opened the center's doors for community organizations. She noted how hospitable Griffin always was and how he would sit in on meetings when the NAACP met at the center. According to Williams, he also supported the issues the NAACP fought for and was a man who ran many programs for Black Niagarans and other interested parties.[211] Williams had great respect for Griffin, a man she described as "a treasure" and a hard worker.

In 1973 community members honored Aaron Griffin by holding a dinner at the local Ramada Inn, commemorating his long service to the city of Niagara Falls.[212] Harwood Bond hosted the event, and over three hundred people attended. Griffin was presented with a scrapbook about his career.[213] Dinner guests were asked to write something in a memento book that was to be given to Griffin. In reflecting on why he stayed in Niagara Falls, considering he had worked in so many places but eventually left, Griffin commented that he felt very much needed in Niagara Falls.[214] Like Ben Bolden, he grew to value the community, and the community in turn valued him as a crucial figure in Black Niagaran history.[215] After Griffin retired, he moved to Buffalo in 1968 from his Haeberle Avenue address in Niagara Falls. Griffin lived in Buffalo another twenty years and died after a long illness at the age of ninety-two.

Ensuring Community Progress by "Helping the Least of These"

The population of Niagara Falls increased significantly from 1950 to 1960 because the economy was booming; people who moved to Niagara Falls could get jobs. In 1950, there were 90,872 individuals living in Niagara Falls, and by 1960 the population had increased to 102,394.[216] This larger population accelerated the demand for more housing and more educational facilities for children. The board of education sought out sections of Niagara Falls where additional schools could be built. The board approached Hooker Chemical Company about purchasing land around Love Canal to accommodate the ever-growing population. Initially Hooker Chemical did not want to sell the land, knowing its history and toxicity. But because of the board's pressure, the company sold the land for $1, provided that if any future lawsuit were initiated Hooker Chemical would be free from liability and that the board, at least to some degree, understood the dangers of building on the property.[217] The board of education had two schools built on the property, the Ninety-Third Street School and the Ninety-Ninth Street School. Because of these new schools, more people purchased homes in the Love Canal neighborhood.

Toward the end of the age of urban renewal, events during the infamous Love Canal crisis involving the Griffon Manor Love Canal residents were related to exclusion and marginalization. The Love Canal neighborhood was part of the LaSalle section of Niagara Falls, an area annexed by the city in 1927,[218] originally a part of the Town of Niagara. White residents' complaints had begun to be publicized in local media by the late 1970s. They complained about foul odors, liquid materials that seeped into their yards, a black substance that surfaced on their basement walls, and mysteriously dying vegetation. Residents experienced a range of serious health issues, such as miscarriages, nervous disorders, cancers, and birth defects. In 1978 Michael Brown, a white reporter for the *Niagara Falls Gazette*, investigated some of the residents' claims and found much validity in them. Brown published his research findings, which captured the media's attention and helped galvanize Love Canal residents to understand the origin and impact of what was happening in their neighborhood and to organize to protect themselves and their families.[219]

Michael Brown's news reports prompted Love Canal residents to connect their health problems to exposure to toxic chemicals. Love Canal residents learned that between 1942 and 1953 Hooker Chemical Company had used the canal as a dumpsite for toxic chemicals.[220] Hooker dumped at least twenty-one thousand tons of chemicals, including caustics, alkalies, fatty acids, and chlorinated hydrocarbons from its manufacture of dyes, perfumes, solvents for rubber, and synthetic resins.[221] Hooker Chemical had buried the toxic substances in drums twenty to twenty-five feet under the ground. The steady construction of schools, the LaSalle Expressway, and sewage systems caused some of the buried chemicals to be exposed on the surface over the years, especially after heavy rainfall.

White resident Ann Hillis, for example, believed that her family's residing in the Love Canal neighborhood caused her son to have bronchitis and a rash.[222] Many other parents made similar claims but were unsure of what to do or whom to contact. Their worries, in conjunction with media attention, motivated people to stand up, organize, and make demands to local, state, and federal officials for assistance.[223] White resident Lois

Gibbs, whose son had had health problems, organized rallies, and helped to form the Love Canal Homeowners' Association, an organization consisting of predominantly working-class whites who owned their homes.²²⁴ They demanded that their homes and surrounding environments be tested for high toxicity levels, that homeowners who decide to leave should be relocated and paid a fair market value for their properties.²²⁵ Through pressure from the Love Canal residents, their allies, and media exposure, New York State and the federal government would soon step in and aid the homeowners in their plight.²²⁶

Griffon Manor, the public housing complex that the irate phone caller had tried to prevent Blacks from moving to was also a part of the Love Canal neighborhood. Located near the canal, Griffon Manor housed about 1,100 tenants, 660 of whom were African American.²²⁷ Heads of households were commonly women with many children. They liked Griffon Manor because the apartments were spacious and suburban. The complex had plenty of grass and trees, along with a neighborly community with a Head Start program for their children.²²⁸ Griffon Manor differed vastly from the old Hyde Park Village of the 1940s and 1950s (see figure 7.7).

Figure 7.7. Griffon Manor, 1980. Courtesy of the Niagara Falls Public Library.

Griffon Manor tenants saw the attention White homeowners received through their struggle versus the lack of consideration they were shown. They maintained that public officials should create a plan to improve conditions for all residents, whether they were homeowners or not, because they were all citizens and, most importantly, human beings. Members of the Love Canal Homeowners' Association and public officials tended to ignore and marginalize the steady complaints of the Griffon Manor tenants due to their race and class (if they were African American) or strictly due to their class (if they were White). Homeowners reasoned that their plight should be top priority because they owned their homes. They had worked hard and put their money into property that was in a chemically contaminated area through no fault of their own. Because of this, they argued that public officials should make aiding them their highest priority.

Griffon Manor tenants organized more extensively, determined to see justice prevail.[229] Their actions, along with those of the property owners, coincided with the environmental protection movement, which began in the early 1970s, concomitant with the modern civil rights movement.[230] The Griffon Manor tenants' struggle signified a continuation of this movement.[231] Agnes Jones, a Black Niagaran, chaired the Tenants of Griffon Manor Association.[232] She walked door to door throughout Griffon Manor to have tenants sign a petition of demands to be presented to state authorities before construction began. In essence, the petition demanded that governmental officials: (1) first and foremost, conduct extensive testing and present the results to the Griffon Manor tenants, (2) improve communication between government officials and Griffon Manor residents, and (3) develop a satisfactory relocation plan for Griffon Manor tenants.[233] Moreover, the residents solicited the aid of the NAACP, which supported them on the local as well as the state level.[234] Barbara Smith, local NAACP branch president during much of the Love Canal crisis, worked tirelessly to ensure that Griffon Manor residents received appropriate consideration and assistance.[235]

Soon a new tenant group formed to fight for the rights of Griffon Manor tenants. They called themselves the Concerned Love Canal Renters Association.[236] Sarah Herbert chaired this group, and Sarah Rich was vice president. They sought and obtained the advice and support of New York State Assemblyman Arthur O. Eve.[237] A white religious group called Ecumenical Task Force also actively aided the Griffon Manor tenants.[238] Directed by effective leadership Griffon Manor tenants, organized an impactful movement consisting of poor families and individuals along with their allies who refused to accept marginalization and exclusion.

In mid-October 1979 the Love Canal Homeowners' Association achieved a major victory. New York State officially agreed to buy out Love Canal homeowners who wanted to leave, which meant purchasing their homes at a fair market value, thus preventing homeowners from suffering major losses.[239] Republican Senator John Daly of Lewiston and Assemblyman Matthew Murphy of Lockport coordinated this plan, which was labeled the Daly-Murphy plan. State representatives initially excluded Griffon Manor because they reasoned that it was a federal housing project; and therefore, the federal government had to solve that problem. A loud protest erupted from Griffon Manor leaders, tenants, and their supporters. The local NAACP branch, led by Barbara Smith, took the state to court.[240] NAACP state representatives kept up the pressure and publicized proceedings, which convinced state representatives to include Griffon Manor tenants in their relocation plan.[241] Still, Griffon Manor residents were marginalized, even when the federal government agreed to assist New York State in purchasing homes and relocating Love Canal residents.[242]

Through the Love Canal Area Revitalization Agency (LCARA), a state group, Griffon Manor tenants were allocated $500,000 for relocation expenses, and homeowners received $17.5 million.[243] Later, LCARA also agreed to purchase stoves and refrigerators for Griffon Manor residents who desired to leave permanently, which triggered complaints from the Love Canal Homeowners' Association. In response, LCARA emphasized that stringent criteria would be used to select tenants choosing this option.[244] Through HUD, the federal government agreed to fund 27 Section 8 certificates for new or substantially rehabilitated HUD homes to accommodate those families needing four or five bedrooms.[245] Niagara Falls's city leaders did not accept these funds until forced to by the federal government, which threatened to hold up $8 million for housing improvement unless the twenty-seven families receiving the Section 8 certificates were relocated throughout the city.[246] Mayor Michael O'Laughlin and Councilman Joseph Smith resisted in participating in a process that would allow Black Niagarans to be relocated in neighborhoods other than African American enclaves.[247] In the end, many Griffon Manor tenants left; some took a risk and stayed because they were unable to find decent comparable housing elsewhere. LCARA eventually demolished the Love Canal complex in 1986.[248]

These cases accentuate that Black Niagarans, throughout much of the urban renewal era, usually were marginalized by city officials who functioned as external change agents. However, directed by their leadership, which functioned as internal change agents, Black Niagarans fought to be properly considered in urban renewal planning. This leadership ranged from conservative to liberal, consisting of institutional, entrepreneurial, and political leaders, with some of them at times operating as community activists. Joe Profit's 1963 electoral victory as Ward 12 supervisor awakened Black Niagarans to their potential political power and inspired several of them to seek broader community positions of public responsibility. All these actions served to strengthen and further develop the Black Niagaran community.

Hence, guided by their leaders, Black Niagarans forced the Urban Renewal Agency to include them in its planning activities, as mandated by the federal government. During the age of urban renewal, Black Niagarans believed that the principles championed in the US Constitution should not work selectively but should apply equally to all citizens. They fought against exclusion and marginalization and strove to gain respect, political power, resources, and opportunities. They worked to maintain parts of their community slated for revitalization not only for themselves and their family members but also for their racial group. They also persisted in their ongoing struggle to sustain and advance community development.

Chapter Eight

A New Reality, 1980 to 1985

Niagara Falls, like Buffalo, experienced steady economic decline in the 1980s. Both metropolitan centers also experienced substantial population loss as a result. Much like their parents and grandparents in the 1940s through the 1960s, many younger Black Niagarans migrated to other cities searching for jobs. Some went to Atlanta, Georgia, which was the latest national hotspot of job opportunities.

The Civil Rights Act of 1968 aided in altering the segregated housing patterns in the city of Niagara Falls. Hence by the mid-1980s Black Niagarans were not only in their old enclaves but also began to appear in many other sections of the city (see table 8.1). Did the Civil Rights Act of 1968 bring about this change? Local residents Barbara Smith, Eddie Palmore, and Ronnie Cunningham made it clear that what brought about more housing integration was a much greater supply of rental properties and homes, due to the significant decline in the population.[1] In other words, they believed that renters and home sellers could make incomes by subleasing or putting their units on the open market. Being exclusive would not have allowed them to rent or sell their properties. Therefore, at this point, dollars and cents influenced the housing market more than the peer pressure and conformity used as exclusionary tactics in the past. By the mid-1980s, a few Black Niagaran families owned homes in the De Veaux section of town, which had been an exclusively White upper-class neighborhood until the 1970s. Even today, this district has remained principally an affluent White community.[2]

By 1980 the city of Niagara Falls population had decreased from its 1960 count of 102,394 to 71,384 Niagarans, a difference of 31,010 people.

Table 8.1. 1980 Niagara Falls Census Tract Population by Race

Census Tracts	Total Population	Whites	Blacks	Other
201	5,080	4,642	396	42
202	3,813	583	3,186	44
203	1,635	1,567	55	13
204	2,519	1,626	833	60
205	3,107	2,661	336	110
206	2,798	1,984	723	91
207	3,319	3,152	131	36
208	1,134	980	125	29
209	3,331	3,111	139	81
210	3,581	3,526	24	31
211	2,544	2,083	311	150
212	3,131	2,708	353	70
213	3,047	2,823	127	97
214	2,579	2,480	66	33
215	806	732	50	24
216	1,263	580	646	37
217	2,399	2,114	248	37
218	2,325	1,914	376	35
219	1,922	1,812	102	8
220	2,605	2,547	29	29
221	3,198	3,155	8	35
222	4,495	4,406	53	36
223	3,143	3,087	20	36
224.01	2,321	2,248	57	16
224.02	1,589	957	597	35
225	3,700	3,587	73	40

Adapted from the 1980 United States Census (Please see page 390, note 1.)

Although Black Niagarans in the past had been restricted and corralled into certain city sections, some changes occurred (table 8.1). Although more Black Niagarans now lived in higher numbers in other city sections, most still lived in old enclaves. Moreover, by 1980 federal officials had again changed how they labeled census tracts. Instead of being labeled 1 to 25, they began labeling the tracts 201 to 225, covering generally the same areas as before but depicted differently than in figure 4.2.

Black Niagarans still predominantly resided in the North Side, South Side, and East Side neighborhoods, but they spread out more in

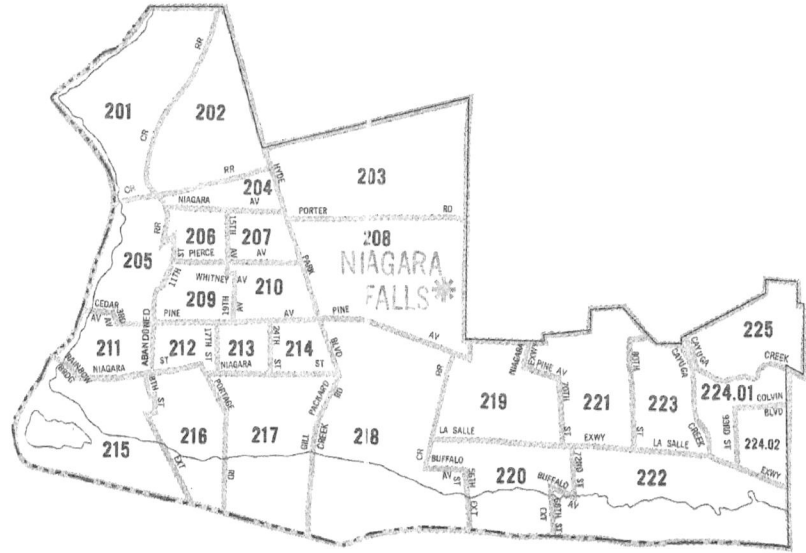

Figure 8.1. Census tract map, 1980. (See note 3, page 390).

the northern and southern sections. Instead of the north clustering being mainly in census tract 202, for example, the neighborhood spread to census tracts 201, 204, and 206, and the south clustering remained and expanded in census tract 216. On the East Side, a small group of Black Niagarans resided mainly in Griffon Manor. They would soon relocate elsewhere, however, because of the Love Canal tragedy. Hence, although integration occurred in degrees, some major enclaves still remained.

By the mid-1980s, Dr. Benjamin F. Bullock, another notable figure, community leader, long-term local NAACP president, and entrepreneur (who was aware of Niagara Falls's housing patterns) probably began to contemplate retirement.[3] He opened his dental office in Niagara Falls in 1950 after receiving his doctor of dentistry degree from Case Western Reserve University in Cleveland. He was a World War II veteran, having served with the famed Tuskegee Airmen as a meteorologist. Dr. Bullock lived in Buffalo but faithfully practiced his profession in the city of Niagara Falls for close to fifty years. As a child, Helen Reed McBride remembers going fearfully to Dr. Bullock's office on East Falls Street. When Dr. Bullock asked her to open her mouth so he could extract a tooth, she began to scream.[4] Before she stopped screaming, Dr. Bullock had the tooth out and asked her, "What's all that screaming for?"[5] It had not hurt at all, and she realized that Dr. Bullock was a master of his craft. Dr. Bullock worked until the late 1990s before moving to Atlanta to live with his sister. He passed away in 2001. Most of the interviewees remembered and commented positively on Dr. Bullock, who was active in community and civic affairs.[6]

Additionally, by the mid-1980s Black Niagarans increasingly noticed a drastic change in the structure of local African American families. For example, as a child, Black Niagaran Gene Simmons grew up in a stable family setting with his mother and father. He and other Blacks had an extended family, in which blood relatives and even fictive kin (people considered relatives who were not related by blood or marriage) looked out for family and community members. Because everyone in the community knew each other, Gene saw the adults in his surrounding community as his guardians. If he and other children misbehaved, they could be chastised and even spanked by adults who were not their parents. Moreover, these guardians would have informed the parents of a child's transgressions, and, according to Simmons, the child might receive an additional parental spanking. Simmons remembered family lessons that his mother taught him. His mother once told him, "Whenever you see the door of a home opened and children going in and out like a community center, there is no structure in that home, and children need and should have structure in their lives."[7] Structure, according to Simmons, is what he saw when growing up in Niagara Falls. Robin L. Jarrett, a family studies scholar, interprets the structure that Simmons described as an essential facet of successful parenting.[8]

Like Gene Simmons, Renee Coates-Smith emphasized family and how family operations had changed. She also was a child in the 1960s.[9] Coates-Smith nostalgically remembered the days of her childhood in Niagara Falls. Her parents and other relatives came to Niagara Falls from the South, later living nearby and reestablishing an extended family network in Niagara Falls. Coates-Smith remembered uncles, aunts, cousins, and a grandmother that lived close by, and all these individuals served as guardians as well. She also remembered an uncle who worked an eight-hour-a-day job and tended an extensive garden when he got home from work. This uncle grew a range of vegetables and readily shared them with his kinfolks, interlinking his southern traits and skills with the northern urban setting he resided in. Coates-Smith remembered always eating plenty of fresh vegetables from her uncle's garden. Because her family frequently ate food directly from the earth, she mentioned that her relatives were rarely sick.

Although her family members were poor, Coates-Smith never heard her relatives mention they were poor; they worked as a collective unit to meet the family's needs. Family members not only monitored and reprimanded the children but also made sure adults acted respectably. If a husband and wife were arguing, other relatives would get involved to defuse the conflict and bring peace; moreover, the reverend of their church might show up to provide spiritual guidance. Coates-Smith remembered that whenever she came home from school her mother was always home; she never had to worry about where her mother was. And her mother's comment "Wait 'til your father gets home; he's going to straighten you out" made her even more inclined to behave herself. Living in this environment made her feel secure growing up. Comparing contemporary African American families to her childhood in Niagara Falls, Coates-Smith remarked that "families [today] often have more material possessions and academic degrees and things; however, something is missing, and what is missing is family."[10] What they describe is the African village concept: the idea that "it takes a village to raise a family."[11]

The family change that several interviewees commented on was the preponderance of female-headed households within African American communities. Several Black Niagarans, particularly those with working-class backgrounds, blamed the welfare system for significantly changing African American family dynamics. Because African American men had to be absent from a household for a mother and her children to receive welfare, the welfare system aided in breaking up African American families.[12] According to community lore, many women felt independent of their children's father, which helped to foster an individualist rather than collectivist attitude.[13]

Sociologist E. Franklin Frazier maintained that the institution of slavery created a matriarchate, an independent female who knew that she had to constantly fend for herself and her family.[14] In her family, she was overwhelmingly dominant.[15] Daniel Patrick Moynihan, a former government official and a liberal researcher in Black family studies, echoed Frazier's work, arguing that slavery not only created a Black matriarchate but also destroyed the Black family.[16] Many scholars refuted Moynihan's thesis, including Herbert G. Gutman, Niara Sudarkasa, Robert Staples, Harold E. Cheatham, and James B. Stewart, noting that the Black family was predominantly nuclear until the early 1970s. At that time, an inordinate number of blue-collar industrial jobs were lost due to de-industrialization, which meant that many Black males were unemployed.[17] This aided in making economics the central stimulus in the transformation of working-class Black families.[18]

In earlier years, when adult males worked, Black Niagaran households tended to have both a father and mother present. This profoundly shaped society's perceptions of what a stable family was. In speaking more about family, all the senior citizens interviewed in this research stated that families were stable from the earliest days and that absent fathers were rare. Zorie Bell Boling stated that "men were men," meaning that they fulfilled their responsibilities. Barbara Smith commented that it was unusual to see fathers not present in households. Eddie Palmore said that families displayed pride in themselves and were unified, while Theodore Williamson commented that he remembered families early on being large but getting increasingly smaller—yet still functioning as effective working units.[19] Accordingly, economics played a crucial role in transforming working-class Black Niagaran families.[20]

Besides economics, changing cultural patterns promoted by the dominant White American culture filtered through and affected other American communities. Such changes included people working two or three jobs, more women working outside the home, a greater acceptance of women having children outside of marriage, and more men staying at home to take care of children while their spouses worked elsewhere. More people were moving long distances from relatives to get jobs. Changing values about attending church services and promotion of ideas such as "do your own thing" exemplify these changing social and religious traditions.[21] Last, and perhaps most profoundly, because African Americans generally do not economically or politically control their communities (and because racism continues), these factors contributed to the transformation of the Black family.

This succinct chapter underlined how economic necessity allowed Black Niagarans to acquire living spaces away from historical enclaves. It also commented on the waning years of Dr. Benjamin Bullock, a community pillar, and the changing undercurrents of a community's most basic structure: the family. Economics compelled White homeowners and White realtors to put their properties on the open market. A common theme that reverberates throughout is leadership. And although by the mid-1980s leadership dynamics had changed in many Black Niagaran families, leadership generally endured, which helped to sustain families and the Black Niagaran community.

Conclusion

This book was written with three central purposes in mind: (1) to demonstrate the proactive role of leadership in effecting community development, (2) to convey a history of Black Niagarans from 1850 to 1985, and (3) to demonstrate that Black Niagarans experienced the same housing discrimination following the Second Great Migration as many African Americans faced in major northeastern and Midwestern cities during the First Great Migration. This further validates that the rapid population expansion of African Americans in Niagara Falls accelerated discriminatory acts. Prior to this study, there was no extensive study of Niagara Falls that covered the history of Black Niagarans. An interesting and useful master's thesis exists but examines only community dimensions mainly during the early 1950s and serves more as a valuable participant observer's report.

In the timeframe of this study, most Black Niagaran leaders could be classified as moderate. This categorization is based on E. Ladd's "Black Leadership Typologies Continuum," in which he defines Black leadership in the context of the surrounding White-controlled milieu.[1] Conservative Black leadership, according to Ladd, regularly concurs with practices and beliefs of the White power structure, conforming to the white paradigm. William Brooks's leadership exemplifies this. Militants are completely unacceptable to the dominant White power structure. Black militants usually strive to control their own environments, independent of White hegemony and governance, believing that this leads to true freedom and equality. The Nation of Islam matches this path. Moderate Black leadership fits somewhere in between conservative and militant Black leadership. Moderate leaders operate within the prevalent White-controlled milieu, yet they seek to reform it. Most of the Black leaders highlighted in this study fit this moderate leadership style.

Furthermore, regardless of class or gender, and impacted by racial barriers, Black Niagaran leaders still operated proactively. Their leadership goals, methods, and rhetoric focused on the collective interests and concerns of their racial group. Black Niagaran leaders, who mainly strove to integrate their racial group into the mainstream of society, often managed institutions that were community funded and/or government funded. After 1940, more so than in any other epoch, Black Niagaran leaders confronted various forms of housing discrimination as their people flooded into overcrowded city sections. Their unending requests for fair housing practices would not be met for decades.

The city of Niagara Falls has only a limited Black Niagaran archive that accounts for the years 1850 to 1985. However, of the available primary sources, leadership and community development themes not only arise but dominate recorded materials; supported by interviews, this allowed a historical narrative to be created. This study employed the framework initiated by W. E. B. Du Bois in his momentous work, *The Philadelphia Negro*, which encouraged evaluation of urban history through the lens of early beginnings, employment, migration, institutional building, inter- and intragroup relations, and political agency. This pattern also fits the mode of most research on African American urban history. In utilizing Du Bois's framework, this study focused on examining how leaders effected Black Niagaran community development from 1850 to 1985. Leaders arose regardless of class, gender, or racial barriers to serve the collective interest of Black Niagarans. Most Black leaders pulled themselves up and achieved success (along with middle-class status) and then directed their efforts toward lifting others up. Alliance leaders assisted fugitive slaves and Black Niagarans by helping them to gain their freedom, citizenship rights, and access to fair treatment and equal opportunities. Hence, many Niagaran leaders, regardless of the racial barriers faced, were tenacious in their efforts to improve Black community development.

In its early years, Niagara Falls was a transnational border, a landmass that connected the northern United States to Canada. Fugitive slaves fled from the United States to Canada or from Canada to the United States, depending on which country they felt they could gain and maintain their freedom. The Niagara River served as a fluid frontier. These fugitive slaves, as historian Larry Gara noted, were often self-liberators, particularly fearful of being seized and returned to slavery. As underscored by Ivan Light in *Ethnic Enterprise in America*, Black leaders working toward group racial advancement or against racism demonstrated collectivist behavior. How Black Niagarans supported enslaved people in their midst, reacted to the Hobbs case, or combated housing discrimination exemplify this cooperative ethos. In serving as role models for their group, Black Niagaran leaders often practiced the Politics of Respectability. They adhered to White society's standards for public decorum and promoted these values both within their families and within their racial group. Charlotte Dett, Alice C. Hayes, John M. Pollard, and several other community leaders epitomized this leadership style.

This study also highlights how external entities aided Black Niagarans and their leaders in their efforts toward advancement. Such forces include the national civil rights movement; the New York State Commissioner of Education; the Federal Department of Housing, and Urban Development and Alliance leaders. As historian Jacquelyn Hall has posited, the local Black Niagaran movements—civil rights, school desegregation, and urban renewal—operated in conjunction with national events.

This study's findings echo those of other historical studies of African American urban northern communities. Most Black Niagarans then and now have family roots in the South or their ancestors came from southern locales, often Alabama. Thus, migration is a dominant theme in this study. When African Americans first arrived and settled in Niagara Falls, they integrated into the general community, but after 1940 they lived mainly in the existing African American community or enclaves to which they were largely restricted. They founded, joined, and expanded churches; they frequented the Niagara Community Center; or they joined a Masonic order. They became northerners and Niagarans, for example, by culturally adjusting to an urban milieu that promoted individualism. They also became northerners by adjusting to working eight hours a day, forty hours per week, in low-level urban industrial plant jobs. They proactively participated in community formation and development, showing a tendency to incorporate southern cultural patterns into their new community.[2] In time, leaders arose among them to provide guidance and to represent their interests, ensuring that Black Niagarans gained opportunities in the surrounding political economic and social structure. These activities were ongoing throughout the decades, as significant numbers of African Americans migrated to Niagara Falls during the nineteenth and twentieth centuries.

This book differs vastly from most African American urban historical studies, first by the number of recorded and unrecorded interviews conducted and, second and most importantly, in how I intermixed with community members over an eighteen-year period. This intensive research method allowed me to learn my interviewees' histories from the inside out. My strategy was both necessary and beneficial for many reasons, principally because mainstream-traditional sources only partially recorded aspects of the lives of Black Niagarans. Therefore, this foundational study includes the limited recorded research combined with what people themselves remembered over the years. My recorded interviews were mainly (but not exclusively) with senior citizens who lived through major events in Niagara Falls in the early to mid-twentieth century.

All interviewees supported having their history told and graciously spent much time telling me their own stories. Several of the interviewees have since passed on (e.g., George Hart, Eugene Hamilton, Zorie Bell Boling, Theodore Williamson, Mildred Isom, Vivian Thompson, Carlyle Miller, Arthur Ray, Mabel Smith, William Williamson, Veedee Price, and others). My deepest regret is that they did not live to see this book completed and published. For years at the Black Pioneers' Annual Picnic, coordinators announced that a book was forthcoming, and many of these people were greatly enthusiastic. I assured them that I would do my utmost to convey Black Niagaran history correctly and share what they disclosed to me. My hope is that their children, grandchildren, friends, and other relatives will appreciate the history.

Black Niagarans from 1850 to 1985 can be generally characterized as a low-income group and active churchgoers who made family and religion integral parts of their lives. They were committed family members and citizens who did whatever was required to sustain themselves. They participated in their communities and also in the broader society, making their mark on history. Fugitive slaves usually arrived in Niagara Falls with just their bodies and a desire to be free; those who stayed joined a budding community in which they eventually felt safe. With time, they became Niagarans by embracing and practicing the cultural norms of their environment. With the expansion of the local economy, more people of African descent came to Cataract City, drawn by the region's job prospects. Some arrived from Canada, and most came from the American South. With an increasing population, people moved away from conducting worship services in their own homes—or sometimes their neighbors' homes—to wanting to establish a church to accommodate and attract more worshippers. By the early 1900s Black Niagarans organized to construct what would have been the first African American church. Although this effort proved unsuccessful, Black Niagarans soon built another church, followed by even more churches. Black Niagarans, therefore, followed a pattern found in most African American urban studies that examines community formation and development—people migrating to towns and cities, obtaining employment, recruiting family members and/or friends, and then establishing or joining places of worship. With further influxes of people, participating in church activities became a vital aspect of an increasing number of people's lives. Family members and neighbors looked out for one another and operated as a village, as highlighted by Helen Reed-McBride, Gene Simmons, and Renee Coates-Smith. With community formation, growth, and development steadily progressing, Black Niagarans then interacted in the broader community to function as leading citizens to ensure that their group received fair representation and its share of opportunities. Black Niagarans, guided by their leaders, who proactively created, developed, and maintained community, rejected marginalization. They strove to live and prosper with the hope that their descendants and community would advance beyond them and leave a meaningful history for future generations. This history of Black Niagarans tells their story.

Appendix A

Template for Interview Questions

Employment

1. What type of work did most Blacks do during the 1920s, 1930s, 1940s, 1950s, 1960s, 1970s, and 1980s?
2. Where did Blacks work?
3. From your memory, what did the Blacks you knew say about their jobs?
4. What type of work did men do in comparison to women?
5. Were there any Blacks in the skilled trades or professions during these periods?
6. Do you remember any Blacks with their own businesses?
7. Who were the elites in the Black community of Niagara Falls, New York?
8. What distinguishing factors made them elites?

Housing

1. From your earliest memories, where did Blacks live in Niagara Falls?
2. Did they live throughout Niagara Falls, or were they clustered in certain areas?
3. Did Blacks own much property? Were Blacks mainly renters?

4. Did Blacks have adequate room space in their homes or rental properties?
5. What were the neighborhoods like in those days?
6. Was housing ever a problem for Blacks in Niagara Falls? If so, when did it become a problem?

Leadership

1. From your earliest memories, who were the leaders of the Black Community of Niagara Falls?
2. In your opinion, what made these people leaders?
3. What were these leaders attempting to do? Did they accomplish their goals?
4. Is there a specific leader that you really admired? If so, who and why?

Community Institutions

1. Were there any community institutions—Black or White—that really aided Blacks? How did these institutions aid Blacks?
2. Were there any community institutions—Black or White—that really harmed Blacks? How did these institutions harm Blacks?
3. What type of events did community institutions sponsor?
4. What were NiaCap, the Niagara Community Center, Friendship House, and others?

Education

1. What was it like for you to attend schools in Niagara Falls?

2. From your earliest memories, where did most Blacks go to school?

3. What did Blacks think of the education they obtained in Niagara Falls?

4. What were some of the educational goals of your family and the Black community?

5. What do you think schools were like for Blacks before and after the integration efforts of the 1960s?

Race Relations

1. From the earliest times, what were race relations like for Blacks in Niagara Falls?

2. How did Blacks and Whites get along in Niagara Falls? Did race relationships change? If so, how and why? Did they change for the better or worse?

3. Did you face discrimination in Niagara Falls? What type of discrimination?

Personal Reflections

1. When you think historically of Blacks in Niagara Falls, what comes to mind?

2. How would you compare life for Blacks in Niagara Falls compared to what you have historically heard about other local areas, including Lockport and Buffalo?

3. If you were writing a book on Blacks in Niagara Falls, what are some subjects you would discuss and why?

Appendix B

Sample Institutional Questions Asked About St. John's AME Church

1. How did St. John's AME Church start?
2. Who were the founding mothers and fathers of the church?
3. What obstacles did St. John's AME Church have to confront to be successful?
4. When would you say St. John's AME was at its height?
5. Who were some of the significant ministers? What made them important?
6. What kinds of social outreach programs did St. John's AME offer to the Niagara Falls community?
7. Has St. John's worked with other churches and denominations for specific community uplift purposes?

Appendix C

Notes on Interviewees

Of the sixty-two recorded interviews, nearly 69 percent were interviews with men, and about 31 percent were with women. Fifty-one of the sixty-two recorded interviews were also from senior citizens (people over the age of sixty-five), most being between the ages of seventy and ninety-five. The job status of the interviewees ranged from low-skilled workers (e.g., domestic servants, laborers, factory laborers, etc.) to clerical and professional workers (e.g., office workers, schoolteachers, construction company owners). Low-skilled workers represented 50 percent of the interviewees.

During the eighteen-year period of this research, the author spoke to more than eighty Black Niagarans to gain a more in-depth knowledge and understanding of their history. These conversations were not recorded by a digital recorder.

Appendix D

*Interview Excerpts from Two Recorded Interviews,
Barbara Smith and Theodore Williamson*

Barbara Smith,
Interview Recorded May 17, 2002, 4:30 p.m.

POINTS

1. Barbara Smith's father came in 1922. The Reverend H. C. Thomas got Barbara Smith's father a job at Carbon Steel Company. Jobs were plentiful in those days. Barbara Smith's other family members came to Niagara Falls in 1923.

2. In 1922 Carbon Steel was hiring African Americans.

3. Barbara Smith was born in 1938 and grew up on the East Side. She attended Niagara Street School.

4. Most African Americans in Barbara Smith's community were related.

5. Barbara Smith's community was a mixed-race community.

6. African Americans in large groups started coming in 1944 and 1945.

7. Housing was a problem for African Americans when they came in large numbers during World War II.

8. Many African Americans worked at Carborundum. Many were maintenance workers. According to Smith, most African Americans worked in factories, and many African American women were domestic workers.

9. Reverend Edgar Huff was head of St. John's AME Church.

10. According to Smith, Teddy Williamson's father had a soda shop.

11. The housing situation, according to Smith, (1) Hyde Park Village was perhaps all African American, (2) Pine Arcs may have been all African American, (3) Griffon Manor became all African American, (4) Center Court was and is all African American, (5) Packard Court was all White and a duplicate of Center Court.

11. St. John's had the first vocational school. Bertha Johnson helped to start New Jerusalem.

12. Barbara Smith said if she were writing a paper on Niagara Falls, New York, her thesis would be that many physical changes have occurred in the area. For example, factories were here, and now they are gone. Strikes existed in the past. Unions were growing. Niagara Falls was a working-class town. A lot of young people have left the city.

13. Most African Americans lived in the North Side and East Side neighborhoods.

14. Niagara Falls, New York, was divided ethnically.

15. A small number of African Americans lived by the waterfalls of Niagara Falls, New York. Those African American families had been living there for a long time.

16. Reverend Whitaker, Ben Bolden, and Reverend Clay were some of the leaders of Niagara Falls, New York.

17. The De Veaux area of Niagara Falls is where many African American domestics worked.

18. The Red Coach and the Niagara Hotel are old hotels that still exist today.

Theodore Williamson, Interview Recorded May 13, 2002, 4:15 p.m.

Points

1. During 1928 and soon after, African Americans were cooks, drivers, and garbage collectors. These were considered good jobs. You were considered prominent if you had one of these jobs.

2. Names of hotels that African Americans worked at during the late 1920s and 1930s:

   a. Cataract Hotel

   b. Henry Hubs Hotel

   c. Prospect House

   d. Mr. Plato's Boarding House on the 400 Block of Erie Avenue

   e. Anna L. Johnson's Boarding House

   f. Tourist Houses: Mr. Alberta Reynolds, The Hamptons, Mr. McDonald, and Mr. Parmey White

3. Red Cab drivers were elite jobs during the late 1920s and 1930s. A person named Hopper was a Red Cab driver.

4. Ben Bolden was a proud man who helped to organize the Niagara Falls Community Center.

5. J. M. Pollard was head of the Niagara Community Center, and Anna Jones was assistant director of the Niagara Community Center.

6. The following were homeowners during the late 1920s and early 1930s (and even after): William Rudolph, who was the first Niagara Falls African American bricklayer. He lived on Livingston Avenue. Rudolph Goffeng and his family lived on North Avenue. The Hershey Family lived on North Avenue. These were African Americans who lived in White communities. Owning a home in the late

1920s and early 1930s (and after for a while) was a big thing. Segregation was in effect in Niagara Falls at this time.

7. An African American holiday during the late 1920s and early 1930s was "Emancipation Day." This occurred the first Thursday in August of every year. It took place at Port Dalhousie, which was on Lake Erie. From a 250-mile radius, African Americans would come and celebrate. More specifically, they came from Buffalo, Rochester, Detroit, Niagara Falls, New York, and other northern cities.

8. The Reverends Johnson and Thomas were ministers in the late 1920s and early 1930s.

9. The African American community of Niagara Falls, New York, was "unified" during the 1920s and early 1930s.

10. Erie Avenue was the center of entertainment and the main business district of the African American community of Niagara Falls. For example, (1) the Niagara Community Center was located at 637 Erie Avenue. (2) Ann Gabriel had a tourist home. (3) Almed Cheatham had a tourist home. (4) Wesley Parker ran a restaurant and boarding house; it was called the Parker House. (5) the Sunset Club was a very popular nightclub. It had New York City–style entertainment. It was for people twenty-one years and older. (6) Murphy's Grill was a restaurant, which had twenty rooms upstairs. 7) A man by the name of Torran operated a pool hall. (8) Emmett Ashford and his wife operated a beauty shop and barbershop.

11. There was a race riot in the mid-1930s. It was over a report that an African American man had bothered some White woman. Theodore Williamson said he remembers being told to stay inside the house.

12. Erie Avenue was on the other side of railroad tracks.

13. The Glorious Church of God and Christ was a prominent church in Niagara Falls, New York, in the late 1920s and early 1930s. It was on Calumet Avenue.

14. The Brinson Family has been in Niagara Falls, New York, for many decades.

15. In 1942 the corporations in the area paid forty-two cents an hour, which was a good hourly rate in those days (according to Theodore Williamson). Union Carbide and Carbon Corporation paid these same wages.

16. Theodore Williamson graduated from Niagara Falls High School in 1941. He was one of five African Americans in his senior class.

17. Ben Bolden was a major leader in Niagara Falls. He attracted people because he was always aware of issues. He read a lot. He looked on the bright side of life.

18. John M. Pollard, according to Theodore Williamson, was normally called J. M. Pollard. He was a great speaker. He was his own boss.

19. The Niagara Fall Community Center was the first center that drew African Americans in Niagara Falls together.

20. Aaron Griffin took over the Niagara Community Center after John M. Pollard.

21. African Americans in Niagara Falls were poor in the 1930s. Milk and bread were given out. Families picked up metals to sell to Jewish junk dealers during the 1930s in Niagara Falls, New York.

22. During the World War II era, African Americans were brought to Niagara Falls to work in factories/corporations. Some examples of them are as follows: Carbon Corporation and Carborundum, both of which hired a lot of African Americans. Du Pont hired only a few African Americans. Hooker hired only a few African Americans. Vanadium hired many African Americans. (They left the area in 1968.) African Americans performed low-level jobs in these companies.

23. From 1940 to 1950, jobs for African Americans were plentiful. Families were large but getting smaller. There were

very few homeowners. Banks would not give a mortgage to African Americans. This was called "redlining."

24. African Americans lived in projects from 1940 to perhaps 1970. Center Court was built in 1941. It was a government housing project that housed 99 percent African Americans, which was against governmental regulations. Packard Court started off White but became an African American project. Harry Jordan was built in the late 1950s and was predominantly African American. Griffon Manor was built before 1950 and was 100 percent African American.

25. Eleventh Street and Erie Avenue were the entertainment spots for African Americans in the 1940s and 1950s. Eleventh Street was a ghetto area for African Americans, Italians, Armenians, and others.

26. According to Theodore Williamson, there was very little interaction between African Americans in Niagara Falls, New York, and African Canadians in Niagara Falls, Canada. (But African American men and White Canadian women had relationships.)

27. The Niagara Falls Community Center was most active between the 1940s and 1950s. The influx of more people made the community center expand according to Theodore Williamson.

28. The Tunnel Area Construction Project (about 1880 nearly 1900) was a very dangerous job for African Americans, according to Theodore Williamson.

Appendix E

*Notable Leaders Who Impacted
Black Niagaran History*

Name	Era	Approach	Ideas	Class	Gender	Race
Colonel P	antebellum	abolitionists	antislavery	upper class—a large farm owner	male	White
Platt H. Skinner	antebellum	abolitionists	antislavery	middle class Dr. Skinner was an educated man.	male	White
Black community members during the slavery era who operated to free slaves brought into their midst.	antebellum	abolitionists	antislavery	mainly working class and probably some middle class	both males and females	Black
Charlotte Dett	1890s to 1930s	Republican Party member and for the uplift of African Americans	integration and uplift of African Americans but work with all groups and treat people how you wish to be treated	middle class; Dett operated a boarding house	female	Black
Jerry Plato	1910 to 1965	self-help Plato, who emigrated from Canada, probably was integration.	self help "An opportunity comes around more than once in a lifetime. It is available as long as you see it and can seize it."	middle class	male	Black

Name	Era	Approach	Ideas	Class	Gender	Race
The Rev. B. B. B. Johnson and his wife	1900	integration; Johnson gave a "patriotic address at the 4th of July Celebration."	collective group work, at least in terms of establishing a church	middle class	male for Rev. Johnson and female for Rev. Johnson's wife	Black
Benjamin W. Bolden	1919 to about 1975	integration	self-help	middle class; Mr. Bolden was the proprietor of a souvenir shop.	male	Black
Theodore Williamson	1920s to 2010	integration	self-help	upper middle class	male	Black
Rev. Donald B. Barton was the minister of St. John's AME Church	1920s	integration	self-help	middle class; Rev. Barton graduated from Howard University in Washington, DC	male	Black
John M. Pollard Sr.	late 1920s	integration	self-help and Blacks benefiting from their taxes	middle class	male	Black
Samuel Dett	1890s to 1962	integration	self-help and Blacks benefiting from their taxes.	middle class	male	Black
Dr. Charles B. Hayes	early 1930s to 1962	integration	self-help and Blacks benefiting from their taxes	upper middle class	male	Black
Alice C. Hayes	early 1930s to 1982	integration	self-help and Blacks benefiting from their taxes	upper middle class	female	Black

continued

Name	Era	Approach	Ideas	Class	Gender	Race
Aaron L. Griffin	early 1940s to 1970s	integration	self-help and Blacks benefiting from their taxes	middle class	male	Black
Willie C. Fields Sr.	1939 to early 2000s	integration	self-help and Blacks benefiting from their taxes	middle class	male	Black
The Rev. Millard Fillmore Clay	1930s, 1940s to ?	integration	?	middle class	male	Black
Rev. H. Edward Whitaker	1952 to about 1962	integration	self-help and Blacks benefiting from their taxes	middle class	male	Black
Bloneva Bond	1943	integration	self-help and Blacks benefiting from their taxes	middle class	male	Black
Otis Cowart	early 1960s	integration	self-help and Blacks benefiting from their taxes	middle class	male	Black
Arthur Ray	civil rights and post–civil rights early 1930s	integration	self-help and Blacks benefiting from their taxes	middle class	male	Black
Joseph Profit	civil rights and post–civil rights early 1940s	integration	Democrat	middle class	male	Black
Rev. Glen Raybon	civil rights	integration	self-help and Blacks benefiting from their taxes	middle class	male	Black
Harwood Bond	civil rights, 1943	integration	self-help and Blacks benefiting from their taxes	middle class, worked as a chemist at Hooker Chemical	male	Black

Name	Era	Approach	Ideas	Class	Gender	Race
Rev. Edgar Huff, pastor of St. John's AME Church	civil rights	integration	self-help and Blacks benefiting from their taxes	middle class	male	Black
Rev. Paul F. Thompson, of Emmanuel Baptist Church	civil rights	integration	self-help and Blacks benefiting from their taxes	middle class	male	Black
Casper L. Jordon	civil rights	integration	self-help and Blacks benefiting from their taxes	middle class	male	Black
Vera Tremier	civil rights	integration	?	middle class	male	Black
Eddie Palmore	1950 to present	integration	self-help and Blacks benefiting from their taxes	middle class	male	Black
Clover Jones	civil rights era and after	integration	self-help and Blacks benefiting from their taxes	middle class	male	Black
Willie Shine	late civil rights era	integration	self-help and community efforts to help racial members	middle class	male	Black
Joe McCoy	civil rights era and after	integration	self-help and Blacks benefiting from their taxes	middle class	male	Black
Ronnie Cunningham	civil rights era and after	integration	self-help and Blacks benefiting from their taxes	middle class	male	Black

continued

Name	Era	Approach	Ideas	Class	Gender	Race
Fred Brown	civil rights era and after	integration	self-help and Blacks benefiting from their taxes	middle class	male	Black
Father Daniel Porter	civil rights era and early 1970s	integration	justice and equality for all	middle class	male	Black
William Brooks	1960s and after	integration	pull yourself up by your bootstraps	middle class	male	Black

Notes

Notes to the Introduction

1. Veedee Price, who was a Vietnam veteran, passed away in August 2017.
2. In creating this foundational study, much of the data gathered for this book was collected in that manner.
3. W. E. B. Du Bois, *The Philadelphia Negro* (Philadelphia: University of Pennsylvania Press, 1996).
4. Gilbert Osofsky, *Harlem: The Making of a Ghetto* (New York: Harper & Row, Publishers, 1971).
5. Joe William Trotter Jr., *Black Milwaukee: The Making of an Industrial Proletariat, 1915–45* (Chicago: University of Illinois Press, 1985).
6. The process of how a significant number of black Milwaukee laborers transformed from southern agricultural laborers to industrial workers and how that impacted community development and progression.
7. Richard W. Thomas, *Life for Us Is What We Make It* (Bloomington: Indiana University Press, 1992); and Lillian Serece Williams, *Strangers in the Land of Paradise* (Bloomington: Indiana University Press, 1999).
8. See table 1.1 of this book.
9. See table 1.1.
10. Afru Cooper, "The Fluid Frontier: Blacks and the Detroit River Region: A Focus on Henry Bibb," *Canadian Review of American Studies* 30, no. 2 (2000): 129–149.
11. Osofsky, *Harlem: The Making of a Ghetto*, 105–158; James R. Grossman, *Land of Hope: Chicago, Black Southerners, and the Great Migration* (Chicago: University of Chicago Press, 1989), 123–207; Kenneth L. Kusmer, *A Ghetto Takes Shape: Black Cleveland, 1870–1930* (Urbana: University of Illinois Press, 1978), 174–189; August Meier and Elliott Rudwick, *From Plantation to Ghetto* (New York: Hill and Wang, 1976), 232–270; Richard W. Thomas, *Life for Us Is What We Make It*, 123–173; and Lillian Serece Williams, *Strangers in the Land of Paradise*, 151–187.

12. Allan Spear, *Black Chicago: The Making of a Negro Ghetto, 1890 to 1920* (Chicago: University of Chicago Press, 1967), 53–54; Trotter, *Black Milwaukee*, 29–31; Meier and Rudwick, *From Plantation to Ghetto*, 252; Kusmer, *A Ghetto Takes Shape*, 113–115, 140–143; and Robert L. Boyd, "Black Enterprise in the Retail Trade During the Early Twentieth Century," *Sociological Focus* 34, no. 3 (August 2001), 242.

13. Throughout the African American urban experience, White entrepreneurs have always had access to (and an ongoing presence in) "the African American market." Their dependence on the African American market made them susceptible to the so-called Don't Buy Where You Can't Work campaigns of the 1930s. Their direct presence would diminish in response to the urban riots of the 1960s.

14. James E. DeVries, *Race and Kinship in a Midwestern Town: The Black Experience in Monroe, Michigan, 1900–1915* (Urbana: University of Illinois Press 1984); Maureen Elgersman Lee, *Black Bangor: African Americans in a Maine Community, 1880–1950* (Durham: University of New Hampshire Press, 2005); and Myra B. Young Armstead, *Lord, Please Don't Take Me in August: African Americans in Newport and Saratoga Springs, 1870–1930* (Urbana: University of Illinois Press, 1999).

15. David B. Landon and Teresa D. Bulger, "Constructing Community: Experiences of Identity, Economic Opportunity, and Institution Building at Boston's African Meeting House," *International Journal of Historical Archaeology*, 17, no. 1 (March), 119–142; and Williams, *Strangers in the Land of Paradise*, 161–170.

16. I formulated this definition to interpret the city of Niagara Falls based on historical analyses of Niagara Falls generally and the Black Niagaran community specifically, in conjunction with my review of the literature involving northern African American community studies.

17. See note 16.

18. Maulana Karenga, "The Crisis of Black Middle Class Leadership: A Critical Analysis," *Black Scholar* 13, no. 6 (Fall 1982), 31; and Jacob U. Gordon, *Black Leadership For Social Change* (Westport, CT: Greenwood, 2000), 23.

19. Ronald W. Walter and Robert C. Smith, *African American Leadership* (Albany: State University of New York Press, 1999), 122.

20. Regarding point three, this study extensively utilizes Booker T. Washington's "captains of industry" concept to accentuate Black Niagaran leaders who succeeded (e.g., educationally, religiously, occupationally, etc.) then energetically and unselfishly helped others succeed, not setting themselves apart from these individuals but aligning themselves with them. Washington's idea epitomizes an infinite range of individuals and organizations within the Black Niagaran community that articulated this uplifting idea. This idea and practice certainly did not originate with Washington. It is a "concept" being employed in this study. Furthermore, his "captains of industry" definition was selected based on its clear and concrete meaning, which elucidates a recurring phenomenon consistent throughout the timeframe of this study.

Where appropriate, this study also employs elements of Booker T. Washington's entrepreneurial philosophy to help describe business activities and ideas of individuals or groups. For the period of this study, 1850 to 1985, a range of economic thought filtered into African American communities nationwide. During the 1850s, Henry Highland Garnet and Martin R. Delany, for example, through the African Civilization Society (ACS), promoted a return to Africa and the pursuit of self-help economic ventures there. Following the Reconstruction era (1865 to 1877), with the abandoning of the federal government's efforts to help rectify the plight of former slaves, an influential self-help movement arose overwhelmingly among African Americans, with business formation and development operating as an integral component of this movement. By 1902 Booker T. Washington, through the establishment of the Tuskegee Institute (1881), the Negro Farmers' Conference (1892), and above all, the National Negro Business League (1900), championed ideas of self-help and business formation and development perhaps more than any leader of his era (1895 to 1915), so much so that he can be characterized as "the father of 20th Century Black Business Development." His economic influence was widespread in communities during his lifetime and after. A survey of available records of urban African American entrepreneurs from 1905 to 1955 will show Washington's broad economic influence, the respect businesspersons held for him, and the tributes they often paid to him.

After Washington's death, Communism and Marcus Garvey's business philosophy filtered into African American communities. Communism, a political, economic, and social philosophy that promotes public ownership of property and communal control of the means of production, was always on the margins within African American communities. Few African Americans embraced it. Conversely, Marcus Garvey's business philosophy made a significant impact in the African American community. However, Garvey's and Washington's philosophies were somewhat similar in this way. Both leaders promoted self-help among African Americans. Both promoted the selling of goods and services for profit and recommended that African Americans support worthy black business ventures. But where Garvey foresaw the elevation of African Americans and other African people to be contingent upon the freedom and elevation of Africa, Washington, of course, saw the potential for salvation within the United States alone. W. E. B. Du Bois, during the Great Depression, advocated a cooperative economic paradigm in which he envisioned African American businesspersons pooling their resources and working collectively for their survival and progression. This was more of a maintenance and uplift strategy rather than a philosophy. During the period of this study, other economic philosophies and strategies arose; for instance, the cooperative economic philosophy of the US Organization, founded by Maulana Karenga and Hakim Jamal during the Black Power era of the 1960s, along with the sort of socialism advocated at one time by the Black Panther Party and the communism encouraged by Angela Davis. Still, African American businesspersons nationally and within the historical milieu of Niagara Falls have traditionally focused on selling goods and services in an effort to make profits, with Booker T. Washington's name resonating often in the available sources as an individual who influenced entrepreneurs and leaders nationwide, particularly from 1905 to 1955.

In summation, with the rationale explicated for using components of Booker T. Washington's business philosophy, along with his "captains of industry" concept as aspects of a framework for leadership analysis, Black Niagaran leaders proactively worked to establish and preserve a vibrant community within the Niagara Falls milieu, which included implementing a range of impactful strategies to influence and respond to changing dynamics within the internal Black Niagaran community as well as the broader external community. How community was established, developed, and maintained centered on the goals of the Black Niagaran community and the extant structural factors created and enforced by the broader community's leadership, which often acted as an impediment but at times could be a source of encouragement. Black Niagaran community goals as well as broader community structural policies, norms, and values often hinged on the changing epochs from the slavery era to the age of urban renewal. See, for instance, Leon Litwack and August Meier, eds., *Black Leaders of the Nineteenth Century* (Urbana: University of Illinois Press, 1991); John Hope Franklin and August Meier, eds., *Black Leaders of the Twentieth Century* (Chicago: University of Illinois Press, 1994); Richard K. MacMaster, "Henry Highland Garnet and the African Civilization Society," *Journal of Presbyterian History* 48, no. 2 (Summer 1970): 95–112; Richard Blackett, "Martin R. Delany and Robert Campbell: Black Americans in Search of an African Colony," *Journal of Negro History* 62, no. 1 (January 1977): 1–25; W. E. B. Du Bois, *Black Reconstruction* (New York: Atheneum, 1969), 711–729; August Meier, *Negro Thought in America, 1880–1915* (Ann Arbor: University of Michigan Press, 1963), 42–58; Chapter 7 of Michael B. Boston, *The Business Strategy of Booker T. Washington* (Gainesville: University Press of Florida, 2010); Daniel Hanglberger, "Marcus Garvey and His Relation to (Black) Socialism and Communism," *American Communist History* 12, no. 2, 200–219; Mark Solomon, *The Cry Was Unity: Communists and African Americans, 1917–1936* (Jackson: University of Mississippi Press, 1998), 3–51; Milfred C. Fierce, "Economic Aspects of the Marcus Garvey Movement," *Black Scholar* 3, nos. 7–8 (March–April 1972), 50–61; Robert J. Norrell, "Booker T. Washington: Understanding the Wizard of Tuskegee," *Journal of Blacks in Higher Education* 42 (Winter 2003–2004), 96–109; Joseph P. DeMarco, "The Rationale and Foundation of Du Bois's Theory of Economic Cooperation," *Phylon* 35, no. 1 (First Quarter 1974): 5–15; Scott Brown, *Fighting for US: Maulana Karenga, The US Organization and Black Cultural Nationalism* (New York: New York University Press, 2005), 6–106; Jessica C. Harris, "Revolutionary Black Nationalism: The Black Panther Party," *Journal of Negro History* 86, no. 3 (Summer 2001): 415–418; Angela Y. Davis, *Angela Davis—an Autobiography* (New York: Random House, 1974); and Angela Davis, *Angela Y. Davis: Women, Race and Class* (New York: Vintage, 1983), 149–171.

21. V. P. Franklin, *Black Self-Determination: A Cultural History of African-American Resistance* (Brooklyn, NY: Lawrence Hill, 1992), 3–9.

22. Although Booker T. Washington died in 1915, his business ideas continued to filter into African American communities throughout the nation until around 1955. See chapter 7 of Boston, *Business Strategy of Booker T. Washington*.

Notes to Chapter 1

1. See Henrietta Buckmaster, *Let My People Go: The Story of the Underground Railroad and the Growth of the Abolition Movement* (Boston: Beacon, 1941), Benjamin Drew, *The Narrative of Fugitive Slaves in Canada* (Boston: John P. Jewett, 1856), William Still, *The Underground Railroad* (Philadelphia: Porter & Coates, 1872, repr., New York: Arno, 1968); and Wilbur H. Siebert, *The Underground Railroad from Slavery to Freedom* (New York: Macmillan, 1899).

2. Siebert, *The Underground Railroad*.

3. William Siener and Thomas Chambers, "Harriet Tubman, the Underground Railroad, and the Bridges at Niagara Falls," *Afro-Americans in New York Life and History* 36 (January 2012), 34–63.

4. "Underground Railroad," *Niagara Falls Gazette*, September 22, 1858.

5. The recorder probably did not mention Joe's last name because he did not want to give Joe's slave master information on his whereabouts. (It is also true that some enslaved individuals had no last names.) See Dann J. Broyld, "Harriet Tubman: Transnationalism and the Land of a Queen in the Late Antebellum," *Meridians* 12, no. 2 (2014): 86.

6. "Tubman Led Slaves to Falls' Freedom Gate," Underground Railroad Clipping Binder, Local History Department, Niagara Falls Public Library; Kate Clifford Larson, "Racing for Freedom: Harriet Tubman's Underground Railroad Network Through New York," *Afro-Americans in New York Life and History* 36 (January 2012), 18–22.

7. William J. Switala, *Underground Railroad in New York and New Jersey* (Mechanicsburg, PA: Stackpole, 2006), 130–131; Don Papson and Tom Calarco, *Secret Lives of the Underground Railroad in New York City* (Jefferson, NC: McFarland, 2015), 151.

8. Switala, *Underground Railroad*, 130.

9. Steven Lubet, *Fugitive Justice: Runaways, Rescuers, and Slavery on Trial* (Cambridge, MA: Harvard University Press, 2010), 11–22.

10. Carl J. Costantino, "History of the Underground Railroad along the Niagara Frontier," (master's thesis, Niagara University, 1947), 52–56.

11. Sharon A. Roger Hepburn, *Crossing the Border: A Free Black Community in Canada* (Urbana: University of Illinois Press, 2007), 12–26; and Robin W. Winks, *The Blacks in Canada* (Montreal: McGill-Queen's University Press, 1971), 178–232.

12. See Frederic Bancroft, *Slave Trading in the Old South* (Columbia: University of South Carolina Press, 1996).

13. Like Platt H. Skinner, Charles T. Torrey saw the effects of slavery in Washington, DC, which influenced him to be an active underground railroad agent in the area. See Stanley Harrold, "On the Borders of Slavery and Race: Charles T. Torrey and the Underground Railroad," *Journal of the Early Republic* 20, no. 2 (Summer 2000), 273–292.

14. *The First Semi-Annual Report of the School for the Instruction of the Colored, Deaf, Dumb, and Blind* (Buffalo: Commercial Advertiser Steam, 1858), 8.

15. "Platt H. Skinner," *The Mute and Blind*, November 3, 1860, Niagara County Historical Society, Lockport, New York, 100.

16. *The Mute and the Blind*, April 26, 1862, Kroch Library at Cornell University, Ithaca, New York, 56–57.

17. Ken Grossi to James M. Boles, October 16, 2009. Ken Grossi is Oberlin College's archivist. He sent Boles a letter verifying that Platt H. Skinner was a student at Oberlin College. (A copy of this letter is in possession of the author.)

18. Fergus M. Bordewich, *Bound for Canaan* (New York: Amistad, 2005), 131; and Robert Bruce Slater, "The American Colleges That led the Abolition Movement," *Journal of Blacks in Higher Education* 9 (Autumn 1995), 97.

19. *First Semi-Annual Report*, 7; H. William Feder, "The Evolution of an Ethnic Neighborhood that Became United in Diversity: The East Side, Niagara Falls, New York 1880–1930" (PhD diss., University of Buffalo, 1999), 601.

20. *The Mute and the Blind*, November 3, 1860, Niagara County Historical Society, Lockport, New York, 99.

21. "House of Many Cellars," *Niagara Falls Gazette*, December 5, 1965.

22. "House of Many Cellars," *Niagara Falls Gazette*.

23. Frederick Douglass, *Narrative of the Life of Frederick Douglass: An American Slave* (Cambridge, MA: Harvard University Press, 1969), 710.

24. Alliance leadership, as defined in the introduction, existed when non-Blacks commonly strove to help elevate the status of Blacks, either by helping them to flee bondage or by assisting them in gaining American citizenship and all its privileges and immunities.

25. David Anderson, *Rochester Region Underground Railroad Network to Freedom: A Guidebook Rochester/Monroe County Freedom Trail Commission* (Rochester, NY: Publication Services, 2003), 48–49, and 56–58.

26. Afua Cooper, "The Fluid Frontier: Blacks and the Detroit River Region, A Focus on Henry Bibb," *Canadian Review of American Studies* 30 (2000): 133.

27. Sigrid Nicole Gallant, "Perspectives on the Motives for the Migration of African Americans to and from Ontario, Canada: From the Abolition of Slavery in Canada to the Abolition of Slavery in the United States," *Journal of Negro History* 86, no. 3 (Summer 2001): 395.

28. Richard Thomas, *Life for Us Is What We Make It* (Bloomington: Indiana University Press, 1992), 2; and Robert Kostoff, *History of Niagara County, New York* (Lewiston, NY: Edwin Mellen, 2011), 63–68.

29. Karolyn Smardz Frost and Veta Smith Tucker, *A Fluid Frontier: Slavery, Resistance, and the Underground Railroad in the Detroit River Borderland* (Detroit: Wayne State University Press, 2016).

30. Judith Wellman, "This Side of the Border: Fugitives from Slavery in Three Central New York Communities," *New York History* 79, no. 4 (October 1998): 359–392.

31. Michael B. Boston, "Blacks in Niagara Falls, New York: 1865 to 1965," *Afro-Americans in New York Life and History* 28 (July 2004): 9; *Population Schedules of the 6th Census of the United States, 1840, New York* (New York census schedules for the year 1840, National Archives microfilm publications), reel 311; *Niagara County Census 1980, Department of Economic Development and Planning for the Niagara County Affiliate Data Center* (Lockport, New York, 1981), 1 of 2; *1990 Census of Population and Housing Summary Population and Housing Characteristics New York* (Washington, DC: US Government Printing Office, 1991), 74.

32. *The Seventh Census of the United States: 1850* (Washington, DC: Robert Armstrong, Public Printer, 1853), 102.

33. Henrietta Buckmaster, *Let My People Go: The Story of the Underground Railroad and the Growth of the Abolition Movement* (Boston: Beacon, 1941), 176–177.

34. Benjamin Quarles, *The Negro in the Making of America* (New York: Touchstone, 1996), 129.

35. *US Census of Population 1870* (Washington, DC: Government Printing Office, 1872), 214. The cities of Buffalo and Detroit experienced a similar pattern. In 1850, 675 Blacks were recorded as residing in Buffalo, while 809 were recorded in 1860. Detroit contained 587 Blacks in 1850 and 1,402 in 1860. See Jean Richardson, "Buffalo's Antebellum African American Community and the Fugitive Slave Law of 1850," *Afro-American in New York Life and History* 27 (July 2003): 42; and David M. Katzman, *Before the Ghetto: Black Detroit in the Nineteenth Century* (Urbana: University of Illinois Press, 1973), 62.

36. Douglass, *Narrative of the Life*, 35–36; Austin Steward, *Austin Steward: Twenty-Two Years a Slave and Forty Years a Freeman* (Reading, MA: Addison-Wesley, 1969), 86; Will Still, *The Underground Railroad: Authentic Narratives and First-Hand Accounts* (Mineola, NY: Dover, 2007), 57–70; Benjamin Quarles, *Black Abolitionists* (New York: Oxford University Press, 1969, 143–167; and Thomas, *Life for Us*, 2.

37. "URR-Niagara County-Niagara Falls, 1847," n.d., Underground Railroad binder, Local History Department, Niagara Falls Public Library; and "Affray at the Falls," n.d., Underground Railroad binder, Local History Department, Niagara Falls Public Library.

38. Michael B. Boston, "Blacks in Niagara Falls, New York: 1865 to 1965," *Afro-Americans in New York Life and History* 28 (July 2004): 11.

39. Stephen Middleton, "The Fugitive Slave Crisis in Cincinnati, 1850–1860: Resistance, Enforcement, and Black Refugees," *Journal of Negro History* 72, no. 1/2 (Winter–Spring, 1987), 22; Cheryl Janifer LaRoche, *Free Black Communities and the Underground Railroad* (Urbana: University of Illinois Press, 2014), 131–133; and Gerald G. Eggert, "The Impact of the Fugitive Slave Law on Harrisburg: A Case Study," *Pennsylvania Magazine of History and Biography*, 109, no. 4 (October 1985): 565–566.

40. *Population of the United States in 1860: Compiled from the Original Returns of the Eighth Census* (Washington, DC: Government Printing Office, 1864), 337.

41. *New York State Census of 1865* (Albany, NY: Charles Van Benthuysen & Sons, 1867), 9; and *US Census of Population 1870* (Washington, DC: Government Printing Office, 1872), 214.

42. *US Census of Population 1870*, 209; and Jean Richardson, "Buffalo's Antebellum African American Community and the Fugitive Slave Law of 1850," *Afro-Americans in New York Life and History* 27 (July 2003), 42.

43. See Larry Gara, *The Liberty Line: The Legend of the Underground Railroad* (Lexington: University of Kentucky Press, 1967).

44. Switala, *Underground Railroad*, 146.

45. John W. Blassingame, *The Slave Community: Plantation Life in the Antebellum South* (New York: Oxford University Press, 1979), 200.

46. Wilbur H. Siebert, *The Underground Railroad from Slavery to Freedom: A Comprehensive History* (New York: Macmillan, 1899), 152.

47. Milton C. Sernett, *Harriet Tubman: Myth, Memory, and History* (Durham, NC: Duke University Press, 2007), 41–104; Josiah Henson, *An Autobiography of the Reverend Josiah Henson* (Reading, MA: Addison, 1969), 82–88; Stuart Seely Sprague, ed., *His Promised Land: The Autobiography of John P. Parker, Former Slave and Conductor on the Underground Railroad* (New York: W.W. Norton, 1998), 71–145; John Hope Franklin and Alfred A. Moss Jr., *From Slavery To Freedom: A History of African Americans*, 8th ed. (New York: McGraw-Hill, 2000), 208; William Still, *The Underground Railroad: Authentic Narratives and First-Hand Accounts* (Mineola, NY: Dover, 2007), 1–23; and Stanley Harrold, "On the Borders of Slavery and Race: Charles T. Torrey and the Underground Railroad," *Journal of the Early Republic* 20, no. 2 (Summer, 2000), 273–292.

48. See Larry Gara, *The Liberty Line: The Legend of the Underground Railroad* (Lexington: University of Kentucky Press, 1967).

49. *New York State Census of 1865*, 5–100.

50. William H. Harris, *The Harder We Run: Black Workers Since the Civil War* (New York: Oxford University Press, 1982), 71–91.

51. "Freedom," *Niagara Gazette*, July 10, 1986.

52. "Freedom," *Niagara Gazette*.

53. *US Census for 1870: Town of Niagara, Village of Niagara City & Village of Niagara Falls*, microfilm, reels 16 and 17, Niagara Falls, NY, Niagara Falls Public Library; *US Census for 1880: Town of Niagara, Village of Niagara Falls & Suspension Bridge*, microfilm, reels 19 and 20, Niagara Falls, NY, Niagara Falls Public Library, microfilm, reels 19 and 20.

54. This fact is apparent throughout the town and village of Niagara Falls censuses for the years 1865 to 1930. These censuses are listed in the bibliography and stored in several archives, including the Niagara Falls, New York Public Library; see "Interesting Reminiscences," *Niagara Falls Gazette*, October 26, 1927.

55. "A Famous Old Hostelry," *Niagara Falls Journal*, January 4, 1918.

56. Orrin E. Dunlap, "The Cataract House," n.d., Local History Hotel folder 647.94, Local History Department, Niagara Falls, New York Public Library.

57. "Interesting Reminiscences."

58. *US Census for 1870*; *US Census for 1880*; and *New York State Census for 1892: Village of Niagara Falls & Village of Suspension Bridge*, microfilm, reel 19, Lockport, NY, Lockport Public Library.

59. *US Census for 1900: Town of Niagara, Niagara Falls City & La Salle Village*, microfilm, reel 23, Niagara Falls, NY, Niagara Falls Public Library.

60. Vivian Flagg McBrier, *R. Nathaniel Dett: His Life and Work* (Washington, DC: Associated, 1977), 1.

61. *US Census for 1910: Town of Niagara, City of Niagara Falls, Village of LaSalle* Niagara Falls, NY, Niagara Falls Public Library, microfilm, reels 28 and 29.

62. Feder, Evolution of an Ethnic Neighborhood," 141.

63. Feder, 135.

64. "John Troy Is No More," *Niagara Falls Gazette*, February 27, 1906.

65. "A Canadian Tunnel," *Niagara Falls Gazette*, August 31, 1893.

66. "A Canadian Tunnel," *Niagara Falls Gazette*.

67. Robin W. Winks, *The Blacks in Canada* (Montreal: McGill-Queen's University Press, 1971), 142–153; and Catherine Clinton, *Harriet Tubman: The Road to Freedom* (New York: Back Bay, 2005), 105.

68. Wilma Morrison, interview by author, June 30, 2002. Morrison is/was director of the Norma Johnson Museum-Library in Niagara Falls, Ontario; and Winks, *Blacks in Canada*, 114–496.

69. Lisa Krissoff Boehm, *Making a Way Out of No Way: African American Women and the Second Great Migration* (Jackson: University Press of Mississippi, 2010).

70. This may have had something to do with the change in classification.

71. *US Census for 1910*, sheet 8.

72. "Former Falls Resident Dies," *Niagara Falls Gazette*, May 18, 1967.

73. *US Census for 1910*, sheet 10.

74. "Faithful," in "326 Blacks in Niagara Falls Notebook," n.d., Local History Department, Niagara Falls Public Library.

75. In my population figures, individuals in the census listed as Mulattoes were counted as Black.
76. Williams, *Strangers in the Land of Paradise*, 11–12.
77. "Colored Republican Meeting," *Niagara Falls Gazette*, September 18, 1872.
78. "The Colored Republicans," *Niagara Falls Gazette*, October 19, 1892.
79. Williams, *Strangers in the Land of Paradise*, 92.
80. "Colored Republicans," *Niagara Falls Gazette*.
81. "Colored '400' Dance," *Niagara Falls Gazette*, April 4, 1897.
82. *US Census for 1900*, sheet 3.
83. Arlene E. Gray, "Nate, My Son, The Story of R. Nathaniel Dett, Mus.D," n.d., Local History Department, Niagara Falls, New York Public Library, 11.
84. Gray, "Nate, My Son," 18.
85. Ibid., 11.
86. Vivian Flagg McBrier, *R. Nathaniel Dett: His Life and Works (1882–1943)* (Washington, DC: Associated, 1977), 2.
87. McBrier, *R. Nathaniel Dett*, 11.
88. "Memorable Day for the Negro Baptists," *Niagara Falls Gazette*, April 9, 1900.
89. "Colored Revivalist," n.d., book 326, Black History, Local History Department, Niagara Falls Public Library.
90. St. Clair Drake and Horace R. Cayton, *Black Metropolis: A Study of Negro Life in a Northern City* (Chicago: University of Chicago Press, 1993), 39–40; David M. Katzman, *Before the Ghetto: Black Detroit in the Nineteenth Century* (Urbana: University of Illinois Press, 1973), 19–20; Kenneth L. Kusmer, *A Ghetto Takes Shape: Black Cleveland, 1870–1930* (Urbana: University of Illinois Press, 1978), 30; and Lillian Serece Williams, *Strangers in the Land of Paradise: The Creation of an African American Community, Buffalo, New York 1900–1940* (Bloomington: Indiana University Press, 1999), 11–12.
91. Harold A. McDougall, *Black Baltimore: A New Theory of Community* (Philadelphia: Temple University Press, 1993), 27.
92. "Rev. and Mrs. B. B. B. Johnson of the Second Baptist Church," *Daily Cataract*, March 24, 1900.
93. "Memorable Day for the Negro Baptists," 1.
94. "Salvation of the Negro Citizen," *Niagara Falls Gazette*, April 16, 1900.
95. Ibid.
96. "Negro Jubilee to be Held on Fourth of July," *Niagara Falls Gazette*, May 5, 1900; and "Plans for Negro Jubilee are Well Underway," *Niagara Falls Gazette*, May 16, 1900.
97. "Rev. and Mrs. B. B. B. Johnson of the Second Baptist Church," *Niagara Falls Gazette*.
98. "Rev. B. B. Johnson Has Given Up His Pulpit," *Niagara Falls Gazette*, June 26, 1900, 1.

99. Ibid.

100. "Negroes Held Big Jubilee Yesterday," *Niagara Falls Gazette*, July 5, 1900.

101. "Rev. B. B. B. Johnson Makes Accounting," *Daily Cataract-Journal*, January 4, 1901.

102. "Wily Colored Pastor Sells Out His Church," *Buffalo Courier*, January 9, 1902; and James Franklin Banks, "Problems Encountered by World War II and Post World War II Negroes, Who Settled in the Niagara Falls, New York Area" (master's thesis, Niagara University, 1958), 73. Banks was a minister himself in Niagara Falls and knew much about the African American religious history of the city.

103. "Negroes Married," *Daily Cataract-Journal*, March 11, 1900; and "Mr. Johnson Is Tired Of It All," *Daily Cataract-Journal*, August 23, 1900.

104. "A History of St. John's A. M. E. Church." A document Barbara Smith gave to the author. Barbara Smith was a longtime active member of St. John's AME Church.

105. Ibid.

106. "One Hundred-Dollar Club Organized to Further Work among Colored Group of Worthy Citizens," *Niagara Falls Gazette*, January 31, 1928.

107. See Stewart E. Tolnay and E. M. Beck, *A Festival of Violence: An Analysis of Southern Lynching, 1882–1930* (Urbana: University of Illinois Press, 1992) and Rayford W. Logan, *The Betrayal of the Negro, from Rutherford B. Hayes to Woodrow Wilson* (New York: Collier, 1965); and C. Vann Woodward, *The Strange Career of Jim Crow* (New York: Oxford University Press, 1973).

108. Maureen Elgersman Lee, *Black Bangor: African Americans in a Maine Community, 1880–1950* (Durham: University of New Hampshire Press, 2005), 88–125; and Myra B. Young Armstead, *"Lord Please Don't Take Me in August"* (Urbana: University of Illinois Press, 1999), 83–110.

109. Douglass S. Massey and Nancy A. Denton, *American Apartheid: Segregation and the Making of the Underclass* (Cambridge, MA: Harvard University Press, 1994), 91–96; Andrew Hacker, *Two Nations: Black and White, Separate, Hostile, Unequal* (New York: Scribner, 2003), 3–86; Richard Rothstein, *The Color of Law: A Forgotten History of How Our Government Segregated America* (New York: Liveright, 2017), 139–151; Williams, *Strangers in the Land of Paradise*, 148; St. Clair Drake and Horace A. Cayton, *Black Metropolis: A Study of Negro Life in a Northern City* (Chicago: University of Chicago Press, 1993), 175–180; Kenneth L. Kusmer, *A Ghetto Takes Shape: Black Cleveland, 1870–1930* (Urbana: University of Illinois Press, 1978), 174–189; William M. Tuttle Jr., *Race Riot: Chicago in the Red Summer of 1919* (New York: Atheneum, 1971), 157–183; James R. Grossman, *Land of Hope: Chicago, Black Southerners, and the Great Migration* (Chicago: University of Chicago Press, 1991), 174–175; and Harvey Amani Whitfield, *Blacks on the Border: The Black Refugees in British North America, 1815–1860* (Burlington: University of Vermont Press, 2006), 45.

110. See Howard N. Rabinowitz, *Race Relations in the Urban South* (New York: Oxford University Press, 1978).

111. Tuttle, *Race Riot*, 3–268.

112. "Negroes Object: Local Men and Buffalo Colored Folk Say if Czol gosz was a Negro His Treatment Would Be Summary," *Niagara Falls Gazette*, September 10, 1901.

113. Ibid.

114. "Row among Colored Gents," *Niagara Falls Gazette*, October 11, 1865; "A Sad Shooting Affair," *Niagara Falls Gazette*, January 8, 1868; "Jail Breaking," *Niagara Falls Gazette*, January 19, 1876; "Poles Shot By Negroes," *New York Times*, March 8, 1892; and "Stabbed by Vicious Negro," *Daily Cataract*, February 27, 1900. Additionally, no interviewee noted hearing of a major racial incident between 1850 and 1914.

115. Williams, *Strangers in the Land of Paradise*, 147. (No major racial conflicts are noted in this study. For the period 1900 to 1920, Buffalo's African American population was extremely small relative to the White population.) See Osofsky, *Harlem*, 3, 46–52.

116. "Row among Colored Gents"; "A Sad Shooting Affair"; "Jail Breaking"; "Poles Shot By Negroes"; "Stabbed by Vicious Negro"; "Were Caught Stealing Coal: Harry Gates and William Briton, Negroes Sent Down for Thirty Days," *Niagara Falls Gazette*, February 27, 1903; "The 'Coke' Habit," *Niagara Falls Gazette*, August 17, 1909; "Woman Burned to Death after Orgy in East Side Hovel with Negroes; Coroner Probes Case," *Niagara Falls Gazette*, December 23, 1925; "Physician Kidnaped Beaten and Robbed As Riots Continue," *Niagara Falls Gazette*, July 14, 1936; "Convict Two Robbery," *Niagara Falls Gazette*, March 12, 1943; "Signing of Negroes Causes Controversy," *Niagara Falls Gazette*, April 3, 1953; "Youth on Rampage," *Niagara Falls Gazette*, April 27, 1968; "Dissatisfaction Seen with Police, Courts," *Niagara Falls Gazette*, September 19, 1975; "Some Blacks See Little Progress in 1970s Housing," *Niagara Falls Gazette*, April 30, 1978; and "Letter about Hiring Blacks," *Niagara Falls Gazette*, August 25, 1985.

117. "Far From Dead Was Mr. Hobbs," *Cataract Journal*, September 21, 1904.

118. Ibid.

119. Ibid.

120. "Niagara Movement: Colored Men Assembled at Fort Erie Form Permanent Organization," *Niagara Falls Gazette*, July 14, 1905; David Levering Lewis, *1868–1919 W. E. B. Du Bois: Biography of a Race* (New York: Henry Holt, 1993), 297–342; and Rayford Logan, *W. E. B. Du Bois: A Profile* (New York: Hill and Wang, 1971), 48–53.

121. Ibid.

122. Melbourne Cummings, "Historical Setting for Booker T. Washington and the Rhetoric of Compromise, 1895," *Journal of Black Studies* 8 (September 1977): 75–82; Charles P. Henry, "Who Won The Great Debate—Booker T. Washington or W. E. B. Du Bois?" *Crisis* 99 (1992): 12–17; David Howard-Pitney, "The Jeremiads

of Frederick Douglass, Booker T. Washington, and W. E. B. Du Bois and Changing Patterns of Black Messianic Rhetoric, 1841–1920." *Journal of American Ethnic History* 6 (Fall 1986): 47–61; and C. Spencer Poxpey, "The Washington-Du Bois Controversy and Its Effect on the Negro Problem,"*History of Education Journal* 8 (1957): 128–152.

123. "Black History Tour" (paper commissioned by Town of Erie, Economic Development Department, Saint Catherine's Historical Museum, 1992), 22.

124. Williams, *Strangers in the Land of Paradise*, 152.

125. "Mossell Spurred Lockport School Integration," *Niagara Falls Gazette*, February 8, 1987.

126. "Wife of A Famous Educator," *Cataract Journal*, July 22, 1904.

127. Williams, *Strangers in the Land of Paradise*, 152.

128. Ibid.

129. "Noted Soloist to Appear in Buffalo," *Chicago Defender*, November 27, 1915.

130. Merline Pitre, "Frederick Douglass: The Politician vs. the Social Reformer," *Phylon* (1960–) 40, no. 3 (Third Quarter 1979), 270.

131. "Colored Man Rode in a Wheelbarrow," *Niagara Falls Gazette*, November 12, 1900.

132. *US Census for 1900*, sheet 22.

133. "Colored Man Rode in a Wheelbarrow."

134. "Negro and Democracy," *Niagara Falls Gazette*, September 28, 1908.

135. Ibid.

136. Ibid.

137. "Mrs. Dett Inspired Sons, Fired GOP Politics," *Niagara Falls Gazette*, February 21, 1987.

138. *US Census for 1900*, sheets 1–25.

139. Williams, *Strangers in the Land of Paradise*, 221.

140. Ibid., 3.

141. "Member of Oldest Black Family Recalls Lost Era," *Niagara Falls Gazette*, February 9, 1987.

142. Ibid.

143. *US Census for 1910*, sheet 8.

144. Ibid., sheets 1, 2, 3, 4, 5, 6, 7, 8, 9, 10, 11, 12, 13, 14, 16, 18, 21, 23, 24, 27, 32.

145. H. William Feder, *The Evolution of an Ethnic Neighborhood that Became United in Diversity: The East Side, Niagara Falls, New York 1880–1930*, 272.

146. *US Census for 1910: Town and Village Census for Niagara Falls*, sheet 9.

147. "Aunty Lee Dead," *Book 326 Black History*, Local History Department, Niagara Falls Public Library.

148. "Remembered Her Former Servant," *Niagara Falls Gazette*, July 23, 1906.

149. Eric Foner, *Reconstruction America's Unfinished Revolution 1863–1877* (New York: Harper & Row, 1988), 81; Leon F. Litwack, *Been in the Storm So*

Long: The Aftermath of Slavery (New York: Vintage, 1980), 292–335. Moreover, immediately after slavery, for example, Booker T. Washington and his mother, brother, and sister left the section of Virginia in which they had been enslaved to go to Malden, West Virginia, a town two hundred miles away. They did this to join Washington Ferguson, who was the stepfather of Washington and his brother and the biological father of his sister. Washington stated that it was not easy to leave the area and people that he and his family knew so well. See Booker T. Washington, *Up From Slavery* (New York: Airmont, 1967), 28.

150. Benjamin Drew, *The Refugee: A North-side View of Slavery* (Reading, MA: Addison-Wesley, 1969), 20.

151. Ibid.

152. "Gideon Lee in Trouble," *Daily Cataract-Journal*, May 10, 1900.

153. "Gid Lee Died at the Hospital," *Niagara Falls Gazette*, April 8, 1912.

154. Arthur Ray, interview with author, April 25, 2010.

155. Ibid.

156. "Colored Masons to Dedicate Hall," *Niagara Falls Gazette*, May 18, 1909.

157. Prince Hall was a man of African descent who came to Massachusetts from Barbados. He strove to make a good life in this country and displayed his appreciation and patriotism by fighting for the patriots in the American Revolution. He was exposed to Masonic practices and highly interested in establishing a lodge. He sought permission to create a Black order of masons from a White-run lodge and was flatly denied. He then applied to the Grand Lodge of England and was immediately granted a warrant. "In 1792 a black Grand Lodge was organized, with Hall as grand master." This was significant because it allowed Hall to grant charters of dispensation to other groups in various locales throughout the United States. Eventually, the Grand Lodge of New York State was granted a charter of dispensation, and they, in time, issued a charter of dispensation to the organizers in Niagara Falls. See John H. Franklin and Alfred A. Moss Jr., *From Slavery to Freedom: A History of African Americans*, 8th ed. (New York: McGraw-Hill, 2000).

158. Chernoh M. Sesay Jr., "The Dialectic of Representation: Black Freemasonry, the Black Public, and Black Historiography," *Journal of African American Studies* 17, no. 3 (September 2013): 382. The term "middle-class respectability," as applied to African American Masons, argues that White racism should be steadily critiqued and fought against and that African Americans should constantly exude upstanding behavior that validates their first-class citizenship rights. See page 382 of Sesay's article.

159. Eddie Palmore, interview by author, April 5, 2010.

160. "Colored Masons Elect Officers," *Niagara Falls Gazette*, December 27, 1912.

161. David G. Hackett, "The Prince Hall Masons and the African American Church: The Labors of Grand Master and Bishop James Walker Hood, 1831–1918,"

Church History 69, no. 4 (December 2000), 801–2. This article helps to explain the relationship between the Prince Hall Masons and the Black Church, a relationship that Jerry Plato valued highly.

162. "Ordered to Leave the City at Once," *Niagara Falls Gazette*, May 28, 1913.
163. Ibid.
164. Lee Rainwater and William L. Yancey, *The Moynihan Report and the Politics of Controversy* (Cambridge, MA: MIT Press, 1967), 47–94.
165. *Thirteenth Census of the United States*, vol. 2: *1910 Population* (Washington, DC: US Government Printing Office, 1913), 219 and 223; John Blassingame, *The Slave Community: Plantation Life in the Antebellum South* (New York: Oxford University Press, 1979); Herbert G. Gutman, *The Black Family in Slavery and Freedom 1750–1925* (New York: Vintage, 1976); Andrew Billingsley, *Climbing Jacob's Ladder: The Enduring Legacy of African American Families* (New York: Touchstone, 1992); and Robert Staples, *The Black Family: Essays and Studies* (Belmont, CA: Wadsworth, 1994).
166. "Gideon Lee In Trouble," *Niagara Falls Gazette*, May 10, 1900.
167. *Thirteenth Census of the United States*, 219.
168. Barbara Smith, interview by author, May 17, 2002.
169. Ibid.
170. "Former Falls Resident Dies," *Niagara Falls Gazette*.
171. McBrier, *R. Nathaniel Dett*, 5–6.
172. Anne Key Simpson, *Follow Me: The Life and Music of R. Nathaniel Dett* (Metuchen, NJ: Scarecrow, 1993), 4.
173. David Levering Lewis, *W.E.B. Du Bois, Biography of Race* (New York: Henry Holt, 1993), 511–513.
174. Charles W. Puttkammer and Ruth Worthy, "William Monroe Trotter, 1872–1934," *Journal of Negro History* 43, no. 4 (October 1958), 306–307.
175. "Our Anvil Chorus," *Niagara Falls Gazette*, September 23, 1912.
176. In 1906 the First Battalion of the Twenty-Fifth Infantry, who were segregated African American troops, was transferred from Fort Niobrara, Nebraska, to Fort Brown in Brownsville, Texas. These African American troops were discriminated against by local Whites and Mexicans. They were not permitted in public parks, and White businesses discriminated against them. A little after midnight on August 14, shooting erupted in Brownsville. Over a hundred shots were fired, resulting in the injury of a policeman and a resident. Without creditable evidence, the African American troops were blamed for this event. None of the African American troops confessed or accused their peers of the incident. With no hearing or trial, President Theodore Roosevelt dismissed three companies of these troops from the army. They were barred from rejoining the forces, denied veterans' benefits or pensions, and could not seek federal jobs. The African American community and much of its leadership vigorously protested this action. President Roosevelt was unmoved.

177. "Repudiating Roosevelt," *Niagara Falls Gazette,* August 12, 1912.
178. Ibid.
179. "Fall from Chair Fatal to Vass," *Niagara Falls Gazette,* June 8, 1915.
180. "Personal," *Niagara Falls Gazette,* August 13, 1912.
181. "Tubman Monument Unveiled in Auburn," *Post-Standard,* July 6, 1915.
182. Evelyn Brooks Higginbotham, *Righteous Discontent: The Women's Movement in the Black Baptist Church, 1880–1920* (Cambridge, MA: Harvard University Press, 1993), 185–229.
183. "Female Smokers Are Criticized, Empire State Federation also Protests against the Chewing of Gum, Women Want to Vote," *New York Age,* July 10, 1913.

Notes to Chapter 2

1. Hamilton B. Mizer, *A City Is Born* (Niagara Falls, NY: Niagara County Historical Society, 1981), 83.
2. Ibid.
3. Most interviewees noted this point when discussing employers of Blacks in the Niagara Frontier, including Eugene Hamilton, Edwardo King, Indiana Martin, Nathaniel McDowell, Carlyle Miller, Eddie Palmore, Arthur Ray, Gene Simmons, James Walker, Theodore Williamson, William Williamson, and others.
4. "History of Carborundum Company at Niagara Covers Half Century of Colorful Industrial Progress," n.d., Industries Reserve Filing Case II, 18 Part 4, Local History Department, Niagara Falls Public Library, 1.
5. Ibid.
6. Ibid.
7. "Union Carbide Company Is Pioneer Manufacturer of Calcium Carbide; Shares Huge Plant With Electro Metallurgical Company, Producing Various Ferro-Alloys," n.d., Industries Reserve Filing Case II, 18 Part 4, Local History Department, Niagara Falls Public Library, 1.
8. George H. Coley, "Facts, Facilities and Industries of Niagara Falls, New York," n.d., Local History Department, Niagara Falls Public Library, 166–167.
9. "National Carbon Company, Inc.," Industries Reserve Filing Case II, 18, Part 4, Local History Department, Niagara Falls Public Library, 1.
10. Coley, "Facts, Facilities and Industries," 145–146.
11. Ibid., 163.
12. Ibid., 132–168.
13. Kimberley L. Phillips, *AlabamaNorth: African American Migrants, Community, and Working-Class Activism in Cleveland, 1915–45* (Urbana: University of Illinois Press, 1999), 57–97; Richard W. Thomas, *Life for Us Is What We Make It: Building Black Community in Detroit, 1915–1945* (Bloomington: Indiana University Press, 1992), 20–48; Trotter, *Black Milwaukee,* 39–79; and Williams, *Strangers in the Land of Paradise,* 65–96.

14. Alphonse Gavin, "Niagara Falls 1918–1929," n.d., Local History Department, Niagara Falls Public Library, 16.
15. Ibid., 17.
16. Ibid., 17–18.
17. Ibid., 18.
18. Ibid., 18.
19. Ibid., 19.
20. Ibid.
21. A ghetto is often referred to as part of a city where minority groups live as a result of social, legal, and economic pressure. Ghettos are often known for being more impoverished than other sections of cities. Ghettos, too, are generally communities neglected by city officials.
22. August Meier and Elliott Rudwick, *From Plantation to Ghetto* (New York: Hill and Wang, 1976), 235.
23. Henderson H. Donald, "Causes of the Recent Negro Migration," *Journal of Negro History* 6, no. 4 (October 1921), 416; and Sam Marullo, "The Migration of Blacks to the North 1911–1918," *Journal of Black Studies* 15, no. 3 (March 1985), 298.
24. James R. Grossman, "Blowing the Trumpet: The Chicago Defender and Black Migration during World War I," *Illinois Historical Journal* 78, no. 2 (Summer 1985), 82.
25. Joe William Trotter Jr., "The Great Migration," *OAH Magazine of History* 17, no. 1 (October 2002), 31.
26. See Jay R. Mandle, *Not Slave, Not Free: The African American Economic Experience Since the Civil War* (Durham, NC: Duke University Press, 1992).
27. Joe W. Trotter Jr., ed., *The Great Migration in Historical Perspective* (Bloomington: Indiana University Press, 1991), 6.
28. "Obituaries: Marie Brinson," n.d., *Obituaries Notebook A-B*, Local History Department, Niagara Falls Public Library, 1.
29. Ibid.
30. Ibid.
31. Ibid.
32. Carl Miller, interview by author, August 2, 2008, and July 10, 2010.
33. Emmett J. Scott, "Letters of Negro Migrants of 1916–1918," *Journal of Negro History* 4, no. 3 (July 1919), 290–340; James R. Grossman, *Land of Hope: Chicago, Black Southerners, and the Great Migration* (Chicago: University of Chicago Press, 1991), 66–97; and Altin Gavranovic, " 'Can't Get My Mind Settle': Black Migrants and the Decision to Leave the South During the First World War," *Australia and New Zealand American Studies* 23, no. 1 (July 2004): 139–148.
34. See W. Fitzhugh Brundage, *Lynching in the New South: 1880–1930* (Urbana: University of Illinois Press, 1993).
35. "Today's Events at Community Center," *Niagara Falls Gazette*, July 9, 1935.

36. *US Census for 1930*, reels 44, 45, and 46, Niagara Falls Public Library, Niagara Falls, New York.

37. Miller, interview.

38. Zorie Bell Boling, interview by author, August 8, 2008

39. Charles Johnson, "Negroes in the Railway Industry: Part II," *Phylon* 3, no. 2 (1940–1956) (Second Quarter, 1942): 200–202.

40. Shepard Krech III, "Black Family Organization in the Nineteenth Century: An Ethnological Perspective," *Journal of Interdisciplinary History* 12 (Winter 1982): 429–452.

41. "Carryover" refers to a family behavioral pattern that is passed on from generation to generation. In the case of African Americans, it commonly refers to family behavioral patterns passed on from the African context to the American setting.

42. Ibid.; Andrew Billingsley, *Climbing Jacob's Ladder: The Enduring Legacy of African American Families* (New York: Touchstone, 1992), 83–95; Leanor Boulin Johnson and Robert Staples, *Black Families at the Crossroad: Challenges and Prospects* (San Francisco: Jossey-Bass, 2005), 1–29; and James Borchert, *Alley Life in Washington: Family, Community, Religion, and Folklife in the City, 1850–1970* (Urbana: University of Illinois Press, 1980), 57–99.

43. Arthur Ray, interview by author, June 27, 2010.

44. Gretchen Lemke-Santangelo, "New Lives in the West," in *Major Problems in African American History*, vol. 2: *From Freedom to "Freedom Now," 1865–1990s* (Boston: Houghton, Mifflin, 2000), 240; *1920 US Census for City of Niagara Falls, Town of Niagara & Village of LaSalle*, reels 33, 34 and 35. Niagara Falls Public Library, Niagara Falls, New York, sheets 1–32.

45. Emmett J. Scott, "Letters of Negro Migrants of 1916–1918," *Journal of Negro History* 4 (July 1919): 290–340; "More Letters of Negro Migrants of 1916–1918," *Journal of Negro History* 4 (October 1919): 412–465; and Henderson H. Donald, "Causes of the Recent Negro Migration," *Journal of Negro History* 6 (October 1921): 410–420.

46. Kenneth L. Kusmer, *A Ghetto Takes Shape: Black Cleveland, 1870–1930* (Urbana: University of Illinois, Press, 1976), 157–173; and Gilbert Osofsky, *Harlem: The Making of a Ghetto* (New York: Harper Torchbooks, 1971), 17–52.

47. Boling, interview.

48. Ibid; *Fourteenth Census of the United States, Volume III, Population 1920: Composition and Characteristics of the Population by States* (Washington, DC: US Government Printing Office, 1922), 717.

49. "Ben Bolden Can Take Pride in Career Here," *Niagara Falls Gazette*, May 25, 1958.

50. "B. W. Bolden Dies; Founded Center Here," *Niagara Falls Gazette*, October 15, 1971.

51. "Ben Bolden Can Take Pride in Career Here," *Niagara Falls Gazette*, 7.

52. Ibid.

53. *US Census for 1930 the City of Niagara Falls*, reels 44, 45, and 46, Niagara Falls Public Library, Niagara Falls, New York.

54. See p. 9 and note 44.

55. Theodore Williamson, interview by author, August 8, 2009.

56. "Ben Bolden: Niagara's Only Negro Souvenir Store," *Buffalo Star*, August 30, 1946.

57. Ibid.

58. Williamson, interview.

59. Robert R. Weyeneth, "The Architecture of Racial Segregation: The Challenges of Preserving the Problematical Past," *Public Historian* 27, no. 4 (Fall 2005), 36.

60. Williamson, interview by author, August 8, 2009.

61. Norwood Hershey Samuel, interview by author, August 2, 2008, and July 10, 2010.

62. Williamson interview; *1920 US Census for City of Niagara Falls, Town of Niagara Falls, & Village of LaSalle*, sheets 1–32. This study uses the labor classifications developed by Kenneth L. Kusmer in *A Ghetto Takes Shape: Black Cleveland, 1870–1930* (Urbana: University of Illinois Press, 1978), 275–80.

63. Barbara Smith, interview by author, May 17, 2002.

64. *1920 US Census for the City of Niagara Falls*, sheets 1–8.

65. Ibid., sheet 16.

66. Ibid., sheet 6.

67. Ibid., sheet 1–8; *US Census for 1910: Town of Niagara, City of Niagara Falls, Village of LaSalle* (Niagara Falls, NY: Niagara Falls Public Library, 1910), microfilm, reels 28 and 29.

68. *US Census for City of Niagara Falls*, sheet 12.

69. Ibid., Sheets 1–8; *US Census for 1910*, reels 28 and 29.

70. Ibid.

71. Ibid.

72. Alphonse Gavin, "Niagara Falls 1918–1929," n.d., Local History Department, Niagara Falls Public Library, 55.

73. *Thirteenth Census of the United States Taken In the Year 1910*, vol. 9: *Manufactures* (Washington, DC: Government Printing Office, 1912), 877.

74. Ibid.

75. Gavin, "Niagara Falls 1918–1929," 55.

76. Ibid.

77. Ibid.

78. Ibid.

79. *Fourteenth Census of the United States*, vol. 11: *Manufactures* (Washington, DC: Government Printing Office, 1923), 1025; *Census of Manufactures: 1929: Industry Classification* (Washington, DC, 1930), 365.

80. *1920 US Census for City of Niagara Falls*, reels 33, 34 and 35, sheets 1–32; *Fourteenth Census of the United States, 1920 Population, General Report and Analytical Tables* (Washington, DC: US Government Printing Office, 19??), 559.
81. Ibid.
82. Ibid.
83. E. Franklin Frazier, *The Negro Family in the United States* (Chicago: University of Chicago Press, 1939).
84. Rainwater and William L. Yancey, *The Moynihan Report and the Politics of Controversy* (Cambridge, MA: MIT Press, 1967), 47–94; Herbert Gutman, *The Black Family in Slavery and Freedom* (New York: Pantheon, 1976); Andrew Billingsley, *Climbing Jacob's Ladder*; Leanor Boulin Johnson and Robert Staples, *Black Families at the Crossroad: Challenges and Prospects* (San Francisco: Jossey-Bass, 2005); and Williams, *Strangers in the Land of Paradise*.
85. Theodore Williamson, interview by author, January 22, 2010; Helen Reed-McBride, interview by author, March 9, 2010; and Arthur B. Ray, interview by author, August 2, 2008.
86. *US Census from 1920 the City of Niagara Falls*, reels 33, 34, and 35, sheets 1–32.
87. *US Census for 1930 the City of Niagara Falls*, reels 44, 45, and 46.
88. Helen Reed-McBride, interview by author, March 9, 2010.
89. Ibid.
90. Ibid.
91. Williamson, interview.
92. Ibid.
93. Ibid.
94. "Rests In Oakwood," *Niagara Falls Gazette*, November 23, 1929.
95. "Die Following Leg Amputation," *Niagara Falls Gazette*, November 20, 1929.
96. Ibid.
97. Niara Sudarkasa, "African American Female-Headed Households: Some Neglected Dimensions," in *Black Families* (Thousand Oaks, CA: SAGE, 2007), 172–183.
98. Ibid.
99. Williams, *Strangers in the Land of Paradise*, 50.
100. *US Census for City of Niagara Falls*, sheets 1–32.
101. Ibid.
102. Mizer, *A City Is Born*, 8.
103. *Fourteenth Census of the United States, 1920 Population*, 691.
104. Albert Raboteau, *Slave Religion: The "Invisible Institution" in the Antebellum South* (New York: Oxford University Press, 1978); C. Eric Lincoln and Lawrence H. Mamiya, *The Black Church in African American Experience* (Durham, NC: Duke University Press, 1990); and Andrew Billingsley, *Mighty Like a River: The Black Church and Social Reform* (New York: Oxford University Press, 1999).

105. Banks, "Problems Encountered," 74.
106. Ibid.
107. Smith, interview.
108. Ibid.
109. Ibid.
110. *US Census for City of Niagara Falls*, sheets 16–17.
111. Ibid.
112. Banks, "Problems Encountered," 74–75.
113. "Shiloh Baptist Church," *Niagara Falls Gazette*, January 10, 1925; "Union Baptist Church," *Niagara Falls Gazette*, January 10, 1925; "Shiloh Baptist Church," *Niagara Falls Gazette*, September 25, 1926; and "Union Baptist Church," *Niagara Falls Gazette*, September 25, 1926.
114. Smith, interview.
115. Banks, "Problems Encountered," 75–76.
116. Ibid.
117. Banks, "Problems Encountered," 75–76.
118. Ibid.
119. "Establishment of Community Center Here for Colored People Suggested as Means of Improving Conditions," *Niagara Falls Gazette*, February 7, 1928, 13; The Community Center Papers were microfilmed by the Afro-American Historical Association of the Niagara Frontier and the Buffalo State College History Department. Referred to hereafter as the microfilmed collection, "The Niagara Community Center Association 1927–1977," 1.
120. W. E. B. Du Bois, *The Philadelphia Negro* (Philadelphia: University of Pennsylvania Press, 1996).
121. "Ben Bolden Can Take Pride." *Niagara Falls Gazette*.
122. "Pollard Opened Door to Community Center," *Niagara Falls Gazette*, February 17, 1987; and Nathan Irvin Huggins, *Harlem Renaissance* (New York: Oxford University Press, 2007).
123. "Establishment of Community Center Here." *Niagara Falls Gazette*.
124. Ibid.
125. See Robert L. Zangrando, *The NAACP Crusade Against Lynching, 1909–1950* (Philadelphia: Temple University Press, 1980).
126. See Stewart E. Tolnay and E. M. Beck, *A Festival of Violence: An Analysis of Southern Lynching, 1882–1930* (Urbana: University of Illinois Press, 1992).
127. Allan Spear, "The Origins of the Urban Ghetto, 1870–1915," in *Key Issues in the Afro-American Experience* (New York: Harcourt Brace Jovanovich, 1971), 164; Osofsky, *Harlem*, 43–44; Williams, *Strangers in the Land of Paradise*, 104–105; and Thomas, *Life for Us*, 10–11, 15, and 17.
128. "Establishment of Community Center Here." *Niagara Falls Gazette*.
129. "From Organization for Advancement of Colored Community: About 150 Negroes Attend Meeting; Will Try to Establish Community Center," *Niagara Falls Gazette*, October 12, 1928.

130. "Selecting Name for New Centre," *Niagara Falls Gazette*, October 17, 1928.

131. *The Niagara Community Center Association 1927-1977* (Buffalo, NY: Butler Library, Buffalo State College, 1978), 6.

132. Ibid., 7.

133. Indiana Martin, interview by author, August 12, 2009.

134. "Activities and Aims of Community Center Topic of Address," *Niagara Falls Gazette*, March 7, 1929.

135. *US Census for 1930*, reels 44, 45, and 46.

136. Williams, *Strangers in the Land of Paradise*, 100-122.

137. "Says Nations Could Borrow Lessons of Peace from Negroes," *Niagara Falls Gazette*, February 22, 1935.

138. Ibid.; "Community Center News," *Niagara Falls Gazette*, November 29, 1931.

139. "News About Negroes," *Niagara Falls Gazette*, June 19, 1934.

140. "Community Center News," *Niagara Falls Gazette*, November 29, 1931.

141. Ibid.

142. "Race Relations to Be Featured," *Niagara Falls Gazette*, February 9, 1939.

143. "Work of Community Center Here Growing Steadily, Report Shows," *Niagara Falls Gazette*, June 8, 1932.

144. "To Address League," *Niagara Falls Gazette*, March 31, 1931.

145. Du Bois, *Philadelphia Negro*, 233.

146. Williamson, interview by author, May 17, 2002.

147. Williamson, interview; and Du Bois, *Philadelphia Negro*, 233.

148. "Negro Leader to Speak at Falls," *Niagara Falls Gazette*, November 3, 1931.

149. "Negro's Advancement During Past 60 Years Phenomenal, Pickens Says," *Niagara Falls Gazette*, November 9, 1931.

150. "About Negroes," *Niagara Falls Gazette*, February 9, 1934.

151. The information in this paragraph is derived from sixty-one recorded interviews conducted by the author as well as from the over eighty persons interviewed concerning Black Niagaran history.

152. The Hodges family, for instance, lived in Niagara Falls, Ontario, during the 1920s but owned property in Niagara Falls, New York, that they rented out to local Blacks. See Arthur Ray, interview by author, July 21, 2010.

153. Wilma Morrison, interview by author, June 30, 2002.

154. William J. Switala, *Underground Railroad in New York and New Jersey* (Mechanicsburg, PA, 2006), 143; and Josiah Henson, *The Life of Josiah Henson, Formerly a Slave* (Boston: Arthur D. Phelps, 1849).

155. Harriet Beecher Stowe, *Uncle Tom's Cabin* (New York: Barnes & Noble, 2003); and Josiah Henson, *An Autobiography of the Reverend Josiah Henson* (Reading, MA: Addison, 1969), 151.

156. Mabel A. Smith, interview by author, May 15, 2010.
157. Ibid.
158. Ibid.
159. "Negro Object: Local Men and Buffalo Colored Folk Say if Czolgosz was a Negro His Treatment Would be Summary," *Niagara Falls Gazette*, September 10, 1901.
160. Williamson, interview.
161. Albert M. Camarillo, "Navigating Segregated Life in American's Racial Borderhood, 1910–1950," *Journal of American History* 100, no. 3 (December 2013): 654–662.
162. William Bradberry, "Black Menagerie: Life Was Anything but Easy for African Americans in 1920s Falls," *Niagara Falls Reporter*, August 19, 2003.
163. Ibid.
164. Boling, interview.
165. Drake and Cayton, *Black Metropolis*, 187–190.

Notes to Chapter 3

1. Studs Terkel, *Hard Times: An Oral History of the Great Depression* (New York: Pantheon, 1970).
2. *Fifteenth Census of the United States: 1930 Population*, vol. 4: *Occupations, By States* (Washington, DC: US Government Printing Office, 1933), 1119.
3. *Sixteenth Census of the United States: 1940 Population*, vol. 2: *Characteristics of the Population* (Washington, DC: United States Government Printing Office, 1943), 133.
4. "Crowds Go To Niagara," *New York Times*, August 18, 1935.
5. Mizer B. Hamilton, *A City Is Born: Niagara Falls A City Matures 1892 A Topical History 1932* (Niagara Falls, NY: Human-Wahl, 1981), 113.
6. "Lehman Proposes Slump Remedies," *New York Times*, October 17, 1930; "Printing Council Asks Extra Session on Idle: Hoover Is Urged at Niagara Falls State Convention to Start Relief Move," *New York Times*, July 30, 1931; "Road Work Distributed Throughout N.Y. State," *New York Times*, January 6, 1935; and "Niagara Plan Presented," *New York Times*, February 27, 1935; and "Allots $13,555,644 For Public Works," *New York Times*, November 24, 1936.
7. *Fifteenth Census of the United States*, 1119; and *Sixteenth Census of the United States*, 133.
8. William Feder, interview by author, June 18, 2015. Nowadays, the term "hobo" is considered by some to be offensive. However, it is used here by William Feder to describe how he and others perceived individuals who illegally traveled on trains from place to place in search of food, shelter, and employment. It is a term commonly used during the Depression era. See Terkel, *Hard Times*.

9. Ibid.

10. Sam Dett Put Efficient Stamp on Post Office," *Niagara Falls Gazette*, February 13, 1987; *US Census for 1930 the City of Niagara Falls*, reels 44, 45, and 46. Niagara Falls Public Library, Niagara Falls, New York.

11. Ibid.

12. Ibid.

13. *US Census for 1930*.

14. "Sam Dett Put Efficient Stamp on Post Office," *Niagara Falls Gazette*.

15. *US Census for 1930*, reels 44, 45, and 46.

16. "Volunteer Committee on Negro Work Announces the Completion of Its Task," n.d., 326 Blacks in Niagara Falls Notebook, Local History Department, Niagara Falls Public Library.

17. Ibid.

18. "Niagara Community Center Association," 4.

19. Barbara Smith, "A History of St. John's A. M. E. Church," n.d. Manuscript given to the author by Barbara Smith, St. John's AME Church historian.

20. "Activities and Aims of Community Center Topics of Address," *Niagara Falls Gazette*, March 7, 1929.

21. *US Census for 1930*, reels 44, 45, and 46.

22. *Niagara Falls City Directory 1941* (Niagara Falls, NY: Wahl, 1941), 527.

23. "Community Center News," *Niagara Falls Gazette*, February 3, 1933.

24. *US Census for 1930*, reels 44, 45, and 46.

25. Ibid.

26. "Edison Tucker Founded Mount Zion Baptist," n.d., Obituaries Notebook S-T, Local History Department, Niagara Falls Public Library, 1; *U.S. Census for 1930*, reels 44, 45, and 46.

27. This statement is based on comments by numerous individuals the author spoke to over the years, particularly Arthur Ray.

28. Boling interview; *Fifteenth Census of the United States, 1930 Population, Volume III* (Washington, DC: US Government Printing Office, 1931), 327.

29. William Bradberry, "Black Menagerie: Life Was Anything but Easy for African Americans in 1920s Falls," *Niagara Falls Reporter*, August 19, 2003.

30. Smith, interview.

31. Norwood Hershey Samuel, interview by author, August 2, 2008 and July 10, 2010.

32. *Report of Real Property Survey, City of Niagara Falls, New York* (Niagara Falls, NY: WPA). This was a report on Official Project #665-21-3-267 conducted under the auspices of the Works Project Administration, October 1939, Local History Department, Niagara Falls Public Library, 40.

33. Ibid.

34. *Fifteenth Census of the United States: 1930 Population*, vol. 6: *Families* (Washington, DC: US Government Printing Office, 1933), 940.

35. *Report of Real Property Survey*, 40.
36. Ibid.
37. Ibid.
38. Ibid.
39. Ibid.
40. "Survey May Show That City Has Nearly 6,000 Sub-standard Homes," *Niagara Falls Gazette*, October 25, 1939.
41. "Large Quarters Are Provided for Community Center Classes," *Niagara Falls Gazette*, March 12, 1935.
42. "Community Center Upholds Morale of Growing Number of Negro Folks," *Niagara Falls Gazette*, April 7, 1932.
43. Ibid.
44. The Niagara Community Center pleased so many Niagarans during an economically depressed era that a patron composed a poem in its honor:

> Community Center—a sonnet to you.
> As a tribute to progress you've made.
> It is pleasing to find every note ringing true.
> In the symphonic action displayed.
> You stand as a beacon for oncoming youth.
> And a guide to ambitions worthwhile.
> The friendship established shall thrive on the truth.
> Of a race God has given a smile.
> The true art of living is finest of themes.
> Inspiring the music of men.
> The joy of real service, like beautiful streams.
> Give wings to the brush and the pen.
> May triumphs be many and failures be few.
> Community Center—a sonnet to you!

Leo M. Dorsey wrote the poem. He was born in St. Catherines, Ontario, but had lived in Niagara Falls, New York, for many years. When he wrote his poem, he lived in Toronto, Canada. He held great respect for the center and especially for Pollard. (See "Young Negro Poet Writes Sonnet To the Niagara Community Center," *Niagara Falls Gazette*, October 29, 1934.)

45. "Distinguished Negro, Educator, Minister Will Speak in City," *Lockport (NY) Union-Sun and Journal*, February 6, 1937.
46. Ibid.
47. Ibid.
48. Ibid.
49. Collectivism here is defined as a group or groups working together to achieve objectives.

50. See chapter 3 of Boston, *Business Strategy of Booker T. Washington*; and Lewis, *W.E.B. Du Bois*. See the section on the "Talented Tenth."

51. This impression was given to the author based on a number of individuals he interviewed who observed John M. Pollard (e.g., Indiana Martin, Theodore Williamson, Vivian Thompson, Norwood Herhsey Samuel, and others.).

52. Dan S. Green, "W. E. B. Du Bois' Talented Tenth: A Strategy for Racial Advancement," *Journal of Negro Education* 46, no. 3 (Summer 1977), 358–366.

53. "Today's Events in Community Center," *Niagara Falls Gazette*, February 8, 1937.

54. Ibid.

55. Ibid.

56. "Prejudice against Negro Definite Hardship, John M. Pollard Declares," *Niagara Falls Gazette*, February 13, 1939.

57. Ibid.

58. Ibid.

59. Ibid.

60. Ibid.

61. "Niagara Falls," *Chicago Defender*, February 27, 1937.

62. "Niagara Falls," *Chicago Defender*, January 23, 1937.

63. "Niagara Falls," *Chicago Defender*, January 30, 1937.

64. "Pollard Urges Square Deal for the Negro," *Citizen-Advertiser, Auburn, N.Y.*, February 11, 1937.

65. Ibid. This was a statement by John M. Pollard. However, it is a historical fact that many enslaved people left farms and plantations when the opportunity presented itself, joining the Union Army when they could or fleeing to Union-held territories.

66. C. Robert Tipton, "The Fisk Jubilee Singers," *Tennessee Historical Quarterly* 29, no. 1 (Spring 1970): 42–48; and "John Hope Franklin: the Fisk Years," *Journal of Blacks in Higher Education* 49 (Autumn 2005), 74–83.

67. "Urges Youth to Think Straight and Use Prayer," *Niagara Falls Gazette*, January 26, 1942.

68. "Physician's Dedication Earned Admiration," *Niagara Falls Gazette*, February 18, 1987.

69. Ibid.

70. "Mrs. Hayes Prominent in Social, Civic Work," *Niagara Falls Gazette*, June 4, 1949.

71. Ibid.

72. This is how a number of interviewees described Dr. Charles B. Hayes.

73. "Civic Group Valued Alice Hayes' Participation," *Niagara Falls Gazette*, February 12, 1987.

74. Ibid.

75. Reed-McBride, interview.

76. Ibid.

77. "Physician's Dedication Earned Admiration," *Niagara Falls Gazette*.
78. Boling, interview; Indiana Martin, interview by author, August 12, 2009; and Arthur Ray, interview with author, June 27, 2010.
79. Evelyn Brooks Higginbotham, *Righteous Discontent: The Women's Movement in the Black Baptist Church, 1880–1920* (Cambridge, MA: Harvard University Press, 1993), 185–229.
80. "Niagara," *Chicago Defender*, December 19, 1936.
81. "Niagara," *Chicago Defender*, April 24, 1937.
82. "Niagara," *Chicago Defender*, February 26, 1938; and "Niagara," *Chicago Defender*, March 6, 1937.
83. "Community Center Members Hear Able Address on Wasserman Test," *Niagara Falls Gazette*, April 15, 1935.
84. "The Reluctance of Black People to Participate in Clinical Medical Research," *Journal of Blacks in Higher Education* 17 (Autumn 1997): 33–34. The Tuskegee Experiment was an unethical medical experiment approved by the US government in which African Americans in Macon County, Alabama, were purposely not treated for their syphilis so they could be studied in order to examine the impact of syphilis on human subjects. An authoritative book on this subject is James Jones, *Bad Blood: The Tuskegee Syphilis Experiment* (New York: Free Press, 1993).
85. "Niagara," *Chicago Defender*, April 17, 1937.
86. "Niagara Falls," *Chicago Defender*, April 24, 1937.
87. Monroe Fordham, "The Buffalo Cooperative Economic Society, Inc., 1928–1961: A Black Self-help Organization," *Niagara Frontier* (Summer 1976): 42.
88. Ibid., 41–49.
89. In discussing their public-school experiences this was a common point echoed by a number of interviewees (e.g., Bill Williamson, Roosevelt Bradberry, Barbara Smith).
90. *Fifteenth Census of the United States 1930: Population*, vol. 3, part 2: *Montana-Wyoming* (Washington, DC: Government Printing Office, 1932), 291.
91. James D. Anderson, *The Education of Blacks in the South 1860–1935* (Chapel Hill: University of North Carolina Press, 1988), 148–185; Gunnar Myrdal, *An American Dilemma: The Negro Problem & Modern Democracy*, vol. 2 (New York: Pantheon, 1972), 893–902.
92. *Fifteenth Census of the United States 1930*, 291.
93. Reed-McBride, interview.
94. Ibid; *US Census for 1930*, reels 44, 45, and 46.
95. Reed-McBride, interview.
96. Ibid.
97. Ibid.
98. Williamson, interview.
99. Reed-McBride, interview.

100. Thomas C. Holt and Elsa Barkley Brown, ed., "The Labor of Politics," *Major Problems in African American History*, vol. 2: *From Freedom to "Freedom Now"* (Boston: Wadsworth Cengage Learning, 2000), 75–84.

101. Myrdal, *An American Dilemma*, 982.

102. Marcus Garvey, *The Philosophy and Opinions of Marcus Garvey* (Dover, MA: Majority, 1986); David Cronon, *Black Moses: The Story of Marcus Garvey and the Universal Negro Improvement Association* (Madison: University of Wisconsin Press, 1969; and Tony Martin, *Marcus Garvey, Hero: A First Biography* (Dover, MA: Majority, 1983).

103. Williamson, interview by author, August 8, 2009.

104. Drake and Cayton. *Black Metropolis*; and Tuttle, *Race Riot*.

105. "Member of Oldest Black Family Recall Lost Era," *Niagara Falls Gazette*, February 9, 1987.

106. Ibid.

107. Williamson, interview.

108. "3000 in Race Riot at Niagara Falls," *New York Times*, August 28, 1934; and Tuttle, *Race Riot,* 157–183.

109. "3000 in Race Riot at Niagara Falls," *New York Times*.

110. Martin, interview.

111. Ibid.

112. Ibid.

113. Ibid.

114. Ibid.

115. Williamson, interview.

116. Reed-McBride, interview.

117. Ibid.

118. Ibid.

119. "3000 in Race Riot at Niagara Falls," *New York Times*.

120. Ibid.

121. Ibid.

122. Ibid.

123. Ibid.

124. "Chronological Review of Events in 1934 in Niagara Falls," *Niagara Falls Gazette*, December 29, 1934.

125. "Fascist Racial Creed Flayed by Educators," *Chicago Defender*, November 5, 1938.

126. Ibid.

127. Ibid.

128. "Formation of the Niagara Civic and Protective Club"; Bill Williamson, Niagara Falls, New York. A copy of this document was given to the author January 30, 2010.

129. This description was formulated after an interview with Bill Williamson. Mr. Joseph Williamson was his father. See Williamson, interview.

130. Mizer, *A City Is Born*, 113.
131. Ibid.
132. Ibid.
133. Williamson, interview; and Williamson, interview, January 23.
134. John H. Franklin and Alfred A. Moss Jr., *From Slavery to Freedom: A History of African Americans*, 7th ed. (New York: McGraw-Hill, 1997), 424.
135. "News about Negroes," *Niagara Falls Gazette*, November 20, 1934.
136. "Negro Democrat Caravan in City," *Niagara Falls Gazette*, October 27, 1936.
137. Ibid.
138. "Negro Who Votes for Democratic Party Will Betray His Race, Says New York Speaker at Rally Here," *Niagara Falls Gazette*, October 31, 1936.
139. Ibid.
140. "Make Plans to Get Out Vote," *Niagara Falls Gazette*, October 29, 1937; Si Sheppard, "If It Wasn't for Roosevelt You Wouldn't Have This Job: The Politics of Patronage and the 1936 Presidential Election in New York," *New York History* 95, no. 1 (Winter 2014): 53 and 63.
141. Anne Key Simpson, *Follow Me: The Life and Music of R. Nathaniel Dett* (Metuchen, NJ: Scarecrow, 1993), 34.
142. Ibid., 151–197.
143. "New York State," *Chicago Defender*, May 3, 1930.
144. Ibid.
145. Ibid.
146. "New York State," *Chicago Defender*, September 20, 1930.
147. Ibid.
148. "Syracuse," *Chicago Defender*, October 4, 1930.
149. Ibid.
150. Ibid.
151. "Niagara Falls," *Chicago Defender*, August 20, 1932.
152. Simpson, *Follow Me*, 210.
153. "Niagara Falls," *Chicago Defender*, September 24, 1932.
154. "New York State," *Chicago Defender*, September 4, 1932.
155. "New York State," *Chicago Defender*, October 8, 1932; "Niagara Falls," *Chicago Defender*, October 29, 1932; "Niagara Falls"; "Niagara Falls," *Chicago Defender*, November 12, 1932; and "Niagara Falls," *Chicago Defender*, April 29, 1933.
156. "New York State," *Chicago Defender*, November 18, 1933.
157. "Niagara Falls," *Chicago Defender*, December 17, 1932.
158. "Rochester, N.Y.," *Chicago Defender*, May 18, 1935.
159. Ibid.
160. Alice C. Hayes, "Niagara Falls," *Chicago Defender*, March 27, 1937, 10; and Alice C. Hayes, "Niagara Falls," *Chicago Defender*, April 10, 1937, 18.
161. "Mourn Death of Mother of Dr. R. N. Dett," *Chicago Defender*, April 24, 1937.

162. Ibid.
163. Ibid.
164. Simpson, *Follow Me*, 233.
165. Ibid.
166. "In Memoriam Dett," *Niagara Falls Gazette*, April 8, 1959.
167. Gray, "Nate, My Son," 13.
168. Compare the percentages of Black Niagaran women working in table 2.4 with table 3.1.
169. The information is this paragraph is derived from interviewees who spoke of the Black Niagaran Community during the Depression years.
170. "Community Center News," *Niagara Falls Gazette*, October 14, 1938.
171. Ibid.
172. Ibid.
173. Ibid.
174. Ibid.
175. Ibid.
176. "Religion Kept Family Strong," *Niagara Falls Gazette*, February 6, 1990; Martin, interview; Smith, interview; and Lawrence Gordon, "A Brief Look at Blacks in Depression Mississippi, 1929–1934: Eyewitness Accounts," *Journal of Negro History* 64, no. 4 (Autumn 1979): 377–390.
177. The "Invisible Institution" refers to secret churches that enslaved people held among themselves often in wooded areas. They acknowledged their preachers and often had lookouts to warn them of approaching overseers, masters, or others that would impede their worship. See Albert J. Raboteau, *Slave Religion: The "Invisible Institution" in the Antebellum South* (New York: Oxford University Press, 1978).
178. C. Eric Lincoln and Lawrence H. Mamiya, *The Black Church in the African American Experience* (Durham, NC: Duke University Press, 1990). See chapter 1 in Sandra L. Barnes, "Priestly and Prophetic Influences on Black Church Social Services," *Social Problems* 51, no. 2 (May 2004): 202–221.
179. " 'Senior' in Age, 'Young' at Heart," n.d., 280 Churches Baptist, vol. 5., Local History Department, Niagara Falls Public Library.
180. Ibid.
181. Andrew Billingsley and Cleopatra Howard Caldwell, "The Church, the Family, and the School in the African American Community," *Journal of Negro Education* 60, no. 3 (Summer 1991), 427–440; and "Religion Kept Family Strong," *Niagara Falls Gazette*, February 6, 1990.
182. Martin, interview.
183. Jacqueline S. Mithum, "Cooperation and Solidarity as Survival Necessities in a Black Urban Community," *Urban Anthropology* 2, no. 1 (Spring 1973): 25–34.
184. "Says Man Must Turn to Spiritual Things to Secure Real Happiness," *Niagara Falls Gazette*, March 5, 1935.

Notes to Chapter 3 | 349

185. Ibid.
186. "Community Center News," *Niagara Falls Gazette*, May 13, 1932.
187. Booker T. Washington, *The Negro in Business* (Wichita, KS: DeVore and Sons, 1992), 1–3.
188. Thomas, *Life for Us*, 17.
189. Shortly after 1900, the date of the formation of the NNBL, to 1955, Washington's business philosophy filtered into African American communities, particularly in urban areas, more than any other Black economic thought. Washington became known as the "Father of 20th Century Black Business Development." See chapter 7 of Boston, *Business Strategy of Booker T. Washington*.
190. Monroe N. Work, *Negro Yearbook, 1914–15* (Tuskegee, AL: Negro Yearbook, 1915), 304–308.
191. See chapter 7 of Boston, *Business Strategy of Booker T. Washington*.
192. "Niagara Falls," *Chicago Defender*, November 28, 1936.
193. "Negro Business League Inspects New C-E Plant," *Buffalo Courier-Express*, February 18, 1931; and "Interesting Items Gleaned by the Age Correspondents," *New York Age*, March 13, 1926.
194. "T. J. Ireland Is Dead at 67," *Niagara Falls Gazette*, September 15, 1970.
195. *US Census for 1930*, reels 44, 45, and 46.
196. Ibid.
197. *US Census for 1900*, microfilm, reel 23; *US Census for 1910*, microfilm, reels 28 and 29; *1920 US Census for the City of Niagara Falls, Town of Niagara Falls and Village of LaSalle* (Washington, DC: US Government Printing Office), reels 33, 34, and 35, sheets 1–32; *US Census for 1930*, reels 44, 45, and 46; *1940 Census.Archives.gov.*, Niagara County, Niagara Falls; Williamson, interview by author, May 13, 2002; and Williamson, interview by author, January 30, 2010.
198. "Niagara Falls," *Chicago Defender*, November 13, 1931.
199. *Annual Report of the Fifteenth Annual Convention: National Negro Business League, Held at Muskogee, Oklahoma, August 19–21, 1914* (Washington, DC: Booker T. Washington Papers, Library of Congress), microfilms, reel 754.
200. "Business Men of Community Center Hold Annual Meeting," *Niagara Falls Gazette*, December 15, 1936.
201. "Community Center News," *Niagara Falls Gazette*, May 13, 1932.
202. Ibid.
203. Ibid.
204. "Falls Men Favor Government Change," *Lockport (NY) Union-Sun and Journal*, February 11, 1932.
205. "Community Center News," *Niagara Falls Gazette*, May 25, 1934.
206. "Niagara Community Center Serves 48 Different Groups of Persons," *Niagara Falls Gazette*, April 13, 1935.
207. "Community Center News," *Niagara Falls Gazette*, January 24, 1939.
208. Louis R. Harlan, *Booker T. Washington: The Wizard of Tuskegee, 1901–1915* (New York: Oxford University Press, 1983), 238–265.

209. "New York State," *Chicago Defender*, October 1, 1938.
210. "Our American Way," *Niagara Falls Gazette*, April 17, 1940.
211. Ibid.
212. See chapter 3 of Boston, *Business Strategy of Booker T. Washington*.
213. "Community Center News," *Niagara Falls Gazette*, May 22, 1936.
214. "Community Center News," *Niagara Falls Gazette*, May 15, 1936.
215. Ibid.
216. "Community Center News," *Niagara Falls Gazette*, May 15, 1936; and Williams, *Strangers in the Land of Paradise*, 95.
217. Ibid.
218. Raymond Wolters, *Negroes and the Great Depression: The Problem of Economic Recovery* (Westport, CT: Greenwood, 1970), 83–90.
219. "Community Center News," *Niagara Falls Gazette*, May 15, 1936.
220. Albon L. Holsey was an author, a Tuskegee Institute employee, the secretary of Tuskegee Institute after Emmett J. Scott left in 1917, and a national organizer for the NNBL. In 1929 he orchestrated a collective business effort for the NNBL. He decided that the NNBL should sponsor a national cooperative grocery store. This was a self-help effort to advance African Americans and to combat the adverse effects of the Great Depression. This national organization was called the Colored Merchants Association (CMA). For more information on the CMA, see Vishnu V. Oak, *The Negro's Adventure in General Business* (Yellow Springs, OH: Antioch, 1949), 62–65; and John Burrows, *The Necessity of Myth: A History of the National Negro Business League, 1900–1945* (Auburn, AL: Auburn University, 1981), 127–149.
221. "Community Center News," *Niagara Falls Gazette*, February 19, 1933.
222. John N. Ingham and Lynne B. Feldman, *African American Business Leaders A Biographical Dictionary* (Westport, CT: Greenwood, 1994), 472; and Burrows, *Necessity of Myth*, 127–149.
223. "News about Negroes," *Niagara Falls Gazette*, March 10, 1937.
224. "T. J. Ireland Is Dead at 67," *Niagara Falls Gazette*.
225. Ibid.
226. See chapter 5 of Boston, *Business Strategy of Booker T. Washington*.
227. Washington, *Negro in Business*, 1–3.
228. "Niagara Falls," *Chicago Defender*, February 27, 1937; "Niagara Falls," *Chicago Defender*, October 1, 1958; "Niagara Falls," *Chicago Defender*, November 28, 1936; "Community Center News," *Niagara Falls Gazette*, May 22, 1936; and "Community Center News," *Niagara Falls Gazette*, May 15, 1936.
229. "Work of Community Center," *Niagara Falls Gazette*, June 8, 1932.
230. Ibid.
231. Jacqueline A. Goggin, *Carter G. Woodson: A Life in Black History* (Baton Rouge: Louisiana State University Press, 1993); L. D. Reddick, "Carter G. Woodson (1875–1950): An Appreciation," *Phylon* 11, no. 2 (Second Quarter,

1950): 177–179; Darlene Clark Hine, "Carter G. Woodson, White Philanthropy and Negro Historiography," *History Teacher* 19, no. 3 (May 1986): 405–425.

232. Young Colored Folk Hear Negro History," *Niagara Falls Gazette*, February 8, 1937.

233. Ibid.

234. "Black Affirmative Action: A Discussion of Economic Strategies towards Self-Help and Self-Determination," *Journal of Social Relation* 14, no. 1/2 (Fall–Winter and Spring–Summer 1987), 184–194; and Ivan H. Light, *Ethnic Enterprise in America: Business and Welfare Among Chinese, Japanese and Blacks* (Berkeley: University of California Press, 1972).

Notes to Chapter 4

1. Osofsky, *Harlem*; and Kenneth L. Kusmer, *A Ghetto Takes Shape: Black Cleveland, 1870–1930* (Urbana: University of Illinois Press, 1978).

2. *Sixteenth Census of the United States: 1940 Population,* vol. 2: *Characteristics of the Population* (Washington, DC: US Government Printing Office, 1943), 133; and *1950 Census of Population,* vol. 2: *Characteristics of the Population Part 32 New York* (Washington, DC: US Government Printing Office, 1952), 94; *Population Schedules of the 6th Census of the United States, 1840, New York*. New York census schedules for the year 1840, National Archives microfilm publications, reel 311; *The Seventh Census of the United States: 1850* (Washington, DC: Robert Armstrong, Public Printer, 1853), 102; *US Census*, Niagara Falls Public Library, Local History Division, Call Number 350.81; *US Census of Population 1870* (Washington, DC: US Government Printing Office, 1872), 214; *US Census of Population 1890* (Washington, DC: US Government Printing Office, 1895), 471; *US Census*, Niagara Falls Public Library, Local History Division, Call Number 350.81; *US Census of Population 1900* (Washington, DC: US Census Office, 1901), 670; *US Census of Population 1910* (Washington, DC: US Government Printing Office, 1913), 179; *Fourteenth Census of the United States, Volume III, Population 1920* (Washington, DC: US Government Printing Office, 1922), 717; *US Census of Population 1930* (Washington, DC: US Government Printing Office, 1932), 276; *US Census of Population 1940* (Washington, DC: US Government Printing Office, 1943), 123; *1950 Census of Population, Volume I, Number of Inhabitants: New York* (Washington, DC: US Government Printing Office, 1952), 15; *Census of the Population: 1960, Volume I, Characteristics of the Population, Part A, Number of Inhabitants for New York State* (Washington, DC: US Department of Commerce, 1961), 34; *1970 Census of Population and Housing* (Washington, DC: US Government Printing Office, 1972), P-1; *Niagara County Census 1980, Department of Economic Development and Planning for Niagara County Affiliate Data Center* (Lockport, NY: 1981), 1; *1990 Census of Population and Housing*

Summary Population and Housing Characteristics, New York (Washington, DC: US Government Printing Office, 1991), 74.

3. "Over $8,000,000 Expended on Private and Public Projects in Niagara Falls during 1942," *Niagara Falls Gazette*, December 31, 1942, 21.

4. Ibid.

5. See table 1.1.

6. This statement was derived from a number of interviewees who reflected on their migration experiences or personal histories that their elders shared with them.

7. Robert C. Weaver, "Employment in the Aircraft Industry," *Quarterly Journal of Economics* 59, no. 4 (August 1945), 600–602; and Andrew E. Kersten, "African Americans and World War II, *OAH Magazine of History* 16, no. 3 (Spring 2002), 13–17.

8. "1942–1943," *Niagara Falls Gazette*, December 31, 1942.

9. "Falls Airport Brought War Plane Plant Here," *Niagara Falls Gazette*, May 7, 1945, 11:3.

10. Boling, interview. Tuskegee Airmen were African American fighter pilots during World War II who escorted American bomber planes to and from their targets. They are known as a unit that never lost an escorted bomber. Initially, due to prejudice, they had to prove their value to the American military.

11. "Dr. Pollard to Take War Job," *Niagara Falls Gazette*, April 10, 1943.

12. "John M. Pollard, Educator, War Worker, Is Dead," *Niagara Falls Gazette*, October 15, 1946.

13. Ibid.

14. *The Carborundum Company: The First 100 Years, 1891–1991, a Commemorative History* (Niagara Falls, NY: Carborundum, 1991).

15. "Jobs Led Blacks to Falls," *Niagara Falls Gazette*, February 5, 1990.

16. Ibid.

17. Williamson, interview with author, August 8, 2009; James Walker, interview by author, May 17, 2010.

18. Ibid.

19. Banks, "Problems Encountered by World War II," 7.

20. Ibid., 5–10; John Modell, Marc Goulden, and Sigurdur Magnusson, "World War II in the Lives of Black Americans: Some Findings and Interpretation," *Journal of American History* 76, no. 3 (December 1989): 839.

21. This information is derived from conversations that the author had with numerous Black Niagarans over an eighteen-year period (e.g., Roosevelt Bradberry, Emma Jean Hunt, Wilbur Hunt, Indiana Martin, Nathaniel McDow, Carlyle Miller, Otis Phelps, Arthur Ray, Minnie Tyler, Theodore Williamson, and others); *Fifteenth Census of the United States: 1930 Population, Volume III, Part 1* (Washington, DC: US Government Printing Office, 1932), 127; *Sixteenth Census*

of the United States: 1940 Population, Volume II, Characteristics of the Population (Washington, DC: US Government Printing Office, 1943), 237 and 313; *Census of Population: 1950, Volume II, Characteristics of the Population, Part 2, Alabama* (Washington, DC: US Government Printing Office, 1952), 63 and 86; *US Census of Population: 1960: Volume I, Characteristics of the Population* (Washington, DC: US Government Printing Office, 1963), 50 and 93; *Census of Population: 1970, Volume I, Characteristics of the Population, Part 2, Alabama* (Washington, DC: US Government Printing Office, 1973), 79 and 113.

22. Rosie Coates, interview by author, July 2, 1981. The author attended one of the Alabama reunions in the city of Buffalo; "Report That Negroes Are Migrating North Alarms Authorities," *Niagara Falls Gazette*, June 16, 1927, 25; and Williams, *Strangers in the Land of Paradise*, 188.

23. Banks, "Problems Encountered by World War II," 7.

24. "Meet Mrs. Wille C. Fields, Beech Racial Imbalance Was Created," *Niagara Falls Gazette*, July 6, 1969; Peter Gottlieb, "The Great Migration," in *Major Problems in African American History*, vol. 2: *From Freedom to "Freedom Now,"* 1865–1990 (Cambridge, MA: Wadsworth, 2000), 138–144. In this work, Peter Gottlieb describes the cyclical pattern in which Black migrants came to Pittsburgh, Pennsylvania, moved back to the South, then returned to Pittsburgh. This cyclical behavior, accord to Gottlieb, was contingent on migrants reobtaining employment after they had been laid off or let go.

25. "Founder of Mount Zion Baptist Church Dead at 64," *280 Churches Baptist*, vol. 5, Local History Department, Niagara Falls Public Library.

26. "Wendel O. Akers," n.d., Obituary Folder A-F, Local History Department, Niagara Falls, New York Public Library.

27. Homer C. Hawkins, "Trends in Black Migration from 1863 to 1960," *Phylon* 34, no. 2 (Second Quarter 1973): 148–152. Johnny R. Anderson, who was born in Colquitt, Georgia, like Wendel O. Akers, migrated to Niagara Falls after the crucial Second Great Migration years, arriving in 1947. He served in the US Air Force from 1942 to 1946 and during World War II was awarded the Victory Medal. Anderson found employment at Union Carbide and Carbon Company and seemed to have been pleased with Niagara Falls because he made a life in the city for his family and himself until 1959. See "Johnnie R. Anderson," n.d., *280 Churches Baptist*, vol. 5, Local History Department, Niagara Falls Public Library; and Irvin H. Lee, *Negro Medal of Honor Men* (New York: Dodd, Mead, 1969).

28. See "Wendel O. Akers," n.d., Obituary Folder A-F, Local History Department, Niagara Falls, New York Public Library; and Homer C. Hawkins, "Trends in Black Migration from 1863 to 1960," *Phylon* 34, no. 2 (Second Quarter 1973), 148–152.

29. "Niagara Personalities: Mr. Griffin Likes Falls as Place to Live, Work," *Niagara Falls Gazette*, November 27, 1948.

30. Daniel T. Kelleher, "The Case of Lloyd Lionel Gaines: The Demise of the Separate but Equal Doctrine," *Journal of Negro History* 56, no. 4 (October 1971): 262–271.

31. Ronald W. Walter and Robert C. Smith, *African American Leadership* (Albany: State University of New York Press, 1999), 223–226.

32. Michael B. Boston, "Bloneva Bond: A Longtime Niagara Falls, New York Activist," *Afro-Americans in New York Life and History*, 38 no. 2 (August 2014), 7–36.

33. Williams, interview by author, March 14, 2010. Mrs. Williams was the secretary of the Niagara Falls Branch of the NAACP under the presidency of both Harwood and Bloneva Bond.

34. Barbara J. Smith, interview by author, January 16, 2010; William Bradberry, "Black Menagerie: Old East Side Was Like United Nations," *Niagara Falls Reporter*, May 7, 2002. Barbara J. Smith taught in the Niagara Public School System for forty-two years.

35. Elizabeth D. Blum, *Love Canal Revisited: Race, Class, and Gender in Environmental Activism* (Lawrence: University of Kansas, 2008), 22.

36. "'Do Unto Others . . .' Her Credo," *Niagara Falls Gazette*.

37. Ibid.

38. Audrey Thomas McCluskey, "Multiple Consciousness in the Leadership of Mary McLeod Bethune," *NWS a Journal* 6, no. 1 (Spring 1994): 69–81.

39. Williams, interview by author, March 14, 2010.

40. Smith, interview by author, January 16, 2010.

41. "Mrs. Bond is a Great Woman," *Niagara Falls Gazette*, August 25, 1971.

42. Boston, "Bloneva Bond," 7–36.

43. "Contractor is Honored for Service," n.d., Black in Niagara Falls Folder, Niagara County Historical Association.

44. Williamson, interview; and Robert Bussel, "The Most Indispensable Man in His Community: African American Entrepreneurs in West Chester, Pennsylvania, 1865–1925," *Pennsylvania History: A Journal of Mid-Atlantic Studies* 65, no. 3 African Americans in Pennsylvania (Summer 1998): 324–349.

45. James R. Grossman, *Land of Hope* (Chicago: University of Chicago Press, 1991); Stewart E. Tolnay, "The African American 'Great Migration' and Beyond," *Annual Review of Sociology* 29 (2003): 209–232; Carole Marks, "Black Workers and the Great Migration North," *Phylon* 46, no. 2 (Second Quarter 1985): 148–161; and Carole Marks, *Farewell—We're Good and Gone: The Great Black Migration* (Bloomington: Indiana University Press, 1989).

46. Ibid; Kenneth Kusmer and Joe Trotter, eds., *African American Urban History since World War II* (Chicago: University of Chicago Press, 2009).

47. Kenneth J. Kusmer, *A Ghetto Takes Shape: Black Cleveland, 1870–1930* (Urbana: University of Illinois Press, 1978), 10–11 and chap. 7 and 8; and Williams, *Strangers in the Land of Paradise*, 100–101.

48. Banks, "Problems Encountered by World War II," 13.

49. Ibid., 14.
50. Williamson, interview by author, May 13, 2002.
51. Williamson, interview by author, May 17, 2002.
52. Banks, "Problems Encountered by World War II," 15.
53. Ibid., 25.
54. Ibid., 16.
55. Ibid.
56. Carlyle Miller, interview by author, August 2, 2008; and Arthur Ray, personal interview, August 2, 2008.
57. 1940 Birch Court Property Inc., and 1955 Birch Court Property Inc., Property Assessor's Office, City Hall, Niagara Falls, New York.
58. 1952 Niagara Place Apartments LLC, Property Assessor's Office, City Hall, Niagara Falls, New York.
59. Douglass S. Massey and Nancy A. Denton, *American Apartheid: Segregation and the Making of the Underclass* (Cambridge, MA: Harvard University Press, 1994), 52–57.
60. Ibid., 52–53; Ira Katznelson, *When Affirmative Action Was White: An Untold History of Racial Inequality in Twentieth-Century America* (New York: W. W. Norton, 2005), 113–141.
61. Massey and Denton, *American Apartheid*, 53–55.
62. Ken Wytsma, *The Myth of Equality: Uncovering the Roots of Injustice and Privilege* (Downers Groves, IL: InterVarsity, 2017), 74–79.
63. James L. Greer, "Historic Home Mortgage Redlining in Chicago," *Journal of the Illinois State Historical Society* 107, no. 2 (Summer 2014): 212–218.
64. Kenneth T. Jackson, *Crabgrass Frontier: The Suburbanization of the United States* (New York: Oxford University Press, 1985), 199.
65. Banks, "Problems Encountered by World War II," 24–25; and Carlyle Miller, interview by author, August 2, 2008.
66. Boling, interview by author, August 8, 2010; Emma Jean Hunt, interview by author, April 8, 2010; Wilbur Hunt, interview by author, April 10, 2010; Willie Thomas Madison, interview by author, March 9, 2010; Indiana Martin, interview by author, August 12, 2009; Minnie Tyler, interview by author, May 22, 2010; Eddie Palmore, interview by author, April 5, 2010; Williamson, interview by author, August 8, 2009.
67. Miller, interview by author, August 2, 2008; Ronnie Cunningham, interview by author August 22, 2017.
68. Banks, "Problems Encountered by World War II," 31–32.
69. "30-Day Stay of Order to Vacate Their Homes Granted to 28 Hyde Park Village Families," *Niagara Falls Gazette*, February 26, 1952.
70. Ibid.
71. Ibid.
72. Ibid.

73. Palmore, interview by author, April 5, 2010.

74. "Housing Segregation Exists at Falls, Negro Leader Says," *Niagara Falls Gazette*, July 10, 1961; and "Lack of Jobs, Housing Plagues Negroes Here," *Niagara Falls Gazette*, August 3, 1962.

75. Banks, "Problems Encountered by World War II," 38-39.

76. Ibid., 40.

77. Ibid.

78. Ibid.

79. Ibid., 40-42;

80. Ibid., 44.

81. 1961 Niagara Place Apartments LLC, 1972 Niagara Place Apartments LLC, and 1982 Niagara Place Apartments LLC., Property Assessor's Office, City Hall, Niagara Falls, New York.

82. "Moonglow Hotel Razing Called for Back in 1937," *Niagara Falls Gazette*, November 17, 1957.

83. Ibid.

84. *Sixteenth Census of the United States*, 138-139; *Fifteenth Census of the United States, 1930 Population, Volume III* (Washington, DC: US Government Printing Office, 1931), 327; *Sixteenth Census of the United States: 1940 Population, Volume II, Characteristics of the Population, Part 5: New York—Oregon* (Washington, DC: US Government Printing Office, 1943), 138-39.

85. *US Censuses of Population and Housing: 1960 Census Tracts, Buffalo, NY* (Washington, DC: US Government Printing Office, 1962), 108-110.

86. "State Solons to Get Plan For More Wards in City," *Niagara Falls Gazette*, February 18, 1955; *US Censuses of Population and Housing: 1960 Census Tracts, Buffalo, N.Y.* (Washington, DC: US Government Printing Office, 1962), 108-9.

87. *US Censuses of Population and Housing*, 30-32.

88. Ibid.

89. This is verified by the accounts of many recorded and unrecorded interviews, along with the author's own eyewitness accounts of the area. For more verification of this, see chapter 7.

90. Karl Taeuber and Alma Taeuber, *Negroes in Cities: Residential Segregation and Neighborhood Change* (New York: Atheneum, 1972).

91. Ibid., 39.

92. Ibid. 54-55; *US Censuses of Population and Housing: 1960 Census Tracts, Buffalo, N.Y.*, 30-32.

93. "We Have Some Race Problems Here Too," *Niagara Falls Gazette*, April 24, 1959.

94. "State Commission Charges Housing Segregation Here," *Niagara Falls Gazette*, November 29, 1961; "Falls Negro Find Democracy Diluted," *Niagara Falls Gazette*, March 17, 1963; "Negro Leader Charges Bias in Housing, Schools, Jobs," *Niagara Falls Gazette*, June 28, 1963; and "Agents Get Blamed for Bias in Housing," *Niagara Falls Gazette*, July 31, 1963.

95. "Project Head Threatened, Warned to Ban Negroes," *Niagara Falls Gazette*, February 16, 1956.

96. A review of local newspapers does not indicate that the threat was carried out.

97. "Lack of Jobs, Housing, Plagues Negroes Here," *Niagara Falls Gazette*, August 3, 1962.

98. "Religious Fellowship Seeks End to Housing Discrimination," *Niagara Falls Gazette*, June 3, 1959.

99. "It Started With the Wartime Migration," *Niagara Falls Gazette*, July 30, 1963.

100. Ibid.

101. Ibid.

102. Ibid.

103. Allan H. Spear, *Black Chicago the Making of a Negro Ghetto 1890–1920* (Chicago: University of Chicago Press, 1967), 167–179; St. Clair Drake and Horace R. Cayton, *Black Metropolis: A Study of Negro Life in a Northern City*, vol. 1 (New York: Harper Torchbooks, 1962), 73–76; and James N. Gregory, *The Southern Diaspora: How the Great Migration of Black and White Southerners Transformed America* (Chapel Hill: University of North Carolina Press, 2005), 117–119.

104. "It Started With the Wartime Migration," *Niagara Falls Gazette*.

105. Ibid.

106. Williams, *Strangers in the Land of Paradise*, 90.

107. See Andrew Hacker, *Two Nations: Black and White, Separate, Hostile, Unequal* (New York: Scribner, 2003).

108. Williamson, interview by author, May 17, 2002.

109. Ibid.

110. "It Started With the Wartime Migration," *Niagara Falls Gazette*; and Palmore, interview by author, April 5, 2010.

111. "Community Center Reaches High Mark in Service to Colored Folk," *Niagara Falls Gazette*, October 2, 1944.

112. "Five Leaders of Community Center Honored: Year's Work of Community Center Reviewed; Larger Quarters Needed," *Niagara Falls Gazette*, February 19, 1946.

113. Edward G. Lindsey, "Survey of the Niagara Community Center Association of Niagara Falls, New York," n.d., Niagara Falls, The Community Chest.

114. "To Seek $120,000 for Community Center Building," *Niagara Falls Gazette*, January 21, 1949.

115. Fifteenth Street is now called Aaron Griffin Way.

116. "Statement of Case of Ernest Lovell Dyett by His Mother," *Papers of the NAACP, Part 3, Series B: 1940–1950*, microfilm, AFR 6, Olin Library, Cornell University.

117. Ibid., 4.

118. "Ernest Lovell Dyett to Walter White," October 6, 1946, *Papers of the NAACP, Part 3, Series B: 1940–1950*, microfilm, AFR 6, Olin Library, Cornell University.

119. "Franklin H. Williams to Reverend William S. Hudson," October 8, 1946, *Papers of the NAACP, Part 3, Series B: 1940–1950*, microfilm, AFR 6, Olin Library, Cornell University, 1–2.

120. "Reverend William S. Hudson to Florence Dyett," October 11, 1946, *Papers of the NAACP, Part 3, Series B: 1940–1950*, microfilm, AFR 6, Olin Library, Cornell University; and "Franklin H. Williams to Florence Dyett," October 14, 1946, *Papers of the NAACP, Part 3, Series B: 1940–1950*, microfilm, AFR 6, Olin Library, Cornell University, 1–2.

121. Joel Kovel, *White Racism* (New York: Columbia University Press, 1984), 177–230; Joe R. Feagin, Hernan Vera, and Pinar Batur, *White Racism* (New York: Routledge, 2001) 1–33.

122. Ernest Dyett, interview by author, February 20, 2010.

123. Joyce A. Hanson, *Mary McLeod Bethune and Black Women's Political Activism* (Columbia: University of Missouri Press, 2003); Audrey Thomas McCluskey and Elaine M. Smith, *Mary McLeod Bethune: Building a Better World, Essays and Selected Documents* (Bloomington: Indiana University Press, 2002); and Sadie Iola Daniel, *Women Builders* (Washington, DC: Associated Press, 1970), 79–110.

124. "Mrs. Baldwin, Restaurant Founder, Dies," *Niagara Falls Gazette*, July 1, 1955.

125. Ibid.

126. "Pristell Anderson," Obituaries Notebook A, Local History Department, Niagara Falls Public Library, 1.

127. Helen Reed-McBride, interview by March 9, 2010.

128. Arthur A. Stukas Jr., "Principled Stands Against Racism," *Race, Gender and Class* 13, no. 1/2 (2006), 118.

129. Palmore, interview by author, March 29, 2010.

130. Carmen Mangion, "Community Voices and 'Community Scripts,'" *Studies: An Irish Quarterly Review* 107, no. 427 (Autumn 2018): 302.

131. Smith, interview by author, May 17, 2002; Smith, interview by author, January 16, 2010; Smith, interview by author, May 18, 2010.

132. Smith, interview by author, January 16, 2010.

133. *US Census for 1930*, Niagara Falls Public Library, Niagara Falls, New York, reels 44, 45, and 46.

134. Ibid.

135. Smith, interview.

136. Ibid.

137. Ibid.; Massey and Denton, *American Apartheid*, 29.

138. Smith, interview.

139. Ibid.

140. Jacqueline Jones, *Labor of Love, Labor of Sorrow* (New York: Vintage, 1995), 44–78; and Sharon Ann Holt, "Making Freedom Pay: Freedpeople Working for Themselves, North Carolina, 1865–1900," *Journal of Southern History* 60 (May 1994): 229–262.

141. Dylan C. Penningroth, *The Claims of Kinfolk: African American Property and Community in the Nineteenth-Century South* (Chapel Hill: University of North Carolina Press, 2003), 163–186; Theodore Rosengarten, *All God's Dangers* (New York: Alfred A. Knopf, 1975), 1–94; and Ann Moody, *Coming of Age in Mississippi* (New York: Dell, 1968), 80–89.

142. William Bradberry, "Black Menagerie: Old East Side Was Like United Nations," *Niagara Falls Reporter*, May 7, 2002.

143. Ibid.

144. Smith, interview.

145. Smith, interview.

146. Scott Holland, "So Many Good Voices in My Head," *CrossCurrents* 49, no. 1 (Spring 1999), 72–83.

147. Joe O'Neal, interview by author, March 20, 2010.

148. Williamson, interview; and Gunnar Myrdal, *An American Dilemma*, vol. 1: *The Negro Problem and Modern Democracy* (New York: Harper Torchbooks, 1962), 194–197.

149. Ibid.

150. Massey and Denton, *American Apartheid*, 34.

151. O'Neal, interview.

152. Robert Joseph Taylor and Linda M. Chatters, "Importance of Religion and Spirituality in the Lives of African Americans," *Journal of Negro Education* 79, no. 3 (Summer 2010): 287.

153. Eugene Hamilton, interview by author, August 4, 2007.

154. The "Black Belt" refers to those mineral-rich sections of the Deep South that slave owners migrated to en masse to grow cotton during the era of the cotton gin. It also refers to that region of the South that had high concentrations of African Americans.

155. This southern cultural value predominated immediately following the slavery era when former enslaved persons sought land from the federal government. See Eric C. Foner, *Reconstruction: America's Unfinished Revolution 1863–1877* (New York: Harper & Row, 1988), 116.

156. Williamson, interview.

157. Hamilton, interview.

158. Palmore, interview by author, March 29, 2010.

159. Drake and Cayton, *Black Metropolis*, 61–64.

160. Palmore, interview.

161. Ibid.

162. Ibid.

163. Ibid.
164. Ibid.
165. Williamson, interview.

Notes to Chapter 5

1. Jacquelyn Dowd Hall, "The Long Civil Rights Movement and the Political Uses of the Past," *Journal of American History* 91, no. 4 (March 2005): 1233–1263.

2. Malcolm X and Alex Haley, *The Autobiography of Malcolm X* (New York: Ballantine, 1992), 394–418; and Andrea McEvoy Spero, "Human Rights: By Any Means Necessary," *OAH Magazine of History* 22, no. 2 (April 2008): 39–45.

3. Ronald W. Walter and Robert C. Smith, *African American Leadership* (Albany: State University of New York Press, 1999), 97–122; and Aldon D. Morris, *The Origins of the Civil Rights Movement: Black Communities Organizing for Change* (New York: Free Press, 1984), ix–xiv.

4. Armstead L Robinson and Patricia Sullivan, eds., *New Directions in Civil Rights Studies* (Charlottesville: University of Virginia Press, 1991), 17–29.

5. Thurgood Marshall, "The Constitution's Bicentennial: Commemorating the Wrong Document?," *Vanderbilt Law Review* 40, no. 6 (November 1987): 1337–1342.

6. The US Constitution was created in 1787. That early document recognized slavery in America as a legal institution.

7. Andrew E. Kersten, "African Americans and World War II," *OAH Magazine of History* 16, no. 3 (Spring 2002), 13–17.

8. Kevin Gaines, "The Civil Rights Movement in World Perspective," *OAH Magazine in History* 21, no. 1 (January 2007): 57–64.

9. Mark Newman, *The Civil Rights Movement* (Edinburgh: Edinburgh University Press, 2004), 45–46.

10. John David Skrentny, "The Effects of the Cold War on African American Civil Rights: American and the World Audience, 1945-1968," *Theory and Society* 27, no. 2 (April 1998): 237–285; and Timothy B. Tyson, *The Blood of Emmett Till* (New York: Simon & Schuster, 2017), 185–189.

11. See Kwame Nkrumah, *Ghana: The Autobiography of Kwame Nkrumah* (New York: International, 1971).

12. Thomas R. Frazier, ed., *Afro-American History: Primary Sources* (New York: Harcourt, Brace & World 1970), 395.

13. Azza Salama Layton, *International Politics and Civil Rights* (New York: Cambridge University Press, 2000), 8. For a broad overview of the American setting during the civil rights era, see Gitlin, *The Sixties*.

14. The Niagara Falls school desegregation movement is covered in chapter 6.

15. Aldon Morris, *The Origins of the Civil Rights Movement, Black Communities Organizing for Change* (New York: Free Press, 1986), 264–274.

16. "The Day Dr. Martin Luther King Jr. Came to New Hope Baptist Church," *Niagara Falls Gazette*, January 19, 2004; and Martin L. King Jr., *Stride Toward Freedom* (New York: Harper & Brothers, 1984).

17. Clayborne Carson, ed., *The Papers of Martin Luther King, Jr.*, Vol. 3: *Birth of a New Age December 1955-December 1956* (Berkeley: University of California Press, 1997), 113.

18. "The Day Dr. Martin Luther King Jr. Came to New Hope Baptist Church," *Niagara Falls Gazette*.

19. "One Man's Dream," *Niagara Falls Gazette*, January 19, 2004.

20. Ibid.

21. Ibid.

22. Ibid.

23. Ibid.

24. Ibid.

25. Taylor Branch, *Parting the Waters: America in the King Years, 1954-63* (New York: Simon & Schuster, 1988), 143-205. The author worked with Mildred Isom in the Black Pioneers of Niagara Falls. He did not find out about her observation of Dr. King until after her death. Therefore, he failed to interview her for more information concerning her interactions and observations of Dr. King.

26. William H. Chafe, *Civilities and Civil Rights: Greensboro, North Carolina, and the Black Struggle for Freedom* (New York: Oxford University Press, 1981), 71-118.

27. "Negroes Urged to Support Passive Resistance Drive," *Niagara Falls Gazette*, April 3, 1960.

28. Ibid.

29. Ibid.

30. "Store Picketing Here To Back Dixie Negroes," *Niagara Falls Gazette*, April 20, 1960; and "Rev. Whitaker Named Head of NAACP," *Niagara Falls Gazette*, December 8, 1959.

31. "NAACP Pickets March at Chain Store Here," *Niagara Falls Gazette*, April 24, 1960.

32. Ibid.

33. Ibid.

34. "Little Rock NAACP Leader Not Ready to Give Up Fight," *Niagara Falls Gazette*, March 20, 1960. See Daisy Bates, *The Long Shadow of Little Rock: A Memoir* (Fayetteville: University of Arkansas Press, 1987).

35. "Little Rock Leader Chides Falls Negroes for Apathy in Politics," *Niagara Falls Gazette*, March 19, 1960.

36. "Falls Called Southern City for Denial of Negro Rights," *Niagara Falls Gazette*, March 31, 1960.

37. C. Eric Lincoln, *The Black Muslims in America* (Trenton, NJ: Africa World, 1994), 1-31 and 130-176. This book was originally published in 1961.

38. "Muslim Cult Now Operating Here," *Niagara Falls Gazette*, January 6, 1962; "Pride & Purpose," *Niagara Falls Gazette*, January 11, 1962. See C. Eric Lincoln, *Black Muslims in America* (Grand Rapids, MI: Eerdmans, 1994). Wallace D. Fard organized the Nation of Islam in Detroit, Michigan, in 1930. This was a nationalist group that embraced and espoused Islamic teachings. This organization expanded significantly during the civil rights years and established mosques throughout the country. Elijah Muhammad headed this group at the height of its powers, while Malcolm X was a key spokesperson.

39. "Shortcomings of Negroes Here Are Cited," *Niagara Falls Gazette*, August 7, 1963.

40. "The Black Muslims, Cult Recruits Following Here," *Democrat and Chronicle*, Thursday, November 15, 1962; and Laura Warren Hill, "'We Are Black Folks First': The Black Freedom Struggle in Rochester, NY and the Making of Malcolm X," *The Sixties: A Journal of History, Politics and Culture* 3, no. 2 (2010): 163–185.

41. Adib Rashad, *Elijah Muhammad & The Ideological Foundation of the Nation of Islam* (Newport News, VA: UB & US Communications Systems, 1993), 187–198. See Mattias Gardell, *In The Name of Elijah Muhammad: Louis Farrakhan and the Nation of Islam* (Durham, NC: Duke University Press, 1996).

42. "Muslim Cult Now Operating at Falls," *Niagara Falls Gazette*.

43. Jabril Shareef, interview by author, March 7, 2010.

44. Ibid.

45. "Muslims Gaining Few Converts," *Niagara Falls Gazette*, January 7, 1962.

46. "Ethical-Problem Solutions Asked of NAACP Panel," *Niagara Falls Gazette*, March 12, 1963.

47. "More about Muslims," *Niagara Falls Gazette*, January 11, 1962.

48. "Falls Seeks to Resolve Problems," *Niagara Falls Gazette*, August 11, 1963.

49. "Muslim Cult Now Operating at Falls."

50. "Pro-Muslim," *Niagara Falls Gazette*, January 18, 1962.

51. Lawrence Tyler, "The Protestant Ethic among the Black Muslims," *Phylon* 27, no. 1 (Spring 1966): 5–14.

52. See chapter 3 of Boston, *Business Strategy of Booker T. Washington*; Elijah Muhammad's economic program was similar to that of Washington's, as Harold Cruse has so eloquently written: "It was nothing but a form of Booker T. Washington's economic self-help, black unity, bourgeois hard work, law-abiding, vocational training, stay-out-of-the-civil-rights-struggle agitation, . . . etc., etc., morality. The only difference was that Elijah Muhammad added the potent factor of the Muslim religion to a race, economic, and social philosophy of which the first prophet was none other than Booker T. Washington." See Harold Cruse, *Rebellion or Revolution?* (New York: William Morrow, 1968), 211; and Rashad, *Elijah Muhammad*, 187–198.

53. "Employment is Major Negro Problem," *Niagara Falls Gazette*, August 4, 1963.

54. Manning Marable, *Malcolm X: A Life of Reinvention* (New York: Viking, 2011), 411–412; and Henry Hampton, Steve Fayer, and Sarah Flynn, *Voices of Freedom* (New York: Bantam, 1990), 221–222 and 241–266.

55. "Housing, Lack of Jobs Plague Negroes Here," *Niagara Falls Gazette*, December 11, 1962; "Negroes Find It Difficult to Find Housing at Falls," *Niagara Falls Gazette*, December 9, 1964; "Negro Leaders Here Cite Bias in Housing, Job Opportunity," *Niagara Fall Gazette*, March 27, 1960; "Finds Housing Intolerable Y-Teen Leader to Leave Falls," *Niagara Falls Gazette*, June 26, 1960; and "NAACP Asks Housing Bill," *Niagara Falls Gazette*, February 16, 1961.

56. Ibid.

57. "City's Stores Are Urged to Hire More Negroes," *Niagara Falls Gazette*, January 8, 1963.

58. Ibid.

59. "Negroes to March Here, Leaders Say," *Niagara Falls Gazette*, August 6, 1963.

60. Clayborne Carson, *In Struggle: SNCC and the Black Awakening of the 1960s* (Cambridge, MA: Harvard University Press, 1981), chap. 1 and 2; and Marvin Rich, "The Congress of Racial Equality and Its Strategy," *Annals of the American Academy of Political and Social Science* 357 (January 1965), 117–118.

61. "CORE Unit Here Picks Grant's for Picketing," *Niagara Falls Gazette*, August 24, 1963.

62. Wendel O. Akers, Obituary Folder A-F, n.d., Local History Department, Niagara Falls, New York Public Library.

63. "CORE Sets Picketing Plans," *Niagara Falls Gazette*, August 27, 1963.

64. Ibid.

65. Arthur B. Ray, interview by author, May 24, 2002.

66. "CORE Picketing Falls Store," *Niagara Falls Gazette*, August 28, 1963.

67. "Management's Policy Stated by Grant Firm," *Niagara Falls Gazette*, August 27, 1963.

68. "CORE Increases Pickets, Starts Boycott at Store," *Niagara Falls Gazette*, August 31, 1963.

69. Ibid.

70. "Main St. Store, CORE End Dispute on Hiring," *Niagara Falls Gazette*, September 21, 1963.

71. Bradberry, "Black Menagerie"; and "Negro Job Gains Called Small," *Niagara Falls Gazette*, January 18, 1964.

72. "32 from Falls Join in Freedom March," *Niagara Falls Gazette*, August 28, 1963.

73. Ibid.

74. Ibid.

75. Ibid.

76. John D'Emilio, "Remembering Bayard Rustin," *OAH Magazine of History* 20, no. 2 (March 2006), 12–14.

77. "32 from Falls Join in Freedom March," *Niagara Falls Gazette*.
78. Lewis, *W. E. B. Du Bois*, 386–407.
79. James L. Crouthamel, "The Springfield Race Riot of 1908," *Journal of Negro History* 45, no. 3 (July 1960): 164–181.
80. "Mrs. Hayes Says NAACP Started Here 25 Years Ago," *Niagara Falls Gazette*, April 3, 1968.
81. "NAACP to Open Drive for 500 Members," *Niagara Falls Gazette*, May 29, 1959.
82. "City Rally Speaker Urges Negroes to Speed Bid for Civil Rights," *Niagara Falls Gazette*, March 28, 1960.
83. "Emancipation Marked by Falls NAACP Unit," *Niagara Falls Gazette*, May 12, 1963.
84. "Forum Deals with Law," *Niagara Falls Gazette*, March 3, 1967.
85. "Voice Sought on Textbooks," *Niagara Falls Gazette*, September 18, 1970.
86. "Meeting set by NAACP," *Niagara Falls Gazette*, May 7, 1972.
87. "Negro Leader Charges Bias in Housing, Schools, Jobs," *Niagara Falls Gazette*, June 28, 1963.
88. "Rally Scores Bias in Housing," *Niagara Falls Gazette*, February 9, 1964.
89. Ibid.
90. Ibid.; Mayor E. Dent Lackey is also discussed in chapter 7.
91. Ibid.
92. Ibid.
93. Ibid.
94. Ibid.
95. Ibid.
96. Ibid.
97. "Schreiber Denies Racial Slur during Interview by Reporters," *Niagara Falls Gazette*, May 31, 1966; "Schreiber Protest Is Planned," *Niagara Falls Gazette*, June 16, 1966; and "Picketing of Schreiber Is Planned," *Niagara Falls Gazette*, June 24, 1966.
98. The Reverend Edgar L. Huff eventually returned to Niagara Falls to again serve as pastor of St. John's AME Church.
99. "Schreiber Denies Racial Slur during Interview by Reporters," *Niagara Falls Gazette*.
100. "Schreiber Protest Is Planned," *Niagara Falls Gazette*.
101. "Schreiber Denies Racial Slur During Interview by Reporters," *Niagara Falls Gazette*.
102. "Schreiber Protest Is Planned," *Niagara Falls Gazette*.
103. "County Welfare Head Is Mum on NAACP March Home," *Niagara Falls Gazette*, June 19, 1966.
104. Ibid.
105. "Picketing of Schreiber Is Planned," *Niagara Falls Gazette*.

106. "Schreiber Denies Racial Slur During Interview by Reporters," *Niagara Falls Gazette*.

107. "'Dutch' Schreiber Ends Long Career; One of Area's Unique Personalities," *Niagara Falls Gazette*, April 25, 1971.

108. See Myrlie Evers-Williams and Manning Marable, *The Autobiography of Medgar Evers: A Hero's Life and Legacy Revealed through His Writings, Letters, and Speeches* (New York: Basic Civitas, 2006).

109. Hampton, Fayer, and Flynn, *Voices of Freedom*, 139–157.

110. Juan Williams, *Eyes on the Prize* (New York: Viking, 1987), 52; and Tyson, *Blood of Emmett Till*, 143.

111. "NAACP Treasurer to Speak," *Niagara Falls Gazette*, June 9, 1967.

112. "City Boycott Is Sought for Mississippi Goods," *Niagara Falls Gazette*, January 12, 1965.

113. Ibid.

114. "Mayor Evers is Given Falls Tour by Lackey," *Niagara Falls Gazette*, August 8, 1972.

115. Bruce J. Dierenfield, *The Civil Rights Movement* (Harlow, UK: Pearson, 2004), 92; and Harvard Sitkoff, *The Struggle For Black Equality* (New York: Hill & Wang, 1993), 172–174.

116. "6 Birmingham Negroes Killed: 4 Girls Die in Church Blast; 2 Boys Are Shot to Death," *Niagara Falls Gazette*, September 16, 1963.

117. Ibid.

118. "Memorial Services Held for 4 Girls," *Niagara Falls Gazette*, September 23, 1963.

119. Ibid.

120. Ibid.

121. Williams, *Eyes on the Prize*, 273.

122. Wilbur Hunt, interview by author, April 10, 2010.

123. "Violence in Selma Protested," *Niagara Falls Gazette*, March 9, 1965.

124. Ibid.

125. "400 Stage Civil Rights March in Falls," *Niagara Falls Gazette*, March 15, 1965.

126. Ibid.
127. Ibid.
128. Ibid.
129. Ibid.
130. Ibid.
131. Ibid.
132. Ibid.
133. Ibid.
134. Ibid.
135. Ibid.

136. Ibid.

137. "$550 Collected Here Will Help Rights Workers," *Niagara Falls Gazette*, March 16, 1965.

138. "Memorial Will Honor Mrs. Lampkin," *Niagara Falls Gazette*, June 5, 1965.

139. Denton L. Watson, "Assessing the Role of the NAACP in the Civil Rights Movement," *Historian* 55, no. 3 (Spring 1993): 453.

140. Barbara Williams, interview by author, March 14, 2010. Mrs. Williams was involved in the NAACP for a long period and served as secretary for a number of years.

141. "NAACP Unit Will Stage Observance," *Niagara Falls Gazette*, January 27, 1965.

142. Carter G. Woodson founded "Black History Week" in 1926. In 1976 Black History Week was changed to "Negro History Month." Both these celebrations took place in February.

143. "NAACP Production to Depict Negro Cultural Achievements," *Niagara Falls Gazette*, February 1, 1965.

144. President Lyndon B. Johnson established "Great Society" programs to rectify poverty in the United States: Head Start, Upward Bound, Community Action Organization, and others. These programs attempted to aid the poor, but the effects were ultimately limited because its projected funding was largely diverted toward the Vietnam War.

145. "NAACP Hits Giving Post to Mrs. Hayes," *Niagara Falls Gazette*, January 25, 1966.

146. Ibid.

147. "Poverty Board Eyes Grievances," *Niagara Falls Gazette*, February 7, 1966.

148. Ibid.

149. "Poverty Board Critics Appeal to Shriver, RFK," *Niagara Falls Gazette*, February 9, 1966.

150. "Local Solution Is Likely in Poverty Unit Dispute," *Niagara Falls Gazette*, February 11, 1966; and "Antipoverty Board Hears Complaints," *Niagara Falls Gazette*, February 24, 1966.

151. Ibid.

152. "Realtors Back 'Open Occupancy,'" *Niagara Falls Gazette*, May 3, 1966.

153. Ibid.

154. Ibid.

155. Ibid.

156. Ibid.

157. Ibid.

158. "State Commission Charges Housing Segregation Here," *Niagara Falls Gazette*, November 29, 1961; "Lack of Jobs, Housing Plagues Negroes Here," *Niagara Falls Gazette*, August 3, 1962; and Arnold R. Hirsch, *Making the Second*

Ghetto: Race & Housing in Chicago 1940–1969 (New York: Cambridge University Press, 1983), 1–39.

159. Jules J. Wanderer, "1967 Riots: A Test of the Congruity of Events," *Social Problems* 16, no. 2 (Autumn 1968): 194.

160. "5 P.M. Meeting Called to Thwart Another Night of Disturbances Here," *Niagara Falls Gazette*, June 29, 1967.

161. Ibid.

162. Ibid.

163. "2nd Night of Tension Here Results in More Meetings," *Niagara Falls Gazette*, June 30, 1967.

164. "Negro Leaders Respond to Disturbance in Falls," n.d., Race Relations Folder, Local History Department, Niagara Falls Public Library, 1 and 2.

165. Ibid.

166. Ibid.

167. Ibid.

168. "Highland Ave. Neglected, Mayor Says," *Niagara Falls Gazette*, June 30, 1967.

169. Ibid.

170. "Mayor's Plan Covers Jobs, Recreation," n.d., Race Relations Folder, Local History Department, Niagara Falls Public Library, 1.

171. Ibid.

172. "Lackey Unveils Ghetto Crash Project," n.d., Race Relations Folder, Local History Department, Niagara Falls Public Library, 1.

173. Ibid.

174. Ibid.

175. Ibid.

176. Ibid.

177. Ibid.

178. Ibid.

179. "Jackie Robinson Warns City to Initiate Solutions," *Niagara Falls Gazette*, July 1, 1967.

180. Ibid.

181. "Falls Negroes to Meet, Discuss Grievances," *Niagara Falls Gazette*, July 3, 1967.

182. Ibid.

183. "Negro Manifesto Readied For Council," *Niagara Falls Gazette*, July 5, 1967.

184. "Negro Unity Cry Rules City Grass Roots Rally," *Niagara Falls Gazette*, July 5, 1967.

185. Ibid.

186. "Negro Speaker Warns City of New Upheaval," *Niagara Falls Gazette*, July 6, 1967.

187. Ibid.

188. William L. Van DeBurg, *New Day in Babylon: The Black Power Movement and American Culture, 1965–1975* (Chicago: University of Chicago Press, 1992), 28.

189. "Negro Speaker Warns City of New Upheaval," *Niagara Falls Gazette*.

190. Ibid.

191. Ibid.

192. "Waiting Stance Indicated by Negroes at Council Session," *Niagara Falls Gazette*, July 7, 1967.

193. Ibid.

194. "Negro" was a term used during the civil rights movement instead of "African American." It is used here in a purely historical context.

195. "Negro Claim Jobs Not Forthcoming," *Niagara Falls Gazette*, July 19, 1967.

196. "Negro Cancel Picketing of Downtown Businesses," *Niagara Falls Gazette*, July 20, 1967.

197. See chapter 6 in Martin L. King Jr., *Stride Toward Freedom* (New York: Harper & Brothers, 1984).

198. "Mayor Raps Race Bias," *Niagara Falls Gazette*, April 10, 1968.

199. "King's Slaying Sign of Sick America, Rights Leader Says," *Niagara Falls Gazette*, April 6, 1968.

200. Ibid.; Mrs. Bond probably meant twelve years earlier instead of eight.

201. "Dr. King Mourned In Area," *Niagara Falls Gazette*, April 9, 1968.

202. Ibid.

203. Ibid.

204. Arthur Ray, interview by author, July 3, 2012.

205. "Staff Is to Be Hired for Friendship House," *Niagara Falls Gazette*, April 12, 1968; and "Friendship House Aided by Board of Education," *Niagara Falls Gazette*, June 21, 1968.

206. "State Grant Expected for Friendship House," *Niagara Falls Gazette*, June 11, 1968; "State May Finance Friendship House," *Niagara Falls Gazette*, June 20, 1968; and "$175,000 to Go Direct to Center," *Niagara Falls Gazette*, June 21, 1968.

207. "Friendship House Will Get $11,800," *Niagara Falls Gazette*, May 9, 1968.

208. Ibid.

209. Niagara Falls leaders and educators used the term "ghetto youth" extensively to define poor, underprivileged African American youths.

210. "Staff Is to Be Hired for Friendship House," *Niagara Falls Gazette*.

211. "Friendship House Head Is Selected," *Niagara Falls Gazette*, April 14, 1968.

212. Ibid.

213. "Friendship House Elects Ray to Post," *Niagara Falls Gazette*, June 12, 1968.

214. "Friendship House Project Has Successful Summer," *Niagara Falls Gazette*, September 8, 1968.
215. "Retiring Friendship House Head Cites Better Civic Attitude," December 14, 1970.
216. "Training Program for Minority Construction Workers Unveiled," *Niagara Falls Gazette*, July 5, 1970.
217. "Training for Construction Inc. Aids Jobless," *Niagara Falls Gazette*, March 11, 1971.
218. "Area Unions, Contractors Told to Hire More Black Trainees," *Niagara Falls Gazette*, November 9, 1970.
219. "Construction Trade Training Program End Expected Nov. 30," *Niagara Falls Gazette*, October 30, 1971.
220. "NiaCAP Drafts Plan to Avert Youth Rumbles," *Niagara Falls Gazette*, May 11, 1967.
221. "NiaCAP Gets $85,265 Grant," *Niagara Falls Gazette*, January 13, 1967.
222. William Grier and Price M. Cobbs, *Black Rage* (New York: Basic Books, 1968).
223. "Niagara Falls Lifts Curfew in Negro Slum Area as Calm Returns to Tense City," *New York Times*, August 24, 1969.
224. Ibid.
225. Ibid.
226. Ibid.
227. "Tension at Niagara Falls," *New York Times*, August 19, 1969.
228. Williams, interview by author, March 14, 2010.
229. Gregg Lee Carter, "Local Police Force Size and the Severity of the 1960s Black Rioting," *Journal of Conflict Resolution* 31, no. 4 (December 1987), 611.
230. "Niagara Falls Lifts Curfew in Negro Slum Area," *Niagara Falls Gazette*.
231. Ibid.
232. Ibid.
233. Hunt, interview by author, April 10, 2010.
234. Bill Williamson, interview by author, January 30, 2010.
235. "Niagara Falls Lifts Curfew in Negro Slum Area," *Niagara Falls Gazette*.
236. Frank Mesiah, interview by author, March 18, 2010.
237. Ibid.
238. "Unique Project, National Black Museum for Niagara Falls," *Daily Defender*, August 6, 1973.
239. "National Black Museum Set," *Chicago Defender*, August 18, 1973.
240. "Unique Project, National Black Museum for Niagara Falls."
241. Ibid.
242. "Unique Project, National Black Museum for Niagara Falls"; and Mesiah, interview by author, March 18, 2010.

243. Ibid.
244. Ibid.
245. Mesiah, interview by author, March 18, 2010.
246. Ibid.
247. Ibid.
248. Ibid.
249. Ibid.; Frank Mesiah resided in neighboring Buffalo, although he had an office in Niagara Falls.
250. Williams, interview by author, March 14, 2010.
251. "New Black Society Asks City for Aid in Ghetto Improvement," *Niagara Falls Gazette*, August 22, 1968.
252. Williams, interview by author, March 14, 2010; and Manning Marable and Leith Mullings, ed., *Let Nobody Turn Us Around* (Lanham, MD: Rowman & Littlefield, 2003), 490.
253. "Equal Opportunity—Zero," *Niagara Falls Gazette*, April 22, 1974; "Bus Jobs Asked for Blacks," *Niagara Falls Gazette*, May 29, 1974; "Man Who Brought Center Avenue School," *Niagara Falls Gazette*, February 23, 1975; and "Black Club to Utilize School for Youth Center," *Niagara Falls Gazette*, August 1, 1975.
254. "Discrimination Encouraged Him to Succeed, Niagara Personality: Fred Brown," *Niagara Falls Gazette*, May 23, 1971; and Mesiah, interview by author, March 18, 2010.
255. Talmadge Anderson, *Introduction to African American Studies* (Dubuque, IA: Kendall/Hunt, 1993), 33; Lerone Bennett Jr., *Before the Mayflower: A History of Black America* (New York: Penguin, 1988), 378; Norman Coombs, *The Black Experience in America* (New York: Hippocrene, 1972), 196; John Hope Franklin and Alfred A. Moss Jr., *From Slavery to Freedom: A History of African Americans* (Boston: McGraw Hill, 2000), 511–512; Benjamin Quarles, *The Negro in the Making of America* (New York: Touchstone, 1996), 291–292; and Joe William Trotter Jr., *The African American Experience*, vol. 2: *From Reconstruction* (Boston: Houghton Mifflin, 2001), 524–526.
256. Clenora Hudson-Weems, "Resurrecting Emmett Till: The Catalyst of the Modern Civil Rights Movement," *Journal of Black Studies* 29, no. 2 (November 1998), 179–188; and Tyson, *Blood of Emmett Till*, 177–209.

Notes to Chapter 6

1. Mark V. Tushnet, *The NAACP Legal Strategy against Segregated Education 1925-1950* (Chapel Hill: University of North Carolina Press, 2005).
2. David Blight, "Charles Hamilton Houston: The Legal Scholar Who Laid the Foundation for Integrated Higher Education in the United States," *Journal*

of Blacks in Higher Education 34 (Winter 2001–2002): 107; and Juan Williams, *Thurgood Marshall: American Revolutionary* (New York: Times Books, 1998).

3. Harvard Sitkoff, *The Struggle for Black Equality* (New York: Hill and Wang, 1993), 3–36.

4. "NAACP Will Ask State to End Bias in Schools," *Niagara Falls Gazette*, September 22, 1967.

5. "Housing Causes School Segregation," *Niagara Falls Gazette*, August 6, 1963, 9.

6. Ibid.

7. Ibid.

8. "NAACP Pickets March at Chain Store Here," *Niagara Falls Gazette*, April 24, 1960; Henry Hampton, Steve Fayer, and Sarah Flynn, *Voices of Freedom: An Oral History of the Civil Rights Movement From the 1950s through the 1980s* (New York: Bantam, 1991), 297–319.

9. "CORE Charges Bias Abuses in Schools," n.d., Folder #370, Local History Department, Niagara Falls, New York Public Library, 1 and 2.

10. Richard H. Kindsvatter and William W. Wilen, "The Dilemma of Racial Imbalance in the Schools," *American Secondary Education* 4, no. 4 (September 1974): 29–33.

11. William W. Beck, Glenn M. Linden, and Michael E. Siegel, "Identifying School Desegregation Leadership Styles," *Journal of Negro Education* 49, no. 2 (Spring 1980): 116; and Charles U. Smith, "Public School Desegregation and the Law," *Social Forces* 54, no. 2 (December 1975): 317–327.

12. Jerrry K. Frye, "The Black Manifesto and the Tactic of Objectification," *Journal of Black Studies* 5, no. 1 (September 1974): 65–76.

13. "Jones Pushes City on Schools," *Niagara Falls Gazette*, July 7, 1967.

14. Ibid.

15. Ibid.

16. Ibid.

17. "NAACP Blasts Program to End School Imbalance," *Niagara Falls Gazette*, August 24, 1967.

18. "NAACP Will Ask State to End Bias in Schools," *Niagara Falls Gazette*.

19. "NAACP Blasts Program to End School Imbalance," *Niagara Falls Gazette*.

20. Ibid.

21. Ibid.

22. Ibid.

23. Ibid.

24. "Housing Causes School Segregation," *Niagara Falls Gazette*.

25. Ellen Goldring, et al., "Schooling Closer to Home: Desegregation Policy and Neighborhood," *American Journal of Education* 112, no. 3 (May 2006): 335–362.

26. "NAACP Blasts Program to End School Imbalance," *Niagara Falls Gazette*.

27. Ibid.

28. "Negroes Outline Objections to Busing," *Niagara Falls Gazette*, August 24, 1967.

29. Jennifer R. Woodward, "How Busing Burdened Blacks: Critical Race Theory and Busing for Desegregation in Nashville-Davidson County," *Journal of Negro Education* 80, no. 1 (Winter 2011): 22–32.

30. Rodney J. Reed, "School Boards, the Community, and School Desegregation," *Journal of Black Studies* 13, no. 2 (December 1982): 189–206.

31. W. F. Collins to Casper L. Jordon, August 22, 1967, Niagara Falls, New York, *Letters of Niagara Falls Branch of the NAACP*, Local History Department, Niagara Falls Public Library.

32. "Ray, Evans Are Elected; Only 5,763 Votes Cast," *Niagara Falls Gazette*, May 6, 1964.

33. Arthur B. Ray, interview by author, July 13, 2012.

34. "NAACP Will Ask State to End Bias in Schools," *Niagara Falls Gazette*.

35. Ibid.

36. "School Racial Imbalance Exists in City Only at Elementary Level," *Niagara Falls Gazette*, November 7, 1967.

37. "NAACP Drafts Briefs to State to Step into Segregation Issue," *Niagara Falls Gazette*, November 6, 1967, 14.

38. "School Racial Imbalance Exists in City Only at Elementary Level," *Niagara Falls Gazette*.

39. Ibid.

40. Melvin J. Knapp and Jon P. Alston, "White Parental Acceptance of Varying Degrees of School Desegregation: 1965 and 1970," *Public Opinion Quarterly* 36, no. 4 (Winter 1972–1973): 585–591.

41. "Parents Argue over Transfer of Children to Beech School," 1970 Desegregation Folder, Local History Department, Niagara Falls Public Library, 1.

42. Ibid.

43. Ibid.

44. Ibid.

45. Douglas Longshore and Jeffrey Prager, "The Impact of School Desegregation: A Situational Analysis," *Annual Review of Sociology* 11 (1985): 83–85.

46. "Oliver Defends Plans for School Integration," 1970 Desegregation Folder, Local History Department, Niagara Falls Public Library, 1.

47. "Pupil Integration Process Gets Off to Smooth Start," 1970 Desegregation Folder, Local History Department, Niagara Falls Public Library, 1.

48. R. W. Irvine and J. J. Irvine, "The Impact of the Desegregation Process on the Education of Black Students: Key Variables," *Journal of Negro Education* 52 (1983): 410–422.

49. "Negroes Fight 'One-Way' Bussing," *Niagara Falls Gazette*, September 11, 1968, 28 and 30.

50. Ibid., 30.
51. Tilman C. Cothran and William Phillips Jr., "Negro Leadership in a Crisis Situation," *Phylon* 22, no. 2 (Second Quarter 1961): 107–118.
52. "Negroes Fight 'One-Way' Bussing."
53. August Meier and John H. Bracey Jr., "The NAACP as a Reform Movement, 1909–1965: 'To Reach the Conscience of America,'" *Journal of Southern History* 59, no. 1 (February 1993): 3–30.
54. "'Dialogue' on School Integration Develops Into a One-Sided Affair," 1970 Desegregation Folder, Local History Department, Niagara Falls Public Library, 1; and William E. Nelson Jr., "School Desegregation and the Black Community," *Theory into Practice* 26 (December 1987): 450–458.
55. "'Dialogue' on School Integration," 1.
56. Ibid.
57. Ibid.; Ronald V. Dellums, "Black Leadership: for Change or for Status Quo?," *Black Scholar* 8, no. 4 (January–February 1977): 2–5.
58. "Black Demand Bias Halt at Beech Avenue School," 1970 Desegregation Folder, Local History Department, Niagara Falls Public Library, 1.
59. "Racial Storm Hits Schools on Busing Termed 'One Way,'" 1970 Desegregation Folder, Local History Department, Niagara Falls Public Library, 1.
60. "Oliver Defends Plans For School Integration."
61. Ibid.
62. Ibid.
63. Ibid.
64. Ibid.
65. Ibid.
66. Ibid.
67. "Boycott, Walkouts Staged at School," *Niagara Falls Gazette*, October 17, 1968.
68. "William Loren Katz, "Black History in Secondary Schools," *Journal of Negro Education* 38, no. 4 (Autumn 1969): 430–434.
69. Ibid.; "Falls Board to Drop Reading Center Plan," 1970 Desegregation Folder, Local History Department, Niagara Falls Public Library, 1.
70. Ibid.
71. "White Parents Hit Two-Way Busing," 1970 Desegregation Folder, Local History Department, Niagara Falls Public Library, 1; and "Negro Parents End Boycott of School," 1970 Desegregation Folder, Local History Department, Niagara Falls Public Library, 1.
72. Gary Orfield, *Must We Bus? Segregated Schools and National Policy* (Washington, DC: Brookings Institution, 1978).
73. "Board Plans to Seek Successor to Oliver," 1970 Desegregation Folder, Local History Department, Niagara Falls Public Library, 1.
74. "White Parents Hit Two-Way Busing," 1.

75. Ibid.
76. Ibid.
77. Ibid.
78. Ibid.
79. Ibid.
80. "New Plans Offered to Integrate Schools," 1969 Desegregation Folder, Local History Department, Niagara Falls Public Library, 1.
81. Janell Drone, "Desegregation and Effective School Leadership: Tracking Success, 1954–1980," *Journal of African American History* 90, no. 4 (Autumn 2005): 410–421; and Jawanza Kunjufu, *There Is Nothing Wrong with Black Students* (Chicago: Images, 2012), 67–90.
82. "Proposals Offered on Integration," 1970 Desegregation Folder, Local History Department, Niagara Falls Public Library, 1.
83. Ibid.
84. Ibid.
85. Ibid.
86. Ibid.
87. "Teachers Assn. Urges Total Falls Integration," 1969 Desegregation Folder, Local History Department, Niagara Falls Public Library, 1.
88. Ibid.
89. Ibid.
90. "New Plans Offered to Integrate Schools," 1.
91. Elmer Enstrom, *Busing, not Integration, Opposed* (Santa Ana, CA: Graphic, 1998).
92. "Integration Aim Put Above Neighborhood School Plan," 1969 Desegregation Folder, Local History Department, Niagara Falls Public Library, 1.
93. Ibid.
94. Ibid.
95. "Parents Hit Falls Integration Plan," 1969 Desegregation Folder, Local History Department, Niagara Falls Public Library, 1.
96. Ibid.
97. Ibid.
98. Ibid.
99. "GOP Is Readying Anti-Busing Law," 1969 Desegregation Folder, Local History Department, Niagara Falls Public Library, 1.
100. Ibid.
101. "Fall Integration Plan Is Hit," 1969 Desegregation Folder, Local History Department, Niagara Falls Public Library, 1.
102. "Fiery Integration Meeting Hammers Away at Plan 18," 1969 Desegregation Folder, Local History Department, Niagara Falls Public Library, 1.
103. "Joint Meeting on Plan 18 Sought with Board," *Niagara Falls Gazette*, July 12, 1969.
104. Ibid.

105. Ibid.
106. Casper L. Jordon to Rev. Ray K. Hallin, September 22, 1967, Niagara Falls, New York, *Letters of Niagara Falls Branch of the NAACP*, Local History Department, Niagara Falls Public Library.
107. "Board Action Postpones Falls School Integration," 1969 Desegregation Folder, Local History Department, Niagara Falls Public Library, 1.
108. "Board Action Postpone Falls School Integration," 1969 Desegregation Folder, Local History Department, Niagara Falls Public Library, 1.
109. Ibid.
110. Ibid.
111. "Black Group Fails in Falls Strategy," 1969 Desegregation Folder, Local History Department, Niagara Falls Public Library, 1; "60 Blacks Charge Board Is Playing with Integration," 1969 Desegregation Folder, Local History Department, Niagara Falls Public Library, 1.
112. "60 Blacks Charge Board Is Playing With Integration," 1.
113. "Voluntary Busing Set at Beech Ave. School," 1969 Desegregation Folder, Local History Department, Niagara Falls Public Library, 1.
114. "Voluntary Busing Set at Beech Ave. School," 1969 Desegregation Folder, 1; and "Beech to Push Integration of Lunch and Play Periods," 1969 Desegregation Folder, Local History Department, Niagara Falls Public Library, 1.
115. "Black Student Rolls Up in High Schools," 1969 Desegregation Folder, Local History Department, Niagara Falls Public Library, 1.
116. Ibid.
117. "Proposal Would Entail Transfer of 372 Pupils," 1970 Desegregation Folder, Local History Department, Niagara Falls Public Library, 1.
118. "Fall Is Target Date, Not Deadline, for Integration," *Niagara Falls Gazette*, February 4, 1970.
119. "School Integration Panel Agrees on 6 Points in Perimeter Plan," 1970 Desegregation Folder, Local History Department, Niagara Falls Public Library, 1.
120. "Integration Plan Gets Tentative Board OK," 1970 Desegregation Folder, Local History Department, Niagara Falls Public Library, 1.
121. "Allen Says Educators Should Lead Equal Education Efforts," 1970 Desegregation Folder, Local History Department, Niagara Falls Public Library, 1.
122. "Falls School Integration Plan Wins Praise of State Official," *Niagara Falls Gazette*, February 18, 1970.
123. Ibid.
124. "Conservatives Oppose Plan 21," 1970 Desegregation Folder, Local History Department, Niagara Falls Public Library, 1.
125. Ibid.
126. Ibid.
127. Ibid.
128. Ibid.

129. "Integration Wins Praise During Plan 21 Discussion," 1970 Desegregation Folder, Local History Department, Niagara Falls Public Library, 1.

130. Ibid.

131. "Plan 21 Wins Approval of City Teachers," *Niagara Falls Gazette*, April 23, 1970.

132. "Citizens Behind Plan 21 Meet Tonight at City Hall," 1970 Desegregation Folder, Local History Department, Niagara Falls Public Library, 1.

133. "Group Named to Promote Plan 21 Here," 1970 Desegregation Folder, Local History Department, Niagara Falls Public Library, 1.

134. Ibid.

135. "Plan 21 Cost Is Set at $49,000," 1970 Desegregation Folder, Local History Department, Niagara Falls Public Library, 1.

136. Ibid.

137. "Lackey Opposed to Forced Busing in Integration Plan," *Niagara Falls Gazette*, May 28, 1970.

138. Ibid.

139. Ibid.

140. Ibid.

141. "Accusations False, Says Mayor," 1970 Desegregation Folder, Local History Department, Niagara Falls Public Library, 1.

142. "Falls Board OKs Integration Plan," 1970 Desegregation Folder, Local History Department, Niagara Falls Public Library, 1.

143. "Integration Plan Adopted for City; to Start in Fall," 1970 Desegregation Folder, Local History Department, Niagara Falls Public Library, 1.

144. "Integration Plan Approval Caps Efforts of 6 Years," 1.

145. Ibid.

146. "Integration Plan Adopted for City; to Start in Fall," 1.

147. "Court Dismisses Plea to Halt Integration," 1970 Desegregation Folder, Local History Department, Niagara Falls Public Library, 1.

148. "Picketing Teachers Block School Buses," 1970 Desegregation Folder, Local History Department, Niagara Falls Public Library, 1.

149. Ibid.

150. Ibid.

151. "School Busing Appeal Slated," 1970 Desegregation Folder, Local History Department, Niagara Falls Public Library, 1.

152. "Court Dismisses Plea to Halt Integration," 1.

153. "Teacher Who Struck Docked," 1970 Desegregation Folder, Local History Department, Niagara Falls Public Library, 1.

154. Ibid.

155. "School Busing Foes Appeal Case," 1970 Desegregation Folder, Local History Department, Niagara Falls Public Library, 1.

156. "Success of Plan 21 Surpasses Backers' Hopes," 1970 Desegregation Folder, Local History Department, Niagara Falls Public Library, 1.

157. "Desegregated City Schools are Rated a 'Prize' by State," 1970 Desegregation Folder, Local History Department, Niagara Falls Public Library, 1.
158. "Attitudes on Falls 'Plan 21' May Be Changing," 1970 Desegregation Folder, Local History Department, Niagara Falls Public Library, 1.
159. "Success of Plan 21 Surpasses Backers' Hopes," 1970 Desegregation Folder, 1.
160. Ibid.
161. "Charts on Racial Breakdown Contain a Flaw," 1970 Desegregation Folder, Local History Department, Niagara Falls Public Library, 1.
162. Ibid.
163. "Beech School Integration Works Well," 1970 Desegregation Folder, Local History Department, Niagara Falls Public Library, 1.
164. "Most Affected in Plan 21 Program is Black Community," 1970 Desegregation Folder, Local History Department, Niagara Falls Public Library, 1.
165. Ibid.
166. Ibid.
167. Ibid.
168. Ibid.
169. "NAACP Protesting Falls School Aid Request," *Niagara Falls Gazette*, April 8, 1973.
170. "Schools Get First Black Top Official," *Niagara Fall Gazette*, August 17, 1973.
171. "NAACP Protesting Falls School Aid Request," *Niagara Falls Gazette*.
172. Ibid.
173. Ibid.
174. "Blacks Don't Receive Top School Posts," *Niagara Falls Gazette*, August 23, 1970.
175. Ibid.
176. Ibid.
177. "Black Faculty and Students Increase Fractionally in City Schools," *Niagara Falls Gazette*, December 4, 1974; and "Blacks Don't Receive Top School Posts," *Niagara Falls Gazette*, August 23, 1970.
178. "No Black on Board Raises Some Concern," *Niagara Falls Gazette*, May 12, 1974.
179. Ibid.
180. Ibid.
181. Ibid.
182. Ibid.
183. Ibid.
184. "58 Blacks to Be Shifted to Hyde Park School," *Niagara Falls Gazette*, June 14, 1974.
185. Steven J. L. Taylor, *Desegregation in Boston and Buffalo: The Influence of Local Leaders* (Albany: State University of New York Press, 1998), 160; and

US Bureau of the Census, Census of Population: 1970, vol. 1: *Characteristics of the Population, Part 34, New York-Section 1* (Washington, DC: US Government Printing Office, 1973), 34.

186. Ibid.
187. Taylor, *Desegregation in Boston and Buffalo*, 54.
188. Ibid.
189. "Falls Cited as School Integration Model," *Niagara Falls Gazette*, September 24, 1971.
190. Taylor, *Desegregation in Boston and Buffalo*, 54.
191. Ibid.
192. Ibid.
193. Ibid., 55.
194. Ibid., 96–97.
195. Ibid., 96.
196. Ibid., 98.
197. Ibid., 100–106.
198. "CORE Charges Bias, Abuses in Schools," 1.
199. Taylor, *Desegregation in Boston and Buffalo*, 53–54.
200. Ibid., 54.
201. Ralph Watkins, "Blacks in Buffalo 1900–1920" (PhD diss., University of Buffalo), 130.
202. Roosevelt Bradberry, interview by author, May 19, 2010. The author interviewed a number of Black Niagarans, and several of them attested to this behavior.
203. Ibid.
204. "We Have Lost the Power," *Niagara Falls Gazette*, May 14, 1974; and "Divided We Fell," *Niagara Falls Gazette*, August 25, 1974.
205. Ronald W. Walter and Robert C. Smith, *African American Leadership* (Albany: State University of New York Press, 1999), 197–221.
206. Taylor, *Desegregation in Boston and Buffalo*, 98.
207. Taylor, 98–99.
208. Waldo E. Martin Jr., *The Mind of Frederick Douglass* (Chapel Hill: University of North Carolina Press, 1984), 124–125; see chapter 1 of James Colaiaco, *Frederick Douglass and the Fourth of July Oration* (New York: Palgrave Macmillan, 2006).

Notes to Chapter 7

1. James Robert Saunders and Renee Nadine Shackelford, *Urban Renewal and the End of Black Culture in Charlottesville, Virginia* (Jefferson, NC: McFarland, 2005); Mindy Thompson Fullilove, *Root Shock: How Tearing Up City Neighborhoods Hurt America, and What We Can Do About It* (New York: Random House,

2009); Mindy Thompson Fullilove, "Root Shock: The Consequences of African American Dispossession," *Journal of Urban Health* 78, no. 1 (March 2001), 72–80; J. Allen Williams Jr., "The Effect of Urban Renewal Upon a Black Community: Evaluation and Recommendations," *Social Science Quarterly* 50, no. 3 (December 1969): 703–712; Niles Williams Niemuth, "Urban Renewal and the Development of Milwaukee's African American Community: 1960–1980 (master's thesis, University of Wisconsin-Milwaukee, 2014); Arnold R. Hirsch, *Making the Second Ghetto: Race & Housing in Chicago 1940–1969* (New York: Cambridge University Press, 1983); Ken Wytsma, *The Myth of Equality: Uncovering the Roots of Injustice and Privilege* (Downers Groves, IL: InterVarsity, 2017), chap. 4.

2. "Corporation Proceedings in Council," *Niagara Falls Gazette*, October 21, 1961.

3. See Hamilton B. Mizer, *A City Is Born* (Niagara Falls, NY: Human-Wahl Printing, 1981.

4. Nathaniel McDowell, interview by author, May 13, 2010.

5. Michael N. Vogel, *Echoes in the Mist: An Illustrated History of the Niagara Falls Area* (Chatsworth, CA: Windsor, 1991), 113.

6. "SPA Refuses to Give Detailed Data on Land to Be Taken in Project," *Niagara Falls Gazette*, October 23, 1957, 27.

7. "Urban Renewal, Jetport Sees Population Boosts," *Niagara Falls Gazette*, May 21, 1970.

8. "Blighted Niagara Falls Works to Rebuild Itself," *New York Times*, October 1, 1973.

9. Urban renewal initiatives began in with the passage of the US Housing Act of 1949 signed into law by President Harry S. Truman; see Richard Rothstein, *The Color of Law: A Forgotten History of How Our Government Segregated America* (New York: Liveright, 2017), 30–31.

10. "City Planners Look Ahead," *Niagara Falls Gazette*, September 17, 1958.

11. "Digest's Attack Hurts 'Useful' Renewal Plan," n.d., Urban Renewal folder 300, Local History Department, Niagara Falls Public Library.

12. Eleanor P. Wolf and Charles N. Lebeaux, "On the Destruction of Poor Neighborhoods by Urban Renewal," *Social Problems* 15, no. 1 (Summer 1967): 3–8.

13. Teron McGrew, "The History of Residential Segregation in the Unites States and Title VIII," *Black Scholar* 27, no. 2 (Summer 1997): 26–27; Douglass S. Massey and Nancy A. Denton, *American Apartheid: Segregation and the Making of the Underclass* (Cambridge, MA: Harvard University Press, 1994), 56–57.

14. James Franklin Banks, "Problems Encountered by World War II and Post World War II Negroes, Who Settled in the Niagara Falls, New York Area" (master's thesis, Niagara University, 1958), 15.

15. "Urban Renewal: Acquisition of Redevelopment Property by Eminent Domain," *Duke Law Journal* 1964, no. 1 (Winter 1964): 123–138.

16. "Pending Slum Clearance Stirs Mixed Feelings," *Niagara Falls Gazette*, October 1, 1961.
17. Ibid.
18. "Lingering Human Problems Seen," *Niagara Falls Gazette*, October 1, 1961.
19. Ibid.
20. "Urban Projects Move Ahead," *Niagara Falls Gazette*, September 6, 1961, 7.
21. "City's Displaced Negroes Relocated in 23 Sections," *Niagara Falls Gazette*, August 22, 1962; and James Q. Wilson, ed., *Urban Renewal: The Record and the Controversy* (Cambridge, MA: MIT Press, 1966), 126–188.
22. "Negroes Moved by Renewal Usually Go to Better Areas," *Niagara Falls Gazette*, May 10, 1965.
23. "Black Menagerie: Race Still a Factor in Housing Here," http://www.niagarafallsreporter.com/menagerie107.html.
24. "Relocated Free to Buy, Rent in City," *Niagara Falls Gazette*, February 16, 1962; and "Negroes Moved by Renewal Usually Go to Better Areas," *Niagara Falls Gazette*, May 10, 1965.
25. Palmore, interview; Banks, "Problems Encountered," 13–45; and Bradberry, "Black Menagerie"; and Massey and Denton, *American Apartheid*, 56–57.
26. "Pending Slum Clearance Stirs Mixed Feelings," *Niagara Falls Gazette*.
27. Bradberry, "Black Menagerie"; and J. Allen Williams Jr., "The Effects of Urban Renewal Upon a Black Community: Evaluation and Recommendations," *Social Science Quarterly* 50, no. 3 (December 1969), 708–709.
28. "Urban Renewal Area Families Relocated in Jordan Gardens," *Niagara Falls Gazette*, February 25, 1962.
29. Ibid.
30. Ibid.
31. Ibid.
32. Eventually, Housing Authority representatives also wanted John Merino to manage the Griffon Manor Projects.
33. Boling, interview.
34. Ibid.
35. "Industrial Park Cost Is $1,075,815," *Niagara Falls Gazette*, October 17, 1962.
36. Ibid.
37. Ibid.
38. Ibid.
39. Ibid.; "Negroes Moved by Renewal Usually Go to Better Areas."
40. Ibid.
41. Ibid.
42. Ibid.
43. Eugene Hamilton, interview by author, August 4, 2007.
44. Wen H. Kuo, "Mayoral Influence in Urban Policy Making," *American Journal of Sociology* 79, no. 3 (November 1973): 620–638.

45. "Blighted Niagara Falls Works to Rebuild Itself," *New York Times*.

46. Vogel, *Echoes in the Mist*, 115.

47. Ibid.; Lizabeth Cohen, "Buying into Downtown Revival: The Centrality of Retail to Postwar Urban Renewal in American Cities," *Annals of the American Academy of Political and Social Science* 611 (May 2007): 82–95.

48. "Breaking Barriers: Black Museums Call for a Truer History," *History News* 36, no. 2 (February 1981): 7.

49. Palmore, interview; William Williamson, interview by author, January 30, 2010; and Edwardo King, interview by author, April 7, 2010.

50. Jane Jacobs, *The Death and Life of Great American Cities* (New York: Random House, 1961).

51. Mayor Lackey died in 1977.

52. "Mayor Lackey Recalls His Role in the Growth of Niagara Falls," Housing folder 300, vol. 1, Local History Department, Niagara Falls Public Library.

53. Ibid.

54. June Manning Thomas, "Urban Displacement: Fruits of a History of Collusion," *Black Scholar* 11, no. 2 (November–December 1979): 68–77; and William Holt and Donald Celmer, "Photo Essay: Urban Renewal in the Model City," *Context* 2, no. 4 (Fall 2003): 50–57.

55. "Advice of Blacks Sought on East Falls Renewal," *Niagara Falls Gazette*, November 9, 1969.

56. Ibid.

57. Chicago Grassroots Curriculum Taskforce, *Urban Renewal or Urban Removal* (Chicago: Chicago Grassroots Curriculum Taskforce, 2012).

58. "E. Falls St. Plan Draws NAACP Ire," *Niagara Falls Gazette*, December 9, 1969.

59. Ibid.

60. Ibid.

61. Ibid.

62. "E. Falls St. Seeks URA Plans," *Niagara Falls Gazette*, May 21, 1973.

63. Palmore, interview.

64. Ibid.

65. Ibid.

66. Ibid.

67. "Lehigh Project May Begin in Summer," n.d., Housing Folder 300, vol. 1, Local History Department, Niagara Falls Public Library.

68. Ibid.; "Falls Building Unity Park," n.d., Housing Folder 300, vol. 1, Local History Department, Niagara Falls Public Library.

69. "Falls Building Unity Park," Niagara Falls Public Library.

70. Ibid.

71. Ibid.

72. "Mrs. Bond Speaks Out on Housing Plan," *Niagara Falls Gazette*, March 14, 1970.

73. "Interfaith Housing Construction Start Slated for October," n.d., Housing Folder 300, vol. 1, Local History Department, Niagara Falls Public Library.

74. "City Rights Unit to Check New Housing Project," *Niagara Falls Gazette*, July 24, 1970.

75. Ibid.

76. Ibid.

77. Ibid.

78. "Falls Building Unity Park," Niagara Falls Public Library.

79. "Some Oppose New Housing," n.d., Housing Folder 300, vol. 1, Local History Department, Niagara Falls Public Library.

80. Ibid.

81. Williamson, interview.

82. "Lehigh Housing—'New Ghetto,'" n.d., Housing Folder 300, vol. 1, Local History Department, Niagara Falls Public Library.

83. "City Rights Unit to Check New Housing Project," *Niagara Falls Gazette*.

84. "Some Opposition Develops at Lehigh Housing Hearing," n.d., Housing Folder 300, vol. 1, Local History Department, Niagara Falls Public Library.

85. Ibid.

86. Drake and Cayton, *Black Metropolis*, 64; Allan H. Spear, *Black Chicago: The Making of a Negro Ghetto, 1890-1920* (Chicago: University of Chicago Press, 1967), 201-222; William M. Tuttle Jr., *Race Riot: Chicago in the Red Summer of 1919* (New York: Atheneum, 1970), 156-183; Richard W. Thomas, *Life for Us Is What We Make It: Building Black Community in Detroit, 1915-1945* (Bloomington: Indiana University Press, 1992), 37-38; Williams, *Strangers in the Land of Paradise*, 30; Andrew Hacker, *Two Nations: Black and White, Separate, Hostile, Unequal* (New York: Charles Scribner's Sons, 1992), 3-16; and Joel Kovel, *White Racism: A Psychohistory* (New York: Columbia University Press, 1984), 51-92.

87. "Unity Park Seeking Mid-income Tenants," *Niagara Falls Gazette*, March 24, 1972.

88. Ibid.

89. Ibid.

90. "Residents Near Unity Park Protest Hill's Swamp, Debris," *Niagara Falls Gazette*, November 5, 1972.

91. Ibid.

92. Ibid.

93. Ibid.

94. Ibid.

95. Ibid.

96. Massey and Denton, *American Apartheid*, 60-83; Hacker, *Two Nations*, 37-39; and Kovel, *White Racism: A Psychohistory*, 51-92.

97. "E. Falls Renewal Up for Discussion," n.d., Housing Folder 300, vol. 1, Local History Department, Niagara Falls Public Library.

98. Ibid.

99. Ibid.
100. Ibid.
101. "E. Falls St. Seeks URA Plan," *Niagara Falls Gazette*.
102. Ibid.
103. Ibid.
104. Ibid.
105. Ibid.
106. "E. Falls Renewal Up for Discussion," *Niagara Falls Gazette*; "E. Falls St. Seeks URA Plan," *Niagara Falls Gazette*.
107. "E. Falls St. Seeks URA Plan," *Niagara Falls Gazette*.
108. "Mrs. Bond Speaks Out on Housing Plan," *Niagara Falls Gazette*.
109. Barbara J. Smith, interview by author, January 16, 2010.
110. E. Falls St. Seeks URA Plan," *Niagara Falls Gazette*.
111. Ibid.
112. "East Falls Street Plan Kept Secret," n.d., Housing Folder 300, vol. 1, Local History Department, Niagara Falls Public Library.
113. Ibid.
114. "URA, East Falls," n.d., Housing Folder 300, vol. 1, Local History Department, Niagara Falls Public Library.
115. "E. Falls St. Procedures Questioned," n.d., Housing Folder 300, vol. 1, Local History Department, Niagara Falls Public Library.
116. Ibid.
117. "Relocation Aid Is Funded," n.d., Housing Folder 300, vol. 1, Local History Department, Niagara Falls Public Library.
118. "East Side to Get Relocation Office," n.d., Housing Folder 300, vol. 1, Local History Department, Niagara Falls Public Library.
119. "Relocation Aid Is Funded," n.d., Housing Folder 300, vol. 1, Local History Department, Niagara Falls Public Library.
120. Ibid.
121. "Relocation Group Defended," *Niagara Falls Gazette*, December 29, 1974.
122. Reverend Harvey L. Kelley, *The 60th Anniversary Journal of New Hope Baptist Church* (Niagara Falls, NY: New Hope Baptist Church, 1997), 4.
123. "Relocation Group Defended," *Niagara Falls Gazette*.
124. Ibid.
125. Thomas, "Urban Displacement," 68–77.
126. "Private Housing Slated for Memorial Pkwy. Block in '74," *Niagara Falls Gazette*, June 12, 1974.
127. "Demolition Drama," n.d., Housing Folder 300, vol. 1, Local History Department, Niagara Falls Public Library.
128. Ibid.
129. "Boom or Bust? Cost Cast Dark Shadow Over Lackey's '65 Dream," n.d., Housing Folder 300, vol. 1, Local History Department, Niagara Falls Public Library.

130. "East Falls Street Groups," *Niagara Falls Gazette*, January 2, 1975.

131. "'RESCUE' Set on 'East Side,'" n.d., Housing Folder 300, vol. 1, Local History Department, Niagara Falls Public Library.

132. "East Falls Street Groups," *Niagara Falls Gazette*.

133. Ibid.

134. "'RESCUE' set on 'East Side,'" Niagara Falls Public Library.

135. Ibid.

136. Ibid.

137. The Black Employees Club started at the Union Carbide Corporation plant. It operated like a union and was an organization that wanted to make improvements for Black Niagaran Union Carbide workers. Willie Brundidge helped to organize the Black Employees Club and had articles published in the *Niagara Falls Gazette* describing their activities.

138. "Falls Street Center to 'Save the Children,'" *Niagara Falls Gazette*, October 13, 1974.

139. The Trust for Public Land, "Healing America's Cities: How Urban Parks Can Make Cities Safe and Healthy," *Children's Environments* 12, no. 1 (March 1995): 65–70.

140. "Black Club Survey Finds Citizens Want Gym, Center," *Niagara Falls Gazette*, February 23, 1975.

141. "East Falls Center," *Niagara Falls Gazette*, December 2, 1974.

142. "Black Club to Utilize School for Youth Center," *Niagara Falls Gazette*, August 1, 1975.

143. "Black Employees Club Receives $5,000 Grant," *Niagara Falls Gazette*, June 8, 1975; and "Development Grant," *Niagara Falls Gazette*, June 9, 1975.

144. "Negro William Brooks Says 'Industrialization Is Only Salvation,'" *Niagara Falls Gazette*, August 27, 1967.

145. The term "Uncle Tom" refers to an African American who denigrates his own racial group to ingratiate himself with White people for purely self-serving reasons.

146. "Negro William Brooks Says 'Industrialization Is Only Salvation,'" *Niagara Falls Gazette*.

147. Ibid.

148. Ibid.

149. Ibid.

150. Ibid.

151. Martin L. King Jr. *Why We Can't Wait* (New York: Harper & Row, 1964). See chap. 8.

152. "First Negro Is Elected to Niagara County Board, *New York Times*, November 6, 1963.

153. See table 1.1.

154. Palmore, interview; Palmore, interview.

155. Ibid.

156. Ibid.
157. "Profit's Win Opened Political Arena to Blacks," *Niagara Fall Gazette*, February 16, 1987.
158. "Many Negroes Don's Bother to Vote," *Niagara Falls Gazette*, August 9, 1963.
159. Ibid.
160. Ibid.
161. Ibid.
162. Williamson, interview.
163. Palmore, interview.
164. Williams, *Strangers in the Land of Paradise*, 152.
165. "Profit's Win Opened Political Arena to Blacks," *Niagara Fall Gazette*.
166. Palmore, interview.
167. "Planners Approve South End Rezoning," *Niagara Falls Gazette*, January 10, 1964; "Corporation Proceedings in Council," *Niagara Falls Gazette*, January 28, 1964; "Corporation Proceedings in Council," *Niagara Falls Gazette*, July 11, 1964; "Train Ride Plan Gets City Study," *Niagara Falls Gazette*, July 8, 1964; "Corporation Proceedings in Council," *Niagara Falls Gazette*, January 23, 1965; and "Pine Arterial Expressway Portion Accepted by City," *Niagara Falls Gazette*, January 20, 1965.
168. "A Black Witch Hunt," *Niagara Falls Gazette*, June 2, 1974.
169. Ibid.
170. "Joe Profit Is Named Public Works Head," *Niagara Falls Gazette*, August 29, 1970.
171. A number of interviewees that discussed Joe Profit and his impact on Niagara Falls attested to this fact.
172. "William Bradberry," *Niagara Falls Reporter*, May 17, 2005.
173. Williams, interview; Palmore, interview; and "Some Kind Words for City Government," *Niagara Falls Gazette*, September 23, 1970.
174. "Resurfacing Job 'A Work of Art,' " *Niagara Falls Gazette*, August 8, 1970.
175. Ibid.
176. Williams, interview. A number of other Niagarans have attested to this.
177. "A Black Witch Hunt," *Niagara Falls Gazette*.
178. "Profit's Win Opened Political Arena to Blacks," *Niagara Falls Gazette*.
179. Ibid.
180. Bill Gallagher, "First Rule Is: All Politics Is Local," *Niagara Falls Reporter*, November 25, 2003, http://www.Niagarafallsreporter.com/gallagher142.html.
181. Herman Boyer Jr., interview by author, June 27, 2020.
182. "4 Republicans, 4 Democrats Seeking Council Nominations," *Niagara Falls Gazette*, September 12, 1971.
183. Arthur B. Ray, interview by author, June 27, 2010; Tom Wicker, *A Time to Die* (Chicago: Haymarket, 2011); and Freedom Archives, *Prison on Fire: Attica, George Jackson and Black Liberation* (Oakland, CA: AK, 2002).

184. Ray, interview.
185. "Prisoners Seek Mrs. Bond's Aid," *Niagara Falls Gazette*, September 10, 1971.
186. Manning Marable and Leith Mullings, *Let Nobody Turn Us Around: Voices of Resistance, Reform, and Renewal* (Lanham, MD: Rowman & Littlefield, 2000), 490.
187. Lillian S. Williams, "Attica Prisoners Seek Aid from the N.A.A.C.P., 1932," *Afro-Americans in New York Life and History* 1 (1977): 211–212.
188. Williams, interview.
189. "Minority Leaders Assail Officials in Handling of Attica," *Niagara Falls Gazette*, September 27, 1971.
190. Ibid.
191. Ibid.
192. Over an eighteen-year period, the author spoke to numerous Black Niagarans who shared these impressions about Fred Brown.
193. "Discrimination Encouraged Him to Succeed," *Niagara Falls Gazette*, May 23, 1971.
194. Ibid.
195. Ibid.
196. Ibid.
197. Washington, *Up From Slavery*; Boston, *Business Strategy of Booker T. Washington*, 57–74.
198. Palmore, interview.
199. "Discrimination Encouraged Him to Succeed," *Niagara Falls Gazette*.
200. Roosevelt Bradberry, interview by author, May 19, 2010.
201. Fred Brown knew Willie C. Fields Sr. Both men started their work lives as employees and became entrepreneurs. Both men migrated from the South. Both men's wives aided them tremendously in their entrepreneurial pursuits. Both involved themselves heavily in community affairs and wanted to contribute to the elevation of Black Niagarans before and during the urban renewal era. Willie C. Fields Sr. worked for the city of Niagara Falls in the Financial Department from 1951 to his retirement in 1981 (See "Willie C. Fields Sr.," http://www.legacy.com/Obituaries.asp?page=lifestory&personid=117871919). In 1946 he built a grocery store on Twentieth Street and Center Avenue. His store was close to Highland Avenue and considered part of the economic structure of the Highland Avenue Business District. Similar to how Ivan H. Light described Asian immigrants out west incorporating their family members into their entrepreneurial ventures in *Ethnic Enterprise in America*, Fields usually worked in the store in the evenings and on weekends, while his wife Doris worked there on weekdays. While growing up, his children also worked in the store. The Fields family operated their grocery store for about twenty years, and due to changing demands, they converted it to a liquor store. See Ivan H. Light, *Ethnic Enterprise in America* (Berkeley: University of California Press, 1972), 62–100.

Willie C. Fields was the first African American in Niagara Falls and Niagara County to obtain a license to sell liquor (see Williamson, interview). Fields is critically important to Black Niagaran History because he was one of the most successful African American entrepreneurs in the city before, during, and after the urban renewal era, and like Fred Brown, he desired to see the economic structure within the Highland Avenue/Center Court area elevated to advance his racial group and the city of Niagara Falls as a whole. See "Willie Fields Honored by Co-workers, Friends and Family Upon Retirement," *Niagara Falls Gazette*, March 14, 1981. Moreover, Fields led quietly both behind the scenes and overtly as a role model for others to emulate. See Williams, interview.

202. "Falls Bids for Macy Store," *Niagara Falls Gazette*, February 1, 1972.

203. "Moore-Donated 'People Center' to Be Dedicated Today," *Niagara Falls Gazette*, August 13, 1972; "Safe Street Act Post for Griffin," *Niagara Falls Gazette*, May 18, 1971.

204. "Aaron Griffin to Be Honored at Testimonial," *Niagara Falls Gazette*, September 23, 1973.

205. "Community Center Viewed as Aid to Black Experience," n.d., 300 Youth Niagara Community Center Binder, Local History Department, Niagara Falls Public Library.

206. Ibid.; and Palmore, interview.

207. "Griffin Made Home for Self, Youth at Center," n.d., Black History Box, Niagara County Historical Society, Lockport, New York.

208. Over fifty individuals were interviewed, and most of them spoke highly of Aaron Griffin.

209. Palmore, interview.

210. Williams, interview.

211. Ibid.

212. "Aaron Griffin to Be Honored at Testimonial," *Niagara Falls Gazette*.

213. "Honoring for Service," *Niagara Falls Gazette*, October 6, 1973.

214. "Griffin Made Home for Self, Youth at Center," *Niagara Falls Gazette*.

215. Aaron Griffin worked throughout his career at the Niagara Community Center to ensure that Black Niagarans received fair and just treatment in the city of Niagara Falls. This was one of the reasons that he and individuals like Alice Hayes, Bloneva Bonds, and others joined so many city-wide organizations and committees. They felt that they were keeping apprised of issues, networking with city leaders, and ensuring their community has access to opportunities distributed by city officials. They did not seem to seek preferential treatment for Black Niagarans but simply justice and equality.

216. *Census of Population*, vol. 1: *Number of Inhabitants: New York* (Washington, DC: US Government Printing Office, 1952), 15; and *1960 Census of Population*, vol. 1: *Characteristics of the Population, Part A Number of Inhabitants for New York State* (Washington, DC: Department of Commerce, 1961), 26 of 34.

217. Jorgette Theophilis, "A Re-examination of the Love Canal Crisis: The Myth and the Reality" (master's thesis, Massachusetts Institute of Technology, 1996), 12.

218. Amy M. Hay, "Recipe for Disaster: Motherhood and Citizenship at Love Canal," *Journal of Women's History* 21 (Spring 2009): 112.

219. Michael Brown, *Laying Waste: The Poisoning of America by Toxic Chemicals* (New York: Washington Square, 1979).

220. Elizabeth D. Blum, *Love Canal Revisited: Race, Class, and Gender in Environmental Activism* (Lawrence: University of Kansas, 2008), 63–85; and Adeline Gordon Levine, *Love Canal: Science, Politics, and People* (Lexington, MA: Lexington, 1982).

221. Blum, *Love Canal Revisited*, 22.

222. Hay, "Recipe for Disaster," 111.

223. Constance Holden, "Love Canal Residents Under Stress," *Science* 208, no. 4449 (June 13, 1980): 1242–1244.

224. Richard Newman, "Making Environmental Politics: Women and Love Canal Activism," *Women's Studies Quarterly* 29, no. 1/2 (Spring–Summer, 2001): 68.

225. Blum, *Love Canal Revisited*, 76–77.

226. Richard S. Newman, *Love Canal: A Toxic History from Colonial Times to Present* (New York: Oxford University Press, 2016), 144–173; and Martha R. Fowlkes and Patricia Y. Miller, *Love Canal: The Social Construction of Disaster* (Washington, DC: Federal Emergency Management Agency, 1983), 19.

227. Hay, "Recipe for Disaster," 112; Amy M. Hay, "A New Earthly Vision: Religious Community Activism in the Love Canal Chemical Disaster," *Environmental History* 14, no. 3 (July 2009): 509.

228. Blum, *Love Canal Revisited*, 70.

229. Rachel D. Godsil, "Remedying Environmental Racism," *Michigan Law Review* 90, no. 2 (November 1991): 394–427.

230. Robert D. Bullard and Beverly H. Wright, "The Quest for Environmental Equity: Mobilizing the Black Community for Social Change," *Race, Poverty and the Environment* 1, no. 2 (July 1990): 14.

231. Newman, "Making Environmental Politics," 66–68; Robert D. Bullard, *Dumping in Dixie: Race, Class, and Environmental Quality* (San Francisco: Westview, 1990), 17–21; Robert D. Bullard, ed., *The Quest for Environmental Justice* (San Francisco: Sierra Club, 2005), 18–42; and Temma Kaplan, "The Changing Face of the Continuing Struggle," in *Major Problems in African American History*, vol. 2: *From Freedom to Freedom Now*, ed. Thomas Holt and Elsa Barkley Brown (Boston: Wadsworth, 2000), 378–387.

232. Blum, *Love Canal Revisited*, 70.

233. Ibid.

234. "NAACP Criticizes Relocation Efforts," *Niagara Falls Gazette*, October 29, 1979.

235. Smith, interview.
236. Blum, *Love Canal Revisited*, 74.
237. Theophilis, "A Re-examination of the Love Canal Crisis," 36.
238. Blum, *Love Canal Revisited*, 76.
239. Ibid., 76–77.
240. Ibid., 76–77; Smith, interview.
241. Blum, *Love Canal Revisited*, 77.
242. Ibid., 78. In 2005 Black victims of Hurricane Katrina in New Orleans experienced a similar sense of marginalization and neglect. See Robert D. Bullard and Beverly Wright, *Race, Place, and Environmental Justice After Hurricane Katrina: Struggles to Reclaim, Rebuild, and Revitalize New Orleans and the Gulf Coast* (Boulder, CO: Westview, 2009), 410–460.
243. Blum, *Love Canal Revisited*, 77.
244. Ibid.
245. Ibid.
246. Ibid., 79.
247. Ibid.
248. In 1981 city officials had shown resistance to Griffon Manor tenants being dispersed throughout the city. At that time, close to the end of the urban renewal era, grassroots community leaders Sam and Albert Rice, Henry Johnson, Zorie Boling, Mable Brooks, and Bernice, William, and Indiana Hunt founded the "Black Pioneers of Niagara Falls." The Black Pioneers were founded to preserve the history of Black Niagarans so their legacy could be recorded for future generations. The Black Pioneers also set out to show their appreciation of the older generations of families who came to Niagara Falls and contributed to local history: these early Black Niagarans were acknowledged at the Pioneers' annual "Old Timers' Picnic" usually held the first Saturday in August. At the 1985 Old Timers' Picnic, for example, a Mr. Uylliss Diggs and Mrs. Joseph Williamson were honored with plaques for their long-term service to their community.

Zorie Boling discussed the incident that helped create the Black Pioneers of Niagara Falls. At the newly built Niagara Falls International Convention Center, administrators agreed to sponsor ethnic festival days. It happened to be the African Americans' turn to demonstrate their cultural heritage. Many people attended and participated in the festivities, thoroughly enjoying themselves. However, Boling noticed the disorganization of the activity. She felt Black Niagarans should have represented themselves much better. Boling and others sought to create and develop something that could competently highlight the history of African Americans in the city of Niagara Falls. In her discussion, Boling gave Mable Brooks tremendous credit for coordinating the formation of the Black Pioneers and encouraging individuals and families to get involved and keep the organization going.

Why else did Black Niagarans strive to keep the Black Pioneers functional? Another crucial reason was because Black Pioneer organizers believed that their histories were not being adequately recorded in mainstream sources, such as the main local newspaper and other forms of media. Moreover, they also noticed that negative events such as crimes often dominated printed sources, which widely damaged their image. In essence, like the Griffon Manor tenants, they felt marginalized. They responded by making a commitment to be proactive in the recording, preserving, and presentation of their important past not only to make their racial group proud but to be an important information source for interested parties and to promote the legacy of their community. See "Black Pioneers Agenda" (unpublished manuscript in possession of author), August 1, 2009; "Black Pioneers Set Annual Picnic Here," *Niagara Falls Gazette*, July 13, 1985; and Boling, interview.

Notes for Chapter 8

1. Smith, interview; Palmore, interview, April 5; Ronnie Cunningham, interview by author, August 22, 2017. *1980 Census of Population and Housing: Census Tracts of Buffalo, N.Y.* (Washington, D.C.: U. S. Government Printing Office, 1983), 52.

2. "Today," meaning the year 2021.

3. Dr. Benjamin F. Bullock Jr., Falls Dentist," *Buffalo News*, October 13, 2001; *1980 Census of Population and Housing Census Tracts Buffalo, N.Y.* (Washington, DC: US Government Printing Office, 1983), last page of book.

4. Reed-McBride, interview.

5. Ibid.

6. "Plan Brotherhood Luncheon," *Niagara Falls Gazette*, February 18, 1963; "Dr. Benjamin F. Bullock Jr., Falls Dentist."

7. Gene Simmons, interview by author, May 17, 2010.

8. Robin L. Jarrett, "Successful Parenting in High-Risk Neighborhoods," *Future of Children* 9, no. 2 (Autumn 1999): 45–50.

9. Renee Coates-Smith, interview by author, March 29, 2010.

10. Ibid.

11. Elaine R. Mohamed, "It Takes a Whole Village to Raise a Child," *Peabody Journal of Education* 71, no. 1 (1996): 57–63.

12. Angela J. Hattery and Earl Smith, *African American Families* (Los Angeles: SAGE, 2007), 48.

13. Edwardo King, interview by author, April 7, 2010.

14. E. Franklin Frazier, *The Negro Family in the United States* (Chicago: University of Chicago Press, 1967), 102–124.

15. Ibid.

16. Lee Rainwater and William L. Yancey, *The Moynihan Report and the Politics of Controversy* (Cambridge, MA: MIT Press 1967), 61–67.

17. Herbert G. Gutman, *The Black Family in Slavery and Freedom 1750–1925* (New York: Vintage, 1976); Harold E. Cheatham and James B. Stewart, eds., *Black*

Families: Interdisciplinary Perspectives (New Brunswick, NJ: Transaction, 1990); Niara Sudarkasa, *The Strength of Our Mothers: African & African American Women & Families: Essays and Speeches* (Trenton, NJ: African World, 1996); and Robert Staples, *The Black Family: Essays and Studies* (Belmont, CA: Wadsworth, 1971).

18. Andrew Billingsley, *Climbing Jacob's Ladder* (New York: Simon & Schuster, 1992), 137–139 and chap. 6; and William Julius Wilson, *When Work Disappears: The World of the New Urban Poor* (New York: Alfred A. Knopf, 1996), chaps. 1–4.

19. Boling, interview; Smith, interview; Palmore, interview, April 5; and Williamson, interview.

20. Angela Davis and Fania Davis, "The Black Family and the Crisis of Capitalism," *Black Scholar* 17, no. 5 (September–October 1986), 35–40; Wilson. *When Work Disappears*, 87–110; Hattery and Smith, *African American Families*, 178–179; Staples, *Black Family*, 254; Leanor Boulin Johnson and Robert Staples, *Black Families at the Crossroad* (San Francisco: Jossey-Bass, 2005), 65–66; and Yanick St. Jean and Joe R. Feagin, *Double Burden: Black Women and Everyday Racism* (Armonk, NY: M. D. Sharpe, 1998), 173.

21. Andrew Billingsley, *Climbing Jacob's Ladder: The Enduring Legacy of African American Families* (New York: Touchstone, 1992), 75.

Notes to Chapter 9

1. Jacob U. Gordon, *Black Leadership For Social Change* (Westport, CT: Greenwood, 2000), 37.

2. Evidence of these statements can be found in the numerous recorded and unrecorded interviews the author had with Black Niagarans over an eighteen-year period.

Bibliography

Primary Sources

ARCHIVES

Local History Department, Niagara Falls Public Library. Niagara Falls, New York.
Niagara County Historical Association. Lockport, New York.

BOOKS AND BOOKLETS

Blockson, Charles L. *The Hippocrene Guide to the Underground Railroad*. New York: Hippocreane, 1994.
Bradberry, Bill. "Meet Mrs. Vivian Virginia Charlotte Ellis Thompson." In *Black Pioneers of Niagara Falls, NY Old Timer's Picnic Silver Anniversary 1981–2006*. Niagara Falls, NY: Black Pioneers of Niagara Falls, 2006.
Carson, Clayborne, ed. *The Papers of Martin Luther King, Jr*. Vol. 3: *Birth of a New Age December 1955–December 1956*. Berkeley: University of California Press, 1997), 113.
Douglass, Fredrick. *Narrative of the Life of Frederick Douglass: An American Slave*. Cambridge, MA: Harvard University Press, 1969.
Drew, Benjamin. *The Refugee: A North-side View of Slavery*. Reading, MA: Addison-Wesley, 1969.
Frazier, Thomas R., ed. *Afro-American History: Primary Sources*. New York: Harcourt, Brace, 1970.
Garvey, Marcus. *The Philosophy and Opinions of Marcus Garvey*. Dover, MA: Majority, 1986.
Henson, Josiah. *An Autobiography of the Reverend Josiah Henson*. Reading, MA: Addison, 1969.
———. *The Life of Josiah Henson, Formerly a Slave*. Boston: Arthur D. Phelps, 1849.
Kelley, Reverend Harvey L. *The 60th Anniversary Journal of New Hope Baptist Church*. Niagara Falls, NY: New Hope Baptist Church, 1997.

King, Martin Luther, Jr. *Why We Can't Wait*. New York: Harper & Row, 1964.
———. *Why We Can't Wait*. New York: Signet Classic, 2000.
Niagara Falls City Directory 1941. Niagara Falls, NY: Wahl, 1941.
Pettit, Eber M. *Sketches in the History of the Underground Railroad, Comprising Many Thrilling Incidents of the Escape of Fugitives from Slavery, and the Perils of Those Who Aided Them*. Fredonia, NY: W. McKinstry and Son, 1879. Reprint, Westfield, NY: Chautauqua Region, 1999.
Still, William. *The Underground Railroad: Authentic Narratives and First-Hand Accounts*. Mineola, NY: Dover, 2007.
———. *The Underground Railroad: A Record of Facts, Authentic Narratives, Letters & Correspondence*. Philadelphia: Porter & Coates, 1872. Reprint, New York: Arno, 1968.
Terkel, Studs. *Hard Times: An Oral History of the Great Depression*. New York: Pantheon, 1971.
Washington, Booker T. *The Negro in Business*. Wichita, Kansas: DeVore and Sons, 1992.
———. *Up From Slavery*. New York: Airmont, 1967.
Work, Monroe N. *Negro Yearbook, 1914–15*. Tuskegee, AL: Negro Yearbook Publishing, 1915.
X, Malcolm, and Alex Haley. *The Autobiography of Malcolm X*. New York: Ballantine, 1992.

Census Reports

Census of Manufactures: 1929 Industry Classifications. Washington, DC: US Government Printing Office, 1929.
Census of Population: 1950 Characteristics of the Population, Part 2 Alabama. Vol. 2. Washington, DC: US Government Printing Office, 1952.
Census of Population: 1960, Characteristics of The Population, Part A Number of Inhabitants for New York State. Vol. 1. Washington, DC: Department of Commerce, 1961.
Fifteenth Census of the United States, 1930 Population. Vol. 3. Washington, DC: US Government Printing Office, 1931.
Fifteenth Census of the United States: 1930 Population. Vol. 3, Part 1. Washington, DC: US Government Printing Office, 1932.
Fifteenth Census of the United States: 1930 Population. Vol. 3, Part 2: *Montana-Wyoming*. Washington, DC: US Government Printing Office, 1932.
Fifteenth Census of the United States: 1930 Population. Vol. 4: *Occupations, By States*. Washington, DC: US Government Printing Office, 1933.
Fifteenth Census of the United States: 1930 Population. Vol. 6: *Families*. Washington, DC: US Government Printing Office, 1933.

Fourteenth Census of the United States: Population 1920. Composition and Characteristics of the Population by States. Vol. 3. Washington, DC: US Government Printing Office, 1922.

Fourteenth Census of the United States: 1920 Population, General Report and Analytical Tables. Washington, DC: US Government Printing Office, 1922.

Fourteenth Census of the United States. Vol. 11: *Manufactures*. Washington, DC: US Government Printing Office, 1923.

New York State Census of 1865. Albany, NY: Charles Van Benthuysen & Sons, 1867.

Niagara County Census 1980: Department of Economic Development and Planning for the Niagara County Affiliate Data Center. Lockport, New York, 1981.

Population of the United States in 1860: Compiled from the Original Returns of the Eighth Census. Washington, DC: US Government Printing Office, 1864.

The Seventh Census of the United States: 1850. Washington, DC: Robert Armstrong, Public Printer, 1853.

Sixteenth Census of the United States: 1940 Population. Vol. 2: *Characteristics of the Population*. Washington, DC: US Government Printing Office, 1943.

Sixteenth Census of the United States: 1940 Population. Vol. 2, Part 5: *Characteristics of the Population: New York—Oregon*. Washington, DC: US Government Printing Office, 1943.

Thirteenth Census of the United States Taken in the Year 1910: Vol. 9, *Manufactures*. Washington, DC: US Government Printing Office, 1912.

Thirteenth Census of the United States: 1910 Population. Vol. 2. Washington, DC: US Government Printing Office, 1913.

US Bureau of the Census, Census of Population: 1970. Vol. 1: *Characteristics of the Population, Part 34, New York-Section 1*. Washington, DC: US Government Printing Office, 1973.

US Census. Niagara Falls Public Library, Local History Division, 350.81.

US Censuses of Population and Housing: 1960 Census Tracts, Buffalo, N.Y. Washington, DC: US Government Printing Office, 1962.

US Census of Population in 1870. Washington, DC: US Government Printing Office, 1872.

US Census of Population 1890. Washington, DC: US Government Printing Office, 1895.

US Census of Population 1900. Washington, DC: US Census Office, 1901.

US Census of Population: 1960: Vol. 1: *Characteristics of the Population*. Washington, DC: US Government Printing Office, 1963.

1950 Census of Population. Vol. 1: *Number of Inhabitants: New York*. Washington, DC: US Government Printing Office, 1952.

1950 Census of Population. Vol. 2: *Characteristics of the Population Part 32, New York*. Washington, DC: US Printing Office, 1952.

1970 Census of Population and Housing. Washington, DC: US Government Printing Office, 1972.
1980 Census of Population and Housing: Census Tracts of Buffalo, NY. Washington, DC: US Government Printing Office, 1983.
1990 Census of Population and Housing Summary Population and Housing Characteristics New York. Washington, DC: US Department of Commerce; U.S. Government Printing Office, 1991.

LETTERS

Grossi, Ken, to James M. Boles, October 16, 2009.
Scott, Emmett J. "Letters of Negro Migrants of 1916–1918," *Journal of Negro History* 4, no. 3 (July 1919): 290–340.

MICROFILM

Annual Report of the Fifteenth Annual Convention: National Negro Business League, Held at Muskogee, Oklahoma, August 19–21, 1914. The Booker T. Washington Papers, The Library of Congress. Microfilms, reel no. 754.
New York State Census for 1892: Village of Niagara Falls & Village of Suspension Bridge. Lockport, NY: Lockport Public Library. Microfilm, reel 19.
The Niagara Community Center Association 1927–1977. By the Afro-American Historical Association of the Niagara Frontier and the Buffalo State College History Department, 1978. Butler Library, Buffalo State College. Microfilm.
Population Schedules of the 6th Census of the United States, 1840, New York. National Archives. Microfilm, reel 311.
Statement of Case of Ernest Lovell Dyett by His Mother. *Papers of the NAACP, Part 3, Series B: 1940–1950.* Olin Library, Cornell University. Microfilm, AFR 6.
US Census 1870 for Niagara County: Village of Niagara City & Village of Niagara Falls. Niagara Falls Public Library, no. 13–14, p. 35. Microfilm.
US Census 1880 for Niagara County: Village of Niagara Falls, Suspension Bridge & Town of Niagara. Niagara Falls Public Library, no. 17–18, p. 9. Microfilm.
US Census for 1900: Town of Niagara, Niagara Falls City & La Salle Village. Niagara Falls, NY: Niagara Falls Public Library. Microfilm, reel 23.
US Census for 1910: Town of Niagara, City of Niagara Falls, Village of LaSalle. Niagara Falls, NY: Niagara Falls Public Library. Microfilm, reels 28 and 29.
US Census for 1930. Niagara Falls, NY: Niagara Falls Public Library. Microfilm, reels 44, 45, and 46.
1920 U.S. Census for City of Niagara Falls, Town of Niagara Falls, & Village of LaSalle. New York: Niagara Falls Public Library. Microfilm, reels 33, 34, and 35.

Newspaper Articles

"A Black Witch Hunt." *Niagara Falls Gazette*, June 2, 1974.
"A Canadian Tunnel." *Niagara Falls Gazette*, August 31, 1893.
"A Famous Old Hostelry." *Niagara Falls Journal*, January 4, 1918.
"A Sad Shooting Affair," *Niagara Falls Gazette*, October 11, 1865.
"Aaron Griffin to Be Honored at Testimonial." *Niagara Falls Gazette*, September 23, 1973.
"About Negroes." *Niagara Falls Gazette*, February 9, 1934.
"Activities and Aims of Community Center Topics of Address." *Niagara Falls Gazette*, March 7, 1929.
"Advice of Blacks Sought on East Falls Renewal." *Niagara Falls Gazette*, November 9, 1969.
"Agents Get Blamed for Bias in Housing." *Niagara Falls Gazette*, July 31, 1963.
"Alice C. Hayes, Niagara Falls." *Chicago Defender*, March 27, 1937.
"Alice C. Hayes, Niagara Falls." *Chicago Defender*, April 10, 1937.
"Allots $13,555,644 for Public Works." *New York Times*, November 24, 1936.
"Antipoverty Board Hears Complaints." *Niagara Falls Gazette*, February 24, 1966.
"Area Unions, Contractors Told to Hire More Black Trainees." *Niagara Falls Gazette*, November 9, 1970.
"B. W. Bolden Dies; Founded Center Here." *Niagara Falls Gazette*, October 15, 1971.
"Barbara Jean Smith Obituary." *Niagara Falls Gazette*, May 2, 2011.
"Beech Racial Imbalance Was Created." *Niagara Falls Gazette*, July 6, 1969.
"Ben Bolden Can Take Pride in Career Here." *Niagara Falls Gazette*, May 25, 1958.
"Ben Bolden: Niagara's Only Negro Souvenir Store." *Buffalo Star*, August 30, 1946.
"Black Club Survey Finds Citizens Want Gym, Center." *Niagara Falls Gazette*, February 23, 1975.
"Black Club to Utilize School for Youth Center." *Niagara Falls Gazette*, August 1, 1975.
"Black Employees Club Receives $5,000 Grant." *Niagara Falls Gazette*, June 8, 1975.
"Black Faculty and Students Increase Fractionally in City Schools." *Niagara Falls Gazette*, December 4, 1974.
"Black Pioneers Set Annual Picnic Here." *Niagara Falls Gazette*, July 13, 1985.
"Blacks at Carbide Are Chagrining Bias." *Niagara Falls Gazette*, October 31, 1971.
"Blacks Don't Receive Top School Posts." *Niagara Falls Gazette*, August 23, 1970.
"Blacks Plan Protest Rally in Girl's Death." *Niagara Falls Gazette*, February 18, 1981.
"Blighted Niagara Falls Works to Rebuild Itself." *New York Times*, October 1, 1973.
"Boycott, Walkouts Staged at School." *Niagara Falls Gazette*, October 17, 1968.
Bradberry, Bill. "Black Menagerie: Life Was Anything But Easy for African Americans in 1920s Falls." *Niagara Falls Reporter*, August 19, 2003.

Bradberry, William. "Black Menagerie: Old East Side Was Like United Nations." *Niagara Falls Reporter*, May 7, 2002.

———. "Black Menagerie: Profit, Williamson, Ray Brought Pride to Black Community in Falls." *Niagara Falls Reporter*, May 17, 2005.

"Bus Jobs Asked for Blacks." *Niagara Falls Gazette*, May 29, 1974.

"Business Men of Community Center Hold Annual Meeting." *Niagara Falls Gazette*, December 15, 1936.

"Chronological Review of Events in 1934 in Niagara Falls." *Niagara Falls Gazette*, December 29, 1934.

"City Boycott Is Sought for Mississippi Goods." *Niagara Falls Gazette*, January 12, 1965.

"City Planners Look Ahead." *Niagara Falls Gazette*, September 17, 1958.

"City Rally Speaker Urges Negroes to Speed Bid for Civil Rights." *Niagara Falls Gazette*, March 28, 1960.

"City Rights Unit to Check New Housing Project." *Niagara Falls Gazette*, July 24, 1970.

"City's Displaced Negroes Relocated in 23 Sections." *Niagara Falls Gazette*, August 22, 1962.

"City's Stores Are Urged to Hire More Negroes." *Niagara Falls Gazette*, January 8, 1963.

"Civic Group Valued Alice Hayes' Participation." *Niagara Falls Gazette*, February 12, 1987.

"Colored Man Rode in a Wheelbarrow." *Niagara Falls Gazette*, November 12, 1900.

"Colored Masons Elect Officers." *Niagara Falls Gazette*, December 27, 1912.

"Colored Masons to Dedicate Hall." *Niagara Falls Gazette*, May 18, 1909.

"Colored Republican Meeting." *Niagara Falls Gazette*, September 18, 1872.

"Colored '400' Dance." *Niagara Falls Gazette*, April 4, 1897.

"Community Center Members Hear Able Address on Wasserman Test." *Niagara Falls Gazette*, April 15, 1935.

"Community Center News." *Niagara Falls Gazette*, February 16, 1932.

"Community Center News." *Niagara Falls Gazette*, November 29, 1931.

"Community Center News." *Niagara Falls Gazette*, May 13, 1932.

"Community Center News." *Niagara Falls Gazette*, February 3, 1933.

"Community Center News." *Niagara Falls Gazette*, May 25, 1934.

"Community Center News." *Niagara Falls Gazette*, May 15, 1936.

"Community Center News." *Niagara Falls Gazette*, May 22, 1936.

"Community Center News." *Niagara Falls Gazette*, October 14, 1938.

"Community Center News." *Niagara Falls Gazette*, January 24, 1939.

"Community Center Reaches High Mark in Service to Colored Folk." *Niagara Falls Gazette*, October 2, 1944.

"Community Center Upholds Morale of Growing Number of Negro Folks." *Niagara Falls Gazette*, April 7, 1932.

"Construction Trade Training Program End Expected Nov. 30." *Niagara Falls Gazette*, October 30, 1971.
"Convict Two of Robbery." *Niagara Falls Gazette*, March 12, 1943.
"CORE Increases Pickets, Starts Boycott at Store." *Niagara Falls Gazette*, August 31, 1963.
"CORE Picketing Falls Store." *Niagara Falls Gazette*, August 28, 1963.
"CORE Sets Picketing Plans." *Niagara Falls Gazette*, August 27, 1963.
"CORE Unit Here Picks Grant's for Picketing." *Niagara Falls Gazette*, August 24, 1963.
"Corporation Proceedings in Council." *Niagara Falls Gazette*, October 21, 1961.
"Corporation Proceedings in Council." *Niagara Falls Gazette*, January 28, 1964.
"Corporation Proceedings in Council." *Niagara Falls Gazette*, July 11, 1964.
"Corporation Proceedings in Council." *Niagara Falls Gazette*, January 23, 1965.
"County Welfare Head is Mum on NAACP March Home." *Niagara Falls Gazette*, June 19, 1966.
"Crowds Go to Niagara." *New York Times*, August 18, 1935.
"Development Grant." *Niagara Falls Gazette*, June 9, 1975.
"Discrimination Encouraged Him to Succeed, Niagara Personality: Fred Brown." *Niagara Falls Gazette*, May 23, 1971.
"Dissatisfaction Seen with Police, Courts." *Niagara Falls Gazette*, September 19, 1975.
"Distinguished Negro Educator, Minister Will Speak in City." *Lockport (N. Y.) Union-Sun and Journal*, February 6, 1937.
"Divided We Fell," *Niagara Falls Gazette*, August 25, 1974.
"Dr. Benjamin F. Bullock Jr., Falls Dentist." *Buffalo News*, October 13, 2001.
"Dr. King Mourned in Area." *Niagara Falls Gazette*, April 9, 1968.
"Dr. Platt H. Skinner." *The Mute and the Blind*, April 26, 1862.
"Dr. Platt H. Skinner," *The Mute and the Blind*. November 3, 1860.
"Dr. Pollard to Take War Job." *Niagara Falls Gazette*, April 10, 1943.
" 'Dutch' Schreiber Ends Long Career; One of Area's Unique Personalities." *Niagara Falls Gazette*, April 25, 1971.
"E. Falls St. Plan Draws NAACP Ire." *Niagara Falls Gazette*, December 9, 1969.
"E. Falls St. Seeks URA Plans." *Niagara Falls Gazette*, May 21, 1973.
"East Falls Center." *Niagara Falls Gazette*, December 2, 1974.
"East Falls Street Groups." *Niagara Falls Gazette*, January 2, 1975.
"Emancipation Marked by Falls NAACP Unit." *Niagara Falls Gazette*, May 12, 1963.
"Employment Is Major Negro Problem." *Niagara Falls Gazette*, August 4, 1963.
"Equal Opportunity—Zero." *Niagara Falls Gazette*, April 22, 1974.
"Establishment of Community Center Here for Colored People Suggested as Means of Improving Conditions." *Niagara Falls Gazette*, February 7, 1928.
"Ethical-Problem Solutions Asked of NAACP Panel." *Niagara Falls Gazette*, March 12, 1963.

"Fall from Chair Fatal to Vass." *Niagara Falls Gazette*, June 8, 1915.
"Fall Is Target Date, Not Deadline, for Integration." *Niagara Falls Gazette*, February 4, 1970.
"Falls Airport Brought War Plane Plant Here." *Niagara Falls Gazette*, May 7, 1945.
"Falls Bids for Macy Store." *Niagara Falls Gazette*, February 1, 1972.
"Falls Called Southern City for Denial of Negro Rights." *Niagara Falls Gazette*, March 31, 1960.
"Falls Cited as School Integration Model." *Niagara Falls Gazette*, September 24, 1971.
"Falls Men Favor Government Change." *Lockport (NY) Union-Sun and Journal*, Feb 11, 1932.
"Falls School Integration Plan Wins Praise of State Official." *Niagara Falls Gazette*, February 18, 1970.
"Falls Negro Find Democracy Diluted." *Niagara Falls Gazette*, March 17, 1963.
"Falls Negroes to Meet, Discuss Grievances." *Niagara Falls Gazette*, July 3, 1967.
"Falls Seeks to Resolve Problems." *Niagara Falls Gazette*, August 11, 1963.
"Falls Street Center to 'Save the Children.'" *Niagara Falls Gazette*, October 13, 1974.
"Family, Education Came First for Williamsons." *Niagara Falls Gazette*, February 26, 1987.
"Far From Dead Was Mr. Hobbs." *Cataract Journal*, September 21, 1904.
"Fascist Racial Creed Flayed by Educators." *Chicago Defender*, November 5, 1938.
"Female Smokers Are Criticized, Empire State Federation also Protests against the Chewing of Gum, Women Want to Vote." *New York Age*, July 10, 1913.
"Finds Housing Intolerable Y-Teen Leader to Leave Falls." *Niagara Falls Gazette*, June 26, 1960.
"Finds Wide Neglect of Jobless Relief." *New York Times*, August 24, 1931.
"First Negro Is Elected to Niagara County Board." *New York Times*, November 6, 1963.
"Five Leaders of Community Center Honored: Year's Work of Community Center Reviewed; Larger Quarters Needed." *Niagara Falls Gazette*, February 19, 1946.
"Former Falls Resident Dies." *Niagara Falls Gazette*, May 18, 1967.
"Forum Deals with Law." *Niagara Falls Gazette*, March 3, 1967.
"Fraternity to Meet." *Niagara Falls Gazette*, January 13, 1936.
"Freedom," *Niagara Falls Gazette*, July 10, 1986.
"Friendship House Aided by Board of Education." *Niagara Falls Gazette*, June 21, 1968.
"Friendship House Elects Ray to Post." *Niagara Falls Gazette*, June 12, 1968.
"Friendship House Head Is Selected." *Niagara Falls Gazette*, April 14, 1968.
"Friendship House Project Has Successful Summer." *Niagara Falls Gazette*, September 8, 1968.
"Friendship House Will Get $11,800." *Niagara Falls Gazette*, May 9, 1968.
From Organization for Advancement of Colored Community: About 150 Negroes Attend Meeting; Will Try to Establish Community Center." *Niagara Falls Gazette*, October 12, 1928.

"Gid Lee Died at the Hospital." *Niagara Falls Gazette*, April 8, 1912.
"Gideon Lee in Trouble." *Niagara Falls Gazette*, May 10, 1900.
"Gideon Lee in Trouble." *Daily Cataract-Journal*, May 10, 1900.
"Highland Ave. Neglected, Mayor Says." *Niagara Falls Gazette*, June 30, 1967.
"Honoring for Service." *Niagara Falls Gazette*, October 6, 1973.
"House of Many Cellars." *Niagara Falls Gazette*, December 5, 1965.
"Housing Causes School Segregation." *Niagara Falls Gazette*, August 6, 1963.
"Housing Lack of Jobs Plague Negroes Here." *Niagara Falls Gazette*, December 11, 1962.
"Housing Segregation Exists at Fall, Negro Leaders Says." *Niagara Falls Gazette*, July 10, 1961.
"Hundreds Attend Rally for Dead Black Girl." *Niagara Falls Gazette*, February 20, 1982.
"Image of Platt H. Skinner Teaching His Students." *The Mute and the Blind*, August 18, 1860.
"In Memoriam Dett." *Niagara Falls Gazette*, April 8, 1959.
"Industrial Park Cost Is $1,075,815." *Niagara Falls Gazette*, October 17, 1962.
"Interesting Items Gleaned by the Age Correspondents." *New York Age*, March 13, 1926.
"Interesting Reminiscences." *Niagara Falls Gazette*, October 26, 1927.
"It Started with the Wartime Migration." *Niagara Falls Gazette*, July 30, 1963.
"Jackie Robinson Warns City to Initiate Solutions." *Niagara Falls Gazette*, July 1, 1967.
"Jail Breaking." *Niagara Falls Gazette*, January 19, 1876.
"Jobs Led Blacks to Falls." *Niagara Falls Gazette*, February 5, 1990.
"Joe Profit Is Named Public Works Head." *Niagara Falls Gazette*, August 29, 1970.
"John M. Pollard, Educator, War Worker, Is Dead." *Niagara Falls Gazette*, October 15, 1946.
"John Troy Is No More." *Niagara Falls Gazette*, February 27, 1906.
"Joint Meeting on Plan 18 Sought with Board." *Niagara Falls Gazette*, July 12, 1969.
"Jones Pushes City on Schools." *Niagara Falls Gazette*, July 7, 1967.
"King's Slaying Sign of Sick America, Rights Leader Says." *Niagara Falls Gazette*, April 6, 1968.
"Lack of Jobs, Housing, Plagues Negroes Here." *Niagara Falls Gazette*, August 3, 1962.
"Lackey Opposed to Forced Busing in Integration Plan." *Niagara Falls Gazette*, May 28, 1970.
"Large Quarters Are Provided for Community Center Classes." *Niagara Falls Gazette*, March 12, 1935.
"Lehman Proposes Slump Remedies." *New York Times*, October 17, 1930.
"Letter About Hiring Blacks." *Niagara Falls Gazette*, August 25, 1985.
"Lingering Human Problems Seen." *Niagara Falls Gazette*, October 1, 1961.

"Little Rock Leader Chides Falls Negroes for Apathy in Politics." *Niagara Falls Gazette*, March 19, 1960.
"Little Rock NAACP Leader Not Ready to Give Up Fight." *Niagara Falls Gazette*, March 20, 1960.
"Local Solution Is Likely in Poverty Unit Dispute." *Niagara Falls Gazette*, February 11, 1966.
"Main St. Store, CORE End Dispute on Hiring." *Niagara Falls Gazette*, September 21, 1963.
"Make Plans to Get Out Vote." *Niagara Falls Gazette*, October 29, 1937.
"Man Who Brought Center Avenue School." *Niagara Falls Gazette*, February 23, 1975.
"Management's Policy Stated by Grant Firm." *Niagara Falls Gazette*, August 27, 1963.
"Many Negroes Don't Bother to Vote." *Niagara Falls Gazette*, August 9, 1963.
"Mayor Evers is Given Falls Tour by Lackey." *Niagara Falls Gazette*, August 8, 1972.
"Mayor Raps Race Bias." *Niagara Falls Gazette*, April 10, 1968.
"Meet Mrs. Willie C. Fields, Beech Racial Imbalance Was Created." *Niagara Falls Gazette*, July 6, 1969.
"Meeting set by NAACP." *Niagara Falls Gazette*, May 7, 1972.
"Member of Oldest Black Family Recall Lost Era." *Niagara Falls Gazette*, February 9, 1987.
"Memorable Day for the Negro Baptists." *Niagara Falls Gazette*, April 9, 1900.
"Memorial Services Held for 4 Girls." *Niagara Falls Gazette*, September 23, 1963.
"Memorial Will Honor Mrs. Lampkin." *Niagara Falls Gazette*, June 5, 1965.
"Minority Leaders Assail Officials in Handling of Attica." *Niagara Falls Gazette*, September 27, 1971.
"Moonglow Hotel Razing Called for Back in 1937." *Niagara Falls Gazette*, November 17, 1957.
"Moore-Donated 'People Center' to Be Dedicated Today." *Niagara Falls Gazette*, August 13, 1972.
"More About Muslims." *Niagara Falls Gazette*, January 11, 1962, 11.
"Mossell Spurred Lockport School Integration." *Niagara Falls Gazette*, February 8, 1987.
"Mourn Death of Mother of Dr. R. N. Dett." *Chicago Defender*, April 24, 1937.
"Mr. Johnson Is Tired of It All." *Daily Cataract-Journal*, August 23, 1900.
"Mrs. Baldwin, Restaurant Founder, Dies." *Niagara Falls Gazette*, July 1, 1955.
"Mrs. Bond Is a Great Woman." *Niagara Falls Gazette*, August 25, 1971.
"Mrs. Bond Speaks Out on Housing Plan." *Niagara Falls Gazette*, March 14, 1970.
"Mrs. Dett Inspired Sons, Fired GOP Politics." *Niagara Falls Gazette*, February 21, 1987.
"Mrs. Hayes Prominent in Social, Civic Work." *Niagara Falls Gazette*, June 4, 1949.
"Mrs. Hays Says NAACP Started Here 25 Years Ago." *Niagara Falls Gazette*, April 3, 1968.
"Muslim Cult Now Operating Here." *Niagara Falls Gazette*, January 6, 1962.

"Muslims Gaining Few Converts." *Niagara Falls Gazette*, January 7, 1962.
"MY PLATFORM IS." *Niagara Falls Gazette*, September 1, 1971.
"NAACP Asks Housing Bill." *Niagara Falls Gazette*, February 16, 1961.
"NAACP Blasts Program to End School Imbalance." *Niagara Falls Gazette*, August 24, 1967.
"NAACP Criticizes Relocation Efforts." *Niagara Falls Gazette*, October 29, 1979.
"NAACP Drafts Briefs to State to Step into Segregation Issue." *Niagara Falls Gazette*, November 6, 1967.
"NAACP Hints Giving Post to Mrs. Hayes." *Niagara Falls Gazette*, January 25, 1966.
"NAACP Pickets March at Chain Store Here." *Niagara Falls Gazette*, April 24, 1960.
"NAACP Production to Depict Negro Cultural Achievements." *Niagara Falls Gazette*, February 1, 1965.
"NAACP Protesting Falls School Aid Request." *Niagara Falls Gazette*, April 8, 1973.
"NAACP to Open Drive for 500 Members." *Niagara Falls Gazette*, May 29, 1959.
"NAACP Treasurer to Speak." *Niagara Falls Gazette*, June 9, 1967.
"NAACP Unit Will Stage Observance." *Niagara Falls Gazette*, January 27, 1965.
"NAACP Will Ask State to End Bias in Schools." *Niagara Falls Gazette*, September 22, 1967.
"National Black Museum Set." *Chicago Defender*, August 18, 1973.
"Negro and Democracy." *Niagara Falls Gazette*, September 28, 1908.
Negro Business League Inspects New C-E Plant." *Buffalo Courier-Express*, February 18, 1931.
"Negro Cancel Picketing of Downtown Businesses." *Niagara Falls Gazette*, July 20, 1967.
"Negro Claim Jobs Not Forthcoming." *Niagara Falls Gazette*, July 19, 1967.
"Negro Democrat Caravan in City." *Niagara Falls Gazette*, October 27, 1936.
"Negro Job Gains Called Small." *Niagara Falls Gazette*, January 18, 1964.
"Negro Jubilee to be Held on Fourth of July." *Niagara Falls Gazette*, May 5, 1900.
"Negro Leader Charges Bias in Housing, Schools, Jobs." *Niagara Falls Gazette*, June 28, 1963.
"Negro Leader to Speak at Falls." *Niagara Falls Gazette*, November 3, 1931.
"Negro Leaders Here Cite Bias in Housing, Job Opportunity." *Niagara Fall Gazette*, March 27, 1960.
"Negro Manifesto Readied for Council." *Niagara Falls Gazette*, July 5, 1967.
"Negro Speaker Warns City of New Upheaval." *Niagara Falls Gazette*, July 6, 1967.
"Negro Unity Cry Rules City Grass Roots Rally." *Niagara Falls Gazette*, July 5, 1967.
"Negro Who Votes for Democratic Party Will Betray His Race, Says New York Speaker at Rally Here." *Niagara Falls Gazette*, October 31, 1936.
"Negro William Brooks Says 'Industrialization Is Only Salvation.'" *Niagara Falls Gazette*, August 27, 1967.
"Negro's Advancement During Past 60 Years Phenomenal, Pickens Says." *Niagara Falls Gazette*, November 9, 1931.
"Negroes Fight 'One-Way' Bussing." *Niagara Falls Gazette*, September 11, 1968.

"Negroes Find it Difficult to Find Housing at Falls." *Niagara Falls Gazette*, December 9, 1964.
"Negroes Held Big Jubilee Yesterday." *Niagara Falls Gazette*, July 5, 1900.
"Negroes Married." *Daily Cataract-Journal*, May 11, 1900.
"Negroes Moved by Renewal Usually Go to Better Areas." *Niagara Falls Gazette*, May 10, 1965.
"Negroes Object: Local Men and Buffalo Colored Folk Say if Czolgosz Was a Negro His Treatment Would Be Summary." *Niagara Falls Gazette*, September 10, 1901.
"Negroes Outline Objections to Busing." *Niagara Falls Gazette*, August 24, 1967.
"Negroes to March Here, Leaders Say." *Niagara Falls Gazette*, August 6, 1963.
"Negroes Urged to Support Passive Resistance Drive." *Niagara Falls Gazette*, April 3, 1960.
"New Black Society Ask City for Aid in Ghetto Improvement." *Niagara Falls Gazette*, August 22, 1968.
"New York State." *Chicago Defender*, May 3, 1930.
"New York State." *Chicago Defender*, September 20, 1930.
"New York State." *Chicago Defender*, October 1, 1938.
"News About Negroes." *Niagara Falls Gazette*, June 19, 1934.
"News About Negroes." *Niagara Falls Gazette*, November 20, 1934.
"News About Negroes." *Niagara Falls Gazette*, March 10, 1937.
"New York State." *Chicago Defender*, September 4, 1932.
"New York State." *Chicago Defender*, October 8, 1932.
"New York State." *Chicago Defender*, November 18, 1933.
"Niagara Community Center Serves 48 Different Groups of Persons." *Niagara Falls Gazette*, April 13, 1935.
"Niagara Falls." *Chicago Defender*, August 20, 1932.
"Niagara Falls." *Chicago Defender*, September 24, 1932.
"Niagara Falls." *Chicago Defender*, October 29, 1932.
"Niagara Falls." *Chicago Defender*, November 12, 1932.
"Niagara Falls." *Chicago Defender*, December 17, 1932.
"Niagara Falls." *Chicago Defender*, April 29, 1933.
"Niagara Falls." *Chicago Defender*, November 28, 1936.
"Niagara Falls." *Chicago Defender*, December 19, 1936.
"Niagara Falls." *Chicago Defender*, January 23, 1937.
"Niagara Falls." *Chicago Defender*, January 30, 1937.
"Niagara Falls." *Chicago Defender*, February 27, 1937.
"Niagara Falls." *Chicago Defender*, March 6, 1937.
"Niagara Falls." *Chicago Defender*, April 17, 1937.
"Niagara Falls." *Chicago Defender*, April 24, 1937.
"Niagara Falls." *Chicago Defender*, November 13, 1937.
"Niagara Falls." *Chicago Defender*, February 26, 1938.

"Niagara Falls." *Chicago Defender*, October 1, 1938.
"Niagara Falls Lifts Curfew in Negro Slum Area as Calm Returns to Tense City." *New York Times*, August 24, 1969.
"Niagara Personalities: Mr. Griffin Likes Falls as Place to Live, Work." *Niagara Falls Gazette*, November 27, 1948.
"Niagara Plan Presented." *New York Times*, February 27, 1935.
"Niagara Throngs at New Peak." *New York Times*, August 16. 1936.
"NiaCAP Drafts Plan to Avert Youth Rumbles." *Niagara Falls Gazette*, May 11, 1967.
"NiaCAP Gets $85,265 Grant." *Niagara Falls Gazette*, January 13, 1967.
"Niagara Movement: Colored Men Assembled at Fort Erie from Permanent Organization." *Niagara Falls Gazette*, July 14, 1905.
"No Black on Board Raises Some Concern." *Niagara Falls Gazette*, May 12, 1974.
"Noted Soloist to Appear In Buffalo." *Chicago Defender*, November 27, 1915.
"Old Cottage, Reminder of Early Niagara and Slavery, Is Wrecked." *Niagara Falls Gazette*, July 20, 1929.
"One Hundred Dollar Club Organized to Further Work among Colored Group of Worthy Citizens." *Niagara Falls Gazette*, January 31, 1928.
"One Man's Dream." *Niagara Falls Gazette*, January 19, 2004.
"Ordered to Leave the City at Once." *Niagara Falls Gazette*, May 28, 1913.
"Our American Way." *Niagara Falls Gazette*, April 17, 1940.
"Our Anvil Chorus." *Niagara Falls Gazette*, September 23, 1912.
"Over $8,000,000 Expended on Private and Public Projects in Niagara Falls during 1942." *Niagara Falls Gazette*, December 31, 1942.
"Pending Slum Clearance Stirs Mixed Feelings." *Niagara Falls Gazette*, October 1, 1961.
"Personal." *Niagara Falls Gazette*, August 13, 1912.
"Physician's Dedication Earned Admiration." *Niagara Falls Gazette*, February 18, 1987.
"Physician Kidnapped Beaten and Robbed as Riots Continue." *Niagara Falls Gazette*, July 14, 1936.
"Picketing of Schreiber Is Planned." *Niagara Falls Gazette*, June 24, 1966.
"Pine Arterial Expressway Portion Accepted by City." *Niagara Falls Gazette*, January 20, 1965.
"Plan Brotherhood Luncheon." *Niagara Falls Gazette*, February 18, 1963.
"Plan 21 Wins Approval of City Teachers." *Niagara Falls Gazette*, April 23, 1970.
"Planners Approve South End Rezoning." *Niagara Falls Gazette*, January 10, 1964.
"Plans for Negro Jubilee Are Well Underway." *Niagara Falls Gazette*, May 16, 1900.
"Poles Shot by Negroes." *New York Times*, March 8, 1892.
"Pollard Opened Door to Community Center." *Niagara Falls Gazette*, February 17, 1987.
"Pollard Urges Square Deal for the Negro." *The Citizen-Advertiser, Auburn, N.Y.*, February 11, 1937.

"Poverty Board Critics Appeal to Shriver, RFK." *Niagara Falls Gazette*, February 9, 1966.
"Poverty Board Eyes Grievances." *Niagara Falls Gazette*, February 7, 1966.
"Prejudice against Negro Definite Hardship, John M. Pollard Declares." *Niagara Falls Gazette*, February 13, 1939.
"Pride & Purpose." *Niagara Falls Gazette*, January 11, 1962.
"Printing Council Asks Extra Session on Idle." *New York Times*, July 30, 1931.
"Prisoners Seek Mrs. Bond's Aid." *Niagara Falls Gazette*, September 10, 1971.
"Private Housing Slated for Memorial Pkwy. Block in '74." *Niagara Falls Gazette*, June 12, 1974.
"Pro-Muslim." *Niagara Falls Gazette*, January 18, 1962.
"Profit's Win Opened Political Arena to Blacks." *Niagara Fall Gazette*, February 16, 1987.
"Project Head Threatened, Warned to Ban Negroes." *Niagara Falls Gazette*, February 16, 1956.
"Race Relations to Be Featured." *Niagara Falls Gazette*, February 9, 1939.
"Rally Scores Bias in Housing." *Niagara Falls Gazette*, February 9, 1964.
"Ray, Evans Are Elected; Only 5,763 Votes Cast." *Niagara Falls Gazette*, May 6, 1964.
"Realtors Back 'Open Occupancy.'" *Niagara Falls Gazette*, May 3, 1966.
"Relates Stories Behind Spirituals." *Niagara Falls Gazette*, December 12, 1935.
"Religion Kept Family Strong." *Niagara Falls Gazette*, February 6, 1990.
"Religious Fellowship Seeks End to Housing Discrimination." *Niagara Falls Gazette*, June 3, 1959.
"Relocated Free to Buy, Rent in City." *Niagara Falls Gazette*, February 16, 1962.
"Relocation Group Defended." *Niagara Falls Gazette*, December 29, 1974.
"Remembered Her Former Servant." *Niagara Falls Gazette*, July 23, 1906.
"Report That Negroes Are Migrating North Alarms Authorities." *Niagara Falls Gazette*, June 16, 1927.
"Repudiating Roosevelt." *Niagara Falls Gazette*, August 12, 1912.
"Residents Near Unity Park Protest Hill's Swamp, Debris." *Niagara Falls Gazette*, November 5, 1972.
"Resurfacing Job 'A Work of Art.'" *Niagara Falls Gazette*, August 8, 1970.
"Retiring Friendship House Head Cites Better Civic Attitude." December 14, 1970.
"Rev. B. B. B. Johnson Makes Accounting." *Daily Cataract-Journal*, January 4, 1901.
"Rev. B. B. Johnson Has Given Up His Pulpit." *Niagara Falls Gazette*, June 26, 1900.
"Rev. and Mrs. B.B.B. Johnson of the Second Baptist Church." *Daily Cataract*, March 24, 1900.
"Rev. Whitaker Named Head of NAACP." *Niagara Falls Gazette*, December 8, 1959.
"Richard Sims Non-Suited." *Niagara Falls Gazette*, October 12, 1905.
"Road Work Distributed Throughout N.Y. State." *New York Times*, January 6, 1935.
"Rochester, N.Y." *Chicago Defender*, May 18, 1935.
"Row among Colored Gents." *Niagara Falls Gazette*, October 11, 1865.

"Safe Street Act Post for Griffin." *Niagara Falls Gazette*, May 18, 1971.
"Salvation of the Negro Citizen." *Niagara Falls Gazette*, April 16, 1900.
"Sam Dett Put Efficient Stamp on Post Office." *Niagara Falls Gazette*, February 13, 1987.
"SPA Refuses to Give Detailed Data on Land to Be Taken in Project." *Niagara Falls Gazette*, October 23, 1957.
"Stabbed by Vicious Negro." *Daily Cataract*, February 27, 1900.
"Staff Is to Be Hired for Friendship House." *Niagara Falls Gazette*, April 12, 1968.
"State Commission Charges Housing Segregation Here." *Niagara Falls Gazette*, November 29, 1961.
"State Grant Expected For Friendship House." *Niagara Falls Gazette*, June 11, 1968.
"State May Finance Friendship House." *Niagara Falls Gazette*, June 20, 1968;
"$175,000 to Go Direct to Center." *Niagara Falls Gazette*, June 21, 1968.
"Says Nations Could Borrow Lessons of Peace from Negroes." *Niagara Falls Gazette*, February 22, 1935.
"School Racial Imbalance Exists in City Only at Elementary Level." *Niagara Falls Gazette*, November 7, 1967.
"Schools Get First Black Top Official." *Niagara Falls Gazette*, August 17, 1973.
"Schreiber Denies Racial Slur During Interview by Reporters." *Niagara Falls Gazette*, May 31, 1966.
"Schreiber Protest is Planned." *Niagara Falls Gazette*, June 16, 1966.
"Selecting Name for New Centre." *Niagara Falls Gazette*, October 17, 1928.
"Shiloh Baptist Church." *Niagara Falls Gazette*, January 10, 1925.
"Shiloh Baptist Church." *Niagara Falls Gazette*, September 25, 1926.
"Shortcomings of Negroes Here Are Cited." *Niagara Falls Gazette*, August 7, 1963.
"Signing of Negroes Causes Controversy." *Niagara Falls Gazette*, April 3, 1953.
"Some Blacks See Little Progress in 1970s Housing." *Niagara Falls Gazette*, April 30, 1978.
"Some Kind Words for City Government." *Niagara Falls Gazette*, September 23, 1970.
"State Commission Charges Housing Segregation Here." *Niagara Falls Gazette*, November 29, 1961.
"State Solons to Get Plan for More Wards in City." *Niagara Falls Gazette*, February 18, 1955.
"Store Picketing Here to Back Dixie Negroes." *Niagara Falls Gazette*, April 20, 1960.
"Survey May Show That City Has Nearly 6,000 Sub-standard Homes." *Niagara Falls Gazette*, October 25, 1939.
"Syracuse." *Chicago Defender*, October 4, 1930.
"T. J. Ireland Is Dead at 67." *Niagara Falls Gazette*, September 15, 1970.
"Tension at Niagara Falls." *New York Times*, August 19, 1969.
"The Black Muslims, Cult Recruits Following Here." *Democrat and Chronicle*, Thursday, November 15, 1962.

"The 'Coke' Habit." *Niagara Falls Gazette*, August 17, 1909.
"The Colored Republicans." *Niagara Falls Gazette*, October 19, 1892.
"The Day Dr. Martin Luther King Jr. Came to New Hope Baptist Church." *Niagara Falls Gazette*, January 19, 2004.
"The Newcomers." *Niagara Falls Gazette*, April 27, 1938.
"To Address League." *Niagara Falls Gazette*, March 31, 1931.
"To Seek $120,000 for Community Center Building." *Niagara Falls Gazette*, January 21, 1949.
"Today's Events at Community Center." *Niagara Falls Gazette*, July 9, 1935.
"Today's Events at Community Center." *Niagara Falls Gazette*, February 8, 1937.
"Train Ride Plan Gets City Study." *Niagara Falls Gazette*, July 8, 1964.
"Training for Construction Inc. Aids Jobless." *Niagara Falls Gazette*, March 11, 1971.
"Training Program for Minority Construction Workers Unveiled." *Niagara Falls Gazette*, July 5, 1970.
"Tubman Monument Unveiled in Auburn." *Post-Standard*, July 6, 1915.
"Underground Railroad." *Niagara Falls Gazette*, September 22, 1858.
"Union Baptist Church." *Niagara Falls Gazette*, September 25, 1926.
"Union Baptist Church." *Niagara Falls Gazette*, January 10, 1925.
"Unique Project, National Black Museum for Niagara Falls." *Daily Defender*, August 6, 1973.
"Unity Park Seeking Mid-income Tenants." *Niagara Falls Gazette*, March 24, 1972.
"Urban Projects Move Ahead." *Niagara Falls Gazette*, September 6, 1961.
"Urban Renewal, Jetport Seen Population Boosts." *Niagara Falls Gazette*, May 21, 1970.
"Urban Renewal Area Families Relocated in Jordan Gardens." *Niagara Falls Gazette*, February 25, 1962.
"Urges Youth to Think Straight and Use Prayer." *Niagara Falls Gazette*, January 26, 1942.
"Violence in Selma Protested." *Niagara Falls Gazette*, March 9, 1965.
"Voice Sought on Textbooks." *Niagara Falls Gazette*, September 18, 1970.
"Waiting Stance Indicated by Negroes at Council Session." *Niagara Falls Gazette*, July 7, 1967.
"We Have Lost the Power." *Niagara Falls Gazette*, May 14, 1974.
"We Have Some Race Problems Here Too." *Niagara Falls Gazette*, April 24, 1959.
"Were Caught Stealing Coal: Harry Gates and William Briton, Negroes Sent Down for Thirty Days." *Niagara Falls Gazette*, February 27, 1903.
"Why Out So Late?" *Niagara Falls Gazette*, February 27, 1981.
"Wife of a Famous Educator." *Cataract Journal*, July 22, 1904.
"Willie Fields Honored by Co-workers, Friends and Family upon Retirement." *Niagara Falls Gazette*, March 14, 1981.
"Wily Colored Pastor Sells Out His Church." *Buffalo Courier*, January 9, 1902.
"Woman Burned to Death After Orgy in East Side Hovel with Negroes; Coroner Probes Case." *Niagara Falls Gazette*, December 23, 1925.

"Work of Community Center Here Growing Steadily, Report Show." *Niagara Falls Gazette*, June 8, 1932.
"Young Colored Folk Hear Negro History." *Niagara Falls Gazette*, February 8, 1937.
"Young Negro Poet Writes Sonnet to the Niagara Community Center." *Niagara Falls Gazette*, October 29, 1934.
"Youths on Rampage." *Niagara Falls Gazette*, April 27, 1968.
"2nd Night of Tension Here Results in More Meetings." *Niagara Falls Gazette*, June 30, 1967.
"4 Republicans, 4 Democrats Seeking Council Nominations." *Niagara Falls Gazette*, September 12, 1971.
"5 P. M. Meeting Called to Thwart Another Night of Disturbances Here." *Niagara Falls Gazette*, June 29, 1967.
"6 Birmingham Negroes Killed: 4 Girls Die in Church Blast; 2 Boys Are Shot to Death." *Niagara Falls Gazette*, September 16, 1963.
"30-day Stay of Order to Vacate Their Homes Granted to 28 Hyde Park Village Families." *Niagara Falls Gazette*, February 26, 1952.
"32 From Falls Join in Freedom March." *Niagara Falls Gazette*, August 28, 1963.
"58 Blacks to Be Shifted to Hyde Park School." *Niagara Falls Gazette*, June 14, 1974.
"400 Stage Civil Rights March in Falls." *Niagara Falls Gazette*, March 15, 1965.
"$550 Collected Here Will Help Rights Workers." *Niagara Falls Gazette*, March 16, 1965.
"1942–1943." *Niagara Falls Gazette*, December 31, 1942.
"3000 in Race Riot at Niagara Falls." *New York Times*, August 28, 1934.

PROPERTY ASSESSOR REPORTS

1940 Birch Court Property Inc. Property Assessor's Office, City Hall, Niagara Falls, New York.
1955 Birch Court Property Inc. Property Assessor's Office, City Hall, Niagara Falls, New York.
1952 Niagara Place Apartments LLC. Property Assessor's Office, City Hall, Niagara Falls, New York.
1961 Niagara Place Apartments LLC. Property Assessor's Office, City Hall, Niagara Falls, New York.
1972 Niagara Place Apartments LLC. Property Assessor's Office, City Hall, Niagara Falls, New York.
1982 Niagara Place Apartments LLC. Property Assessor's Office, City Hall, Niagara Falls, New York.

REPORTS

The First Semi-Annual Report of the School for the Instruction of the Colored, Deaf, Dumb, and Blind. Buffalo: Commercial Advertiser Steam, 1858.

SPEECHES

Marshall, Thurgood. "The Constitution's Bicentennial: Commemorating the Wrong Document?" *Vanderbilt Law Review* 40, no. 6 (November 1987): 1337–1342.

UNPUBLISHED DOCUMENTS

Ray, Arthur. "Black Pioneers Agenda." Unpublished manuscript, August 1, 2009.
Smith, Barbara. "A History of St. John's A. M. E. Church." Unpublished manuscript given to the author by Barbara Smith, St. John's AME Church historian.
Williamson, Bill. "Formation of the Niagara Civic and Protective Club." Unpublished manuscript of Bill Williamson, Niagara Falls, New York. A copy of this document was given to the author January 30, 2010.

WEBSITES

Ancestry.com. http://www.ancestry.com/1940-census/usa/New-York/ArthurRay_4yqhq.
Bradberry, Bill. "Black Menagerie: Neighborhoods Are the People, Not the Buildings." http://www.niagarafallsreporter.com/menagerie17.html.
———. "Black Menagerie: Race Still A Factor In Housing Here." http://www.niagarafallsreporter.com/menagerie107.html.
Densmore, Christopher. "Underground Railroad Agents in Western New York." Ublib.buffalo.edu/libraries/units/archives/urr/agents.html.
Gallagher, Bill. "First Rule Is: All Politics Is Local." http://www.Niagarafallsreporter.com/gallagher142.html.
"Willie C. Fields Sr." http://www.legacy.com/Obituaries.asp?page=lifestory&personid=117871919.

Secondary Sources

ARCHIVAL MATERIALS

"A History of St. John's A. M. E. Church." A document given to the author from Barbara Smith, January 16, 2010.
"Black History Tour." Commissioned by Town of Erie, Economic Development Department 1992. Saint Catherine's Historical Museum.
Local History Department, Niagara Falls Public Library, New York

BOOKS

Anderson, David. *Rochester Region Underground Railroad Network to Freedom: A Guidebook Rochester/Monroe County Freedom Trail Commission.* Rochester, NY: Publication Services, 2003.

Anderson, James D. *The Education of Blacks in the South, 1860–1935*. Chapel Hill: University of North Carolina Press, 1988.

Anderson, Talmadge, and James Stewart. *Introduction to African American Studies: Transdisciplinary Approaches and Implications* (Baltimore, MD: Black Classic, 2007.

Anderson, Talmadge. *Introduction to African American Studies*. Dubuque, IA: Kendall/Hunt, 1993.

Armstead, Myra B. Young. *Lord, Please Don't Take Me in August: African Americans in Newport and Saratoga Springs, 1870–1930*. Urbana: University of Illinois Press, 1999.

Ayers, Edward L. *The Promise of the New South: Life After Reconstruction*. New York: Oxford University Press, 1992.

Bancroft, Frederic. *Slave Trading in the Old South*. Columbia: University of South Carolina Press, 1996.

Barr, Alwyn. *Black Texans: A History of Negroes in Texas 1528–1971*. Austin: Jenkins, 1973.

Bates, Daisy. *The Long Shadow of Little Rock: A Memoir*. Fayetteville: University of Arkansas Press, 1987.

Bennett, Lerone, Jr. *Before the Mayflower: A History of Black America*. New York: Penguin, 1993.

———. *The Shaping of Black America: The Struggles and Triumphs of African Americans, 1619 to the 1990s*. New York: Penguin, 1993.

Bigham, Darrel E. *We Ask Only a Fair Trial: A History of the Black Community of Evansville, Indiana*. Bloomington: Indiana University Press, 1987.

Billingsley, Andrew, *Mighty Like a River: The Black Church and Social Reform*. New York: Oxford University Press, 1999.

———. *Climbing Jacob's Ladder: The Enduring Legacy of African American Families*. New York: Touchstone, 1992,

Blassingame, John W. *The Slave Community: Plantation Life in the Antebellum South*. New York: Oxford University Press, 1979.

Blum, Elizabeth D. *Love Canal Revisited: Race, Class, and Gender in Environmental Activism*. Lawrence: University of Kansas Press, 2008.

Bodnar, John, Roger Simon, and Michael P. Weber. *Lives of Their Own: Blacks, Italians, and Poles in Pittsburgh, 1900–1960*. Urbana: University of Illinois Press, 1982.

Boehm, Lisa Krissoff. *Making a Way Out of No Way: African American Women and the Second Great Migration*. Jackson: University Press of Mississippi, 2010.

Boles, Ed D., and Michael B. Boston. *Dr. Skinner's Remarkable School for "Colored Deaf, Dumb, and Blind Children" 1857–1860*. Buffalo, NY: People Ink, 2010.

Borchert, James. *Alley Life in Washington: Family, Community, Religion, and Folklife in the City, 1850–1970*. Urbana: University of Illinois Press, 1980.

Bordewich, Fergus M. *Bound for Canaan*. New York: Amistad, 2005.

Boston, Michael B. *The Business Strategy of Booker T. Washington.* Gainesville: University Press of Florida, 2010.
Branch, Taylor. *Parting the Waters: America in the King Years 1954–63.* New York: Simon and Schuster, 1988.
Brown, Elsa Barkley, and Thomas C. Holt. *Major Problems in African American History.* Vol. 2: *From Freedom to "Freedom Now," 1865–1990s.* Boston: Houghton Mifflin, 2000.
Brown, Michael. *Laying Waste: The Poisoning of America by Toxic Chemicals.* New York: Washington Square, 1979.
Brown, Scott. *Fighting for US: Maulana Karenga, The US Organization and Black Cultural Nationalism.* New York: New York University Press, 2005.
Brundage, W. Fitzhugh. *Lynching in the New South: Georgia and Virginia, 1880–1930.* Urbana: University of Illinois Press, 1993.
Buckmaster, Henrietta. *Let My People Go: The Story of the Underground Railroad and the Growth of the Abolition Movement.* Boston: Beacon, 1941.
Bullard, Robert D., and Beverly Wright. *Race, Place, and Environmental Justice After Hurricane Katrina: Struggles to Reclaim, Rebuild, and Revitalize New Orleans and the Gulf Coast.* Boulder, CO: Westview, 2009.
Bullard, Robert D. *The Quest for Environmental Justice: Human Rights and the Politics of Pollution.* San Francisco: Sierra Club, 2005.
———. *Dumping in Dixie: Race, Class, and Environmental Quality.* San Francisco: Westview, 1990.
Butler, John S. *Entrepreneurship and Self-Help Among Black Americans: A Reconsideration of Race and Economics.* Albany, New York: State University of New York Press, 1991.
Carson, Clayborne. *In Struggle: SNCC and the Black Awakening of the 1960s.* Cambridge, MA: Harvard University Press, 1981.
Chafe, William H. *Civilities and Civil Rights: Greensboro, North Carolina, and the Black Struggle for Freedom.* New York: Oxford University Press, 1981.
Cheatham, Harold E., and James B. Stewart. *Black Families: Interdisciplinary Perspectives.* New Brunswick, NJ: Transaction, 1990.
Chicago Grassroots Curriculum Taskforce. *Urban Renewal or Urban Removal.* Chicago: Chicago Grassroots Curriculum Taskforce, 2012.
Coombs, Norman. *The Black Experience in America.* New York: Hippocrene, 1972.
Cronon, E. David. *Black Moses: The Story of Marcus Garvey and the Universal Negro Improvement Association.* Madison: University of Wisconsin Press, 1969.
Cruse, Harold. *Plural But Equal: a Critical Study of Blacks and Minorities and America's Plural Society.* New York: William Morrow, 1987.
———. *Rebellion or Revolution?* New York: William Morrow, 1968.
———. *The Crisis of the Negro Intellectual.* New York: William Morrow, 1967.
Daniel, Sadie Iola. *Women Builders.* Washington, DC: Associated Press, 1970.
Davis, Angela Y. *Angela Y. Davis: Women, Race and Class.* New York: Vintage, 1983.

———. *Angela Davis—an Autobiography.* New York: Random House, 1974.
DeVries, James E. *Race and Kinship in a Midwestern Town: The Black Experience in Monroe, Michigan, 1900–1915.* Urbana: University of Illinois Press, 1984.
Dierenfield, Bruce J. *The Civil Rights Movement.* Harlow, UK: Pearson, 2004.
Drake, St. Clair, and Horace A. Cayton. *Black Metropolis: A Study of Negro Life in a Northern City.* Chicago: University of Chicago Press, 1993.
Du Bois, W. E. B. *Black Reconstruction in America 1860–1880.* New York: Atheneum, 1969.
———. *The Philadelphia Negro.* Philadelphia: University of Pennsylvania Press, 1996.
Enstrom, Elmer. *Busing, Not Integration, Opposed.* Santa Ana, CA: Graphic, 1998.
Evers-Williams, Myrlie, and Manning Marable. *The Autobiography of Medgar Evers: A Hero's Life and Legacy Revealed through His Writings, Letters, and Speeches.* New York: Basic Civitas Books, 2006.
Feagin, Joe R., Hernan Vera, and Pinar Batur. *White Racism.* New York: Routledge, 2001.
Filler, Louis. *The Crusade Against Slavery, 1830–1860.* New York: Harper and Brothers, 1960.
Foner, Eric. *Reconstruction America's Unfinished Revolution 1863–1877.* New York: Harper & Row, 1988.
Fowlkes, Martha R., and Patricia Y. Miller. *Love Canal: The Social Construction of Disaster.* Washington, DC: Federal Emergency Management Agency, 1983.
Franklin, John Hope, and August Meier, eds. *Black Leaders of the Twentieth Century.* Chicago: University of Illinois Press, 1994.
Franklin, John Hope, and Alfred A. Moss, Jr. *From Slavery to Freedom: A History of African Americans.* 8th ed. New York: McGraw Hill, 2000.
Franklin, V. P. *Black Self-Determination: A Cultural History of African American Resistance.* Brooklyn, NY: Lawrence Hill, 1992.
Frazier, E. Franklin. *The Negro Family in the United States.* Chicago: University of Chicago Press, 1967.
Freedom Archives. *Prison on Fire: Attica, George Jackson and Black Liberation.* Oakland, CA: AK, 2002.
Frost, Karolyn Smardz. *Steal Away Home: One Woman's Epic Flight to Freedom—and Her Long Road Back to the South.* Toronto, ON: HarperCollins, 2017.
Frost, Karolyn Smardz, and Veta Smith Tucker. *A Fluid Frontier: Slavery, Resistance, and the Underground Railroad in the Detroit River Borderland.* Detroit: Wayne State University Press, 2016.
Fullilove, Mindy, *America, and What We Can Do About It.* New York: Random House, 2009.
Gaines, Kevin K. *Uplifting the Race: Black Leadership, Politics, and Culture in the Twentieth Century.* Chapel Hill: University of North Carolina Press, 1996.

Gara, Larry. *The Liberty Line: The Legend of the Underground Railroad*. Lexington: University of Kentucky Press, 1967.
Gardell, Mattias. *In the Name of Elijah Muhammad: Louis Farrakhan and the Nation of Islam*. Durham, NC: Duke University Press, 1996.
Gerber, David A. *Black Ohio and the Color Line 1860–1915*. Urbana: University of Illinois Press, 1976.
Gitlin, Todd. *The Sixties: Years of Hope, Days of Rage*. New York: Bantam, 1987.
Goggin, Jacqueline A. *Carter G. Woodson: A Life in Black History*. Baton Rouge: Louisiana State University Press, 1993.
Gordon, Jacob U. *Black Leadership for Social Change*. Westport, CT: Greenwood, 2000.
Gottlieb, Peter. *Making Their Own Way: Southern Blacks' Migration to Pittsburgh, 1916–1930*. Champaign: University of Illinois Press, 1987.
Greenberg, Cheryl. *"Or Does It Explode?": Black Harlem in the Great Depression*. New York: Oxford University Press, 1997.
Gregory, James N. *The Southern Diaspora: How the Great Migration of Black and White Southerners Transformed America*. Chapel Hill: University of North Carolina Press, 2005.
Grier, William, and Price M. Cobbs. *Black Rage*. New York: Basic Books, 1968.
Grossman, James R. *Land of Hope*. Chicago: University of Chicago Press, 1991.
Gutman, Herbert G. *The Black Family in Slavery and Freedom 1750–1925*. New York: Vintage, 1976.
Hacker, Andrew. *Two Nations: Black and White, Separate, Hostile, Unequal*. New York: Scribner, 2003.
Hampton, Henry, Steve Fayer, and Sarah Flynn. *Voices of Freedom*. New York: Bantam, 1990.
Hanson, Joyce A. *Mary McLeod Bethune and Black Women's Political Activism*. Columbia: University of Missouri Press, 2003.
Harlan, Louis R. *Booker T. Washington: The Wizard of Tuskegee, 1901–1915*. New York: Oxford University Press, 1983.
Harris, H. William. *The Harder We Run: Black Workers since the Civil War*. New York: Oxford University Press, 1982.
Hattery, Angela J., and Earl Smith. *African American Families*. Los Angeles: SAGE, 2007.
Higgs, Robert. *Competition and Coercion: Blacks in the American Economy, 1865–1914*. Chicago: University of Chicago Press, 1980.
Hirsch, Arnold R. *Making the Second Ghetto: Race & Housing in Chicago 1940–1960*. New York: Cambridge University Press, 1983.
Holt, Thomas C., and Elsa Barkley Brown, eds. *Major Problems in African American History*. Vol. 2: *From Freedom to "Freedom Now," 1865–1990*. Boston: Wadsworth, 2000.
Huggins, Nathan Irvin. *Harlem Renaissance*. New York: Oxford University Press, 2007.

Jacobs, Jane. *The Death and Life of Great American Cities.* New York: Random House, 1961.
Jackson, Kenneth, T. *Crabgrass Frontier: The Suburbanization of the United States.* New York: Oxford University Press, 1985.
Johnson, Leanor Boulin, and Robert Staples, *Black Families at the Crossroad: Challenges and Prospects.* San Francisco: Jossey-Bass, 2005.
Jones, E. Michael. *Slaughter of Cities: Urban Renewal As Ethnic Cleansing.* South Bend, IN: St. Augustine, 2004.
Jones, Jacqueline. *Labor of Love, Labor of Sorrow.* New York: Vintage, 1995.
Jones, James. *Bad Blood: The Tuskegee Syphilis Experiment.* New York: Free Press, 1993.
Katznelson, Ira. *When Affirmative Action Was White: An Untold History of Racial Inequality in Twentieth-Century America.* New York: W. W. Norton, 2005.
King, Martin L., Jr. *Stride Toward Freedom.* New York: Harper & Brothers, 1984.
Kostoff, Robert. *History of Niagara County, New York.* Lewiston, NY: Edwin Mellen, 2011.
Kovel, Joel. *White Racism: A Psychohistory.* New York: Columbia University Press, 1984.
Kunjufu, Jawanza. *There Is Nothing Wrong with Black Students.* Chicago: Images, 2012.
Kusmer, Kenneth, and Joe Trotter, eds. *African American Urban History since World War II.* Chicago: University of Chicago Press, 2009.
Kusmer, Kenneth L. *A Ghetto Takes Shape: Black Cleveland, 1870–1930.* Urbana: University of Illinois, Press, 1976.
Ladd, E. *Negro Political Leadership.* Ithaca, NY: Cornell University Press, 1966.
Lamon, Lester C. *Black Tennesseans 1900–1930.* Knoxville: University of Tennessee Press, 1977.
LaRoche, Cheryl Janifer. *Free Black Communities and the Underground Railroad: The Geography of Resistance.* Urbana: University of Illinois Press, 2014.
Lawn, George W. *Race, Religion and Urban Renewal Jamestown in the Sixties.* Jamestown, NY: Kwik Kopy Printing, 2001.
Layton, Azza Salama. *International Politics and Civil Rights.* New York: Cambridge University Press, 2000.
Lee, Irvin H. *Negro Medal of Honor Men.* New York: Dodd, Mead, 1969.
Lee, Maureen Elgersman. *Black Bangor: African Americans in a Maine Community, 1880–1950.* Durham: University of New Hampshire Press, 2005.
Lemak, Jennifer A. *Southern Life, Northern City: The History of Albany's Rapp Road.* Albany: State University of New York Press, 2008.
Levine, Adeline Gordon. *Love Canal: Science, Politics, and People.* Lexington, MA: Lexington, 1982.
Lewis, David Levering. *W.E.B. Du Bois, Biography of Race.* New York: Henry Holt, 1993.
Lewis, Earl. *In Their Own Interests.* Oakland: University of California Press, 1993.

Light, Ivan H. *Ethnic Enterprise in America: Business and Welfare among Chinese, Japanese and Blacks.* Berkeley: University of California Press, 1972.

Lincoln, C. Eric. *The Black Muslims in America.* Trenton, NJ: Africa World, 1994.

Lincoln, C. Eric, and Lawrence H. Mamiya. *The Black Church in the African American Experience.* Durham, NC: Duke University Press, 1990.

Litwack, Leon, and August Meier, eds. *Black Leaders of the Nineteenth Century.* Urbana: University of Illinois Press, 1991.

Litwack, Leon F. *Been in the Storm So Long: The Aftermath of Slavery.* New York: Vintage, 1980.

Logan, Rayford W. *W. E. B. Du Bois: A Profile.* New York: Hill and Wang, 1971.

———. *The Betrayal of the Negro, from Rutherford B. Hayes to Woodrow Wilson.* New York: Collier, 1965.

Lubet, Steven. *Fugitive Justice: Runaways, Rescuers, and Slavery on Trial.* Cambridge, MA: Harvard University Press, 2010.

Mandle, Jay R. *Not Slave, Not Free: The African American Economic Experience since the Civil War.* Durham, NC: Duke University Press, 1992.

———. *The Roots of Black Poverty.* Philadelphia: Temple University Press, 1978.

Marable, Manning. *Malcolm X: A Life of Reinvention.* New York: Viking, 2011.

Marable, Manning, and Leith Mullings, eds. *Let Nobody Turn Us Around.* Lanham, MD: Rowman & Littlefield, 2003.

Marable, Manning. *Black Leadership.* New York: Columbia University Press, 1998.

———. *How Capitalism Underdeveloped Black America.* Boston: South End, 1983.

Marks, Carle. *Farewell—We're Good and Gone: The Great Black Migration.* Bloomington: Indiana University Press, 1989.

Martin, Tony. *Marcus Garvey, Hero: A First Biography.* Dover, MA: Majority, 1983.

Martin, Waldo E., Jr. *The Mind of Frederick Douglass.* Chapel Hill: University of North Carolina Press, 1984.

Massey, Douglas S., and Nancy A. Denton. *American Apartheid: Segregation and the Making of the Underclass.* Cambridge, MA: Harvard University Press, 1994.

McBrier, Vivian Flagg. *R. Nathaniel Dett: His Life and Work.* Washington, DC: Associated, 1977.

McCluskey, Audrey Thomas, and Elaine M. Smith. *Mary McLeod Bethune: Building a Better World, Essays and Selected Documents.* Bloomington: Indiana University Press, 2002.

McDougall, Harold. *Black Baltimore: A New Theory of Community.* Philadelphia: Temple University Press, 1993.

Meier, August. *Negro Thought in America, 1880–1915.* Ann Arbor: University of Michigan Press, 1963.

Meier, August, and Elliott Rudwick. *From Plantation to Ghetto.* New York: Hill and Wang, 1970.

Mizer, Hamilton B. *A City Is Born.* Niagara Falls, NY: Human-Wahl, 1981.

Moody, Anne. *Coming of Age in Mississippi.* New York: Dell, 1968.

Morris, Aldon. *The Origins of the Civil Rights Movement, Black Communities Organizing for Change*. New York: Free Press, 1986.
Myrdal, Gunnar. *An American Dilemma Volume I: The Negro Problem and Modern Democracy*. New York: Harper Torchbooks, 1962.
———. *An American Dilemma: The Negro Problem & Modern Democracy*, Vol. 2. New York: Pantheon, 1972.
Newman, Mark. *The Civil Rights Movement*. Edinburgh: Edinburgh University Press, 2004.
Newman, Richard, S. *Love Canal: A Toxic History from Colonial Times to Present*. New York: Oxford University Press, 2016.
Nkrumah, Kwame. *Ghana: The Autobiography of Kwame Nkrumah*. New York: International, 1971.
Oak, Vishnu V. *The Negro's Adventure in General Business*. Westport, CT: Negro University Press, 1970.
Orfield, Gary. *Must We Bus? Segregated Schools and National Policy*. Washington, DC: Brookings Institution, 1978.
Osofsky, Gilbert. *Harlem: The Making of a Ghetto*. New York: Harper Torchbooks, 1971.
Papson, Don, and Tom Calarco. *Secret Lives of the Underground Railroad in New York City*. Jefferson, NC: McFarland, 2015.
Penningroth, Dylan C. *The Claims of Kinfolk: African American Property and Community in the Nineteenth-Century South*. Chapel Hill: University of North Carolina Press, 2003.
Quarles, Benjamin. *The Negro in the Making of America*. New York: Touchstone, 1996.
———. *Black Abolitionists*. New York: Oxford University Press, 1969.
Rabinowitz, Howard N. *Race Relations in the Urban South 1865–1890*. New York: Oxford University Press, 1978.
Raboteau, Albert J. *Slave Religion: The "Invisible Institution" in the Antebellum South*. New York: Oxford University Press, 1978.
Rainwater, Lee, and William L. Yancey. *The Moynihan Report and the Politics of Controversy*. Cambridge, MA: MIT Press, 1967.
Rashad, Adib. *Elijah Muhammad & The Ideological Foundation of The Nation of Islam*. Newport News, VA: UB & US Communications Systems, 1993.
Robinson, Armstead L., and Patricia Sullivan, eds. *New Directions in Civil Rights Studies*. Charlottesville: University of Virginia Press, 1991.
Roger Hepburn, Sharon A. *Crossing the Border: A Free Black Community in Canada*. Urbana: University of Illinois Press, 2007.
Rosengarten, Theodore. *All God's Dangers: The Life of Nate Shaw*. New York: Alfred A. Knopf, 1975.
Rothstein, Richard. *The Color of Law: A Forgotten History of How Our Government Segregated America*. New York: Liveright, 2017.

Saunders, James Robert, and Renae Nadine Shackelford. *Urban Renewal and the End of Black Culture in Charlottesville, Virginia*. Jefferson, NC: McFarland, 2005.

Sernett, Milton. *Harriet Tubman: Myth, Memory, and History*. Durham, NC: Duke University Press, 2007.

———. *North Star Country: Upstate New York and the Crusade for African American Freedom*. Syracuse, NY: Syracuse University Press, 2002.

Siebert, Wilbur H. *The Underground Railroad from Slavery to Freedom: A Comprehensive History*. New York: Macmillan, 1899.

Simpson, Anne Key. *Follow Me: The Life and Music of R. Nathaniel Dett*. Metuchen, NJ: Scarecrow, 1993.

Sitkoff, Harvard. *The Struggle for Black Equality*. New York: Hill and Wang, 1993.

Solomon, Mark. *The Cry Was Unity: Communists and African Americans, 1917–1936*. Jackson: University of Mississippi Press, 1998.

Spear, Allen. *Black Chicago: The Making of a Negro Ghetto, 1890–1920*. Chicago: University of Chicago Press, 1967.

Sprague, Stuart Seely, ed. *His Promised Land: The Autobiography of John P. Parker, Former Slave and Conductor on the Underground Railroad*. New York: W.W. Norton, 1998.

Staples, Robert. *The Black Family: Essays and Studies*. Belmont, CA: Wadsworth, 1971.

———. *The Black Family: Essays and Studies* Belmont, CA: Wadsworth, 1994.

St. Jean, Yanick, and Joe R. Feagin, *Double Burden: Black Women and Everyday Racism*. Armonk, NY: M. D. Sharpe, 1998.

Steward, Austin. *Austin Steward: Twenty-two Years a Slave and Forty Years a Freeman*. Reading, MA: Addison-Wesley, 1969.

Stowe, Harriet Beecher. *Uncle Tom's Cabin* (New York: Barnes & Noble, 2003).

Sudarkasa, Niara. *The Strength of Our Mothers: African & African American Women & Families: Essays and Speeches*. Trenton, NJ: Africa World, 1996.

Switala, William J. *Underground Railroad in New York and New Jersey*. Mechanicsburg, PA: Stackpole, 2006.

Taylor, Henry L. *Race and the City: Work, Community and Protest in Cincinnati, 1820–1970*. Champaign: University of Illinois Press, 1993.

Taylor, Steven J. L. *Desegregation in Boston and Buffalo: The Influence of Local Leaders*. Albany: State University of New York Press, 1998.

The Carborundum Company: The First 100 Years, 1891–1991, a Commemorative History Niagara Falls, NY: Carborundum, 1991.

Thomas, Richard W. *Life for Us Is What We Make It: Building Black Community in Detroit, 1915–1945*. Bloomington: Indiana University Press, 1992.

Tolnay, Stewart E., and E. M. Beck. *A Festival of Violence: An Analysis of Southern Lynching, 1882–1930*. Urbana: University of Illinois Press, 1992.

Travis, Dempsey J. *An Autobiography of Black Chicago*. Berkeley: Agate, 2013.
Trotter, Joe W., Jr. *The Great Migration in Historical Perspective*. Bloomington: Indiana University Press, 1991.

———. Trotter, Joe W. Jr., and Eric Ledell Smith. *African Americans in Pennsylvania: Shifting Historical Perspectives*. University Park: Pennsylvania State University Press, 1997.

———. *The African American Experience*. Vol. 2: *From Reconstruction*. Boston: Houghton Mifflin, 2001.

———. *Black Milwaukee: The Making of an Industrial Proletariate, 1915–1945*. Champaign: University of Illinois Press, 2006.

Tushnet, Mark V. *The NAACP Legal Strategy against Segregated Education 1925–1950*. Chapel Hill: University of North Carolina Press, 2005.

Tuttle, William M., Jr. *Race Riot: Chicago in the Red Summer of 1919*. New York: Atheneum, 1971.

Tyson, Timothy B. *The Blood of Emmett Till*. New York: Simon & Schuster, 2017.

Van DeBurg, William L. *New Day in Babylon: The Black Power Movement and American Culture, 1965–1975*. Chicago: University of Chicago Press, 1992.

Vogel, Michael N. *Echoes in the Mist: An Illustrated History of the Niagara Falls Area*. Chatsworth, CA: Windsor, 1991.

Walter, Ronald W., and Robert C. Smith. *African American Leadership*. Albany: State University of New York Press, 1999.

Washington, Booker T. *Up From Slavery*. New York: Doubleday and Page, 1901.

Whitfield, Harvey Amani, *Blacks on the Border: The Black Refugees in British North America 1815–1860*. Burlington: University of Vermont Press, 2006.

Wicker, Tom. *A Time to Die*. Chicago: Haymarket, 2011.

Wilkerson, Isabel. *The Warmth of Other Suns: The Epic Story of America's Great Migration*. New York: Vintage, 2011.

Williams, Charles. *African American Life and Culture in Orange Mound: Case Study of a Black Community in Memphis, Tennessee, 1890–1980*. Lanham, MD: Lexington, 2013.

Williams, Juan. *Thurgood Marshall: American Revolutionary*. New York: Times Books, 1998.

———. *Eyes on the Prize*. New York: Viking, 1987.

Williams, Lillian S. *Strangers in the Land of Paradise*. Bloomington: Indiana University Press, 1999.

Wilson, James Q., ed. *Urban Renewal: The Record and the Controversy*. Cambridge, MA: MIT Press, 1966.

Wilson, William Julius. *When Work Disappears: The World of the New Urban Poor*. New York: Alfred A. Knopf, 1996.

Winks, Robin W. *The Blacks in Canada A History*. Montreal: McGill-Queen's University Press, 1971.

Wolters, Raymond. *Negroes and the Great Depression: The Problem of Economic Recovery.* Westport, CT: Greenwood, 1970.

Woodward, C. Vann. *The Strange Career of Jim Crow.* New York: Oxford University Press, 1973.

Wytsma, Ken. *The Myth of Equality: Uncovering the Roots of Injustice and Privilege.* Downers Grove, IL: InterVarsity, 2017.

DISSERTATIONS AND THESES

Banks, James Franklin. "Problems Encountered by World War II and Post World War II Negroes, Who Settled in the Niagara Falls, New York Area." Master's thesis, Niagara University, 1958.

Costantino, Carl J. "History of the Underground Railroad along the Niagara Frontier." Master's thesis, Niagara University, 1947.

Feder, H. William. "The Evolution of an Ethnic Neighborhood that Became United in Diversity: The East Side, Niagara Falls, New York 1880–1930." PhD diss., University of Buffalo, 1999.

Niemuth, Niles Williams. "Urban Renewal and the Development of Milwaukee's African American Community: 1960–1980." Master's thesis, University of Wisconsin-Milwaukee, 2014.

Theophilis, Jorgette. "A Re-Examination of the Love Canal Crisis: The Myth and the Reality." Master's thesis, Massachusetts Institute of Technology, 1996.

Watkins, Ralph. "Blacks in Buffalo 1900–1920." PhD diss., University of Buffalo, 1978.

JOURNAL ARTICLES

Anderson, Talmadge, "Black Affirmative Action: A Discussion of Economic Strategies Toward Self-Help and Self-Determination." *Journal of Social Relations* 14, no. 1/2 (Fall–Winter and Spring–Summer 1987) 185–194.

Baber, M. Yvette. "Urban Renewal Policy and Community Change." *Practicing Anthropology* 20, no. 1 (Winter 1998): 15–17.

Barnes, Sandra L. "Priestly and Prophetic Influences on Black Church Social Services," *Social Problems* 51, no. 2 (May 2004): 202–221.

Beck, William W., Glenn M. Linden, and Michael E. Siegel. "Identifying School Desegregation Leadership Styles," *Journal of Negro Education* 49, no. 2 (Spring 1980): 115–133.

Billingsley, Andrew, and Cleopatra Howard Caldwell. "The Church, the Family, and the School in the African American Community." *Journal of Negro Education* 60, no. 3 (Summer 1991): 427–440.

Blackett, Richard. "Martin R. Delany and Robert Campbell: Black Americans in Search of an African Colony." *Journal of Negro History* 62, no. 1 (January 1977): 1–25.

Blight, David. "Charles Hamilton Houston: The Legal Scholar Who Laid the Foundation for Integrated Higher Education in the United States." *Journal of Blacks in Higher Education* 34 (Winter 2001-2002): 107.

Boston, Michael B. "Bloneva Bond—a Longtime Niagara Falls, New York Activist." *Afro-Americans in New York Life and History* 38, no. 2 (August 2014): 7-36.

———."Dr. P. H. Skinner: Controversial Educator of the Deaf, Blind and Mute, and Niagara Falls, New York Abolitionist." *Afro-Americans in New York Life and History* 29 (July 2005): 45-66.

———. "Blacks in Niagara Falls, New York: 1865 to 1965." *Afro-Americans in New York Life and History* 28 (July 2004): 7-49.

Boyd, Robert L. "Black Enterprise in the Retail Trade during the Early Twentieth Century," *Sociological Focus* 34, no. 3 (August 2001): 242-250.

"Breaking Barriers: Black Museums Call for a Truer History." *History News* 36, no. 2 (February 1981): 7.

Brewer, William M. "Poor Whites and Negroes in the South since the Civil War." *Journal of Negro History* 15 (1930): 26-37.

Broyld, Dann J., "Harriet Tubman: Transnationalism and the Land of a Queen in the Late Antebellum," *Meridians* 12, no. 2 (2014): 78-98.

Bullard, Robert D., and Beverly H. Wright. "The Quest for Environmental Equity: Mobilizing the Black Community for Social Change." *Race, Poverty and the Environment* 1, no. 2 (July 1990): 14-17.

Bussel, Robert. " 'The Most Indispensable Man in His Community'; African American Entrepreneurs in West Chester, Pennsylvania, 1865-1925." *Pennsylvania History: A Journal of Mid-Atlantic Studies* 65, no. 3 (Summer 1998): 324-349.

Camarillo, Albert M. "Navigating Segregated Life in American's Racial Borderhood, 1910-1950." *Journal of American History* 100, no. 3 (December 2013): 645-662.

Carter, Gregg Lee. "Local Police Force Size and the Severity of the 1960s Black Rioting." *Journal of Conflict Resolution* 31, no. 4 (December 1987): 601-614.

Cohen, Lizabeth. "Buying into Downtown revival: The Centrality of Retail to Postwar Urban Renewal in American Cities," *Annals of the American Academy of Political and Social Science* 611 (May 2007): 82-95.

Cooper, Afua. "The Fluid Frontier: Blacks and the Detroit River Region, A Focus on Henry Bibb." *Canadian Review of American Studies* 30 (2000): 129-149.

Cothran, Tilman C., and William Phillips, Jr. "Negro Leadership in a Crisis Situation." *Phylon* 22, no. 2 (Second Quarter 1961): 107-118.

Crouthamel, James L. "The Springfield Race Riot of 1908." *Journal of Negro History* 45, no. 3 (July 1960): 164-181.

Cummings, Melbourne. "Historical Setting for Booker T. Washington and the Rhetoric of Compromise, 1895." *Journal of Black Studies* 8 (September 1977): 75-82.

Davis, Angela, and Fania Davis. "The Black Family and the Crisis of Capitalism." *Black Scholar* 17, no. 5 (September-October 1986): 33-40.

Dellums, Ronald V. "Black Leadership: For Change or for Status Quo?," *Black Scholar* 8, no. 4 (January–February 1977): 2–5.
D'Emilio, John. "Remembering Bayard Rustin," *OAH Magazine of History* 20, no. 2 (March 2006): 12–14.
Drone, Janell. "Desegregation and Effective School Leadership: Tracking Success, 1954–1980." *Journal of African American History* 90, no. 4 (Autumn 2005): 410–421.
Eggert, Gerald G. "The Impact of the Fugitive Slave Law on Harrisburg: A Case Study." *Pennsylvania Magazine of History and Biography* 109, no. 4 (October 1985): 537–569.
Farley, Reynolds. "The Urbanization of Negroes in the United States." *Journal of Social History* 1 (Spring 1968): 241–258.
Fierce, Milfred, C. "Economic Aspects of the Marcus Garvey Movement." *Black Scholar* 3, no. 7–8 (March–April 1972): 50–61.
Fordham, Monroe. "The Buffalo Cooperative Economic Society, Inc., 1928–1961: A Black Self-help Organization." *Niagara Frontier* (Summer 1976): 41–49.
Franklin, John Hope. "John Hope Franklin: The Fisk Years." *Journal of Blacks in Higher Education* 49 (Autumn 2005): 74–83.
Frye, Jerry K. "The Black Manifesto and the Tactic of Objectification." *Journal of Black Studies* 5, no. 1 (September 1974): 65–76.
Fullilove, Mindy Thompson. "Root Shock: The Consequences of African American Dispossession." *Journal of Urban Health* 78, no. 1 (March 2001): 1–9.
Gaines, Kevin. "The Civil Rights Movement in World Perspective." *OAH Magazine in History* 21, no. 1 (January 2007): 57–64.
Gallant, Sigrid Nicole. "Perspectives on the Motives for the Migration of African-Americans to and from Ontario, Canada: From the Abolition of Slavery in Canada to the Abolition of Slavery in the United States." *Journal of Negro History* 86, no. 3 (Summer 2001): 391–408.
Gavranovic, Altin. "'Can't Get My Mind Settle': Black Migrants and the Decision to Leave the South during the First World War." *Australia and New Zealand American Studies* 23, no. 1 (July 2004): 139–148.
Godsil, Rachel, D. "Remedying Environmental Racism." *Michigan Law Review* 90, no. 2 (November 1991): 394–427.
Goldring, Ellen Lora Cohen-Vogel, Claire Smrekar, and Cynthia Taylor. "Schooling Closer to Home: Desegregation Policy and Neighborhood." *American Journal of Education* 112, no. 3 (May 2006): 335–362.
Gordon, Lawrence. "A Brief Look at Blacks in Depression Mississippi, 1929–1934: Eyewitness Accounts." *Journal of Negro History* 64, no. 4 (Autumn 1979): 377–390.
Green, Dan S. "W. E. B. Du Bois' Talented Tenth: A Strategy for Racial Advancement." *Journal of Negro Education* 46, no. 3 (Summer 1977): 358–366.
Greer, James L. "Historic Home Mortgage Redlining in Chicago." *Journal of the Illinois State Historical Society* 107, no. 2 (Summer 2014): 204–233.

Grossman, James R. "Blowing the Trumpet: The Chicago Defender and Black Migration during World War I." *Illinois Historical Journal* 78, no. 2 (Summer 1985): 82–96.

Hackett, David G. "The Prince Hall Masons and the African American Church: The Labors of Grand Master and Bishop James Walker Hood, 1831–1918." *Church History* 69, no. 4 (December 2000): 770–802.

Hall, Jacquelyn Dowd. "The Long Civil Rights Movement and the Political Uses of the Past." *Journal of American History* 91, no. 4 (March 2005): 1233–1263.

Hanglberger, Daniel. "Marcus Garvey and His Relation to (Black) Socialism and Communism." *American Communist History* 12, no. 2 (June 2018): 200–219.

Harris, Jessica C. "Revolutionary Black Nationalism: The Black Panther Party." *Journal of Negro History* 86, no. 3 (Summer 2001): 409–421.

Harrold, Stanley. "On the Borders of Slavery and Race: Charles T. Torrey and the Underground Railroad." *Journal of the Early Republic* 20, no. 2 (Summer 2000): 273–292.

Hawkins, Homer C. "Trends in Black Migration from 1863 to 1960." *Phylon* 34, no. 2 (Second Quarter 1973): 148–152.

Hay, Amy M. "Recipe for Disaster: Motherhood and Citizenship at Love Canal." *Journal of Women's History* 21 (Spring 2009): 111–134.

———. "A New Earthly Vision: Religious Community Activism in the Love Canal Chemical Disaster." *Environmental History* 14, no. 3 (July 2009): 502–526.

Henderson, Donald H. "Causes of the Recent Negro Migration." *Journal of Negro History* 6 (October 1921): 410–420.

Henry, Charles P. "Who Won the Great Debate: Booker T. Washington or W. E. B. Du Bois?" *Crisis* 99 (1992): 12–17.

Hill, Laura Warren. "'We Are Black Folks First': The Black Freedom Struggle in Rochester, NY and the Making of Malcolm X." *The Sixties: A Journal of History, Politics and Culture* 3, no. 2 (2010): 163–185.

Hine, Darlene C. "Black Professionals and Race Consciousness: Origins of the Civil Rights Movement, 1890–1950." *Journal of American History* 89, no. 4 (March 2003): 1279–1294.

Hine, Darlene C. "Carter G. Woodson, White Philanthropy and Negro Historiography." *History Teacher* 19, no. 3 (May 1986): 405–425.

Hines, Revathi, I. "African Americans' Struggle for Environmental Justice and the Case of the Shintech Plant: Lessons Learned from a War Waged." *Journal of Black Studies* 31, no. 6 (July 2001): 777–789.

Holden, Constance. "Love Canal Residents Under Stress." *Science, New Series* 208, no. 4449 (June 13, 1980): 1242–1244.

Holland, Scott. "So Many Good Voices in My Head," *Cross Currents* 49, no. 1 (Spring 1999): 72–83.

Holt, Sharon Ann. "Making Freedom Pay: Freedpeople Working for Themselves, North Carolina, 1865–1900." *Journal of Southern History* 60 (May 1994): 229–262.

Holt, William, and Donald Celmer. "Photo Essay: Urban Renewal in the Model City." *Context* 2, no. 4 (Fall 2003): 50–57.
Howard-Pitney, David. "The Jeremiads of Frederick Douglass, Booker T. Washington, and W. E. B. Du Bois and Changing Patterns of Black Messianic Rhetoric, 1841–1920." *Journal of American Ethnic History* 6 (Fall 1986): 47–61.
Hudson-Weems, Clenora, "Resurrecting Emmett Till: The Catalyst of the Modern Civil Rights Movement." *Journal of Black Studies* 29, no. 2 (November 1998): 179–188.
Irvine, R. W., and J. J. Irvine, "The Impact of the Desegregation Process on the Education of Black Students: Key Variables." *Journal of Negro Education* 52 (1983): 410–422.
Jarrett, Robin L. "Successful Parenting in High-Risk Neighborhoods." *Future of Children* 9, no. 2 (Autumn 1999): 45–50.
Johnson, Charles. "Negroes in the Railway Industry: Part II." *Phylon (1940–1956)* 3, no. 2 (Second Quarter 1942): 196–205.
Karenga, Maulana. "The Crisis of Black Middle Class Leadership: A Critical Analysis." *Black Scholar* 13, no. 6 (Fall 1982): 16–32.
Katz, William Loren. "Black History in Secondary Schools." *Journal of Negro Education* 38, no. 4 (Autumn 1969): 430–434.
Kelleher, Daniel T. "The Case of Lloyd Lionel Gaines: The Demise of the Separate but Equal Doctrine," *Journal of Negro History* 56, no. 4 (October 1971): 262–271.
Kersten, Andrew E. "African Americans and World War II." *OAH Magazine of History* 16, no. 3 (Spring 2002): 13–17.
Kindsvatter, Richard H., and William W. Wilen. "The Dilemma of Racial Imbalance in the Schools." *American Secondary Education* 4, no. 4 (September 1974): 29–33.
Knapp, Melvin J., and Jon P. Alston. "White Parental Acceptance of Varying Degrees of School Desegregation: 1965 and 1970." *Public Opinion Quarterly* 36, no. 4 (Winter 1972–1973): 585–591.
Krech, Shepard, III. "Black Family Organization in the Nineteenth Century: An Ethnological Perspective." *Journal of Interdisciplinary History* 12 (Winter 1982): 429–452.
Kuo, Wen H. "Mayoral Influence in Urban Policy Making." *American Journal of Sociology* 79, no. 3 (November 1973): 620–638.
Landon, David B., and Teresa D. Bulger. " 'Constructing Community': Experiences of Identity, Economic Opportunity, and Institution Building at Boston's African Meeting House." *International Journal of Historical Archaeology* 17, no. 1 (March 2013): 119–142.
Larson, Kate Clifford. "Racing for Freedom: Harriet Tubman's Underground Railroad Network Through New York." *Afro-Americans in New York Life and History* 36 (January 2012): 7–33.

Longshore, Douglas, and Jeffrey Prager. "The Impact of School Desegregation: A Situational Analysis." *Annual Review of Sociology* 11 (1985): 75-91.
MacMaster, Richard K., "Henry Highland Garnet and the African Civilization Society." *Journal of Presbyterian History* 48, no. 2 (Summer 1970): 95-112.
Mangion, Carmen. "Community Voices and 'Community Scripts.'" *Studies: An Irish Quarterly Review* 107, no. 427 (Autumn 2018): 302-313.
Marks. Carole. "Black Workers and the Great Migration." *Phylon* 46, no. 2 (Second Quarter 1985): 148-161.
Marullo, Sam. "The Migration of Blacks to the North 1911-1918," *Journal of Black Studies* 15, no. 3 (March 1985): 291-306.
McCluskey, Audrey Thomas. "Multiple Consciousness in the Leadership of Mary McLeod Bethune." *NWSA Journal* 6, no. 1 (Spring 1994): 69-81.
McGrew, Teron. "The History of Residential Segregation in the Unites States and Title VIII." *Black Scholar* 27, no. 2 (Summer 1997): 22-30.
McIntyre, Wallace. "Niagara Falls Power Redevelopment," *Economic Geography* 8, no. 3 (July 1952): 261-273.
Meier, August, and John H. Bracey, Jr. "The NAACP as a Reform Movement, 1909-1965: 'To Reach the Conscience of America.'" *Journal of Southern History* 59, no. 1 (February 1993): 3-30.
Middleton, Stephen. "The Fugitive Slave Crisis in Cincinnati, 1850-1860: Resistance, Enforcement, and Black Refugees." *Journal of Negro History* 72, no. 1/2 (Winter-Spring, 1987): 20-32.
Mithum, Jacqueline S. "Cooperation and Solidarity as Survival Necessities in a Black Urban Community." *Urban Anthropology* 2, no. 1 (Spring 1973): 25-34.
Modell, John Marc Goulden, and Sigurdur Magnusson. "World War II in the Lives of Black Americans: Some Findings and Interpretation." *Journal of American History* 76, no. 3 (December 1989): 838-848.
Mohamed, Elaine R. "It Takes a Whole Village to Raise a Child," *Peabody Journal of Education* 71, no. 1 (1996): 57-63.
"More Letters of Negro Migrants of 1916-1918." *Journal of Negro History* 4 (October 1919): 412-465.
Nelson, William E., Jr. "School Desegregation and the Black Community." *Theory into Practice* 26 (December 1987): 450-458.
Newman, Richard. "Making Environmental Politics: Women and Love Canal Activism." *Women's Studies Quarterly* 29, no. 1/2 (Spring-Summer, 2001): 65-84.
Norrell, Robert J. "Booker T. Washington: Understanding the Wizard of Tuskegee." *Journal of Blacks in Higher Education* 42 (Winter 2003-2004): 96-109.
Pitre, Merline. "Frederick Douglass: The Politician vs. the Social Reformer." *Phylon (1960-)* 40, no. 3 (Third Quarter 1979): 270-277.
Poxpey, C. Spencer. "The Washington—Du Bois Controversy and Its Effect on the Negro Problem." *History of Education Journal* 8 (1957): 128-152.

Puttkammer, Charles W., and Ruth Worthy. "William Monroe Trotter, 1872–1934." *Journal of Negro History* 43, no. 4 (October 1958): 306–307.

Reddick, L. D. "Carter G. Woodson (1875–1950): An Appreciation." *Phylon* 11, no. 2 (Second Quarter, 1950): 177–179.

Reed, Rodney J. "School Boards, the Community, and School Desegregation." *Journal of Black Studies* 13, no. 2 (December 1982): 189–206.

"The Reluctance of Black People to Participate in Clinical Medical Research." *Journal of Blacks in Higher Education* 17 (Autumn 1997): 33–34.

Rich, Marvin. "The Congress of Racial Equality and Its Strategy." *Annals of the American Academy of Political and Social Science* 357 (January 1965): 113–118.

Richardson, Jean. "Buffalo's Antebellum African American Community and the Fugitive Slave Law of 1859." *Afro-Americans in New York Life and History* 27 (July 2003): 29–46.

Scott, Emmett J. "Letters of Negro Migrants of 1916–1918," *Journal of Negro History* 4 (July 1919): 290–340.

Sheppard, Si. "If It Wasn't for Roosevelt You Wouldn't Have This Job: The Politics of Patronage and the 1936 Presidential Election in New York." *New York History* 95, no. 1 (Winter 2014): 41–69.

Siener, William H., and Thomas A. Chambers. "Harriet Tubman, the Underground Railroad, and the Bridges at Niagara Falls." *Afro-Americans in New York Life and History* 36 (January 2012): 34–63.

Skrentny, John David. "The Effects of the Cold War on African American Civil Rights: American and the World Audience, 1945–1968," *Theory and Society* 27, no. 2 (April 1998): 237–285.

Slater, Robert Bruce. "The American Colleges That Led the Abolition Movement." *Journal of Blacks in Higher Education* 9 (Autumn 1995): 95–97.

Smith, Charles U. "Public School Desegregation and the Law." *Social Forces* 54, no. 2 (December 1975): 317–327.

Spero, Andrea McEvoy. "Human Rights: By Any Means Necessary." *OAH Magazine of History* 22, no. 2 (April 2008): 39–45.

Steele, Eric. "A Conspiracy Afoot? The Sham of Urban Renewal." *Umoja Sasa* (October–November 1980): 8–9.

Stukas, Arthur A., Jr. "Principled Stands against Racism." *Race, Gender and Class* 13, no. 1/2 (2006): 108–123.

Swezey, Kenneth M. "Nikola Tesla," *Science* 127, no. 3307 (May 1958): 1147–1159.

Taylor, Robert Joseph, and Linda M. Chatters. "Importance of Religion and Spirituality in the Lives of African Americans." *Journal of Negro Education* 79, no. 3 (Summer 2010): 280–294.

Thomas, June Manning. "Urban Displacement: Fruits of a History of Collusion." *Black Scholar* 11, no. 2 (November–December 1979): 68–77.

Thompson Fullilove, Mindy. "Root Shock: The Consequences of African American Dispossession." *Journal of Urban Health* 78, no. 1 (March 2001): 72–80.

Tipton, Robert C. "The Fisk Jubilee Singers." *Tennessee Historical Quarterly* 29, no. 1 (Spring 1970): 42–48.
Tolnay, Stewart E. "The African American 'Great Migration' and Beyond." *Annual Review of Sociology* 29 (2003): 209–232.
Trotter, Joe William, Jr. "The Great Migration." *OAH Magazine of History* 17, no. 1 (October 2002): 31–33.
Trust for Public Land. "Healing America's Cities: How Urban Parks Can Make Cities Safe and Healthy." *Children's Environments* 12, no. 1 (March 1995): 65–70.
Tyler, Lawrence. "The Protestant Ethic among the Black Muslims." *Phylon* 27, no. 1 (Spring 1966): 5–14.
"Urban Renewal: Acquisition of Redevelopment Property by Eminent Domain." *Duke Law Journal* 1964, no. 1 (Winter 1964): 123–138.
Wanderer, Jules J. "1967 Riots: A Test of the Congruity of Events." *Social Problems* 16, no. 2 (Autumn 1968): 193–198.
Watson, Denton L. "Assessing the Role of the NAACP in the Civil Rights Movement." *Historian* 55, no. 3 (Spring 1993): 453–468.
Weaver, Robert C. "Employment in the Aircraft Industry." *Quarterly Journal of Economics* 59, no. 4 (August 1945): 597–625.
Wellman, Judith. "This Side of the Border: Fugitives from Slavery in Three Central New York Communities." *New York History* 79, no. 4 (October 1998): 359–392.
Weyeneth, Robert R. "The Architecture of Racial Segregation: The Challenges of Preserving the Problematical Past." *Public Historian* 27, no. 4 (Fall 2005): 11–44.
Williams, J. Allen, Jr. "The Effects of Urban Renewal Upon a Black Community: Evaluation and Recommendations." *Social Science Quarterly* 50, no. 3 (December 1969): 703–712.
Williams, Lillian S. "Attica Prisoners Seek Aid from the N.A.A.C.P., 1932." *Afro-Americans in New York Life and History* 1 (1977): 211–212.
Wolf, Eleanor P., and Charles N. Lebeaux. "On the Destruction of Poor Neighborhoods by Urban Renewal." *Social Problems* 15, no. 1 (Summer 1967): 3–8.
Woodward, Jennifer R. "How Busing Burdened Blacks: Critical Race Theory and Busing for Desegregation in Nashville-Davidson County." *Journal of Negro Education* 80, no. 1 (Winter 2011): 22–32.
Wurst, Lou Ann. "Human Accumulation: Class and Tourism." *International Journal of Historical Archaeology* 15, no. 2 (June 2011): 254–266.

Recorded Interviews

Beaman, Henry. Personal interview, June 12, 2010.
Boling, Zorie Bell. Personal interview, August 8, 2008.

Boyer, Herman (Chuck), Jr. Personal interview, August 14, 2017.
Bradberry, Roosevelt. Personal interview, May 19, 2010.
Coates, Rosie. Personal interview, July 2, 1981.
Coates-Smith, Renee. Personal interview, March 29, 2010.
Cunningham, Ronnie. Personal interview, August 22, 2017.
Dyett (Lovell), Ernest. Personal interview, February 20, 2010.
Feder, William. Personal interview, June 18, 2015.
Hamilton, Eugene. Personal interview, August 4, 2007.
Hooper, Michael. Personal interview, August 23, 2017.
Hunt, Emma Jean. Personal interview, April 8, 2010.
Hunt, Wilbur. Personal interview, April 10, 2010.
King, Edwardo. Personal interview, April 10, 2010.
———. Personal interview, April 7, 2010.
Madison, Willie Thomas. Personal interview, March 9, 2010.
Martin, Indiana. Personal interview, August 12, 2009.
McCoy, Joe. Personal interview, April 5, 2010.
———. Personal interview, April 11, 2010.
McDowell, Nathaniel. Personal interview, May 13, 2010.
Mesiah, Frank. Personal interview, March 18, 2010.
Miller, Carlyle. Personal interview, August 2, 2008.
———. Personal interview, January 15, 2010.
———. Personal interview, July 10, 2010.
Morrison, Wilma. Personal interview, June 30, 2002.
O'Neal, Joe. Personal interview, March 20, 2010.
Palmore, Eddie. Personal interview, March 29, 2010.
———. Personal interview, April 5, 2010.
Phelps, Otis. Personal interview, May 25, 2010.
Ray, Arthur. Personal interview, May 24, 2002.
———. Personal interview, August 2, 2008.
———. Personal interview, April 24, 2010.
———. Personal interview, April 25, 2010.
———. Personal interview, June 27, 2010.
———. Personal interview, July 3, 2010.
———. Personal interview, July 13, 2010.
———. Personal interview, July 21, 2010.
Reed-McBride, Helen. Personal interview, March 9, 2010.
Samuel Hershey. Personal interview, August 2, 2008.
———. Personal interview, July 10, 2010.
Shareef, Jabril. Personal interview, March 7, 2010.
Simmons, Gene. Personal interview, May 17, 2010.
Smith, Barbara. Personal interview, May 17, 2002.
———. Personal interview, January 16, 2010.

———. Personal interview, May 18, 2010.
Smith, Mable A. Personal interview, May 15, 2010.
Tannehill, Tomas. Personal interview, June 16, 2010.
Tyler, Minnie. Personal interview, May 22, 2010.
Walker, James. Personal interview, May 17, 2010.
Williams, Barbara. Personal interview, March 14, 2010.
Williamson, Barbara. Personal interview, May 2, 2015.
———. Personal interview, August 17, 2015.
Williamson, Bill. Personal interview, January 30, 2010.
———. Personal interview, May 2, 2015.
———. Personal interview, August 17, 2015.
Williamson, Thelma. Personal interview, May 2, 2015.
———. Personal interview, August 17, 2015.
Williamson, Theodore. Personal interview, May 13, 2002.
———. Personal interview, August 8, 2009.
———. Personal interview, January 22, 2010.
———. Personal interview, January 23, 2010.

Index

Abate, Harry F., 210
Abramowitz, Morton H., 272
Acheson, Dr. Edward G., 52
Acosta, John W., 215
Africans: movements for independence by, 168–69
African Americans, 2; advancement of, 77, 78, 100, 117–21, 167, 294–95; and the church, 71; and Communism, 321n20; contributions to America, 79, 168, 187, 200, 201; divisions among, 48; European perceptions of, 110; and employment, 54, 157; entrepreneurialism among, 8, 31f, 115, 120, 127; fight for equal status, 167–68; foodways of, 125, 148; and "ghettos," 6, 54, 189, 194, 335n21; growing population of in US, 48; historiography of, 3, 7, 8; housing discrimination against, 12, 123, 133–34, 143, 189–90; job discrimination against, 189–90; and the "politics of respectability," 9, 48–49, 99, 129, 133, 158, 241, 295; population shifts among, 55, 124–27; racism against, 43, 292, 333n176; recreational activities among, 102, 191–92; and the United Nations, 168; and White American culture, 292; Whites' misconceptions of, 201
"African American market," 320n13
African American urban studies, 31; and intragroup relations, 74; and *Blacks in Niagara Falls*, 3, 6, 8–9, 295–96; and community formation, 297; and the First Great Migration, 123
African Canadians, 7
Afro-Americans in New York Life and History (journal), 1, 3
"Aunty Lee," 42
Akers, Wendel O., 127
Albond, Harvey N., 252, 253
Allen, James E., Jr., 206, 214, 225, 237, 239, 240
Allen MacKenna Avenue project, 246–50
Allen, Richard, 178
Anderson, Pristell, 148
Anderson, Robert, 274
Anglin, Milton, 210
Ashely, Eddie L., 211
Ashford, Emmett, 132, 310

Baker, William, 64
Baldwin, James, 250

Baldwin, Mary H., 148
Banks, Reverend James, 130–31, 179, 246, 248
Banneker, Benjamin, 107
Barkley-Brown, Elsa, 102
Barton, Reverend Donald B., 72, 74, 89, 315
Barton, Sally, 17
Bash, L. Paul, 129
Bates, Daisy, 173
Baugh, Florence, 238, 241
Beckwith, Byron de la, 183
Bell, Zorie, 56
Belw, B., 64
Bennett, Charlette, 178
Berlin, Ira, 1
Bethune, Dr. Mary M., 78, 147
Bibb, Henry, 80
Billingsley, Andrew, 44, 71
Black Bangor: African Americans in a Maine Community, 1880–1950 (Lee), 8
Black Chicago: The Making of a Negro Ghetto, 1890 to 1920 (Spear), 8
Black churches (in Niagara Falls), 29, 77, 82, 295–96, 310; activism by, 175; Black Baptists, 31–32; as historical repositories, 6; as community hubs, 31; role in Black community, 71–72, 113–14, 121, 296; and spiritual belief, 115
Black Coalition, 221–22
Black Employee Club, 203, 266–67, 383n137
"Black Leadership Typologies Continuum" (Ladd), 293
Black Milwaukee: The Making of an Industrial Proletariat, 1915–45 (Trotter), 7
Black Niagarans, 3–4, 28–29, 88, 148–49; activism by, 10–11, 95, 129, 135–36, 162–63, 165, 179, 192–96, 203–204, 243, 271, 283–85, 294; alliances with non-Black Niagarans, 11, 17–18, 22, 43, 95, 117, 121, 128, 161–62, 164, 167, 172, 177–78, 180, 185, 186, 187, 265, 324n24; in the antebellum era, 18; anti-slavery activism among, 49; arrival and settlement in Niagara Falls, 10–13, 41, 54–61, 72, 81–82, 92, 125–30, 142–44, 148, 152, 154, 160–61, 164, 295, 296; on the Board of Education, 236–37; citizenship rights of, 9, 16–17, 129; "clustering" of, 6–7, 72, 82, 85, 91–92, 101–102, 130–32, 134–35, 138–43, 151, 180, 207, 239, 243–44, 246–48, 249, 250, 287–89, 295, 299, 308; daily life among, 39, 72; demographics of, 2, 18, 22, 29, 34, 35, 44–45, 48–49, 51, 55, 65–66, 81, 82, 90–91, 104, 120, 124–25, 134, 142; economic/social aspirations of, 11, 12, 55, 102, 114–15, 120, 152, 155–56, 167, 285, 294; economic status of, 63, 80, 114–15, 174, 193; and education (as desideratum), 70, 100, 102, 114, 120, 152, 156, 163, 303; and the education system, 12, 15, 45, 70, 101, 156, 167–68, 205–42; and employment, 22–29, 51–58, 62–65, 72, 73, 78, 81, 82, 87–88, 93, 95, 112, 116, 117–18, 120, 125–27, 130, 150–52, 154, 157, 160, 164, 175–76, 191, 193, 255, 291–92, 295, 299, 305, 307, 309; entrepreneurship among, 61, 62, 63, 66, 89, 92, 116, 120, 127, 129, 132, 151, 161–62, 164, 277, 287, 309, 310, 385n201; family dynamics of, 44, 65–70, 151–53, 290–92; family networks among, 57, 290–91; fighting spirit of, 9, 10, 102, 149, 160, 294, 297;

Index | 433

flourishing of, 49, 51, 53, 65, 83, 95; growth of community, 7, 18, 25, 29–33, 81, 82, 83, 85–88, 91, 94, 104, 120–21, 124–25, 128, 132, 135, 138, 141–43, 151, 165, 179, 203, 207, 243, 257–58, 269, 293, 295, 296, 303, 307, 313; historiography of, 1–4, 6, 295, 320n16; and home ownership, 5, 142–43, 156–58, 160, 309–10, 311–12; and housing, 3, 25, 57–59, 62, 66, 72, 81–82, 91–93, 95–96, 130, 132–33, 138, 142, 157, 161, 175, 192, 216, 221, 299–300, 308; housing discrimination against, 12, 51, 82, 89, 123, 130, 134–38, 142–43, 154, 161, 165, 167–68, 175, 180–81, 189, 193, 198–200, 205–206, 228, 238, 243, 247, 248, 282, 287–88, 293, 294, 295; illiteracy among, 70; job discrimination against, 117, 149, 167–68, 176–77, 189, 191, 193, 198–200, 228, 31; in leadership roles, 9–11, 24, 28–29, 32, 43–44, 48–49, 53, 55, 61, 68, 72, 73, 74, 76, 85, 88, 89, 90, 93–96, 99, 100, 106–107, 111, 119, 121, 123, 128, 148, 157, 163, 164, 167–68, 173, 177, 198, 203, 260, 268, 273, 276, 285, 292–94, 300, 314–18, 320–21n20; integrationist spirit of, 73–74, 78, 82–83, 95, 99, 121, 123, 128, 129–30, 167, 173, 213, 271, 294, 315–18; and leisure travel, 45; and the March on Washington, 178; marginal status of, 34, 48, 49, 65, 81, 98, 146, 389n248; marital status of, 65–66; marriage to Canadians, 45–46; police mistreatment of, 35–36, 103, 174, 190, 193, 200; population data on, 18, 19, 20, 29, 41, 60, 63, 80, 82, 124–25, 138; population distribution of, 101–102, 130–32, 134–35, 138–43, 145, 151, 180, 207, 239, 243, 287, 295; poverty among, 62, 80, 86, 93, 95–96, 102, 112–13, 132–33, 135–36, 188, 193, 246, 264, 291, 311; racial pride among, 120, 271, 388–89n248; recreational activities among, 102, 104, 131–33, 151, 157–58, 192–93, 196–98, 265–67, 312; and "self-determinism," 11–12; shrinking of community, 27, 277, 287; solidarity among, 19–20, 22, 35–36, 43, 49, 56, 68, 72, 79–80, 86, 89, 100, 102, 104, 107, 113–14, 116–17, 127, 149, 162–63, 290, 294–95, 297, 310; and "slum clearance," 245–48, 250, 268, 272; and slum creation, 258–59; and sporting teams, 95; stable family/professional lives of, 151–52, 163, 164; tension/conflict among, 143, 150–51, 153, 195, 268; and tourist trade, 62, 132; as a voting bloc, 48

Black Pioneers of Niagara Falls: author's involvement with, 5, 296; mission of, 4, 388–89n248; and Taylor Branch, 306n25

Black workers: in Niagara Falls, 24; population of in US, 25, 28, 87

Blacks in Niagara Falls (book): conceptual framework of, 9, 294, 320n16; genesis of, 1–3; emphasis of, 6; research methodology of, 3, 7–9, 294–96, 299–301, 303, 305, 319n2, 340n152

Black Masons of Niagara Falls, 43
Black Power movement, 194, 200
Black Women's Club Movement, 38
Blassingame, John, 1, 44
Blumenthal, Ralph, 183
Bolden, Benjamin W., 60–62, 72, 73, 74, 89, 121, 280; as community

Bolden, Benjamin W. *(continued)*
  leader, 311, 315; activism of, 137–38, 173; and the NF Community Center, 310
Boling, Zorie Bell, 82, 91, 125, 296; on Black families in NF, 292; and the Black Pioneers, 388–89n248; family history of, 56, 59–60; and the Jordan Garden housing project, 249
Bond, Bloneva, 5, 154, 165, 240, 268, 276, 316, 386–87n215; and the Attica prison uprising, 274–76; on Martin Luther King, Jr., 196; and the NAACP, 174, 178–80, 203, 235–36, 260–61, 263, 353n33; on the Nation of Islam, 173–74; and the Niagara Community Center, 128–29; arrival in Niagara Falls, 126, 128; personality of, 278; on urban renewal, 256, 261–62
Bond, Harwood, 125, 165, 178, 193, 205, 240, 316; as NAACP president, 179–80, 203, 211, 235, 253, 353n33; and school desegregation, 207, 217, 235
Booth, Dr. Clayburn, 180
Boutwell, Albert, 184–85
Bowman, Francis D., 117
Boyer, George K., 270
Boys' Handicraft Club, the, 95
Bradberry, Ramona, 177
Bradberry, Roosevelt, 240
Bradberry, William: advice for author (Boston), 3, 5; and segregation, 247–48
Bradley, Reverend James M., 181
Bridges, Earl, Jr., 180
Brinson, Reverend Arthur L., Sr., 55, 311
Brinson, Marie, 55, 311

British Methodist Episcopal Church, 45
Brooks, William, 81, 264, 267–69, 271, 293, 318
Brown, Alma, 276, 277
Brown, Arthur, 28–29
Brown, Benny, 160
Brown, Charles, 41
Brown, Elijah, 105
Brown, Fred, 203, 211–12, 240, 276–77, 318, 385n201; vision of NF's renewal, 277–78
Brown, Gertrude, 41
Brown, Maggie, 64
Brown, Michael, 281
Brown v. Board of Education, 203, 241
Bradberry, Roosevelt, 240
Bryan, William Jennings, 38–39
Bryant, Turner, 92, 163
Bryant, William, 64
Brydges, Earl W., Jr., 183, 219
Buchalski, Mathew V., 229, 232
"Bucket of Blood" (bar), 133
Buckford, William, 106
Buffalo (NY), 21; Black population of, 330n115; desegregation of schools, 237–39, 241; racial boundaries in, 239–40; racial unrest in, 196
Bullock, Dr. Benjamin F., 172–73, 289–90, 292
Butler, Al, 192–93
Butler, William F., 30
Byrd, Irene, 110

Campbell, James, 23
Canada, 102; as destination for fugitive slaves, 17, 20, 21, 27, 30, 36, 80, 294; fugitive slave communities in, 16, 80; interracial mixing in, 80–81; racism in, 27, 80; segregation in, 80

Canes, F., 64
Caprio, James R., 229, 236
Carborundum Corporation, 117, 124, 127, 152, 159, 219, 248, 250, 277; hiring of Blacks, 52, 125–26, 150, 308, 311; racism at, 150, 158–59
Carlo, Reverend Joseph, 228
Carmichael, Frank, 176
Carr, Alexander, 178
Carr, Judge J. D., 135
Carter, Robert L., 187
Cassey, 14–15
Catalano, Michael, 230
Cataract House (hotel), 20, 23
"Cathcart," 14
Cayton, Horace R., 161
Center Court (housing project), 132, 151, 157, 160, 312
Chang, Li Hung, 23
Cheatham, Almed, 132, 310
Cheatham, Harold E., 291
Childs, W. H., 14
Chille, Joseph, 207, 221, 229, 230
civil rights (pre-1950s), 46, 147, 226; activism on behalf of, 36, 129, 142, 165, 177; advancement of, 150; hopes for, 38
Civil Rights Act, the, 197, 287
Civil Rights League, Inc., 135
civil rights movement, the, 2, 9, 142, 175, 179, 180, 247; birth of, 115, 167, 203, 269; Black Niagarans' involvement in, 5–6, 12, 142, 165, 167–72, 175–76, 178, 180–83, 185–87, 203–204; impact of, 150, 200, 203, 295; inspiration for, 169; tactics of, 171, 184, 187, 269–70
Civil War, the, 16, 20, 23, 29, 34, 109, 202
Clark, Mildred C., 88
Clark, James, 186

Clarke, John Henrik, 1
Clay, Reverend Millard Fillmore, 156–57, 179, 317
Cloud, John, 185
Coates-Smith, Renee, 290–91, 297
Cody, Carol D., 216
Cold War, the, 9
Coleman, Elizabeth Brown, 41, 69
Coles, Robert, 202
Collins, Addie Mae, 184
Collins, Daniel, 261, 265
Collins, William F., 206–207, 229
Colonel P., 14–15, 49, 314
Colored Dance, 30
Colored Merchants Association (CMA), 119–20
Colored Republicans, 29–30
Community Chest, the, 72–74, 78, 144
Congress of Racial Equality (CORE), 188; and housing discrimination, 180; and job discrimination, 176–78, 277; and education reform, 239
Conklin, Seth, 22
Connor, Theophilus Eugene, 184
Cook, Barbara, 178
Cook, Eugene, 127
Council of Mother's Club, 115
Covatta, Richard L., 220
Cowart, Otis, 176–77, 181, 186, 316
Cronin, Joseph, 47
Cross, John, 185
Cunningham, Ronnie, 287, 317
Current, Gloster, 179
Curto, Ernest, 93
Czolgosz, Leon, 34

D., Robert, 64
Daily Cataract-Journal, 33
Daly, John, 284

Daniels, Alexander, 106–107
Daniels, John, Sr., 149, 152
Davis, Alphonso, 105
Davis, Angela, 321n20
Davis, Ariel, 178
Davis, Ben, 14, 18
Davis, Deacon W. B., 71, 117
Davis, Helen, 178
Davis, Olivia, 178
Davis, T. R., 163
Davis, W. H., 116, 119
Death and Life of Great American Cities, The (Jacobs), 251
Delany, Martin R., 321n20
Democratic Party: Black Niagarans' attitude toward, 48, 109, 270: Blacks' disdain for, 108–109: Blacks' support for, 107–108; and Black interests, 39
Denton, Nancy A., 248
DePriest, Oscar, 108
Desegregation of NF schools, 244, 260, 262; Blacks' frustration over, 209–11, 214, 216, 221–22, 234–35, 241–42; implementation of, 211, 223–24, 229–30, 237, 242; postponement of, 220–22; progress toward, 214, 223, 229–34, 237–38; proposals regarding, 206–10, 216–29; teachers' responses to, 230–31, 233; unforeseen consequences of, 230; Whites' cooperation with, 222, 227–28, 230–31; Whites' resistance to, 215–19, 226–27, 230, 232, 241
Dett, Arthur, 30
Dett, Charlotte, 23–25, 28, 30, 37, 89, 113; and Black tourism, 62; as gadfly/engagé, 48–49, 75, 96, 111–12, 314; leadership style of, 295; political involvement by, 31, 39, 99, 109; trip to Europe, 110

Dett, Harriet, 30
Dett, R. Nathaniel, 2, 45, 75; achievements of, 88; as actor in NAACP drama, 187; grief over mother's death, 112; and Negro spirituals, 23, 30; renown as musician, 75, 89, 109–11
Dett, Robert, 23–24, 30, 32–33, 112
Dett, Samuel, 24, 88–89, 110–12, 121, 315
De Veaux School, 146–47, 181
Dick, Rabbi Irvin, 228
Dietz, William, 136
Diggs, Ulysses, 178
Doerr, John H., 230
Double V-Campaign, 125
Douglass, Frederick, 75; on power, 242;
and the Republican Party, 38; and the Underground Railroad, 14, 17
Douglass, James, 43
Drake, St. Clair, 161
Drew, Benjamin, 42
Du Bois, W. E. B., 6; influence of, 77–78, 117; leadership traits of, 94; and the Niagara Movement, 36, 38, 179; on racial advancement, 79, 94–95, 100, 121, 153, 321n20; research methods of, 73, 294; support for William Howard Taft, 46–47; support for Woodrow Wilson, 46, 48
Dunbar, Paul Laurence, 75, 187
Dyett, Ernest, 146–47
Dyett, Florence Lovell, 146–47

Earl W. Bridges Public Library, 2
Echols, Diane, 178
Echols, Reverend Walter M., 186
Edward Dean Adams Power Plant, 26–27, 33

Electric City Lodge No. 49, 29, 43, 95, 120, 130, 279
Ellis, Eugene, 72
Ellis, Vivian, 110
Emancipation Day Celebration, 102–103, 310
Emmanuel Baptist Church of Niagara Falls, 130, 156–57, 178
Erias, Bo, 236
Ethnic Enterprise in America (Light), 294–95
Eve, Arthur O., 275
Evers, Charles, 183–84
Evers, Medgar, 183

Fairfield, John, 22
Farrakhan, Louis, 275
Faulk, Bertha, 137
Fayette, Anderson, 23, 24, 28, 30, 64
Fayette, Henry, 23, 24, 43
Feder, William, 86
Federation of Colored Women's Clubs, 49
Ferguson, Washington, 332n149
Fields, Willie C., Sr., 127, 317, 385–85n201
Fiener, Matthew, 253
Fillman, John, 109
Fillmore, Millard, 18, 23
First Presbyterian Church of Niagara Falls, 111
Fisher, William, 106
Fisk University, 96
First Great Migration, 8, 12, 55–58, 71, 125, 127, 130, 293
Flakes, Josephine, 69
Flanagan, Matthew P., 189, 253
Flay, Frank, 271
Ford, Frederick, 119
Fordham, Monroe, 1, 3
Franklin, John Hope, 1

Franz, T., 23
Frazier, E. Franklin, 44, 291
Friendship House, 196–98, 203, 266, 303; support for NF school integration, 227
Frisch, Dr. Michael, 4
Fugitive Slave Act(s), 18–19
fugitive slaves: courage of, 22; in Canada, 42; in Niagara Falls, 18–22, 294, 296; in upstate NY, 21; risks undertaken by, 20–21; scholarship on, 21–22

Gabriel, Anna, 89–90, 131, 310
Gainor, Guy, 178
Gallagher, Bill, 274
Gara, Larry, 294
Garey, Robert, 163
Garey, W. A., 109
Garnet, Henry Highland, 321n20
Garrison, William Lloyd, 179
Garvey, Marcus Mosiah, 102–103, 321n20
George, David K., 229
Gibbs, Lois, 281–82
Gillespie, Dizzy, 158
Gipson, Charles, 178
Glad, Priscilla, 76
Goat Island, 41
Goffeng, Rudolph, 310
Goodman, Bernard, 258
Gottlieb, Peter, 127
Grant, Ulysses S., 23
Greenberg, Jack, 187
Griffin, Aaron L., 165, 268, 317; on integration, 173; on the Nation of Islam, 174; and the Niagara Community Center, 98, 128–29, 163, 197, 278–80, 311, 386–87n215; and the Unity Park project, 253
Griffon Manor, 142, 282–84

Grisby, Romania L., 76
Grossman, Stanley, 270–71
Gutman, Herbert, 44, 291

Hall, Jacquelyn Dow, 167, 295
Hall, Prince, 43, 332n157
Hallin, Reverend Ray, 220–21, 229
Hamilton, Eugene, 4–5, 157, 164, 296
Hampton Institute, 96, 109
Hard Times (Terkel), 85
Harlan, Ashlan, 258
Harlan, Louis R., 1
Harlem: The Making of a Ghetto (Osofsky), 6–7
Harlem Renaissance, 73
Harper, Frances Watkins, 187
Harriet Tubman Club, the, 95, 120
Harris, Charlotte, 5
Harrison, J. Bradley, 229
Hart, George, 3, 296
Hart, Reid, 193–94
Hatchet (Reverend), 33
Haugabook, Elizata, 178
Hayes, Alice C., 121, 129, 165, 240, 315; advocacy for Black Niagarans, 386–87n215; and the civil rights struggle, 186–87; and the Community Center, 97; and the Community Action Program, 188–89; eadership style of, 295
Hayes, Dr. Charles B., 97–99, 116, 121, 127, 151, 163, 240, 315; as NAACP president, 179
Haynes, Austin, 106–107
Henry F. Abate School, 153
Henson, Josiah, 22, 80
Higginbotham, Evelyn Brooks, 48
Hillis, Ann, 281
Hobbs, Galleon, 35–36, 43, 49
Holloman, Frank W., 116
Holloway, Reverend Luther, 71, 82
Hoover, Herbert, 107
Hoover, J. Edgar, 184

Hoskins (Deacon), 71
Holsey, Albon L., 119
Howard, Ruby, 265
Hudson, Reverend William S., 146–47
Huff, Reverend Edgar, 178, 181, 185–86, 193, 271, 308, 317, 363n98
Hughes, Langston, 187
Hunt, Wilbur, 3
Hunt, William, 81–82, 91
Hyde Park Village, 132–36, 140, 143, 151, 156, 161, 282, 308

International Hotel, 22–23
Ireland, T. J., 116, 119, 121
Isom, Geraldine, 178
Isom, Hazel, 178
Isom, Jerry, 109
Isom, Mildred, 171, 296

Jackson, Ben, 14
Jackson, Chasa, 64
Jackson, Mary, 69
Jamal, Hakim, 321n20
Jarrett, Robin L., 290
Javits, Jacob K., 237
Jefferson, Jesse, 202
Jenss, Frank A., 117
Jim Crow, 34, 94
"Joe," 13–14, 323n5
Johnson, Annie, 79, 310
Johnson, Bertha, 308
Johnson, Donald C., 205, 217
Johnson, Fredrick, 116
Johnson, Gertrude, 63
Johnson, Jack, 137
Johnson, John, 55–56
Johnson, Lyndon B., 185, 188, 225, 365n44
Johnson, Maggie, 43
Johnson, Reverend B. B. B., 31–33, 315
Johnston, Reverend J. Donald, 186
Johnson, Reverend Sydney O. B., 118

Johnson, Reverend William H., 29, 72, 82
Johnson, Richard, 137
Jones, Agnes, 283
Jones, Anna, 310
Jones, Clarence, 275
Jones, Clover, 193–95, 198, 317; and NF school desegregation, 205–207
Jones, Georgia, 57
Jones, John J, 32
Jones, Leeland, 171–72
Jones, Peter, 46
Jordan, Harry S., 248
Jordon, Casper L., 240, 317; on desegregation, 205, 221; NAACP leadership, 179, 187–89, 209
Jordan Garden housing project, 248–59, 272
Jubilee Celebration (1900), 32–33
Judge Piper, 43–44
Junior Girls' Club, the, 95

Kalfas, Henry J., 216, 217, 221, 227, 229–30, 233
Karenga, Maulana, 321n20
Kedzie, John and Lemira, 17
Kennedy, John F, 185
Kennedy, Robert F., 188
Kimble, Renae, 274
King, Edwardo, 3
King, Dr. Martin Luther, Jr., 269, 360n25; assassination of, 195–98; "I Have a Dream" speech, 178; "Letter from a Birmingham Jail," 184; visit to Niagara Falls, 169–71, 196
Knights of Pythias, 68
Konitz, Lee, 158
Korpolinski, Walter, 106
Ku Klux Klan, 81

Lackey, E. Dent, 178, 180–81, 183, 186; and the Black museum, 202–203; on desegregation, 228–29; and the 1967 unrest in Niagara Falls, 191–93; on racial prejudice in NF, 196; and urban renewal, 245, 250–52, 254, 264, 274
Lafferty, James A., 135
Lalone (police officer), 35–36
Lane College, 109
Larke, Russell G., 93
Laster, Robert E., 278
Laughlin, Mayor William, 89
Layton, Azza Salama, 169
Lee, Donald, 193
Lee, Gideon, 42
Lee, Judge Thomas B., 117, 135
Lemke-Santangelo, Gretchen, 57
Level (Commissioner), 35
Lewis, Janie, 57
Lewis, H. H., 30
Liberty Line: The Legend of the Underground Railroad, The (Gara), 22
Life for Us Is What We Make It: Building Black Community in Detroit, 1915–1945 (Trotter), 7
Life of Josiah Henson, Formerly a Slave, The (Henson), 80
Lincoln, Abraham (evangelist), 43–44
Lincoln, Abraham (president), 23, 182; and the Emancipation Proclamation, 46; influence on Black Niagarans, 77–78; legacy among African Americans, 39
Lincoln, C. Eric, 71
Lincoln Institute, 109
Lindsey, Edward G., 144
Lingo, Anita, 260
Little, Frank, 43
Littlewood, Arnold, 257
Lodge 34 FM and AM, Free and Accepted Masons, 5
Long, Dr. Charles M., 226, 228

Lord, Please Don't Take Me in August: African Americans in Newport and Saratoga Springs, 1870–1930 (Young), 8
Love, Sylvia, 269

Mabry, George, 178
Magner (police officer), 35–36
Malcolm X, 167, 173
Mann, Geraldine, 210
Marable, James, 270
Mariano, Charlie, 158
Marigold Restaurant, 148
Marshall, William, Jr., 193
Marshall, Thurgood, 187
Martin, George, 25, 64
Martin, Indiana (aka Indiana Hunt), 75–76, 105, 113
Martin, Johnny and Pappy (brothers), 158
Martin, Sadie, 178
Martin, William, 116
Mary B. Talbert Club, the, 95
Mason, Ollie, 163
Massaro, Angelo, 265–66
Massey, Douglass S., 248
McCaskill, Reverend Randall, 261–64
McClain, Patricia, 178
McClendon, William F., 129–30
McConnaughey, Charles, 232
McConnaughey, Dawn, 232
McConnaughey, Garnet, 232
McCoy, Joe, 198, 255, 262, 317
McGlynn, Gerald, 217
McKinley, William, 23, 34, 38, 81
McNair, Denise, 184
Mein Kampf (Hitler), 106
Memphis, University of, 1
Men's Club of Niagara Falls (Ontario), 117
Menter, Theodore L., 186
Meranto, Ralph R., 216–17

Merino, John F., 249
Mesiah, Frank, 200–201
Michigan Avenue Baptist Church, 37
Miles, Jimmy, 193, 200
Miller, Carlyle, 4, 5, 55–56, 92, 296
Miller, Clayton R., 226
Miller, Eugene, 55–56
Mills, Leamon, 178
"Miss Townsend," 42
Mithum, Jacqueline, 114
Mizer, Hamilton B., 98
Moonglow Hotel, 136–37, 142, 163–64, 248
Morreale, Carmen, 236
Moses, Robert, 251
Mossell, Nathan, 37
Mothers' Club, the, 95
Mount Zion Baptist Church, 90, 127
Moynihan, Daniel P., 44, 291
"Mrs. Fields," 127
"mulattoes" (in NF), 29, 49, 69, 328n75
Murphy, Bill, 173
Murphy, Calvin, 192–93
Murphy, Matthew, 284
Mute and the Blind, The (newspaper), 15–16
Myrdal, Gunnar, 102
Myles, Larry, 256–58, 261

NAACP, 5, 37, 79, 171, 201; and Black Niagarans, 162–63, 172; Buffalo branch of, 38, 200, 275; and the civil rights movement, 171–73, 178–89, 193, 199, 203; and desegregation efforts, 205–209, 212, 217, 221, 227, 235–36, 239; and the Dyett case, 146–47; mission of, 179; Niagara Falls branch of, 147, 153, 172–73, 178–85, 187–89, 193, 199, 206–209, 212, 217, 221, 227, 235–36, 239, 252, 253, 260, 279;

support for NF school integration, 227; and urban renewal in NF, 252, 263
Narkiewicz, Robert, 265
Nash, Reverend Jesse, Sr., 115
National Association of Colored Women, 37
National Black American Museum and Cultural Center, 200-203, 278
National Negro Business League (NNBL), 8, 38, 350n220; Niagara Falls branch, 115-20, 174
Nation of Islam, 361n38; presence in Niagara Falls, 173-75
Negro History Week, 120
Negro Manifesto, 193-95, 206
Neighborhood Council, the, 95
Nelson, Dr. Ezekiel E., 100
New Black Society, 203, 221
New Hope Baptist Church, 6, 113, 127, 142, 161, 179; MLK's visit to, 169-71, 196
Newton, Huey P., 275
New York Institute for the Instruction of the Deaf and Dumb, 15
New York State Federation of Colored Women's Clubs, 48
Niagara Community Action Program (NiaCAP), 198, 228, 260, 264, 277, 303
Niagara Civic and Protective Club, 106-107
Niagara Community Center, 29, 81, 88, 96, 203, 280, 300; and desegregation, 221; formation of, 12, 72-75, 89, 94; flourishing of, 77-78, 82, 85, 95, 121, 144-46, 313; importance of, 51, 113, 120-21, 311, 343n44; leadership of, 97-98, 100, 128-29, 135-36, 144-45, 163, 309, 310; location of, 131, 145-46, 310; NAACP meeting at, 179, 280; purpose of, 6, 75, 100, 115, 120, 266, 295; services offered by, 93-94, 110, 111, 113, 117, 163, 278-79; strain on, 144-45
Niagara Falls (city), 3, 73, 102, 186; abolitionism in, 18, 19; Black "ghettos" in, 39, 194, 250, 255, 258, 312; civil rights activities in, 169, 172-73, 175-79, 181-83, 186, 203-205; cosmopolitanism of, 143; desegregation of schools, 12, 192, 205-42; dissimilarity index of, 141; economic decline of, 85-86, 107, 124, 243-45, 287-88, 308; economy of (general), 7, 51-54, 65, 107, 243, 250, 280, 308; home ownership / renting in, 139; housing conditions in, 93, 221, 280, 287; immigrant population of (non-Black), 42; inter-racial relationships in, 69, 70, 104-105, 149, 312; and the Love Canal crisis, 281-83, 289; and the Niagara Community Center, 79; non-Black minorities in, 6, 63, 138-41, 143, 198, 312; population of, 70, 124-25, 141, 280, 288; prosperous years in, 164, 243, 251, 280; race riot in, 105-106, 109, 190-93, 199-200, 252, 257, 310; racism in, 3, 11, 35, 62, 74, 82, 89, 91, 95, 142, 146-48, 198-200, 206, 257; race relations in, 34-35, 80-83, 89, 96, 104, 113, 142-44, 189-96, 303; segregation in, 62, 81, 101, 139, 141-42, 149-50, 245-48, 287; and slavery, 1-2, 11-13, 16-20; stagnation of, 153-54, 287; and tourism, 23, 51-52, 86, 89, 162, 245, 250-51, 277; urban renewal in, 12, 226, 243-85, 385n201; waterfalls in, 14, 17, 37, 51, 60, 61, 86, 92, 104, 170, 201, 251, 308; White

Niagara Falls (city) *(continued)*
residents of, 33, 41, 48, 66, 78, 96, 97–98, 117, 143, 174, 194, 206, 248, 267–68, 272, 292, 308, 312; White supremacy, in 106
Niagara Falls Colored Moosevelt Club, 46
Niagara Falls Gazette, 2, 3, 4, 98, 108, 113, 217, 225, 249, 275; coverage of Black Niagarans, 5–6, 13, 31–32, 34, 76, 78–79, 88, 99, 112, 118, 136–37, 173, 175, 177, 186–87, 221, 229, 262, 276, 277; on the "Love Canal" crisis, 280–81; on Teddy Roosevelt, 46–47; on urban renewal, 246–47, 257; voting advice for Black Niagarans, 39
Niagara Falls Housing Authority, 137
Niagara Falls public school system, 78, 79, 153; Black alumnae of, 45, 160; Black faculty in, 128, 235–36; Blacks' experiences in, 301–302; desegregation of, 205–42; expansion of, 280–81; and multicultural education, 180
Niagara Falls Public Library, xiii
Niagara Falls Senior High School, 128, 153, 161
Niagara Falls Teachers Association, 220, 227
Niagara Frontier region, 2
Niagara Movement, 36–37
Niagara Peace Council, 95, 115
Niagara Reservation, 32
Niagara River, 17
Niagara Street School, 152–53
Niagara University, 2, 106, 130
Niso, Bertha, 69
Niso, John, 69
Nixon, Richard, 225, 275
Nkrumah, Dr. Kwame, 169
Noonan, Reverend Joseph M., 106

Nordos, Wilbur R., 211–12, 216
Nunn, Washington, 190–91
Nyquist, Ewald J., 222, 237

O'Hara, Donald J., 194, 199–200, 252
Oliver, Weldon R., 189, 197, 207–10, 213–15
O'Neal, Joe, 154–57
Oswald, Russell, 274, 275

Pafazzo, Onofrio Murphy, 272
Palmer, Ann, 76
Palmer, Bessie, 74, 89
Palmer, Howard, 270
Palmer, Royal, 43, 62, 89, 92, 163
Palmer, Terrell, 62, 92
Palmore, Eddie, 148, 160–61, 163–65, 240, 253, 270–71, 317; arrival in NF, 279–80; on Black families in NF, 292; on housing integration, 287
Park, Robert, 73
Parker, James B., 34
Parker, John, 22
Parker, John J., 107
Parker, Wesley, 132, 310
Paterson, William M., 197
Patterson, Henry, 116, 163
Patterson, Louisa, 23
Payne, Juanita, 178
Peabody, George F., 109
Peck, Reverend Donald, 228
Pendergast, Mrs. Thomas, 117–18
Penn, Rabbi Alan L., 186
Perry, Sandy, 278–79
Pettaway, Thomas, 193
Philadelphia Negro, The (Du Bois), 6, 73, 294
Pickens, William O., 79
Pickett, Moses, 181–83
Pitarresi, Murphy J., 273
Plampton, Gorton, 191

Plarsick, Molen, 64
Plato, Jerry, 8–29, 43–45, 163; as community leader, 49, 89, 314
Plessy vs. Ferguson, 205
Pollard, John Magnus, Sr.: as Black leader/advocate, 94–97, 99–100, 108, 121, 173, 295, 315; as columnist for *Niagara Falls Gazette*, 78–79, 110; on housing conditions in NF, 93; and the Niagara Community Center, 76–79, 82–83, 85, 113, 116, 120–21, 125, 128, 309, 311; report on Black Niagarans, 73–74
Ponn, Rabbi Alan, 228
Porter, Daniel, 221–22, 240, 260–63, 318
Porter, Samuel and Susan, 17
Post, Amy and Isaac, 17
Potters House Church, 68
Poulos, George, 262
Powell, Adam Clayton, 188
Pratt, R. R., 93
Price, Veedee, 3, 5, 296, 319n1
Profit, Joe, 178, 193, 240, 276, 278, 316; firing of, 190, 273; and racial unrest in NF, 191; political career of, 5, 269–74, 285

Quarles, Benjamin, 1

Raboteau, Albert, 71
racial separatism, 173–74
Race and Kinship in a Midwestern Town: The Black Experience in Monroe, Michigan, 1900–1915 (DeVries), 8
racism: and the Brownville, Texas incident, 96; in Niagara Falls, 2, 6–9, 11–13, 27, 34, 35, 41, 49, 52, 62, 72, 81, 82–83, 85, 89, 91, 95, 101, 104–105, 113, 117, 121, 146–48, 154, 156, 164, 165, 181, 189, 199, 204, 206, 210, 257–60, 268, 273, 284–85, 303; organized opposition to, 36–37; in the US Armed Forces, 351n10; in the US (generally), 10, 34; in the US South, 4, 39, 55–57, 74, 81, 92, 108–109, 130, 173, 183–86
Rainbow Centre Project, 250–53
Rainville, Lucy, 153
Rakeshaw, Dr. W. E., 108–109
Randolph, A. Phillip, 125, 178
Ray, Arthur B., 268, 270, 274, 276, 296, 316; assistance to author, xiii, 3–6; civil rights activism by, 176–77; and desegregation, 205; and Friendship House, 197; membership in Masons, 163; and the NF Board of Education, 209, 213, 220–21, 229, 236–37, 240, 271
Raybon, Reverend Glen, 316; and Friendship House, 198; and housing in NF, 180, 229, 240, 254; and integration of public schools, 211; and the March on Washington, 178; and the Negro Manifesto, 193
Reconstruction, 34, 221n20
redlining, 9, 133–34, 311–12
Reed, Dr. Eugene, 182
Reed, Reverend Thomas, 72, 82, 101, 310
Reed-McBride, Helen, 98–99, 114, 289–90; on Blacks' solidarity in NF, 102, 107, 297; on racism in NF, 101, 105–106, 148
Reefer, William J., 108
Reid, Paul H., Jr., 207
Reiehert, Reverend David, 178
Republican Party, 111; and Black interests, 39; Black Niagarans' attitude toward, 270; Blacks' support for, 38, 39, 46, 107–109;

Republican Party *(continued)*
  Blacks' waning support for, 107–109; and integration of NF schools, 219; neglect of African Americans, 48, 107
RESCUE (Rebuild East Side through Cooperation, Unity and Effort), 265
Reynolds, Alberta, 310
Rice, David, 106–107
Richmond, Robert, 38–39
Rider, Edna Florence, 105
Rizzo, Nunzio, 181
Robinson, Jackie, 192–93, 271
Robinson, Sugar Ray, 154
Roberson, Carol, 184
Rockefeller, Nelson A., 192, 274, 275
Roots (Haley), 200
Roosevelt, Franklin D., 38, 118, 133; Blacks' allegiance to, 107–108; Black Niagarans' support for, 109
Roosevelt, Theodore, 34; betrayal of African Americans, 46–47, 96, 333–34n176
Rosa, Parks, 203, 269
Roth, Richard J., 275
Roundtree, Elizabeth William, 68
Roundtree, Ernie, 68
Roundtree, Estella, 68
Roundtree, Ethel, 67–68
Roundtree, Heredia, 68
Roundtree, James, 68
Roundtree, Ramon
Roundtree, Timothy, 68
Roundtree, William (Bill), 67–68
Roundtree, Winifred, 68
Rudolph, William, 143–44, 310
Rustin, Bayard, 178

Samuel, Norwood Hershey, 62, 92
Schnadelbach, R. T., 259–60
Schoninger, Helen, 205, 216, 232, 233
Schreiber, Norman J., 181–83
Schwartzeenbeg, Edith A., 78
Scott, A. A., 71 Searcy, Walter, 178
Seals, Hewer K., 270
Second Baptist Church, 6, 32–33, 72, 100
Second Great Migration, 8, 12, 27, 121, 125–28, 130, 132, 142–43, 154, 292
Second Street Baptist Church, 100
segregation: in the army, 333n176; in Canadian schools, 80; in economies, 8; in Federal buildings and agencies, 46; in Niagara Falls, 149, 206; and the *Plessy* case, 205; in restaurants, 171; in schools, 167, 189, 206; in the US South, 125, 128, 184, 241, 270
Shackford, Elenie, 57
Shareef, Jabril, 174
Shiloh Baptist Church, 6, 71, 89
Shine, Willie, 197, 198, 317
Shriver, R. Sargent, 188
Simmons, Gene, 290, 297
Skinner, Platt H., 14–17, 49, 314, 321n17
slavery, 2, 10, 42, 80, 113–14, 167; in Canada, 18, 149–50; and Christianity, 16; after the Civil War, 109; eradication of, 18, 20, 46; injustice of, 17; legacy of, 44; loyalty of slaves, 96; sharecropping as form of, 58; in the US South, 14
Slominski, Alfreda, 238
Smith, Barbara J., xiii, 92, 151–53, 163, 164, 292, 307–308; activism of, 153, 165, 283–84; on Black Niagaran families, 151–52, 292; on Black Niagarans during WWII, 152; on housing integration, 287; on racial mixing, 149–50; and St. John's AME Church, 329n104; youth of, 152–53, 154

Smith, Daisy, 150, 152
Smith, George, 259
Smith, John, Jr., 150–51, 152
Smith, Mabel A., 80–81, 104, 296
Smith, Rosie B., 178
Snead, Patrick, 20
Sobel, Dr. Morton, 225
Spencer, Henry A., 43
Springfield Race Riot, The, 178–79
Staples, Robert, 44, 291
Stephens, John Q., 236
Stephens, Lillie P., 236
Stewart, James B., 291
Stiwark, Jack, 64
Stovall, Deacon Benjamin, 71
Still, William, 14
St. John's AME Church, 6, 29, 61, 72, 78, 89, 96, 130, 178, 189, 303; establishment of, 33–34; NAACP rally at, 180; role in Black community, 49; and the civil rights movement, 185
Stovall, Early, 57
Stovall, Richard Ben, 57
Stowe, Harriet Beecher, 80
Straker, D. Augustus, 32
Styles, Reverend Joseph, 33
Sudarkasa, Niara, 68–69, 291
Sunset Lodge No. 295, 120
Swensson, Gerda, 185

Taeuber, Karl and Alma, 141–42
Talbert, Mary, 37–38, 48–49, 111
Talbert, William H., 37
Taft, William, 46, 47
Tatory, John, 98
Tatory, Mary, 98
Taylor, Johnny, 163
Terkel, Studs (85)
Terrell, Mary Church, 38
Terry-Berry's Saloon, 39
Third Street School, 45

Thomas, Dan, 219–20
Thomas, H. C., 92, 307
Thomas, Harry, 106
Thomas, Howard, 64
Thomas, Minerva L., 90
Thomas, Reverend H. C., 71
Thomas, Richard W., 115
Thompson, Reverend Paul F., 178, 179, 181, 317
Thompson, Vivian V. C., 113, 115, 296
Thorton, Ralph, 178
Till, Emmett, 183, 203
Titus, Richard, 38–39
"Torran," 132
Torrey, Charles, 22
Towns, Charles, 178
Tremier, Vera, 178, 181–82, 317
Trinity Baptist Church, 6, 72
Trotter, Joe, 55
Trotter, William Monroe, 36; and Theodore Roosevelt, 46–47; and Woodrow Wilson, 46, 48
Troy, John, 27
Tryon, Amos, 17
Tryon, Josiah, 17, 49
Tryon's Folly, 17
Tucker, Edison, 90, 163
Tucker, Helen, 90
Turnipseed, Reverend Dr. Andrew S., 186
Tuskegee Airmen, 125, 289, 351n10
Tuskegee experiment, 100, 345n84
Tuskegee Institute, 96, 119
Tubman, Harriet, 42; legacy of, 48; and the Underground Railroad, 13–14, 22, 202
Tucker, Edison, 90
Tunnel District, 33
Tunnel District Blues Band, 33
Tweed, William Boss, 23

Udut, Michael, Jr., 230

Uncle Tom's Cabin (Stowe), 80
Underground Railroad from Slavery to Freedom, The (Siebert), 21
Underground Railroad, the, 1–2, 16, 17, 324n13; and Canada, 18, 30, 201; and Niagara Falls, 13–14, 18, 37, 201; representations of in modern culture, 21
Understanding Each Other (activist group), 180
Union Baptist Church, 6, 71
Union Carbide and Carbon Corporation, 124, 244–45, 311; establishment of, 52–53; hiring of black employees, 52, 81, 90, 118, 126, 154–57, 159, 352n27, 383n137
Unity Park project, 253–59, 261
Universal Negro Improvement Association (UNIA), 102–103
University of Buffalo, 3

Van Liew, 145
Vass, Spencer, 48
Venters, Joseph, 64
Villard, Oswald Garrison, 178–79
Voice of the Fugitive (newspaper), 80

Walker, Charles, 274
Walker, James, 5
Wallace, George, 185, 187
Ware, Annie, 71
Ware, Reverend William, 71, 82
Warren, Helen M., 127
Washington, Booker T., 98, 332n149; on Black success and solidarity, 149; "captains of industry" concept, 99, 121, 129, 267, 272, 320n20; economic philosophy of, 8, 115–16, 120, 174, 321–22n20, 349n189, 361–62n52; influence on Black Niagarans, 12, 77–78, 94–95, 120, 321–22n20; leadership traits of, 94; and the National Negro Business League (NNBL), 115, 117; opposition to, 36; scheduled appearance in Niagara Falls, 32; supporters of, 37–38, 46; women's advice for, 119
Washington, Harriet, 30
Washington, Margret Murray, 37–38
Waters, Ray, 116, 119
Watkins, James, 64
Watson, Denton L., 187
Weaver, Perc, 272
Webb, Orace, 68
Webb, Samuel, 68
Wendel, William H., 250
Wesby, Virginia, 178
Weyeneth, Robert, 62
Wheatley, Phillis, 187
Whitaker, Reverend H. Edward, 142, 165, 169–70, 172, 317; on integration, 173; as NAACP president, 179; on racial discrimination in NF, 175
White abolitionists, 17–18
White communities: response to civil rights activism, 172, 182, 185, 210; response to growing Black populations, 130, 133, 143, 257, 293
White, John, 43
White, Mabel, 110
White, Parmey, 310
White society: rules and norms of, 292, 295
White, Walter, 146–47
Wicker, Tom, 274
Wilkins, Roy, 182
Williams, Barbara: and the NAACP, 5, 187, 280
Williams, Franklin H., 146–47
Williams, Lillian, 29, 69, 77
Williams, Robert, 64

Williamson, Bill, 200, 296
Williamson, Joseph, 106–107, 154–55
Williamson, Theodore, xiii, 296, 309–12; on Black entrepreneurs in NF, 61, 62; on Black families in NF, 292; as leader, 315; on the NF race riots, 105
Wilson, Gussy, 153
Wilson, Reverend A. L., 33; as community leader, 49
Wilson, Woodrow, 46–48, 168
Woodson, Carter G., 120
Woodward, C. Vann, 1
Wright, Bill, 160
Wright, Franklin, 43
Wyman, George K., 182

YMCA (Niagara Falls), 88, 96, 227; black membership in, 72, 104
Young, Elizabeth, 128

www.ingramcontent.com/pod-product-compliance
Lightning Source LLC
Chambersburg PA
CBHW020257240426

43673CB00039B/623